# Brief Contents

# Contents

# Illustrated Series™

# Microsoft® 365®
# Excel®

Comprehensive

**First Edition**

Lynn Wermers

Cengage

Australia • Brazil • Canada • Mexico • Singapore • United Kingdom • United States

Cengage

***Illustrated Microsoft® 365® Excel® Comprehensive*, First Edition**

**Lynn Wermers**

SVP, Product Management: Cheryl Costantini

VP, Product Management & Marketing: Thais Alencar

Senior Product Director, Portfolio Product Management: Mark Santee

Portfolio Product Director: Rita Lombard

Senior Portfolio Product Manager: Amy Savino

Senior Product Assistant: Ciara Boynton

Learning Designer: Zenya Molnar

Senior Content Manager: Samantha Rundle

Digital Project Manager: Jim Vaughey

Developmental Editor: Mary-Terese Cozzola

Senior Director, Product Marketing: Danae April

Senior Marketing Manager: Mackenzie Paine

Portfolio Specialist: Matt Schiesl

Content Acquisition Analyst: Callum Panno

Production Service: Lumina Datamatics Ltd.

Senior Designer: Erin Griffin

Cover Image Source: Novendi Prasetya/ Shutterstock.com



Mac Users: If you're working through this product using a Mac, some of the steps may vary. Additional information for Mac users is included with the Data files for this product.

Disclaimer: This text is intended for instructional purposes only; data is fictional and does not belong to any real persons or companies.

Disclaimer: The material in this text was written using Microsoft Windows 11 and Office 365 Professional Plus and was Quality Assurance tested before the publication date. As Microsoft continually updates the Windows operating system and Office 365, your software experience may vary slightly from what is presented in the printed text.



For product information and technology assistance, contact us at **Cengage Customer & Sales Support, 1-800-354-9706 or support.cengage.com.**

For permission to use material from this text or product, submit all requests online at **www.copyright.com.**

Library of Congress Control Number: 2024915466

Student Edition ISBN: 978-0-357-88283-2

Looseleaf ISBN: 978-0-357-88284-9

**Cengage**
5191 Natorp Boulevard
Mason, OH 45040
USA

Cengage is a leading provider of customized learning solutions. Our employees reside in nearly 40 different countries and serve digital learners in 165 countries around the world. Find your local representative at **www.cengage.com**.

To learn more about Cengage platforms and services, register or access your online learning solution, or purchase materials for your course, visit **www.cengage.com**.

**Notice to the Reader**

Publisher does not warrant or guarantee any of the products described herein or perform any independent analysis in connection with any of the product information contained herein. Publisher does not assume, and expressly disclaims, any obligation to obtain and include information other than that provided to it by the manufacturer. The reader is expressly warned to consider and adopt all safety precautions that might be indicated by the activities described herein and to avoid all potential hazards. By following the instructions contained herein, the reader willingly assumes all risks in connection with such instructions. The publisher makes no representations or warranties of any kind, including but not limited to, the warranties of fitness for particular purpose or merchantability, nor are any such representations implied with respect to the material set forth herein, and the publisher takes no responsibility with respect to such material. The publisher shall not be liable for any special, consequential, or exemplary damages resulting, in whole or part, from the readers' use of, or reliance upon, this material.

Printed at CLDPC, USA, 11-24

# Preface: The Illustrated Series®: Microsoft® 365® and Office®

## About the Authors

**Access:** Robert S. Wilson has a Computer Science degree from the University of Waterloo, holds numerous certifications from CompTIA, Microsoft, and Cisco, and has over 40 years of experience in the computing field. Rob has expertise in many areas including database development and administration. He has built complex applications using Microsoft® Access® as its foundation, including production control and project management systems. He is also the co-founder and chief technical officer of Got Your Six Cybersecurity Solutions, a cybersecurity firm offering services covering the entire cybersecurity spectrum.

**Excel:** Lynn Wermers is a professor in the Computer Science Department at North Shore Community College in Massachusetts, where she teaches IT, data management, data analysis, and web development courses. She also teaches part-time in the math department for the College of Professional Studies at Northeastern University. Professor Wermers has authored numerous leading Cengage books focusing on Excel.

**PowerPoint:** David W. Beskeen has authored or co-authored over 65 successful computer books since 1992 for Microsoft Press and other publishers, including more than 40 educational titles for Course Technology, Thomson Learning, and Cengage. Over the years he has guided readers in mastering PowerPoint®, Word®, Excel®, Internet Explorer, Outlook®, Windows®, LiveMotion, and other leading proprietary software packages. An expert in applied technology, Beskeen has extensive teaching and consulting experience in today's computer technology.

**Integration and Word:** Carol M. Cram is the author of more than 35 textbooks on computer applications, business communications, and Internet-related subjects. Ms. Cram was also a long-time faculty member at Capilano College in North Vancouver, where she served as the Convenor of the Executive Support Program and the Program Consultant for Business and Computers in Continuing Education as well as instructor of business and computer-related courses.

**Word:** Jennifer Duffy is the author of nine editions of Microsoft® Word® Illustrated and many other textbooks on computer applications for the popular Office series. An award-winning writer and educator, she has worked successfully in the business world as a content creator and communications consultant and in colleges and universities as an effective instructor of writing. She combines her expertise in Word with her strong business and teaching knowledge to create compelling learning tools for students.

## Preface for the Instructor

The Illustrated series' concise, student-friendly approach uses a proven two-page layout that enables learners to focus on discrete Office skills as they complete module readings. Each module begins with a brief overview of the principles covered in the lesson while large, full-color screen images reflect what students see on their computers. Distinctive to *Illustrated*, Tips and Clues boxes are incorporated throughout the text, while Trouble elements help students troubleshoot or explain common errors to strengthen their confidence. Module learning objectives are mapped to Microsoft Office Specialist (MOS) certification objectives, preparing students to take the MOS exam, which they can leverage in their careers. In addition, MindTap and updated SAM (Skills Assessment Manager) online resources are available to guide additional studies and ensure successful results.

*The Illustrated Series* is designed for students at two- and four-year schools as well as in continuing education programs. Skill levels range from experienced—for those with a foundational understanding from prior exposure to technology—to introductory—for those using a computer or technology device for the first time. The Illustrated Series is comprised of three parts: introductory, intermediate, and advanced. The series offers a comprehensive title that includes the four main Microsoft applications (Word, Excel, PowerPoint, and Access) at the introductory level. The MindTap Collection includes additional module coverage, including Outlook, Operating Systems, and Teams.

Market research is conducted semi-annually with both current Cengage users and those who use other learning materials. The focus of our market research is to gain insights into the user experience and overall learner needs so we can continuously evolve our content to exceed user expectations. We survey hundreds of instructors to ensure we gather insights from a large and varied demographic.

## New to This Edition

The Illustrated Series provides thoroughly updated coverage that reflects current Microsoft 365 features. Narrative content has been authored using Microsoft 365 Business Standard. Module projects incorporate career topics that apply diversity, equity, and inclusion principles and ensure accessibility. All projects, assignments, and lessons have been refreshed with authentic case scenarios that focus on practical skills and employability.

**Access:** New features in the Access content include an updated, real-world scenario from a leading industry that illustrates the relevance of Access databases in today's businesses. Completely updated projects use gapped Start and Solution files to ensure students use new, authentic files for each project from one module to the next.

**Excel:** With the thoroughly updated coverage in the Excel modules, students learn both long-standing Excel functions and tools as well as the most recent innovations. New Microsoft® Excel 365® features include dynamic arrays and related functions such as FILTER, RANDARRAY, SEQUENCE, SORT, SORTBY, TRANSPOSE, and UNIQUE. This edition also introduces new Excel data types and the Analyze Data feature for spotting trends and gaining insight into data. With co-authoring, threaded comments, and Notes, users can collaborate with colleagues on workbooks, annotate data, and have useful discussions about the data.

**Integration:** Along with understanding how to leverage Microsoft Word, Excel, PowerPoint, and Access individually, the Illustrated Series offers further opportunities for users to learn how these applications work together. This knowledge enables students to leverage the full potential of these applications and create comprehensive, professional, and visually appealing documents, spreadsheets, presentations, and databases. By integrating these tools, students can seamlessly transfer data between applications, analyze and visualize data in Excel, import charts and graphs into Word or PowerPoint, and create interactive databases in Access. This knowledge not only enhances their productivity and communication skills but also prepares them for real-world scenarios where the ability to work with these applications in an integrated manner is highly valued in academic and professional settings.

**PowerPoint:** The PowerPoint coverage introduces the new commenting experience, which lets users display comments in a contextual view or the Comments pane. The comment anchor helps reviewers identify specific slide elements with comments and place the comment bubble anywhere on the slide. With the revised search feature, users can enter a word or phrase in the Search box to find the definition. Microsoft Search also provides support articles to help perform tasks. Users can record and save a presentation that includes digital inking to capture text, drawings, and annotations, and then play back animated drawings. The Speaker Coach uses artificial intelligence (AI) to improve presentation skills by giving feedback on body language, the use of sensitive and filler words, and perceived mispronounced words.

**Word:** New features in the Word content include the enhanced Accessibility Checker, which identifies potential accessibility issues and presents suggestions to make documents more inclusive. The Word modules also introduce Focus mode, the updated collaboration experience, Microsoft's expanded search tool, and voice options. The Immersive Reader is covered, as is the ability to create a private document copy and use Word's screen reader.

## Organization of the Text

*The Illustrated Series: Microsoft 365 & Office, First Edition* is a comprehensive introduction to Microsoft applications—Word, Excel, PowerPoint, and Access—and is intended for students in introductory computing courses. Each application is divided into modules within the three levels—introductory, intermediate, and advanced. Each module introduces a topic through a real-world case scenario and presents content that aligns directly with the learning objectives stated at the beginning of the module and the more specific learning objectives in each lesson. Skills are taught progressively in visually rich lessons to encourage student learning as they proceed through the modules.

To enable students to practice and apply skills learned and to assess their mastery of the learning objectives, each module ends with three types of exercises: Skills Review, Independent Challenge, and Visual Workshop. The Skills Review contains hands-on exercises that mirror the progression of the lesson material. Each step matches a lesson title or learning objective and provides practice in the skills learned in the module lessons. To encourage critical and creative thinking, modules include two Independent Challenges, with the second more challenging than the first. Each exercise uses a different case scenario based on a real-life application in a top industry. The Visual Workshop provides a figure or screenshot showing a completed document, worksheet, presentation, or part of a database and asks the student to recreate it independently, without following step-by-step instructions.

## Features of the text

The features of the text, which are found consistently throughout all modules, are designed to aid the student in a specific way.

The projects are centered around authentic case scenarios focused on employability and based on research and data to motivate students to perform the steps in the module.

---

Lesson titles organize topics within a module.

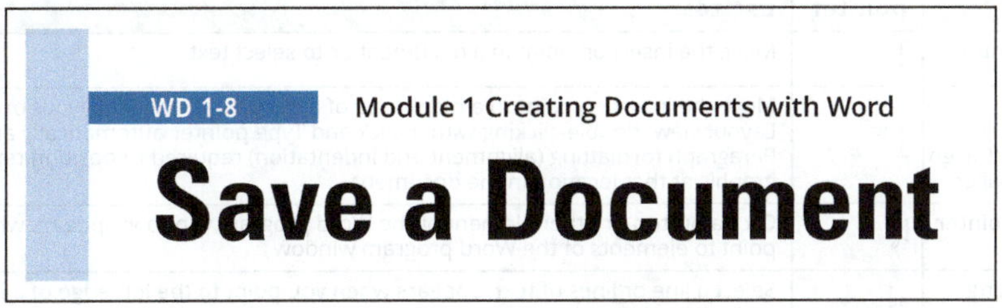

Numbered steps lead students through the process of completing a task while bullets in a Details section provide a planning lesson or, in the case of a challenging topic, a conceptual lesson.

Numbered steps include the following features:

**QuickTips** provide shortcuts and hints for using the app more effectively. A QuickTip points to a numbered step and is directly related to the corresponding action.

**Quick Tip**
You can also type a font size in the Font Size text box.

**4. Click the Font Size list arrow in the Font group, drag the pointer slowly up and down the Font Size list, then click 18**
As you drag the pointer over a font size, a preview of the font size is applied to the selected text. Clicking 18 increases the font size of the selected text to 18 points.

**Troubles** are marginal elements that anticipate common errors or provide troubleshooting advice to fix problems that might occur while completing the steps. The troubleshooting advice is related to the numbered step to which it points.

**Trouble**
If the Mini toolbar disappears, right-click the selection to display it again.

**1. Select Fall Career Fair**
The Mini toolbar appears over the selected text, as shown in **Figure 1-9**. You click a formatting option on the Mini toolbar to apply it to the selected text. **Table 1-5** describes the function of the buttons on the Mini toolbar. Yours may differ. The buttons on the Mini toolbar are also available on the Ribbon.

**Clues** boxes provide information that either expands on one component of the lesson skill or describes an independent task related to the lesson skill.

**Planning a document**

Before you create a new document, it's a good idea to spend time planning it. Identify the audience for your document, the message you want to convey, and the elements, such as tables or charts, you want to include. You should also think about the tone and appearance of your document—are you writing a business letter, which should be written in a pleasant, but serious, tone and have a formal appearance, or are you creating a flyer that must be colorful, eye-catching, and fun to read? The purpose and audience for your document determine the appropriate design. Planning the layout and design of a document involves deciding how to organize the text, selecting the fonts to use, identifying the graphics to include, and selecting the formatting elements that will enhance the message and appeal of the document. For longer documents, such as newsletters, it can be useful to sketch the layout and design of each page before you begin.

Other in-text pedagogical elements include the following:

**Tables** provide a quick summary of features that relate to the lesson task, such as identifying pointer shapes and what they do.

**Table 1-1:** Common mouse pointers in Word

| name | pointer | use to |
|---|---|---|
| I-beam pointer | | Move the insertion point in a document or to select text |
| Click and Type pointers, including left-align and center-align | | Move the insertion point to a blank area of a document in Print Layout or Web Layout view; double-clicking with a Click and Type pointer automatically applies the Paragraph formatting (alignment and indentation) required to position text or a graphic at that location in the document |
| Selection pointer | | Click a button or other element of the Word program window; appears when you point to elements of the Word program window |
| Right-pointing arrow pointer | | Select a line or lines of text; appears when you point to the left edge of a line of text in the document window |
| Hand pointer | | Open a hyperlink; appears when you point to a hyperlink in a task pane or when you press CTRL and point to a hyperlink in a document |
| Hide white space pointer | | Hide the white space in the top and bottom margins of a document in Print Layout view |
| Show white space pointer | | Show the white space in the top and bottom margins of a document in Print Layout view |

**Icons** are included throughout the steps to show students examples of what buttons look like within the app.

> 8. **Click the Save button** on the Quick Access toolbar
> Your change to the notice is saved. After you save a document for the first time, you must continue to save the changes you make to the document.

**Key terms** appear in blue and bold font. The bold text appears as a clickable link in MindTap.

> - The **title bar** displays the name of the document and the name of the program. Until you give a new document a different name, its temporary name is Document1. The left side of the title bar contains the **Quick Access toolbar**, which includes buttons for saving a document. The middle of the title bar contains the **Search box**, which you can use to find a command or access the Word Help system. The right side of the title bar contains the resizing buttons and the program Close button.

**SAM Upload and Download Icons** are for SAM users. A SAM download icon appears next to any step where students download a Data File to begin a SAM Project.

> 1. **sam** Start Word, then click **Blank document**
> A blank document opens in the **Word program window**, as shown in **Figure 1-2**. The blinking vertical line in the document window is the **insertion point**. It indicates where text appears as you type.

A SAM upload icon appears next to any step where students submit a file to SAM for a completed SAM project.

> 9. **sam** Click the **File tab**, then click **Close**
> The document closes, but the Word program window remains open.

---

# Course Solutions

## Online Learning Platform: MindTap with SAM

*The Illustrated Series MindTap Collection*, powered by *SAM* (Skills Assessment Manager), enables proficiency in Microsoft Office and computing concepts for your Introductory Computing courses. With a library of renowned course materials, including ready-to-assign, auto-graded learning modules, you can easily adapt your course to best prepare students for the evolving job market. In addition to an eReader that includes the full content of the printed book, the Illustrated Collection, First Edition MindTap course includes the following:

- SAM Textbook Projects: Follow the steps and scenarios outlined in the textbook readings; enable students to complete projects based on a real-world scenario live in Microsoft Office applications and submit them in SAM for automatic grading and feedback.
- SAM Training and Exam: Trainings teach students to complete specific skills in a simulated Microsoft application environment while exams allow students to demonstrate their proficiency (also in a simulated environment).
- SAM Projects: Students complete projects based on real-world scenarios live in Microsoft applications and submit the projects in SAM for automatic grading and feedback. SAM offers several types of projects, each with a unique purpose: 1A and 1B, critical thinking, end of module, capstone, and integration.

- Microsoft Office Specialist (MOS) resources: Training and exams are based on the Microsoft Office 365 Objective Domains for the MOS Exam and exam simulation that replicates the test-taking environment of the MOS exam for Word, Excel, Access, PowerPoint, and Outlook.

To learn more, go to https://www.cengage.com/mindtap-collections/

## Ancillary Package

Additional instructor and student resources for this product are available online. Instructor assets include an Instructor Manual, an Educator Guide, PowerPoint® slides, a Guide to Teaching Online, Solution Files, a test bank powered by Cognero®, and a Transition Guide. Student assets include data files and a glossary. Sign up or sign in at www.cengage.com to search for and access this product and its online resources. The instructor and student companion sites contain ancillary material for the full New Perspectives Series Collection, along with instructions on how to find specific content within the companion site.

- Instructor Manual: This guide provides additional instructional material to assist in class preparation, including module objectives, module outline, discussion questions, and additional activities and assignments. Each outline corresponds directly with the content in each module and additional discussion questions and activities are aligned to headings in the book.
- Educator Guide: The MindTap Educator Guide contains a detailed outline of the corresponding MindTap course, including activity types and time on task. The SAM Educator Guide explains how to use SAM functionality to maximize your course.
- PowerPoint slides: The slides may be used to guide classroom presentations, to provide to students for module review, or to print as classroom handouts. The slides align closely with the book while activities and the self-assessment align with module learning objectives and supplement the content in the book.
- Guide to Teaching Online: This guide presents technological and pedagogical considerations and suggestions for teaching the Introductory Computing course when you can't be in the same room with students.
- Solution Files: These files provide solutions to all textbook projects for instructors to use to grade student work.
  - Instructors using SAM do not need solution files since projects are auto-graded within SAM.
  - Solution files are provided on the instructor companion site for instructors *not* using SAM.
- Data Files: These files are provided for students to complete the projects in each module. Students using SAM to complete the projects download the required data files directly from SAM.
  - Students who are *not* using SAM to complete the projects can find data files on the student companion site and within MindTap.
- Test banks: A comprehensive test bank, offered in Cognero, Word, Blackboard, Moodle, Desire2Learn, Canvas, and SAM formats, contains questions aligned with each module's learning objectives and are written by subject matter experts. Powered by Cognero, Cengage Testing is a flexible, online system that allows you to author, edit, and manage test bank content from multiple Cengage solutions and to create multiple test versions that you can deliver from your LMS, your classroom, or wherever you want.
- Transition Guide: This guide highlights all the changes in the text and the digital offerings from the previous edition to the current one so that instructors know what to expect.

## Acknowledgments

**Lynn Wermers:** I am extremely grateful for the creative talent, good judgment, and editing savvy that Mary-Terese Cozzola brought to the development of this publication. MT, thank you for your support, guidance, good humor and always finding the right words for every situation. Thanks also to Samantha Rundle for bringing her outstanding management skills to this project. Zenya Molnar's comprehensive feedback and suggestions for bringing together the concepts with the best learning experience have improved this edition greatly. Thank you also to Amy Savino for getting this project going and supporting it throughout its duration.

**David W. Beskeen:** The content of this book has evolved significantly since the first edition was published in 1994 and I am proud to have been given the opportunity since then to write and revise this book for the benefit of students. I want to thank Cengage for the opportunity to write this latest edition and to the whole Cengage team for their hard work on this project. Finally, I want to acknowledge my editor Barbara Clemens for her fine work, her diligence to detail, and her patience with me.

**Carol M. Cram:** Thank you to the wonderful team at Cengage and my developmental editor Michael Sanford for their expertise, support, and dedication. And, as always, my deepest thanks to my husband Gregg and our daughter Julia who make everything I do possible.

**Jennifer Duffy:** It is always a pleasure to work with a talented team of professionals to create a book. Thank you to Michael Sanford for his careful editing, and to the Cengage team—Amy Savino, Samantha Rundle, Zenya Molnar, and all the others—for their expertise and guidance.

# Getting to Know Microsoft Office Versions

Cengage is proud to bring you the next edition of Microsoft Office. This edition was designed to provide a robust learning experience that is not dependent upon a specific version of Office.

Microsoft supports several versions and editions of Office: (Refer to Table 1 below for more information)

- **Microsoft 365 (formerly known as Office 365):** A service that delivers the most up-to-date, feature-rich, modern Microsoft productivity applications direct to your device. There are several combinations of Microsoft 365 programs for business, educational, and personal use. Microsoft 365 is cloud-based, meaning it is stored, managed, and processed on a network of remote servers hosted on the Internet, rather than on local servers or personal computers. Microsoft 365 offers extra online storage and cloud-connected features, as well as updates with the latest features, fixes, and security updates. Microsoft 365 is purchased for a monthly subscription fee that keeps your software up to date with the latest features.
- **Office 2021:** The Microsoft "on-premises" version of the Office apps, available for both PCs and Macintosh computers, offered as a static, one-time purchase and outside of the subscription model. Unlike Microsoft 365, Office 2021 does not include online product updates with new features.
- **Microsoft 365 Online (formerly known as Office Online):** A free, simplified version of Microsoft web applications (Teams, Access, Word, Excel, PowerPoint, and OneNote) that lets users create and edit files collaboratively.
- **Office 365 Education:** A free subscription including Word, Excel, PowerPoint, OneNote, and now Microsoft Teams, plus additional classroom tools. Only available for students and educators at select institutions.

Table 1 Microsoft Office applications — uses and availability

| Application | Use | Availability/Editions |
|---|---|---|
| Word | Create documents and improve your writing with intelligent assistance features. | Microsoft 365 Family, Home, Business, Office 2021, Office 365 Education |
| Excel | Simplify complex data into easy-to-read spreadsheets. | Microsoft 365 Personal, Home, Business, Office 2021, Office 365 Education |
| PowerPoint | Create presentations that stand out. | Home, Business, Office 2021, Office 365 Education |
| OneNote | A digital notebook for all your note-taking needs. | Home, Office 365 Education |
| OneDrive | Save and share your files and photos wherever you are. | Home, Business |
| Outlook | Manage your email, calendar, tasks, and contacts all in one place. | Home, Business |
| SharePoint | Create team sites to share information, files, and resources. | Business |
| Publisher | Create polished, professional layouts without the hassle. | Home, Business, Office 2021 (PC only) |
| Access | Create your own database apps easily in formats that serve your business best. | Home, Business, Office 2021 (PC only) |
| Teams | Bring everyone together in one place to meet, chat, call, and collaborate. | Business, Office 365 Education |
| Exchange | Business-class email and calendaring. | Business |

Over time, the Microsoft 365 cloud interface will continuously update using its web connection, offering new application features and functions, while Office 2021 will remain static.

Because Microsoft 365 releases updates continuously, your onscreen experience may differ from what you see in this product. For example, the more advanced features and functionalities covered in this product may not be available in Microsoft 365 Online, may have updated from what you see in Office 2021, or may be from a post-publication update of Microsoft 365.

For up-to-date information on the differences between Microsoft 365, Office 2021, and Microsoft 365 Online, please visit the Microsoft Support website.

Cengage is committed to providing high-quality learning solutions for you to gain the knowledge and skills that will empower you throughout your educational and professional careers.

Thank you for using our product, and we look forward to exploring the future of Microsoft Office with you!

# Using SAM Projects and Textbook Projects

**SAM** (Skills Assessment Manager) **Projects** allow you to actively apply the skills you learned in Microsoft Word, Excel, PowerPoint, or Access. You can also submit your work to SAM for online grading. You can use SAM Projects to become a more productive student and use these skills throughout your career.

**To complete SAM Textbook Projects, please follow these steps:**

SAM Textbook Projects allow you to complete a project as you follow along with the steps in the textbook. As you read the module, look for icons that indicate when you should download **sam**↓ your SAM Start file(s) and when to upload **sam**↑ your solution file to SAM for grading.

Everything you need to complete this project is provided within SAM. You can launch the eBook directly from SAM, which will allow you to take notes, highlight, and create a custom study guide, or you can use a print textbook or your mobile app. Download IOS or Download Android.

To get started, launch your SAM Project assignment from SAM, MindTap, or a link within your learning management system.

1. Step 1:
   **Download Files**
   - Click the "Download All" button or the individual links to download your **Start File** and **Support File(s)** (when available). You must use the SAM Start file.
   - Click the Instructions link to launch the eBook (or use the print textbook or mobile app).
   - Disregard any steps in the textbook that ask you to create a new file or to use a file from a location outside of SAM.
   - Look for the SAM Download icon **sam**↓ to begin working with your start file.
   - Follow the module's step-by-step instructions until you reach the SAM Upload icon **sam**↑.
   - Save and close the file.

2. Step 2:
   **Save Work to SAM**
   - Ensure you rename your project file to match the Expected File Name.
   - Upload your in-progress or completed file to SAM. You can download the file to continue working or submit it for grading in the next step.
3. Step 3:
   **Submit for Grading**
   - Upload your completed solution file to SAM for immediate feedback and to view the available Reports.
     - The **Graded Summary Report** provides a detailed list of project steps, your score, and feedback to aid you in revising and resubmitting the project.
     - The **Study Guide** provides your score for each project step and links to the associated training and textbook pages.
   - If additional attempts are allowed, use your reports to assist with revising and resubmitting your project.
   - To re-submit your project, download the file you saved in step 2.
   - Edit, save, and close the file, then re-upload and submit it again.

**For all other SAM Projects, please follow these steps:**

To get started, launch your SAM Project assignment from SAM, MindTap, or a link within your learning management system.

1. Step 1:
   **Download Files**
   - Click the "Download All" button or the individual links to download your **Instruction File**, **Start File**, and **Support File(s)** (when available). You must use the SAM Start file.
   - Open the Instruction file and follow the step-by-step instructions. Ensure you rename your project file to match the Expected File Name (change _1 to _2 at the end of the file name).

2. Step 2:
   **Save Work to SAM**
   - Upload your in-progress or completed file to SAM. You can download the file to continue working or submit it for grading in the next step.
3. Step 3:
   **Submit for Grading**
   - Upload the completed file to SAM for immediate feedback and to view available Reports.
     - The **Graded Summary Report** provides a detailed list of project steps, your score, and feedback to aid you in revising and resubmitting the project.
     - The **Study Guide** provides your score for each project step and links to the associated training and textbook pages.
   - If additional attempts are allowed, use your reports to assist with revising and resubmitting your project.
   - To re-submit the project, download the file saved in step 2.
   - Edit, save, and close the file, then re-upload and submit it again.

For additional tips to successfully complete your SAM Projects, please view our SAM Video Tutorials.

# Getting Started with Excel

## Case

You have been hired as an Executive Assistant at Bayside Consulting, a company that provides IT services for small and medium-sized companies. You report to Jamia Arias, the CEO of the company. One of your responsibilities in this role is creating and analyzing worksheet data from various company offices to help Jamia make sound decisions on expansion, investments, and new recruiting opportunities.

## Module Objectives

After completing this module, you will be able to:

- Describe an Excel workbook
- Enter data
- Edit data
- Copy and move cell data
- Enter formulas
- Enter a formula with multiple operators
- Insert a function
- Change worksheet views
- Customize print options

## Files You Will Need

IL_EX_1-1.xlsx
IL_EX_1-2.xlsx
IL_EX_1-3.xlsx
IL_EX_1-4.xlsx
IL_EX_1-5.xlsx

# Describe an Excel Workbook

**Case** Maria Lopez, Director of the IT Consulting Division, submitted preliminary data on consulting position postings and asked for your help in analyzing this data. You will begin by reviewing the postings in the southern region.

**Objectives**
- Define key spreadsheet terms
- Save an Excel file
- Identify Excel window elements

Microsoft Excel is an **electronic spreadsheet program**, a computer program used to perform calculations and analyze and present numeric data. An Excel file, a **workbook**, is a collection of related worksheets contained within a single file with the file extension xlsx. A workbook is made up of one or more worksheets. A **worksheet** contains a grid of columns and rows where you can enter and manipulate data, perform calculations with data, and analyze data.

## Steps

**Trouble**
If the extension .xlsx doesn't appear after the filenames in the Save As dialog box, don't worry; Windows can be set up to display or not to display the file extensions.

**Quick Tip**
You can open a blank workbook by clicking Blank workbook rather than Open.

**Quick Tip**
Depending on the installation of your software, the title bar may include a Quick Access Toolbar, which can be customized to provide easier access to the tools you use frequently. To display or hide it, click the Ribbon Display Options button, located in the lower-right of the ribbon, then click Show Quick Access Toolbar or Hide Quick Access Toolbar.

**Quick Tip**
The button that opens in the bottom-right corner of a range is the Quick Analysis tool.

1. **sam Click the Start button on the Windows taskbar, type Excel, click Excel, click Open, navigate to the location where you store your Data Files, click IL_EX_1-1.xlsx, then click Open**
2. **Click the File tab, click Save As on the navigation bar, click Browse, navigate to the location where you store your Data Files, if necessary, type IL_EX_1_Postings in the File name box, then click Save**

   Referring to **Figure 1-1**, identify the following items:
   - The **Name box** is the box to the left of the formula bar that shows the cell reference or name of the active cell. "A1" appears in the Name box.
   - The **formula bar** is the area above the worksheet grid where you enter or edit data in the active cell.
   - The **worksheet window** is an area of the program window that displays part of the current worksheet, which can contain a total of 1,048,576 rows and 16,384 columns. The columns and rows intersect to form cells, where you can enter and manipulate text, numbers, formulas, or a combination of all three. Every cell has its own unique location or **cell address**, expressed by combining its column letter and row number such as A1.
   - The **cell pointer** is a dark rectangle that outlines the active cell in a worksheet. In the figure, the cell pointer outlines cell A1, so A1 is the active cell.
   - By default, a workbook file contains one worksheet named Sheet1—but you can have as many sheets as your computer's memory allows in a workbook. The New sheet button to the right of Sheet1 allows you to add worksheets to a workbook. **Sheet tab scrolling buttons** are triangles that let you navigate to additional sheet tabs when available; they're located to the left of the sheet tabs.
   - The status bar provides a brief description of the active command or task in progress. The **mode indicator** on the left end of the status bar indicates the program's status, such as the Edit mode in Excel. You are in Edit mode any time you are entering or changing the contents of a cell. You can use the Zoom In and Zoom Out buttons on the status bar to increase or decrease the scale of the displayed worksheet.
   - You can use the **Search box** on the title bar to find a command or access the Excel Help system.
   - The AutoSave button on the title bar is on if you are working on a file saved on OneDrive. When AutoSave is on, your file will be automatically saved as you make changes.
3. **Click cell B4**

   Cell B4 becomes the active cell. To activate a different cell, you can click the cell or press the arrow keys on your keyboard to move to it.
4. **Click cell B4, press and hold the mouse button, drag the pointer to cell E4, then release the mouse button**

   You selected a group of cells, and they are highlighted, as shown in **Figure 1-2**. A series of two or more adjacent cells in a column, row, or rectangular group of cells, notated using the cell address of its upper-left and lower-right corners, such as B4:B4, is called a **range**; you select a range when you want to perform an action on a group of cells at once, such as moving them or formatting them. When you select a range, the status bar displays the average, count (or number of items selected), and sum of the selected cells as a quick reference.

**Figure 1-1:** Open workbook

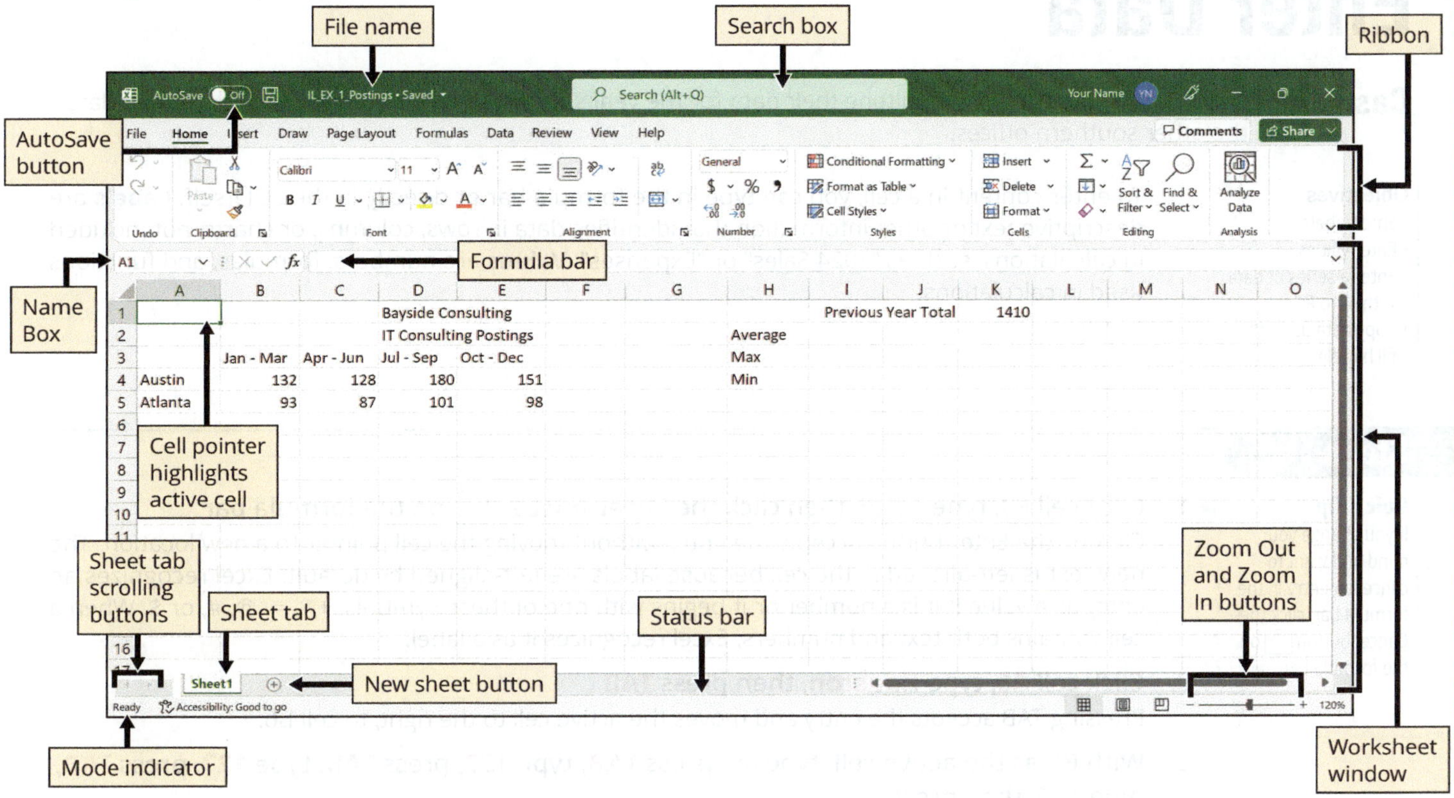


**Figure 1-2:** Selected range

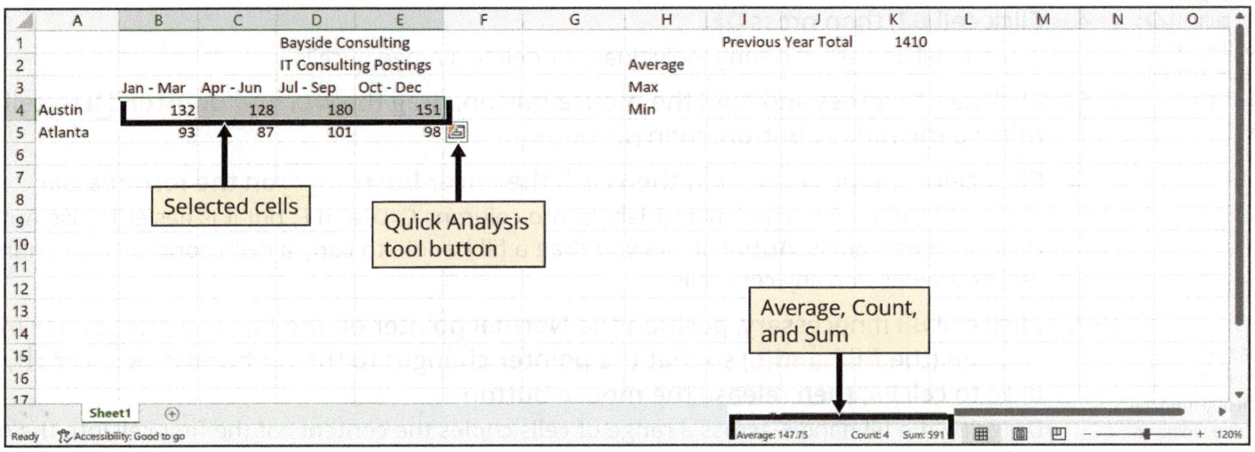


## Navigating a worksheet

With over a million cells available in a worksheet, it is important to know how to move around in, or navigate, a worksheet. You can use the arrow keys on the keyboard ↑, ↓, →, or ← to move one cell at a time, or press PAGE UP or PAGE DOWN to move one screen at a time. To move one screen to the left, press ALT+PAGE UP; to move one screen to the right, press ALT+PAGE DOWN. You can also use the mouse pointer to click the desired cell. If the desired cell is not visible in the worksheet window, use the scroll bars or use the Go To command by clicking the Find & Select button in the Editing group on the Home tab on the ribbon. To quickly jump to the first cell in a worksheet, press CTRL+HOME; to jump to the last cell, press CTRL+END.

# Enter Data

**Case** The Houston office was late in submitting their data for the year's four quarters. You need to add it to the data from the other southern offices.

**Objectives**
- Enter labels
- Enter values
- Enter a series of data with Auto Fill
- Copy data using the fill handle

To enter content in a cell, you can type in the formula bar or directly in the cell itself. **Labels** are descriptive text or other information that identifies data in rows, columns, or charts, not included in calculations, such as "2024 Sales" or "Expenses". **Values** are numbers, formulas, and functions used in calculations.

## Steps

**Quick Tip**
If you change your mind and want to cancel an entry in the formula bar, click the Cancel button on the formula bar.

1. **Click cell F3, type Total, then click the Enter button on the formula bar**
   Clicking the Enter button accepts the entry without moving the cell pointer to a new location. The new text is left-aligned in the cell because labels are left-aligned by default. Excel recognizes an entry as a value if it is a number or it begins with one of these symbols: +, -, =, @, #, or $. When a cell contains both text and numbers, Excel recognizes it as a label.

2. **Click cell A6, type Houston, then press TAB**
   Pressing TAB accepts the entry and moves the active cell to the right, to cell B6.

3. **With B6 as the active cell, type 89, press TAB, type 132, press TAB, type 127, press TAB, type 125, then press TAB**
   The quarterly data is displayed for the Houston office, as shown in **Figure 1-3**. The numbers are right-aligned because values are right-aligned by default. You want to replace the monthly labels in row 3 with quarter labels.

**Quick Tip**
If you want to clear a cell's content, including its formatting, click the Clear button in the Editing group on the Home tab on the ribbon, then click Clear All.

4. **Click cell B3, then press DEL**
   You can delete each cell entry individually or delete a range of cells.

5. **Click cell C3, press and hold the mouse button, drag the Normal pointer to cell E3, release the mouse button, then press DEL**

6. **Click cell B3, type Quarter 1, then click the Enter button on the formula bar**
   You could continue to type quarter labels into columns C, D, and E, but it is easier to use Auto Fill to enter these labels. **Auto Fill** lets you drag a fill handle to copy a cell's contents or continue a selected series into adjacent cells.

**Trouble**
On your screen, column widths may differ slightly from the figures, depending on your screen resolution and display settings.

7. **Click cell B3 if necessary, position the Normal pointer on the lower-right corner of the cell (the fill handle) so that the pointer changes to the fill handle pointer +, drag to cell E3, then release the mouse button**
   Dragging the fill handle across a range of cells copies the contents of the first cell into the other cells in the range or completes a data series. In this case, since Excel detected a data pattern in the selected cells, it filled the remaining selected cells with a series of annual quarters.

8. **Click the Auto Fill Options button**
   Options for filling the selected range include Fill Series, which is selected, as shown in **Figure 1-4**. The other available options allow you to change to copying cells, fill the cells with formatting only, or fill the cells without formatting.

9. **Save your work**

**Figure 1-3:** Houston data entered

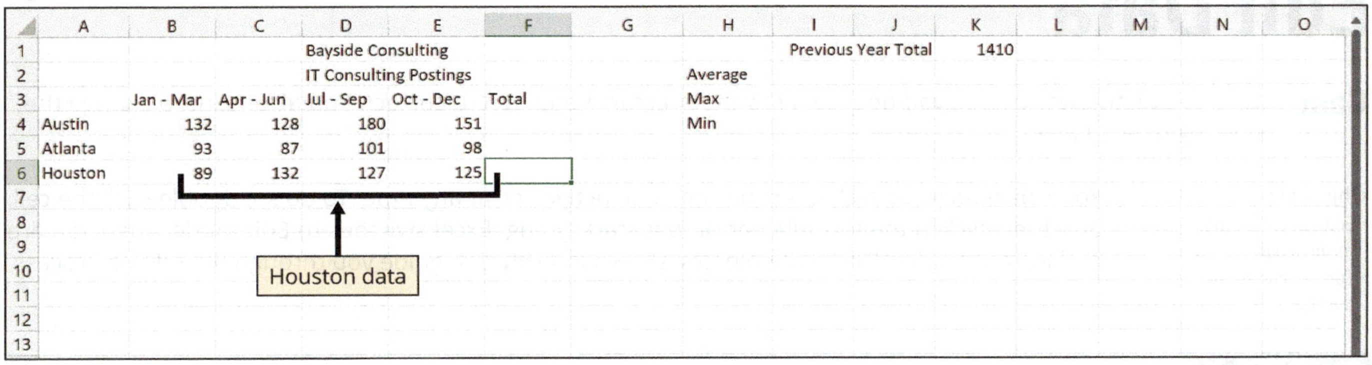


**Figure 1-4:** Auto Fill options

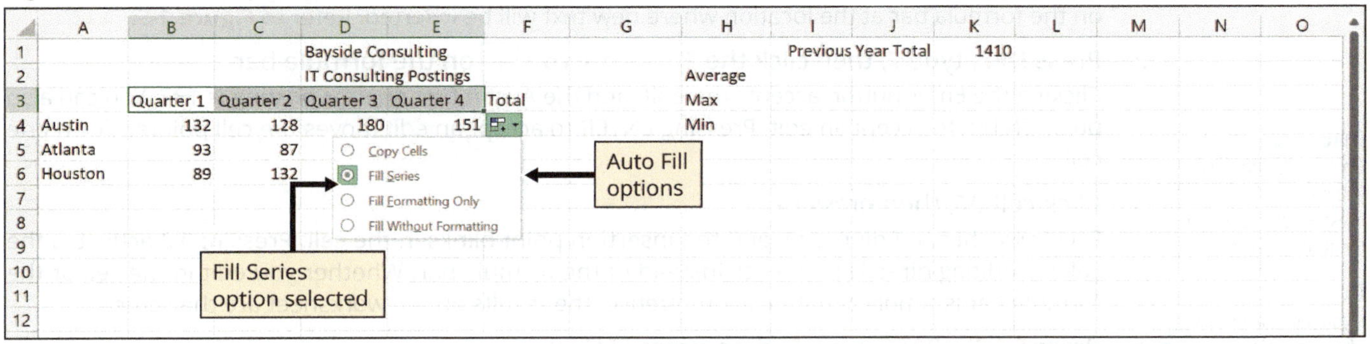


### Inserting and deleting selected cells

As you add formulas to your workbook, you may need to insert or delete cells. To insert cells, click the Insert arrow in the Cells group on the Home tab on the ribbon, then click Insert Cells. The Insert dialog box opens, asking if you want to insert a cell and move the current active cell down or to the right of the new one. To delete one or more selected cells, click the Delete arrow in the Cells group, click Delete Cells, and in the Delete dialog box, indicate which way you want to move the adjacent cells. When using this option, be careful not to disturb row or column alignment that may be necessary to maintain the accuracy of cell references on the worksheet. You can also click the Insert button or Delete button in the Cells group to insert or delete a single cell. Excel automatically adjusts cell references within the formulas of any moved cells to reflect their new locations.

# Edit Data

**Case** In reviewing the worksheet, you noticed a few input errors you need to correct. You also want to change the wording of two labels.

**Objectives**
- Edit cell entries in the formula bar
- Edit cell entries in the cell

You can change, or edit, the contents of an active cell at any time. To do so, double-click the cell, and then click in the formula bar or just start typing. Excel switches to Edit mode when you are making cell entries. Different pointers, shown in **Table 1-1**, guide you through the editing process.

## Steps

1. **Click cell B4, then click to the left of 2 in the formula bar**
   As soon as you click in the formula bar, a blinking vertical line called the **insertion point** appears on the formula bar at the location where new text will be inserted. Refer to **Figure 1-5**.
2. **Press DEL, type 7, then click the Enter button ✓ on the formula bar**
   Clicking the Enter button accepts the edit, and the Austin first quarter posting is 137. You can also press ENTER to accept an edit. Pressing ENTER to accept an edit moves the cell pointer down one cell.

**Quick Tip**
On some keyboards, you might need to press F-LOCK to enable the function keys.

3. **Click cell B6, then press F2**
   Excel switches to Edit mode, and the insertion point blinks in the cell. Pressing F2 activates the cell for editing directly in the cell instead of the formula bar. Whether you edit in the cell or the formula bar is simply a matter of preference; the results on the worksheet are the same.

**Quick Tip**
If you notice a mistake *after* confirming a cell entry, click the Undo button ↶ in the Undo group on the Home tab. The Undo button allows you to reverse up to 100 previous actions, one at a time. If you mistakenly undo an action, you can click the Redo button ↷ in the Undo group on the Home tab.

4. **Press BACKSPACE, type 5, then press ENTER**
   The value in the cell changes from 89 to 85, and cell B7 becomes the active cell.
5. **Click cell H3, then double-click the word Max in the formula bar**
   Double-clicking a word in a cell selects it. When you selected the word, the Mini toolbar automatically opened.
6. **Type Maximum, then press ENTER**
   When text is selected, typing deletes it and replaces it with the new text.
7. **Double-click cell H4, click to the right of n, type imum, then click the Enter button ✓**
   Double-clicking a cell activates it for editing directly in the cell. Compare your screen to **Figure 1-6**.
8. **Save your work**

### Recovering unsaved changes to a workbook file

You can use Excel's AutoRecover feature to automatically save your work as often as you want. This means that if you suddenly lose power or if Excel closes unexpectedly while you're working, you can recover all or some of the changes you made since you saved it last. (This is added insurance and not a substitute for regularly saving your work.) To customize the AutoRecover settings, click the File tab, click More, click Options, then click Save. AutoRecover lets you decide how often and into which location it should save files. When you restart Excel after an unexpected close, a Recovered files section may open above the listing of recent files. You can click Show Recovered Files to access the saved versions of files that were open when Excel closed.

**Figure 1-5:** Worksheet in Edit mode

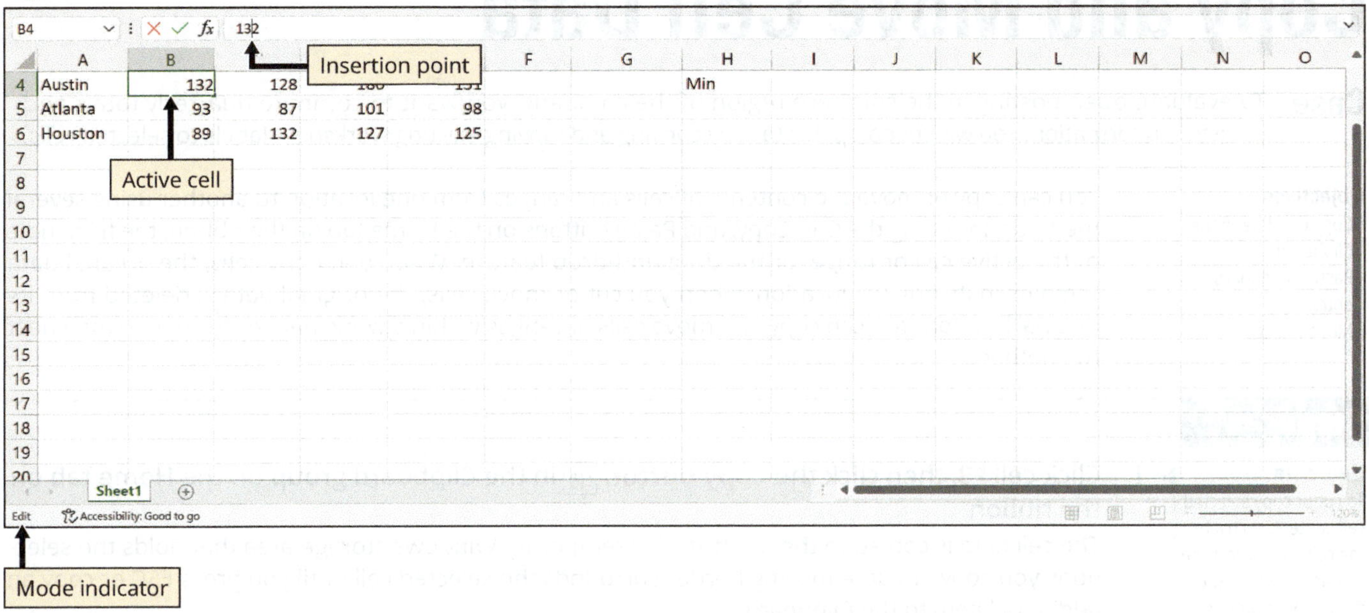


**Figure 1-6:** Edited worksheet

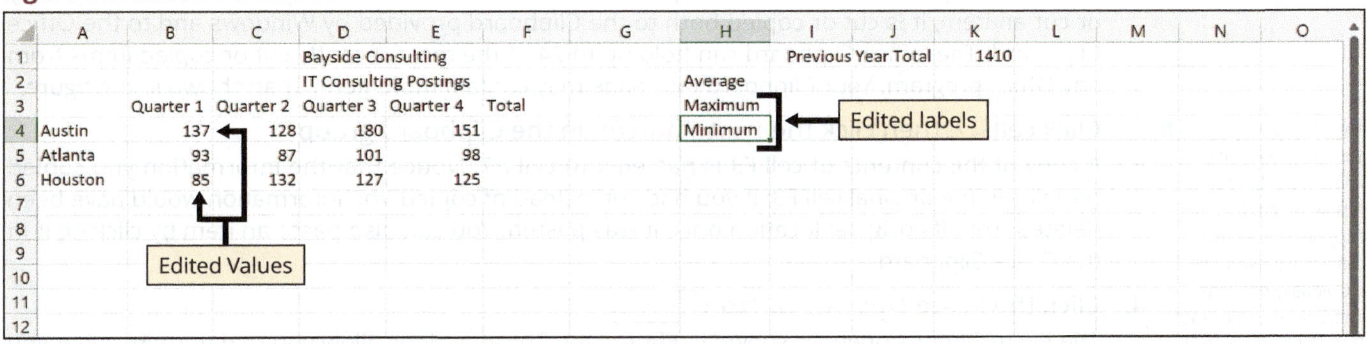


**Table 1-1:** Common pointers in Excel

| name | pointer | use to | visible over the |
|---|---|---|---|
| Normal |  | Select a cell or range; indicates Ready mode | Active worksheet |
| Fill handle |  | Copy cell contents or series to adjacent cells | Lower-right corner of the active cell or range |
| I-beam |  | Edit cell contents in active cell or formula bar | Active cell in Edit mode or over the formula bar |
| Move |  | Change the location of the selected cell(s) | Perimeter of the active cell(s) |
| Copy | 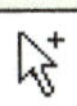 | Create a duplicate of the selected cell(s) | Perimeter of the active cell(s) when CTRL is pressed |
| Column resize | 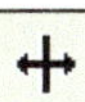 | Change the width of a column | Border between column heading indicators |

# Copy and Move Cell Data

**Case** To evaluate open posting in the southern region of the company, you want to compare quarterly totals and statistical information. You will speed up this task by copying and moving existing worksheet labels to selected cells.

**Objectives**
- Copy cell data to the Clipboard
- Paste a Clipboard entry
- Move a range

You can copy or move the contents of cells and ranges from one location to another using several methods, including the Cut, Copy, and Paste buttons on the Home tab on the ribbon, the fill handle of the active cell or range, or the drag-and-drop feature. When you copy cells, the original data remains in its original location; when you cut or move cells, the original data is deleted from its original location. You can copy and move cells or ranges within a worksheet or from one worksheet to another.

## Steps

**Quick Tip**
To cut or copy selected cell contents, activate the cell, then select the characters within the cell that you want to cut or copy.

**Quick Tip**
You can have multiple items in the Clipboard resulting from multiple copy operations. You can paste these items individually or all the items at the same time by clicking the Paste All button.

1. **Click cell F3, then click the Copy button in the Clipboard group on the Home tab on the ribbon**
   The cell data is copied to the **Clipboard**, a temporary Windows storage area that holds the selections you copy or cut. A moving border surrounds the selected cell until you press ESC or copy an additional item to the Clipboard.
2. **Click the dialog box launcher in the Clipboard group**
   The Office Clipboard opens in the Clipboard task pane, as shown in **Figure 1-7**. When you copy or cut an item, it is cut or copied both to the Clipboard provided by Windows and to the Office Clipboard. The Office Clipboard can hold up to 24 of the most recently cut or copied items from any Office program. Your Clipboard task pane may contain more items than shown in the figure.
3. **Click cell A7, then click the Paste button in the Clipboard group**
   A copy of the contents of cell F3 is pasted into cell A7. Notice that the information you copied remains in the original cell F3; if you had cut instead of copied, the information would have been deleted from its original location once it was pasted. You can also paste an item by clicking it in the Office Clipboard.
4. **Click the Paste Options button (Ctrl)**
   The Paste Options open, as shown in **Figure 1-8**. These options allow you to determine what you want pasted and how you want the pasted data to appear on the worksheet. Review the three categories, Paste, Paste Values, and Other Paste Options. The current pasted data doesn't need any change in formatting.
5. **Press ESC twice, then click the Close button on the Clipboard task pane**
6. **Select the range H2:H4, point to any edge of the selected range until the Normal pointer changes to the Move pointer, drag the range to cell A9, then release the mouse button**
   The move pointer displays an outline of the range you are dragging. When you release the mouse button, you "drop" the selection to the range A9:A11. When pasting an item from the Clipboard, you only need to specify the upper-left cell of the range where you want to paste the selection. If you press and hold CTRL while dragging and dropping, the information is copied instead of moved. The Quick Analysis tool to the right of the copied content offers some useful tools in Excel.
7. **Save your work**

**Figure 1-7:** Copied data in Office Clipboard

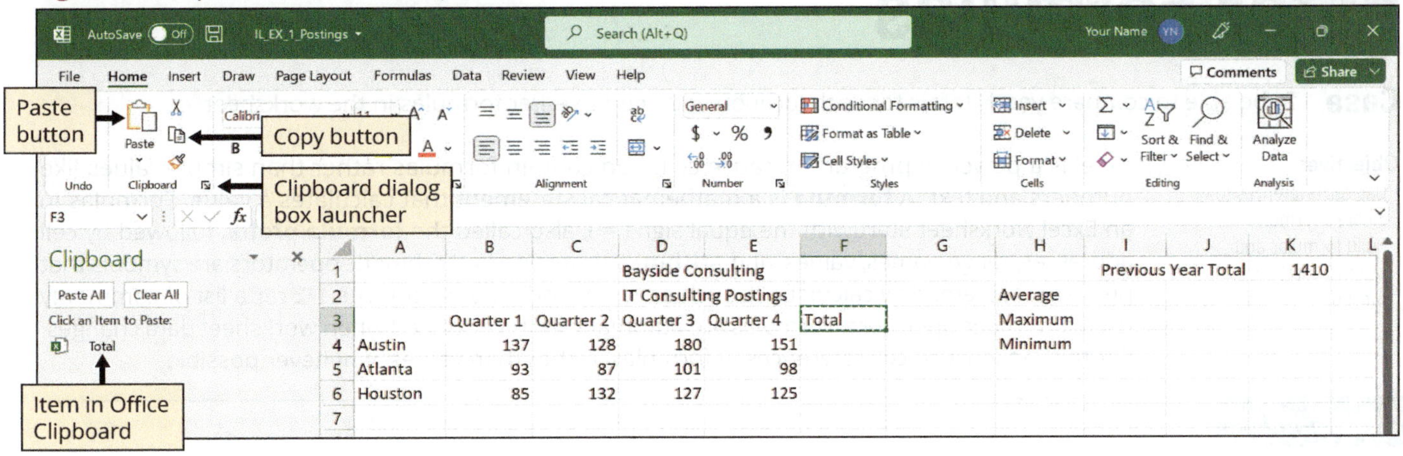


**Figure 1-8:** Paste options

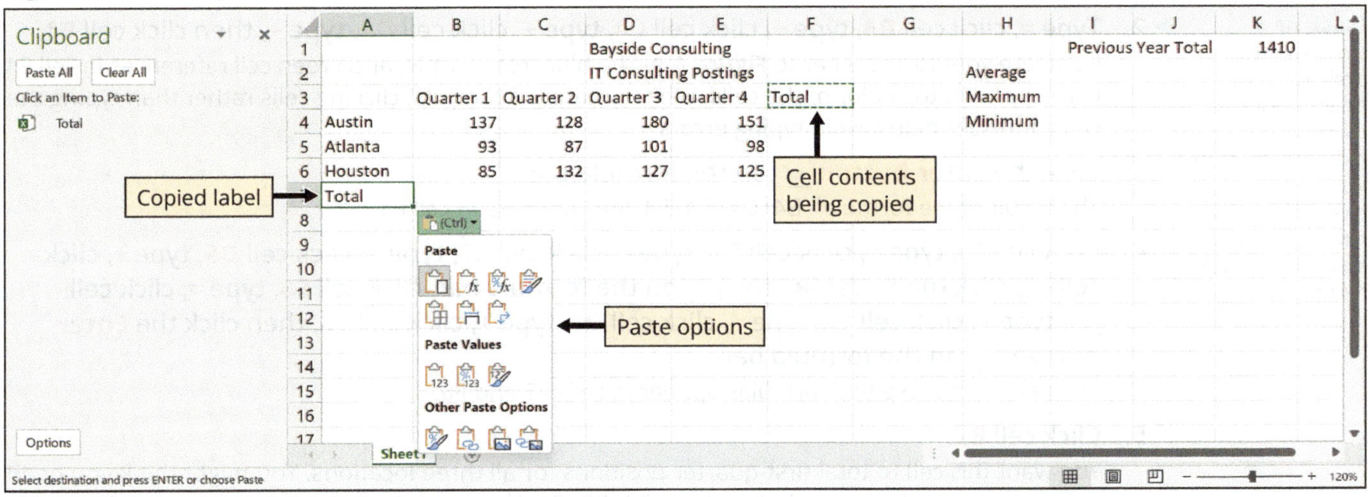


### Using Paste Options and Paste Preview

You can selectively paste copied or cut formulas, values, or other data by using the Paste Options button that opens on the worksheet after you paste data or clicking the Paste arrow in the Clipboard. The Paste Preview feature shows how the current selection will look when pasted. When you click the Paste Options button (or simply press [Ctrl] or the Paste arrow, a gallery of paste option icons opens, organized by category. The Paste category includes pasting formulas, pasting formulas and number formatting, pasting using the source formatting, pasting with no borders (to remove any borders around pasted cells), pasting with the source column widths, and pasting transposed data so that column data appears in rows and row data appears in columns. The Paste Values category includes pasting values only (without formatting), pasting values and number formatting, and pasting values with source formatting. The Other Paste Options category includes pasting formatting, links, pictures, and linked pictures. Clicking Paste Link in this category creates a link to the source data so that in the future, changes to the copied data update the pasted data. Clicking Picture in this category pastes the data as a picture where the picture tools can be used to format it, resize it, or move it.

# Enter Formulas

**Case** To be able to compare yearly totals for each location you need to enter formulas in the worksheet.

**Objectives**
- Use cell references to create a formula
- Build formulas and use the AutoSum function

Excel is a powerful program because cells can contain formulas rather than simply values like numbers and text. A **formula** is a mathematical statement that calculates a value. Formulas in an Excel worksheet start with the equal sign ( = ), also called the **formula prefix**, followed by cell addresses, range names, values, and **arithmetic operators**. Arithmetic operators are symbols that perform mathematical calculations such as +, -, *, and /. Refer to **Table 1-2** for a list of commonly used arithmetic operators. Formulas are automatically recalculated when worksheet data changes. For this reason, use cell references in formulas, rather than values, whenever possible.

## Steps

**Quick Tip**
You can reference a cell in a formula either by typing the cell reference or clicking the cell on the worksheet; when you click a cell to add a reference, the Mode indicator changes to "Point."

**Trouble**
Your button may only be displaying the Sum ScreenTip. Not all display devices show the AutoSum label.

1. **Click cell F4**
   This is the first cell where you want to insert a formula. To calculate the yearly total for the Austin location, you need to add the quarterly totals.
2. **Type =, click cell B4, type +, click cell C4, type +, click cell D4, type +, then click cell E4**
   Compare your formula bar to **Figure 1-9**. The blue, red, purple, and green cell references in cell F4 correspond to the color of the cells. When entering a formula, clicking cells rather than typing the cell addresses helps avoid typing errors.
3. **Click the Enter button ✓ on the formula bar**
   The result of the formula =B4+C4+D4+E4, 596, appears in cell F4.
4. **Click cell F5, type =, click cell B5, type +, click cell C5, type +, click cell D5, type +, click cell E5, click the Enter button ✓ on the formula bar, click cell F6, type =, click cell B6, type +, click cell C6, type +, click cell D6, type +, click cell E6, then click the Enter button ✓ on the formula bar**
   The results of these two formulas appear in cells F5 and F6.
5. **Click cell B7**
   You want this cell to total first-quarter positions for all three locations. You might think you need to create a formula that looks like this: =B4+B5+B6. However, there's an easier way to achieve this result.
6. **On the ribbon, click the AutoSum button Σ in the Editing group on the Home tab**
   The SUM function is inserted in the cell, and a suggested range appears in parentheses. A **function** is a predefined procedure that returns a value; it includes the **arguments** (the information necessary to calculate an answer) as well as cell references and other unique information. Clicking the AutoSum button sums the adjacent range (that is, the cells next to the active cell) above or to the left, although you can adjust the range if necessary by selecting a different range before accepting the cell entry. Using the SUM function is quicker than entering a formula, and using the range B4:B6 is more efficient than entering individual cell references.
7. **Click the Enter button ✓ on the formula bar**
   Excel calculates the total contained in cells B4:B6 and displays the result, 315, in cell B7. The cell actually contains the formula =SUM(B4:B6), but it displays the result.
8. **Click cell C7, click the AutoSum button Σ, click the Enter button ✓, click cell D7, click the AutoSum button Σ, click the Enter button ✓, click cell E7, click the AutoSum button Σ, click the Enter button ✓, click cell F7, click the AutoSum button Σ, click the Enter button ✓, compare your screen to Figure 1-10, then save your work**

**Figure 1-9:** Entering a formula

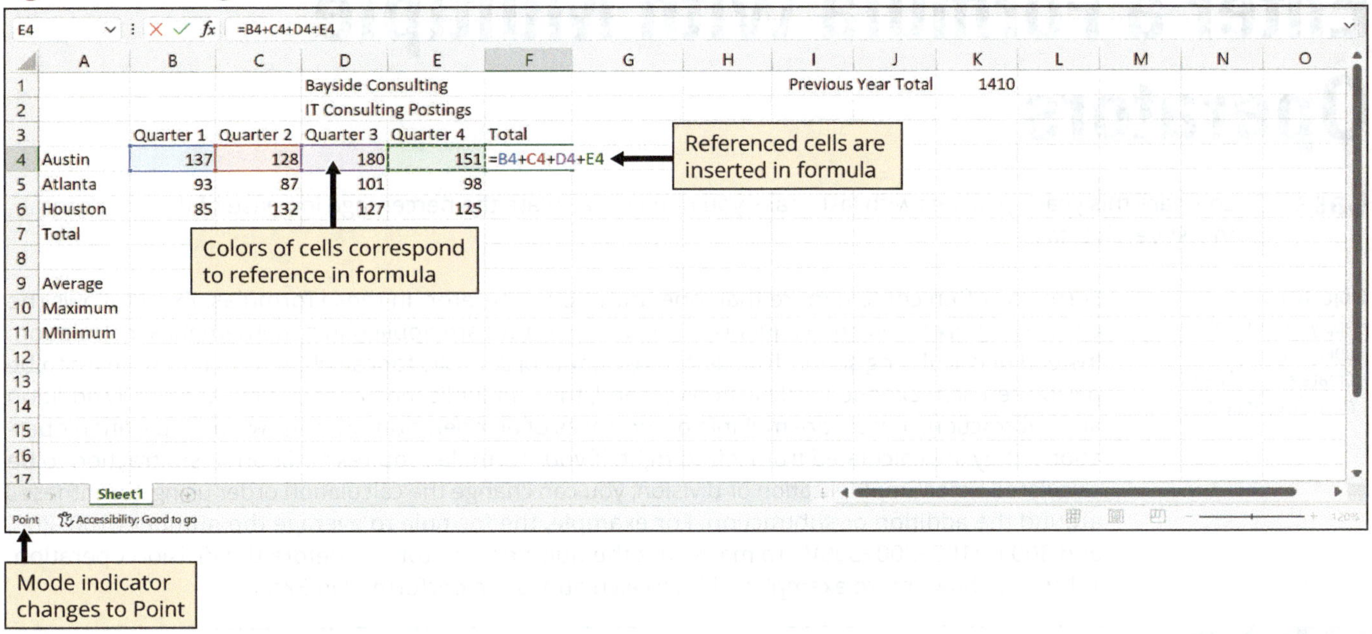


**Figure 1-10:** SUM functions in a worksheet

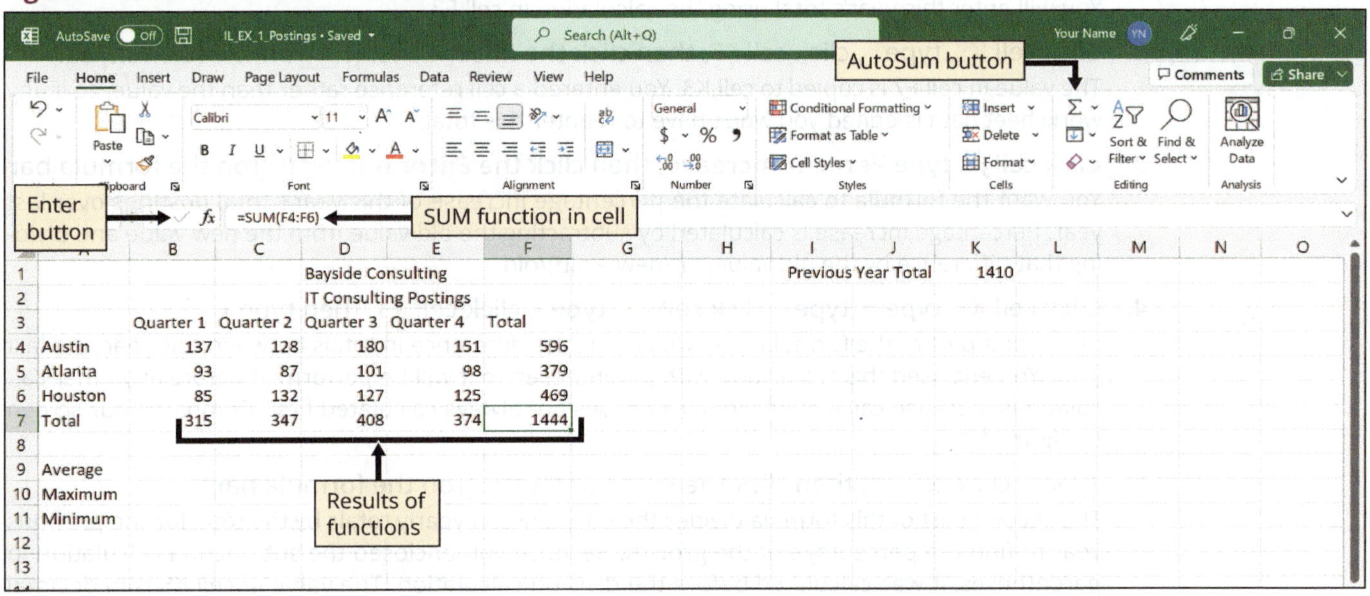


**Table 1-2:** Excel arithmetic operators

| operator | purpose | example |
|---|---|---|
| + | Addition | =A5+A7 |
| - | Subtraction or negation | =A5-10 |
| * | Multiplication | =A5*A7 |
| / | Division | =A5/A7 |
| % | Percent | =35% |
| ^ (caret) | Exponent | =6^2 (same as $6^2$) |

# Enter a Formula with Multiple Operators

**Case** To compare this year's postings with last year's you need to calculate the percentage increase of this year's total from last year's total.

**Objectives**
- Apply the order of operations
- Create a formula with multiple operators

Formulas often contain more than one arithmetic operator. In these formulas, Excel follows the **order of operations**, the sequence in which operators are applied in a mathematical calculation. Instead of calculating simply from left to right, this order calls for calculations in parentheses to be performed first, exponent calculations second, then multiplication and division, and finally addition and subtraction. If there are multiple occurrences of an operation, such as two multiplication operations, they are calculated from left to right. If your formula requires addition or subtraction to be calculated before multiplication or division, you can change the calculation order using parentheses around the addition or subtraction. For example, the formula to average the numbers 100, 200, and 300 is (100+200+300)/3 to make sure the numbers are totaled before the division operation. **Table 1-3** shows more examples of how calculations are performed in Excel.

## Steps

1. **Click cell J3, type This Year, then click the Enter button ✓ on the formula bar**
   You will enter this year's total using the calculation in cell F7.
2. **Click cell K3, type =, click cell F7, then click the Enter button ✓ on the formula bar**
   The value in cell F7 is copied to cell K3. You entered a cell reference rather than the value, so if any worksheet data is edited you won't have to reenter this total.
3. **Click cell J5, type Percent Increase, then click the Enter button ✓ on the formula bar**
   You want the formula to calculate the percentage increase of this year's total postings over last year. Percentage increase is calculated by subtracting the old value from the new value and dividing that difference by the old value, or (new – old)/old.
4. **Click cell K5, type =, type (, click cell K3, type -, click cell K1, then type )**
   In this first part of the formula, you are finding the difference in totals between this year and last year. You enclosed this calculation with parentheses so it will be performed before any other calculations, because calculations in parentheses are always calculated first. Compare your screen to **Figure 1-11**.
5. **Type /, click cell K1, then click the Enter button ✓ on the formula bar**
   The second part of this formula divides the difference in yearly totals by the total for the previous year to find the percentage of the growth. Because you enclosed the subtraction calculation in parentheses, it was calculated before the division calculation. The value in cell K5 is in decimal format. You want to display this value as a percentage with two decimal places.
6. **Click the Percent Style button % in the Number group on the Home tab, then click the Increase Decimal button in the Number group twice**
   The percentage increase in cell K5 is 2.41%, as shown in **Figure 1-12**.
7. **Save your work**

**Figure 1-11:** Formula with parentheses

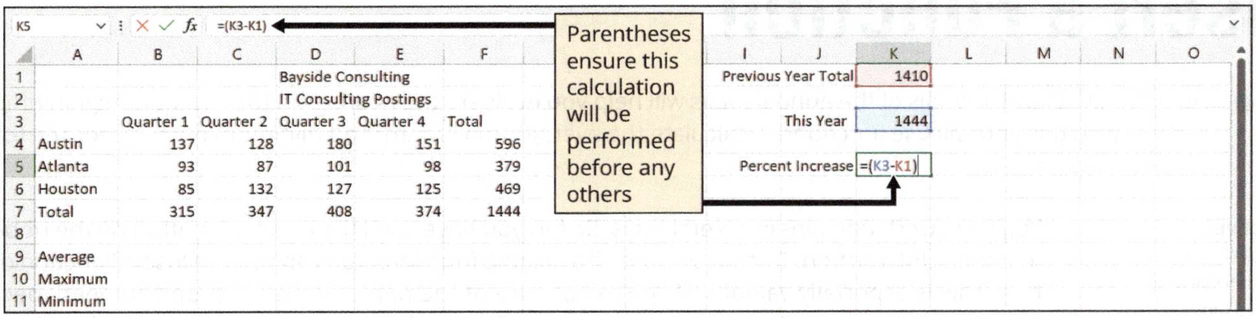


**Figure 1-12:** Formula with percentage increase

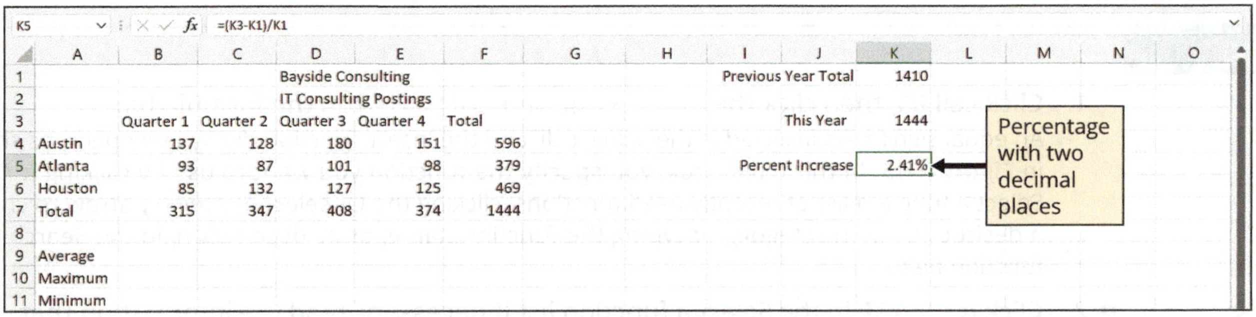


**Table 1-3:** Calculation results in Excel formulas

| formula | result |
|---|---|
| 10+20+40/2 | 50 |
| (10+20+40)/2 | 35 |
| 10+5*2 | 20 |
| (10+5)*2 | 30 |
| 20-10/2 | 15 |
| (20-10)/2 | 5 |

# Insert a Function

**Case** Adding a statistical analysis of the annual totals will help you evaluate the postings in the southern region offices. To help with this you will use functions to calculate the average, maximum, and minimum postings for the totals for the locations.

**Objectives**
- Use the Insert Function dialog box
- Insert a function manually

You can insert functions in several ways. So far, you have used the AutoSum button on the ribbon to add the SUM function. To choose from all available functions you can use the Insert Function dialog box. This is especially valuable if you're not sure of the name of the function you need, because functions are organized into categories, such as Financial, Date & Time, and Statistical, and you are guided through the process. Other ways to insert a function include manually typing it in a cell and using the AutoSum arrow to insert commonly used functions.

## Steps

1. **Click cell B9, then click the Insert Function button on the formula bar**
   An equal sign ( = ) is inserted in the active cell, and the Insert Function dialog box opens, as shown in **Figure 1-13**. In this dialog box, you specify the function you want to use by clicking it in the Select a function list of recently used functions, clicking the Or select a category arrow to choose a desired function category, or typing the function name, or its description, in the Search for a function field.

**Trouble**
If AVERAGE is not in the function list, type AVERAGE in the Search for a function box, then click Go.

2. **Click AVERAGE in the Select a function list if necessary, read the information that appears under the list, then click OK**
   The Function Arguments dialog box opens, as shown in **Figure 1-14**.
3. **Click the Collapse button in the Number1 field of the Function Arguments dialog box, select the range F4:F6 on the worksheet, then click the Expand button in the Function Arguments dialog box**
   Clicking the Collapse button minimizes the dialog box so that you can select cells on the worksheet. When you click the Expand button, the dialog box is restored. You can also begin dragging on the worksheet to automatically minimize the dialog box; after you select the desired range, the dialog box is restored.
4. **Click OK**
   The Function Arguments dialog box closes, and the calculated value is displayed in cell B9. The average number of postings for the year is 481.3333.
5. **Click cell B10, type =, then type m**
   Because you are manually typing this function, you must manually type the opening equal sign ( = ). Once you type an equal sign in a cell, each letter you type acts as a trigger to activate the Excel **Formula AutoComplete**, a feature that automatically suggests text, numbers, or dates to insert based on previous entries. Because you entered the letter *m*, this feature suggests a list of function names beginning with "M."

**Quick Tip**
In the AutoComplete list, if you click a function instead of double-clicking, a ScreenTip displays more detailed information about the function.

6. **Double-click MAX in the list, select the range F4:F6, then click the Enter button on the formula bar**
   The result, 596, appears in cell B10. When you completed the entry, the closing parenthesis was automatically added to the formula.
7. **Click cell B11, type =, type m, double-click MIN in the list of function names, select the range F4:F6, then press ENTER**
   The result, 379, appears in cell B11.
8. **Click cell A8, type Annual Statistics, press ENTER, then save your work**
   Compare your worksheet to **Figure 1-15**.

**Figure 1-13:** Insert Function dialog box

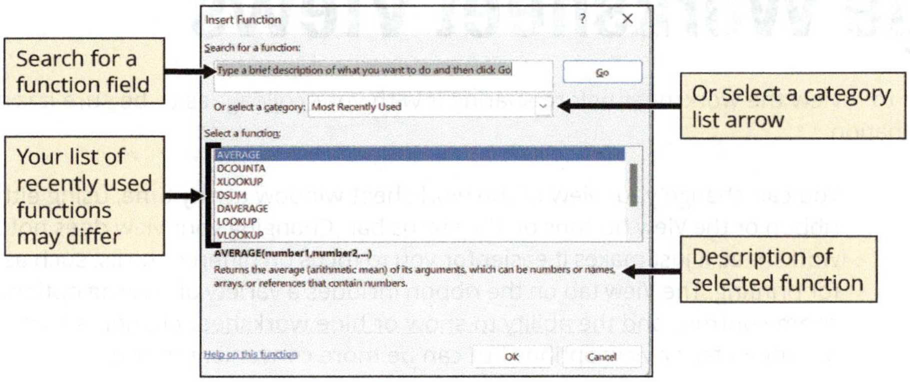


**Figure 1-14:** Function Arguments dialog box

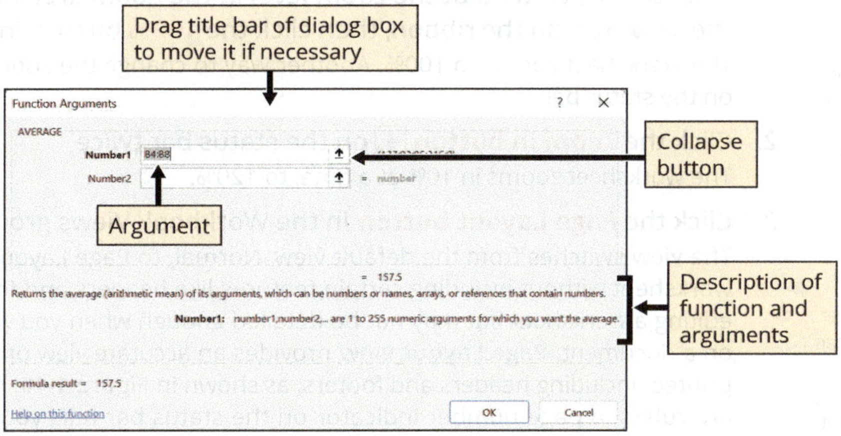


**Figure 1-15:** Worksheet with annual statistics

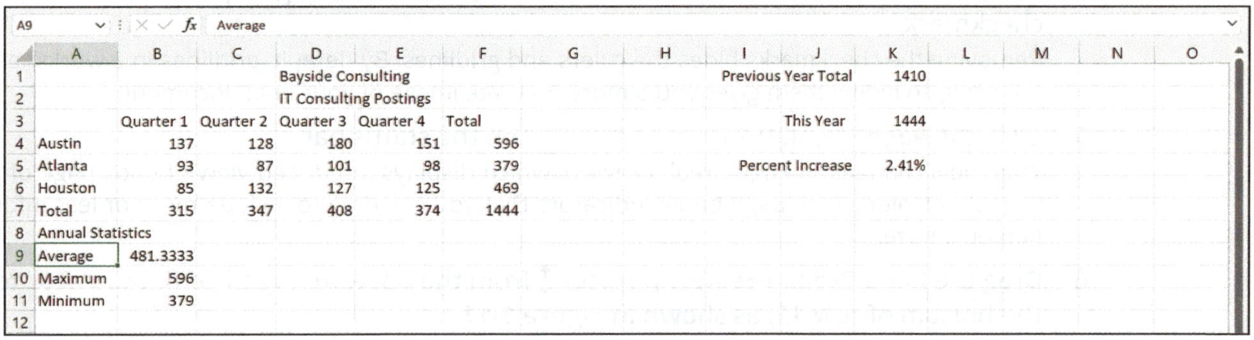


| | A | B | C | D | E | F | G | H | I | J | K |
|---|---|---|---|---|---|---|---|---|---|---|---|
| 1 | | | | Bayside Consulting | | | | | | Previous Year Total | 1410 |
| 2 | | | | IT Consulting Postings | | | | | | | |
| 3 | | Quarter 1 | Quarter 2 | Quarter 3 | Quarter 4 | Total | | | | This Year | 1444 |
| 4 | Austin | 137 | 128 | 180 | 151 | 596 | | | | | |
| 5 | Atlanta | 93 | 87 | 101 | 98 | 379 | | | | Percent Increase | 2.41% |
| 6 | Houston | 85 | 132 | 127 | 125 | 469 | | | | | |
| 7 | Total | 315 | 347 | 408 | 374 | 1444 | | | | | |
| 8 | Annual Statistics | | | | | | | | | | |
| 9 | Average | 481.3333 | | | | | | | | | |
| 10 | Maximum | 596 | | | | | | | | | |
| 11 | Minimum | 379 | | | | | | | | | |
| 12 | | | | | | | | | | | |

# Change Worksheet Views

**Case** You want to review the worksheet before sharing it with your colleagues to be sure it is easy for them to view the information.

**Objectives**
- Use the Zoom option on a worksheet
- Change worksheet views
- Adjust page breaks in a worksheet

You can change your view of the worksheet window at any time, using either the View tab on the ribbon or the View buttons on the status bar. Changing your view does not affect the contents of a worksheet; it just makes it easier for you to focus on different tasks, such as preparing a worksheet for printing. The View tab on the ribbon includes a variety of viewing options, such as View buttons, zoom controls, and the ability to show or hide worksheet elements such as gridlines. The status bar offers fewer view options but can be more convenient to use.

## Steps

**Quick Tip**
You can use the Zoom button to select the worksheet magnification level or the Zoom to Selection button to zoom into the cell or range that is selected on the worksheet.

**Quick Tip**
Although a worksheet can contain more than a million rows and thousands of columns, the current document contains only as many pages as necessary for the current project.

**Quick Tip**
Once you view a worksheet in Page Break Preview, the page break indicators appear as lines after you switch back to Normal view or Page Layout view.

1. **Click cell A1, verify that the zoom level in the Zoom area of the status bar is 120%, click the View tab on the ribbon, then click the 100% button in the Zoom group**
   The worksheet zooms to 100%. Another way to change the zoom level is to use the Zoom slider on the status bar.
2. **Click the Zoom in button [+] on the status bar twice**
   The worksheet zooms in 10% at a time, to 120%.
3. **Click the Page Layout button in the Workbook Views group on the View tab**
   The view switches from the default view, Normal, to Page Layout view. **Normal view** shows the worksheet without including certain features like headers and footers; it's ideal for creating and editing a worksheet but may not be detailed enough when you want to put the finishing touches on a document. **Page Layout view** provides an accurate view of how a worksheet will look when printed, including headers and footers, as shown in **Figure 1-16**. Above and to the left of the page are rulers. A page number indicator on the status bar tells you the current page and the total number of pages in this worksheet.
4. **Click the Ruler check box in the Show group on the View tab to remove the checkmark, then click the Gridlines check box in the Show group to remove the checkmark**
   Removing the checkmarks hides the rulers and gridlines. By default, gridlines in a worksheet do not print, so hiding them gives you a more accurate image of your final document.
5. **Click the Page Break Preview button on the status bar**
   Your view changes to Page Break Preview, which displays a reduced view of each page of your worksheet, along with page break indicators that you can drag to include more or less information on a page.
6. **Drag the Page Break Preview pointer ↕ from the bottom page break indicator to the bottom of row 15, as shown in Figure 1-17**
   When you're working on a large worksheet with multiple pages, sometimes you need to adjust where pages break; in this worksheet, however, the information all fits comfortably on one page.
7. **Click the Page Layout button in the Workbook Views group, click the Ruler box in the Show group, then click the Gridlines box in the Show group**
   Adding checkmarks to the check boxes displays the rulers and gridlines. You can show or hide View tab items in any view.
8. **Click the Normal button in the Workbook Views group, then save your work**

**Figure 1-16:** Page Layout view

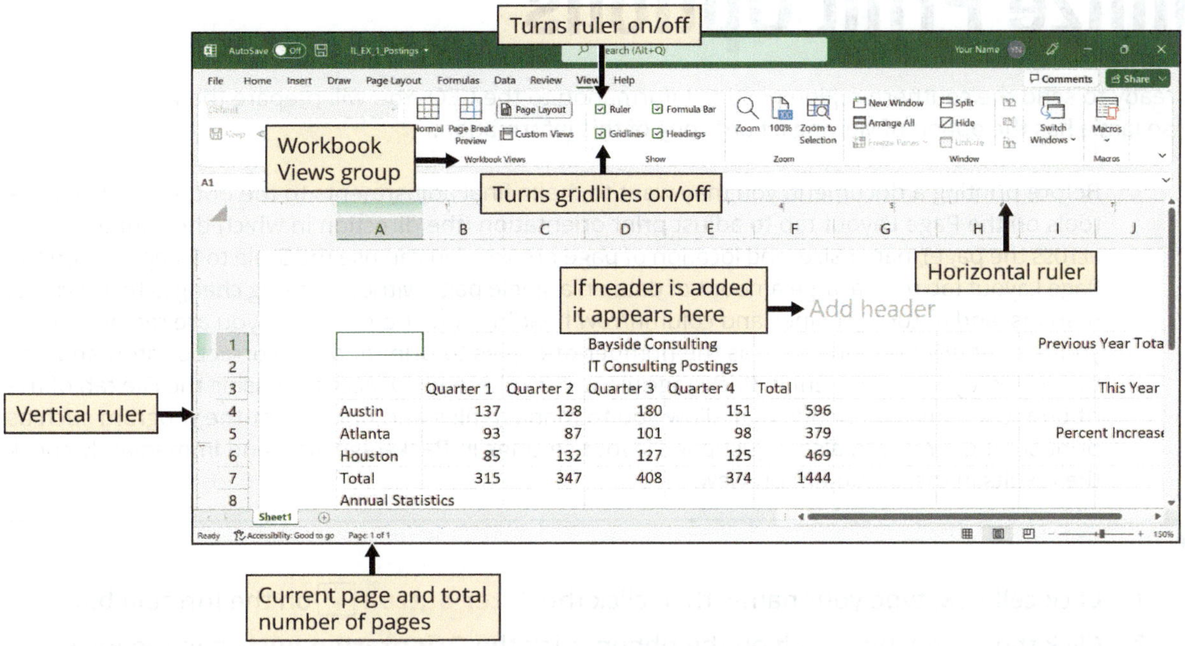


**Figure 1-17:** Page Break Preview

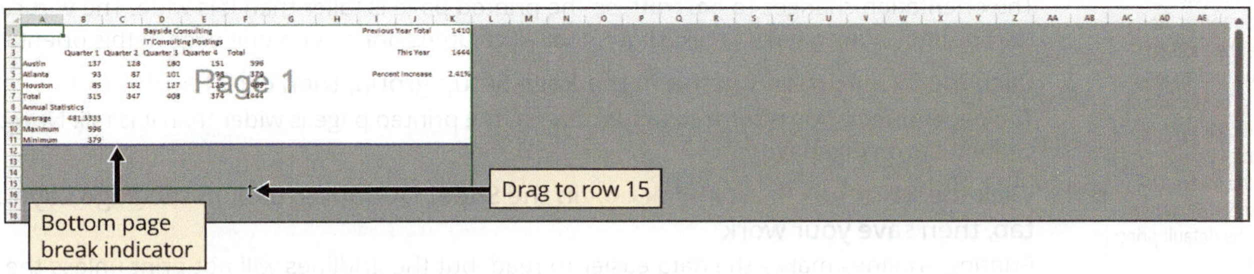


## Working with Sheet View options

If you are collaborating with others on a worksheet containing a large amount of data, you can use a Sheet View to view and work with only the columns and rows you need. A Sheet View allows you to work with the data you need without being interrupted by others changing their view of the worksheet. Any changes you make to the worksheet will automatically be saved with the workbook.

The New button is available in the Sheet View group of the View tab on the ribbon when a workbook is saved on OneDrive, as shown in **Figure 1-18**. To create a Sheet View, click the View tab, click the New button in the Sheet View group, then click Exit guide if necessary. Your new view is named Temporary View because it hasn't been saved yet. You can save a Sheet View by selecting the name Temporary View, entering a new name, then pressing ENTER. An eye symbol is displayed next to the worksheet tab name; hovering over this will display the name of the Sheet View. You can delete a Sheet View by selecting it in the Sheet View group, clicking the Options button in the Sheet View group, clicking Delete, then clicking Delete again to confirm the action.

**Figure 1-18:** Sheet View options

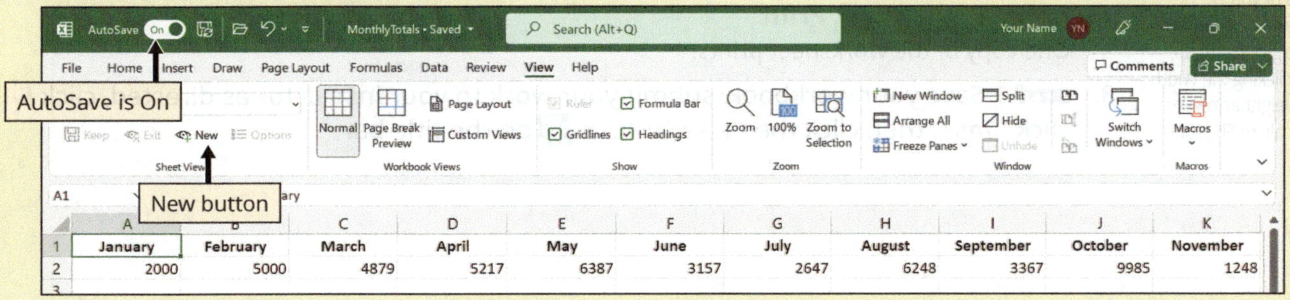

# Customize Print Options

**Case** You are ready to send the southern region posting information to the CEO. You will prepare the worksheet for printing so Jamia has the option of viewing a hard copy of this information.

**Objectives**
- Change the page orientation
- Change print options for gridlines
- Change the Page Setup options for a worksheet
- Print a worksheet

Before printing a document, you may want to make final adjustments to the output. You can use tools on the Page Layout tab to adjust print orientation (the direction in which the content prints across the page), paper size, and location of page breaks. You can use the Scale to Fit options on the Page Layout tab to fit a large amount of data on a single page without making changes to individual margins, and to turn gridlines and column/row headings on and off. When you are ready to print, you can set print options such as the number of copies to print and the correct printer, and you can preview your document in Backstage view. **Backstage view**, accessed using the File tab of the ribbon, contains commands that allow you to manage files and options for the program such as print settings. You can also adjust page layout settings in Backstage view and immediately check the results in the document preview.

## Steps

**Quick Tip**
If you choose to display the Quick Access Toolbar, you can add a Quick Print button to the toolbar by clicking the Customize Quick Access Toolbar button and choosing the Quick Print item from the menu. The worksheet will print using the default print settings.

**Quick Tip**
You can choose to print an entire workbook or a selected area of the worksheet by clicking the Print Active Sheets button in the Settings list, then clicking Print Entire Workbook or Print Selection.

**Quick Tip**
You can change the number of printed pages of your worksheet by clicking the Page Layout tab, then clicking the Width and Height arrows in the Scale to Fit group.

1. **Click cell A13, type your name, then click the Enter button on the formula bar**
2. **Click the Page Layout tab on the ribbon, click the Orientation button in the Page Setup group, then click Portrait**
   The orientation changes to **portrait**, so the printed page is taller than it is wide. The vertical dotted line, indicating a page break, shows that all columns don't fit on one page in this orientation.
3. **Click the Orientation button in the Page Setup group, then click Landscape**
   The paper orientation returns to **landscape**, so the printed page is wider than it is tall. Now all the content fits on one page.
4. **Click the Gridlines Print check box in the Sheet Options group on the Page Layout tab, then save your work**
   Printing gridlines makes the data easier to read, but the gridlines will not print unless the Gridlines Print check box contains a checkmark. You can also print row numbers and column letters by clicking the Headings Print box. If you don't want to print gridlines or headings, make sure these boxes do not contain checkmarks.
5. **Click the File tab, in Backstage view click Print on the navigation bar, then select an active printer if necessary**
   The Print screen in Backstage view displays a preview of your worksheet exactly as it will look when it is printed. To the left of the preview, you can also change several document settings and print options. Compare your screen to **Figure 1-19**. You can print from this view by clicking Print, or you can return to the worksheet without printing by clicking the Back button.
6. **Click the Page Setup link in the Settings list, click the Margins tab in the Page Setup dialog box, click the Horizontally check box in the Center on page section, click the Vertically check box in the Center on page section, then compare your screen to Figure 1-20**
   The printed worksheet will be centered on the page.
7. **Click OK, then click Print**
   One copy of the worksheet prints.
8. **sam Save your workbook, submit your work to your instructor as directed, click File, click Close, then click the Close button on the title bar**

**Figure 1-19:** Worksheet in Backstage view

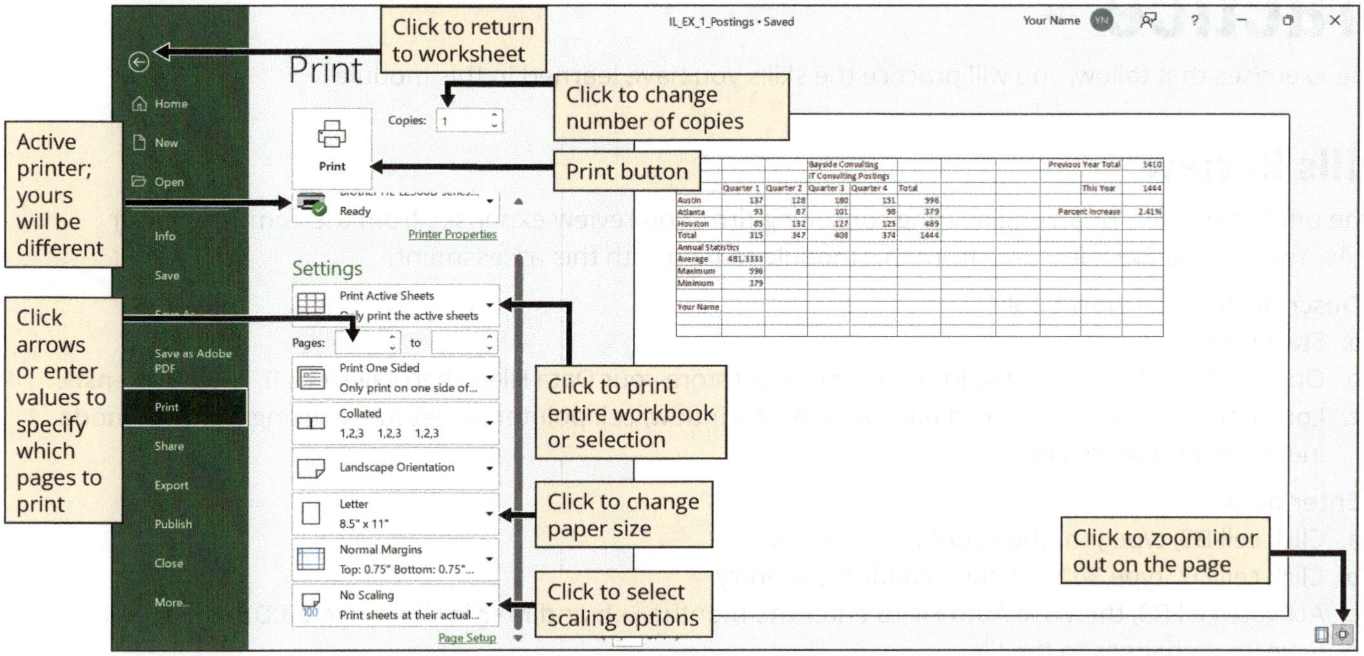


**Figure 1-20:** Page Setup dialog box

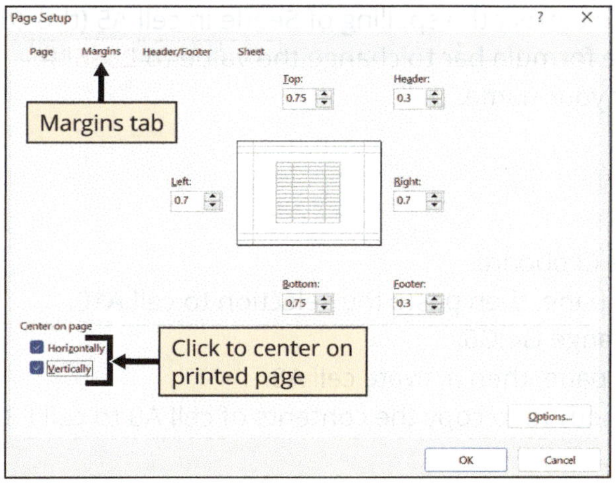


## Setting a print area

If you want to print a selected worksheet area repeatedly, it's best to define a **print area**, so that the Quick Print feature prints only that portion of the worksheet area. To define a print area, select the range you want to print on the worksheet, click the Page Layout tab on the ribbon, click the Print Area button in the Page Setup group, then click Set Print Area. A print area can consist of one contiguous range of cells or multiple ranges in different parts of a worksheet. To clear a print area, click the Page Layout tab on the ribbon, click the Print Area button in the Page Setup group, then click Clear Print Area.

## Scaling to fit

If you have a large amount of data that you want to fit onto a single sheet of paper, you can control how much of your work to print on a single sheet by clicking the No Scaling arrow in the Settings list in the Print screen in Backstage view, then clicking Fit Sheet on One Page, Fit All Columns on One Page, or Fit All Rows on One Page. Another method for fitting worksheet content onto one page is to click the Page Layout tab on the ribbon, then change the Width and Height settings in the Scale to Fit group to 1 page each. You can also click the Page Setup link in the Print tab in Backstage view, click the Page tab if necessary in the Page Setup dialog box, click the Fit to option button, then enter 1 in the page(s) wide by and tall fields.

# Practice

In the exercises that follow, you will practice the skills you have learned in this module.

## Skills Review

As the office manager for an engineering consulting firm, you review expenses from the company's four offices. You will use Excel features from this module to help with this assessment.

1. **Describe an Excel workbook.**
   a. Start Excel.
   b. Open IL_EX_1-2.xlsx from the location where you store your Data Files, then save it as **IL_EX_1_Expenses**.
   c. Locate the Name box, formula bar, worksheet window, cell pointer, sheet tab scrolling buttons, mode indicator, and Search box.
2. **Enter data.**
   a. Click cell B3, type **Jan**, then confirm the entry.
   b. Click cell D7, type **302497**, then confirm the entry.
   c. Activate cell B3, then use Auto Fill to enter the months **Feb** and **Mar** in the range C3:D3.
   d. Save your changes to the file.
3. **Edit data.**
   a. Use the F2 function key to correct the spelling of Seatle in cell A5 (the correct spelling is Seattle).
   b. Click cell C6, then use the formula bar to change the value to **288610**.
   c. Click cell A14, then enter your name.
   d. Save your changes.
4. **Copy and move cell data.**
   a. Select the range G4:G6.
   b. Copy the selection to the Clipboard.
   c. Open the Clipboard task pane, then paste the selection to cell A10.
   d. Delete the labels in the range G4:G6.
   e. Close the Clipboard task pane, then activate cell A8.
   f. Use the drag-and-drop method to copy the contents of cell A8 to cell E3. (**Hint**: Press and hold CTRL while dragging.)
   g. Save your work.
5. **Enter formulas.**
   a. Activate cell E4, then enter a formula that adds cells B4, C4, and D4.
   b. Activate cell E5, then enter a formula that adds cells B5, C5, and D5.
   c. Activate cell E6, then enter a formula that adds cells B6, C6, and D6.
   d. Activate cell E7, then enter a formula that adds cells B7, C7, and D7.
   e. Use AutoSum to enter the total expenses for the month of January in cell B8.
   f. Use AutoSum to enter the total expenses for the month of February in cell C8.
   g. Use AutoSum to enter the total expenses for the month of March in cell D8.
   h. Save your changes.
6. **Enter a formula with multiple operators.**
   a. Enter a formula in cell B10 that calculates the average office expenses for the month of January. Use a formula that contains cell references and not a function. (**Hint**: The formula is =(B4+B5+B6+B7)/4.)
   b. Enter a formula in cell C10 that calculates the average office expenses for the month of February. Use a formula that contains cell references and not a function.

c. Enter a formula in cell D10 that calculates the average office expenses for the month of March. Use a formula that contains cell references and not a function.
d. Review the use of the parentheses in the formulas.
e. Save your work.

7. **Insert a function.**
   a. Use the Insert Function button to enter a function in cell B11 that calculates the maximum office expense for January.
   b. Use the Insert Function button to enter a function in cell C11 that calculates the maximum office expense for February.
   c. Use the Insert Function button to enter a function in cell D11 that calculates the maximum office expense for March.
   d. In cell B12, enter a function to calculate the minimum office expenses for January.
   e. In cell C12, enter a function to calculate the minimum office expenses for February.
   f. In cell D12, enter a function to calculate the minimum office expenses for March.
   g. Save your work.

8. **Change worksheet views.**
   a. Click the View tab on the ribbon, then switch to Page Layout view.
   b. Verify that the Ruler and Gridlines check boxes contain checkmarks.
   c. Switch the view to Page Break Preview and adjust the page break so it comes at the bottom of row 16.
   d. Switch to Normal View, use a button in the Zoom group of the View tab to zoom the worksheet to 100%, then use the Zoom buttons on the status bar to zoom the worksheet back to 120%.
   e. Save your changes.

9. **Customize print options.**
   a. Use the Page Layout tab to change the orientation to Portrait.
   b. Turn on gridlines for printing using a check box in the Sheet Options group of the Page Layout tab.
   c. Preview the worksheet in Backstage view, then use the Page Setup dialog box to center the worksheet vertically and horizontally on the page. (**Hint**: The commands are located on the Margins tab.)
   d. Exit Backstage view. Compare your screen to **Figure 1-21**.
   e. Save your changes, submit your work to your instructor as directed, close the workbook, then exit Excel.

**Figure 1-21**

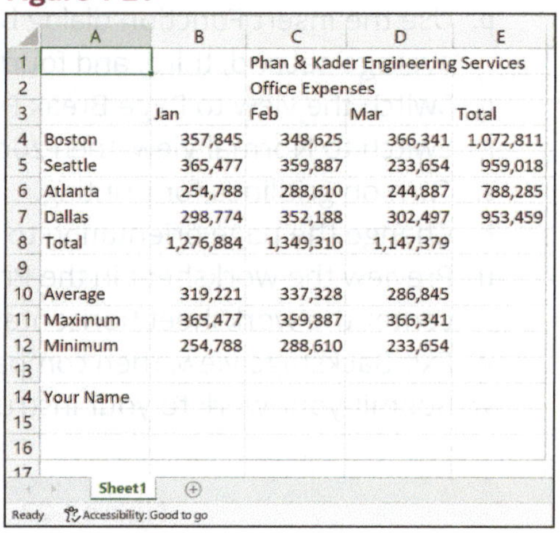


# Independent Challenge 1

The manager at Westbank Urgent Care has hired you to help analyze departmental insurance reimbursements. The clinic management would like to review the quarterly totals and averages as well as check what each quarter's revenue would be with a 20% reimbursement increase. The worksheet provided by management is missing some of the data required for a complete analysis.

a. Open IL_EX_1-3.xlsx from the location where you store your Data Files, then save it as **IL_EX_1_Reimbursements**.
b. Enter the data shown in **Table 1-4** in the range E4:E11.
c. Type your name in cell A17.
d. Move the label in cell F2 to cell A15.
e. Use the Clipboard to copy and paste the label in cell F3 to cell A12, then delete the label in cell F3.

# Independent Challenge 1 (Continued)

f. Use the formula bar to correct the spelling error in the label in cell A11. (**Hint**: The correct spelling is Immunizations.)

g. Edit cell A10 to change the cell entry from Pediatric to Pediatrics.

h. Type **Quarter 1** in cell B3, then use Auto Fill to enter Quarter 2, Quarter 3, and Quarter 4 in the range C3:E3.

i. Using AutoSum, enter a function in cell B12 that totals the reimbursements for Quarter 1.

j. Using AutoSum, enter a function in cell C12 that totals the second quarter reimbursements for all the departments.

k. Using AutoSum, enter a function in cell D12 that totals the third quarter reimbursements for all the departments.

l. Using AutoSum, enter a function in cell E12 that totals the fourth quarter reimbursements for all the departments.

m. Enter a formula in cell B14 to calculate a 20% increase in the first quarter reimbursement total in cell B12. (**Hint**: You need to add B12 to B12 multiplied by .20. Use parentheses if necessary to follow the order of operations.)

n. Enter formulas in cells C14, D14, and E14 that calculate a 20% increase in the second, third, and fourth quarters, respectively.

o. Enter a function, using the help of AutoComplete, in cell B15 that calculates the average first quarter reimbursement amount for the departments.

p. Use the Insert Function dialog box to enter functions in cells C15, D15, and E15 that calculate the average second, third, and fourth quarter reimbursements for the departments.

q. Switch the view to Page Break Preview and adjust the page break so it is the bottom of row 18.

r. Switch to Normal View, then zoom the worksheet to 130%.

s. Turn on gridlines for printing.

t. Change the page orientation to landscape.

u. Preview the worksheet in the Print pane of Backstage view, then use the Page Setup dialog box to center the worksheet horizontally and vertically on the page.

v. Exit Backstage view, then compare your screen to **Figure 1-22**.

w. Submit your work to your instructor as directed, close the workbook, then exit Excel.

**Table 1-4:**

| cell address | value |
|---|---|
| E4 | 57854 |
| E5 | 29874 |
| E6 | 36874 |
| E7 | 42157 |
| E8 | 41859 |
| E9 | 35241 |
| E10 | 37548 |
| E11 | 49847 |

**Figure 1-22**

| | A | B | C | D | E | F |
|---|---|---|---|---|---|---|
| 1 | | Westbank Urgent Care | | | | |
| 2 | | Insurance Reimbursements | | | | |
| 3 | | Quarter 1 | Quarter 2 | Quarter 3 | Quarter 4 | |
| 4 | Examinations | 57,562.00 | 58,745.00 | 69,847.00 | 57,854.00 | |
| 5 | Lab | 41,587.00 | 39,584.00 | 42,327.00 | 29,874.00 | |
| 6 | Cardiac | 42,987.00 | 45,147.00 | 45,877.00 | 36,874.00 | |
| 7 | Imaging | 40,257.00 | 44,517.00 | 45,874.00 | 42,157.00 | |
| 8 | Pharmacy | 48,795.00 | 24,789.00 | 27,457.00 | 41,859.00 | |
| 9 | Orthopedics | 33,257.00 | 48,747.00 | 32,874.00 | 35,241.00 | |
| 10 | Pediatrics | 29,847.00 | 31,487.00 | 29,847.00 | 37,548.00 | |
| 11 | Immunizations | 68,457.00 | 67,201.00 | 32,147.00 | 49,847.00 | |
| 12 | Total | 362,749.00 | 360,217.00 | 326,250.00 | 331,254.00 | |
| 13 | | | | | | |
| 14 | 20% increase | 435,298.80 | 432,260.40 | 391,500.00 | 397,504.80 | |
| 15 | Average | 45,343.63 | 45,027.13 | 40,781.25 | 41,406.75 | |
| 16 | | | | | | |
| 17 | Your Name | | | | | |
| 18 | | | | | | |
| 19 | | | | | | |

Sheet1

## Independent Challenge 2

As the assistant to the Provost at North County College, it is your responsibility to review the budgets of the academic divisions to plan for the upcoming academic year. You've decided to use Excel formulas and functions to help with this analysis.

a. Open IL_EX_1-4.xlsx from the location where you store your Data Files, then save it as **IL_EX_1_Budgets**.

b. Move the labels in the range A6:A10 to the range A5:A9.

c. Enter **Total** in cell A10, then use AutoSum to calculate the total Year 1 budgeted amounts for all divisions in cell B10.

d. Use AutoSum to calculate the total Year 2 expenses in cell C10.

e. Enter **Average** in cell A11, then use the AutoSum arrow to enter a function in cell B11 that calculates the average Year 1 budgeted amount for all divisions. (**Hint**: Make sure you include only the division data and not the total.)

f. Enter a function in cell C11 that calculates the average Year 2 budgeted amount for all divisions.

g. Enter a formula in cell D2 that calculates the percentage increase in total expenses from Year 1 to Year 2. (**Hint**: The Year 1 total is in cell B10 and the Year 2 total is in cell C10.) Display the value in cell D2 as a percentage with two decimal places.

h. Using cell references, enter a formula in cell G2 that calculates the Projected Year 3 total, using the percent increase shown in cell D2 over the Year 2 total shown in cell C10. (**Hint**: Multiply the percentage in cell D2 by the Year 2 total expenses in cell C10, then add that amount to the Year 2 total shown in cell C10.)

i. Using cell references, enter a formula in cell J2 that calculates the Projected Year 3 average, using the percent increase shown in cell D2 over the Year 2 average shown in cell C11. (**Hint**: Multiply the percentage in cell D2 by the Year 2 average in cell C11, then add that amount to the Year 2 average shown in cell C11.)

j. Change the page orientation to landscape, then turn on gridlines for printing.

k. Enter your name in cell A13.

l. Preview the worksheet in Backstage view, exit Backstage view, then compare your screen to **Figure 1-23**.

m. Save your work, then submit the worksheet to your instructor as directed.

n. Close the workbook and exit Excel.

**Figure 1-23**

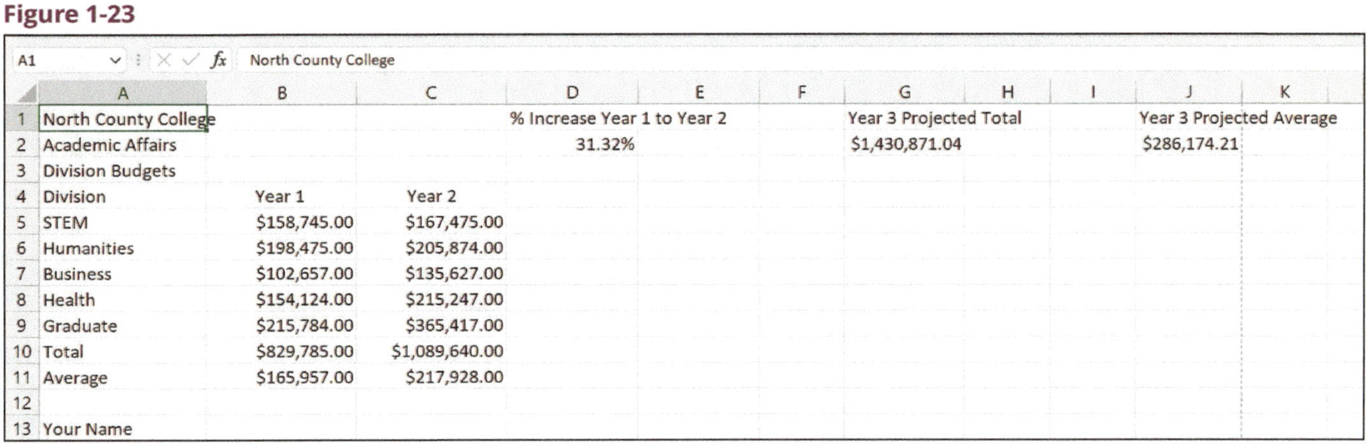
A1 fx North County College

| | A | B | C | D | E | F | G | H | I | J | K |
|---|---|---|---|---|---|---|---|---|---|---|---|
| 1 | North County College | | | % Increase Year 1 to Year 2 | | | Year 3 Projected Total | | | Year 3 Projected Average | |
| 2 | Academic Affairs | | | 31.32% | | | $1,430,871.04 | | | $286,174.21 | |
| 3 | Division Budgets | | | | | | | | | | |
| 4 | Division | Year 1 | Year 2 | | | | | | | | |
| 5 | STEM | $158,745.00 | $167,475.00 | | | | | | | | |
| 6 | Humanities | $198,475.00 | $205,874.00 | | | | | | | | |
| 7 | Business | $102,657.00 | $135,627.00 | | | | | | | | |
| 8 | Health | $154,124.00 | $215,247.00 | | | | | | | | |
| 9 | Graduate | $215,784.00 | $365,417.00 | | | | | | | | |
| 10 | Total | $829,785.00 | $1,089,640.00 | | | | | | | | |
| 11 | Average | $165,957.00 | $217,928.00 | | | | | | | | |
| 12 | | | | | | | | | | | |
| 13 | Your Name | | | | | | | | | | |

# Visual Workshop

Open IL_EX_1-5.xlsx from the location where you store your Data Files, then save it as **IL_EX_1_Sales**. Modify the content and view using the skills you learned in this module so that your worksheet and zoom level match **Figure 1-24**. Use functions in cells B8:B11 to calculate the values described in cells A8:A11. Enter formulas in cells C4:C8 to calculate the commissions. (**Hint**: Multiply each revenue in column B by the commission percentage in cell E2.) Enter your name in cell A14. Submit your work to your instructor as directed.

**Figure 1-24**

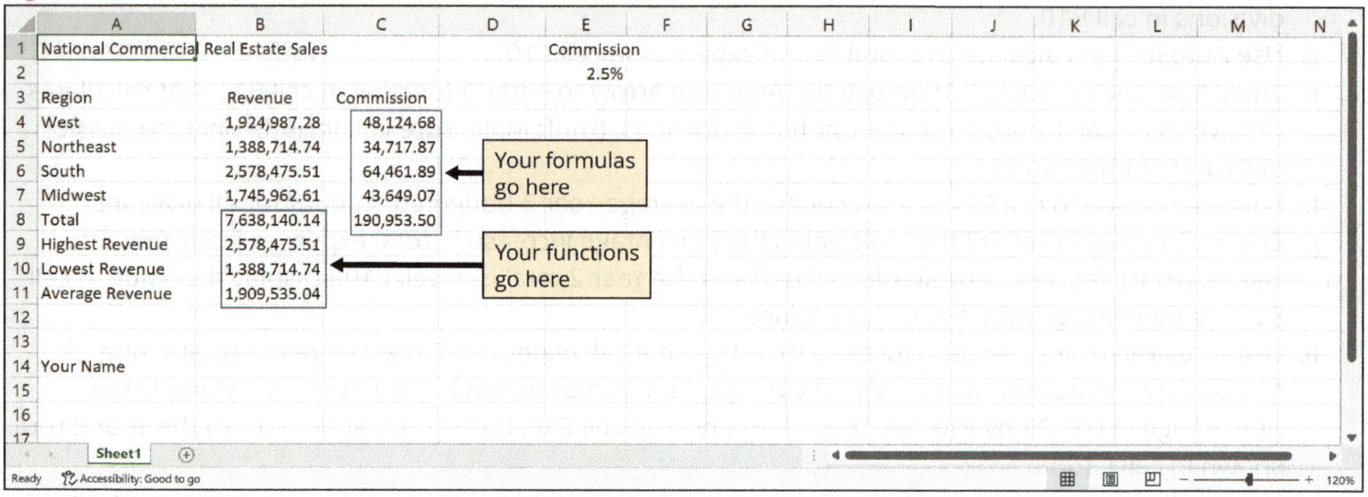

# Formatting a Worksheet

## Case

Luis Herrero, the manager of Bayside Consulting's Houston office, has gathered data on technology job postings for the first quarter of the year. Luis submitted this data to you in a worksheet. To make it easier to view and analyze the position postings, you will format the worksheet.

## Module Objectives

After completing this module, you will be able to:

- Format values
- Change font attributes
- Modify font styles and alignment
- Adjust column width and row height
- Insert and delete rows and columns
- Modify data formatting and documentation
- Apply conditional formatting
- Modify worksheet tabs
- Check spelling and find text

## Files You Will Need

IL_EX_2-1.xlsx
IL_EX_2-2.xlsx
IL_EX_2-3.xlsx
IL_EX_2-4.xlsx
IL_EX_2-5.xlsx

# Format Values

**Case** Luis has provided you with a worksheet that details first-quarter postings. You decide to format several cells to reflect the type of values they contain, such as currency, percentages, and dates, so the worksheet is easier to understand.

**Objectives**
- Format a number
- Increase/decrease decimal places
- Format a date

When you **format** a cell, you enhance the appearance of information by changing its font, size, color, or alignment. Formatting changes only the appearance of a value or label; it does not alter the actual data in any way. To format a cell or range, first, you select it, then you apply the formatting using the ribbon, Mini toolbar, or a keyboard shortcut. You can apply formatting before or after you enter data in a cell or range.

## Steps

**Quick Tip**
You can format values with a custom number format using format symbols. Right-click a cell range, click Format Cells on the shortcut menu, in the Category box of the Format Cells dialog box, click Custom, select the number format you want to use in the Type list, make changes to the format symbols in the Type box, then click OK.

**Quick Tip**
You can also apply formatting to a range of cells by clicking the Number Format arrow, then choosing the desired number format.

**Quick Tip**
If you want numeric values to be treated as text, click Text in the Category list. Cells formatted in this way are treated as text even if they contain numeric data. You can also precede a number with an apostrophe to treat the value as text.

1. **sam Start Excel, open IL_EX_2-1.xlsx from the location where you store your Data Files, then save it as IL_EX_2_Openings**
   This worksheet is difficult to interpret because all the information is crowded and looks the same. In some columns, the contents appear cut off because there is too much data to fit given the current column width. You decide not to widen the columns yet, because the other changes you plan to make might affect column width and row height.
2. **Select the range H3:H15, then click the Accounting Number Format button [$] in the Number group on the Home tab on the ribbon**
   A **number format** is applied to values to express numeric concepts, such as currency, date, and percentage. The default Accounting number format adds dollar signs and two decimal places to the expense data, as shown in **Figure 2-1**.
3. **Select the range I3:I15, then click the Comma Style button [,] in the Number group**
   The values in column I display the Comma Style format, which does not include a dollar sign but can be useful for some types of accounting data.
4. **Select cell B17, click the Percent Style button [%] in the number group, then click the Increase Decimal button in the Number group**
   The bonus rate is now formatted with a percent sign (%) and one decimal place. Each time you click the Increase Decimal button, you add one decimal place; clicking the button twice would add two decimal places.
5. **Click the Decrease Decimal button in the Number group**
   The decimal place is removed from the bonus value.
6. **Select the range C3:C15, then click the dialog box launcher in the Number group**
   The Format Cells dialog box opens.
7. **Click the Number tab if necessary, click Date in the Category list box, select the 3/14 format in the Type list box, as shown in Figure 2-2, then click OK**
   The dates in column C appear in the 3/14 format.
8. **Select the range H3:I15, right-click the range, click Format Cells on the shortcut menu, in the Category list of the Number tab in the Format Cells dialog box click Currency, in the Decimal places box type 2 if necessary, then click OK**
   This number format looks similar to the Accounting format but aligns currency symbols and decimal points slightly differently. Compare your worksheet to **Figure 2-3**.
9. **Click the Decrease Decimal button in the Number group twice, press CTRL+HOME, then save your work**
   The cell values in this range now use a custom format that doesn't display decimal places. This format is applied to all cells in the selected range.

**Figure 2-1:** Accounting number format applied to range

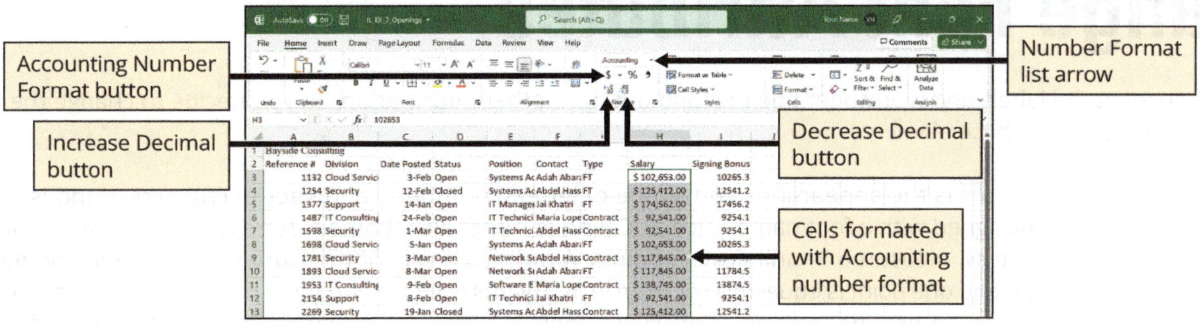


**Figure 2-2:** Format Cells dialog box

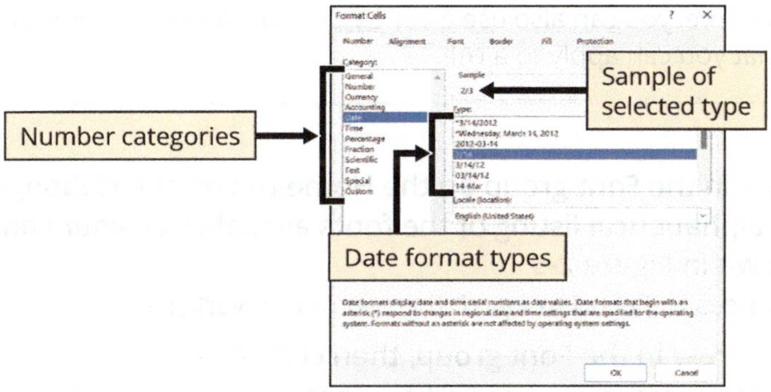


**Figure 2-3:** Worksheet with formatted values

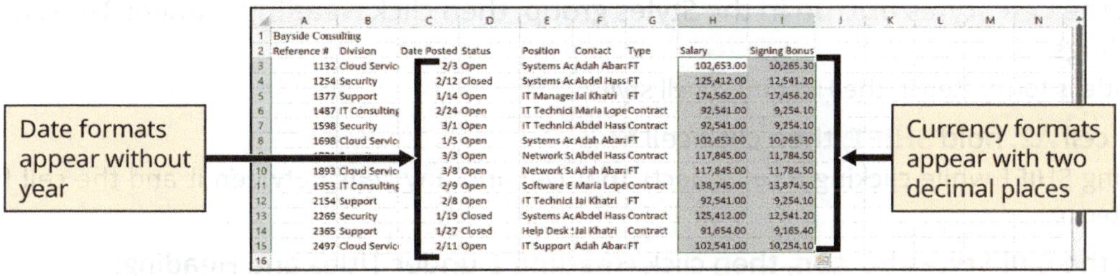


## Working with online pictures, other images, and symbols

You can illustrate your worksheets using online pictures and other images. To add a picture to a worksheet, click the Pictures button in the Illustrations group on the Insert tab on the ribbon, then choose the location of the picture. Clicking Online Pictures opens the Online Pictures dialog box where you can search for online pictures using the Bing search engine, as shown in **Figure 2-4**. To search, type one or more keywords in the search box, then press ENTER. When you double-click an image in the Search Results window, the image is inserted at the location of the active cell. Clicking an image selects it and adds resizing handles. To resize an image proportionally, drag any corner sizing handle. If you drag an edge sizing handle, the image will be resized non-proportionally. You can add alternative text to an image by right-clicking it, clicking Edit Alt Text on the shortcut menu, then entering the text in the Alt Text pane. To move an image, point inside the image until the pointer changes to the Move pointer, then drag it to a new location. To delete a picture, select it, then press DEL. To work with an image, it must be selected. You can select an image, or any object, by clicking it. To work with multiple images at once, hold CTRL while clicking each image. You can insert a symbol in a worksheet by clicking the Insert tab, clicking the Symbols button in the Symbols group, Clicking Symbol, clicking a symbol from the Symbols tab in the Symbol dialog box, clicking Insert, then clicking Close to close the Symbol dialog box.

**Figure 2-4:** Results of Online Picture search

# Change Font Attributes

**Case** You want the labels and worksheet title to stand out from other information, so you decide to change the font and font size of these elements.

**Objectives**
- Change a font
- Apply a cell style

A **font** is the appearance and shape of letters, numbers, and special characters and is usually designed with a font name, such as Calibri or Times New Roman. The **font size** is the size of characters, measured in units called points. A **point** is a unit of measure used for font size and row height; one point is equal to 1/72 of an inch. The default font and font size in Excel is 11-point Calibri. **Table 2-1** provides examples of several fonts in different font sizes. You can change the font and font size of any cell or range using the Font and Font Size arrows. The Font and Font Size arrows are located on the Home tab on the ribbon and on the Mini toolbar, which opens when you right-click a cell or range. To save time, you can also use a **cell style**, a predesigned combination of font, font size, and font color that you can apply to a cell.

## Steps

**Quick Tip**
You can also use the Increase Font Size button A^ to increase the font size by one point or the Decrease Font Size button A˅ to decrease it by one point.

**Quick Tip**
Holding CTRL while selecting cells allows you to select multiple nonadjacent cells.

1. **Click the Font arrow in the Font group on the Home tab on the ribbon, scroll down in the Font list for an alphabetical listing of the fonts available on your computer, then click Calibri, as shown in Figure 2-5**
   The font in cell A1 changes to Calibri to match the rest of the worksheet.
2. **Click the Font Size arrow in the Font group, then click 20**
   The worksheet title is formatted in 20-point Calibri, and the Font and Font Size boxes on the Home tab display the new font and font size information.
3. **Click the Cell Styles button in the Styles group, then click Heading 1 under Titles and Headings**
   The title is formatted in the Heading 1 cell style.
4. **Click cell A2, hold SHIFT, then click cell I2**
   Holding SHIFT while clicking a cell selects that cell and any cells between it and the cell first selected.
5. **Click the Cell Styles button, then click Heading 2 under Titles and Headings**
   Notice that some of the column labels are now too wide to appear fully in the column. Excel does not automatically adjust column widths to accommodate cell formatting; these column widths must be adjusted manually. You'll learn to do this in a later lesson.
6. **Click cell A17, click the Cell Styles button, then click Heading 4 under Titles and Headings**
   The worksheet's title and labels are formatted in different font sizes using consistent styles.
7. **Compare your worksheet to Figure 2-6, then save your work**

**Table 2-1:** Examples of fonts and font sizes

| font name | 12 point | 24 point |
|---|---|---|
| Calibri | Excel | Excel |
| Playbill | Excel | Excel |
| Comic Sans MS | Excel | Excel |
| Times New Roman | Excel | Excel |

**Figure 2-5:** Font list

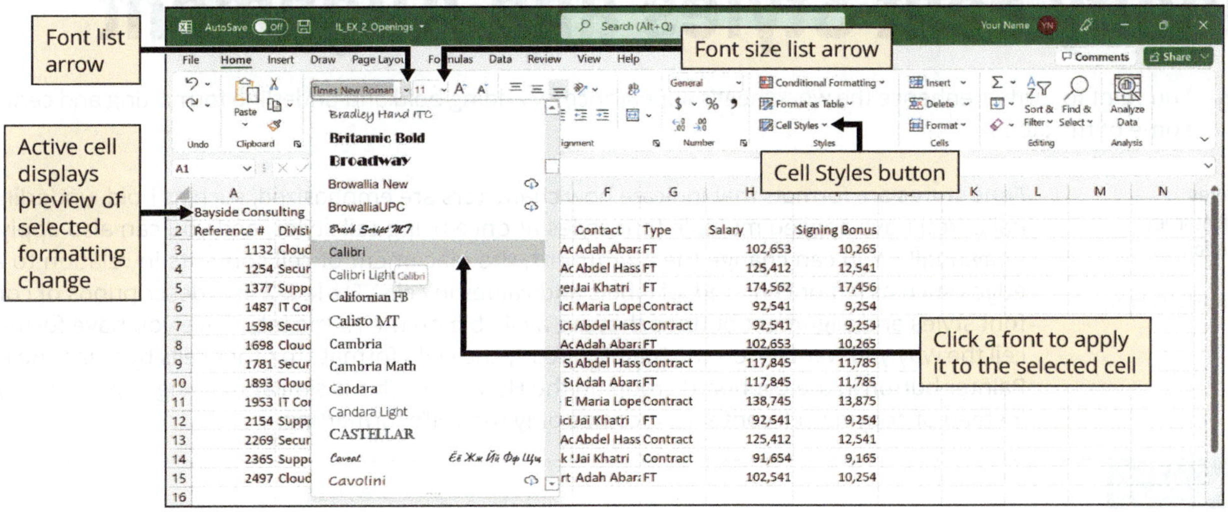


**Figure 2-6:** Worksheet with formatted headings and column labels

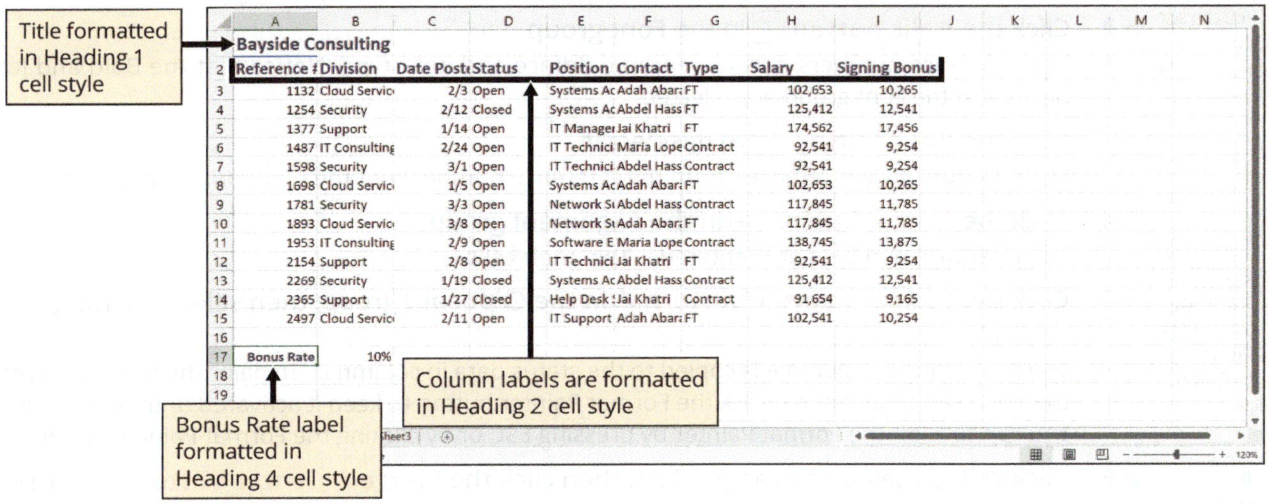


## Modify, create, and merge styles

You can modify any style in the Cell Styles gallery. In the Cell Styles gallery, right-click the cell style that you want to modify, on the shortcut menu shown in **Figure 2-7**, click Modify, select the style options from the Style includes list in the Style dialog box, click the Format button to choose new customized formatting, then click OK twice. To create a new cell style, click New Cell Style at the bottom of the Cell Styles gallery, enter a name in the Style name box, select style options from the Style includes list, click the Format button to choose customized formatting for your style, then click OK twice. You can merge styles from a different workbook by opening the workbook that contains the cell styles that you want to copy, clicking Merge Styles at the bottom of the Cell Styles gallery, clicking the workbook in the Merge styles from list, then clicking OK. If styles in the workbooks have the same name, you will be asked if you want to merge those styles.

**Figure 2-7:** Shortcut menu in Cell Styles gallery

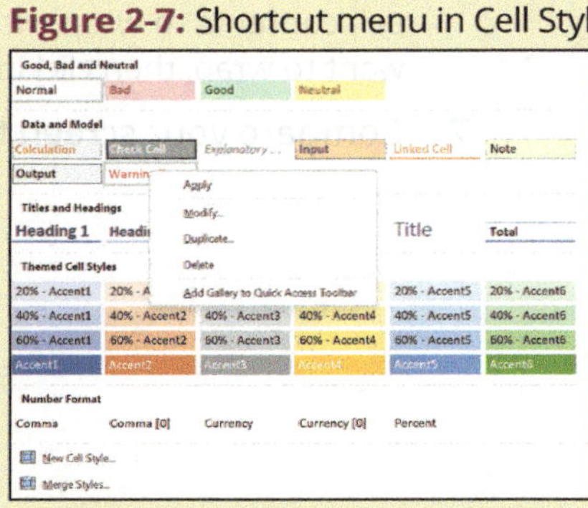

# Modify Font Styles and Alignment

**Case** You want to further enhance the worksheet's appearance by adding bold and underline formatting and centering some of the labels.

**Objectives**
- Apply font styles
- Use the Format Painter
- Change cell alignment

**Font styles** are formats that indicate how characters are emphasized, such as bold, underline, and italic. You have applied multiple font styles at once using cell styles, and you can also apply them individually. You can change the **alignment**, the placement of cell contents in relation to a cell's edges such as left or centered, of labels and values in cells. **Table 2-2** lists descriptions of common font styles and alignment buttons that are available on the Home tab. Once you have formatted a cell the way you want it, you can "paint" or copy the cell's formats to other cells by using the Format Painter button in the Clipboard group on the Home tab. This is similar to using copy and paste, but instead of copying cell contents, it copies only the cell's formatting.

## Steps

**Quick Tip**
You can use the Underline button [U] to underline cell contents. You can also use the Mini toolbar to format text by right-clicking selected cells.

**Quick Tip**
To format a selected cell or range using keyboard shortcuts, you can press CTRL+B to bold, CTRL+I to italicize, and CTRL+U to underline.

**Quick Tip**
To clear all formatting from a selected range, click the Clear button in the Editing group on the Home tab, then click Clear Formats.

1. **Select the range A3:A15, then click the Bold button [B] in the Font group on the Home tab on the ribbon**
   The reference numbers in column A appear in bold.
2. **Click the Italic button [I] in the Font group**
   The reference numbers now appear in boldface and italic type. Notice that the Bold and Italic buttons in the Font group are selected.
3. **Click the Italic button [I] to deselect it**
   The italic font style is removed from the reference numbers but the bold font style remains.
4. **Click the Center button in the Alignment group**
   The reference numbers are centered within their cells.
5. **Click the Format Painter button in the Clipboard group, then select the range D3:D15**
   The formatting in column A is copied to the status data in column D. To paint the formats to more than one selection, double-click the Format Painter button to keep it activated until you turn it off. You can turn off the Format Painter by pressing ESC or by clicking the Format Painter button.
6. **Click cell A1, select the range A1:I1, then click the Merge & Center button in the Alignment group**
   The Merge & Center button creates one cell out of the nine cells across the row, then centers the text in that newly created, merged cell. The title "Bayside Consulting" is centered across the nine columns you selected. To split a merged cell into its original components, select the merged cell, then click the Merge & Center button to deselect it. Occasionally, you may find that you want cell contents to wrap within a cell. You can do this by selecting the cells containing the text you want to wrap, then clicking the Wrap Text button in the Alignment group on the Home tab.
7. **Compare your screen to Figure 2-8, then save your work**

**Figure 2-8:** Worksheet with font styles and alignment applied

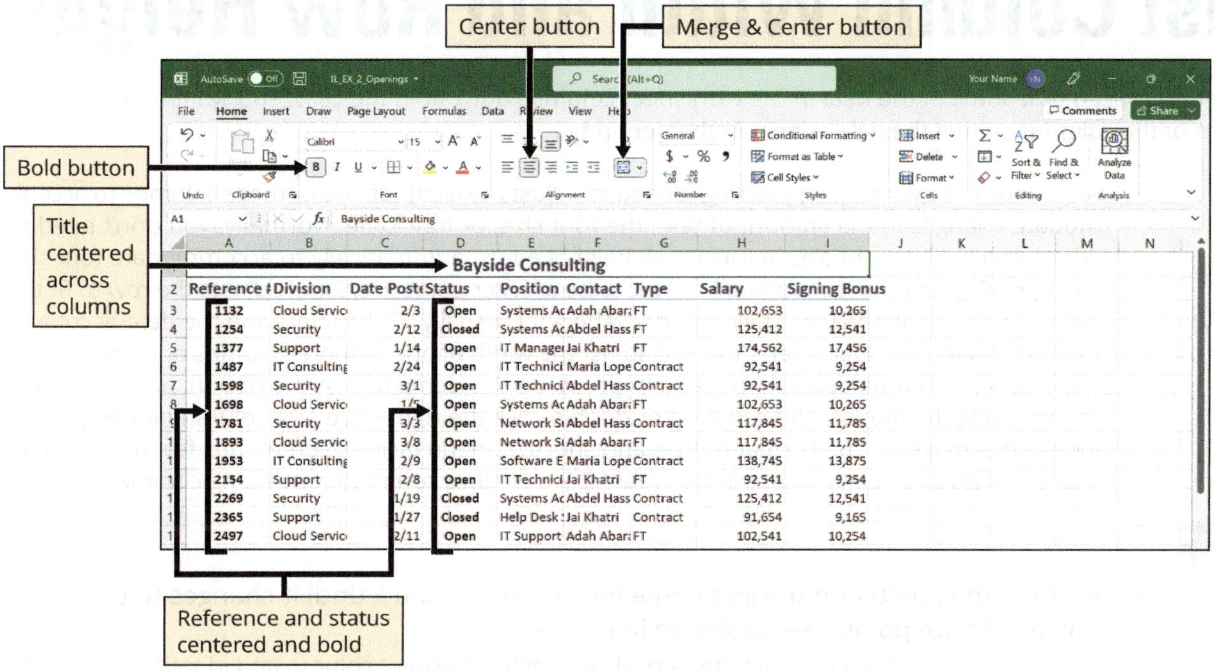


**Table 2-2:** Common font style and alignment buttons

| button | button name | description |
|---|---|---|
| B | Bold | Bolds cell content |
| I | Italic | Italicizes cell content |
| U | Underline | Underlines cell content |
| | Merge & Center | Centers content across columns; also merges two or more selected, adjacent cells into one cell; also unmerges previously merged cells |
| | Align Left | Aligns content at the left edge of the cell |
| | Center Align | Centers content horizontally within the cell |
| | Align Right | Aligns content at the right edge of the cell |
| ab | Wrap Text | Wraps long text into multiple lines to fit within a column |
| | Top Align | Aligns content at the top of a cell |
| | Bottom Align | Aligns content at the bottom of a cell |
| | Middle Align | Aligns content in the middle of a cell |

**Rotating and indenting cell entries**

In addition to applying fonts and font styles, you can rotate or indent data within a cell. To rotate text within a cell, click the Home tab on the ribbon, select the cells you want to modify, then click the dialog box launcher in the Alignment group to open the Alignment tab of the Format Cells dialog box. Click a position in the Orientation box or type a number in the Degrees box to rotate text from its default horizontal orientation, then click OK. You can indent cell contents by clicking the Increase Indent button in the Alignment group, which moves cell contents to the right, or the Decrease Indent button, which moves cell contents to the left.

# Adjust Column Width and Row Height

**Case** You have noticed that some of the data in the worksheet columns don't fit in the cells. You want to adjust the widths of the columns so that the data appear in their entirety.

**Objectives**
- Change a column width by dragging
- Resize a column with AutoFit
- Change the width of multiple columns

As you format a worksheet, you might need to adjust the width of one or more columns to accommodate changes in the amount of text, the font size, or font style. Normally, you don't need to adjust row height manually, because row heights adjust automatically to accommodate font size changes. If you format something in a row to be a larger point size, Excel adjusts the row to fit the largest point size in the row. The default row height is usually 12.75 points and the default column width is usually 8.43 characters. You can adjust the width of one or more columns or rows by using the mouse, the Format button in the Cells group on the Home tab on the ribbon, or the shortcut menu. Using the mouse, you can drag or double-click the right edge of a column heading or the lower edge of a row. The Format button and shortcut menu include commands for making more precise width and height adjustments. **Table 2-3** describes common formatting commands.

## Steps

1. **Position the pointer on the line between columns E and F until it changes to the Column Resize pointer ✛ as shown in Figure 2-9**

   A **column heading** is a box that appears above each worksheet column and identifies it by a letter. You positioned the mouse pointer here because to adjust column width using the mouse, you need to position the pointer on the right edge of the column heading for the column you want to adjust.

2. **Double-click**

   Column E automatically widens to fit the widest entry. Double-clicking the right edge of a column heading activates **AutoFit**. This feature adjusts column width or row height to accommodate its widest or tallest entry.

3. **Position the mouse pointer on the line between the column B and column C headings until it changes to the Column Resize pointer ✛**

4. **Click and drag the Column Resize pointer ✛ to the right slightly so there's room to fully display the names in the Division column (approximately 12.09 characters or 140 pixels)**

   Due to differences in Windows resolution and scaling from device to device, your measurements may vary slightly. As you change the column width, a ScreenTip opens displaying the column width.

5. **Use AutoFit to resize columns A, C, and F**

6. **Position the mouse pointer in the column heading area for column H until it changes to the Column Select pointer ⬇, then drag to select columns H and I**

7. **Click the Format button in the Cells group on the Home tab on the ribbon, then click Column Width**

   The Column Width dialog box opens. Column width measurement is based on the number of characters that will fit in the column when formatted in the Normal font and font size.

8. **Type 9 in the Column width box, then click OK**

   The widths of columns H and I change to reflect the new setting. You will format the label for column I for a better fit.

9. **Click cell I2, click the Wrap Text button in the Alignment group, click cell A1, compare your screen to Figure 2-10, then save your work**

   The height of row 2 automatically adjusts to accommodate the required size for the wrapped text.

**Trouble**
If you have difficulty dragging to the specified width, double-click the right edge of column B.

**Quick Tip**
If "#######" appears after you adjust a column of values, the column is too narrow to display the values completely; increase the column width until the values appear.

**Trouble**
In the last lesson of this module, you will fix spelling errors that may be now visible on the worksheet.

**Figure 2-9:** Preparing to change the column width

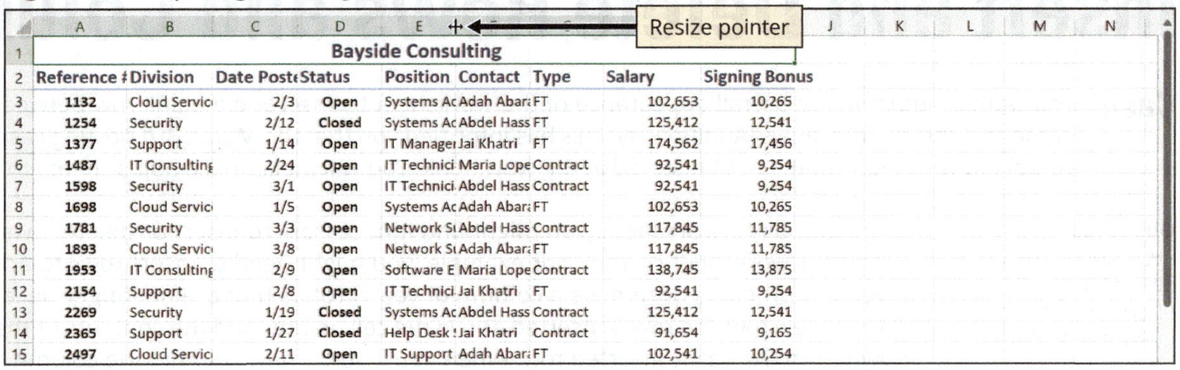


| | A | B | C | D | E | F | G | H | I |
|---|---|---|---|---|---|---|---|---|---|
| 1 | Bayside Consulting | | | | | | | | |
| 2 | Reference # | Division | Date Poste | Status | Position | Contact | Type | Salary | Signing Bonus |
| 3 | 1132 | Cloud Servic | 2/3 | Open | Systems Ac | Adah Abar | FT | 102,653 | 10,265 |
| 4 | 1254 | Security | 2/12 | Closed | Systems Ac | Abdel Hass | FT | 125,412 | 12,541 |
| 5 | 1377 | Support | 1/14 | Open | IT Manager | Jai Khatri | FT | 174,562 | 17,456 |
| 6 | 1487 | IT Consulting | 2/24 | Open | IT Technici | Maria Lope | Contract | 92,541 | 9,254 |
| 7 | 1598 | Security | 3/1 | Open | IT Technici | Abdel Hass | Contract | 92,541 | 9,254 |
| 8 | 1698 | Cloud Servic | 1/5 | Open | Systems Ac | Adah Abar | FT | 102,653 | 10,265 |
| 9 | 1781 | Security | 3/3 | Open | Network Su | Abdel Hass | Contract | 117,845 | 11,785 |
| 10 | 1893 | Cloud Servic | 3/8 | Open | Network Su | Adah Abar | FT | 117,845 | 11,785 |
| 11 | 1953 | IT Consulting | 2/9 | Open | Software E | Maria Lope | Contract | 138,745 | 13,875 |
| 12 | 2154 | Support | 2/8 | Open | IT Technici | Jai Khatri | FT | 92,541 | 9,254 |
| 13 | 2269 | Security | 1/19 | Closed | Systems Ac | Abdel Hass | Contract | 125,412 | 12,541 |
| 14 | 2365 | Support | 1/27 | Closed | Help Desk S | Jai Khatri | Contract | 91,654 | 9,165 |
| 15 | 2497 | Cloud Servic | 2/11 | Open | IT Support | Adah Abar | FT | 102,541 | 10,254 |

**Figure 2-10:** Worksheet with column widths and row height adjusted

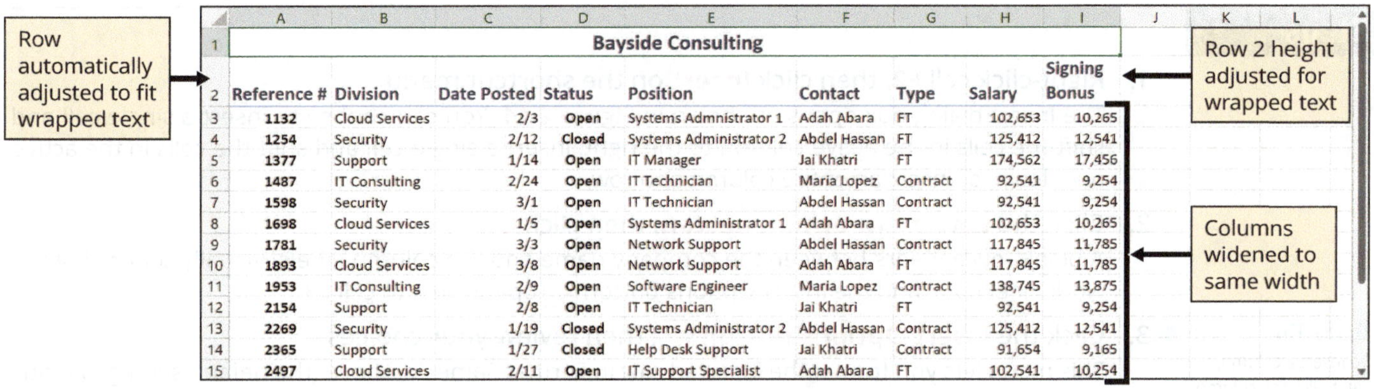


| | A | B | C | D | E | F | G | H | I |
|---|---|---|---|---|---|---|---|---|---|
| 1 | Bayside Consulting | | | | | | | | |
| 2 | Reference # | Division | Date Posted | Status | Position | Contact | Type | Salary | Signing Bonus |
| 3 | 1132 | Cloud Services | 2/3 | Open | Systems Admnistrator 1 | Adah Abara | FT | 102,653 | 10,265 |
| 4 | 1254 | Security | 2/12 | Closed | Systems Administrator 2 | Abdel Hassan | FT | 125,412 | 12,541 |
| 5 | 1377 | Support | 1/14 | Open | IT Manager | Jai Khatri | FT | 174,562 | 17,456 |
| 6 | 1487 | IT Consulting | 2/24 | Open | IT Technician | Maria Lopez | Contract | 92,541 | 9,254 |
| 7 | 1598 | Security | 3/1 | Open | IT Technician | Abdel Hassan | Contract | 92,541 | 9,254 |
| 8 | 1698 | Cloud Services | 1/5 | Open | Systems Administrator 1 | Adah Abara | FT | 102,653 | 10,265 |
| 9 | 1781 | Security | 3/3 | Open | Network Support | Abdel Hassan | Contract | 117,845 | 11,785 |
| 10 | 1893 | Cloud Services | 3/8 | Open | Network Support | Adah Abara | FT | 117,845 | 11,785 |
| 11 | 1953 | IT Consulting | 2/9 | Open | Software Engineer | Maria Lopez | Contract | 138,745 | 13,875 |
| 12 | 2154 | Support | 2/8 | Open | IT Technician | Jai Khatri | FT | 92,541 | 9,254 |
| 13 | 2269 | Security | 1/19 | Closed | Systems Administrator 2 | Abdel Hassan | Contract | 125,412 | 12,541 |
| 14 | 2365 | Support | 1/27 | Closed | Help Desk Support | Jai Khatri | Contract | 91,654 | 9,165 |
| 15 | 2497 | Cloud Services | 2/11 | Open | IT Support Specialist | Adah Abara | FT | 102,541 | 10,254 |

**Table 2-3:** Common formatting commands

| command | description | available using |
|---|---|---|
| Column Width | Sets the width to a specific number of characters | Format button; shortcut menu |
| Row Height | Sets the height to a specific number of points | Format button; shortcut menu |
| AutoFit Column Width | Fits to the widest entry in a column | Format button; mouse |
| AutoFit Row Height | Fits to the highest entry in a row | Format button; mouse |
| Hide & Unhide | Hides or displays selected column(s) or row(s) | Format button; shortcut menu |
| Default Width | Resets column to worksheet's default column width | Format button |

### Changing row height

You have just as many options for changing row height as you do column width. The row height must exceed the size of the font you are using to make a change. Using the mouse, you can place the ✢ pointer on the line dividing a row heading from the heading below it, and then drag to the desired height; double-clicking the line AutoFits the row height where necessary. You can also select one or more rows, right-click the selection, then use the Row Height command on the shortcut menu. Row height can also be changed by clicking the Format button on the Home tab on the ribbon, then clicking the Row Height or AutoFit Row Height command.

# Insert and Delete Rows and Columns

**Case** You want to improve the overall appearance of the worksheet by inserting a blank row between the company name and the column labels. Additionally, Luis has informed you that the March 3rd posting is an error and that contact information should not be stored in the workbook. You will make these adjustments to the worksheet.

**Objectives**
- Use the Insert dialog box to insert a row
- Modify columns and rows using heading buttons

As you modify a worksheet, you might find it necessary to insert or delete rows and columns to keep your worksheet current. For example, you might need to insert rows to accommodate new inventory products or remove a column of yearly totals that are no longer necessary. When you insert a new row, the row is inserted above the cell pointer and the contents of the worksheet shift down from the newly inserted row. When you insert a new column, the column is inserted to the left of the cell pointer, and the contents of the worksheet shift to the right of the new column. To insert multiple rows, select the same number of row headings as you want to insert before using the Insert command.

## Steps

1. **Right-click cell F2, then click Insert on the shortcut menu**
   The Insert dialog box opens as shown in **Figure 2-11**. You can choose to insert a single cell and shift the cells in the active column to the right, insert a single cell and shift the cells in the active row down, or insert an entire column or a row.
2. **Click the Entire row option button, then click OK**
   A blank row appears between the company name and the column labels, visually separating the worksheet data, and the Insert Options button opens next to cell F3.
3. **Click the Insert Options button, then review your choices**
   This menu lets you format the inserted row in Format Same As Above (the default setting, already selected), Format Same As Below, or Clear Formatting.
4. **Click the Insert Options button to close the menu without making changes, then click the row 10 heading**
   All of row 10 is selected, as shown in **Figure 2-12**.
5. **Click the Delete button in the Cells group on the Home tab on the ribbon; do not click the Delete arrow**
   Excel deletes row 10, and all rows below it shift up one row, making Reference # 1893 the new row 10. You must use the Delete button or the Delete command on the shortcut menu to delete a row or column; pressing DEL on the keyboard removes only the *contents* of a selected row or column.
6. **Click the column F heading**
   The contact information is in this column and it is saved on a separate worksheet.
7. **Click the Delete button in the Cells group**
   Excel deletes column F. The remaining columns to the right shift left one column, and the Type column is now column F.
8. **Save your work**

**Quick Tip**
To insert a column, right-click the column heading to the right of where you want the new column, click Insert on the shortcut menu, then click the Entire column option button.

Figure 2-11: Insert dialog box

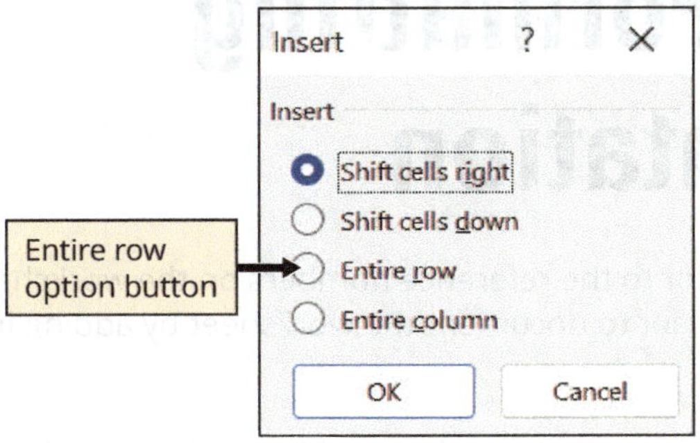


Figure 2-12: Worksheet with row 10 selected

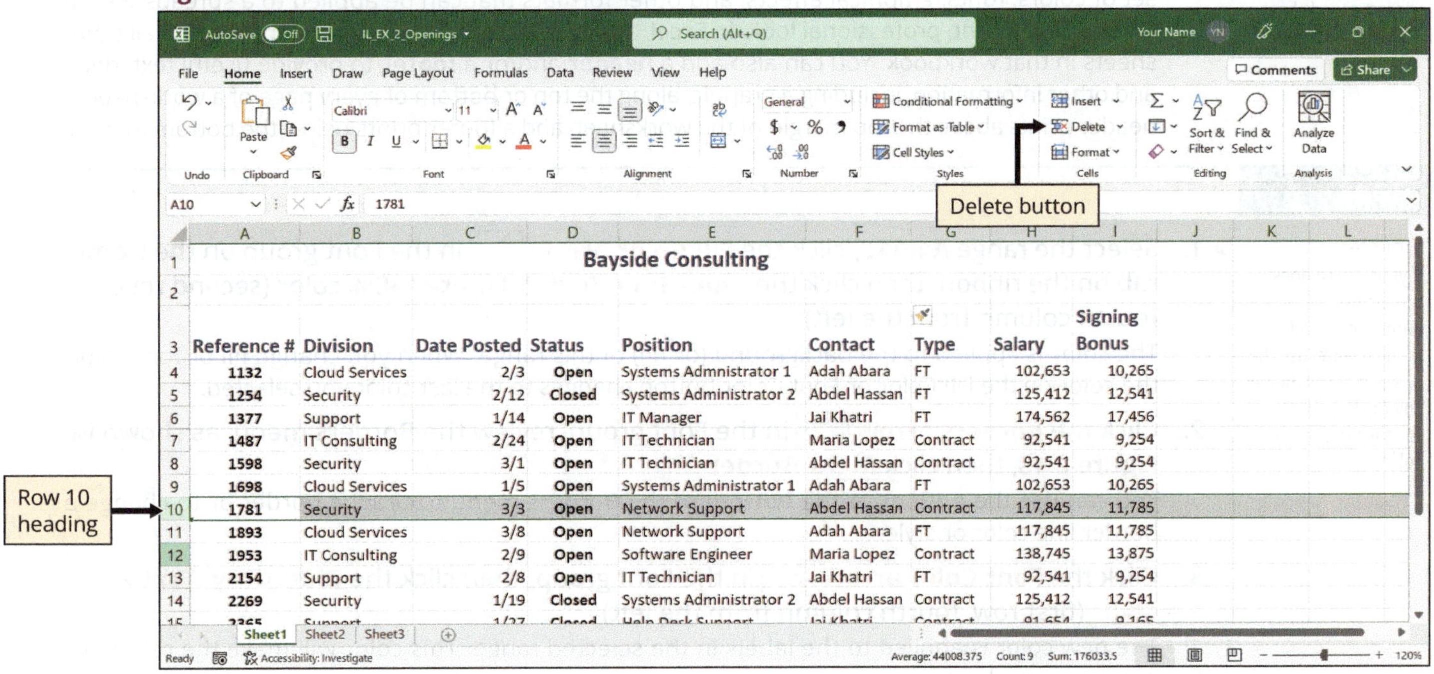


### Hiding and unhiding columns and rows

When you don't want data in a column or row to be visible, but you don't want to delete it, you can hide the column or row. To hide a selected column, click the Format button in the Cells group on the Home tab on the ribbon, point to Hide & Unhide, then click Hide Columns. A hidden column is indicated by a dark green vertical line in its original position. This green line is removed when you click elsewhere on the worksheet, but a thin double line remains between the column heading to remind you that one or more columns are hidden. You can display a hidden column by selecting the column headings on either side of the hidden column, clicking the Format button in the Cells group, pointing to Hide & Unhide, then clicking Unhide Columns. (To hide or unhide one or more rows, substitute Hide Rows and Unhide Rows for the Hide Columns and Unhide Columns instructions.)

# Modify Data Formatting and Documentation

**Case** You want to add a border and color to the reference numbers on the worksheet to make them stand out from the other information. You also want to document the worksheet by adding information about the worksheet in a header and footer.

**Objectives**
- Change text and fill color
- Apply a border to a cell
- Insert a worksheet header and footer

You have used cell styles to add predesigned formatting, including colors and borders to a worksheet. If a cell style doesn't capture the formatting you need for a worksheet, you can add this formatting individually. Color options are based on the worksheet theme. A **theme** is a predefined, coordinated set of colors, fonts, graphical effects, and other formats that can be applied to a spreadsheet to give it a consistent, professional look. In Excel, applying a theme to one sheet applies it to all other sheets in that workbook. You can also add a **header** and/or a **footer** to provide useful text, date, and other information, including a graphic, along the top or bottom of every page of a worksheet. A header prints above the top margin of the worksheet, and a footer prints below the bottom margin.

## Steps

**Trouble**
If your device does not display the names of the colors in the palette, use the position of the theme color in the palette to select the correct color.

1. **Select the range A4:A15, click the Fill Color arrow in the Font group on the Home tab on the ribbon, then click the Blue-Gray, Text 2, Lighter 80% color (second row, fourth column from the left)**
   The color is applied to the background (or fill) of this range. When you change fill or font color, the color on the Fill Color or Font Color button changes to the last color you selected.
2. **Click the Borders arrow in the Font group, review the Borders menu, as shown in Figure 2-13, then click Right Border**
   You can use the options at the bottom of the Borders menu to draw a border or to change a border line color or style.
3. **Click the Font Color arrow in the Font group, then click the Blue-Gray, Text 2 color (first row, fourth column from the left)**
   The new color is applied to the labels in the selected range. This color will make the reference numbers stand out.

**Quick Tip**
You can use the settings in the Options group on the Header & Footer tab to set a different header or footer for the first page of a worksheet. You can also use an option in this group to set different headers or footers for odd and even worksheet pages.

4. **Click the Insert tab on the ribbon, click the Text button, then click the Header & Footer button**
   The header is divided into three sections, as shown in Figure 2-14, where you can enter or edit text. The Header & Footer tab includes elements and options for customizing the header or footer.
5. **Click the Sheet Name button in the Header & Footer Elements group on the Header & Footer tab**
   The & [Tab] code is added, which will display the current sheet name in this location. Using codes instead of manually typing the information ensures this information is always up to date. In a later lesson, you will rename the worksheet to a more descriptive name.
6. **Click the Go to Footer button in the Navigation group, enter your name in the center footer section, click any cell on the worksheet, click the Normal button on the status bar, then press CTRL+HOME**
   The header and footer are only visible in Page Layout view and Print Preview.
7. **Click File, then click Print**
   Your header and footer will provide useful information to others viewing the worksheet.
8. **Click the Back button to return to your worksheet, then save your work**

**Figure 2-13:** Borders menu

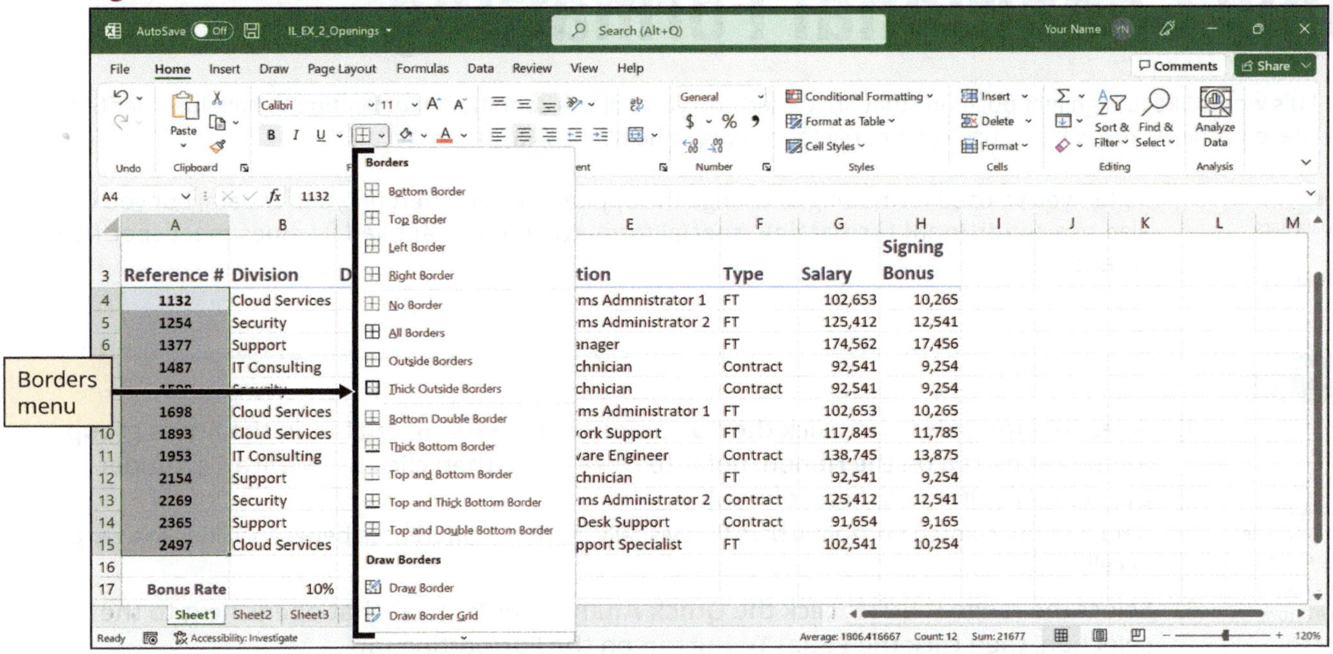


**Figure 2-14:** Header & Footer tab

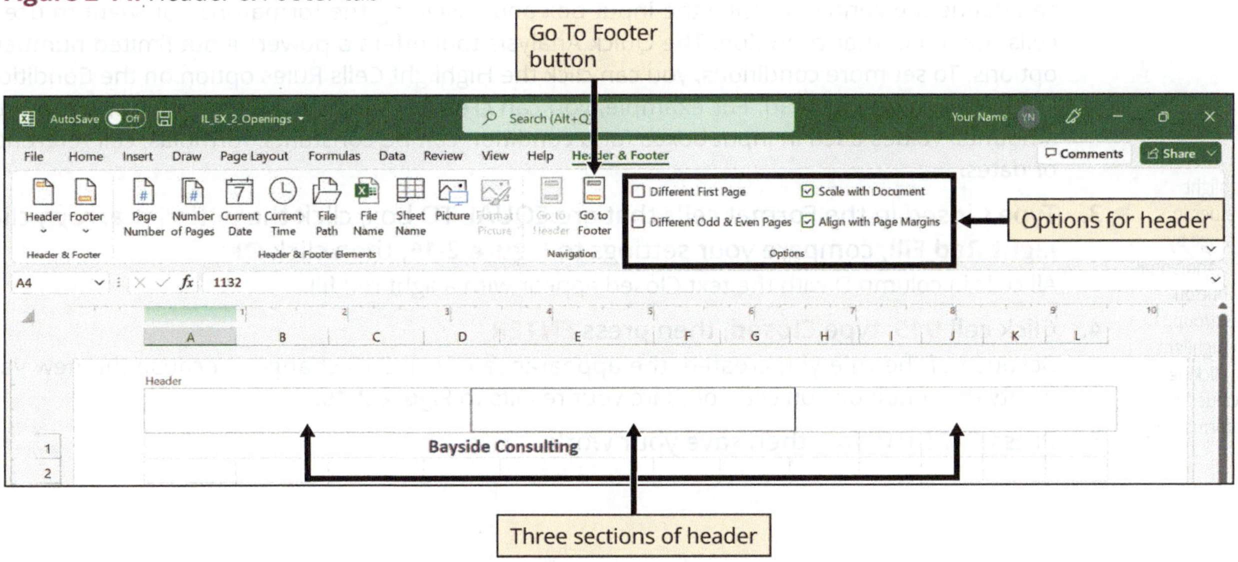


## Working with Microsoft Office color palettes

Microsoft Office color palettes are divided into two main sections: Theme Colors and Standard Colors. The colors in the first row of theme colors each have a name, such as Blue or Green, and a description of their suggested use, such as Background 1, Text 1, or Accent 2. For most devices, this name is displayed when you hover over each color. The colors in the rows below the first row are shades of the theme colors. The first row of shades is the lightest with the colors labeled by percentage of intensity, such as Lighter 80% or Darker 5%. Each row gets progressively darker as you move down the palette and is named according to the intensity of shading, such as Lighter 60%. The last row in the palette displays the standard colors with names such as Light Blue and Orange. These colors are common to all themes but might vary according to factors such as color palette, screen resolution, and Office version. Screen resolution might also affect the location of the standard colors within the color palette.

# Apply Conditional Formatting

**Case** Luis would like to highlight positions that are closed and you will use conditional formatting to help him identify these postings. You will also use conditional formatting to highlight salary patterns.

**Objectives**
- Create a Data Bars rule
- Create a Highlight Cells rule

So far, you've used formatting to change the appearance of different types of data, but you can also use **conditional formatting**, special formatting that is applied if values meet specified criteria.

## Steps

**Quick Tip**
You can create a custom data bar rule by clicking the Conditional Formatting button, clicking New Rule, clicking the Format Style arrow, clicking Data Bar, adjusting the options in the New Formatting Rule dialog box, then clicking OK.

1. **Select the range H4:H15, click the Conditional Formatting button in the Styles group on the Home tab on the ribbon, point to Data Bars, then click Blue Data Bar under Gradient Fill (first row, first column)**
   Data bars are colored horizontal bars that visually illustrate differences between values in a range of cells.

2. **Select the range D4:D15, click the Quick Analysis button that opens next to the selection, then click the Equal To button on the Formatting tab**
   The Equal To dialog box opens, displaying an input box you can use to define the condition and a default format (Light Red Fill with Dark Red Text) selected for cells that meet that condition. You can define the condition using the input box and assigning the formatting you want to use for cells that meet that condition. The Quick Analysis tool offers a powerful but limited number of options. To set more conditions, you can click the Highlight Cells Rules option on the Conditional Formatting menu instead. For example, you can create a rule for values that are between two amounts. Values used in input boxes for a condition can be constants, formulas, cell references, or dates.

**Quick Tip**
You can highlight duplicate values in a selected range by clicking the Conditional Formatting button in the Styles group, pointing to Highlight Cells Rules, clicking Duplicate Values, then selecting a formatting option.

3. **Type Closed in the Format cells that are EQUAL TO box, click the with list arrow, click Light Red Fill, compare your settings to Figure 2-15, then click OK**
   All cells in column D with the text Closed appear with a light red fill.

4. **Click cell D15, type Closed, then press ENTER**
   Because of the rule you created, the appearance of cell D15 changes because the new value meets the condition you set. Compare your results to **Figure 2-16**.

5. **Press CTRL+HOME, then save your work**

### Formatting data with icon sets

**Icon sets** are a conditional format in which different icons are displayed in a cell based on the cell's value. In one group of cells, for example, upward-pointing green arrows might represent the highest values, while downward-pointing red arrows represent the lower values. To add an icon set to a data range, select a data range, click the Conditional Formatting button in the Styles group, point to Icon Sets, then click an icon set. You can customize the values that are used as thresholds for an applied icon set by clicking the Conditional Formatting button in the Styles group, clicking Manage Rules, clicking the rule in the Conditional Formatting Rules Manager dialog box, clicking Edit Rule, entering new values, clicking OK, clicking Apply, then clicking OK to close the dialog box.

**Figure 2-15:** Equal To dialog box

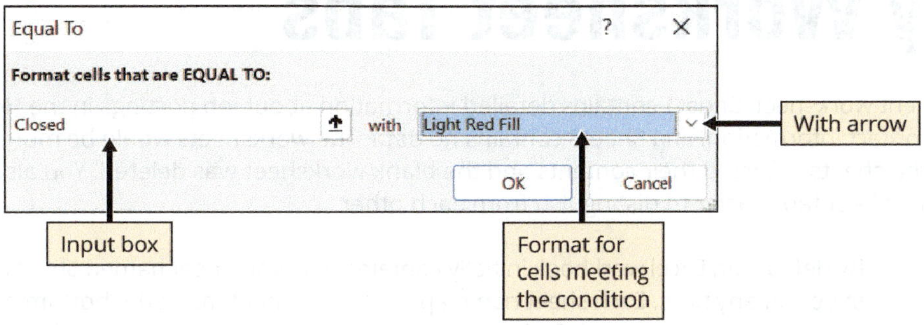


**Figure 2-16:** Worksheet with conditional formatting

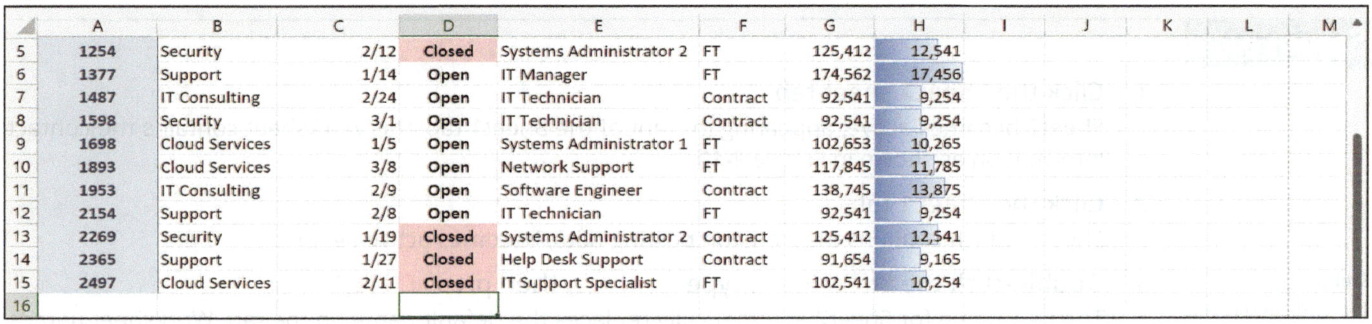

| | A | B | C | D | E | F | G | H | I | J | K | L | M |
|---|---|---|---|---|---|---|---|---|---|---|---|---|---|
| 5 | 1254 | Security | 2/12 | Closed | Systems Administrator 2 | FT | 125,412 | 12,541 | | | | | |
| 6 | 1377 | Support | 1/14 | Open | IT Manager | FT | 174,562 | 17,456 | | | | | |
| 7 | 1487 | IT Consulting | 2/24 | Open | IT Technician | Contract | 92,541 | 9,254 | | | | | |
| 8 | 1598 | Security | 3/1 | Open | IT Technician | Contract | 92,541 | 9,254 | | | | | |
| 9 | 1698 | Cloud Services | 1/5 | Open | Systems Administrator 1 | FT | 102,653 | 10,265 | | | | | |
| 10 | 1893 | Cloud Services | 3/8 | Open | Network Support | FT | 117,845 | 11,785 | | | | | |
| 11 | 1953 | IT Consulting | 2/9 | Open | Software Engineer | Contract | 138,745 | 13,875 | | | | | |
| 12 | 2154 | Support | 2/8 | Open | IT Technician | FT | 92,541 | 9,254 | | | | | |
| 13 | 2269 | Security | 1/19 | Closed | Systems Administrator 2 | Contract | 125,412 | 12,541 | | | | | |
| 14 | 2365 | Support | 1/27 | Closed | Help Desk Support | Contract | 91,654 | 9,165 | | | | | |
| 15 | 2497 | Cloud Services | 2/11 | Closed | IT Support Specialist | FT | 102,541 | 10,254 | | | | | |
| 16 | | | | | | | | | | | | | |

### Managing conditional formatting rules

If you create a conditional formatting rule and then want to change a condition, you don't need to create a new rule; instead, you can edit the rule using the Rules Manager. Select the cells containing the conditional formatting you want to change, click the Conditional Formatting button in the Styles group, then click Manage Rules. The Conditional Formatting Rules Manager dialog box opens where you can use the Show formatting rules for arrow to display rules for the current selection, the worksheet, or for other sheets in the workbook. Selecting This Worksheet displays the rules for the worksheet, as shown in **Figure 2-17.** Select the rule you want to edit, click Edit Rule, then modify the settings in the Edit the Rule Description area in the Edit Formatting Rule dialog box. To change the formatting for a rule, click the Format button in the Edit the Rule Description area, select the formatting styles you want the cells to have, then click OK three times to close the Format Cells dialog box, the Edit Formatting Rule dialog box, and the Conditional Formatting Rules Manager dialog box. To delete a rule, select the rule in the Conditional Formatting Rules Manager dialog box, click the Delete Rule button, then click OK. You can quickly clear conditional formatting rules by clicking the Conditional Formatting button in the Styles group, pointing to Clear Rules, then clicking Clear Rules from Selected Cells or Clear Rules from Entire Worksheet.

**Figure 2-17:** Conditional Formatting Rules Manager dialog box

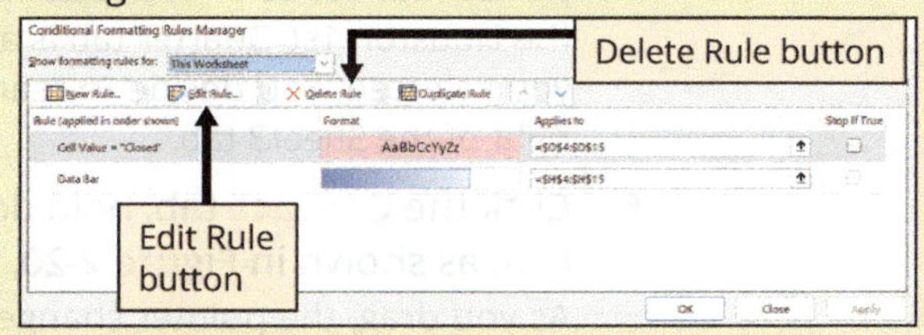

# Modify Worksheet Tabs

**Case** In the current worksheet, Sheet1 contains detailed information about job postings in the Houston office. Sheet2 contains contact information, and Sheet3 contains no data. The worksheets would be more accessible and identifiable if the sheets reflected their contents and the blank worksheet was deleted. You also decide to add color to make the sheet tabs easier to distinguish from each other.

**Objectives**
- Rename a sheet
- Apply color to a sheet tab
- Reorder sheets in a workbook

By default, an Excel workbook initially contains one worksheet named Sheet1, although you can add sheets at any time. Each sheet name appears on a sheet tab at the bottom of the worksheet. Worksheets are initially given default names such as Sheet1. Renaming worksheet default names to more descriptive names can help people using screen readers to understand the worksheet contents. Worksheets are easier to identify if you add color to the tabs and organize them in a logical order. To move from sheet to sheet, you can click any sheet tab at the bottom of the worksheet window.

## Steps

1. **Click the Sheet2 sheet tab**
   Sheet2 becomes active, appearing in front of the Sheet1 tab; this worksheet contains the contact information as shown in **Figure 2-18**.

2. **Click the Sheet1 tab**
   Sheet1, which contains the Houston posting data, becomes active again.

**Quick Tip**
If a workbook contains more sheet tabs than are visible, you can navigate between sheets by using the tab scrolling buttons to the left of the sheet tabs: the Previous Worksheet button ◄ and the Next Worksheet button ►.

3. **Double-click the Sheet2 tab, type Contact, then press ENTER**
   The new name for Sheet2 automatically replaces the default name on the tab. Worksheet names can have up to 31 characters, including spaces and punctuation.

4. **Right-click the Contact tab, point to Tab Color on the shortcut menu, then click the Blue, Accent 5, Darker 25% color (fifth row, second column from the right), as shown in Figure 2-19**

5. **Right-click the Sheet1 tab, click Rename on the shortcut menu, type Houston 1st Quarter, then press ENTER**
   Notice that the color of the Contact tab changes depending on whether it is the active tab; when the Houston 1st Quarter tab is active, the color of the Contact tab changes to the blue tab color you selected. You decide to rearrange the order of the sheets so that the Contact tab is to the right of the Sheet3 tab.

6. **Click the Contact tab, hold down the mouse button, drag it to the right of the Sheet3 tab, as shown in Figure 2-20, then release the mouse button**
   As you drag, the pointer changes to the Move sheet pointer, and a small black triangle just above the tabs shows the position where the moved sheet will be when you release the mouse button. The last sheet in the workbook is now the Contact sheet as shown in **Figure 2-21**. You can move multiple sheets by pressing and holding SHIFT while clicking the sheets you want to move, then dragging the sheets to their new location.

**Quick Tip**
To insert a worksheet, click the New sheet button ⊕ to the right of the sheet tabs.

7. **Right-click the Sheet3 tab, click Delete on the shortcut menu, press CTRL+HOME, then save your work**
   The sheet is deleted. With the sheet tabs renamed from their default to descriptive names, the Accessibility status on the status bar changes from Investigate to Good to go.

**Figure 2-18:** Sheet tabs in workbook

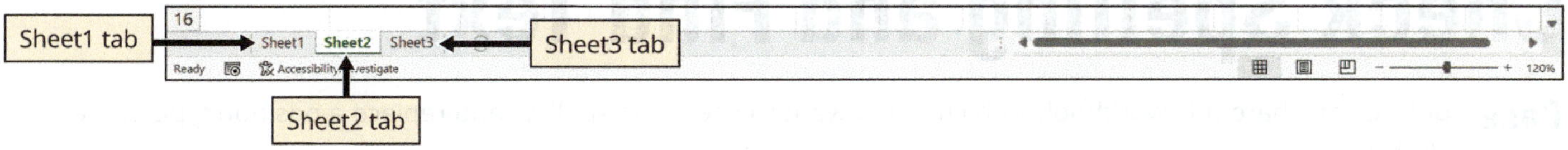


**Figure 2-19:** Tab Color palette

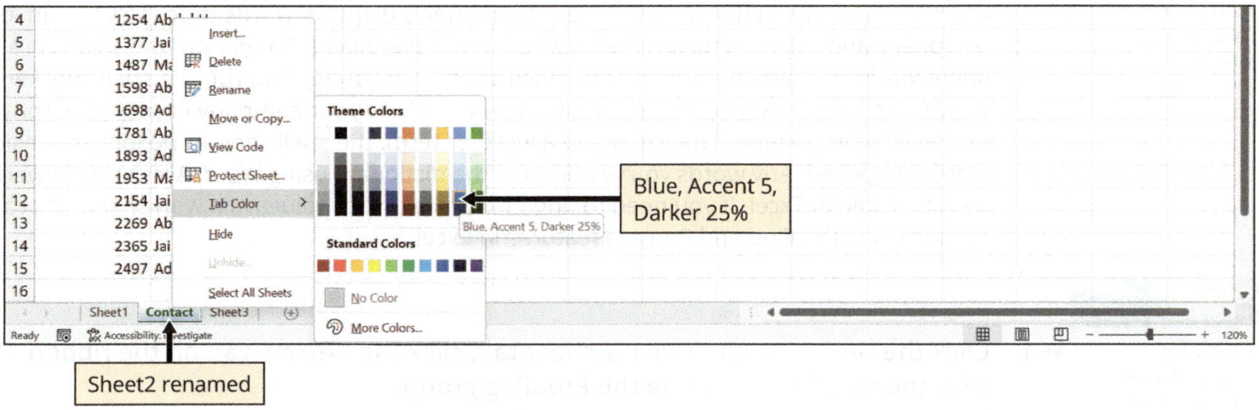


**Figure 2-20:** Moving the Contact sheet

**Figure 2-21:** Reordered sheets

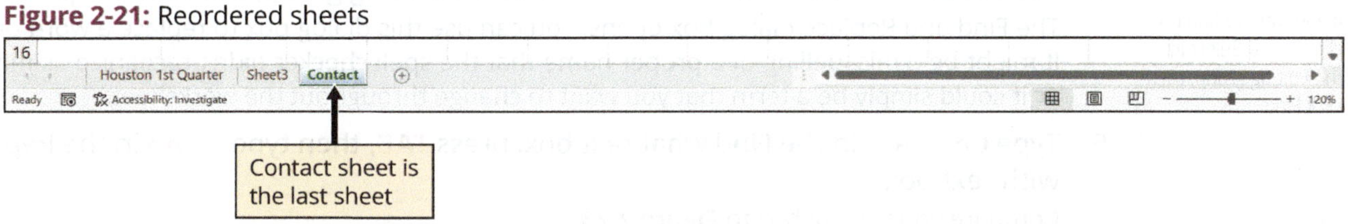


## Copying, adding, and deleting worksheets

There are times when you may want to copy a worksheet. For example, a workbook might contain a sheet with Quarter 1 expenses, and you want to use that sheet as the basis for a sheet containing Quarter 2 expenses. To copy a sheet within the same workbook, press and hold CTRL, drag the sheet tab to the desired tab location, release the mouse button, then release CTRL. A duplicate sheet appears with the same name as the copied sheet followed by "(2)," indicating that it is a copy. You can then rename the sheet to a more meaningful name. To copy a sheet to a different workbook, both the source and destination workbooks must be open. Select the sheet to copy or move, right-click the sheet tab, click Move or Copy in the shortcut menu, then complete the information in the Move or Copy dialog box. Be sure to click the Create a copy check box if you want to copy rather than move the worksheet. Carefully check your calculation results whenever you move or copy a worksheet. You can add multiple worksheets quickly by pressing and holding SHIFT, clicking the number of existing worksheet tabs that correspond with the number of sheets you want to add, clicking the Insert arrow in the Cells group on the Home tab, then clicking Insert Sheet. You can delete multiple worksheets from a workbook by clicking the Home tab on the ribbon, pressing and holding SHIFT, clicking the sheet tabs of the worksheets you want to delete, clicking the Delete arrow in the Cells group, clicking Delete Sheet, then clicking Delete to confirm.

# Check Spelling and Find Text

**Case** Before you share this workbook with Luis, you want to check the spelling and replace a position type in the worksheet.

**Objectives**
- Change spelling using a suggestion
- Replace text using Find & Select

Excel includes a spell checker to help you ensure that the words in your worksheet are spelled correctly. The spell checker scans your worksheet, displays words it doesn't find in its built-in dictionary, and suggests replacements when they are available. To check all the sheets in a multiple-sheet workbook, you need to display each sheet individually and run the spell checker for each one. You can also add words to the dictionary, such as your company name, an acronym, or an unusual technical term. Once you add a word or term, the spell checker no longer considers that word misspelled. Any words you've added to the dictionary using Word, Access, or PowerPoint are also available in Excel. If you need to find or replace text or values in a worksheet, you can quickly do this using the Find and Replace features in Excel.

## Steps

**Quick Tip**
You can click the Thesaurus button in the Proofing group to open a Thesaurus pane with a list of synonyms for a selected word in a cell.

1. **Click the Houston 1st Quarter sheet tab, click the Review tab on the ribbon, then click the Spelling button in the Proofing group**
   The Spelling: English (United States) dialog box opens, as shown in **Figure 2-22**, with "Administrator" selected as the first misspelled word on the worksheet, and with "Administrator" selected in the Suggestions list as a possible replacement. For any word, you have the option to Ignore this case of the flagged word, Ignore All cases of the flagged word, Change the word to the selected suggestion, Change All instances of the flagged word to the selected suggestion, AutoCorrect the word, or Add to Dictionary to add the flagged word to the dictionary.
2. **Click Change**
   When no more incorrect words are found, Excel displays a message indicating that the spell check is complete.
3. **Click OK**

**Quick Tip**
If you want to find text, click Find & Select in the Editing group, then click Find.

4. **Click the Home tab, click Find & Select in the Editing group, then click Replace**
   The Find and Replace dialog box opens. You can use this dialog box to replace a word or phrase. It might be a misspelling of a proper name that the spell checker didn't recognize as misspelled, or it could simply be a term that you want to change throughout the worksheet.
5. **Type Contract in the Find what text box, press TAB, then type Temp in the Replace with text box**
   Compare your dialog box to **Figure 2-23**.

**Quick Tip**
You can find and replace cell formatting by clicking the Options button in the Find and Replace dialog box, then clicking the Format arrows to select the desired formatting.

6. **Click Replace All, click OK to close the Microsoft Excel dialog box, then click Close to close the Find and Replace dialog box**
   Excel made five replacements, changing each instance of "Contract" on the worksheet to "Temp."
7. **Compare your screen to Figure 2-24, save your workbook, then submit your work to your instructor as directed**
8. **sam Close the workbook, then close Excel**

### Translating text

You can translate text in a worksheet by clicking the Review tab, clicking the Translate button in the Language group, then, if necessary, clicking Turn on when asked if you want to use intelligent services. The Translator pane opens and allows you to select the From language and the To language from menus of world languages. The translated text appears in the To language box.

**Figure 2-22:** Spelling: English (United States) dialog box

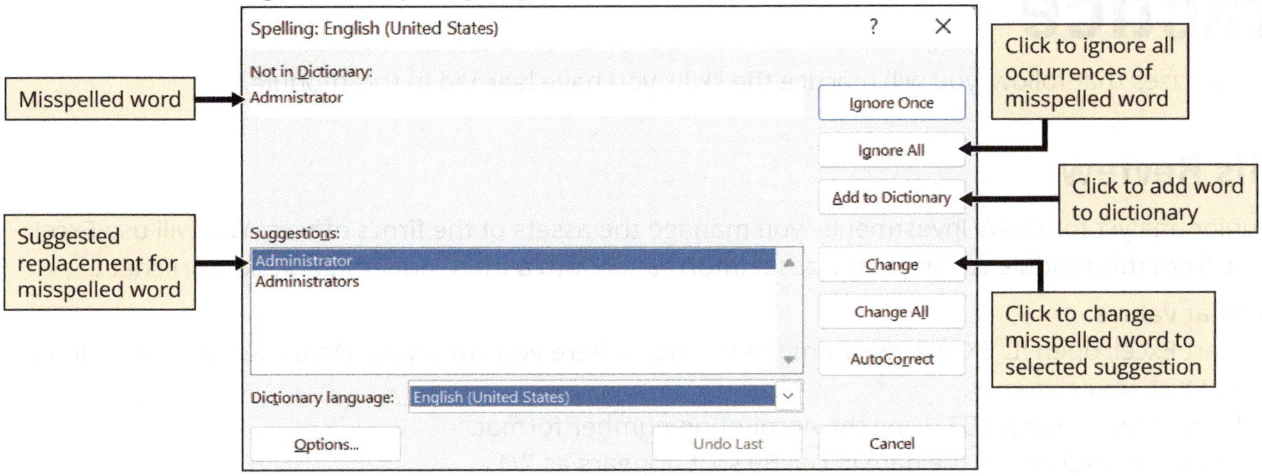


**Figure 2-23:** Find and Replace dialog box

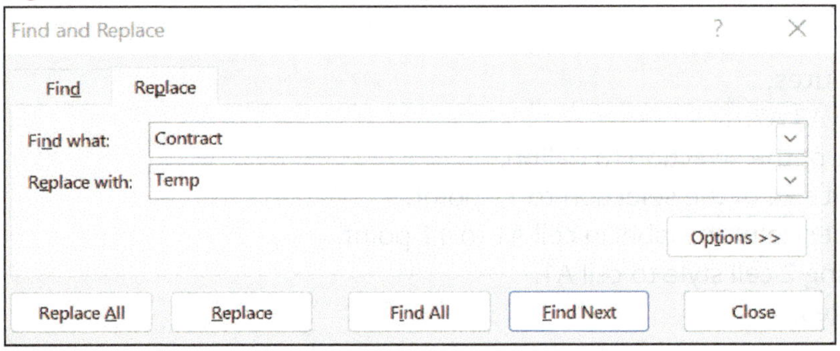


**Figure 2-24:** Completed worksheet

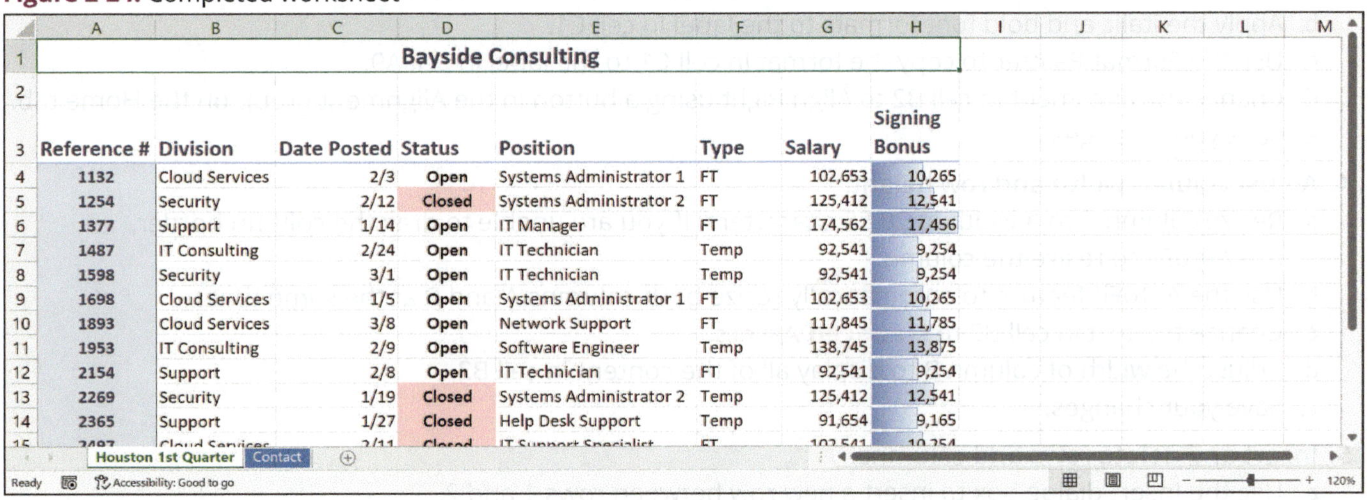

| Reference # | Division | Date Posted | Status | Position | Type | Salary | Signing Bonus |
|---|---|---|---|---|---|---|---|
| 1132 | Cloud Services | 2/3 | Open | Systems Administrator 1 | FT | 102,653 | 10,265 |
| 1254 | Security | 2/12 | Closed | Systems Administrator 2 | FT | 125,412 | 12,541 |
| 1377 | Support | 1/14 | Open | IT Manager | FT | 174,562 | 17,456 |
| 1487 | IT Consulting | 2/24 | Open | IT Technician | Temp | 92,541 | 9,254 |
| 1598 | Security | 3/1 | Open | IT Technician | Temp | 92,541 | 9,254 |
| 1698 | Cloud Services | 1/5 | Open | Systems Administrator 1 | FT | 102,653 | 10,265 |
| 1893 | Cloud Services | 3/8 | Open | Network Support | FT | 117,845 | 11,785 |
| 1953 | IT Consulting | 2/9 | Open | Software Engineer | Temp | 138,745 | 13,875 |
| 2154 | Support | 2/8 | Open | IT Technician | FT | 92,541 | 9,254 |
| 2269 | Security | 1/19 | Closed | Systems Administrator 2 | Temp | 125,412 | 12,541 |
| 2365 | Support | 1/27 | Closed | Help Desk Support | Temp | 91,654 | 9,165 |



## Using Find & Select features

You can navigate to a specific place in a workbook by clicking the Find & Select button in the Editing group on the Home tab, clicking Go To, typing a cell address, then clicking OK. Clicking the Find & Select button also allows you to quickly go to notes, formulas, constants, data validation, and conditional formatting in a worksheet. You can use the Go to Special dialog box to navigate to cells with special elements such as different types of formulas or objects. Some Go to Special commands also appear on the Find & Select menu. Using this Find & Select menu, you can also change the mouse pointer shape to the Select Objects pointer so you can quickly select drawing objects when necessary. To return to the standard Excel pointer, press ESC.

# Practice

In the exercises that follow, you will practice the skills you have learned in this module.

## Skills Review

As a junior analyst for GWW Investments, you manage the assets of the firm's offices. You will use Excel features from this module to format the asset information into a more understandable worksheet.

1. **Format values.**
   a. Start Excel, open IL_EX_2-2.xlsx from the location where you store your Data Files, then save it as **IL_EX_2_Investments**.
   b. Format the range B3:B7 using the Accounting number format.
   c. Change the format of the date in cell B9 so it appears as 7/1.
   d. Increase the number of decimals in cell D1 to 1, using a button in the Number group on the Home tab on the ribbon.
   e. Save your work.
2. **Change font attributes.**
   a. Select the range A3:A7.
   b. Change the font of the selection to Calibri.
   c. Increase the font size of the selection to 11 point.
   d. Increase the font size of the label in cell A1 to 11 point.
   e. Apply the Heading 2 cell style to cell A1.
   f. Save your changes.
3. **Modify font styles and alignment.**
   a. Use the Merge & Center button to center the label in cell A1 over columns A and B.
   b. Apply the italic and bold font formats to the label in cell C1.
   c. Use the Format Painter to copy the format in cell C1 to the label in cell A9.
   d. Change the alignment of cell B2 to Align Right using a button in the Alignment group on the Home tab.
   e. Save your changes.
4. **Adjust column width and row height.**
   a. Resize column C to a width of 20.55 characters. If you are unable to drag the column border, use AutoFit to resize the column.
   b. Use the AutoFit feature to automatically resize both columns A and B at the same time.
   c. Change the text in cell B2 to **Managed Assets**.
   d. Adjust the width of column B to display all of the content in cell B2.
   e. Save your changes.
5. **Insert and delete rows and columns.**
   a. Use the Insert dialog box to insert a new row between rows 1 and 2.
   b. Use a column heading to insert a new column between columns B and C.
   c. Type **Fee** in cell C3 and center the label in the cell.
   d. Use a row heading to delete the Philadelphia row from the worksheet.
   e. Create a formula in cell C4 that calculates the fee for the New York office by multiplying the total managed assets in cell B4 by the annual fee percentage in cell E1. (**Hint**: Use the correct type of cell reference for the annual fee percentage that will enable you to copy the formula.)
   f. Insert formulas in cells C5, C6, and C7 to calculate the fees for the Los Angeles, Miami, and Chicago offices.
   g. Save your changes.

6. **Modify data formatting and documentation.**
   a. Add an outside border around the range A3:C7.
   b. Apply the Green, Accent 6, Lighter 80% fill color (second row, last column under Theme Colors) to the range D1:E1.
   c. Change the color of the font in the range A9:B9 to Green, Accent 6, Darker 50% (last row, last column under Theme Colors).
   d. Add a header in the center section of the worksheet that contains the sheet name.
   e. Enter your name in the center section of the worksheet footer, then return to Normal view.
   f. Save your changes.
7. **Apply conditional formatting.**
   a. Select the range C4:C7, then create a Highlight Cells rule that changes cell contents to green fill with dark green text if the value is greater than 75000.
   b. Select the range B4:B7, then apply Gradient Fill green data bars. (**Hint**: Click Green Data Bar in the Gradient Fill section.)
   c. Open the Conditional Formatting Rules Manager dialog box and view the conditional formatting rules for the worksheet. (**Hint**: Click Manage Rules on the Conditional Formatting menu, then click the Show formatting rules for arrow.)
   d. Review the rules for the worksheet, making sure your rules are correct, then close the dialog box.
   e. Save your changes.
8. **Modify worksheet tabs.**
   a. Rename the Sheet1 tab to **Active Management** and rename the Sheet2 tab to **Passive Management**.
   b. Add a sheet to the workbook, then name the new sheet **Total Fees**.
   c. Change the Active Management tab color to Green, Accent 6, Darker 50% (last row, last column under Theme Colors).
   d. Change the Passive Management tab color to Blue, Accent 5, Darker 50% (last row, second to last column under Theme Colors).
   e. Reorder the sheets so that the Total Fees sheet comes before (to the left of) the Active Management sheet.
   f. Delete the Total Fees sheet.
   g. Activate the Active Management sheet, then save your work.
9. **Check spelling and find text.**
   a. Move the cell pointer to cell A1.
   b. Use the Find & Select feature to replace the word "New York" with **Boston**.
   c. Use the Spelling tool to check the spelling on the worksheet and correct any spelling errors, using suggestions as appropriate. (**Hint**: The label in cell A9 should be Report date.)
   d. Save your changes, then compare your Active Management sheet to **Figure 2-25**.
   e. Preview the Active Management sheet in Backstage view, submit your work to your instructor as directed, close the workbook, then close Excel.

**Figure 2-25**

| | A | B | C | D | E | F |
|---|---|---|---|---|---|---|
| 1 | GWW | | | *Annual Fee Percentage* | 1.1% | |
| 2 | | | | | | |
| 3 | Office | Managed Assets | Fee | | | |
| 4 | Boston | $ 7,842,634.35 | $ 86,268.98 | | | |
| 5 | Los Angeles | $ 6,695,714.77 | $ 73,652.86 | | | |
| 6 | Miami | $ 4,815,981.19 | $ 52,975.79 | | | |
| 7 | Chicago | $ 7,713,257.23 | $ 84,845.83 | | | |
| 8 | | | | | | |
| 9 | *Report date:* | 7/1 | | | | |
| 10 | | | | | | |

# Independent Challenge 1

As an accountant for Albuquerque Urgent Care, you have been asked to review the expenses for the facility. You have organized the data in an Excel workbook, and now you want to format the data to improve its readability and highlight trends in expenses.

a. Start Excel, open IL_EX_2-3.xlsx from the location where you store your Data Files, then save it as **IL_EX_2_Expenses**.
b. Format the values in the Total column in the Accounting number format.
c. Format the value in cell I1 as Percent format with two decimal places.
d. Format the values in the Inv. Date column with the Date format 14-Mar.
e. Apply bold formatting to the column labels in row two and increase the font size of the labels to 12.
f. Italicize the Departments in column A.
g. Change the font of the Sales Tax label in cell H1 to Calibri.
h. Apply the Title cell style to cell A1.
i. Delete column G, then delete row 13.
j. Merge and center the title in cell A1 over columns A1:F1.
k. Resize column widths as necessary using AutoFit so that all columns are wide enough to display the data and labels.
l. Use the Format Painter to copy the date format in the Inv. Date column to the dates in the Inv. Due column.
m. Change the fill color of the sales tax information in the range G1:H1 to the Blue, Accent 1, Lighter 80% color (second row, fifth column from the left), and the font color to the Blue, Accent 1, Darker 50% color (last row under Theme colors, fifth column from the left).
n. Add a bottom border to the column labels in row 2.
o. Use conditional formatting to apply blue gradient data bars to the Total column data.
p. Rename Sheet3 to **Budget** and rename Sheet1 to **Actual**.
q. Change the tab color of the Budget sheet to Red in the Standard colors. Change the tab color of the Actual sheet to Purple in the Standard colors.
r. Move Sheet2 to the right of the Budget sheet.
s. Activate the Actual Sheet and spell check the worksheet. Correct any spelling errors.
t. Using Find & Select, replace all instances of X-ray on the worksheet with Imaging.
u. Delete Sheet2, enter the sheet name in the center section of the Actual worksheet header, enter your name in the center section of the worksheet footer, then save the file.
v. Activate cell A1, switch to Normal view, then compare your worksheet to **Figure 2-26**.
w. Submit your work to your instructor as directed, close the workbook, then close Excel.

**Figure 2-26**

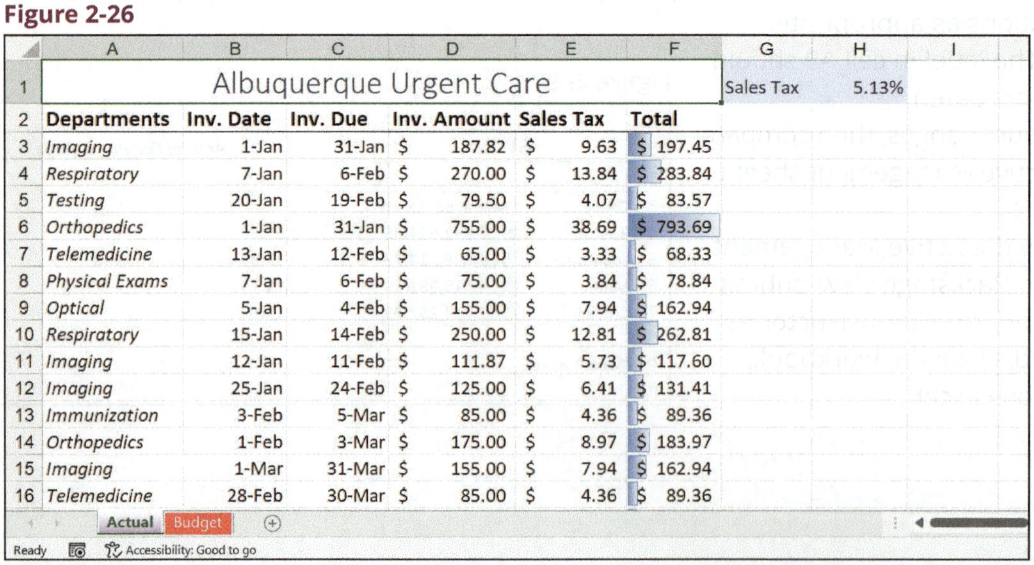

| | A | B | C | D | E | F | G | H |
|---|---|---|---|---|---|---|---|---|
| 1 | Albuquerque Urgent Care | | | | | | Sales Tax | 5.13% |
| 2 | Departments | Inv. Date | Inv. Due | Inv. Amount | Sales Tax | Total | | |
| 3 | Imaging | 1-Jan | 31-Jan | $ 187.82 | $ 9.63 | $ 197.45 | | |
| 4 | Respiratory | 7-Jan | 6-Feb | $ 270.00 | $ 13.84 | $ 283.84 | | |
| 5 | Testing | 20-Jan | 19-Feb | $ 79.50 | $ 4.07 | $ 83.57 | | |
| 6 | Orthopedics | 1-Jan | 31-Jan | $ 755.00 | $ 38.69 | $ 793.69 | | |
| 7 | Telemedicine | 13-Jan | 12-Feb | $ 65.00 | $ 3.33 | $ 68.33 | | |
| 8 | Physical Exams | 7-Jan | 6-Feb | $ 75.00 | $ 3.84 | $ 78.84 | | |
| 9 | Optical | 5-Jan | 4-Feb | $ 155.00 | $ 7.94 | $ 162.94 | | |
| 10 | Respiratory | 15-Jan | 14-Feb | $ 250.00 | $ 12.81 | $ 262.81 | | |
| 11 | Imaging | 12-Jan | 11-Feb | $ 111.87 | $ 5.73 | $ 117.60 | | |
| 12 | Imaging | 25-Jan | 24-Feb | $ 125.00 | $ 6.41 | $ 131.41 | | |
| 13 | Immunization | 3-Feb | 5-Mar | $ 85.00 | $ 4.36 | $ 89.36 | | |
| 14 | Orthopedics | 1-Feb | 3-Mar | $ 175.00 | $ 8.97 | $ 183.97 | | |
| 15 | Imaging | 1-Mar | 31-Mar | $ 155.00 | $ 7.94 | $ 162.94 | | |
| 16 | Telemedicine | 28-Feb | 30-Mar | $ 85.00 | $ 4.36 | $ 89.36 | | |

## Independent Challenge 2

You are assisting the head of business operations at CGS Merchant Services. You have been asked to format a worksheet showing the first-quarter business services for the company's five branches. As part of this effort, you want to illustrate trends among the branches.

a. Start Excel, open IL_EX_2-4.xlsx from the location where you store your Data Files, then save it as **IL_EX_2_Services**.
b. Apply the Title cell style to cell A1, apply the Heading 4 cell style to the column headings in row 2, and apply the Total cell style to the range A8:G8.
c. Merge and center the title in cell A1 across the range A1:G1.
d. Format the range B3:G8 using the Accounting number format. AutoFit the widths of all columns and format the range with no decimal places.
e. Format the date in cell B9 using the 14-Mar date format.
f. Rotate the label in cell A2 up by 45 degrees. Copy this rotated format to the other column headings in row two. Center the rotated labels in their cells.
g. Format the range A9:B9 with a Blue-Gray, Text 2, Lighter 60% fill (third row, fourth column from the left, under Theme Colors).
h. Format the range A9:B9 with a Blue, Accent 1, Darker 50% font color (last row, fifth column from the left, under Theme Colors).
i. Create a conditional format in the range G3:G7 so that entries less than 30,000,000 appear in light red fill with dark red text.
j. Create a conditional format in the range B8:F8 to add the 3 Stars Ratings icon set. Widen the columns as necessary to fully display the data and formatting.
k. Use the Spelling tool to check spelling in the sheet. Make all necessary spelling corrections.
l. Rename Sheet1 to **First Quarter**. Copy the First Quarter sheet and rename the copied sheet **Second Quarter**. Move the Second Quarter sheet if necessary so it is to the right of the First Quarter sheet.
m. On the Second Quarter sheet, delete the data in the range B3:F7 and delete the date in cell B9.
n. Activate the First Quarter sheet. Compare your worksheet to **Figure 2-27**.
o. Enter your name in the center header section, change the worksheet orientation to landscape, then save your work.
p. Preview the worksheet, make any final changes you think are necessary, then submit your work to your instructor as directed.
q. Close the workbook, then close Excel.

**Figure 2-27**

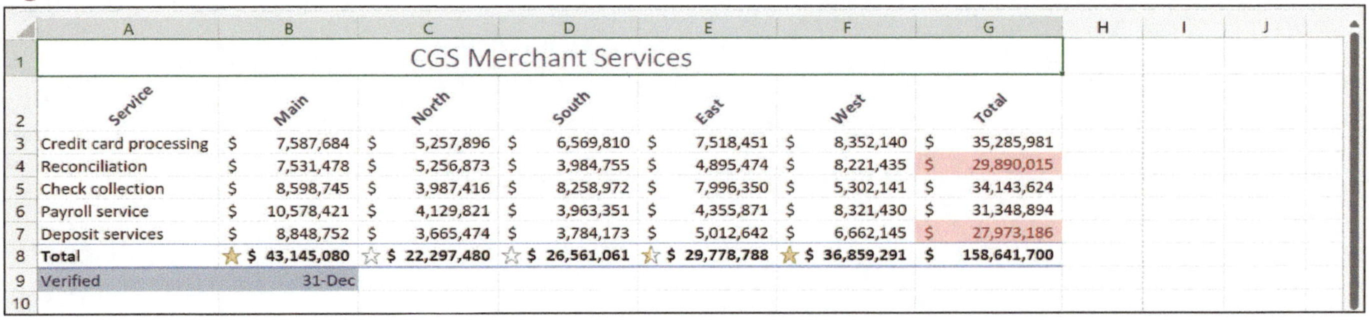

| | A | B | C | D | E | F | G |
|---|---|---|---|---|---|---|---|
| 1 | CGS Merchant Services | | | | | | |
| 2 | Service | Main | North | South | East | West | Total |
| 3 | Credit card processing | $ 7,587,684 | $ 5,257,896 | $ 6,569,810 | $ 7,518,451 | $ 8,352,140 | $ 35,285,981 |
| 4 | Reconciliation | $ 7,531,478 | $ 5,256,873 | $ 3,984,755 | $ 4,895,474 | $ 8,221,435 | $ 29,890,015 |
| 5 | Check collection | $ 8,598,745 | $ 3,987,416 | $ 8,258,972 | $ 7,996,350 | $ 5,302,141 | $ 34,143,624 |
| 6 | Payroll service | $ 10,578,421 | $ 4,129,821 | $ 3,963,351 | $ 4,355,871 | $ 8,321,430 | $ 31,348,894 |
| 7 | Deposit services | $ 8,848,752 | $ 3,665,474 | $ 3,784,173 | $ 5,012,642 | $ 6,662,145 | $ 27,973,186 |
| 8 | Total | $ 43,145,080 | $ 22,297,480 | $ 26,561,061 | $ 29,778,788 | $ 36,859,291 | $ 158,641,700 |
| 9 | Verified | 31-Dec | | | | | |
| 10 | | | | | | | |

# Visual Workshop

Open IL_EX_2-5.xlsx from the location where you store your Data Files, then save it as **IL_EX_2_Northbridge**. Use the skills you learned in this module to modify the worksheet as necessary so the content and formatting matches **Figure 2-28**. (Note that cell A1 is selected in the figure.) Use the blue gradient fill for the data bars in the Total column. Use the Title cell style for the company name in cell A1, the Heading 1 cell style for the column labels in row 2, and the Total cell style for the total values in the last row. The font color for the service packages listed in column A is Blue in the standard colors and the font is formatted in bold. (**Hint**: A row has been deleted from the worksheet.) Enter your name in the upper-left section of the header, check the spelling on the worksheet, change the worksheet orientation to landscape, save your changes, then submit your work to your instructor as directed.

**Figure 2-28**

| | A | B | C | D | E | F | G | H | I | J | K | L | M |
|---|---|---|---|---|---|---|---|---|---|---|---|---|---|
| 1 | Northbridge Data Center Services | | | | | | | | | | | | |
| 2 | Service Packages | January | February | March | April | May | June | Total | | | | | |
| 3 | Support | $ 858,840 | $ 547,891 | $ 732,171 | $ 583,658 | $ 596,556 | $ 383,847 | $ 3,702,963 | | | | | |
| 4 | Outsourcing | $ 510,123 | $ 664,399 | $ 508,911 | $ 673,112 | $ 773,259 | $ 967,453 | $ 4,097,257 | | | | | |
| 5 | Applications | $ 794,366 | $ 462,919 | $ 629,686 | $ 533,313 | $ 755,231 | $ 518,836 | $ 3,694,351 | | | | | |
| 6 | Training | $ 681,339 | $ 641,158 | $ 575,496 | $ 562,181 | $ 345,542 | $ 752,138 | $ 3,557,854 | | | | | |
| 7 | Total | $ 2,844,668 | $ 2,316,367 | $ 2,446,264 | $ 2,352,264 | $ 2,470,588 | $ 2,622,274 | $ 15,052,425 | | | | | |
| 8 | | | | | | | | | | | | | |

# Analyzing Data Using Formulas

## Case

Elena Fuentes, Vice President of Finance at Bayside Consulting, wants to know how U.S. revenues have performed compared to last year and relative to projected targets. She asks you to prepare a worksheet that summarizes and analyzes this revenue data.

## Module Objectives

After completing this module, you will be able to:

- Enter a formula using the Quick Analysis tool
- Copy formulas with relative cell references
- Build a logical formula with the IF function
- Copy formulas with absolute cell references
- Build a logical formula with the AND function
- Use a function to round a value
- Build a statistical formula with the COUNTA function
- Enter a date function
- Control worksheet calculations

### Files You Will Need

IL_EX_3-1.xlsx
IL_EX_3-2.xlsx
IL_EX_3-3.xlsx
IL_EX_3-4.xlsx
IL_EX_3-5.xlsx

# Enter a Formula Using the Quick Analysis Tool

**Case** To help Elena evaluate revenues at Bayside, you want to calculate yearly revenue totals for each U.S. office and compare the yearly performance of each office to the previous year.

**Objectives**
- Create a formula using the Quick Analysis tool
- Create a formula to find a percentage increase

So far, you have used the AutoSum button on the ribbon to quickly add simple formulas that sum and average selected data. You can also add formulas using the Quick Analysis tool, which opens when you select a range of cells. This tool allows you to quickly format, chart, or analyze data by calculating sums, averages, and other selected totals.

## Steps

1. **sam Start Excel, open IL_EX_3-1.xlsx from the location where you store your Data Files, then save it as IL_EX_3_Revenue**
2. **Select the range B3:E11, click the Quick Analysis button that appears below the selection, then click the Totals tab**

   The Totals tab in the Quick Analysis tool displays commonly used functions, as shown in **Figure 3-1**. This tab includes two Sum buttons. The first Sum button, with displays a blue row, inserts the SUM function in a row beneath the selected range. The second button, which displays a gold column, inserts the SUM function in the column to the right of the range.
3. **Click the second Sum button, which displays the gold column**

   The newly calculated totals are displayed in the column to the right of the selected range, in cells F3:F11.

**Quick Tip**
Clicking the first Sum button enters totals in a row below a selected range.

4. **Click cell H3, type =(, click cell F3, type -, click cell G3, then type )**

   This first part of the formula finds the difference in total revenue from the previous year to this year. You enclosed this operation in parentheses to make sure this difference is calculated first.
5. **Type /, then click cell G3**

   The second part of this formula divides the difference in revenue by the total revenue for the previous year, to calculate the increase or decrease.
6. **Click the Enter button on the formula bar**

   The result, .82868268, appears in cell H3. The column isn't wide enough to fully display this value but the number of decimal places will be adjusted in the next formatting step.
7. **Click the Percent Style button in the Number group on the Home tab on the ribbon, then click the Increase Decimal button in the Number group twice**

   The formatted percentage, 82.87%, appears in cell H3, as shown in **Figure 3-2**.
8. **Save the workbook**

**Figure 3-1:** Quick Analysis tool

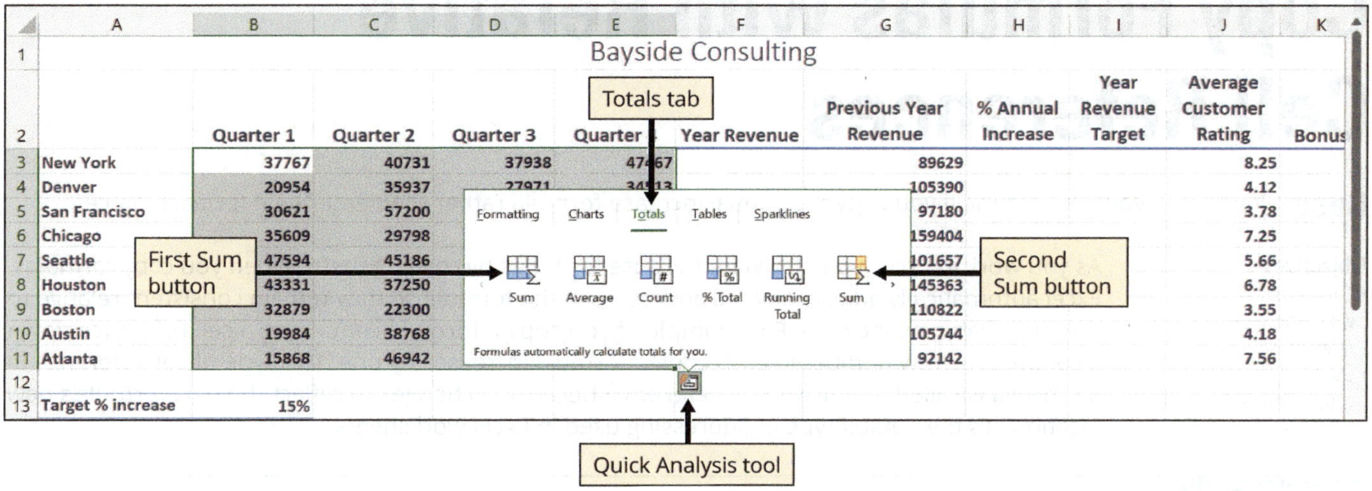


**Figure 3-2:** Formatted annual increase percentage

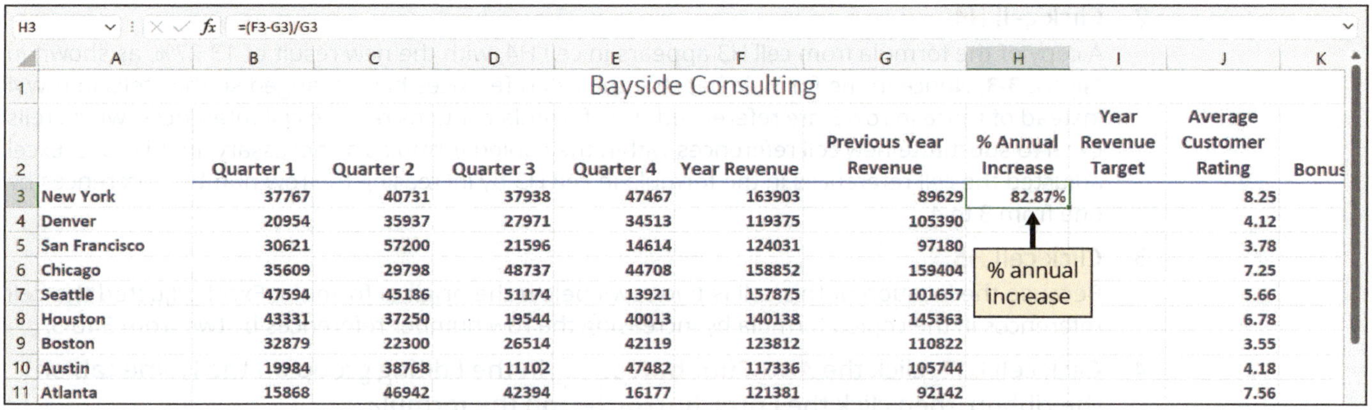

# Copy Formulas with Relative Cell References

**Case** It will save you a lot of time if you copy the annual increase formula rather than entering it for each office.

**Objectives**
- Copy formulas with relative cell references
- Use the fill handle to copy formulas

As you work in Excel, you may want to reuse formulas by copying them. When you copy formulas, Excel automatically adjusts any cell addresses in the formula so they remain consistent relative to the formula's new location. For example, if you copy a formula containing a cell reference down a column, the row number in each copied formula increases by one. This type of cell reference in a formula is called a **relative cell reference** because it changes to reflect the new formula's new location; it's the default type of addressing used in Excel worksheets.

## Steps

1. **Click cell H3 if necessary, drag the fill handle from cell H3 down to cell H11**
   The formula for calculating the percentage increase is copied into the range H3:H11.
2. **Click cell H4**
   A copy of the formula from cell H3 appears in cell H4, with the new result of 13.27%, as shown in **Figure 3-3**. Notice in the formula bar that the cell references have changed so that cells in row 4 instead of those in row 3 are referenced. This formula contains relative cell references, which tells Excel to substitute new cell references within the copied formulas as necessary. In this case, Excel adjusted the cell references in the formula in cell H3 by increasing the row number references by one from 3 to 4.
3. **Click cell H5**
   Because the location of this cell is two rows below the original formula, Excel adjusted the cell references in the copied formula by increasing the row number references by two from 3 to 5.
4. **Click cell B12, click the AutoSum button Σ in the Editing group on the Home tab on the ribbon, then click the Enter button ✓ on the formula**
5. **Drag the fill handle to the right to cell E12**
   A formula similar to the one in cell B12 now appears in the range C12:E12.
6. **Click cell C12**
   In copying the formula one cell to the right, the cell references are adjusted by increasing the column letter references by one from B to C. Compare your worksheet to **Figure 3-4**.
7. **Save your work**

**Figure 3-3:** Formula copied using the fill handle

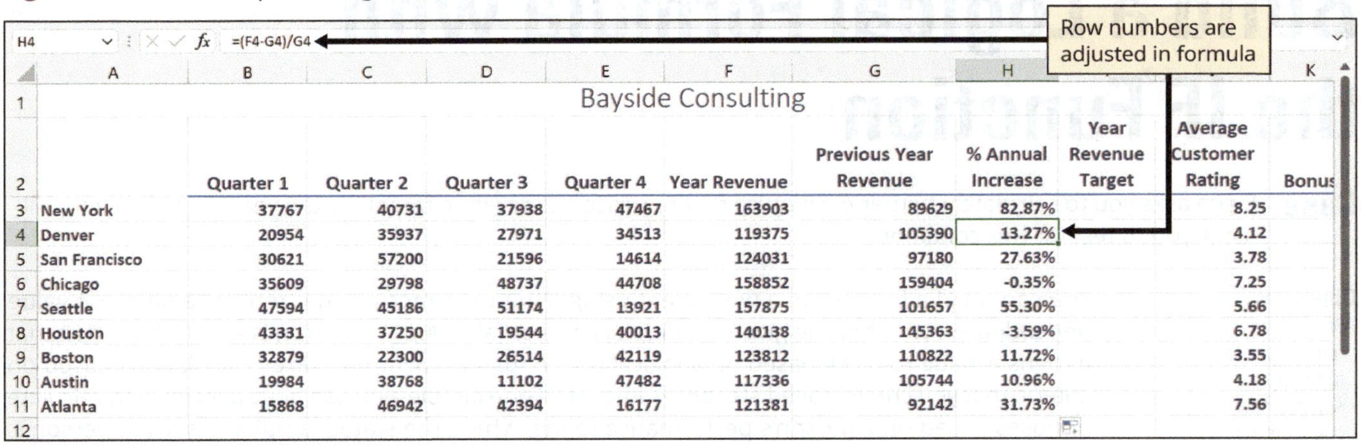


| | A | B | C | D | E | F | G | H | I | J | K |
|---|---|---|---|---|---|---|---|---|---|---|---|
| 1 | | | | | Bayside Consulting | | | | | | |
| 2 | | Quarter 1 | Quarter 2 | Quarter 3 | Quarter 4 | Year Revenue | Previous Year Revenue | % Annual Increase | Year Revenue Target | Average Customer Rating | Bonus |
| 3 | New York | 37767 | 40731 | 37938 | 47467 | 163903 | 89629 | 82.87% | | 8.25 | |
| 4 | Denver | 20954 | 35937 | 27971 | 34513 | 119375 | 105390 | 13.27% | | 4.12 | |
| 5 | San Francisco | 30621 | 57200 | 21596 | 14614 | 124031 | 97180 | 27.63% | | 3.78 | |
| 6 | Chicago | 35609 | 29798 | 48737 | 44708 | 158852 | 159404 | -0.35% | | 7.25 | |
| 7 | Seattle | 47594 | 45186 | 51174 | 13921 | 157875 | 101657 | 55.30% | | 5.66 | |
| 8 | Houston | 43331 | 37250 | 19544 | 40013 | 140138 | 145363 | -3.59% | | 6.78 | |
| 9 | Boston | 32879 | 22300 | 26514 | 42119 | 123812 | 110822 | 11.72% | | 3.55 | |
| 10 | Austin | 19984 | 38768 | 11102 | 47482 | 117336 | 105744 | 10.96% | | 4.18 | |
| 11 | Atlanta | 15868 | 46942 | 42394 | 16177 | 121381 | 92142 | 31.73% | | 7.56 | |
| 12 | | | | | | | | | | | |

**Figure 3-4:** Formula column references changed

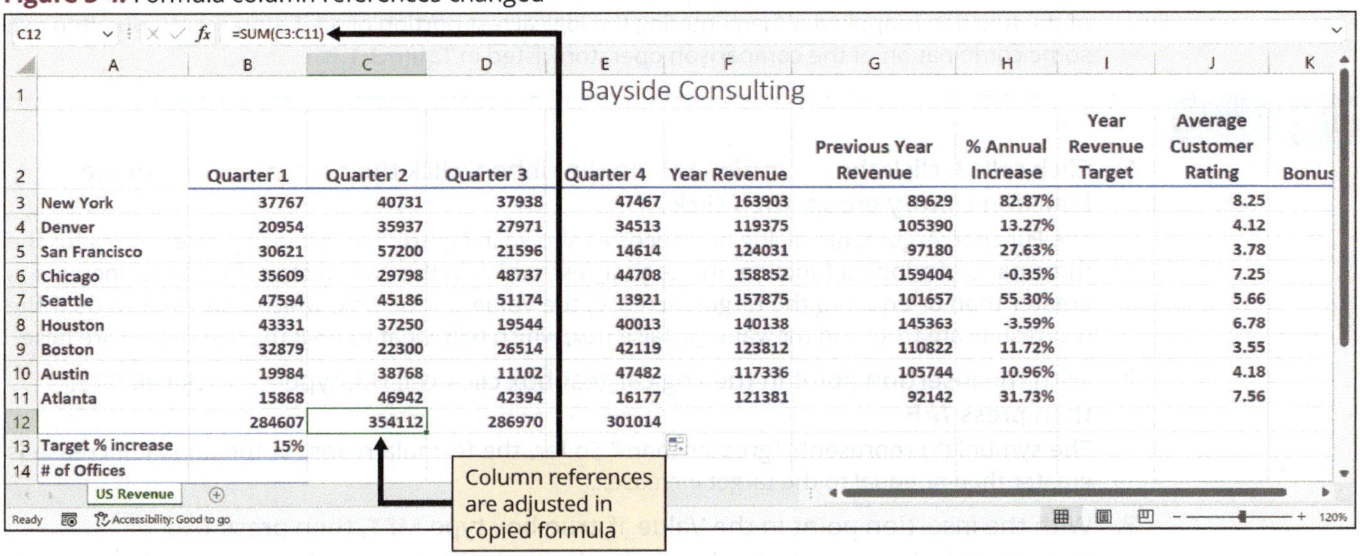


| | A | B | C | D | E | F | G | H | I | J | K |
|---|---|---|---|---|---|---|---|---|---|---|---|
| 1 | | | | | Bayside Consulting | | | | | | |
| 2 | | Quarter 1 | Quarter 2 | Quarter 3 | Quarter 4 | Year Revenue | Previous Year Revenue | % Annual Increase | Year Revenue Target | Average Customer Rating | Bonus |
| 3 | New York | 37767 | 40731 | 37938 | 47467 | 163903 | 89629 | 82.87% | | 8.25 | |
| 4 | Denver | 20954 | 35937 | 27971 | 34513 | 119375 | 105390 | 13.27% | | 4.12 | |
| 5 | San Francisco | 30621 | 57200 | 21596 | 14614 | 124031 | 97180 | 27.63% | | 3.78 | |
| 6 | Chicago | 35609 | 29798 | 48737 | 44708 | 158852 | 159404 | -0.35% | | 7.25 | |
| 7 | Seattle | 47594 | 45186 | 51174 | 13921 | 157875 | 101657 | 55.30% | | 5.66 | |
| 8 | Houston | 43331 | 37250 | 19544 | 40013 | 140138 | 145363 | -3.59% | | 6.78 | |
| 9 | Boston | 32879 | 22300 | 26514 | 42119 | 123812 | 110822 | 11.72% | | 3.55 | |
| 10 | Austin | 19984 | 38768 | 11102 | 47482 | 117336 | 105744 | 10.96% | | 4.18 | |
| 11 | Atlanta | 15868 | 46942 | 42394 | 16177 | 121381 | 92142 | 31.73% | | 7.56 | |
| 12 | | 284607 | 354112 | 286970 | 301014 | | | | | | |
| 13 | Target % increase | 15% | | | | | | | | | |
| 14 | # of Offices | | | | | | | | | | |

### Inserting functions into formulas

You can insert a function on its own or as part of another formula. For example, you have used the SUM function on its own to sum a range of cells—for example, =SUM(B5:B9). You could also use the SUM function within a formula that adds a range of cells and then multiplies the total by a decimal—for example, =SUM(B5:B9)*.5.

# Build a Logical Formula with the IF Function

**Case** Elena asks you to calculate whether each office met or missed its revenue target for the year. An IF function will allow you to test for this condition.

**Objectives**
- Build a logical formula using the IF function
- Apply comparison operators in a logical test

You can build a formula in a worksheet using a **logical function** that returns a different value depending on whether the given condition is true or false. An **IF function** is a logical function that assigns a value to a cell based on a logical test. A **logical formula** makes calculations based on criteria that you create, called **stated conditions**. For example, you can build a formula to calculate bonuses based on a person's performance rating, where the stated condition is 5. If a person is rated a 5 on a scale of 1 to 5, they receive an additional 10% of their salary as a bonus; otherwise, there is no bonus. The IF function has three parts, including the **logical test**, which is the first part of the function. This test is a condition that can be answered with a true or false response. If the logical test is true, then the second part of the function is applied; if it is false, then the third part of the function is applied. When entering the logical test portion of an IF statement, you often use some combination of the comparison operators listed in **Table 3-1**.

## Steps

1. **Click cell I3, click the Formulas tab on the ribbon, click the Logical button in the Function Library group, then click IF**

   The Function Arguments dialog box opens as shown in **Figure 3-5**, displaying three boxes for the three parts of a logical function: the Logical_test, which in this case tests if the annual increase is greater than or equal to the target increase; the Value_if_true box, which tells what to do if the test results are true; and the Value_if_false box, which tells what to do if the test results are false.

2. **With the insertion point in the Logical_test box click cell H3, type >=, click cell B13, then press TAB**

   The symbol (>) represents "greater than." So far, the formula reads, "If the annual increase is greater than or equal to the target increase..."

3. **With the insertion point in the Value_if_true box type MET, then press TAB**

   This part of the function tells Excel to display the text MET if the annual increase equals or exceeds the target increase of 15%. Quotation marks are automatically added around the text you entered.

4. **Type MISSED in the Value_if_false box, then click OK**

   This part tells Excel to display the text MISSED if the results of the logical test are false—that is, if the increase does not equal or exceed the target. The function is complete, and the result, MET, appears in cell I3, as shown in **Figure 3-6**.

5. **Click the Home tab, click the Center ☰ button in the Alignment group, then save the workbook**

   The status of the year revenue target in cell I3 is centered in the cell.

**Figure 3-5:** Function Arguments dialog box

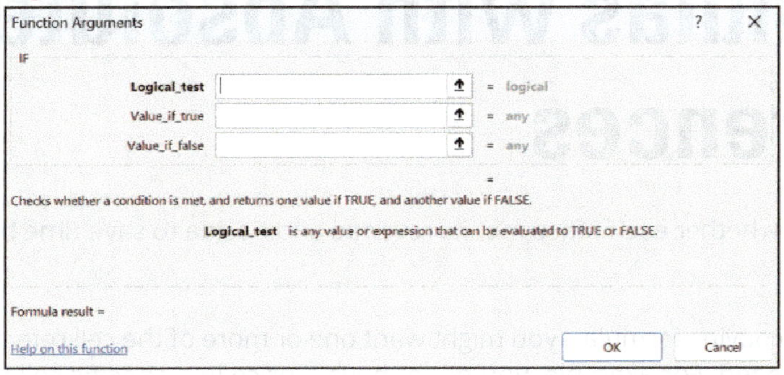


**Figure 3-6:** Worksheet with IF function

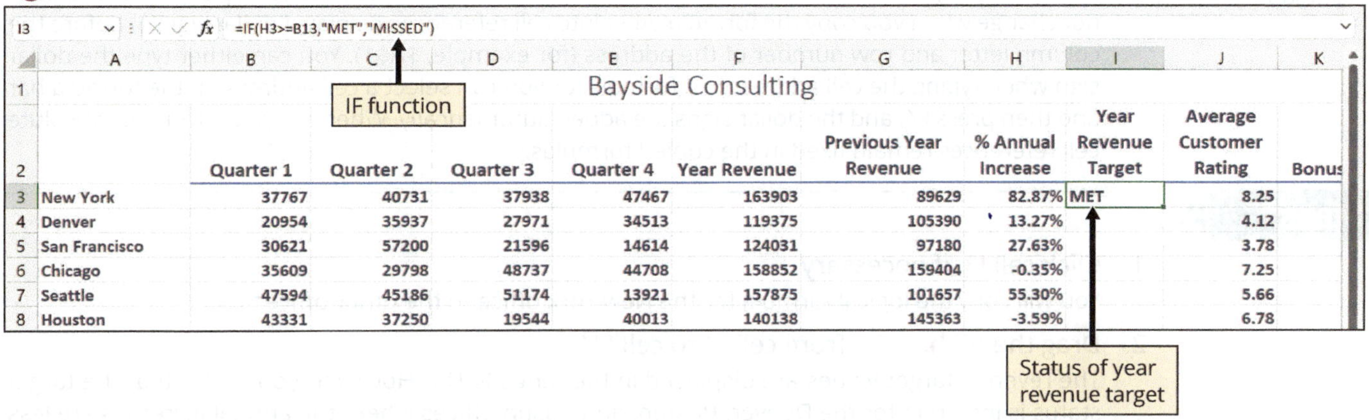


Bayside Consulting

| | Quarter 1 | Quarter 2 | Quarter 3 | Quarter 4 | Year Revenue | Previous Year Revenue | % Annual Increase | Year Revenue Target | Average Customer Rating | Bonus |
|---|---|---|---|---|---|---|---|---|---|---|
| New York | 37767 | 40731 | 37938 | 47467 | 163903 | 89629 | 82.87% | MET | 8.25 | |
| Denver | 20954 | 35937 | 27971 | 34513 | 119375 | 105390 | 13.27% | | 4.12 | |
| San Francisco | 30621 | 57200 | 21596 | 14614 | 124031 | 97180 | 27.63% | | 3.78 | |
| Chicago | 35609 | 29798 | 48737 | 44708 | 158852 | 159404 | -0.35% | | 7.25 | |
| Seattle | 47594 | 45186 | 51174 | 13921 | 157875 | 101657 | 55.30% | | 5.66 | |
| Houston | 43331 | 37250 | 19544 | 40013 | 140138 | 145363 | -3.59% | | 6.78 | |

**Table 3-1:** Comparison operators

| operator | meaning | operator | meaning |
|---|---|---|---|
| < | Less than | <= | Less than or equal to |
| > | Greater than | >= | Greater than or equal to |
| = | Equal to | <> | Not equal to |

## Nesting IF functions

You can nest IF functions to test several conditions in a formula. A **nested IF function** contains IF functions inside other IF functions to test these multiple conditions. To create a nested IF function, enter the second IF statement in the value_if_false argument of the first IF statement. For example, the nested statement =IF(H3<0%,"Warning",IF(H3<50%,"No Bonus","Bonus") tests whether a warning should be issued based on the percentage increases for an office. Assuming the percentage increase of an office is in cell H3, the nested IF statement first evaluates whether the increase was less than 0. If that first test is true, the text "Warning" will display. If the first test is false, a second test will be performed to check to evaluate whether the increase is less than 50%. If that second test is true (values are less than 50%), the text "No Bonus" will display. If that second test is false, the text "Bonus" will display.

# Copy Formulas with Absolute Cell References

**Case** You want to calculate whether each office met its revenue and decide to save time by copying the logical formula for the New York office.

**Objectives**
- Create an absolute cell reference
- Use the fill handle to copy absolute cell references

When copying formulas, you might want one or more of the cell references in the formula to remain unchanged. For example, you might have a price in a specific cell that you want to use in all the copied formulas, regardless of their location. If you used relative cell referencing, the formula results would be incorrect, because the formula would reference a different cell every time you copy it. In this situation, you need to use an **absolute cell reference**, which refers to a specific cell and does not change when you copy the formula. Absolute cell references display a dollar sign ($) before the column letter and row number of the address (for example, $A$1). You can either type the dollar sign when typing the cell address in a formula, or you can select a cell address on the formula bar and then press F4, and the dollar signs are added automatically. When copying a formula, absolute cell references remain fixed in the copied formulas.

## Steps

1. **Click cell I3, if necessary**
   You will copy the logical formula for the New York office to the other offices.
2. **Drag the fill handle from cell I3 to cell I11**
   The revenue target values are displayed in the range I4:I11. However, you notice that the target status is incorrect for the Denver, Boston, and Austin offices where the annual increases are less than the target for the year.
3. **Click cell I4**
   Because you used relative cell addressing in the formula in cell I3, the copied formula adjusted so that the logical test in the formula in cell I4 is H4>=B14 because there is no value in cell B14, it has a value of zero. You need to use an absolute reference for cell B13 in the IF formula to keep the value in from adjusting in a relative way as the formula is copied. That way, the formula will always reference the target increase in cell B13.
4. **Click cell I3, press F2 to change to Edit mode, select B13 in the formula, then press F4**
   When you press F4, dollar signs are inserted in the B13 cell reference, making it an absolute reference as shown in **Figure 3-7**.
5. **Click the Enter button ✓, then drag the fill handle from cell I3 to cell I11**
   Because the formula correctly contains an absolute cell reference, the correct target status appears for each location in cells I4:I11. Compare your worksheet to **Figure 3-8**.
6. **Save your work**

**Quick Tip**
Before you copy or move a formula, always check whether you need to use an absolute cell reference.

**Quick Tip**
When changing a cell reference to an absolute reference, make sure the reference is selected or the insertion point is to the left of the reference you want to change before pressing F4.

**Figure 3-7:** Absolute reference created in formula

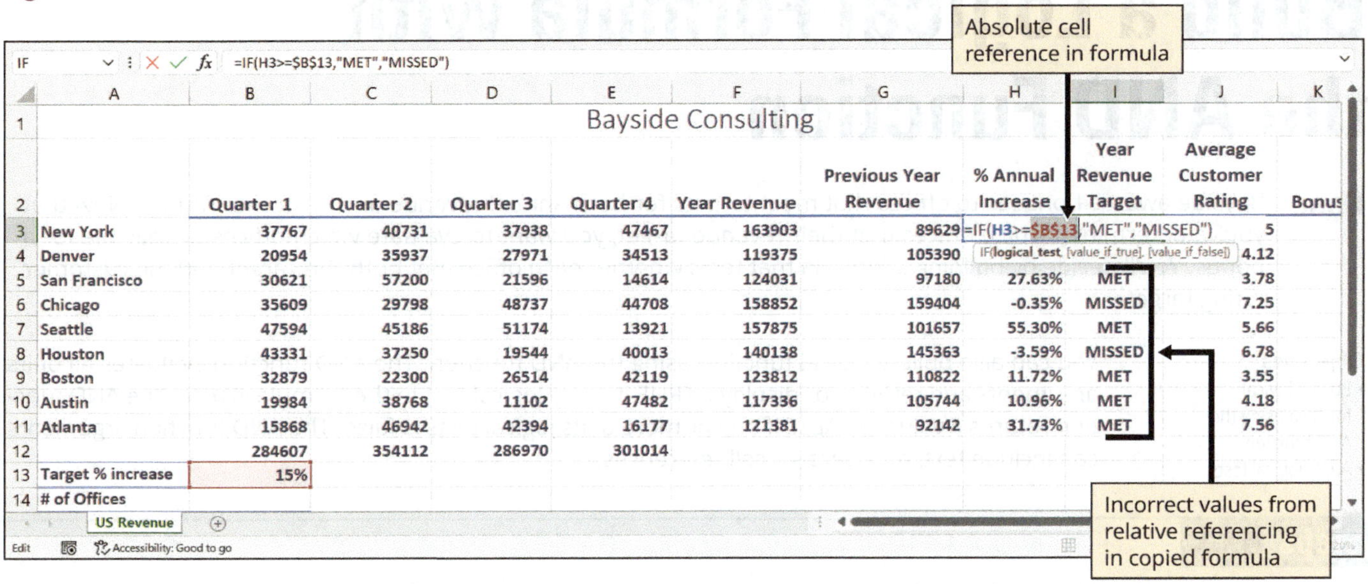


**Figure 3-8:** Correct percentages calculated

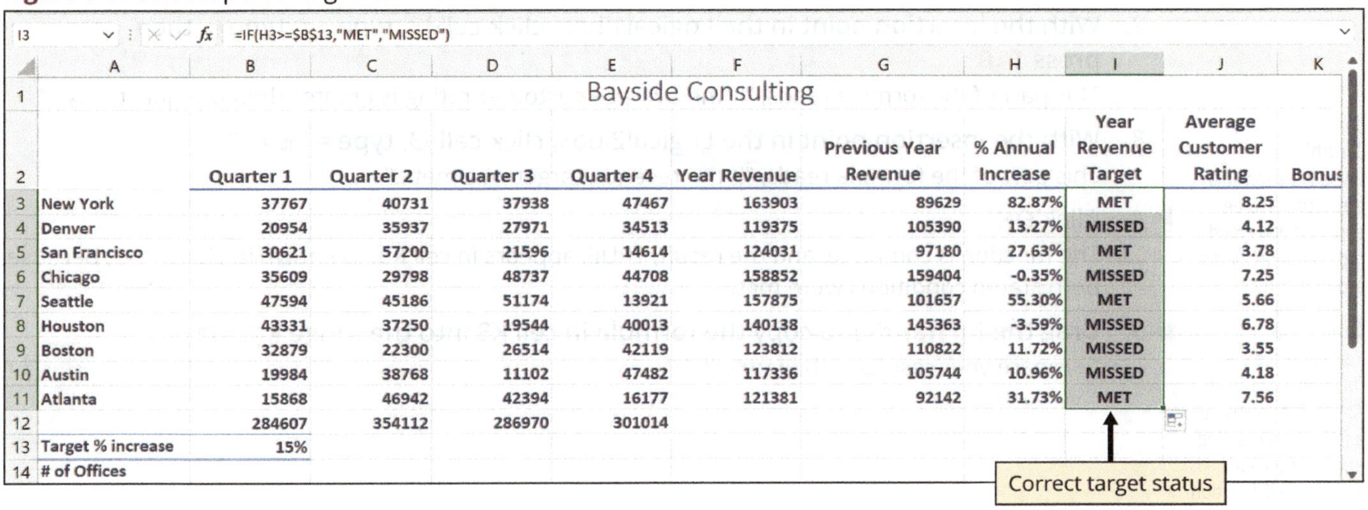


## Using a mixed reference

Sometimes when you copy a formula, you want to change the row reference but keep the column reference the same. This type of cell referencing, where one factor remains constant and the other one varies, is a **mixed reference**. For example, when copied, a formula containing the mixed reference C$14 would change the column letter relative to its new location, but not the row number. In the mixed reference $C14, the column letter would not change, but the row number would be updated relative to its location. Like an absolute reference, a mixed reference can be created by pressing F4 with the cell reference selected. With each press of the F4 key, you cycle through all the possible combinations of relative, absolute, and mixed references (C14, $C$14, C$14, and $C14).

# Build a Logical Formula with the AND Function

**Case** Bayside awards bonuses to offices that meet targets for both annual revenue and customer ratings. Now that you've determined which offices met their revenue target, you want to evaluate which offices are eligible for a bonus. You'll decide by building a formula that tests whether each office met both this target and the customer rating target.

**Objectives**
- Build a logical formula using the AND function
- Apply logical tests

You can also build a logical function using the AND function. The AND function evaluates all of its arguments and returns, or displays, TRUE if every logical test in the formula is true. The AND function returns a value of FALSE if one or more of its logical tests is false. The AND function arguments can include text, numbers, or cell references.

## Steps

1. **Click cell K3, click the Formulas tab on the ribbon, click the Logical button in the Function Library group, then click AND**
   The Function Arguments dialog box opens.
2. **With the insertion point in the Logical1 box, click cell J3, type >=, type 6, then press TAB**
   This part of the formula reads, "If the average customer rating is greater than or equal to six..."
3. **With the insertion point in the Logical2 box, click cell I3, type = "MET"**
   This part of the formula reads, "If the revenue target was met..."
4. **Click OK**
   The function is complete, and the result, TRUE, appears in cell K3, as shown in **Figure 3-9**, because both stated conditions were met.
5. **Drag the fill handle to copy the formula in cell K3 into the range K4:K11**
   Compare your results with **Figure 3-10**.

**Trouble**
If you get a formula error, check to be sure that you typed the quotation marks around MET.

**Quick Tip**
You can place one function, such as an AND function, inside a formula containing another function, such as an IF function. For example, you could replace the formulas in cell I3 and K3 with one formula in K3 that reads =IF(AND(H3>=$B$13, J3>=6),"TRUE", "FALSE").

### Using the OR and NOT logical functions

The **OR logical function** follows the same syntax as the AND function, but rather than returning TRUE if every argument is true, the OR function will return TRUE if any of its arguments are true. It will only return FALSE if all of its arguments are false. The **NOT logical function** reverses the value of its argument. For example, NOT(TRUE) reverses its argument of TRUE and returns FALSE. You might want to use this function in a worksheet to ensure that a cell is not equal to a particular value. **Table 3-2** lists examples of the AND, OR, and NOT functions.

**Figure 3-9:** Worksheet with AND function

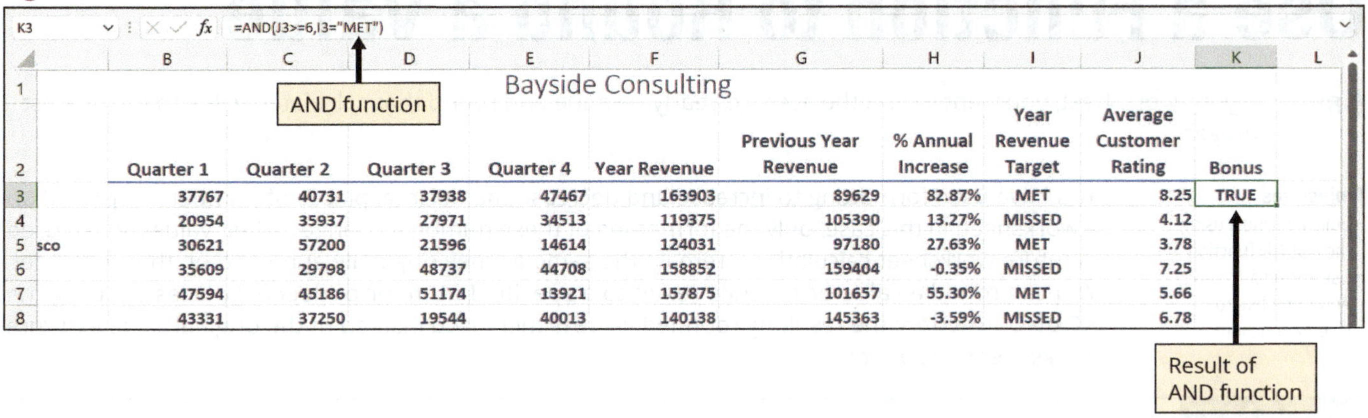


| | A | B | C | D | E | F | G | H | I | J | K |
|---|---|---|---|---|---|---|---|---|---|---|---|
| 1 | | | | | | Bayside Consulting | | | | | |
| 2 | | Quarter 1 | Quarter 2 | Quarter 3 | Quarter 4 | Year Revenue | Previous Year Revenue | % Annual Increase | Year Revenue Target | Average Customer Rating | Bonus |
| 3 | | 37767 | 40731 | 37938 | 47467 | 163903 | 89629 | 82.87% | MET | 8.25 | TRUE |
| 4 | | 20954 | 35937 | 27971 | 34513 | 119375 | 105390 | 13.27% | MISSED | 4.12 | |
| 5 | sco | 30621 | 57200 | 21596 | 14614 | 124031 | 97180 | 27.63% | MET | 3.78 | |
| 6 | | 35609 | 29798 | 48737 | 44708 | 158852 | 159404 | -0.35% | MISSED | 7.25 | |
| 7 | | 47594 | 45186 | 51174 | 13921 | 157875 | 101657 | 55.30% | MET | 5.66 | |
| 8 | | 43331 | 37250 | 19544 | 40013 | 140138 | 145363 | -3.59% | MISSED | 6.78 | |

**Figure 3-10:** Worksheet with bonus status for all offices

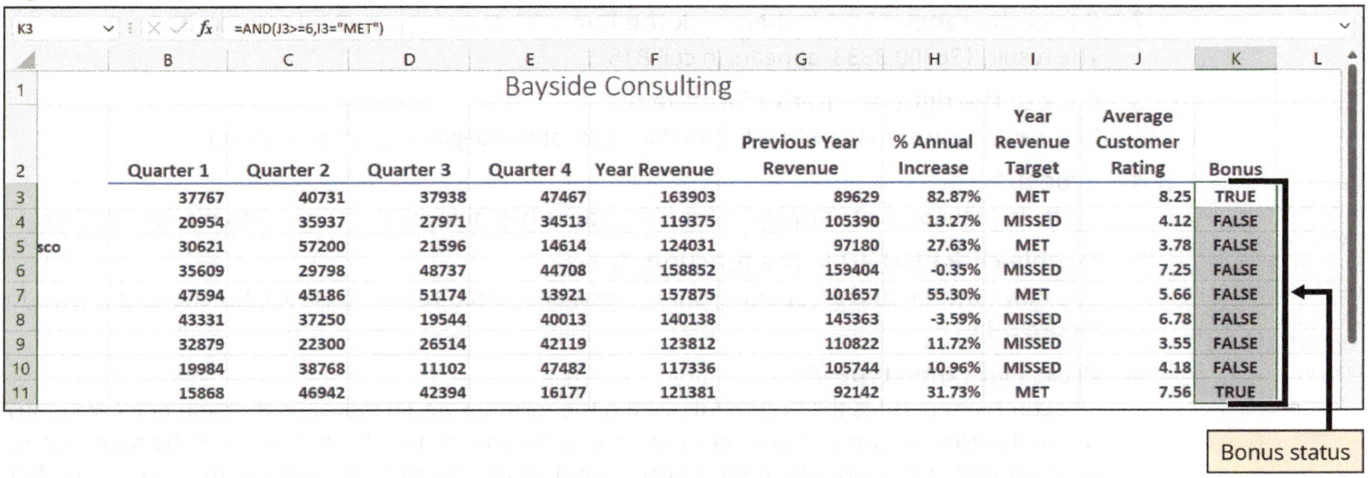


| | A | B | C | D | E | F | G | H | I | J | K |
|---|---|---|---|---|---|---|---|---|---|---|---|
| 1 | | | | | | Bayside Consulting | | | | | |
| 2 | | Quarter 1 | Quarter 2 | Quarter 3 | Quarter 4 | Year Revenue | Previous Year Revenue | % Annual Increase | Year Revenue Target | Average Customer Rating | Bonus |
| 3 | | 37767 | 40731 | 37938 | 47467 | 163903 | 89629 | 82.87% | MET | 8.25 | TRUE |
| 4 | | 20954 | 35937 | 27971 | 34513 | 119375 | 105390 | 13.27% | MISSED | 4.12 | FALSE |
| 5 | sco | 30621 | 57200 | 21596 | 14614 | 124031 | 97180 | 27.63% | MET | 3.78 | FALSE |
| 6 | | 35609 | 29798 | 48737 | 44708 | 158852 | 159404 | -0.35% | MISSED | 7.25 | FALSE |
| 7 | | 47594 | 45186 | 51174 | 13921 | 157875 | 101657 | 55.30% | MET | 5.66 | FALSE |
| 8 | | 43331 | 37250 | 19544 | 40013 | 140138 | 145363 | -3.59% | MISSED | 6.78 | FALSE |
| 9 | | 32879 | 22300 | 26514 | 42119 | 123812 | 110822 | 11.72% | MISSED | 3.55 | FALSE |
| 10 | | 19984 | 38768 | 11102 | 47482 | 117336 | 105744 | 10.96% | MISSED | 4.18 | FALSE |
| 11 | | 15868 | 46942 | 42394 | 16177 | 121381 | 92142 | 31.73% | MET | 7.56 | TRUE |

**Table 3-2:** Examples of AND, OR, and NOT functions with cell values A1=10 and B1=20

| function | formula | result |
|---|---|---|
| AND | =AND(A1>5,B1>25) | FALSE |
| OR | =OR(A1>5,B1>25) | TRUE |
| NOT | =NOT(A1=0) | TRUE |

# Use a Function to Round a Value

**Case** In your worksheet, you want to find the average yearly revenue and round that calculated value to the nearest integer.

**Objectives**
- Build a formula using the ROUND function
- Use Formula AutoComplete to insert a function

You have used formatting to increase and decrease the decimal places of numbers displayed on a worksheet. In this case, only the formatting of these numbers changes. Their values, when used in future worksheet calculations, remain the same as they originally appeared on the worksheet. You can round a value or formula result to a specified number of decimal places by using the **ROUND function**; the resulting rounded value is then used instead of the original value in future worksheet calculations.

## Steps

1. **Click cell B15, if necessary click the Home tab on the ribbon, click the AutoSum arrow Σ▾ in the Editing group, then click Average**
2. **Select the range F3:F11, then click the Enter button ✓ on the formula bar**
   The result, 136300.3333, appears in cell B15.
3. **Click to the right of = in the formula bar**
   You want to position the ROUND function here, at the beginning of the formula.
4. **Type RO**
   Formula AutoComplete displays a list of functions beginning with RO beneath the formula bar.
5. **Double-click ROUND in the functions list**
   The new function and an opening parenthesis are added to the AVERAGE function, as shown in **Figure 3-11**.
6. **Press END, then type ,0)**
   The comma separates the arguments within the formula, and 0 indicates that you don't want any decimal places to appear in the calculated value. You may have also noticed that the parentheses at either end of the formula briefly became bold, indicating that you entered the correct number of open and closed parentheses so the formula is balanced. Rounding the average to zero decimal places changes the actual value in cell B15. On the other hand, using decimal place formatting would only affect the appearance of the value.
7. **Click the Enter button ✓ on the formula bar**
8. **Compare your worksheet to Figure 3-12, then save your work**

**Quick Tip**
In the Insert Function dialog box and Function Library on the Formulas tab, the ROUND function is in the Math & Trig category.

**Trouble**
If you have too many or too few parentheses, the extraneous parenthesis is displayed in red, or a warning dialog box opens with a suggested solution to the error.

**Figure 3-11:** ROUND function added to an existing function

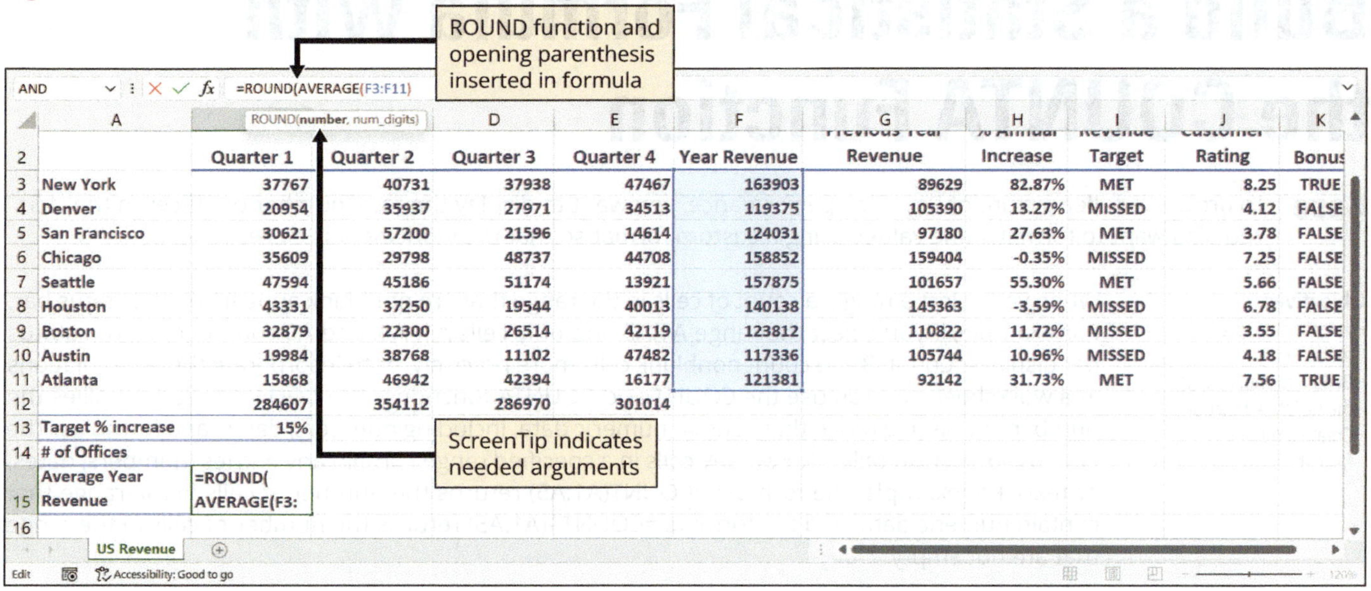


**Figure 3-12:** Rounded year average

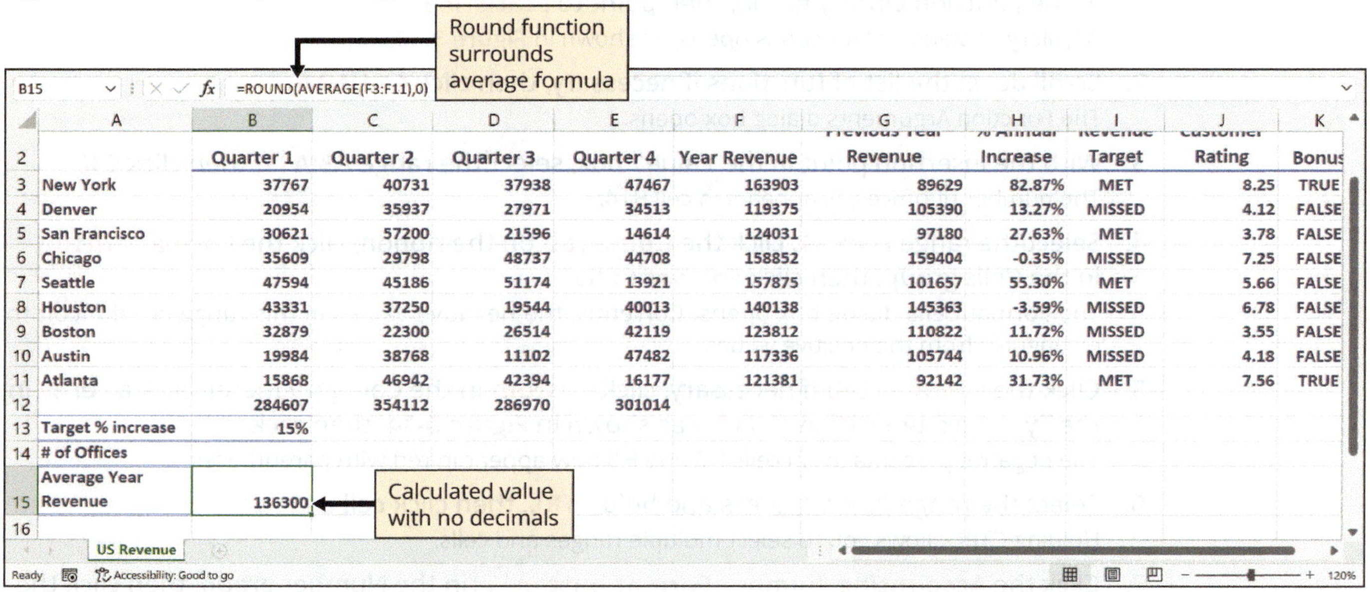


## Using Excel rounding functions

You can use other rounding functions besides ROUND to fine-tune the rounding results you want to display. The **MROUND function** rounds a number to the nearest multiple of another number. The syntax is: MROUND(number, multiple). For example, MROUND(14,3) returns the value 15 because 15 is the nearest multiple of 3 to 14. The **ROUNDDOWN function** works like the ROUND function except that rather than rounding a number to the next closest value, it always rounds down. The syntax is ROUNDDOWN(number, num_digits). For example, =ROUNDDOWN(15.778, 2) returns a value of 15.77 because this is the nearest two-digit number below 15.778. The **ROUNDUP function** works similarly but rounds a number up. The syntax is ROUNDUP(number, num_digits). For example, =ROUNDUP(15.778, 2) returns a value of 15.78.

# Build a Statistical Formula with the COUNTA Function

**Case** To provide a fuller picture of Bayside's performance, you want to display the total number of offices in the U.S. You also want to format some values using a custom format so that the worksheet is easier to read.

**Objectives**
- Insert a statistical function
- Build a formula using the COUNTA function
- Create a number format

When you select a range, a count of cells in the range that are not blank appears on the status bar. For example, if you select the range A1:A5 and only cells A1, A4, and A5 contain data, the status bar displays "Count: 3." To count nonblank cells more precisely, or to incorporate these calculations in a worksheet, you can use the COUNT and COUNTA functions. The **COUNT function** tallies the number of cells in a range that contain numeric data, including numbers, dates, and formulas. The **COUNTA function** tallies how many cells in a specified range contain any entries (numbers, dates, or text). For example, the formula =COUNT(A1:A5) returns the number of cells in the range that contain numeric data, and the formula =COUNTA(A1:A5) returns the number of cells in the range that are not empty.

## Steps

1. **Click cell B14, click the Formulas tab on the ribbon, click the More Functions button in the Function Library group, then point to Statistical**
   A gallery of statistical functions opens, as shown in **Figure 3-13**.
2. **Scroll down the list of functions if necessary, then click COUNTA**
   The Function Arguments dialog box opens.
3. **With the insertion point in the Value1 box, select the range A3:A11, then click OK**
   The number of offices, 9, appears in cell B14.
4. **Select the range H3:H11, click the Home tab on the ribbon, click the Format button in the Cells group, then click Format Cells**
   The Format Cells dialog box opens. Currently, the negative values in this range are difficult to distinguish from the positive values.
5. **Click the Number tab if necessary, click Custom in the Category menu, click after % in the Type box, type ;[Red](0.00%) as shown in Figure 3-14, then click OK**
   The negative percentages in cells H6 and H8 now appear in red with parentheses.
6. **Select the range B3:G11, press and hold CTRL, then click cell B15**
   Holding CTRL allows you to select multiple ranges and cells.
7. **Click the Accounting Number Format button [$] in the Number group, then click the Decrease Decimal button [.00→.0] twice**
   Formatting these revenue figures makes them easier to read. Compare your worksheet to **Figure 3-15**.
8. **Save your work**

**Figure 3-13:** Statistical functions

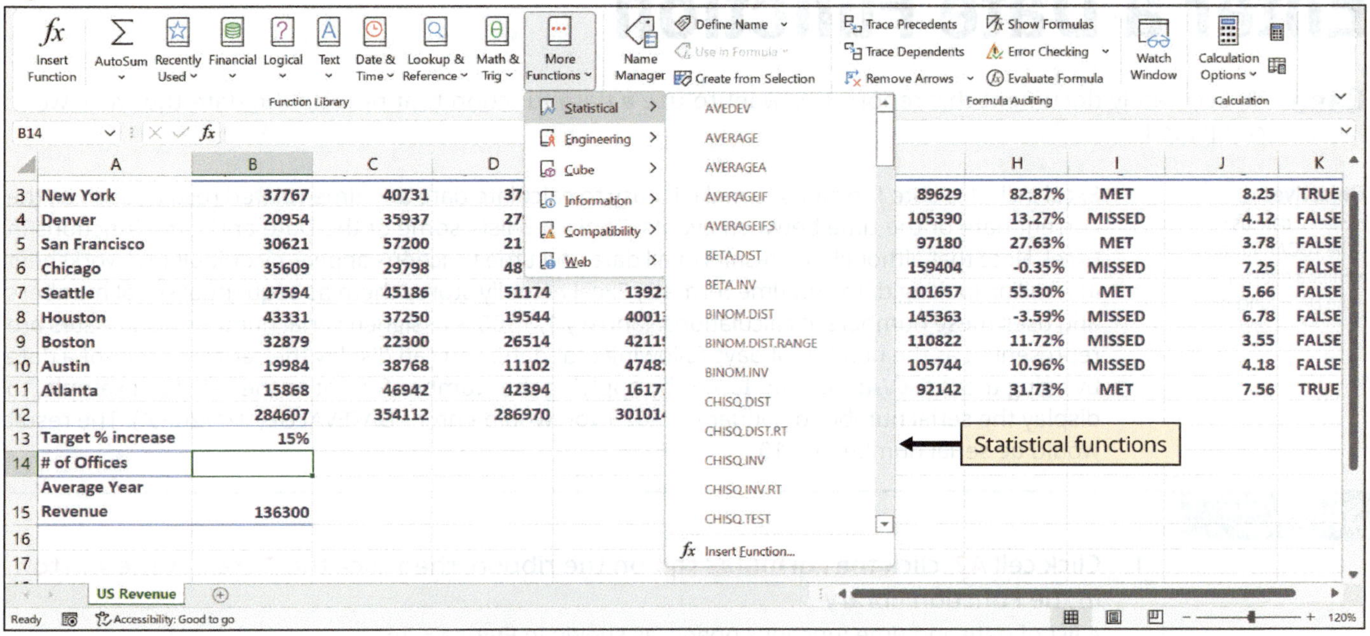


**Figure 3-14:** Custom number format

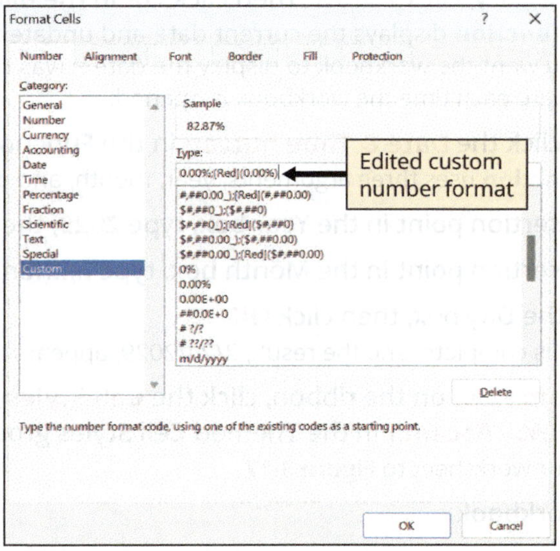


**Figure 3-15:** Formatted worksheet

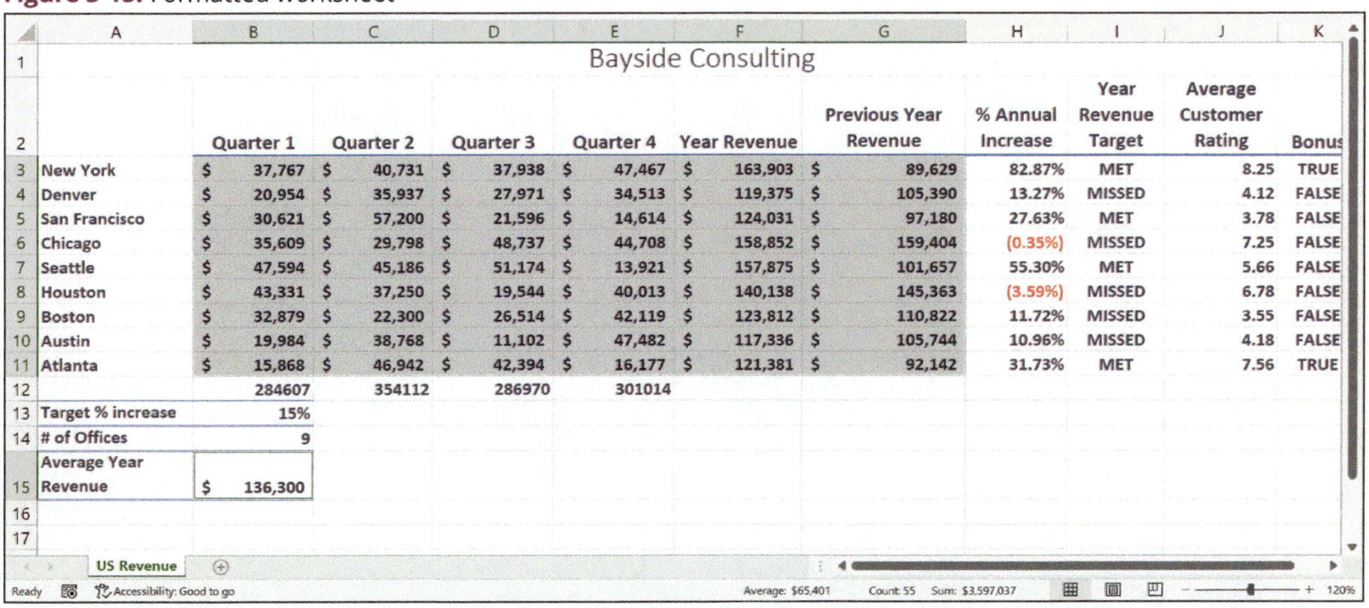

| | A | B | C | D | E | F | G | H | I | J | K |
|---|---|---|---|---|---|---|---|---|---|---|---|
| 1 | | | | | Bayside Consulting | | | | | | |
| 2 | | Quarter 1 | Quarter 2 | Quarter 3 | Quarter 4 | Year Revenue | Previous Year Revenue | % Annual Increase | Year Revenue Target | Average Customer Rating | Bonus |
| 3 | New York | $ 37,767 | $ 40,731 | $ 37,938 | $ 47,467 | $ 163,903 | $ 89,629 | 82.87% | MET | 8.25 | TRUE |
| 4 | Denver | $ 20,954 | $ 35,937 | $ 27,971 | $ 34,513 | $ 119,375 | $ 105,390 | 13.27% | MISSED | 4.12 | FALSE |
| 5 | San Francisco | $ 30,621 | $ 57,200 | $ 21,596 | $ 14,614 | $ 124,031 | $ 97,180 | 27.63% | MET | 3.78 | FALSE |
| 6 | Chicago | $ 35,609 | $ 29,798 | $ 48,737 | $ 44,708 | $ 158,852 | $ 159,404 | (0.35%) | MISSED | 7.25 | FALSE |
| 7 | Seattle | $ 47,594 | $ 45,186 | $ 51,174 | $ 13,921 | $ 157,875 | $ 101,657 | 55.30% | MET | 5.66 | FALSE |
| 8 | Houston | $ 43,331 | $ 37,250 | $ 19,544 | $ 40,013 | $ 140,138 | $ 145,363 | (3.59%) | MISSED | 6.78 | FALSE |
| 9 | Boston | $ 32,879 | $ 22,300 | $ 26,514 | $ 42,119 | $ 123,812 | $ 110,822 | 11.72% | MISSED | 3.55 | FALSE |
| 10 | Austin | $ 19,984 | $ 38,768 | $ 11,102 | $ 47,482 | $ 117,336 | $ 105,744 | 10.96% | MISSED | 4.18 | FALSE |
| 11 | Atlanta | $ 15,868 | $ 46,942 | $ 42,394 | $ 16,177 | $ 121,381 | $ 92,142 | 31.73% | MET | 7.56 | TRUE |
| 12 | | 284607 | 354112 | 286970 | 301014 | | | | | | |
| 13 | Target % increase | 15% | | | | | | | | | |
| 14 | # of Offices | 9 | | | | | | | | | |
| 15 | Average Year Revenue | $ 136,300 | | | | | | | | | |
| 16 | | | | | | | | | | | |
| 17 | | | | | | | | | | | |

# Enter a Date Function

**Case** To accurately document this report, you want to use a date function that reflects the date the work was completed.

**Objectives**
- Enter a date using the TODAY function
- Enter a date using the DATE function

Excel includes date functions to make it easy to calculate date and time-related results, such as the current date or the time between events. **Table 3-3** lists some of the Date and Time functions in Excel. Note that although the results of all date and time functions appear by default in a worksheet in familiar-looking date and time formats, Excel actually stores them as sequential serial numbers and uses these numbers in calculations. January 1, 1900 is assigned serial number 1 and dates are represented as the number of days following that date. You can display the serial number of a date by using the **DATEVALUE function** or by applying the Number format to the cell. For example, to display the serial number of January 1, 2029 you would enter =DATEVALUE("1/1/2029"). The result would be serial number 47119.

## Steps

1. **Click cell A2, click the Formulas tab on the ribbon, then click the Date & Time button in the Function library**
   A list of date and time functions opens, as shown in **Figure 3-16**.
2. **Scroll if necessary, click TODAY, then click OK in the dialog box**
   The **TODAY function** displays the current date and updates each time a worksheet is opened. However, you want the workbook to display the date it was completed, rather than adjusting for the current date each time the workbook is opened.

**Quick Tip**
To apply a format to a selection of time data, you can click the Format button in the Cells group, click Format Cells, click Time in the Category list, select the time format in the Type list, then click OK. For example, choosing the 13:30 type would display the time of 11:15 PM as 23:15.

3. **Press DEL, click the Date & Time button in the Function Library, then click DATE**
   The **DATE function** uses three arguments, year, month, and day, to enter a date.
4. **With the insertion point in the Year box, type 2029, then press TAB**
5. **With the insertion point in the Month box, type 2, then press TAB**
6. **Type 24 in the Day box, then click OK**
   The function is complete, and the result, 2/24/2029, appears in cell A2.
7. **Click the Home tab on the ribbon, click the Cell Styles button in the Styles group, then click 20% - Accent1 in the Themed Cell Styles group**
   Compare your worksheet to **Figure 3-17**.
8. **Save the workbook**

**Figure 3-16:** Date & Time functions

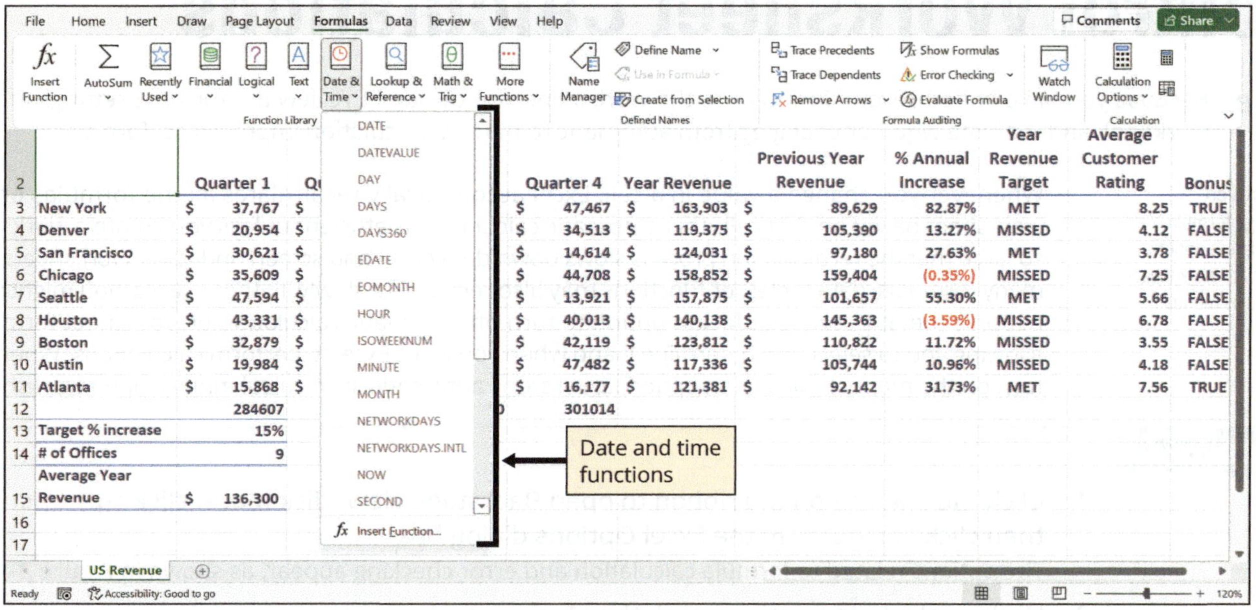


**Figure 3-17:** Formatted date

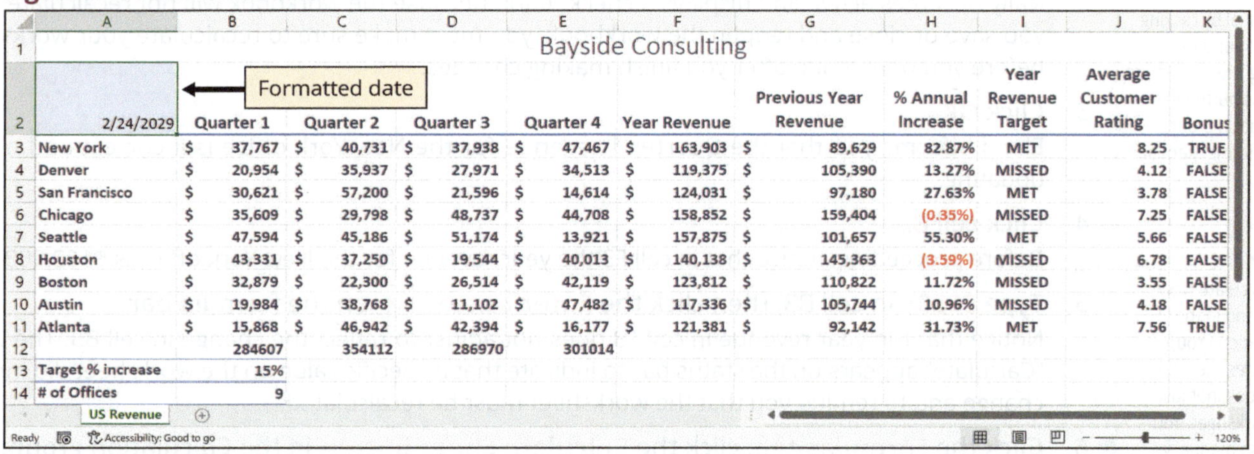


**Table 3-3:** Date and Time functions

| function | calculates | example formula | example result |
|---|---|---|---|
| DAY | The day of the month using a date serial number | =DAY(47297) | 28 |
| NOW | The current date and time | =NOW() | 1/1/2029 10:00 |
| MONTH | The month number using a date serial number | =MONTH(47297) | 6 |
| TIME | A serial number in time format from hours, minutes, and seconds | =TIME(5,12,20) | 0.216898 |
| TIMEVALUE | A serial time in text format | =TIMEVALUE("5:15:24") | .219028 |
| YEAR | The year portion of a date | =YEAR(47297) | 2029 |
| HOUR | The hour portion of a time | =HOUR("6:45:21 PM") | 18 |
| MINUTE | The minute portion of a time | =MINUTE("6:45:21 PM") | 45 |
| SECOND | The second portion of a time | =SECOND("6:45:21 PM") | 21 |
| WEEKDAY | The day of the week from a serial date ( 1 = Sunday, 2 = Monday...) | =WEEKDAY("6/21/2029") | 5 |
| WORKDAY | A serial number in date format after a certain number of working days | =WORKDAY(47297,5) | 47304 (When formatted as a date: 1/8/2029) |

# Control Worksheet Calculations

**Case** Because you have added several formulas to the worksheet, you decide to review the formula settings in the workbook and evaluate whether changing from automatic to manual calculation improves performance.

**Objectives**
- Change formula calculation options
- Calculate worksheet formulas manually

Whenever you change a value in a cell, Excel automatically recalculates all the formulas on the worksheet based on that cell. This automatic calculation is efficient unless you create a worksheet so large that the recalculation process slows down data entry and screen updating. Worksheets with many formulas, data tables, or functions may also recalculate slowly. In these cases, you might want to apply the **manual calculation** option to turn off automatic calculation of worksheet formulas, allowing you to selectively determine if and when you want Excel to perform calculations. When you turn on the manual calculation option, Excel stops automatically recalculating all open worksheets.

## Steps

1. **Click the File tab on the ribbon to open Backstage view, click More, click Options, then click Formulas in the Excel Options dialog box**
   The options related to formula calculation and error checking appear, as shown in **Figure 3-18**.

**Quick Tip**
You can also change the formula calculation to manual by clicking the Formulas tab, clicking the Calculation Options button in the Calculation group, then clicking Manual.

2. **Under Calculation options, click the Manual option button**
   When you select the Manual option, the Recalculate workbook before saving check box automatically becomes active and displays a check mark. Because the workbook will not recalculate until you save or close and reopen the workbook, you must make sure to recalculate your worksheet before you print it and after you finish making changes.

3. **Click OK**
   Elena informs you that the Quarter 1 revenue for the New York office is incorrect and needs updating.

4. **Click cell B3**
   Before proceeding, notice that in cell F3 the year revenue for the New York office is $163,903.

**Quick Tip**
The Calculate Now command in the Calculation group calculates the entire workbook, not just the worksheet. You can also manually recalculate a workbook by pressing F9. Pressing SHIFT+F9 recalculates only the current worksheet.

5. **Type 36305 in cell B3, then click the Enter button ✓ on the formula bar**
   Notice that the year revenue in cell F3 does not adjust to reflect the change in cell B3. The word "Calculate" appears on the status bar to indicate that a specific value on the worksheet did indeed change and to remind you that the worksheet must be recalculated.

6. **Click the Formulas tab, click the Calculate Sheet button in the Calculation group, click cell A1, then save the workbook**
   The year revenue in cell F3 is now $162,441. The other formulas on the worksheet affected by the value in cell B3 changed as well, as shown in **Figure 3-19**. Because this is a relatively small worksheet that recalculates quickly, you decide that the manual calculation option is not necessary.

**Quick Tip**
If your worksheet contains a table, such as a complex payment schedule, you may want to use manual recalculation just for the table. To do so, click the Automatic Except for Data Tables option in the list of calculation options.

7. **Click the Calculation Options button in the Calculation group, then click Automatic**
   Using the commands on the Calculation Options button is a quick alternative to opening the Options dialog box. Now any additional changes you make will automatically recalculate the worksheet formulas.

8. **Enter your name in the center section of the worksheet footer, save your changes, activate cell A1, submit the workbook to your instructor as directed, close the workbook, then close Excel**

**Figure 3-18:** Excel formula options

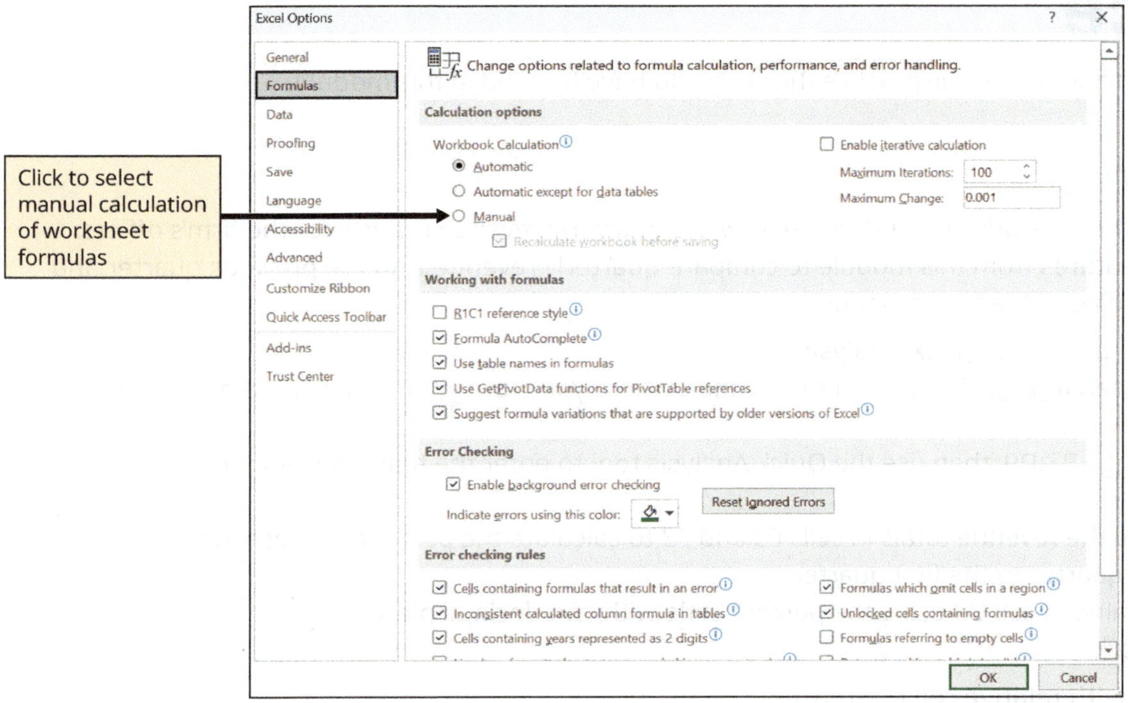


**Figure 3-19:** Worksheet with updated values

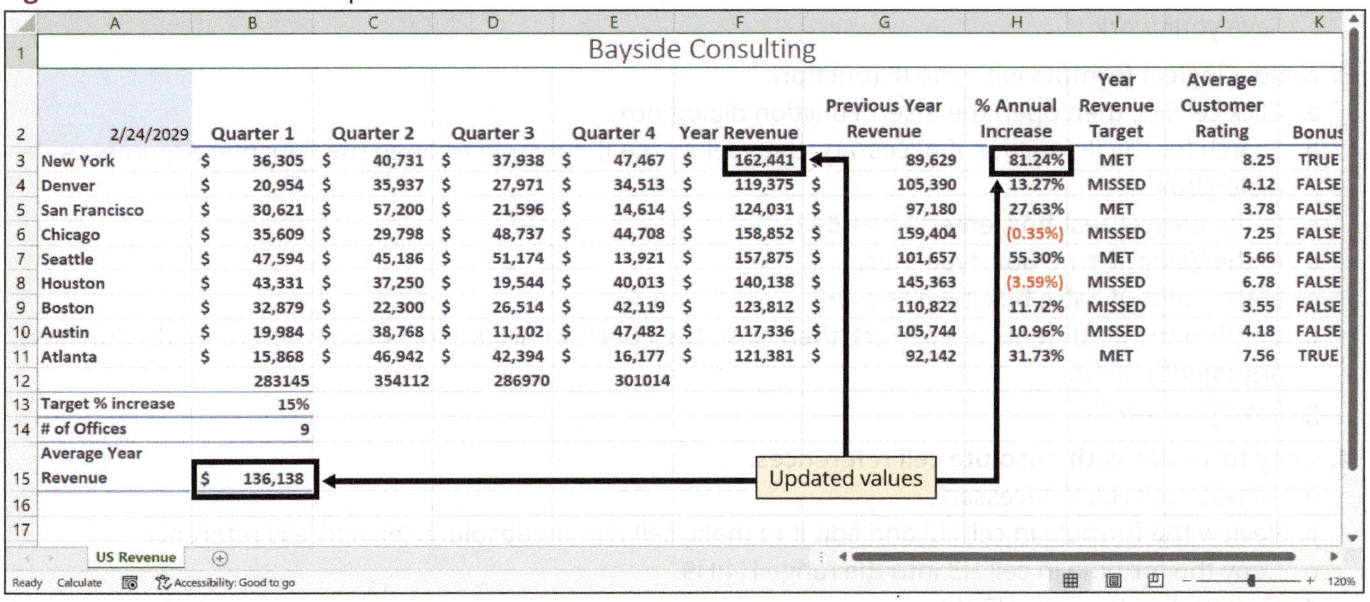

| | A | B | C | D | E | F | G | H | I | J | K |
|---|---|---|---|---|---|---|---|---|---|---|---|
| 1 | Bayside Consulting | | | | | | | | | | |
| 2 | 2/24/2029 | Quarter 1 | Quarter 2 | Quarter 3 | Quarter 4 | Year Revenue | Previous Year Revenue | % Annual Increase | Year Revenue Target | Average Customer Rating | Bonus |
| 3 | New York | $ 36,305 | $ 40,731 | $ 37,938 | $ 47,467 | $ 162,441 | 89,629 | 81.24% | MET | 8.25 | TRUE |
| 4 | Denver | $ 20,954 | $ 35,937 | $ 27,971 | $ 34,513 | $ 119,375 | $ 105,390 | 13.27% | MISSED | 4.12 | FALSE |
| 5 | San Francisco | $ 30,621 | $ 57,200 | $ 21,596 | $ 14,614 | $ 124,031 | $ 97,180 | 27.63% | MET | 3.78 | FALSE |
| 6 | Chicago | $ 35,609 | $ 29,798 | $ 48,737 | $ 44,708 | $ 158,852 | $ 159,404 | (0.35%) | MISSED | 7.25 | FALSE |
| 7 | Seattle | $ 47,594 | $ 45,186 | $ 51,174 | $ 13,921 | $ 157,875 | $ 101,657 | 55.30% | MET | 5.66 | FALSE |
| 8 | Houston | $ 43,331 | $ 37,250 | $ 19,544 | $ 40,013 | $ 140,138 | $ 145,363 | (3.59%) | MISSED | 6.78 | FALSE |
| 9 | Boston | $ 32,879 | $ 22,300 | $ 26,514 | $ 42,119 | $ 123,812 | $ 110,822 | 11.72% | MISSED | 3.55 | FALSE |
| 10 | Austin | $ 19,984 | $ 38,768 | $ 11,102 | $ 47,482 | $ 117,336 | $ 105,744 | 10.96% | MISSED | 4.18 | FALSE |
| 11 | Atlanta | $ 15,868 | $ 46,942 | $ 42,394 | $ 16,177 | $ 121,381 | $ 92,142 | 31.73% | MET | 7.56 | TRUE |
| 12 | | 283145 | 354112 | 286970 | 301014 | | | | | | |
| 13 | Target % increase | 15% | | | | | | | | | |
| 14 | # of Offices | 9 | | | | | | | | | |
| 15 | Average Year Revenue | $ 136,138 | | | | | | | | | |
| 16 | | | | | | | | | | | |
| 17 | | | | | | | | | | | |



## Showing and printing worksheet formulas

Sometimes you need to display or keep a record of all the formulas in a worksheet. You might want to do this to display a complex calculation, so you can explain it to others. To display formulas rather than results in a worksheet, first, open the workbook. Click the Formulas tab on the ribbon, then click the Show Formulas button in the Formula Auditing group to select it. When the Show Formulas button is selected, formulas rather than resulting values are displayed on the worksheet, and any entered values appear without number formatting. You can print the worksheet to save a record of all the formulas. The Show Formulas button is a toggle: click it again to display the values, rather than the formulas, on the worksheet. You can also display a formula in a cell using the syntax =FORMULATEXT(Cell address). For example, entering =FORMULATEXT(A1) in a cell would display the text of the formula in cell A1.

# Practice

In the exercises that follow, you will practice the skills you have learned in this module.

## Skills Review

As a junior analyst for Enterprise Capital, you review the quarterly revenue reports for the firm's offices. You will use Excel features from this module to compare quarterly revenue with the previous quarter and determine if each office will receive a bonus.

1. **Enter a formula using the Quick Analysis tool.**
   a. Start Excel, open IL_EX_3-2.xlsx from the location where you store your Data Files, then save it as **IL_EX_3_Enterprise**.
   b. Select the range B3:D9, then use the Quick Analysis tool to enter the first quarter revenue totals in column E.
   c. In cell G3, use the revenue totals in cells E3 and F3 to calculate the percent increase in revenue from the previous quarter to the first quarter.
   d. Format the value in cell G3 using the percent style with two decimal places.
   e. Save your work.
2. **Copy formulas with relative cell references.**
   a. In cell G3, use the fill handle to copy the formula in cell G3 to the range G4:G9.
   b. Click cell G4 and review the copied formula making sure the cell references are correct.
   c. Save your work.
3. **Build a logical formula with the IF function.**
   a. Click cell H3, then open the Insert Function dialog box.
   b. Search for the IF function if necessary, then select the IF function to open the Function Arguments dialog box.
   c. In the Logical_test box, enter **G3 >= B11**.
   d. In the Value_if_true box, type **Met**.
   e. In the Value_if_false box, type **Missed**.
   f. Confirm the arguments are correct, then close the Function Arguments dialog, accepting the function argument entries.
   g. Save your work.
4. **Copy formulas with absolute cell references.**
   a. Activate cell H3, if necessary.
   b. Review the formula in cell H3 and edit it to make cell B11 an absolute cell address reference.
   c. Copy the formula in cell H3 into the range H4:H9.
   d. Center align the cells H3:H9.
   e. Save your work.
5. **Build a logical formula with the AND function.**
   a. In cell J3, use the Function Arguments dialog box to enter the formula **=AND(H3="Met",I3>=4)**.
   b. Copy the formula in cell J3 into the range J4:J9.
   c. Save your work.
6. **Round a value with a function.**
   a. In cell B13, use the AutoSum list arrow to enter a function to average the first quarter revenue values in column E.
   b. Use Formula AutoComplete to edit this formula to include the ROUND function showing zero decimal places.

c. Correct any errors in the formula.
d. Save your work.

**7. Build a statistical formula with the COUNTA function.**

a. In cell B12, use a statistical formula to calculate the number of office locations in column A.
b. Create a custom format for the percentages in column G so that the negative values appear in red with parentheses.
c. Format the revenue values in the range B3:F9 and in cell B13 using the Accounting Number Format with no decimal places.
d. Save your work.

**8. Enter a date function.**

a. In cell D12, enter **Report Date**.
b. In cell E12, use the TODAY function to enter today's date.
c. Delete the TODAY function in cell E12, then use the DATE function to enter the date **4/3/2029**.
d. Use the Cell Style Light Blue, 20% - Accent 1, (the first row and first column in the Themed Cell Styles group) to format the range D12:E12.
e. Activate cell A1, then save your work.

**9. Control worksheet calculations.**

a. Open the Formulas category of the Excel Options dialog box.
b. Change the worksheet calculations to manual.
c. Change the value in cell B3 to **70000**.
d. Recalculate the worksheet manually.
e. Change the worksheet calculation back to automatic using the Calculation Options button on the Formulas tab of the ribbon, then save the workbook.
f. Compare your screen to **Figure 3-20**.
g. Save your changes, enter your name in the center section of the footer for the First Quarter sheet, submit your work to your instructor as directed, close the workbook, then close Excel.

**Figure 3-20**

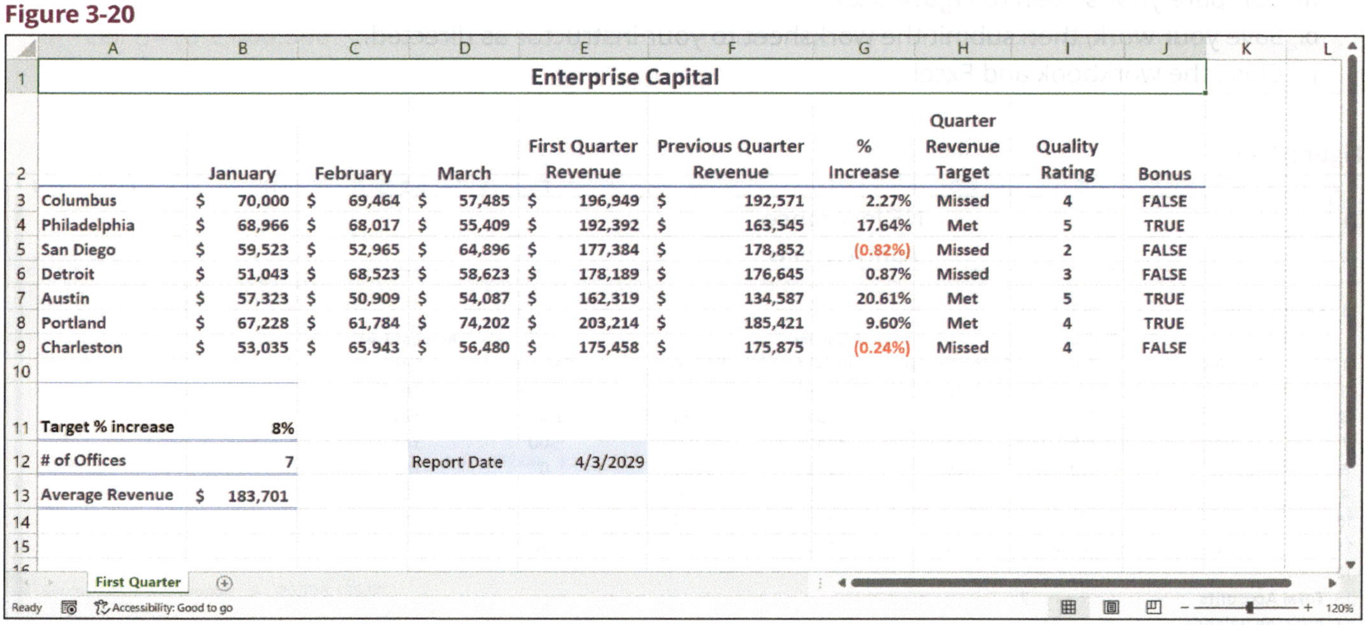

| | A | B | C | D | E | F | G | H | I | J |
|---|---|---|---|---|---|---|---|---|---|---|
| 1 | Enterprise Capital | | | | | | | | | |
| 2 | | January | February | March | First Quarter Revenue | Previous Quarter Revenue | % Increase | Quarter Revenue Target | Quality Rating | Bonus |
| 3 | Columbus | $ 70,000 | $ 69,464 | $ 57,485 | $ 196,949 | $ 192,571 | 2.27% | Missed | 4 | FALSE |
| 4 | Philadelphia | $ 68,966 | $ 68,017 | $ 55,409 | $ 192,392 | $ 163,545 | 17.64% | Met | 5 | TRUE |
| 5 | San Diego | $ 59,523 | $ 52,965 | $ 64,896 | $ 177,384 | $ 178,852 | (0.82%) | Missed | 2 | FALSE |
| 6 | Detroit | $ 51,043 | $ 68,523 | $ 58,623 | $ 178,189 | $ 176,645 | 0.87% | Missed | 3 | FALSE |
| 7 | Austin | $ 57,323 | $ 50,909 | $ 54,087 | $ 162,319 | $ 134,587 | 20.61% | Met | 5 | TRUE |
| 8 | Portland | $ 67,228 | $ 61,784 | $ 74,202 | $ 203,214 | $ 185,421 | 9.60% | Met | 4 | TRUE |
| 9 | Charleston | $ 53,035 | $ 65,943 | $ 56,480 | $ 175,458 | $ 175,875 | (0.24%) | Missed | 4 | FALSE |
| 10 | | | | | | | | | | |
| 11 | Target % increase | 8% | | | | | | | | |
| 12 | # of Offices | 7 | | Report Date | 4/3/2029 | | | | | |
| 13 | Average Revenue | $ 183,701 | | | | | | | | |
| 14 | | | | | | | | | | |
| 15 | | | | | | | | | | |

## Visual Workshop

Open IL_EX_3-5.xlsx from the location where you store your Data Files, then save it as **IL_EX_3_Freight**. Use the skills you learned in this module to complete the worksheet so it looks like the one shown in **Figure 3-23**. To build the formulas in column G, calculate the percentage increase of the fourth quarter revenue over the third quarter revenue. (**Hint**: The percentage increases in column G must be calculated before calculating the average increase in cell B10.) To build the formulas in column I, issue a warning of TRUE if the percentage increase is less than the average increase shown in cell B10 AND the on-time delivery is less than 70%. (**Hint**: Remember to use an absolute cell reference where necessary.) When you are finished, enter your name in the center footer section, then submit your work to your instructor as directed.

**Figure 3-23**

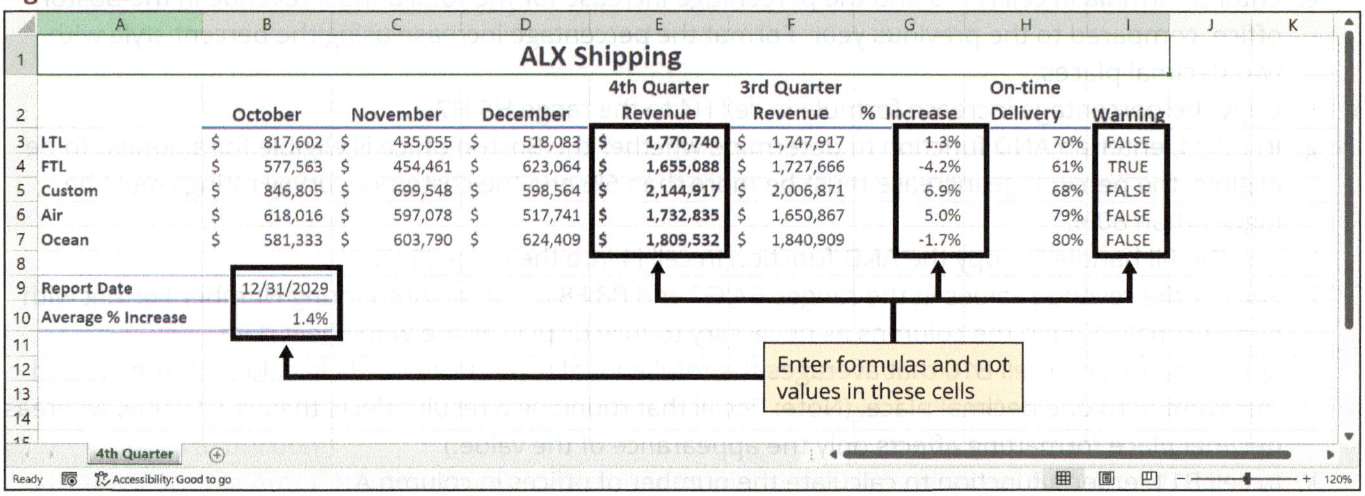

# Working with Charts

## Case

At the upcoming annual meeting, Elena Fuentes, vice president of finance, wants to review revenue at Bayside's U.S. offices. She asks you to create charts illustrating the revenue trends in these offices over the past four quarters.

## Module Objectives

After completing this module, you will be able to:

- Identify chart features
- Create a chart with a title
- Position a chart
- Modify a chart
- Change the chart layout
- Format a chart
- Create a pie chart
- Summarize data with sparklines
- Identify data trends

## Files You Will Need

IL_EX_4-1.xlsx
IL_EX_4-2.xlsx
IL_EX_4-3.xlsx
IL_EX_4-4.xlsx
IL_EX_4-5.xlsx

# Identify Chart Features

**Case** In preparation for creating the charts for Elena's presentation, you review the purpose of the charts and decide how to organize the data to convey the information most effectively.

**Objectives**
- Identify chart elements
- Identify common chart types

The process of creating a chart involves deciding which data to use and what type of chart best highlights the trends or patterns that are most important, such as steady increases over time or stellar performance by one sales rep compared to others in the same division. Understanding the parts of a chart makes it easier to evaluate specific elements to make sure the chart effectively illustrates your data.

## Details

**Use the following guidelines to plan the chart:**

**Quick Tip**
To display the available charts in Excel, select the worksheet data, click the Insert tab on the ribbon, click the Recommended Charts button in the Charts group, then click the All Charts tab.

- **Determine the purpose of the chart, and identify the data relationships you want to graphically communicate**
  You want to create a chart that displays quarterly revenue for Bayside's U.S. offices. You also want to illustrate whether the quarterly revenue for each office increased or decreased from quarter to quarter.
- **Determine the results you want to display, and decide which chart type is most appropriate**
  Different chart types display data in distinctive ways. For example, a pie chart compares parts of a whole, whereas a line chart is best for displaying trends over time. To choose the best chart type for your data, first decide how you want your data to be interpreted. **Figure 4-1** displays the available chart types in Excel, listed by category on the All Charts tab of the Insert Chart dialog box. **Table 4-1** describes the most frequently-used categories. Because you want to compare Bayside's revenue in multiple offices over a period of four quarters, you decide to use a column chart, which is ideal for comparing parts to each other.
- **Identify the worksheet data you want the chart to illustrate**
  Sometimes you use all the data in a worksheet to create a chart, while at other times you may need to select a range within the sheet. The worksheet from which you are creating your chart contains revenue data for each of the past four quarters and the totals for the past year. To create a column chart, you will need to use all the quarterly data except the quarterly totals.
- **Understand the elements of a chart**
  The chart displayed in **Figure 4-2** contains basic elements of a chart. In the figure, Bayside's offices are on the category axis and revenue dollar amounts are on the value axis. The **category axis**, also called the x-axis, is the horizontal axis in a chart, usually containing the names of data categories. The **value axis**, also called the vertical axis, contains numerical values. In a 2-dimensional chart, it is also known as the y-axis. (Three-dimensional charts contain a **z-axis**, for comparing data across both categories and values.) The area inside the horizontal and vertical axes that contains the graphical representation of the data series is the **plot area**. **Gridlines**, the horizontal and vertical lines, make a chart easier to read. Each piece of data plotted in a chart is a **data point**. In any chart, a **data marker** is a graphical representation of a data point, such as a bar or column. A set of values represented in a chart is a **data series**. In this chart, there are four data series: Quarter 1, Quarter 2, Quarter 3, and Quarter 4. Each is made up of columns of a different color. To differentiate each data series, information called a **legend** or a legend key identifies how the data is represented using colors and/or patterns.

**Figure 4-1:** Insert Chart dialog box lists available charts by category

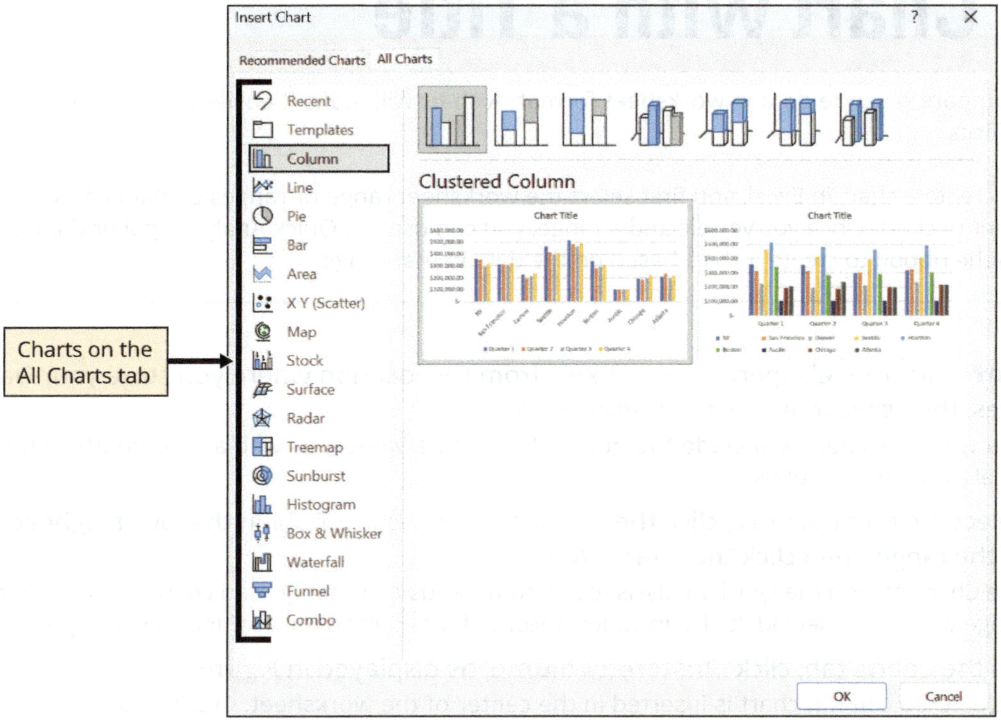


**Figure 4-2:** Chart elements

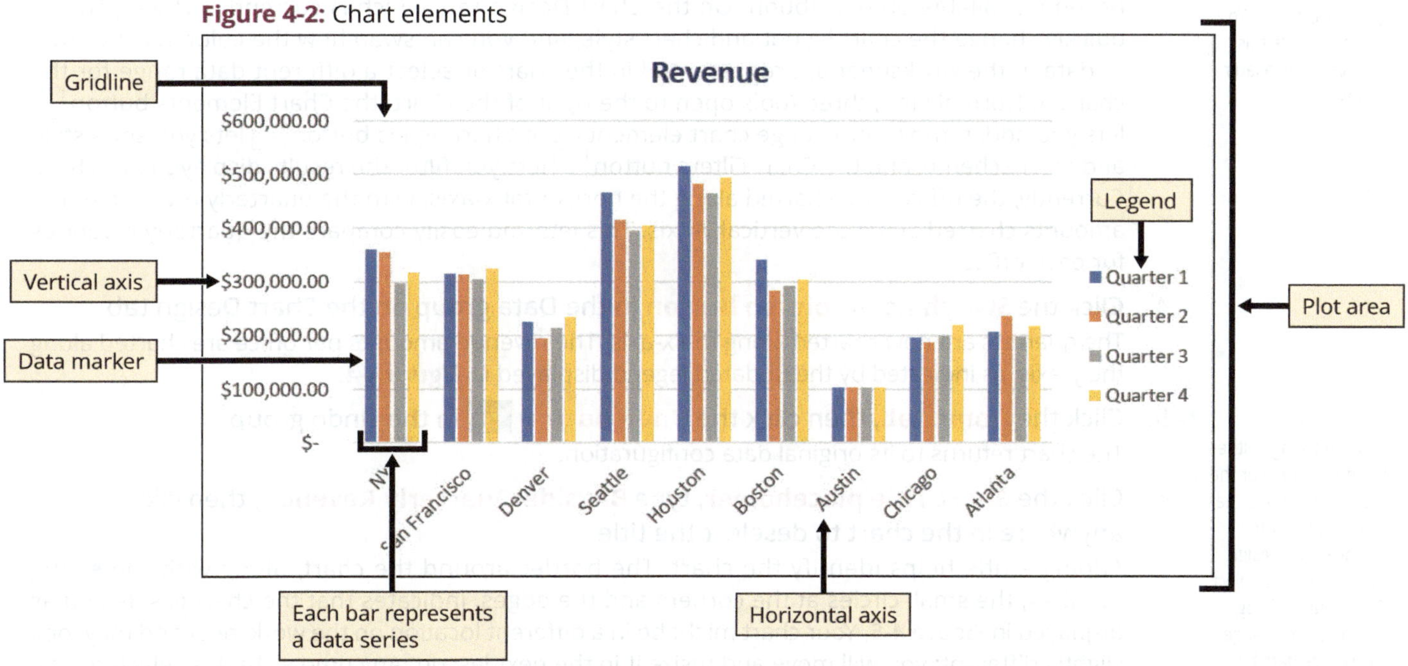


**Table 4-1:** Common chart types

| type | description |
|---|---|
| Column | Displays data values as columns; column height represents its value |
| Line | Displays data as separate lines across categories |
| Pie | Is shaped in a circle and divided into slices like a pie, which displays data values as percentages of the whole |
| Bar | Displays data values in horizontal bars; the length of each bar represents its value |
| Area | Displays how individual volume changes over time in relation to total volume |
| Line with Markers | Compares trends over time by displaying data markers that represent worksheet data values |

# Create a Chart with a Title

**Case** It is difficult to compare revenue data in worksheet format. A chart will make it easier to compare revenues across the U.S. offices.

**Objectives**
- Create a chart
- Add a title to a chart

To create a chart in Excel, you first select the worksheet range or ranges containing the data you want to chart. Once you've selected a range, you can use the Quick Analysis tool or the Insert tab on the ribbon to create a chart based on the data in that range.

## Steps

1. **sam Start Excel, open IL_EX_4-1.xlsx from the location where you store your Data Files, then save it as IL_EX_4_USRevenue**
   You want the chart to include the quarterly revenue values, as well as the quarter and office labels, but not any totals.
2. **Select the range A3:E12, click the Quick Analysis button in the lower-right corner of the range, then click the Charts tab**
   The Charts tab on the Quick Analysis tool recommends commonly used chart types based on the range you have selected. It also includes a More Charts button for additional chart types.
3. **On the Charts tab, click Clustered Column, as displayed in Figure 4-3**
   A clustered column chart is inserted in the center of the worksheet. **Clustered column charts** display data values in side-by-side columns. Two contextual tabs, Chart Design and Format, become available on the ribbon. On the Chart Design tab, which is currently active, you can quickly change the chart layout and chart style, and you can swap how the columns and rows of data in the worksheet are represented in the chart or select a different data range for the chart. In Normal view, three tools open to the right of the chart: the Chart Elements button lets you add, remove, or change chart elements, the Chart Styles button lets you set a style and color scheme, and the Chart Filters button lets you filter the results displayed in a chart. Currently, the offices are charted along the horizontal x-axis, with the quarterly revenue dollar amounts charted along the vertical y-axis. This lets you easily compare the quarterly revenues for each office.
4. **Click the Switch Row/Column button in the Data group on the Chart Design tab**
   The quarters are now charted along the x-axis. The revenue amounts per office are charted along the y-axis, as indicated by the updated legend displayed in Figure 4-4.
5. **Click the Home tab, then click the Undo button in the Undo group**
   The chart returns to its original data configuration.
6. **Click the Chart Title placeholder, type Bayside Quarterly Revenue, then click anywhere in the chart to deselect the title**
   Adding a title helps identify the chart. The border around the chart, along with the **sizing handles**, the small circles at the corners and the edges, indicates that the chart is selected as displayed in Figure 4-5. Your chart might be in a different location on the worksheet and may look slightly different; you will move and resize it in the next lesson. Any time a chart is selected, as it is now, a blue border surrounds the worksheet data range on which the chart is based, a purple border surrounds the cells containing the category axis labels, and a red border surrounds the cells containing the data series labels. This chart is known as an **embedded chart** because it is displayed as an object in the worksheet. Embedding a chart in the current sheet is the default selection when creating a chart, but you can also embed a chart on a different sheet in the workbook or a newly created chart sheet. A **chart sheet** is a separate sheet in a workbook that contains only a chart that is linked to the workbook data.
7. **Save your work**

**Trouble**
The Accessibility notice on the status bar has changed from Good to go to Investigate. You will investigate this notification in a later lesson.

**Quick Tip**
You can change either the data source or the legend by clicking the Select Data button on the Chart Design tab to open the Select Data Source dialog box. You can change the source data by editing the data range in the Chart data range box. Clicking Add, Edit, or Remove under Legend Entries (Series) allows you to change the legend labels. When you finish making changes, click OK to close the dialog box.

**Figure 4-3:** Charts tab in Quick Analysis tool

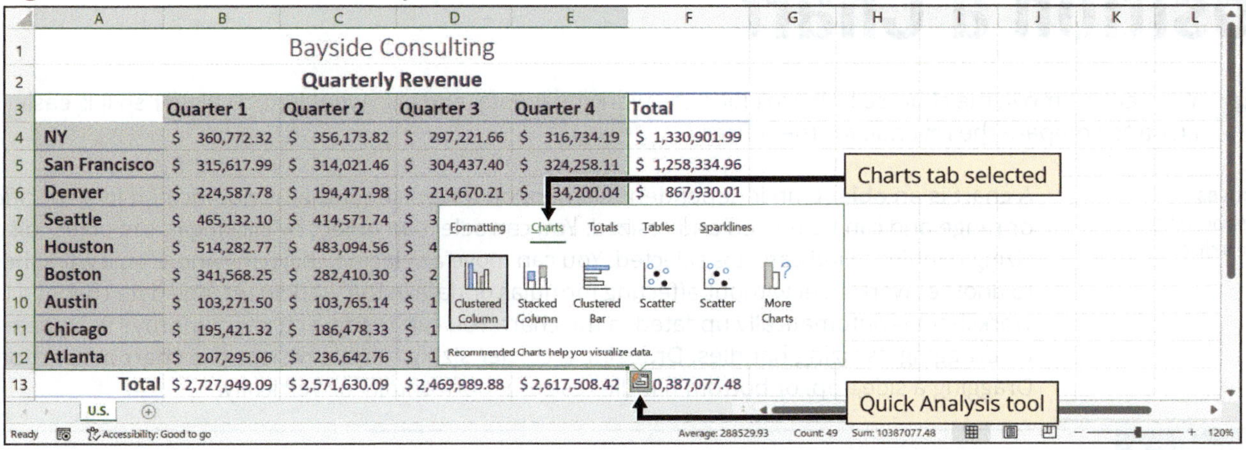


**Figure 4-4:** Clustered Column chart with different configuration of rows and columns

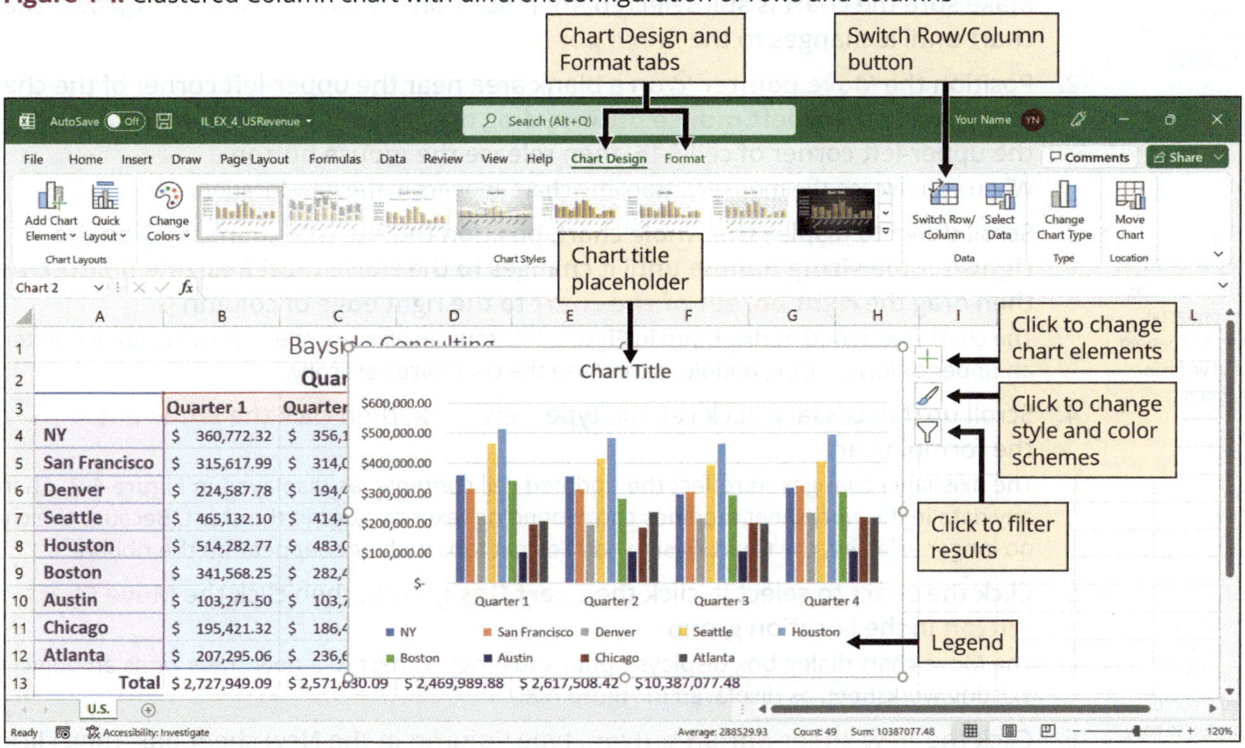


**Figure 4-5:** Chart with original configuration restored and title added

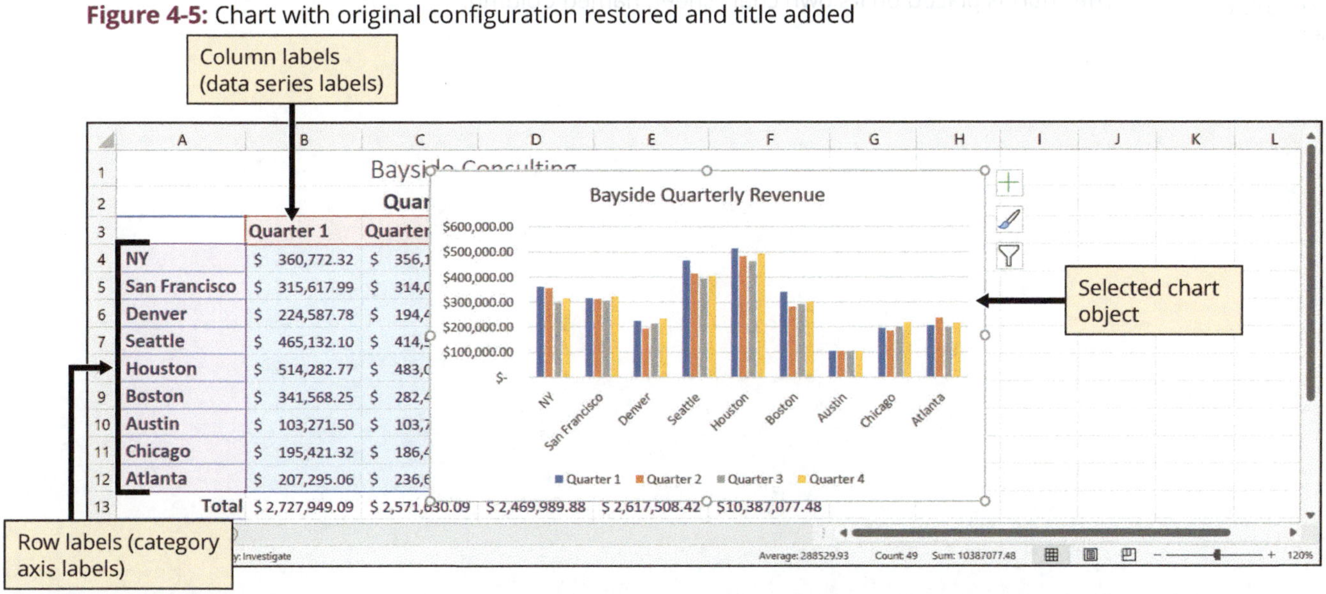

# Position a Chart

**Case** You need to move the chart so it doesn't hide the worksheet data, and also want it to be bigger so it is easier for Elena to compare the revenue for the offices.

**Objectives**
- Reposition a chart
- Resize a chart

A chart is an **object**, an independent element on a worksheet that is not located in a specific cell or range and can be moved and resized. You can select an object by clicking it; the object displays sizing handles to indicate it is selected. You can move a selected chart anywhere on a worksheet or to another worksheet without affecting formulas or data in the worksheet. Any data changed in the worksheet is automatically updated in the chart. You can resize a chart to improve its appearance by dragging its sizing handles. Dragging a corner sizing handle resizes the chart proportionally. Dragging a side, top, or bottom handle resizes it horizontally or vertically.

## Steps

**Quick Tip**
To delete a selected chart, press DEL.

**1. Make sure the chart is still selected, then position the Normal pointer over the chart until it changes to the Move pointer**

**2. Position the Move pointer on a blank area near the upper-left corner of the chart, press and hold the left mouse button, drag the chart until its upper-left corner is at the upper-left corner of cell A15, then release the mouse button**

When you release the mouse button, the chart appears in the new location.

**Quick Tip**
To resize a selected chart to an exact size, click the Format tab, then enter the desired height and width in the Size group.

**3. Scroll down to display the whole chart, position the Normal pointer on the right-middle sizing handle until it changes to the Horizontal Resizing pointer, then drag the right border of the chart to the right edge of column G**

The chart is widened as displayed in **Figure 4-6**. You can also use the Vertical Resizing pointer on an upper or lower sizing handle to increase the chart size vertically.

**4. Scroll up if necessary, click cell A4, type New York, then click the Enter button on the formula bar**

The axis label changes to reflect the updated cell contents, as displayed in **Figure 4-7**. Changing any data in the worksheet modifies corresponding text or values in the chart. Because the chart is no longer selected, the Chart Design and Format tabs no longer appear on the ribbon.

**Quick Tip**
You can also use the Copy and Paste buttons in the Clipboard group of the Home tab to copy a selected chart and paste it on a different worksheet.

**5. Click the chart to select it, click the Chart Design tab, then click the Move Chart button in the Location group**

The Move chart dialog box displays options to move a chart to a new sheet or as an object in an existing worksheet, as displayed in **Figure 4-8**.

**6. Click the New sheet option button, type Column in the New sheet box, then click OK**

The chart is placed on its own chart sheet, named Column.

**Figure 4-6:** Moved and resized chart

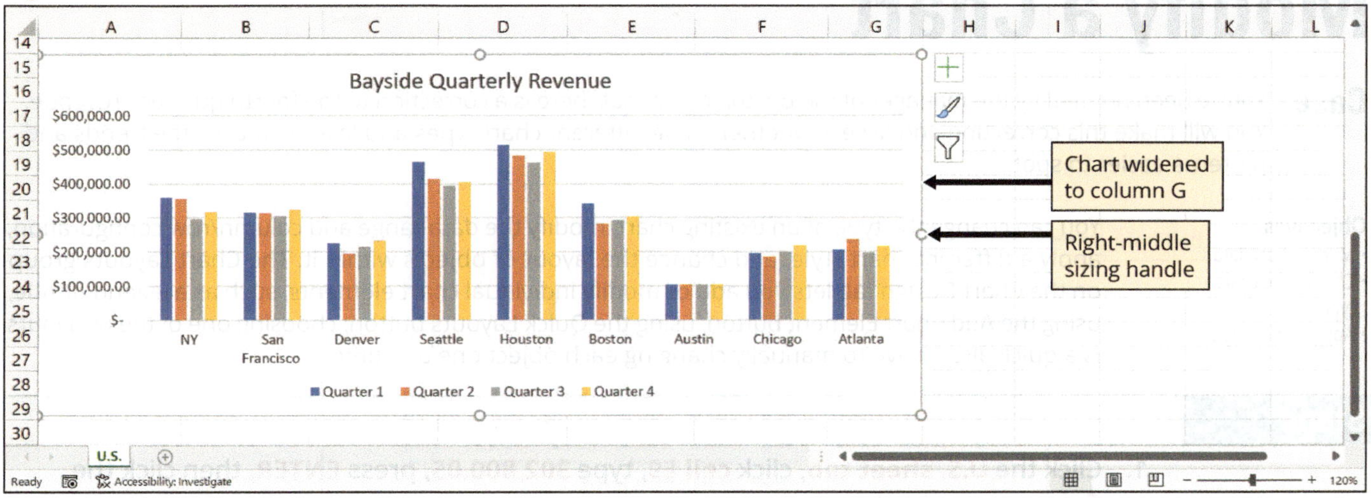


**Figure 4-7:** Worksheet with modified label

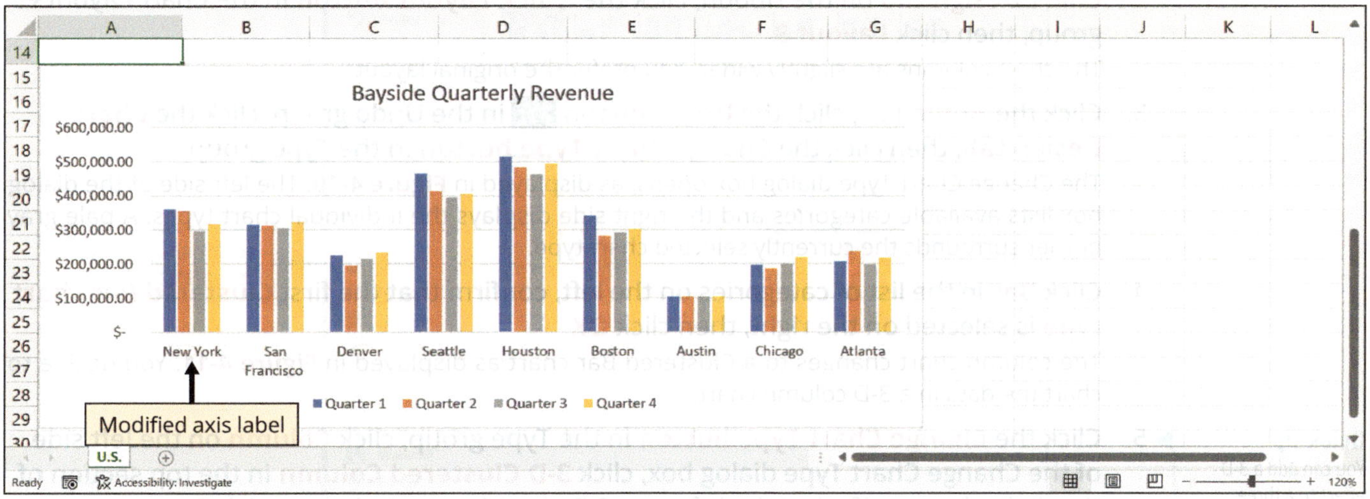


**Figure 4-8:** Move Chart dialog box

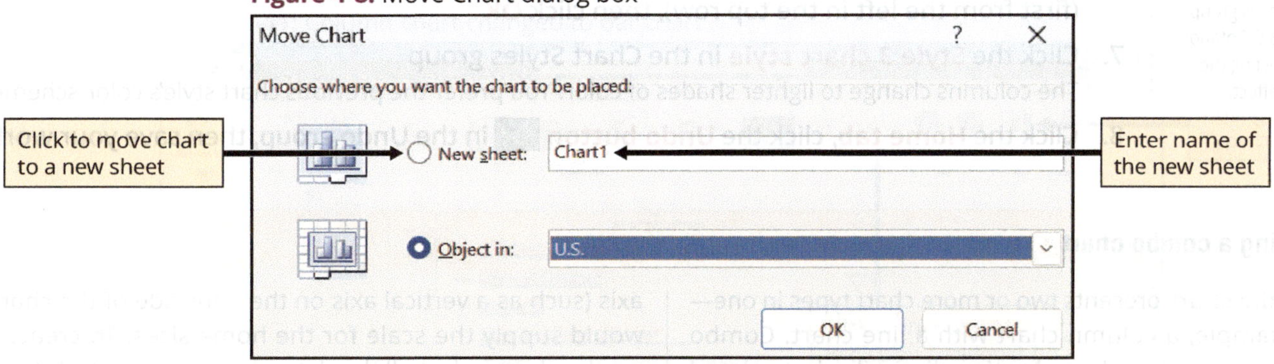

# Change the Chart Layout

**Case** You want to make the chart easier to understand with horizontal and vertical axes titles. You also want to add a data table to provide more information about the charted data.

**Objectives**
- Change the gridlines display
- Add axis titles
- Add a data table

While the Chart Design tab contains preconfigured chart layouts you can apply to a chart, the Chart Elements button makes it easy to add, remove, and modify individual chart objects such as a chart title, gridlines, or legend. Using options on this shortcut menu, you can also add a **data table**, a grid containing the chart data, to the chart.

## Steps

1. **With the chart still selected, click the Chart Design tab, click the Chart Elements button ⊞ in the upper-right corner of the chart, click the Gridlines arrow on the Chart Elements fly-out menu, click Primary Major Horizontal to deselect it, then click the Chart Elements button to close the menu**
   The gridlines that extend across the chart's plot area are removed, as displayed in **Figure 4-12**.
2. **Click the Chart Elements button ⊞, click the Axis Titles check box to add a checkmark, click the Chart Elements button to close the Chart Elements fly-out menu, with the vertical axis title on the chart selected, type Revenue, click the Enter button ✓, then click the chart area to deselect the title**
   Descriptive text on the category axis helps readers understand the chart.
3. **Click the horizontal axis title on the chart, type U.S. Offices, then click the Enter button ✓**
   The horizontal title is added, as displayed in **Figure 4-13**.
4. **Right-click the horizontal axis labels ("New York," "San Francisco," etc.), click Font on the shortcut menu, click the Latin text font arrow in the Font dialog box, scroll down the font list, click Arial, select the value in the Size box, type 12, then click OK**
   The font of the horizontal axis labels changes to Arial, and the font size increases, making the labels easier to read.
5. **With the horizontal axis labels still selected, click the Home tab on the ribbon, click the Format Painter button in the Clipboard group, then click the area within the vertical axis labels**
6. **Double-click the chart title (Bayside Quarterly Revenue), click Border in the Format Chart Title pane if necessary to display the Border options, then click the Solid line option button**
   The default color (Blue, Accent 1) appears around the chart title.
7. **Click the Effects button in the Format Chart Title pane, click Shadow, click the Presets arrow, click Offset: Bottom Right in the Outer group (first row, first from the left), then close the Format Chart Title pane**
   A border with a drop shadow surrounds the title.
8. **Click the Chart Elements button ⊞, click the Data Table check box to add a data table to the chart, in the list of chart elements, click the Legend check box to deselect it and remove the legend, close the Chart Elements menu, then save your work**
   A data table with its own legend displays the chart data. Compare your work to **Figure 4-14**.

**Quick Tip**
You can also apply a border to a chart by double-clicking the Chart Area, clicking Border in the Format Chart Area pane, then selecting from the available border options.

**Quick Tip**
You can apply a shadow, glow, or outline to title text by clicking Text Options in the Format Chart Title pane. Clicking the Text Effects button allows you to select from the available shadow and glow options; clicking the Text Fill & Outline button displays outline options for chart text.

**Figure 4-12:** Gridlines removed from chart

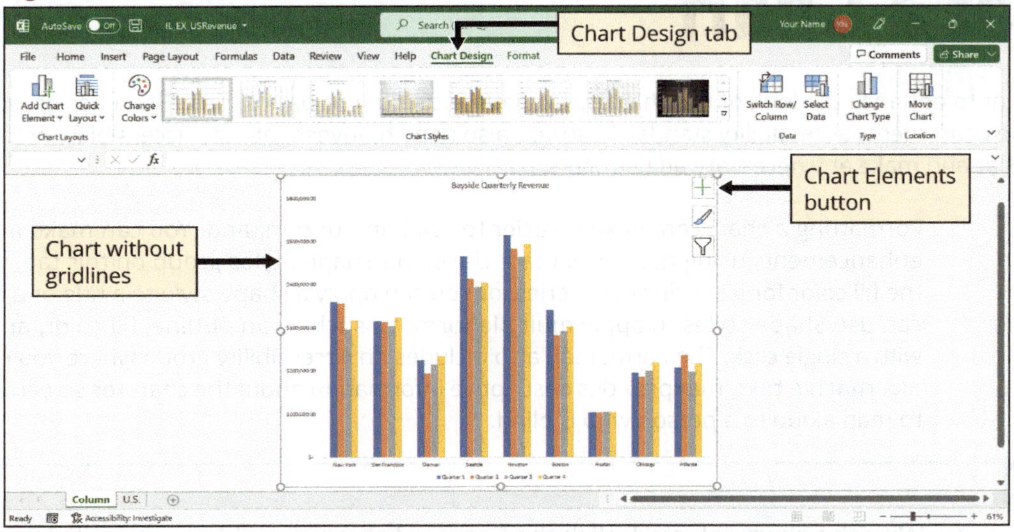


**Figure 4-13:** Axis titles added to chart

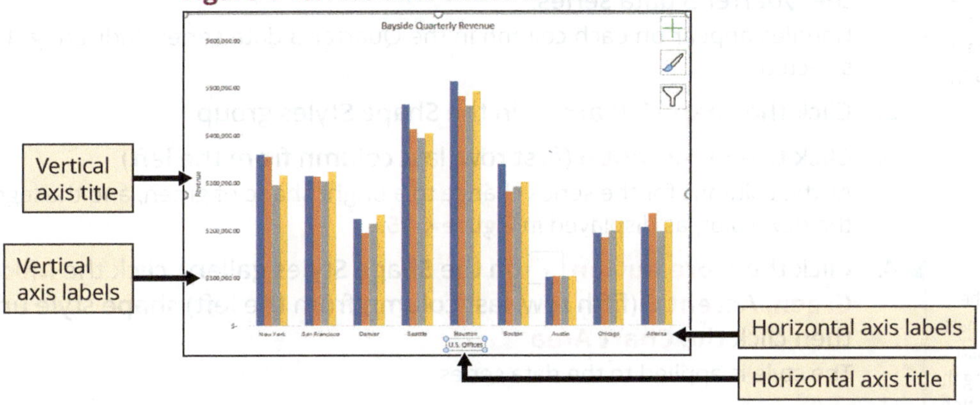


**Figure 4-14:** Enhanced chart

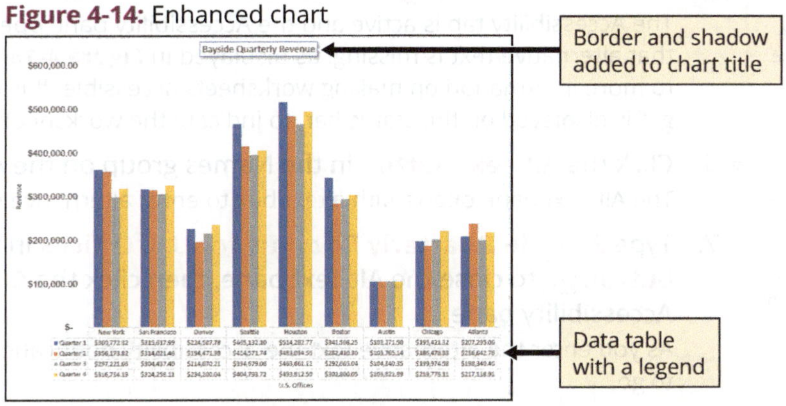


### Working with chart axes

You can change both the number format and text formatting of a chart's axes. For example, you may want to change the starting and ending values of an axis. You can do this by double-clicking the axis, clicking Axis Options in the Format Axis pane if necessary, then entering new values in the Minimum and Maximum boxes under the Bounds headings. To change the number format of the values on an axis, scroll down in the Axis Options pane, click Number to display the options, if necessary, then select from the available number formats. In the Number area, you also can create a number format code by typing a custom code in the Format Code box, then clicking Add. In addition to these axis options, you can work with axis text by clicking the Text Options button at the top of the pane, then clicking the Text box button. The Text Box group includes options for changing the vertical alignment of the data labels on the axis and the text direction of axis data labels from horizontal to stacked or rotated.

# Format a Chart

**Case** You want to enhance the look of the chart by formatting one of the data series. Elena has asked you to make sure the chart meets accessibility standards, so you also need to investigate the accessibility notification on the status bar and make any necessary adjustments.

**Objectives**
- Change the fill of a data series
- Apply a style to a data series

Formatting a chart can make it easier to read and understand. You can make many formatting enhancements using the Format tab. Using the Shape Styles group on this tab, you can change the fill color for a specific data series, or you can apply a shape style to a title or a data series. You can use Shape styles to apply multiple formats, such as an outline, fill color, and text color, all with a single click. The Format tab also includes an Accessibility group where you can add Alt Text, **alternative text**, that provides descriptive information about the chart for screen reader software to read aloud to a person who is blind.

## Steps

**Quick Tip**
You can remove a data series from a chart by selecting the data series, then pressing DEL.

1. **With the chart selected, click the Format tab on the ribbon, then click any column in the Quarter 3 data series**
   Handles appear on each column in the Quarter 3 data series, indicating that the entire series is selected.
2. **Click the Shape Fill arrow in the Shape Styles group**
3. **Click Green, Accent 6 (first row, last column from the left)**
   All the columns for the series change to a bright shade of green, and the legend changes to match the new color, as displayed in **Figure 4-15**.

**Quick Tip**
You can change the colors used in a chart by clicking the Chart Design tab, clicking the Change Colors button in the Chart Styles group, then clicking a color palette in the gallery.

4. **Click the More button on the Shape Styles gallery, click the Moderate Effect – Green, Accent 6 (fifth row, last column from the left) shape style under Theme Styles, then click the Chart Area**
   The style is applied to the data series.
5. **Click the Accessibility checker on the status bar**
   The Accessibility tab is active and the Accessibility pane opens with the Inspection Results noting that alternative text is missing, as displayed in **Figure 4-16**. The Inspection Results include a link to more information on making worksheets accessible. It is important that the message "Good to go" is displayed on the status bar, to indicate the worksheet is accessible.

**Quick Tip**
You can also click the Alt Text button in the Accessibility group on the Format tab to open the Alt Text pane.

6. **Click the Alt Text button in the Names group on the Accessibility pane**
   The Alt Text pane opens with a text box to enter alternative text for the chart
7. **Type Bayside Quarterly Revenue for U.S. Offices in the text box, click the Close button to close the Alt Text pane, then click the Close button to close the Accessibility pane**
   As you enter the alternative text the accessibility notification on the status bar changes to Good to go.
8. **Click the Insert tab on the ribbon, click the Text button, click the Header & Footer button, click Custom Footer, type your name in the center section, click OK, click OK again, then save your work**

### Working with WordArt

You can insert WordArt into a worksheet or a chart. To insert WordArt in a worksheet, click the Insert tab on the ribbon, click the Text button in the Text group, click WordArt, then select the WordArt style from the gallery. You can change a WordArt style by clicking the WordArt to select it, clicking the WordArt Styles More button on the Shape Format tab, then selecting a new WordArt style. You can change the fill color of the WordArt by clicking the Text Fill button in the WordArt Styles group and choosing a fill color, texture, gradient, or picture.

**Figure 4-15:** New shape fill applied to data series

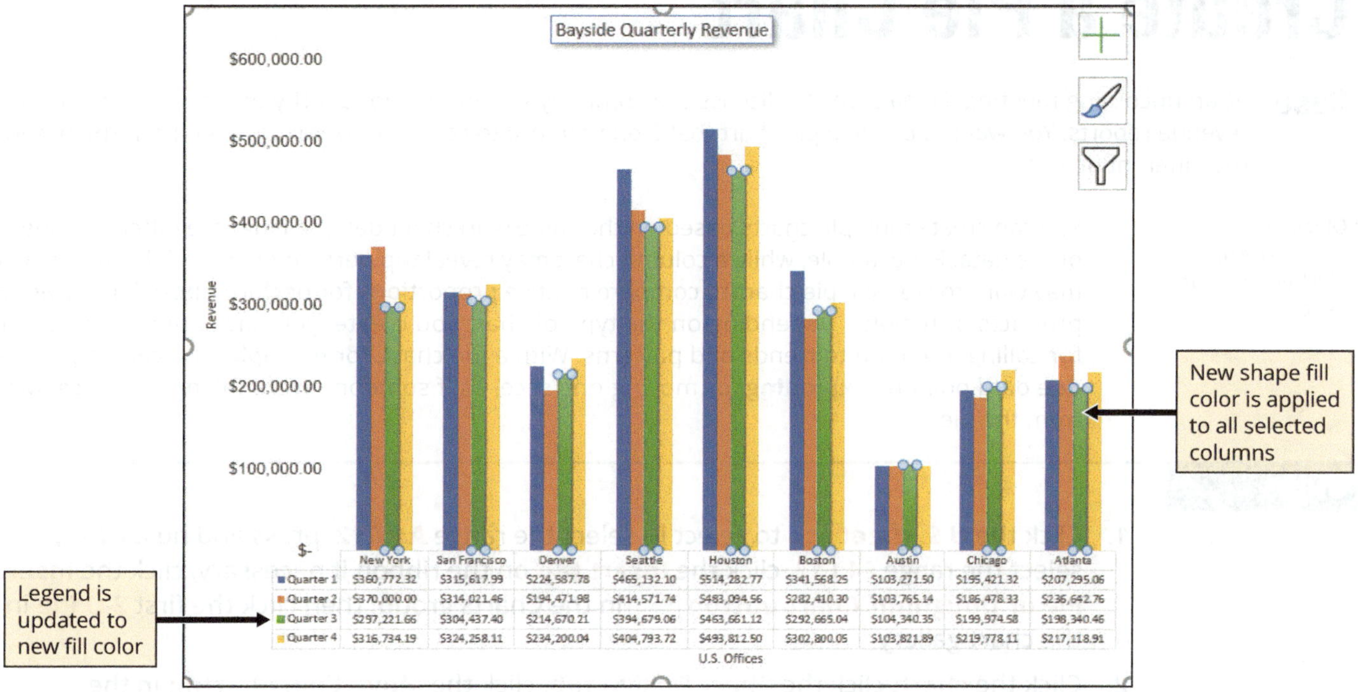


**Figure 4-16:** Accessibility pane

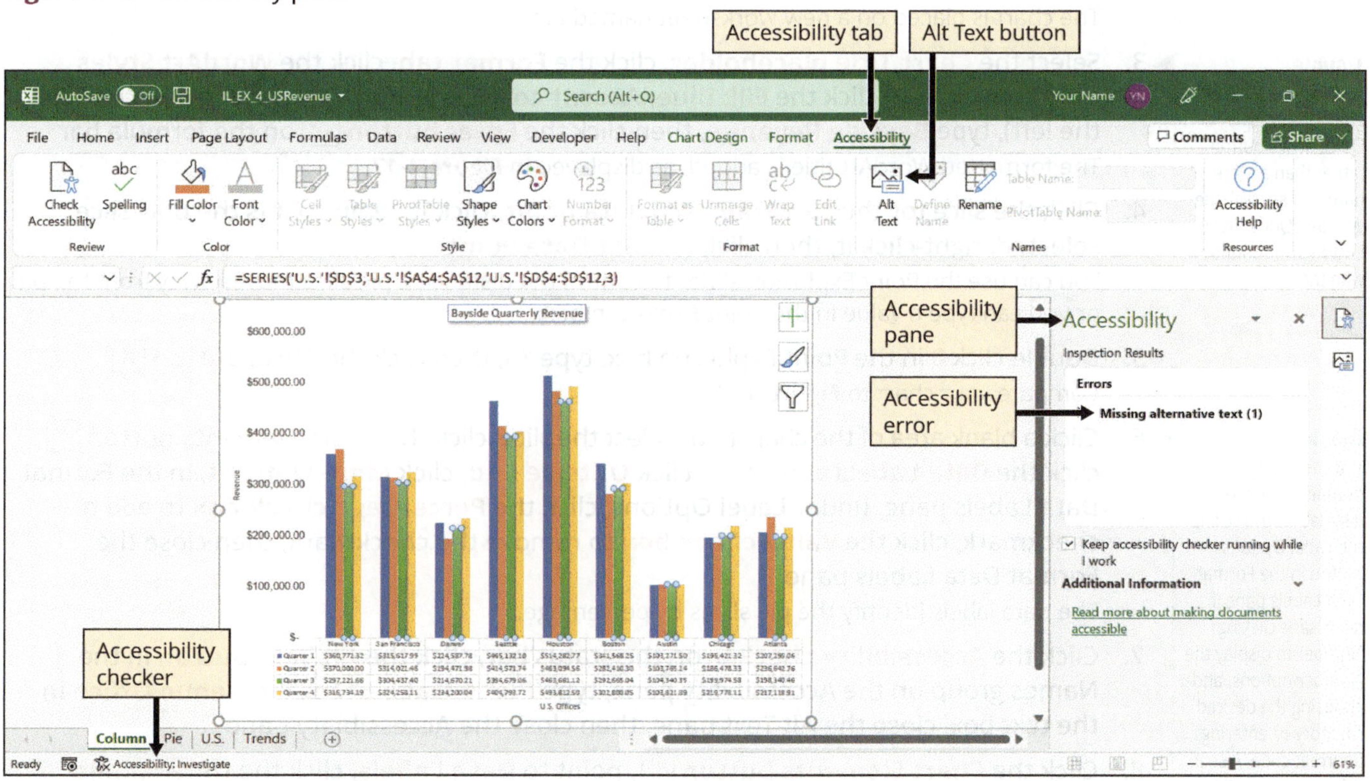


## Aligning charts

If you have two or more embedded charts on a worksheet, you can line them up to make them easier to view. First, select the charts by clicking the first chart and holding CTRL, then click the other chart(s). With the charts selected, click the Shape Format tab, click the Align button in the Arrange group, then choose the alignment position for the charts.

# Create a Pie Chart

**Case** At an upcoming meeting, Elena plans to discuss the company's revenue and identify offices that have weak revenue reports. You want to create a pie chart that Elena can use to compare overall revenue performance in the different offices.

**Objectives**
- Create a pie chart
- Explode a pie chart slice

You can create multiple charts based on the same worksheet data, to illustrate different aspects of the data. For example, while a column chart may reveal top performers month by month, you may want to create a pie chart to compare relative proportions for performances for individual products or regions. Depending on the type of chart you create, you have additional options for calling attention to trends and patterns. With a pie chart, for example, you can emphasize one data point by **exploding**, or moving one slice, as if someone were taking the piece away from the pie.

## Steps

1. Click the **U.S. sheet tab** to select it, select the range **A4:A12**, press and hold **CTRL**, select the range **F4:F12**, click the **Insert tab** on the ribbon if necessary, click the **Insert Pie or Doughnut Chart button** in the Charts group, then click the first **2-D Pie** in the chart gallery
2. Click the **chart**, click the **Chart Design tab**, click the **Move Chart button** in the Location group, click the **New sheet option button**, type **Pie** in the New sheet box, then click **OK**
   The chart is placed on a new worksheet named Pie.
3. Select the **Chart Title placeholder**, click the **Format tab**, click the **WordArt Styles More button**, click the **Fill: Blue, Accent color 1; Shadow** fill (first row, second from the left), type **Bayside Revenue**, then click the **Enter button** on the formula bar
   The formatted WordArt title is added, as displayed in **Figure 4-17**.
4. Click the slice for the **San Francisco data point**, click it again so it is the only slice selected, right-click it, then click **Format Data Point**
   You can use the Point Explosion slider to control the distance a pie slice moves away from the pie, or you can type a value in the Point Explosion box.
5. Double-click **0** in the Point Explosion box, type **10**, then click the **Close button**
   Compare your chart to **Figure 4-18**.
6. Click a blank area of the chart to deselect the slice, click the **Chart Elements button**, click the **Data Labels arrow**, click **Outside End**, click **More Options**, in the Format Data Labels pane, under Label Options, click the **Percentage check box** to add a checkmark, click the **Value check box** to remove the checkmark, then close the Format Data Labels pane
   The data labels identify the pie slices by percentage.
7. Click the **Accessibility checker** on the status bar, click the **Alt Text button** in the Names group on the Accessibility pane, type **Percentage of total revenue Office** in the text box, close the Alt Text pane, then close the Accessibility pane
8. Click the **Chart Elements button**, point to **Data Labels**, click the **Data Labels arrow**, click **Data Callout**, click the **Legend check box** to deselect it, click the **Chart Elements button**, click the **Bold button** on the Home tab, then click a blank area of the chart to deselect the callouts
   The data is labeled using percentage callouts in bold formatting, as displayed in **Figure 4-19**.
9. Click the **Insert tab** on the ribbon, click the **Text button**, click the **Header & Footer button** in the Text group, click the **Custom Footer button**, enter your name in the center section, click **OK**, click **OK** again, then save your work

**Trouble**
Your WordArt Styles group may display a Quick Styles button rather than a More button; if so, click the WordArt Quick Styles button and continue with the step.

**Quick Tip**
You can change the number format of the data labels by clicking the Label Options button in the Format Data Labels pane if necessary, clicking Number to display the Number options, and choosing the desired category or entering a format code. Also in this pane are options under Label Position to change the position of the data labels to Center, Inside End, and Best Fit.

**Figure 4-17:** Title Formatted using WordArt

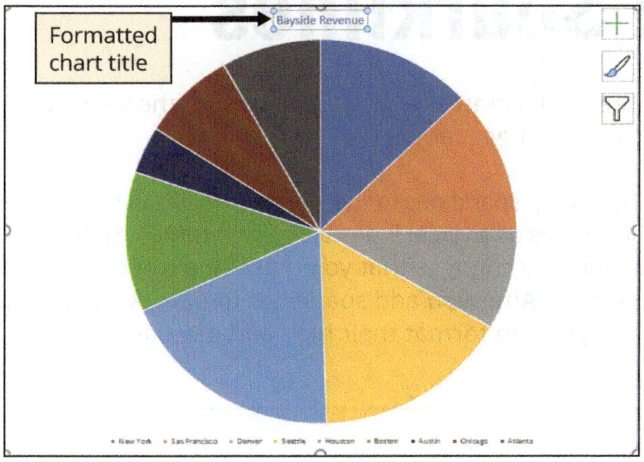


**Figure 4-18:** Exploded pie slice

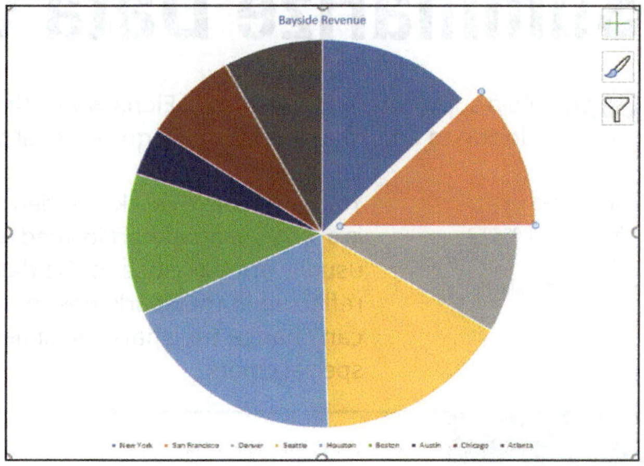


**Figure 4-19:** Pie chart with percentages

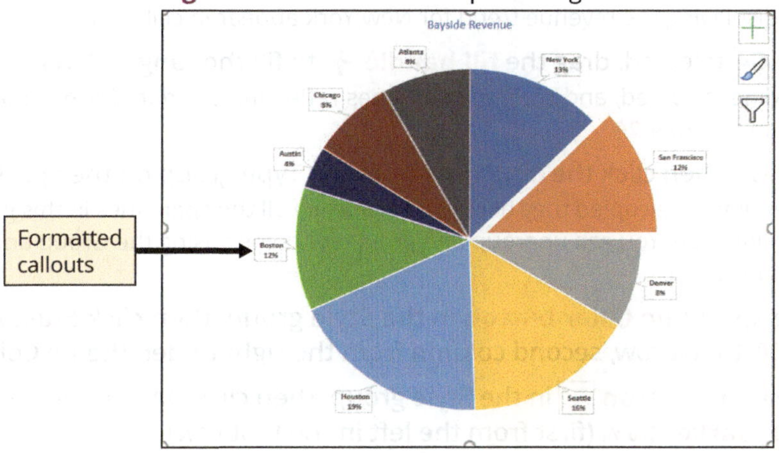


### Working with other chart types

Excel includes chart types that are useful for illustrating highly specific types of data. These include Waterfall, Histogram, Funnel, Box & Whisker, Treemap, Scatter, and Sunburst. A **treemap chart** is a hierarchy chart in which each category is placed within a rectangle and subcategories are nested as rectangles within those rectangles. A **sunburst chart** is also a hierarchy chart, but it groups categories within a series of concentric rings, with the upper levels of the hierarchy placed in the innermost rings. To insert one of these chart types, click the Insert tab, click the Insert Hierarchy Chart button in the Charts group, click More Hierarchy Charts, then click the chart type. **Waterfall charts** are used to track the addition and subtraction of values within a sum and **funnel charts** are used to chart the progressive stages of a process. To insert a waterfall or funnel chart, click the Insert tab, click the Insert Waterfall, Funnel, Stock, Surface, or Radar Chart button in the Charts group, then click Waterfall or Funnel. A **histogram chart** displays the distribution of data grouped in bins. These charts look similar to column charts, but each column (or bin) represents a range of values. To insert a histogram chart, click the Insert tab on the ribbon, click the Insert Statistic Chart button in the Charts group, then click the Histogram chart button. You can edit the bins in a histogram chart by double-clicking the x-axis, clicking to expand the Axis Options group on the Format Axis pane, then choosing options under Bins.

A **scatter chart** displays the correlation between two numeric variables. It is a type of **XY scatter chart**, which displays the pattern or relationship between two or more sets of values. Scatter charts look similar to line charts but have two value axes. The data points on a scatter chart display the intersection of the horizontal and vertical axes values. To insert a scatter chart, select the data you want to chart, click the Insert tab, click the Insert Scatter (X,Y) or Bubble Chart button in the Charts group, then choose a scatter chart type.

# Summarize Data with Sparklines

**Case** As a supplement to the charts, Elena wants the U.S. worksheet to illustrate the revenue trends for the year. You decide to add sparklines to tell a quick visual story within the worksheet cells.

**Objectives**
- Add sparklines to a worksheet
- Format sparklines

You can create a quick overview of your data by adding sparklines to the worksheet cells. A **sparkline** is a small, simple chart located within a cell that serves as a visual indicator of data trends. Sparklines usually appear close to the data they represent. Any changes that you make to a worksheet are reflected in the sparklines that represent the data. After you add sparklines to a worksheet, you can change the sparkline style and color, and you can format their high and low data points in special colors.

## Steps

**Trouble**
You may have to move the Create Sparklines dialog box to select the data range.

1. **Click the U.S. sheet tab, click cell G4, click the Insert tab on the ribbon if necessary, click the Column button in the Sparklines group, verify that the insertion point is in the Data Range box, select the range B4:E4 on the worksheet, then click OK**
   Columns displaying the revenue trend for New York appear in cell G4.
2. **With cell G4 selected, drag the fill handle + to fill the range G5:G12**
   The sparkline is copied, and column sparklines reflecting the data for each office are added, as displayed in **Figure 4-20**.

**Quick Tip**
To insert Win/Loss sparklines, which display upward column symbols for positive values and downward symbols for negative values, click the Win/Loss button in the Type group.

3. **Click cell G4, then click the Line button in the Type group on the Sparkline tab**
   When sparklines are copied they become a group, so all the sparklines in this group change to the Line sparkline type. You can ungroup and group sparklines using the Group and Ungroup buttons in the Group group.
4. **Click the Sparkline Color button in the Style group, then click Blue, Accent 5, Darker 50% (last row, second column from the right under Theme Colors)**
5. **Click the More button in the Style group, then click Dark Blue, Sparkline Style Accent 1, Darker 50% (first from the left in the first row)**
   The sparkline colors and styles are consistent with the colors on the worksheet.
6. **Click the Marker Color button in the Style group, point to High Point, select Green Accent 6, (first row, last column from the left), then click the Markers check box in the Show group to add a checkmark**
   Data markers indicate each quarter's revenue.

**Quick Tip**
To clear sparklines, select the sparklines, then click the Clear button in the Group group.

7. **Click cell C4 type 370,000.00, click the Enter button ✓, then compare your screen to Figure 4-21**
   The sparklines update to reflect the new worksheet data.
8. **Click the Insert tab on the ribbon, click the Text button, click the Header & Footer button in the Text group, click the Go to Footer button in the Navigation group, enter your name in the center footer section, click any cell on the worksheet, click the Normal button on the status bar, then press CTRL+HOME**
9. **Save your changes**

**Figure 4-20:** Revenue trend sparklines

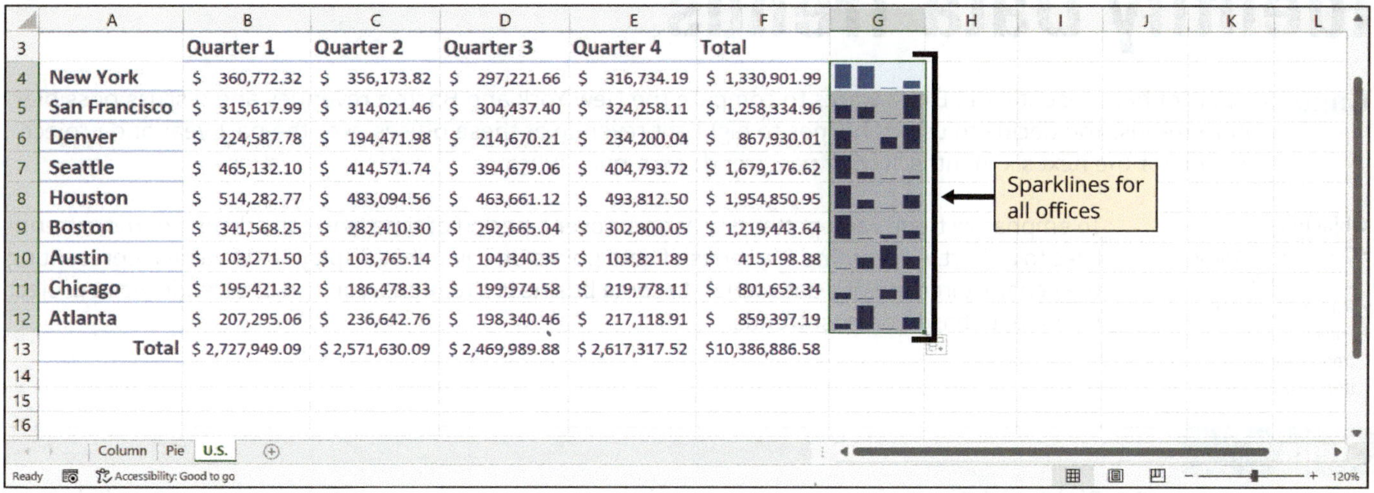

| | A | B | C | D | E | F | G |
|---|---|---|---|---|---|---|---|
| 3 | | Quarter 1 | Quarter 2 | Quarter 3 | Quarter 4 | Total | |
| 4 | New York | $ 360,772.32 | $ 356,173.82 | $ 297,221.66 | $ 316,734.19 | $ 1,330,901.99 | |
| 5 | San Francisco | $ 315,617.99 | $ 314,021.46 | $ 304,437.40 | $ 324,258.11 | $ 1,258,334.96 | |
| 6 | Denver | $ 224,587.78 | $ 194,471.98 | $ 214,670.21 | $ 234,200.04 | $ 867,930.01 | |
| 7 | Seattle | $ 465,132.10 | $ 414,571.74 | $ 394,679.06 | $ 404,793.72 | $ 1,679,176.62 | |
| 8 | Houston | $ 514,282.77 | $ 483,094.56 | $ 463,661.12 | $ 493,812.50 | $ 1,954,850.95 | |
| 9 | Boston | $ 341,568.25 | $ 282,410.30 | $ 292,665.04 | $ 302,800.05 | $ 1,219,443.64 | |
| 10 | Austin | $ 103,271.50 | $ 103,765.14 | $ 104,340.35 | $ 103,821.89 | $ 415,198.88 | |
| 11 | Chicago | $ 195,421.32 | $ 186,478.33 | $ 199,974.58 | $ 219,778.11 | $ 801,652.34 | |
| 12 | Atlanta | $ 207,295.06 | $ 236,642.76 | $ 198,340.46 | $ 217,118.91 | $ 859,397.19 | |
| 13 | Total | $ 2,727,949.09 | $ 2,571,630.09 | $ 2,469,989.88 | $ 2,617,317.52 | $10,386,886.58 | |



**Figure 4-21:** Formatted sparklines

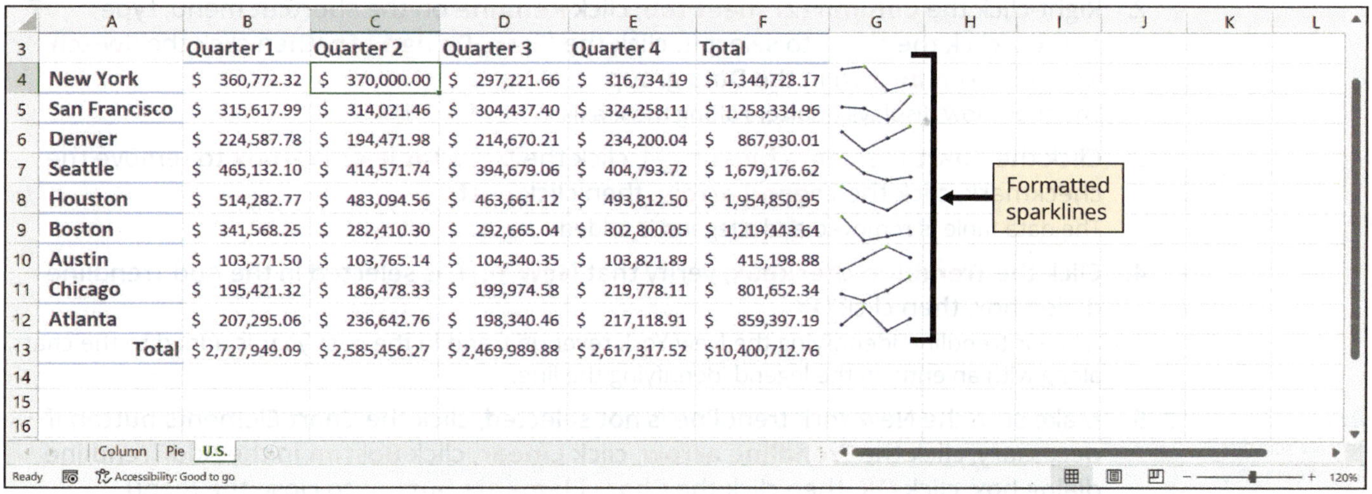

| | A | B | C | D | E | F | G |
|---|---|---|---|---|---|---|---|
| 3 | | Quarter 1 | Quarter 2 | Quarter 3 | Quarter 4 | Total | |
| 4 | New York | $ 360,772.32 | $ 370,000.00 | $ 297,221.66 | $ 316,734.19 | $ 1,344,728.17 | |
| 5 | San Francisco | $ 315,617.99 | $ 314,021.46 | $ 304,437.40 | $ 324,258.11 | $ 1,258,334.96 | |
| 6 | Denver | $ 224,587.78 | $ 194,471.98 | $ 214,670.21 | $ 234,200.04 | $ 867,930.01 | |
| 7 | Seattle | $ 465,132.10 | $ 414,571.74 | $ 394,679.06 | $ 404,793.72 | $ 1,679,176.62 | |
| 8 | Houston | $ 514,282.77 | $ 483,094.56 | $ 463,661.12 | $ 493,812.50 | $ 1,954,850.95 | |
| 9 | Boston | $ 341,568.25 | $ 282,410.30 | $ 292,665.04 | $ 302,800.05 | $ 1,219,443.64 | |
| 10 | Austin | $ 103,271.50 | $ 103,765.14 | $ 104,340.35 | $ 103,821.89 | $ 415,198.88 | |
| 11 | Chicago | $ 195,421.32 | $ 186,478.33 | $ 199,974.58 | $ 219,778.11 | $ 801,652.34 | |
| 12 | Atlanta | $ 207,295.06 | $ 236,642.76 | $ 198,340.46 | $ 217,118.91 | $ 859,397.19 | |
| 13 | Total | $ 2,727,949.09 | $ 2,585,456.27 | $ 2,469,989.88 | $ 2,617,317.52 | $10,400,712.76 | |

# Identify Data Trends

**Case** As part of her presentation, Elena wants to compare the New York and Boston revenues and discuss possible future trends. You decide to use trendlines to highlight revenue at these offices over the past year and project revenue for the next six months, if their past trends continue.

**Objectives**
- Compare chart data using trendlines
- Format a trendline
- Forecast future trends using trendlines

To emphasize trends and patterns that occur over a period of time, you can add one or more trendlines to a chart. A **trendline** is a series of data points on a line that displays data values representing the general direction of a data series. In some business situations, you can use trendlines to project future data based on past trends.

## Steps

1. **Right-click the Column sheet tab, click Move or Copy on the shortcut menu, click (move to end) in the Before sheet box, click the Create a copy check box to add a checkmark, then click OK**
   The new worksheet Column (2) is a copy of the Column sheet.
2. **Right-click the Column (2) sheet tab, click Rename on the shortcut menu, type Trends, click the chart to select it, click the Chart Design tab, then click the Switch Row/Column button in the Data group**
   The chart now displays quarters along the x-axis.
3. **Click the Chart Elements button, click the Data Table check box to remove the checkmark, click the Legend arrow, then click Bottom**
   The data table is removed and a legend is added.
4. **Click the Trendline checkbox, verify that New York is selected in the Add Trendline dialog box, then click OK**
   A linear trendline identifying the New York revenue trend in the past year is added to the chart, along with an entry in the legend identifying the line.
5. **Make sure the New York trendline is not selected, click the Chart Elements button if necessary, click the Trendline arrow, click Linear, click Boston in the Add Trendline dialog box, click OK, then click the Chart Elements button to close the menu**
   The chart now has two trendlines, making it easy to compare the revenue trends of the New York and Boston offices, as displayed in **Figure 4-22**.

   **Quick Tip**
   To make sure that a chart element is not selected, simply click away from the element.
6. **Double-click the New York data series trendline, in the Format Trendline pane click the Trendline Options button if necessary, select 0.0 in the Forward box, type 1, press ENTER, click the Fill & Line button, select 1.5 in the Width box, type 2.5, then close the Format Trendline pane**
   Trendlines are often used to project future trends. The formatted New York trendline projects an additional quarter of future revenue trends for the office, assuming past trends continue.
7. **Double-click the Boston data series trendline, click the Trendline Options button in the Format Trendline pane if necessary, select 0.0 in the Forward box, type 1, press ENTER, click the Fill & Line button, select 1.5 in the Width box, type 2.5, then close the Format Trendline pane**
   The formatted Boston trendline also projects an additional quarter of future revenue, if past trends continue.
8. **sam Compare your chart to Figure 4-23, save your work, preview the Trends sheet, close the workbook, submit the workbook to your instructor, then close Excel**

**Figure 4-22:** Chart with two trendlines

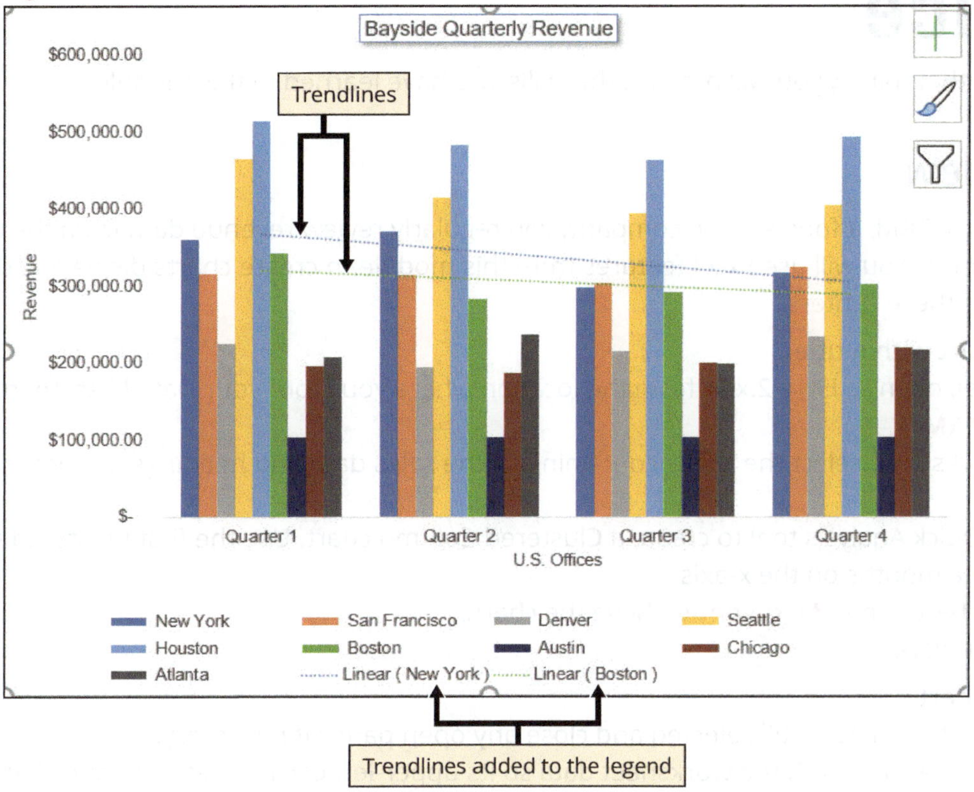


**Figure 4-23:** Revenue chart with trendlines for New York and Boston

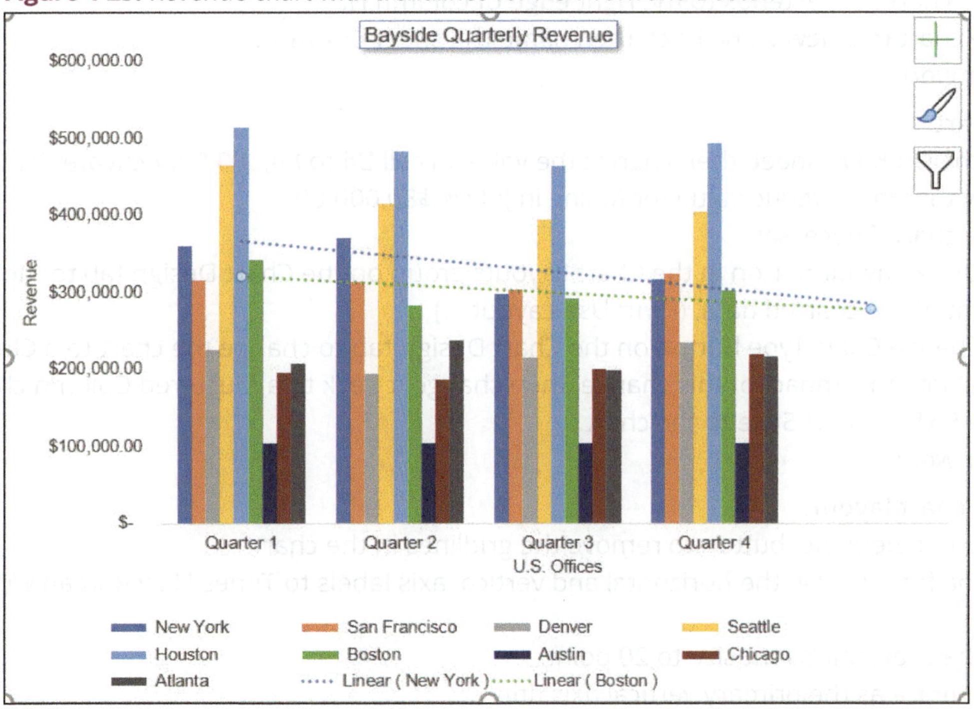


### Choosing the right trendline options for your chart

When choosing a trendline, it is important to know which one is best for the information you want to communicate. If the data progression follows a straight line, using a linear trendline helps to emphasize that. If the pattern of a chart's data is linear but the data points don't follow a straight line, you can use a linear forecast trendline to chart a best-fit straight line. When data values increase or decrease in an arc shape, consider using an exponential or power trendline to illustrate this. A two-period moving average smooths out fluctuations in data by averaging the data points.

# Practice

In the exercises that follow, you will practice the skills you have learned in this module.

## Skills Review

As the manager of TRM, a food service company, you regularly review revenue data from the regional distribution centers. You will use Excel features from this module to create charts displaying the revenue relationships for these centers.

1. **Create a chart with a title.**
   a. Start Excel, open IL_EX_4-2.xlsx from the location where you store your Data Files, then save it as **IL_EX_4_TRM**.
   b. In the worksheet, select the range containing all the sales data and headings. Do not include the totals.
   c. Use the Quick Analysis tool to create a Clustered Column chart. Use the first Clustered Column option, placing the months on the x-axis.
   d. Add the chart title **TRM Revenue** above the chart.
   e. Save your work.
2. **Position a chart.**
   a. Make sure the chart is still selected and close any open panes if necessary.
   b. Move the chart beneath the worksheet data so its upper-left corner is at the upper-left corner of cell A11.
   c. Widen the chart so it extends to the right edge of column H.
   d. Move the chart to a new worksheet, then name the sheet **Column**.
   e. Save your work.
3. **Modify a chart.**
   a. Activate the Q3 & Q4 sheet, then change the value in cell B4 to **80,000.00**. Activate the Column sheet and verify that the revenue value for Maine in July is $80,000.00.
   b. Select the chart if necessary.
   c. Use the Quick Layout button in the Chart Layouts group on the Chart Design tab to move the legend to the right of the charted data. (**Hint**: Use Layout 1.)
   d. Use the Change Chart Type button on the Chart Design tab to change the chart to a Clustered Bar chart, evaluate the impact of this change, then change it back to a Clustered Column chart.
   e. Apply the Style 6 Chart Style to the chart.
   f. Save your work.
4. **Change the chart layout.**
   a. Use the Chart Elements button to remove the gridlines in the chart.
   b. Change the font used in the horizontal and vertical axis labels to Times New Roman with a font size of 11 point.
   c. Change the chart title's font size to 20 point.
   d. Insert **Revenue** as the primary vertical axis title.
   e. Change the font size of the vertical axis title to 16 point.
   f. Add a solid line border to the chart title, using the Orange, Accent 2 color (first row, sixth from left) and a preset shadow of Outer Offset: Bottom Right.
   g. Add a data table to the chart with a legend key, then remove the chart legend.
   h. Save your work.

5. **Format a chart.**
   a. Use the Format tab to change the shape fill of the Vermont data series to Green, Accent 6 (first row of Theme Colors, last column from the left).
   b. Change the shape style of the Vermont data series to Colored Fill – Green, Accent 6 (second row, last column from the left), then click the chart area to deselect the Vermont data series.
   c. Use the Alt Text pane to add the alternative text **Revenue for July through December**, then close the Alt Text and Accessibility panes.
   d. Enter your name in the center footer section, then save your work.

6. **Create a pie chart.**
   a. Switch to the Q3 & Q4 sheet, then select the range A4:A8 and H4:H8. (**Hint**: Holding CTRL allows you to select multiple nonadjacent ranges.)
   b. Create a 2-D pie chart, then move the chart beneath the worksheet data so the upper-left corner is at the upper-left corner of cell A11.
   c. Resize the chart so its bottom border is at the bottom edge of row 20 and its right border is at the right edge of column E.
   d. Add data labels in the outside end position with only category names and percentage options. Do not display the legend.
   e. Change the chart title to **Region by Region Comparison** and format the title using the WordArt style Fill: Blue, Accent color 1, Shadow (second style in the first row).
   f. Explode the New Hampshire slice from the pie chart at **20%**.
   g. Select the chart area then add the alternative text of **Revenue percentage by region** to the chart.
   h. Save your work.

7. **Summarize data with sparklines.**
   a. Add a Column sparkline to cell I4 that represents the data in the range B4:G4.
   b. Copy the sparkline in cell I4 into the range I5:I8.
   c. Apply the Sparkline style Dark Blue, Sparkline Style Accent 1, Darker 25% (second row, first column) to the group.
   d. Add high point markers with the color Orange, Accent 2 (first row, sixth from the left).
   e. Compare your worksheet to **Figure 4-24**.
   f. Add your name to the center footer section of the worksheet, then save the workbook.

**Figure 4-24**

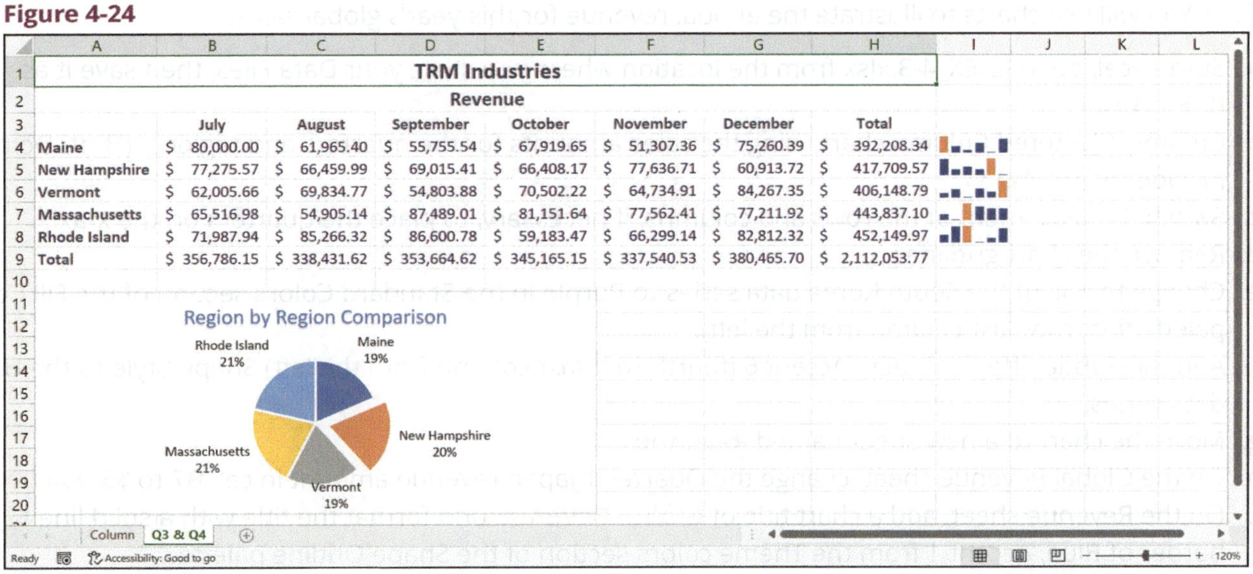

## Skills Review (Continued)

8. **Identify data trends.**
   a. Switch to the Column sheet.
   b. Add linear trendlines to the New Hampshire and Massachusetts data series.
   c. Set the forward option to 2.0 periods for both trendlines.
   d. Change the width of both trendlines to 3.
   e. Compare your screen to **Figure 4-25**.
   f. Save the workbook, close the workbook, then submit the workbook to your instructor.
   g. Close Excel.

**Figure 4-25**

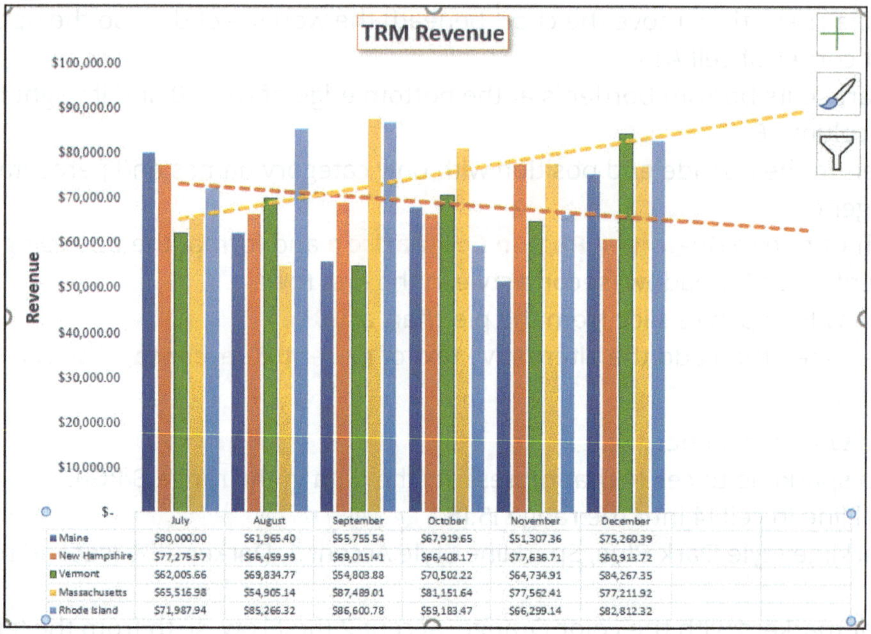


## Independent Challenge 1

As an executive assistant for GSI, a global semiconductor engineering firm, you prepare revenue reports for the CEO. You will use charts to illustrate the annual revenue for this year's global sales.

a. Start Excel, open IL_EX_4-3.xlsx from the location where you store your Data Files, then save it as **IL_EX_4_GSI**.
b. Create a Clustered Column chart using the sales amounts for the quarters and regions. (**Hint**: Do not include the totals.)
c. Switch the placement of the rows and columns, if necessary, to place the quarters on the x-axis.
d. Remove the chart gridlines.
e. Change the fill of the South Korea data series to Purple in the Standard Colors section of the Fill Color palette (last row, last column from the left).
f. Add the Subtle effect – Green, Accent 6 (fourth row, last column from the left) Shape Style to the U.S. data series.
g. Move the chart to a new sheet named **Revenue**.
h. On the Global Revenue sheet, change the Quarter 1 Japan revenue amount in cell B7 to **$5,000,000**.
i. On the Revenue sheet, add a chart title of **Global Revenue** and format the title with a solid line border of Blue, Accent 1 from the Theme colors section of the Shape Outline palette.
j. Add a data table, then remove the chart legend.
k. Add trendlines to the Taiwan and U.S. revenue data, with a width of 3 points forecasting one period ahead.
l. Change the chart type to a line chart, then apply the Style 12 chart Style to the chart.

m. Add the alternative text **Global Revenue for all regions** to the chart. Compare your chart to **Figure 4-26**.
n. Enter your name in the center section of the worksheet footer of the Revenue sheet, then save your work.
o. Submit your work to your instructor as directed.
p. Close the workbook, then close Excel.

**Figure 4-26**

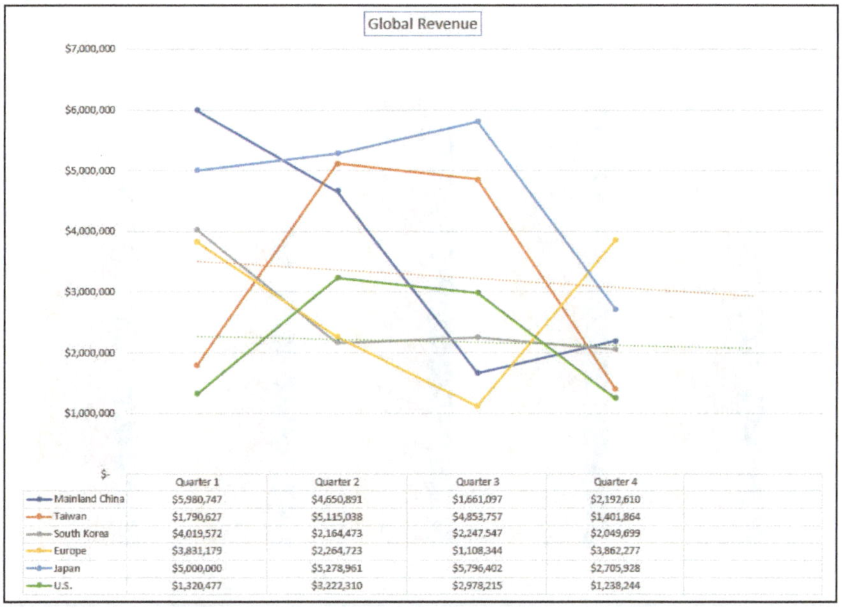


## Independent Challenge 2

One of your responsibilities as the director of operations at Quest Adventures is to present occupancy rate data to the executive staff at the end of the year. Your assistant has organized the company's occupancy data by region in a worksheet. You will review the data and create charts to visually represent the occupancy for the year.

a. Start Excel, open IL_EX_4-4.xlsx from the location where you store your Data Files, then save it as **IL_EX_4_Occupancy**.
b. Create a 3-D Clustered Column chart in the worksheet displaying the occupancy data for all four quarters. (**Hint**: The regions, such as Northeast, Mid-Atlantic, and so forth, should appear on the x-axis.)
c. Add a chart title of **Occupancy**, then format the title with the WordArt Quick Style of Fill: Blue, Accent color 1; Shadow (first row, second from left).
d. Move the chart so its upper-left corner is at the upper-left corner of cell H3.
e. On the worksheet, type **Average** in cell F3, then use the Average function to calculate the average Northeast occupancy for the year. Format the average in cell F4 as a percentage with two decimal places.
f. Copy the average formula in cell F4 to the range F5:F8.
g. Add the average data from column F to the chart. (**Hint**: Use the Select Data button on the Chart Design tab to select the new chart data, including the average data.)
h. Change the chart type to Combo Clustered Column - Line chart (first option of combo charts) with the Average data series charted as a line. (**Hint**: After selecting the chart type in the Change Chart Type dialog box, scroll down to make sure all four quarter series are charted as clustered columns and the Average data series is charted as a line. You may need to change the fourth quarter chart type. Do not use the secondary axis options.)
i. Add the alternative text **Occupancy for regions by quarter with average for each region** to the chart.
j. Move the chart to a new sheet named **Occupancy**.
k. Using **Figure 4-27** as a guide, add data labels to the Average data series only. (**Hint**: Select the Average data series on the chart before adding data labels.)

## Independent Challenge 2 (Continued)

l. Enter your name in the center footer section of both sheets, then preview the worksheet.
m. Save your work.
n. Submit your work to your instructor as directed, close the workbook, then close Excel.

**Figure 4-27**

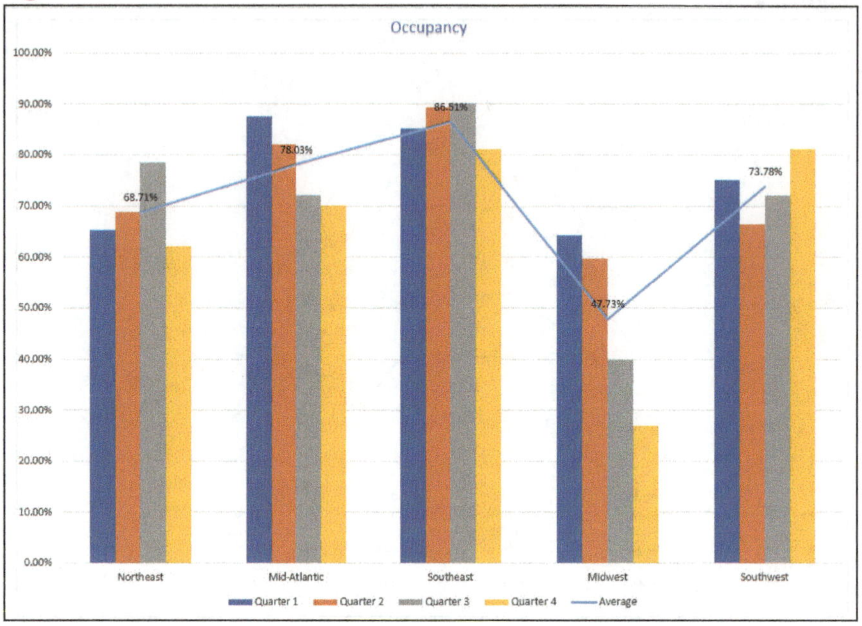

# Visual Workshop

Open IL_EX_4-5.xlsx from the location where you store your Data Files, then save it as **IL_EX_4_SUV**. Create, modify, and position the charts to match those in **Figure 4-28**. (**Hint**: Use the CTRL key as needed to select nonadjacent ranges.) You will need to make design changes once you create the chart. (**Hints**: The WordArt used in the pie chart title is Fill: Blue, Accent color 1: Shadow. The Full-size data point in the pie chart is exploded 20%. The sparkline color is Green, Accent 6) The Alternative text for the pie chart is **Annual deliveries for four categories of SUVs**, without a period at the end of the text. Enter your name in the center section of the footer, then save and preview the worksheet. Submit your work to your instructor as directed, then close the workbook and close Excel.

**Figure 4-28**

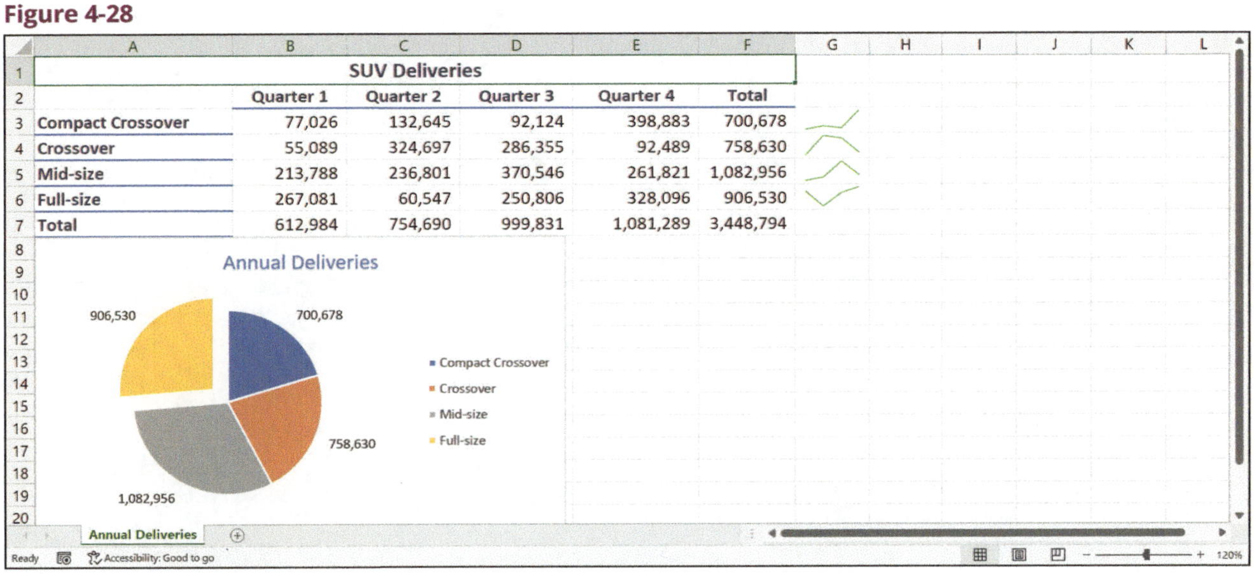

| | Quarter 1 | Quarter 2 | Quarter 3 | Quarter 4 | Total |
|---|---|---|---|---|---|
| **SUV Deliveries** | | | | | |
| Compact Crossover | 77,026 | 132,645 | 92,124 | 398,883 | 700,678 |
| Crossover | 55,089 | 324,697 | 286,355 | 92,489 | 758,630 |
| Mid-size | 213,788 | 236,801 | 370,546 | 261,821 | 1,082,956 |
| Full-size | 267,081 | 60,547 | 250,806 | 328,096 | 906,530 |
| Total | 612,984 | 754,690 | 999,831 | 1,081,289 | 3,448,794 |

# Working with Tables

## Case

Bayside Consulting uses tables to organize invoice data so that they can analyze information and make decisions. The manager of the Boston office, Naya Patel, asks you to help her build and manage a table of information about the office's invoices for the month of January. You will create the table, add information including dates, divisions, and commissions, organize it so it is easy to view, and perform calculations that help Naya compare invoicing differences among the divisions in the Boston office.

## Module Objectives

After completing this module, you will be able to:

- Create a table
- Change table data
- Sort table data
- Use formulas in a table
- Filter a table
- Use LOOKUP functions
- Summarize table data
- Validate table data

## Files You Will Need

IL_EX_5-1.xlsx
IL_EX_5-2.xlsx
IL_EX_5-3.xlsx
IL_EX_5-4.xlsx
IL_EX_5-5.xlsx

# Create a Table

**Case** You begin building the analysis of January invoices by creating and formatting a table using worksheet data.

**Objectives**
- Create a table
- Format a table

You can analyze and manipulate data in a table structure to take advantage of Excel tools and features designed specifically for tables. An Excel **table** is an organized collection of rows and columns of similarly structured data on a worksheet. Tables are a convenient way to understand and manage large amounts of information. A table is organized into rows of data called **records**, each of which represents a complete set of field values for a specific person, place, object, event, or idea. A **field** is a column containing a specific property for each record, such as a person's last name or street address. Each field has a field name, which is a column label, such as "Address," that describes its contents. The **header row** is the first row of the table, and it contains the field names. After you create a table you can add preset formatting combinations of fill color, borders, type style, and type color by applying a table style.

## Steps

1. **sam Start Excel, open IL_EX_5-1.xlsx from the location where you store your Data Files, then save it as IL_EX_5_Boston**

> **Quick Tip**
> You can change a table back to a worksheet range by clicking the Convert to Range button in the Tools group on the Table Design tab.

2. **With cell A1 selected, click the Insert tab on the ribbon, click the Table button in the Tables group, in the Create Table dialog box verify that the range $A$1:$F$65 appears in the Where is the data for your table? box and the My table has headers check box contains a checkmark, as shown in Figure 5-1, then click OK**

   The data range is now defined as a table and is selected. **Filter list arrows**, which let you display portions of your data, appear next to each field name in the table. When you create a table, Excel automatically applies a table style. The default table style has a dark blue header row and alternating light and dark blue data rows. The Table Design tab appears, and the Table Styles group displays a gallery of table formatting options.

3. **Click the Table Styles More button on the Table Design tab, scroll and view all the table styles, then move the Excel pointer over several styles without clicking**

   The Table Styles gallery on the Table Design tab contains three style categories—Light, Medium, and Dark—each of which includes numerous designs. The designs use the current workbook theme colors so the table coordinates with your existing workbook content. If you select a different workbook theme and color scheme in the Themes group on the Page Layout tab, the Table Styles gallery uses those colors.

> **Quick Tip**
> You can make a table more accessible by selecting a table style that has strong contrasting colors.

4. **Click the Blue, Table Style Light 9 table style (the third style in the second row under Light), then click cell A1**

5. **Position the Column Select pointer in the column heading area for column A, then drag to select columns A through F, click the Home tab, click the Format button in the Cells group, click Column Width, in the Column Width dialog box type 12 in the Column width box, click OK, then click the Wrap Text button in the Alignment group**

   To make the table accessible, you decide to enter a table name in the Table Name text box in the Properties group on the Table Design tab.

> **Quick Tip**
> This table name will enable screen readers to refer to the table in a more meaningful way.

6. **Click the Table Design tab, select the table name in the Table Name text box in the Properties group, type January, then press ENTER**

7. **Click cell A1, compare your table to Figure 5-2, then save your work**

Figure 5-1: Create Table dialog box

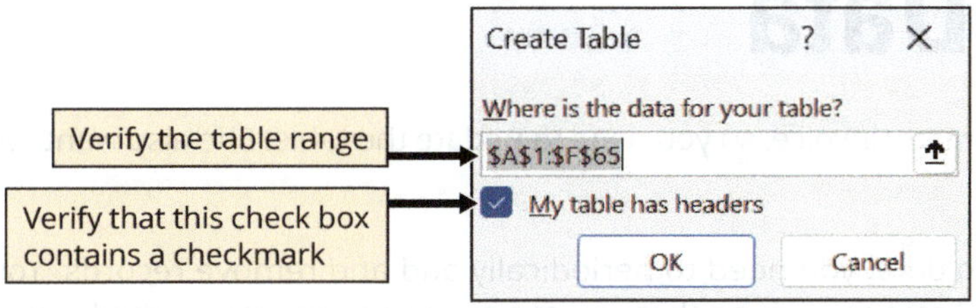


Figure 5-2: Formatted table

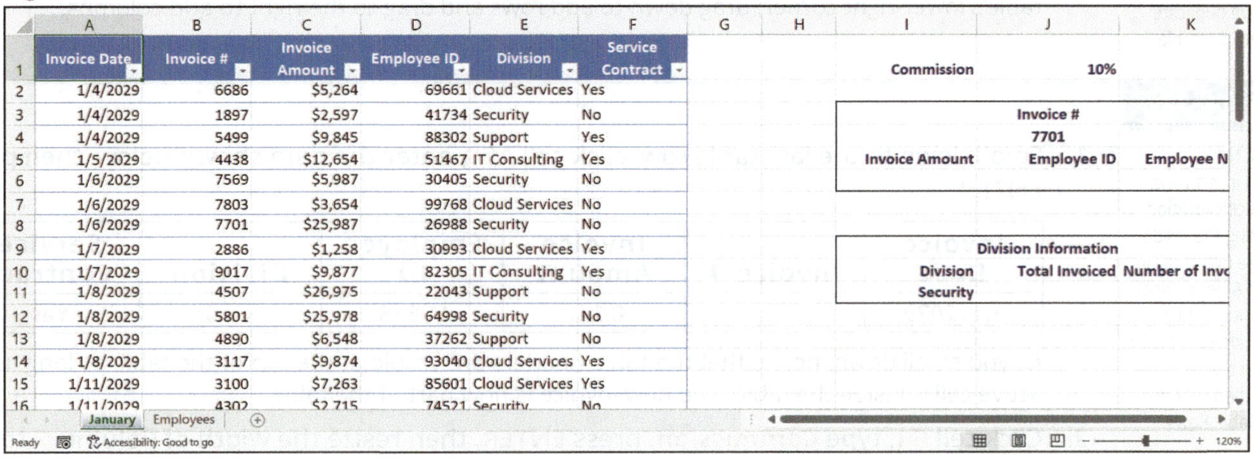


## Changing table style options

You can change a table's appearance by using the check boxes in the Table Style Options group on the Table Design tab, as shown in **Figure 5-3**. You can use the check boxes to turn on or turn off the following options: Header Row, which displays or hides the header row; Total Row, which calculates totals for each column; Banded Rows, which controls **banding**, a type of formatting in which adjacent rows and columns are formatted differently; Banded Columns; and First Column and Last Column, which applies special formatting to the first and last columns. You can display or remove the filter arrows on a table using the Filter Button check box; removing the checkmark removes the arrows.

You can also create your own table style by clicking the Table Styles More button, then clicking New Table Style at the bottom of the Table Styles Gallery. In the New Table Style dialog box, enter a name for the style in the Name box, click an item in the Table Element list, then click Format to format the selected element.

Figure 5-3: Table Style Options group

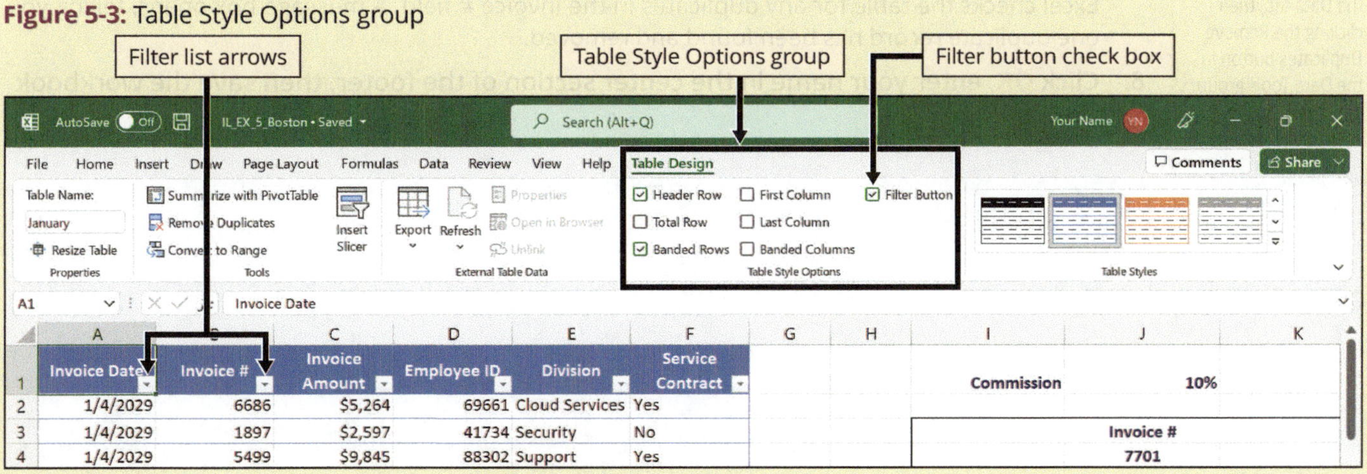

# Change Table Data

**Case** Naya informs you of an additional January invoice, so you need to update the table. She also wants you to remove any duplicate data from the table.

**Objectives**
- Add a row to a table
- Add a column to a table
- Delete a table row
- Remove duplicate data from a table

To keep a table up to date, you need to periodically add and remove records. You also need to check a table for duplicate records so that you can remove unnecessary duplication. You can add records and columns to a table by typing data directly below the last row of the table or directly to the right of the last table column. You can also expand a table by dragging the sizing handle in a table's lower-right corner; drag down to add rows and drag to the right to add columns.

## Steps

**Quick Tip** You can insert rows in a specific location by clicking the inside left edge of the cell in column A below where you want to add a row, clicking the Insert arrow in the Cells group, then clicking Insert Table Rows Above.

1. **Scroll down to the last table row, click cell A66, enter the data shown below, then press ENTER**

| Invoice Date | Invoice # | Invoice Amount | Employee ID | Division | Service Contract |
|---|---|---|---|---|---|
| 1/8/2029 | 8001 | 8,243 | 80848 | Security | Yes |

As you scroll down, notice that the table headers are visible at the top of the table as long as the active cell is inside the table. The new invoice is now part of the table.

2. **Click cell G1, type Commission, press ENTER, then resize the width of Column G to 14.00**

The new field becomes part of the table, and the header formatting extends to the new field name, as shown in **Figure 5-4**. The table range is now A1:G66.

3. **Click the inside left edge of cell A3 to select the table row, click the Delete arrow in the Cells group, then click Delete Table Rows**

The invoice in row 3 is deleted, and the invoice in row 4 moves up to row 3. You can also delete a table row or a column by right-clicking the row or column and then clicking Delete.

4. **Click any cell in the table, click the Table Design tab on the ribbon, then click the Remove Duplicates button in the Tools group**

The table is selected, and the Remove Duplicates dialog box opens, as shown in **Figure 5-5**.

**Quick Tip** You can also remove duplicate rows from a worksheet by clicking the Data tab, then clicking the Remove Duplicates button in the Data Tools group.

5. **Make sure the My data has headers check box contains a checkmark, click Unselect All to deselect all the check boxes, click the Invoice # check box to add a checkmark, then click OK**

Excel checks the table for any duplicates in the Invoice # field. A message box opens, telling you one duplicate record has been found and removed.

6. **Click OK, enter your name in the center section of the footer, then save the workbook**

**Figure 5-4:** New table column

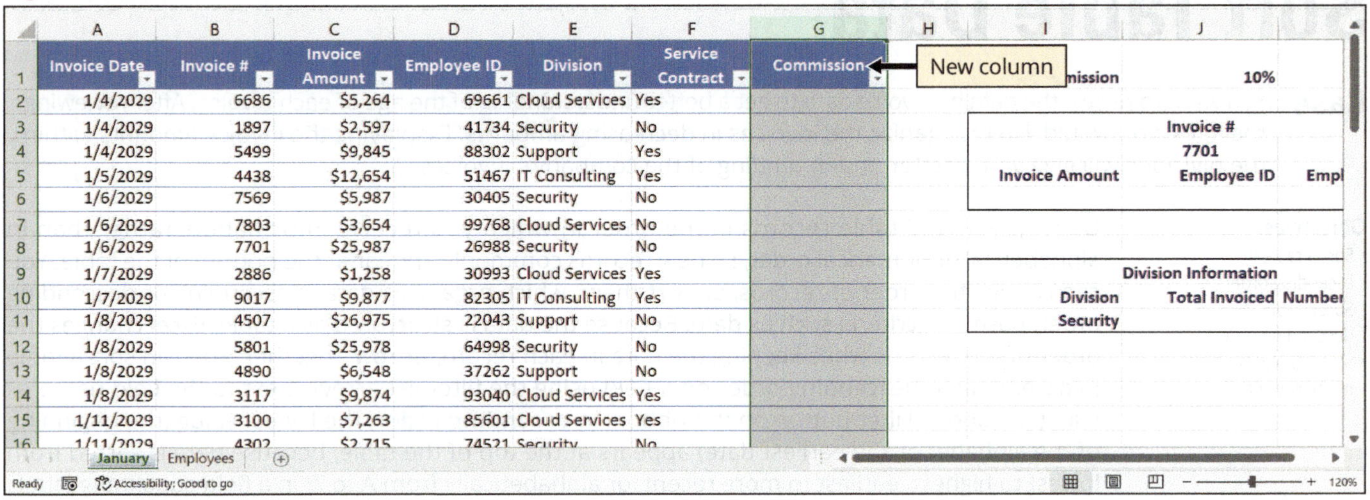


**Figure 5-5:** Remove Duplicates dialog box

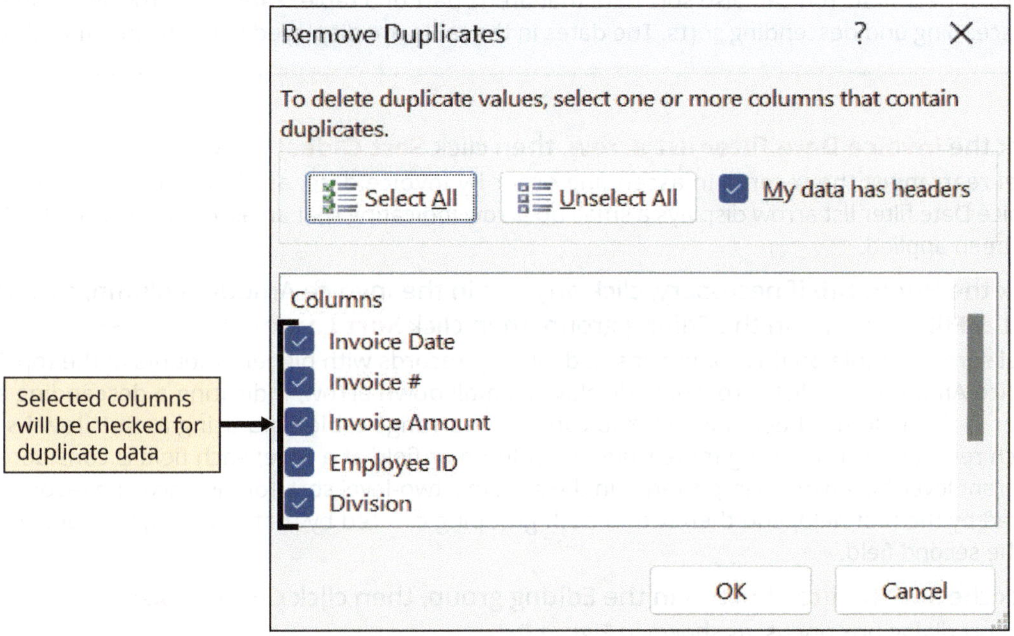


## Selecting table elements

When working with tables you often need to select rows, columns, and even the entire table. Clicking to the right of a row number, just inside the left border of column A, selects the table row. You can select a table column by clicking the top edge of the column. Be careful not to click a column letter or row number, however, because this selects the entire worksheet row or column. You can select the entire table by clicking the upper-left corner of the top-left table cell. When selecting a column or a table, the first click selects only the data in the column or table. If you click a second time, you add the headers to the selection.

# Sort Table Data

**Case** You want to review the data by invoice date to get a better understanding of the age of each invoice. After reviewing the ages, you would like to organize the invoices in decreasing amounts. Displaying the invoice amounts within the divisions will give you a better understanding of the company's invoices.

**Objectives**
- Sort a table in ascending order
- Sort a table in descending order
- Sort a table using a multilevel sort

Usually, you add table records in the order in which you receive information, rather than in alphabetical or numerical order, so new records commonly appear at the bottom of the table. You can change the order of records, or **sort** them, which organizes data in ascending or descending order, based on criteria such as date. Because the data is structured as a table, Excel changes the order of the records while keeping the data in each record, or row, together. You can sort a table in ascending or descending order on a field using the filter list arrows next to the field name or using the Sort & Filter button on the ribbon. In **ascending order**, the lowest value (the beginning of the alphabet or the earliest date) appears at the top of the table, because data is sorted from lowest to highest, earliest to more recent, or alphabetically from A to Z; in a field containing labels and numbers, numbers appear first in the sorted list. In **descending order**, the highest value (the end of the alphabet or the latest date) appears at the top of the table because data is sorted from highest to lowest, most recent to earliest, or from Z to A; in a field containing labels and numbers, labels appear first. You can also sort data that aren't part of a table. **Table 5-1** provides examples of ascending and descending sorts. The dates in the table are displayed in the format month/day.

## Steps

1. **Click the Invoice Date filter list arrow, then click Sort Oldest to Newest**
   Excel rearranges the records in ascending order by invoice date, as shown in **Figure 5-6**. The Invoice Date filter list arrow displays a small up arrow indicating that an ascending sort in this field has been applied.

**Quick Tip**
You can also sort worksheet data that isn't part of a table. To do so, select a cell in the column you want to sort on, then either click the Sort & Filter button in the Editing group on the Home tab, or click the Data tab, then click a button in the Sort & Filter group, such as the Sort A to Z button or Sort Z to A button.

2. **Click the Home tab if necessary, click any cell in the Invoice Amount column, click the Sort & Filter button in the Editing group, then click Sort Largest to Smallest**
   Excel sorts the table on this column instead, placing records with higher amounts at the top. The Invoice Amount filter list arrow now displays a small down arrow, indicating a descending sort order in this field has been applied. You can also rearrange table data using a **multilevel sort**, which reorders records using more than one column or field at a time; each field is considered a different level, based on its importance in the sort. In a two-level sort, for instance, the records are sorted by the first field, and then within each grouping created by that first sort, they are sorted by the second field.
3. **Click the Sort & Filter button in the Editing group, then click Custom Sort**
   The Sort dialog box opens, as shown in **Figure 5-7**.

**Quick Tip**
You can also add a multilevel sort by clicking the Sort button in the Sort & Filter group on the Data tab.

4. **Click the Sort by arrow, click Division, click the Order arrow, click A to Z, click Add Level, click the Then by arrow, click Invoice Amount, click the second Order arrow, click Smallest to Largest if necessary, then click OK**
   As shown in **Figure 5-8**, the table is sorted alphabetically in ascending order (A–Z) by Division and, within each division grouping, in ascending order by the invoice amount (smallest amount to largest).
5. **Save the workbook**

**Table 5-1:** Sort order options and examples

| option | alphabetic | numeric | date | alphanumeric |
|---|---|---|---|---|
| Ascending | A, B, C | 7, 8, 9 | 1/1, 2/1, 3/1 | 12A, 99B, DX8, QT7 |
| Descending | C, B, A | 9, 8, 7 | 3/1, 2/1, 1/1 | QT7, DX8, 99B, 12A |

Figure 5-6: Table sorted by invoice date

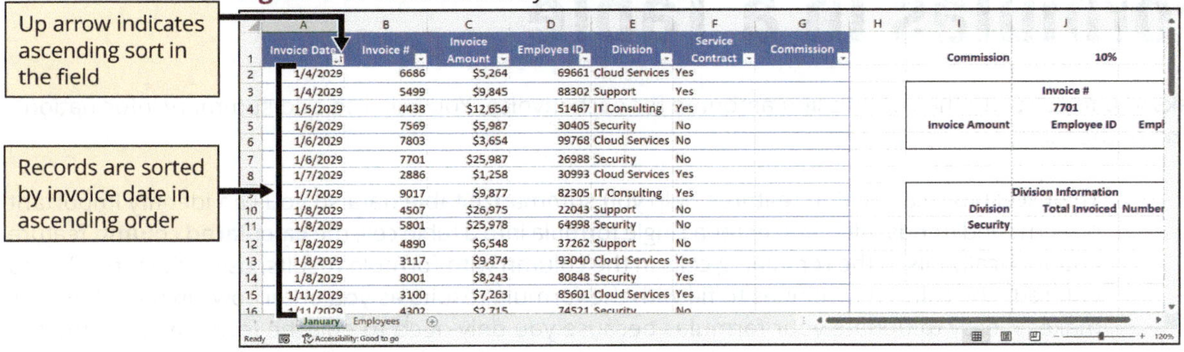


Figure 5-7: Sort dialog box

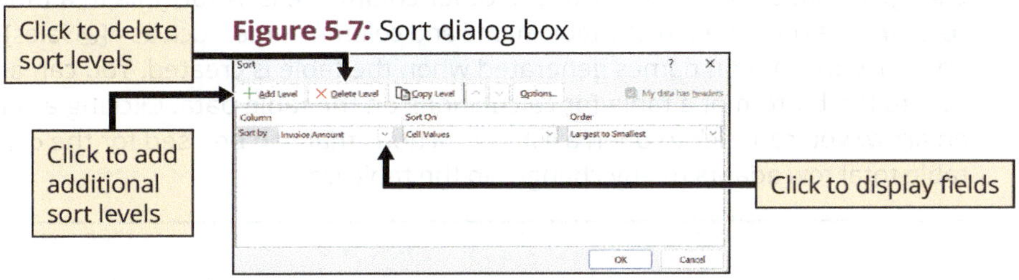


Figure 5-8: Table sorted using two levels

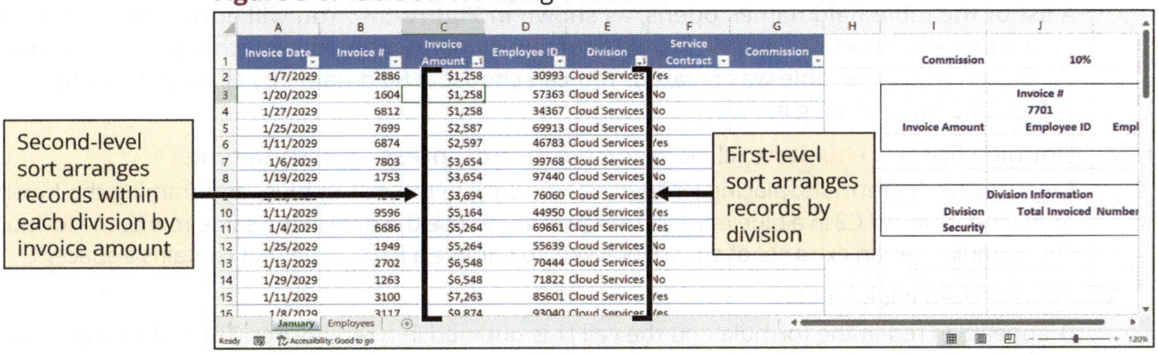


### Sorting conditional formatted data

You can emphasize top-ranked or bottom-ranked values in a field or column by applying conditional formatting to the sorted data. To highlight the top or bottom values in a field, select the field data, click the Conditional Formatting button in the Styles group on the Home tab, point to Top/Bottom Rules, click a rule, and if necessary modify the percentage or number of cells you want to format, select the desired formatting, then click OK. You can also format your worksheet or table data using color scales based on the cell values. A **color scale** is a formatting scheme that uses a color set or gradients of color to convey relative values of data. For example, you could use the Green – Yellow – Red Color Scale to indicate cells with higher values in red, medium values in yellow, and lower values in green. To add a color scale, select a data range, click the Home tab, click the Conditional Formatting button in the Styles group, then point to Color Scales. On the submenu, you can select preformatted color sets or click More Rules to create your own color sets. If conditional formats have been applied to a table or worksheet data, you can sort the table using conditional formatting to arrange the rows. For example, if cells are conditionally formatted with color, you can use the Sort dialog box to sort a field on Cell Color, using the color with the order of On Top or On Bottom in the Sort dialog box.

### Specifying a custom sort order

You can identify a custom sort order in the Sort dialog box if the standard alphabetic and numeric sort orders do not meet your needs. For example, you might want to sort records by days of the week (Sun, Mon, Tues, Wed, etc.); an alphabetic sort would not sort these items properly. In the Sort dialog box, first specify the field you want to sort on, click the Order arrow, then click Custom List. In the Custom Lists dialog box that opens, click an item under Custom lists, view the list entries, then click OK. To build your own custom list, click NEW LIST, click Add, type the desired list order under List entries, then click OK.

# Use Formulas in a Table

**Case** Naya asks you to calculate the commission amounts for each invoice. You will also add summary information to the end of the table.

**Objectives**
- Use structured references in a formula
- Use calculated columns to display formula results
- Use the table style options to add summary information

The Excel table calculation features help you summarize table data so you can identify important patterns and trends. After you enter a single formula into a table cell, the **calculated column** feature automatically fills in the remaining cells in the column with formula results, using the formula you entered. The column continues to fill with the formula results as you enter rows in the table. This makes it easy to update your formulas because you only need to edit the formula once, and the change is made automatically to the other column cells. A formula in a table uses a **structured reference**, a combination of a table name and column name, such as =[@Sales]–[@Cost] where Sales and Cost are column names generated when the table is created. You can also add a **table total row** to the bottom of a table for calculations on the table data. Clicking a cell in this row displays an arrow you can click to open a list of functions that can be used for the column calculation. The table total row adapts to any changes in the table size.

## Steps

1. **Click cell G2, then type =[**
   A list of the table field names opens, as shown in **Figure 5-9**. You will enter a formula using structured references to refer to the table column by name using this list that was automatically generated when the table was created. You can choose a field name by clicking it and pressing TAB or by double-clicking it.
2. **Double-click @ - This Row, click Invoice Amount, press TAB, then type ]**
   Excel begins the formula, placing [@[Invoice Amount]] in the cell, in blue, and framing the Invoice Amount data in cell C2 in a blue border. The @ means to use the data in the same row as the formula. The formula uses an extra set of square brackets to enclose a field name that contains a space.
3. **Type *, then click cell J1**
   J1 appears in red in the formula and the cell J1 is outlined in a red border. The cell reference to J1 in the formula needs absolute referencing
4. **Press F4, then click the Enter button ✓ on the formula bar**
   The formula result, $126, is displayed in cell G2. The table column also fills with the formula, displaying the commission for each invoice. The AutoCorrect Options button provides an option to turn off calculated columns. Because the calculated columns option saves time, you decide to leave the feature on.
5. **Click the Table Design tab, then click the Total Row check box in the Table Style Options group to add a checkmark**
   A total row appears at the bottom of the table, and the sum of the commissions, $75,889, is displayed in cell G65.
6. **Click cell G65, click the cell list arrow on the right side of the cell, then click Average**
   The average commission, $1,205, is displayed in cell G65.
7. **Click cell A65, type Average, then click the Enter button ✓ on the formula bar**
   The total row shows the average commission on the January invoices.
8. **Compare your total row to Figure 5-10, then save your work.**

**Figure 5-9:** Table field names

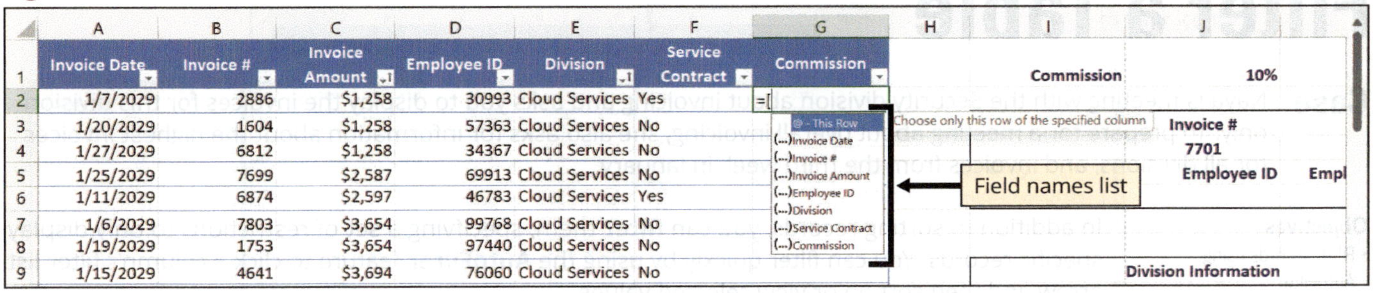

| | Invoice Date | Invoice # | Invoice Amount | Employee ID | Division | Service Contract | Commission |
|---|---|---|---|---|---|---|---|
| 2 | 1/7/2029 | 2886 | $1,258 | 30993 | Cloud Services | Yes | =[ |
| 3 | 1/20/2029 | 1604 | $1,258 | 57363 | Cloud Services | No | |
| 4 | 1/27/2029 | 6812 | $1,258 | 34367 | Cloud Services | No | |
| 5 | 1/25/2029 | 7699 | $2,587 | 69913 | Cloud Services | No | |
| 6 | 1/11/2029 | 6874 | $2,597 | 46783 | Cloud Services | Yes | |
| 7 | 1/6/2029 | 7803 | $3,654 | 99768 | Cloud Services | No | |
| 8 | 1/19/2029 | 1753 | $3,654 | 97440 | Cloud Services | No | |
| 9 | 1/15/2029 | 4641 | $3,694 | 76060 | Cloud Services | No | |



**Figure 5-10:** Table with total row

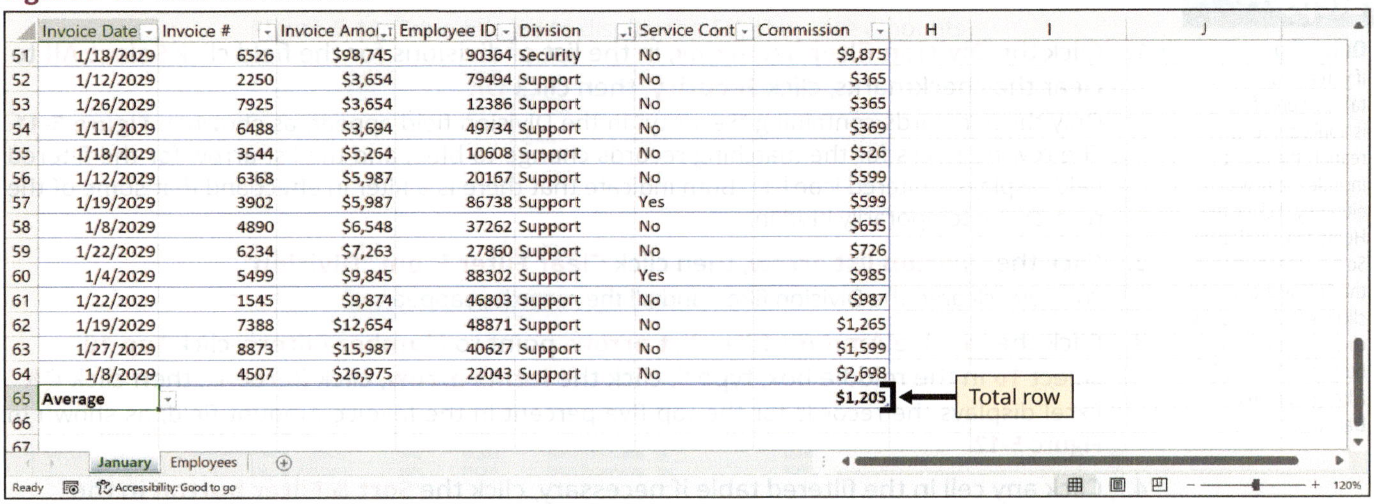

| | Invoice Date | Invoice # | Invoice Amount | Employee ID | Division | Service Cont | Commission |
|---|---|---|---|---|---|---|---|
| 51 | 1/18/2029 | 6526 | $98,745 | 90364 | Security | No | $9,875 |
| 52 | 1/12/2029 | 2250 | $3,654 | 79494 | Support | No | $365 |
| 53 | 1/26/2029 | 7925 | $3,654 | 12386 | Support | No | $365 |
| 54 | 1/11/2029 | 6488 | $3,694 | 49734 | Support | No | $369 |
| 55 | 1/18/2029 | 3544 | $5,264 | 10608 | Support | No | $526 |
| 56 | 1/12/2029 | 6368 | $5,987 | 20167 | Support | No | $599 |
| 57 | 1/19/2029 | 3902 | $5,987 | 86738 | Support | Yes | $599 |
| 58 | 1/8/2029 | 4890 | $6,548 | 37262 | Support | No | $655 |
| 59 | 1/22/2029 | 6234 | $7,263 | 27860 | Support | No | $726 |
| 60 | 1/4/2029 | 5499 | $9,845 | 88302 | Support | Yes | $985 |
| 61 | 1/22/2029 | 1545 | $9,874 | 46803 | Support | No | $987 |
| 62 | 1/19/2029 | 7388 | $12,654 | 48871 | Support | No | $1,265 |
| 63 | 1/27/2029 | 8873 | $15,987 | 40627 | Support | No | $1,599 |
| 64 | 1/8/2029 | 4507 | $26,975 | 22043 | Support | No | $2,698 |
| 65 | Average | | | | | | $1,205 |

# Summarize Table Data

**Case** Naya is reviewing the yearly performance of each division. She needs your help in analyzing the total number of invoices and invoice amounts for each division.

**Objectives**
- Select a database for a database function
- Summarize table data using a database function

An Excel table acts as a simple type of database, and you can use database functions to summarize table data in a variety of ways. When working with a sales activity table, for example, you can use Excel to count the number of client contacts by sales representative or to total the amount sold to specific accounts by month. **Table 5-3** lists commonly used database functions for summarizing table data.

## Steps

1. **Review the criteria range for the Security division in the range I10:I11**
   The criteria range in I10:I11 will be used to tell Excel to summarize records with the entry "Security" in the Division column.
2. **Click cell J11, if necessary click the Formulas tab on the ribbon, click the Insert Function button in the Function Library group, in the Search for a function text box type database, click Go, click DSUM under Select a function, then click OK**
3. **In the Function Arguments dialog box, with the insertion point in the Database text box move the pointer over the upper-left corner of cell A1 until the pointer changes to the Arrow pointer ➘, click once, then click again**
   The first argument of the DSUM function is the table or database. The first click selects the table's data range, and the second click selects the entire table, including the header row. Because the DSUM formula uses column headings to locate and sum the table data, you need to include the header row in the database range.
4. **Click the Field text box, click cell C1 (the Invoice Amount heading), click the Criteria text box, then select the range I10:I11**
   The second argument of the DSUM function is the label for the column that you want to sum. You want to total the invoice amounts. The last argument for the DSUM function is the criteria that will be used to determine which values to total. Your completed Function Arguments dialog box should match **Figure 5-17**.
5. **Click OK, click the Home tab on the ribbon, click the Accounting Number Format button [$] in the Number group, then click the Decrease Decimal button [.00→.0] twice**
   The result in cell J11 is $249,276. Excel totaled the information in the Invoice Amount column for those records that meet the criterion of Division equals Security.
6. **Click cell K11, click the Insert Function button [fx] on the formula bar, in the Search for a function text box type database, click Go, then double-click DCOUNTA in the Select a function list, then click OK**
   The DCOUNT and the DCOUNTA functions can help you determine the number of records meeting specified criteria in a database field. DCOUNTA counts the number of nonblank cells.
7. **With the insertion point in the Database text box move the pointer over the upper-left corner of cell A1 until it changes to the Arrow pointer ➘, click once, click again to include the header row, click the Field text box, click cell C1, click the Criteria text box and select the range I10:I11, then click OK**
   The result in cell K11 is 16 and indicates that the security division had 16 invoices in January.
8. **Click cell I11, type Support, click the Enter button [✓] on the formula bar, then save your work**
   The formulas in cells J11 and K11 are updated to reflect the new criteria. **Figure 5-18** shows that the support division had 13 invoices and a total invoice amount of $117,386 over the past year.

**Trouble** (step 3)
Your second arrow may look more like the diagonal pointer ⤡.

**Trouble** (step 7)
As an alternative to clicking to select a table, you can type the database argument, Table1[#All], in the Database text box.

**Figure 5-17:** Completed Function Arguments dialog box for DSUM

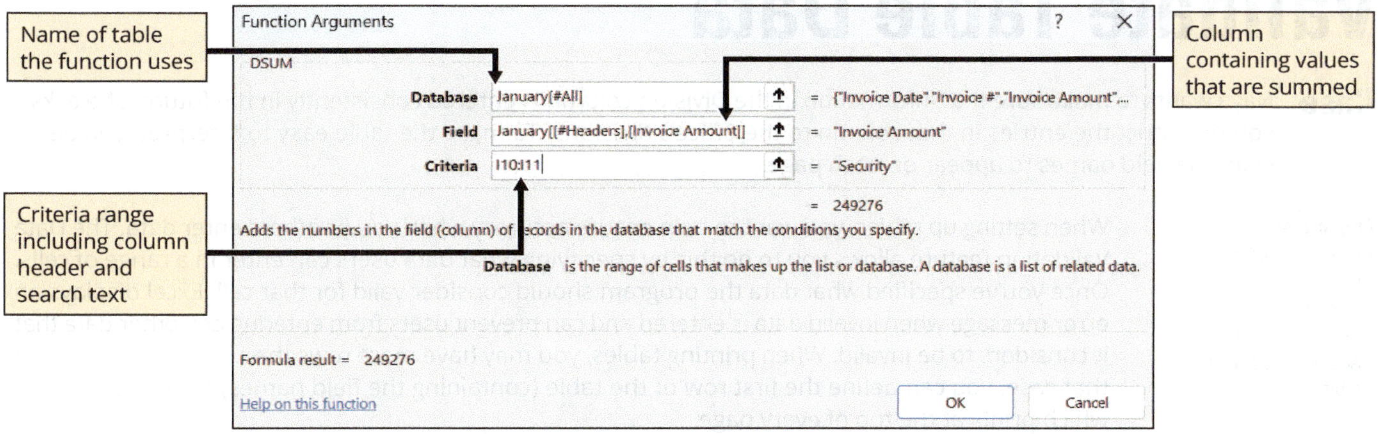


**Figure 5-18:** Result generated by database functions

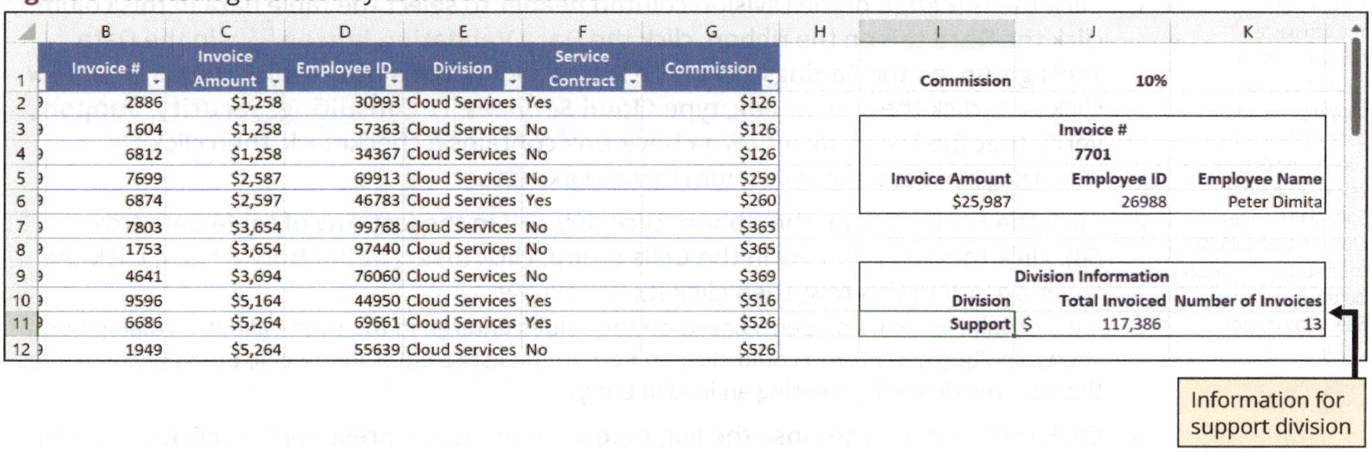


**Table 5-3:** Common database functions

| function | result |
|---|---|
| DGET | Extracts a single record from a table that matches criteria you specify |
| DSUM | Totals numbers in a given table column that match criteria you specify |
| DAVERAGE | Averages numbers in a given table column that match criteria you specify |
| DCOUNT | Counts the cells that contain numbers in a given table column that match criteria you specify |
| DCOUNTA | Counts the cells that contain nonblank data in a given table column that match criteria you specify |

# Validate Table Data

**Case** Naya wants to make sure that information in the Division column is entered consistently in the future. She asks you to restrict the entries in that column to the office's divisions. To make the table easy to interpret, you also want the field names to appear on each page.

**Objectives**
- Use data validation to restrict data entry
- Insert table data using data validation
- Add print titles to a table

When setting up tables, you want to help ensure accuracy when you or others enter data. The Data Validation feature allows you to do this by specifying what data users can enter in a range of cells. Once you've specified what data the program should consider valid for that cell, Excel displays an error message when invalid data is entered and can prevent users from entering any other data that it considers to be invalid. When printing tables, you may have more rows than can fit on a page. In that case, you can define the first row of the table (containing the field names) as the **print title**, which prints at the top of every page.

## Steps

**Quick Tip**
You can paste cell validation in a worksheet by copying a cell with data validation, right-clicking the destination cell, clicking Paste Special in the Paste Options, then clicking to select the Validation button in the Paste Special dialog box.

1. **Click the top edge of the Division column header to select the table data in this column, click the Data tab on the ribbon, click the Data Validation button in the Data Tools group, on the Settings tab of the Data Validation dialog box click the Allow arrow, click List, click the Source box, type Cloud Services, IT Consulting, Security, Support, verify that the In-cell dropdown check box contains a checkmark, then click OK**
   The dialog box closes, and you return to the worksheet.
2. **Click the Home tab on the ribbon, click any cell in the last row of table data (row 64), click the Insert arrow in the Cells group, click Insert Table Row Below, click the Division cell in this row, then click its list arrow**
   A list of valid list entries opens, based on the values entered in the Data Validation dialog box, as shown in **Figure 5-19**. You could click an item in the list to enter in the cell, but you want to test the data restriction by entering an invalid entry.
3. **Click the list arrow to close the list, type Management, press ENTER, click Cancel in the warning dialog box, click the list arrow, then click Security**
   The cell accepts the valid entry.
4. **Click the Delete arrow in the Cells group, click Delete Table Rows, click the File tab on the ribbon, click Print, in the Preview window click No Scaling under Settings, then click Fit All Columns on One Page**
   Below the table, the text 1 of 2 indicates that this is page 1 of a 2-page document.
5. **Click the Next Page button in the Preview area**
   The rows continue onto page 2, though the field names are not displayed.

**Quick Tip**
You can choose to print an entire workbook or a selected area of the worksheet by clicking the Print Active Sheets button in the Settings list, then clicking Print Entire Workbook or Print Selection.

6. **Return to the worksheet, click the Page Layout tab on the ribbon, click the Print Titles button in the Page Setup group, click inside the Rows to repeat at top text box under Print titles, in the worksheet scroll up to row 1 if necessary, click any cell in row 1 on the table, click the Print Preview button in the Page Setup dialog box, then click in the preview window to view the second page**
   A print title that repeats row 1 shows the field names at the top of each printed page.
7. **Return to the worksheet, click the Insert tab, click the Text button, click the Header & Footer button, click the left header section text box if necessary, type Boston January Invoices, click any cell on the worksheet, click the Normal button in the status bar, then press CTRL+HOME**
8. **Click the top edge of the Invoice # column header, hold CTRL, click the top edges of the Employee ID and Service Contract column headers, then release CTRL**
9. **sam Click the Home tab, click the Center button in the Alignment group, save the table, close the workbook, close Excel, then submit the workbook to your instructor**
   Compare your printed table with **Figure 5-20**.

**Figure 5-19:** Entering data in restricted cells

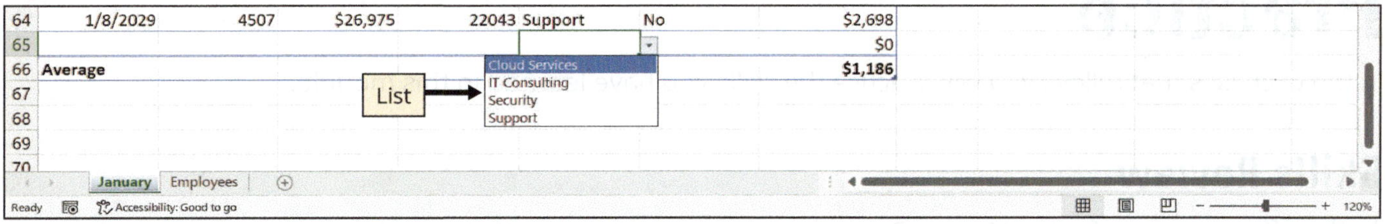


**Figure 5-20:** Printed table

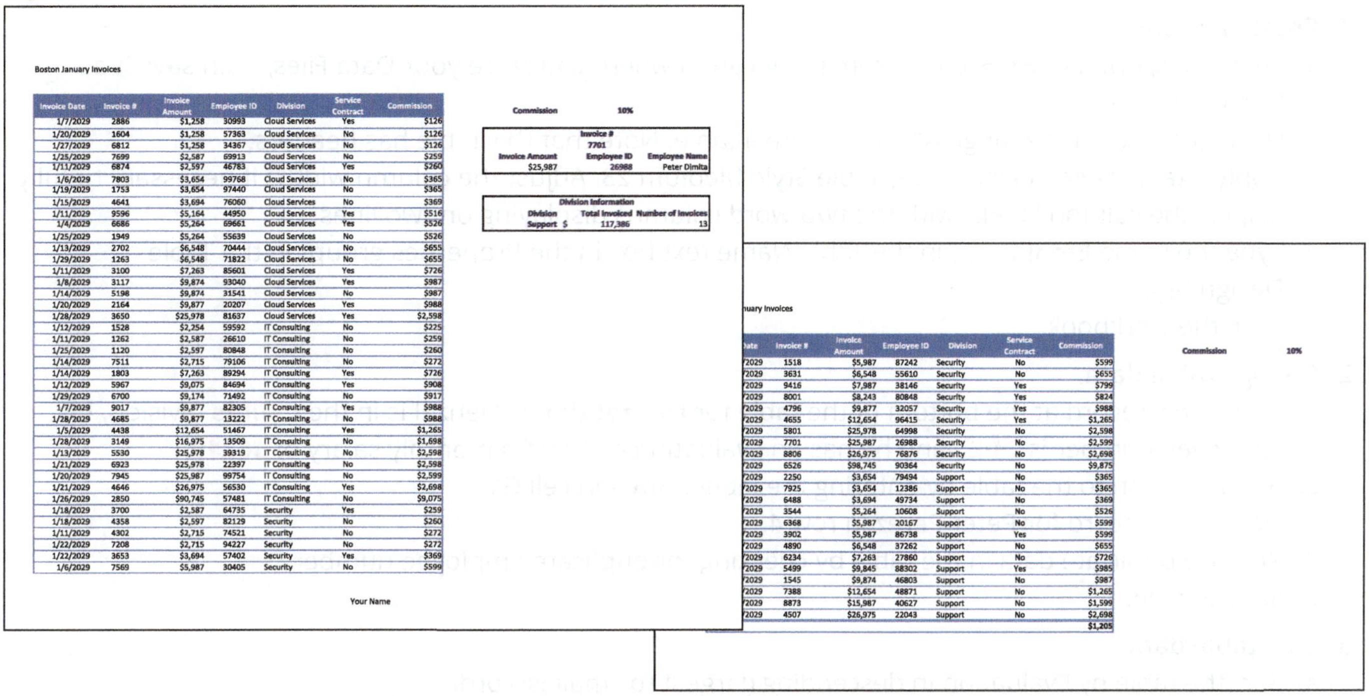

## Restricting cell values and data lengths

In addition to providing an in-cell list for data entry, you can use data validation to restrict the values that are entered into cells. For example, you might want to restrict cells in a selected range to values less than a certain number, date, or time. To do so, click the Data tab, click the Data Validation button in the Data Tools group, on the Settings tab click the Allow arrow, select Whole number, Decimal, Date, or Time, click the Data arrow, select less than, then in the bottom text box, enter the maximum value. You can also limit the length of data entered into cells by choosing Text length in the Allow list, clicking the Data arrow and selecting less than, then entering the maximum length in the Maximum text box.

## Adding input messages and error alerts

You can customize the way data validation works by adding input messages and setting alert styles. For example, you might want to add a message with instructions about what type of data a user should enter. To do so, click the Input Message tab in the Data Validation dialog box, enter a message title and message, then click OK. To set an alert style, which controls how a user can proceed when entering invalid data, click the Error Alert tab, then click the Style arrow. The Information style displays your message with the information icon but allows the user to proceed with data entry. The Warning style displays your information with the warning icon and gives the user the option to proceed with data entry or not. The Stop style, which you used in this lesson, is the default; it displays your message and only lets the user retry or cancel data entry for that cell.

# Practice

In the exercises that follow, you will practice the skills you have learned in this module.

## Skills Review

As the office manager for the Human Resources Department at a west coast insurance company, you manage employee information for the company's four divisions. You will use Excel features from this module to locate and summarize employee and division data.

1. **Create a table.**
   a. Start Excel, open IL_EX_5-2.xlsx from the location where you store your Data Files, then save it as **IL_EX_5_Bonus**.
   b. Using the data in the range A1:F13, create a table. Note that this table has headers.
   c. Apply a table style of Light Blue, Table Style Medium 23. Adjust the column widths if necessary to fully display the column labels, with the two-word columns displaying on two lines.
   d. Type the name **Employees** in the Table Name text box in the Properties group on the Table Design tab.
   e. Save the workbook.
2. **Change table data.**
   a. Add a new record at the bottom of the table for **Denzel Davis**. Denzel is in the **Claims** division, his employee number is **2442**, and he has an evaluation of **4** and a monthly salary of **$6210**.
   b. Add a column to the table by entering the label **Bonus** in cell G1.
   c. Delete the record for Peter Perez in row 4.
   d. Remove duplicate data in the table by checking for duplicate employee numbers.
   e. Save the file.
3. **Sort table data.**
   a. Sort the table by Evaluation in descending (largest to smallest) order.
   b. Sort the table again by Last Name in ascending (A to Z) order.
   c. Perform a custom, multilevel sort by sorting the table first by Division in A to Z order, and then by Evaluation in Smallest to Largest order.
   d. Review the results of the multilevel sort to make sure the records are sorted first by Division and then by Evaluation.
   e. Save the file.
4. **Use formulas in a table.**
   a. In cell G2, enter a formula, using structured references, to calculate an employee's bonus assuming an evaluation must be greater than or equal to three to receive a $5000 bonus payment. (**Hint**: Use a formula with IF. The formula IF([@Evaluation]>=3,5000,0) should be entered in cell G2.)
   b. Check the table to make sure that the formula from cell G2 is filled into the cells in column G, and that the bonus is calculated for the cells in the column.
   c. Format all bonus values in the Accounting format and with no decimal places.
   d. Add a total row to display the total bonus amount for all employees.
   e. Save your work.

5. **Filter a table.**
   a. Filter the table to list only records for employees in the Legal Division.
   b. Clear the filter.
   c. Use AutoFilter to list only the three employees with the highest monthly earnings. (**Hint**: Find the top three items.)
   d. Clear the filter to redisplay all the records.
   e. Create a Custom AutoFilter showing employees with monthly earnings between $5,000 and $8,000. (**Hint**: Use both rows in the Custom AutoFilter dialog box to set the criteria.)
   f. Redisplay all the records and save your work.

6. **Use LOOKUP functions.**
   a. Open the Name Manager using a button on the Formulas tab, view named tables in the workbook, then close the Name Manager.
   b. Enter the employee number **1688** in cell A16.
   c. In cell B16, use the XLOOKUP function to display the name and division for a given employee number. To accomplish this, enter **A16** as the Lookup_value, **D2:D12** as the Lookup_array, **A2:C12** as the Return_array; observe the First Name, Last Name, and Division displayed for that employee number, then check these values against the table to make sure they are correct.
   d. Replace the existing Employee Number in cell A16 with **1987**, then view the First Name, Last Name, and Division for that employee.
   e. In cell E16, use the XLOOKUP function to return the office for a given employee number. To accomplish this, enter **A16** as the Lookup_value, **Offices!A:A** as the Lookup_array, and **Offices!B:B** as the Return_array; observe the Office displayed for that employee number, then check this value against the Offices table on the Offices sheet to make sure it is correct. (**Hint**: You can select the Lookup_array and Return_array on the Offices worksheet by clicking the column headings.)
   f. Save the workbook.

7. **Summarize table data.**
   a. In cell A19 of the Employees sheet, enter **Finance**
   b. In cell B19, use the DAVERAGE function to find the average evaluation for the Finance Division. (**Hint**: Click the upper-left corner of cell A1 twice to select the table and its header row as the Database, select cell E1 for the Field, and select the range A18:A19 for the Criteria.
   c. Verify that the average evaluation for employees in the Finance Division is 4.3333.
   d. Test the function further by entering **Claims** in cell A19. When the criterion is entered, verify that the average evaluation for employees in the Legal Division is 4.0000.
   e. Save the workbook.

8. **Validate table data.**
   a. Select the table data in column C and set a validation criterion specifying that you want to allow a list of valid options.
   b. Enter a list of valid options that restricts the entries to **Claims**, **Finance**, **Legal**, and **Underwriting**. Remember to use a comma between each item in the list.
   c. Test the data validation by changing the division of Amaya Mele in row 5 from Finance to Legal.
   d. Compare your screen to **Figure 5-21**.
   e. Add columns A and B as print titles that repeat at the left of each printed page. (**Hint**: The Columns to repeat at left text box should display $A:$B.)
   f. Enter your name in the center section of the Employees worksheet footer.
   g. Save the worksheet, then preview the worksheet to verify that the first and last name columns appear on both pages.
   h. Submit your workbook to your instructor. Close the workbook, then close Excel.

# Skills Review (Continued)

**Figure 5-21**

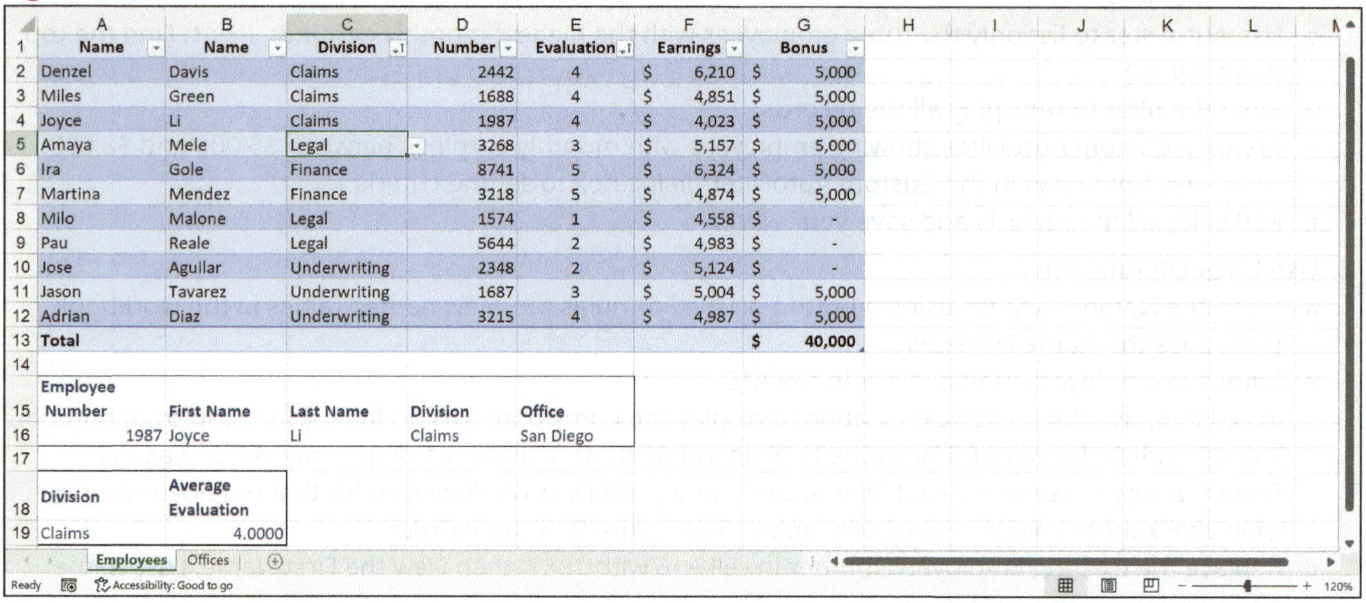

| | A | B | C | D | E | F | G |
|---|---|---|---|---|---|---|---|
| 1 | Name | Name | Division | Number | Evaluation | Earnings | Bonus |
| 2 | Denzel | Davis | Claims | 2442 | 4 | $ 6,210 | $ 5,000 |
| 3 | Miles | Green | Claims | 1688 | 4 | $ 4,851 | $ 5,000 |
| 4 | Joyce | Li | Claims | 1987 | 4 | $ 4,023 | $ 5,000 |
| 5 | Amaya | Mele | Legal | 3268 | 3 | $ 5,157 | $ 5,000 |
| 6 | Ira | Gole | Finance | 8741 | 5 | $ 6,324 | $ 5,000 |
| 7 | Martina | Mendez | Finance | 3218 | 5 | $ 4,874 | $ 5,000 |
| 8 | Milo | Malone | Legal | 1574 | 1 | $ 4,558 | $ - |
| 9 | Pau | Reale | Legal | 5644 | 2 | $ 4,983 | $ - |
| 10 | Jose | Aguilar | Underwriting | 2348 | 2 | $ 5,124 | $ - |
| 11 | Jason | Tavarez | Underwriting | 1687 | 3 | $ 5,004 | $ 5,000 |
| 12 | Adrian | Diaz | Underwriting | 3215 | 4 | $ 4,987 | $ 5,000 |
| 13 | Total | | | | | | $ 40,000 |
| 14 | | | | | | | |
| 15 | Employee Number | First Name | Last Name | Division | Office | | |
| 16 | 1987 | Joyce | Li | Claims | San Diego | | |
| 17 | | | | | | | |
| 18 | Division | Average Evaluation | | | | | |
| 19 | Claims | 4.0000 | | | | | |



# Independent Challenge 1

You are the assistant to the director of the Accounts Receivable Department at HWQ, a travel wholesale company, that puts together packages for travel agents to sell to their clients. As part of your job, you review invoice data of the travel agencies for whom you provide travel services. You will use table features to analyze data for invoices with outstanding balances.

a. Start Excel, open IL_EX_5-3.xlsx from the location where you store your Data Files, then save it as **IL_EX_5_HWQ**.
b. Using the data in the range A1:E57, create a table, name the table **Invoices**, then widen the columns as necessary to fully display the field names.
c. Remove the banding of the table rows. (**Hint**: Deselect a check box in the Table Style Options group on the Table Design tab.)
d. Add the record shown below to the end of the table:

| Invoice # | Invoice Date | Company | Amount | Payment |
|---|---|---|---|---|
| 500 | 2/7/2029 | Adventure Travel | 3000 | 1000 |

e. Delete the record in row 8 for invoice # 184.
f. Remove any duplicate records by checking for matching invoice numbers.
g. Add a new column to the table by entering a field named **Balance** in cell F1. Widen the column as necessary to fully display the column name. Calculate the balance for each invoice using structured references to subtract the payment from the amount invoiced.
h. Sort the table by Balance in ascending order.
i. Use a custom sort to sort the table first by the company in descending order (Z to A), and then, within each category, by the balance in ascending order (Smallest to Largest).
j. Filter the table to show only Pacific Cruises invoices, then copy the filtered records and header row to the Pacific Cruises sheet. Widen the columns on the Pacific Cruises worksheet as necessary to fully display the data and field names.
k. Return to the Invoice sheet, then clear the filter.

l. Filter the table to show only invoices for the first quarter. (**Hint**: The invoice dates must be after or equal to 1/1/2029 and before or equal to 3/31/2029.) Copy the filtered records and the header row to the First Quarter worksheet. Widen the columns on the worksheet as necessary to fully display the data and field names, with the field names on one line.

m. Remove the filter from the Invoice Date field on the Invoice worksheet.

n. Enter **275** in cell I3. Using table references, enter an XLOOKUP function in cell H5 to retrieve the company, amount, payment, and balance for this invoice and place this information in the range H5:K5. Format the balance in cell K5 in the Accounting format with the $ symbol and no decimal places.

o. Use the database function DSUM in cell H11 to total the amount invoiced for Adventure Travel using the criteria in H8:H9. Format cell H11 in the Accounting format with the $ symbol and no decimal places.

p. Using the criteria in H8:H9, enter a database function in cell I11 to count the number of Adventure Travel invoices. (**Hint**: Use the DCOUNTA function.)

q. Use the Data Validation dialog box to add an in-cell dropdown list to the cells in the Company column, and restrict entries to **Adventure Travel**, **Leisure Experiences**, **Pacific Cruises**, **Luxury Getaways**, and **A & L Events**. Check the list by clicking cell C2. Compare your table to **Figure 5-22**.

r. Add print titles to repeat the first row at the top of each printed page of the Invoice sheet, enter your name in the center section of all three worksheet footers, enter the sheet names in the center section of all three worksheet headers, then activate cell A1.

s. Save the workbook, preview it, then submit the workbook to your instructor.

t. Close the workbook, then close Excel.

**Figure 5-22**

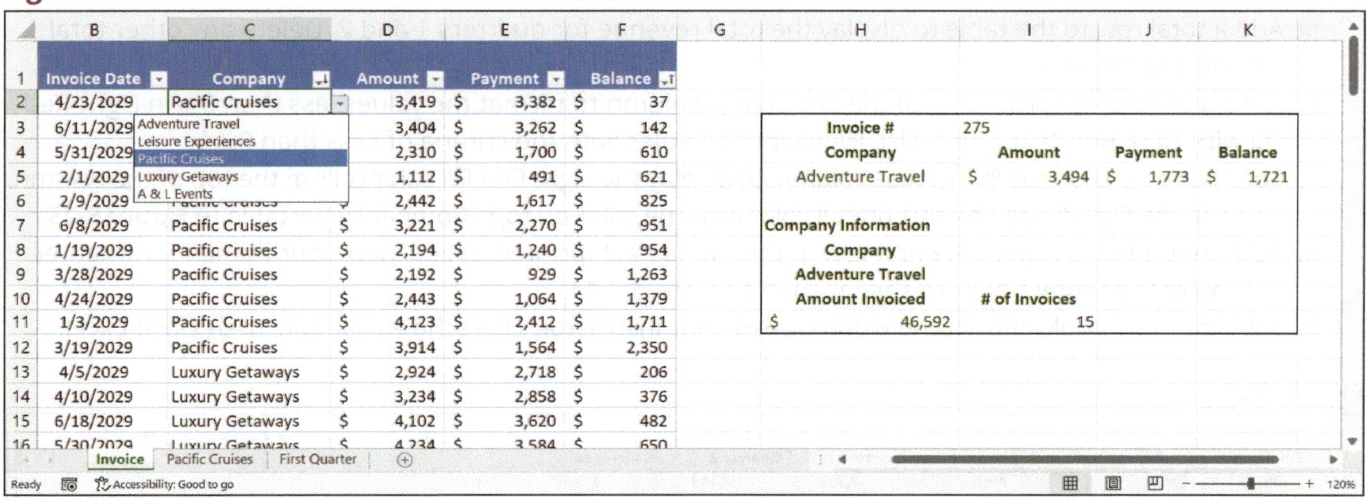


## Independent Challenge 2

As the assistant manager of a food services company, you are responsible for analyzing department revenue. The past two-quarters of revenue data are listed in a worksheet. You will analyze this data using table features.

a. Start Excel, open IL_EX_5-4.xlsx from the location where you store your Data Files, then save it as **IL_EX_5_Revenue**.

b. Using the data in the range A1:E92, create a table and format the table with the table style Light Orange, Table Style Medium 24. Widen the columns as necessary to fully display the field names.

c. Delete the record in row 5 for employee #18574. Check the table for duplicates, using the Employee # field, and remove any duplicate records.

## Independent Challenge 2 (Continued)

d. Add a field named **% Increase** in cell F1.

e. Enter a table formula in cell F2 that calculates the percent increase in the revenue from Quarter 1 to Quarter 2. (**Hint**: A % increase is calculated by subtracting the old value—in this case, the Quarter 1 value—from the new value—in this case, Quarter 2, and then dividing that difference by the old value. Remember to use parentheses when calculating the difference between the old and new values.)

f. Check that the formula was filled into the other column cells. Format the values in column F in the Percent Style format with two decimal places.

g. Use a number filter to find employee records where the % increase is less than zero. Copy the results and paste them into a new sheet named Negative Growth. Widen the columns on the new sheet as necessary to fully display the field names.

h. Return to the Revenue sheet and remove the filter from the % Increase field.

i. Use the Data Validation dialog box to create an in-cell drop-down list that restricts entries in the Division column to **North**, **South**, **East**, and **West**.

j. Use the Error Alert tab of the Data Validation dialog box to set the alert style to the Warning style, and enter the error message **Data is not valid**. Use the Input Message tab to add an input message of **Select the division**.

k. Add a new row at the end of the table and test the validation in the table with a valid entry. Use the new row to add a record with the following data: **99999** in the Employee # column, **Quality** in the Department column, **North** in the Division column, **5000** in the Quarter 1 column, and **5100** in the Quarter 2 column.

l. Test the data validation by entering **Southwest** in cell C91. Verify the correct error message is displayed, then click Cancel to keep the existing valid data.

m. Add a total row to the table to display the total revenue for quarters 1 and 2. Delete any other total amounts in the row.

n. Apply conditional formatting to the % Increase column to format the values less than 0% in Light Red Fill with Dark Red Text. (**Hint**: Use Highlight Cell Rules with the criteria of Less than 0%.)

o. Sort the records on the % Increase column, to display the Light Red Fill color cells at the top of the column. (**Hint**: In the Sort dialog box sort on cell color with the color on top.) Compare your table to **Figure 5-23**.

p. Add print titles to repeat the first row at the top of each printed page. Enter your name in the center section of the footers of both sheets, then activate cell A1.

q. Save the workbook, submit the workbook to your instructor, close the workbook, then close Excel.

**Figure 5-23**

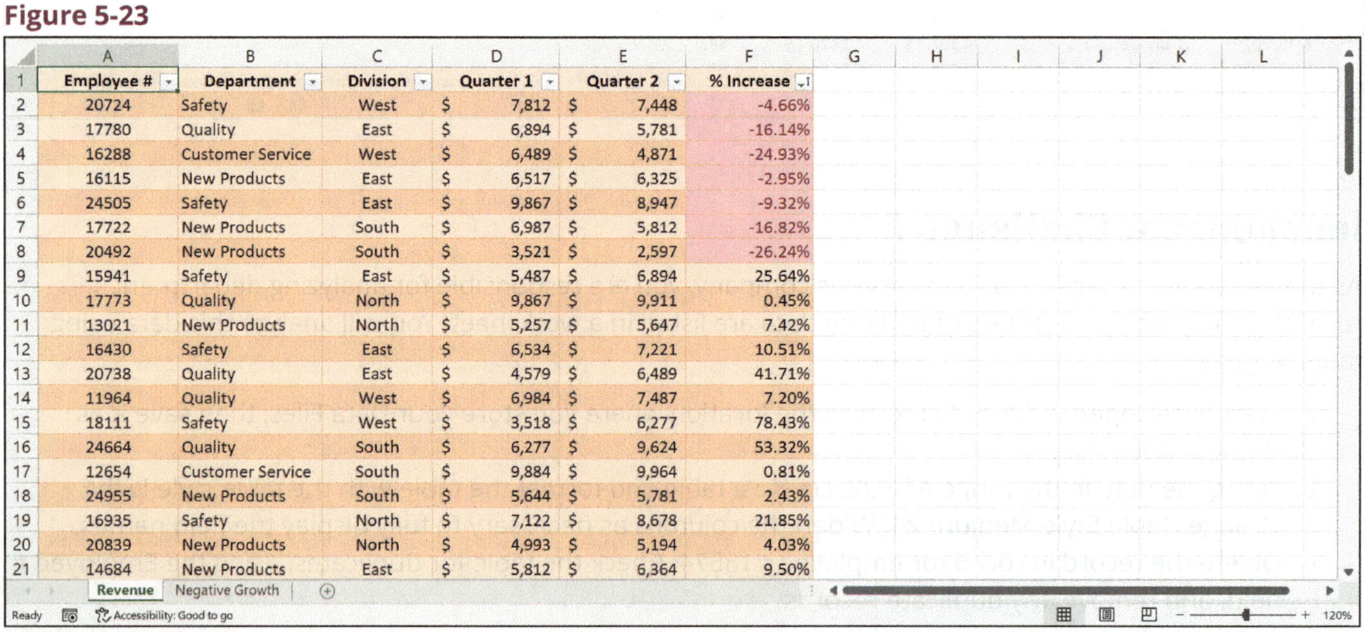

| | A | B | C | D | E | F |
|---|---|---|---|---|---|---|
| 1 | Employee # | Department | Division | Quarter 1 | Quarter 2 | % Increase |
| 2 | 20724 | Safety | West | $ 7,812 | $ 7,448 | -4.66% |
| 3 | 17780 | Quality | East | $ 6,894 | $ 5,781 | -16.14% |
| 4 | 16288 | Customer Service | West | $ 6,489 | $ 4,871 | -24.93% |
| 5 | 16115 | New Products | East | $ 6,517 | $ 6,325 | -2.95% |
| 6 | 24505 | Safety | East | $ 9,867 | $ 8,947 | -9.32% |
| 7 | 17722 | New Products | South | $ 6,987 | $ 5,812 | -16.82% |
| 8 | 20492 | New Products | South | $ 3,521 | $ 2,597 | -26.24% |
| 9 | 15941 | Safety | East | $ 5,487 | $ 6,894 | 25.64% |
| 10 | 17773 | Quality | North | $ 9,867 | $ 9,911 | 0.45% |
| 11 | 13021 | New Products | North | $ 5,257 | $ 5,647 | 7.42% |
| 12 | 16430 | Safety | East | $ 6,534 | $ 7,221 | 10.51% |
| 13 | 20738 | Quality | East | $ 4,579 | $ 6,489 | 41.71% |
| 14 | 11964 | Quality | West | $ 6,984 | $ 7,487 | 7.20% |
| 15 | 18111 | Safety | West | $ 3,518 | $ 6,277 | 78.43% |
| 16 | 24664 | Quality | South | $ 6,277 | $ 9,624 | 53.32% |
| 17 | 12654 | Customer Service | South | $ 9,884 | $ 9,964 | 0.81% |
| 18 | 24955 | New Products | South | $ 5,644 | $ 5,781 | 2.43% |
| 19 | 16935 | Safety | North | $ 7,122 | $ 8,678 | 21.85% |
| 20 | 20839 | New Products | North | $ 4,993 | $ 5,194 | 4.03% |
| 21 | 14684 | New Products | East | $ 5,812 | $ 6,364 | 9.50% |

# Visual Workshop

Open IL_EX_5-5.xlsx from the location where you store your Data Files, then save it as **IL_EX_5_Assets**. Create a table based on the data, and use the default table style. Sort, summarize, add a column, build a table formula, and add data validation so that your screen matches the table shown in **Figure 5-24**. (**Hints**: The table name is Accounts; the fee is calculated by multiplying the assets by the management fee percentage; the XLOOKUP function is used to find the assets in cell K3; the DSUM function is used to calculate the total assets in cell K9.) Enter your name in the center section of the worksheet footer. Save the workbook, preview the table, close the workbook, submit the workbook to your instructor, then close Excel.

**Figure 5-24**

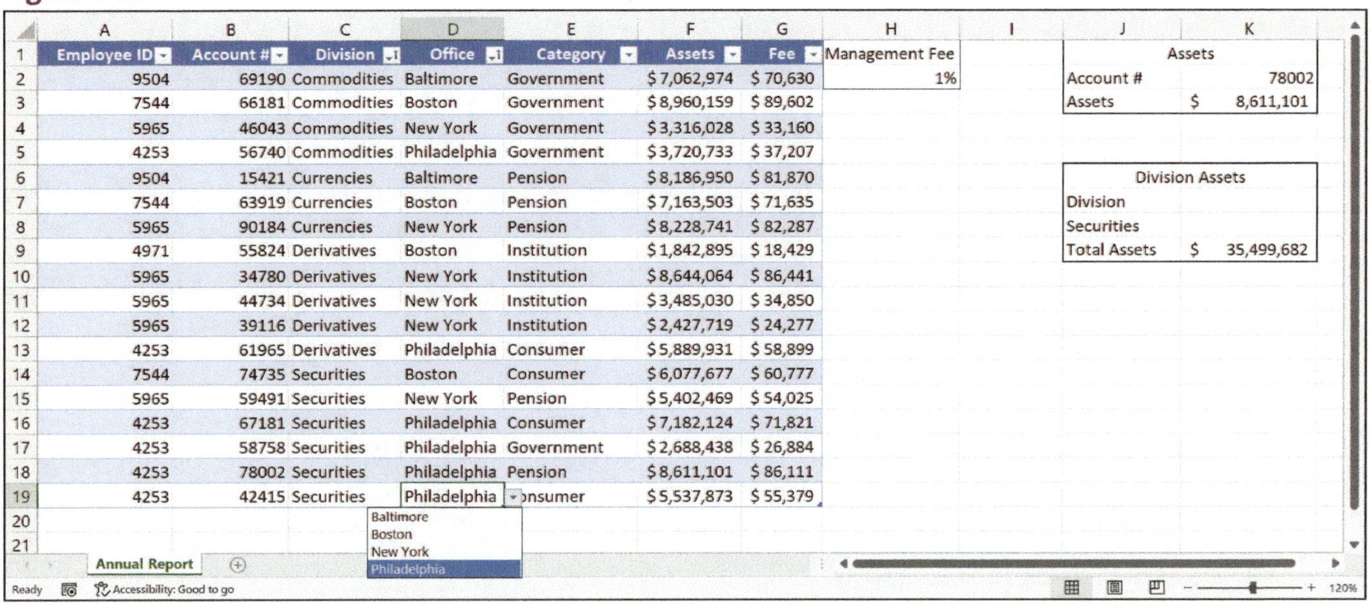

| | A | B | C | D | E | F | G | H | I | J | K |
|---|---|---|---|---|---|---|---|---|---|---|---|
| 1 | Employee ID | Account # | Division | Office | Category | Assets | Fee | Management Fee | | Assets | |
| 2 | 9504 | 69190 | Commodities | Baltimore | Government | $ 7,062,974 | $ 70,630 | 1% | | Account # | 78002 |
| 3 | 7544 | 66181 | Commodities | Boston | Government | $ 8,960,159 | $ 89,602 | | | Assets | $ 8,611,101 |
| 4 | 5965 | 46043 | Commodities | New York | Government | $ 3,316,028 | $ 33,160 | | | | |
| 5 | 4253 | 56740 | Commodities | Philadelphia | Government | $ 3,720,733 | $ 37,207 | | | | |
| 6 | 9504 | 15421 | Currencies | Baltimore | Pension | $ 8,186,950 | $ 81,870 | | | Division Assets | |
| 7 | 7544 | 63919 | Currencies | Boston | Pension | $ 7,163,503 | $ 71,635 | | | Division | |
| 8 | 5965 | 90184 | Currencies | New York | Pension | $ 8,228,741 | $ 82,287 | | | Securities | |
| 9 | 4971 | 55824 | Derivatives | Boston | Institution | $ 1,842,895 | $ 18,429 | | | Total Assets | $ 35,499,682 |
| 10 | 5965 | 34780 | Derivatives | New York | Institution | $ 8,644,064 | $ 86,441 | | | | |
| 11 | 5965 | 44734 | Derivatives | New York | Institution | $ 3,485,030 | $ 34,850 | | | | |
| 12 | 5965 | 39116 | Derivatives | New York | Institution | $ 2,427,719 | $ 24,277 | | | | |
| 13 | 4253 | 61965 | Derivatives | Philadelphia | Consumer | $ 5,889,931 | $ 58,899 | | | | |
| 14 | 7544 | 74735 | Securities | Boston | Consumer | $ 6,077,677 | $ 60,777 | | | | |
| 15 | 5965 | 59491 | Securities | New York | Pension | $ 5,402,469 | $ 54,025 | | | | |
| 16 | 4253 | 67181 | Securities | Philadelphia | Consumer | $ 7,182,124 | $ 71,821 | | | | |
| 17 | 4253 | 58758 | Securities | Philadelphia | Government | $ 2,688,438 | $ 26,884 | | | | |
| 18 | 4253 | 78002 | Securities | Philadelphia | Pension | $ 8,611,101 | $ 86,111 | | | | |
| 19 | 4253 | 42415 | Securities | Philadelphia | onsumer | $ 5,537,873 | $ 55,379 | | | | |
| 20 | | | | Baltimore | | | | | | | |
| 21 | | | | Boston | | | | | | | |
| | | | | New York | | | | | | | |
| | | | | Philadelphia | | | | | | | |

# Managing Workbook Data

## Case

Elena Fuentes, the vice president of finance at Bayside, asks for your help analyzing revenues from the U.S. and Canada divisions. When the analysis is complete, she will distribute the workbook to the office managers in the North America region and present the summary information to the executive leadership group.

## Module Objectives

After completing this module, you will be able to:

- Arrange worksheets
- Protect workbook data
- Save custom views of a worksheet
- Insert hyperlinks
- Group worksheet data
- Group worksheets
- Prepare a workbook for distribution
- Save a workbook for distribution

## Files You Will Need

IL_EX_6-1.xlsx
IL_EX_6-2.xlsx
IL_EX_6-3.xlsx
IL_EX_6-4.xlsx
IL_EX_6-5.xlsx

# Save Custom Views of a Worksheet

**Case** Elena is interested in the revenue for the offices in the southern region of the United States. You decide to create a custom view of Bayside's revenue data that displays only the southern offices, to provide to Elena.

**Objectives**
- Create a custom view of worksheet data
- Display different views of worksheet data

A **view** is a set of display and/or print settings that you can name and save, and then access at a later time. By using the Custom Views feature, you can create several different views of a worksheet without having to create separate sheets. For example, if you often hide columns in a worksheet, you can create two views, one that displays all the columns and another with the columns hidden. You set the worksheet display first, then name the view. Then you can open the view whenever you want, using the name.

## Steps

1. **With the U.S. sheet active, click cell A1, click the View tab on the ribbon, then click the Custom Views button in the Workbook Views group**
   The Custom Views dialog box opens, as displayed in **Figure 6-8**. Any previously defined views for the active worksheet appear in the Views box. No views are currently defined for the U.S. worksheet.
2. **Click Add**
   The Add View dialog box opens. Here, you enter a name for the view and decide whether to include print settings and/or hidden rows, columns, and filter settings. By default, these settings will be included in the new view.
3. **In the Name box type All Regions, then click OK**
   You have created a view called All Regions that displays revenues for all U.S. offices.
4. **Select rows 3 through 8, right-click the selected area, then click Hide on the shortcut menu**
   The offices in rows three through eight are hidden.
5. **Click cell A1, click the Custom Views button in the Workbook Views group, click Add, in the Name box type Southern Region, then click OK**
6. **Click the Custom Views button in the Workbook Views group, click All Regions in the Views list, then click Show**
   The All Regions custom view displays all the offices' revenue data.
7. **Click the Custom Views button in the Workbook Views group, then with Southern Region in the Custom Views dialog box selected, click Show**
   Only the Austin, Atlanta, and Houston revenue figures appear on the screen, as displayed in **Figure 6-9**.
8. **Click the Custom Views button, click All Regions, click Show, then save your work**

**Quick Tip**
Clicking Hide on the shortcut menu will similarly hide selected worksheet columns. To unhide columns and rows, select the columns or rows on both sides of the hidden ones, right-click the selected area, then click Unhide on the shortcut menu.

**Trouble**
If you receive the message "Some view settings could not be applied," turn off worksheet protection by clicking the Unprotect Sheet button in the Protect group on the Review tab.

**Figure 6-8:** Custom Views dialog box

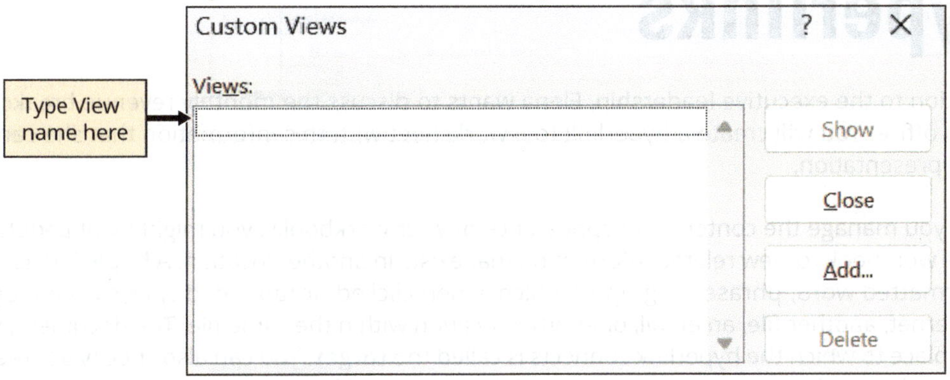


**Figure 6-9:** Southern Region view

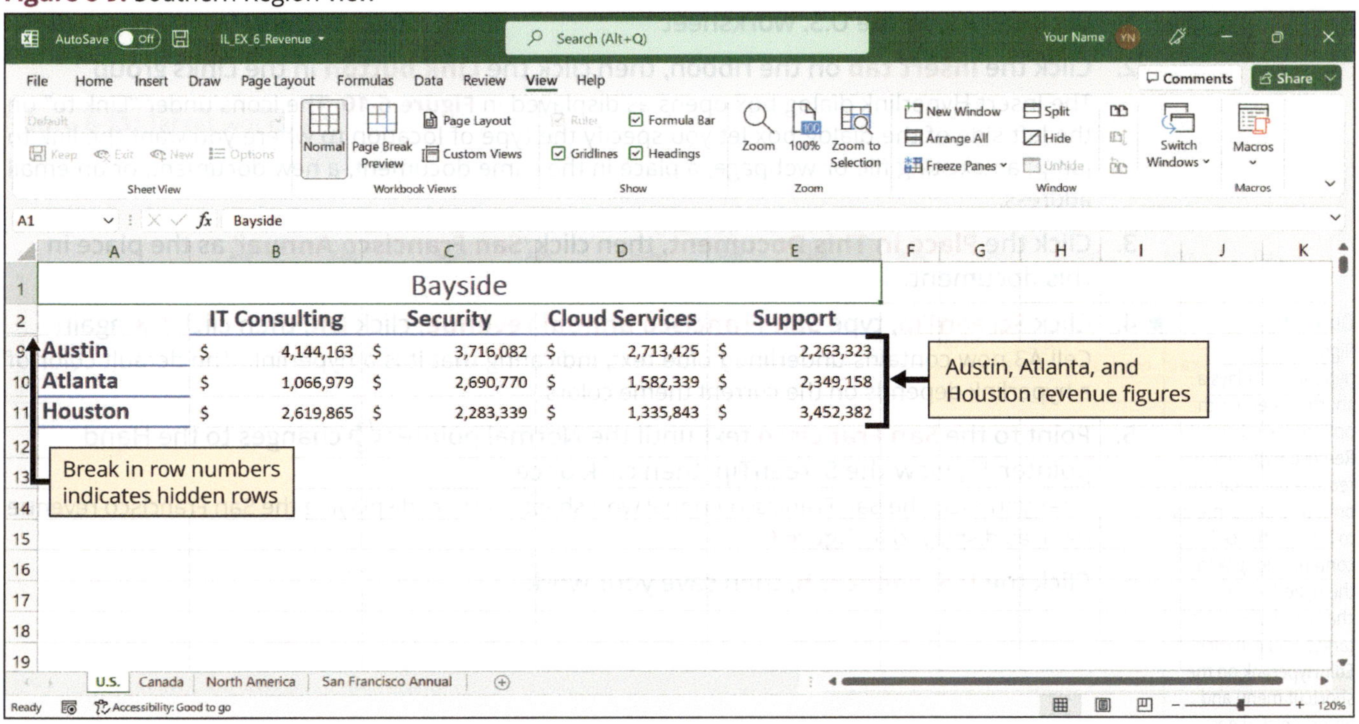


## Using Page Break Preview

Excel automatically inserts a page break when your worksheet data doesn't fit on one page. These page breaks are **dynamic**, which means they adjust automatically when workbook content changes, such as when rows and columns are added, deleted, or resized. In Normal view, these page breaks are displayed as vertical and horizontal dashed lines. Everything to the left of the first vertical dashed line and above the first horizontal dashed line is printed on the first page. You can manually add or remove page breaks by clicking the Page Layout tab on the ribbon, clicking the Breaks button in the Page Setup group, then clicking Insert Page Break, Remove Page Break, or Reset All Page Breaks. Clicking Insert Page Break adds a page break above and to the left of a selected cell, and clicking Remove Page Break removes page breaks above and to the left of a cell. Reset All Page Breaks resets page breaks back to the default setting. You can also view and change page breaks manually by clicking the View tab on the ribbon, then clicking the Page Break Preview button in the Workbook Views group.

# Group Worksheet Data

**Case** Elena asks you for a report displaying the North America revenue summarized by the United States and Canada offices. To accomplish this, you decide to create two groups, one with data for the U.S. offices and one for the Canadian offices so that you can collapse the details of these data for Elena's report. You will begin by grouping the data for the U.S. offices so you can collapse them to show only the total for all U.S. offices in the final report.

**Objectives**
- Group worksheet data
- Change the level of detail in worksheet data

You can create groups of rows and columns on a worksheet to manage your data and make it easier to work with and view. The Excel grouping feature displays outline symbols that allow you to easily expand and collapse groups to display or hide selected worksheet data. You can hide the outline symbols if you are using the condensed data in a report and do not want the symbols to distract from the information. When working with levels of detail in a worksheet, you can use an option to hide outline symbols that can be distracting when presenting information.

## Steps

1. **Click the North America sheet tab, select the range B3:E11, click the Data tab on the ribbon, click the Group button in the Outline group, in the Group dialog box click the Rows option button if necessary, then click OK**
   The rows containing revenue for the individual U.S. offices are grouped. The **outline symbols** that let you hide and display details appear to the left of the grouped rows, as displayed in **Figure 6-12**.

**Trouble**
If the dialog box doesn't open you can continue with the grouped data.

2. **Select the range B13:E14, click the Group button in the Outline group, in the Group dialog box click the Rows option button if necessary, click OK, then click cell A1**
   The U.S. and Canada revenue data are grouped.
3. **Click the Collapse Outline button [−] to the left of the row 12 label, then click the Expand Outline button [+] to the left of the row 12 label**
   Clicking the ( – ) symbol temporarily hides the U.S. detail rows, and the ( – ) symbol changes to a ( + ) symbol. Clicking the ( + ) symbol expands the U.S. details and redisplays the hidden rows. The numbered Outline symbols in the upper-left corner of the worksheet are used to display and hide levels of detail across the entire worksheet.

**Quick Tip**
You can create an outline of a range using the Auto Outline feature by clicking the Group arrow in the Outline group, then clicking Auto Outline.

4. **Click the level 1 Outline Symbol button [1]**
   All the grouped detail rows, considered Level 2, collapse, and only the U.S. and Canada totals, considered Level 1, are displayed.
5. **Click the level 2 Outline Symbol button [2]**
   The office details are displayed again. Elena asks you to hide the office details and the outline symbols for the summary report.

**Quick Tip**
You can ungroup a range of cells by clicking Ungroup in the Outline group. You can clear an outline by clicking the Ungroup arrow and clicking Clear Outline.

6. **Click the level 1 Outline Symbol button [1], click the File tab, click Options, click Advanced in the category list, scroll down to Display options for this worksheet, verify that North America is displayed as the worksheet name, click the Show outline symbols if an outline is applied check box to deselect it, then click OK**
   The worksheet displays the North America revenue totals without outline symbols, as displayed in **Figure 6-13**.
7. **Save the workbook**

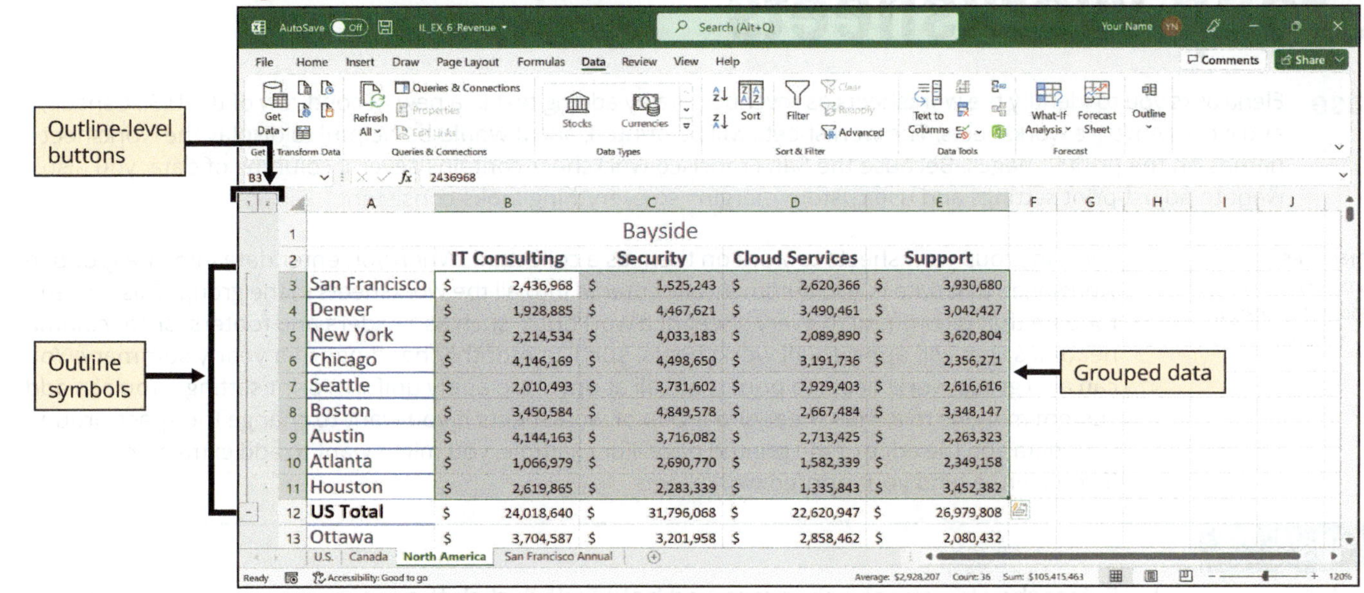


| | A | B | C | D | E |
|---|---|---|---|---|---|
| 1 | | | Bayside | | |
| 2 | | IT Consulting | Security | Cloud Services | Support |
| 3 | San Francisco | $ 2,436,968 | $ 1,525,243 | $ 2,620,366 | $ 3,930,680 |
| 4 | Denver | $ 1,928,885 | $ 4,467,621 | $ 3,490,461 | $ 3,042,427 |
| 5 | New York | $ 2,214,534 | $ 4,033,183 | $ 2,089,890 | $ 3,620,804 |
| 6 | Chicago | $ 4,146,169 | $ 4,498,650 | $ 3,191,736 | $ 2,356,271 |
| 7 | Seattle | $ 2,010,493 | $ 3,731,602 | $ 2,929,403 | $ 2,616,616 |
| 8 | Boston | $ 3,450,584 | $ 4,849,578 | $ 2,667,484 | $ 3,348,147 |
| 9 | Austin | $ 4,144,163 | $ 3,716,082 | $ 2,713,425 | $ 2,263,323 |
| 10 | Atlanta | $ 1,066,979 | $ 2,690,770 | $ 1,582,339 | $ 2,349,158 |
| 11 | Houston | $ 2,619,865 | $ 2,283,339 | $ 1,335,843 | $ 3,452,382 |
| 12 | **US Total** | $ 24,018,640 | $ 31,796,068 | $ 22,620,947 | $ 26,979,808 |
| 13 | Ottawa | $ 3,704,587 | $ 3,201,958 | $ 2,858,462 | $ 2,080,432 |

**Figure 6-12:** U.S. revenue grouped

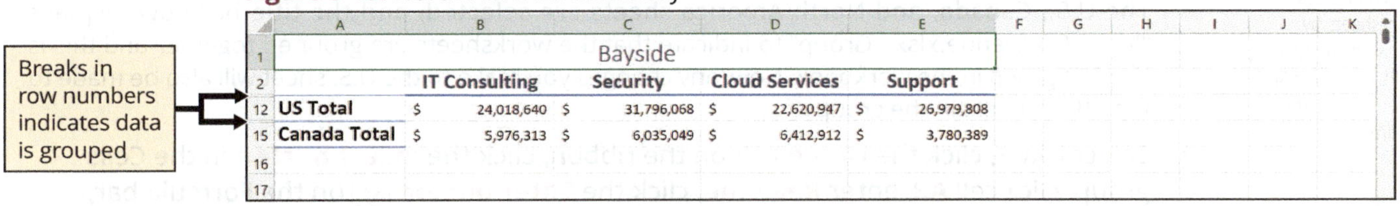


| | A | B | C | D | E |
|---|---|---|---|---|---|
| 1 | | | Bayside | | |
| 2 | | IT Consulting | Security | Cloud Services | Support |
| 12 | **US Total** | $ 24,018,640 | $ 31,796,068 | $ 22,620,947 | $ 26,979,808 |
| 15 | **Canada Total** | $ 5,976,313 | $ 6,035,049 | $ 6,412,912 | $ 3,780,389 |

**Figure 6-13:** North America summary

## Creating Subtotals

The Excel Subtotals feature provides a quick, easy way to group and summarize a range of data. It lets you create not only subtotals using the SUM function, but other statistics as well, including COUNT, AVERAGE, MAX, and MIN. To get meaningful statistics, data must be sorted on the field on which you will group. To create subtotals, first select the range of data you want to subtotal, click the Data tab on the ribbon, click the Subtotal button in the Outline group, click the At each change in arrow in the Subtotal dialog box, select the field by which you want to group the data, such as region, click the Use function arrow, click the function you want to use, select the fields that you want to subtotal in the "Add subtotal to" list, then click OK. **Figure 6-14** displays data grouped by region and summed on each quarter.

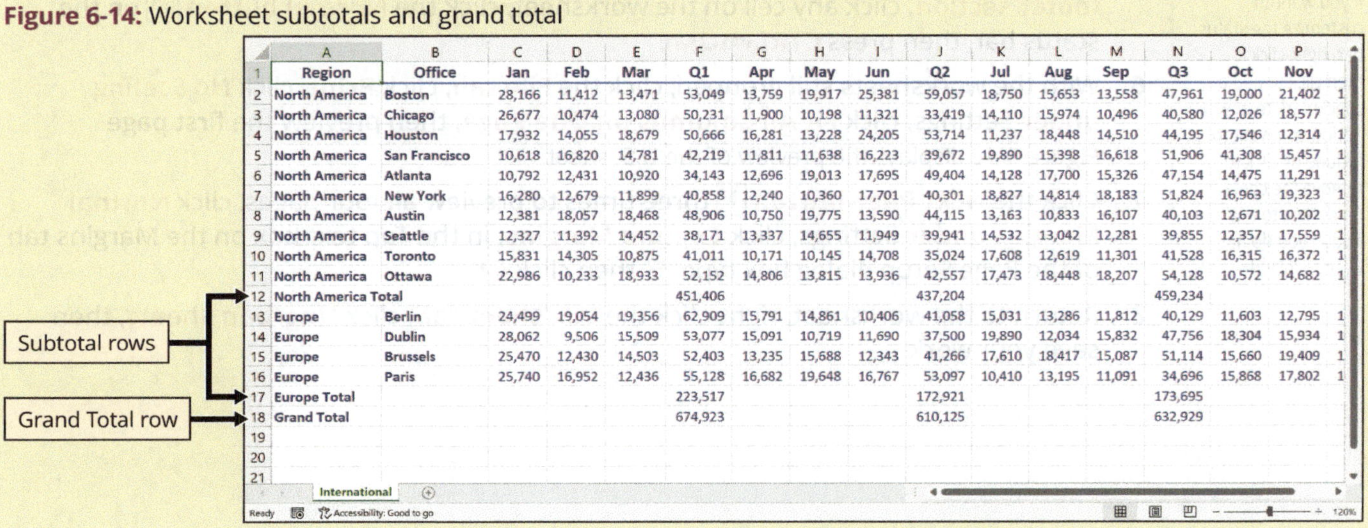


| | Region | Office | Jan | Feb | Mar | Q1 | Apr | May | Jun | Q2 | Jul | Aug | Sep | Q3 | Oct | Nov |
|---|---|---|---|---|---|---|---|---|---|---|---|---|---|---|---|---|
| 2 | North America | Boston | 28,166 | 11,412 | 13,471 | 53,049 | 13,759 | 19,917 | 25,381 | 59,057 | 18,750 | 15,653 | 13,558 | 47,961 | 19,000 | 21,402 |
| 3 | North America | Chicago | 26,677 | 10,474 | 13,080 | 50,231 | 11,900 | 10,198 | 11,321 | 33,419 | 14,110 | 15,974 | 10,496 | 40,580 | 12,026 | 18,577 |
| 4 | North America | Houston | 17,932 | 14,055 | 18,679 | 50,666 | 16,281 | 13,228 | 24,205 | 53,714 | 11,237 | 18,448 | 14,510 | 44,195 | 17,546 | 12,314 |
| 5 | North America | San Francisco | 10,618 | 16,820 | 14,781 | 42,219 | 11,811 | 11,638 | 16,223 | 39,672 | 19,890 | 15,398 | 16,618 | 51,906 | 41,308 | 15,457 |
| 6 | North America | Atlanta | 10,792 | 12,431 | 10,920 | 34,143 | 12,696 | 19,013 | 17,695 | 49,404 | 14,128 | 17,700 | 15,326 | 47,154 | 14,475 | 11,291 |
| 7 | North America | New York | 16,280 | 12,679 | 11,899 | 40,858 | 12,240 | 10,360 | 17,701 | 40,301 | 18,827 | 14,814 | 18,183 | 51,824 | 16,963 | 19,323 |
| 8 | North America | Austin | 12,381 | 18,057 | 18,468 | 48,906 | 10,750 | 19,775 | 13,590 | 44,115 | 13,163 | 10,833 | 16,107 | 40,103 | 12,671 | 10,202 |
| 9 | North America | Seattle | 12,327 | 11,392 | 14,452 | 38,171 | 13,337 | 14,655 | 11,949 | 39,941 | 14,532 | 13,042 | 12,281 | 39,855 | 12,357 | 17,559 |
| 10 | North America | Toronto | 15,831 | 14,305 | 10,875 | 41,011 | 10,171 | 10,145 | 14,708 | 35,024 | 17,608 | 12,619 | 11,301 | 41,528 | 16,315 | 16,372 |
| 11 | North America | Ottawa | 22,986 | 10,233 | 18,933 | 52,152 | 14,806 | 13,815 | 13,936 | 42,557 | 17,473 | 18,448 | 18,207 | 54,128 | 10,572 | 14,682 |
| 12 | North America Total | | | | | 451,406 | | | | 437,204 | | | | 459,234 | | |
| 13 | Europe | Berlin | 24,499 | 19,054 | 19,356 | 62,909 | 15,791 | 14,861 | 10,406 | 41,058 | 15,031 | 13,286 | 11,812 | 40,129 | 11,603 | 12,795 |
| 14 | Europe | Dublin | 28,062 | 9,506 | 15,509 | 53,077 | 15,091 | 10,719 | 11,690 | 37,500 | 19,890 | 12,034 | 15,832 | 47,756 | 18,304 | 15,934 |
| 15 | Europe | Brussels | 25,470 | 12,430 | 14,503 | 52,403 | 13,235 | 15,688 | 12,343 | 41,266 | 17,610 | 18,417 | 15,087 | 51,114 | 15,660 | 19,409 |
| 16 | Europe | Paris | 25,740 | 16,952 | 12,436 | 55,128 | 16,682 | 19,648 | 16,767 | 53,097 | 10,410 | 13,195 | 11,091 | 34,696 | 15,868 | 17,802 |
| 17 | Europe Total | | | | | 223,517 | | | | 172,921 | | | | 173,695 | | |
| 18 | Grand Total | | | | | 674,923 | | | | 610,125 | | | | 632,929 | | |

**Figure 6-14:** Worksheet subtotals and grand total

# Group Worksheets

**Case** Elena asks you to identify the worksheets as revenue data by adding text in a new, second row of the U.S., Canada, and North America worksheets. The worksheets will be printed, and it would be helpful to display the worksheet names on the printed pages. Because the San Francisco worksheet contains several columns of data, you also want to adjust print settings and use custom margins so everything looks consistent.

**Objectives**
- Group worksheets
- Add custom margins to worksheets

You can group worksheets to work on them as a collection. When you enter data into one grouped worksheet, that data is also automatically entered into all the worksheets in the group. This is useful for data that is common to every sheet of a workbook, such as headers and footers, or for column headings that will apply to all worksheets, such as monthly headings in a yearly summary. You can also group worksheets to print them all at once and apply uniform print settings. You can add custom margins to a worksheet or a group of worksheets if you want to change the space around your data and the edge of the printed page. For example, you might want to add extra margin space if you plan to bind your printed worksheets.

## Steps

**Quick Tip**
You can group noncontiguous worksheets by pressing and holding CTRL instead of SHIFT while clicking the desired sheet tabs.

1. **Select the U.S. sheet tab, press and hold SHIFT, click the North America sheet tab, then release SHIFT**
   The U.S., Canada, and North America sheets are selected, and the title bar now displays "IL_EX_6_Revenue.xlsx - Group" to indicate that the worksheets are grouped together and this is the first group in the workbook. Now, any changes you make to the U.S. sheet will also be made to the other sheets in the group.
2. **Select row 2, click the Home tab on the ribbon, click the Insert button in the Cells group, click cell A2, enter Revenue, click the Enter button on the Formula bar, select the range A2:E2, then click the Merge & Center button in the Alignment group**
   Figure 6-15 displays the U.S. worksheet with the new Revenue row.
3. **Right-click the U.S. sheet tab, click Ungroup Sheets on the shortcut menu, then verify the revenue label appears on the Canada and North America sheets**
4. **Select the U.S. sheet tab, press and hold SHIFT, click the San Francisco Annual sheet, release SHIFT, click the Insert tab on the ribbon, click the Header & Footer button in the Text group, then with the cursor in the center header section click the Sheet Name button in the Header & Footer Elements group of the Header & Footer tab**

**Quick Tip**
If you want to customize the status bar, right-click it, then click to add a checkmark to any option you want to include or click to remove the check mark next to any option you do not want to include.

5. **Click the Go to Footer button in the Navigation group, enter your name in the center footer section, click any cell on the worksheet, click the Normal button on the status bar, then press CTRL+HOME**
6. **With the worksheets still grouped, click the File tab, click Print, click No Scaling under Settings, click Fit All Columns on One Page, then preview the first page**
   Figure 6-16 displays the preview of the U.S. sheet.
7. **Click the Next Page button three times to preview all four pages, click Normal Margins under Settings, click Custom Margins, in the Top text box on the Margins tab of the Page Setup dialog box type .5, then click OK**
8. **Return to the worksheet, right-click the U.S. sheet tab, click Ungroup Sheets, then save your work**

**Figure 6-15:** U.S. worksheet with Revenue label

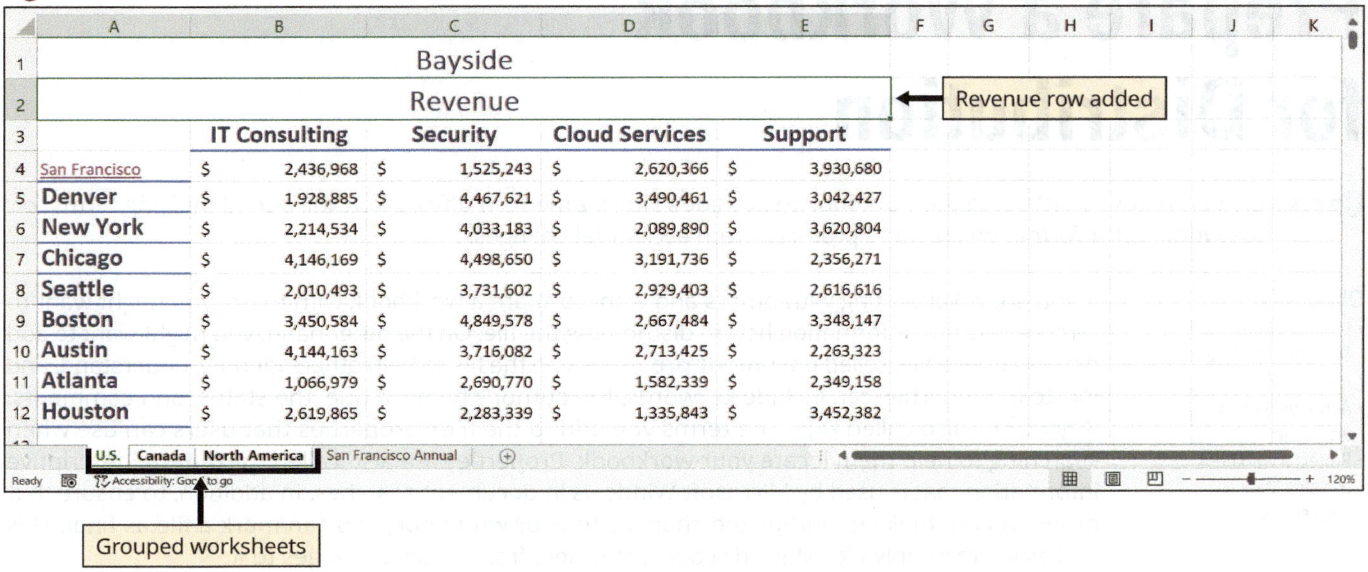

| | IT Consulting | Security | Cloud Services | Support |
|---|---|---|---|---|
| San Francisco | $ 2,436,968 | $ 1,525,243 | $ 2,620,366 | $ 3,930,680 |
| Denver | $ 1,928,885 | $ 4,467,621 | $ 3,490,461 | $ 3,042,427 |
| New York | $ 2,214,534 | $ 4,033,183 | $ 2,089,890 | $ 3,620,804 |
| Chicago | $ 4,146,169 | $ 4,498,650 | $ 3,191,736 | $ 2,356,271 |
| Seattle | $ 2,010,493 | $ 3,731,602 | $ 2,929,403 | $ 2,616,616 |
| Boston | $ 3,450,584 | $ 4,849,578 | $ 2,667,484 | $ 3,348,147 |
| Austin | $ 4,144,163 | $ 3,716,082 | $ 2,713,425 | $ 2,263,323 |
| Atlanta | $ 1,066,979 | $ 2,690,770 | $ 1,582,339 | $ 2,349,158 |
| Houston | $ 2,619,865 | $ 2,283,339 | $ 1,335,843 | $ 3,452,382 |



**Figure 6-16:** Preview of U.S. worksheet

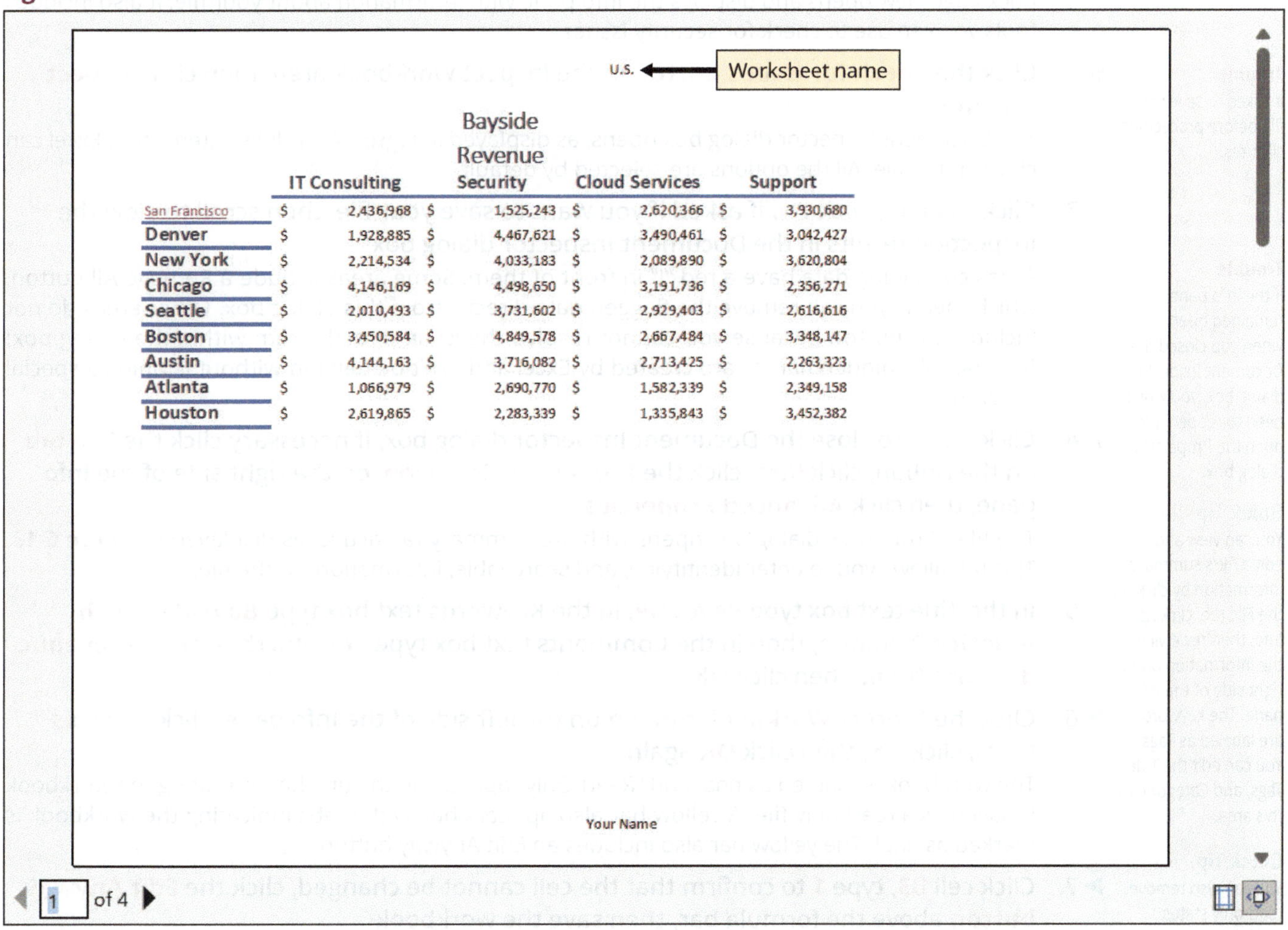

| | IT Consulting | Security | Cloud Services | Support |
|---|---|---|---|---|
| San Francisco | $ 2,436,968 | $ 1,525,243 | $ 2,620,366 | $ 3,930,680 |
| Denver | $ 1,928,885 | $ 4,467,621 | $ 3,490,461 | $ 3,042,427 |
| New York | $ 2,214,534 | $ 4,033,183 | $ 2,089,890 | $ 3,620,804 |
| Chicago | $ 4,146,169 | $ 4,498,650 | $ 3,191,736 | $ 2,356,271 |
| Seattle | $ 2,010,493 | $ 3,731,602 | $ 2,929,403 | $ 2,616,616 |
| Boston | $ 3,450,584 | $ 4,849,578 | $ 2,667,484 | $ 3,348,147 |
| Austin | $ 4,144,163 | $ 3,716,082 | $ 2,713,425 | $ 2,263,323 |
| Atlanta | $ 1,066,979 | $ 2,690,770 | $ 1,582,339 | $ 2,349,158 |
| Houston | $ 2,619,865 | $ 2,283,339 | $ 1,335,843 | $ 3,452,382 |

# Prepare a Workbook for Distribution

**Case** Elena is ready to distribute the workbook to Bayside's North American offices. You will add identifying terms to the workbook information area and protect it from accidental changes.

**Objectives**
- Use the Inspect Document feature to review a file
- Add keywords to a worksheet
- Protect a workbook by using Mark as Final status

If you are collaborating with others and want to share a workbook with them, you might want to remove sensitive information before distributing the file. On the other hand, you might want to add details about a file, called **document properties**, to the file to help others identify, understand, and locate it. Properties can include keywords, the author's name, a title, the status, and comments. **Keywords**, also called **tags**, are terms you add to the file's properties that users can use when searching to help them locate your workbook. Properties are also called **metadata**, descriptive information that is used by Microsoft Windows in document searches. In addition, to ensure that others do not make unauthorized changes to your workbook, you can mark a file as final. This makes it a read-only file, which discourages others from making changes to it.

## Steps

1. **Click the File tab on the ribbon, then click Info on the navigation bar**
   Backstage view opens and displays the Info pane with information about your file. It also includes tools you can use to check for security issues.

2. **Click the Check for Issues button in the Inspect Workbook area, then click Inspect Document**
   The Document Inspector dialog box opens, as displayed in **Figure 6-17**. It lists items that Excel can check in the file. All the options are selected by default.

   **Trouble**
   If asked to save your file before proceeding, click Yes.

3. **Click Inspect, click Yes if asked if you want to save your file, then scroll to view the inspection results in the Document Inspector dialog box**
   Areas containing data have a red "!" in front of them. Some areas include a Remove All button, which means you can remove the flagged data directly from this dialog box. Other areas do not include this button because you cannot resolve the issue directly from within the dialog box; for example, hidden names are created by Excel and can't be deleted without running a special program.

4. **Click Close to close the Document Inspector dialog box, if necessary click the File tab on the ribbon, click Info, click the Properties list arrow on the right side of the Info pane, then click Advanced Properties**
   The file's Properties dialog box opens with the Summary tab active, as displayed in **Figure 6-18**. This tab allows you to enter identifying, and searchable, information for the file.

   **Trouble**
   If the Info pane remained open when you closed the Document Inspector dialog box, you won't need to reopen it to open the Properties dialog box.

5. **In the Title text box type Revenue, in the Keywords text box type Bayside North America Revenue, then in the Comments text box type The North America revenue data are final., then click OK**

6. **Click the Protect Workbook button on the left side of the Info pane, click Mark as Final, click OK, then click OK again**
   The workbook is marked as final and "Read-Only" appears in the title bar indicating the workbook is saved as a read-only file. A yellow bar also appears below the tabs indicating the workbook is marked as final. The yellow bar also includes an Edit Anyway button.

   **Quick Tip**
   You can view and edit a file's summary information by clicking the File tab, clicking Info, then reviewing the information on the right side of the Info pane. The keywords are labeled as Tags. You can edit the Title, Tags, and Categories in this area.

7. **Click cell B3, type 1 to confirm that the cell cannot be changed, click the Edit Anyway button above the formula bar, then save the workbook**
   By clicking Edit Anyway, you removed the read-only status, making the workbook editable again. Marking a workbook as final is not a strong form of workbook protection because a workbook recipient can remove this Final status.

   **Quick Tip**
   You can also remove read-only status by clicking Mark as Final in the Protect Workbook menu, to toggle the setting off.

**Figure 6-17:** Document Inspector dialog box

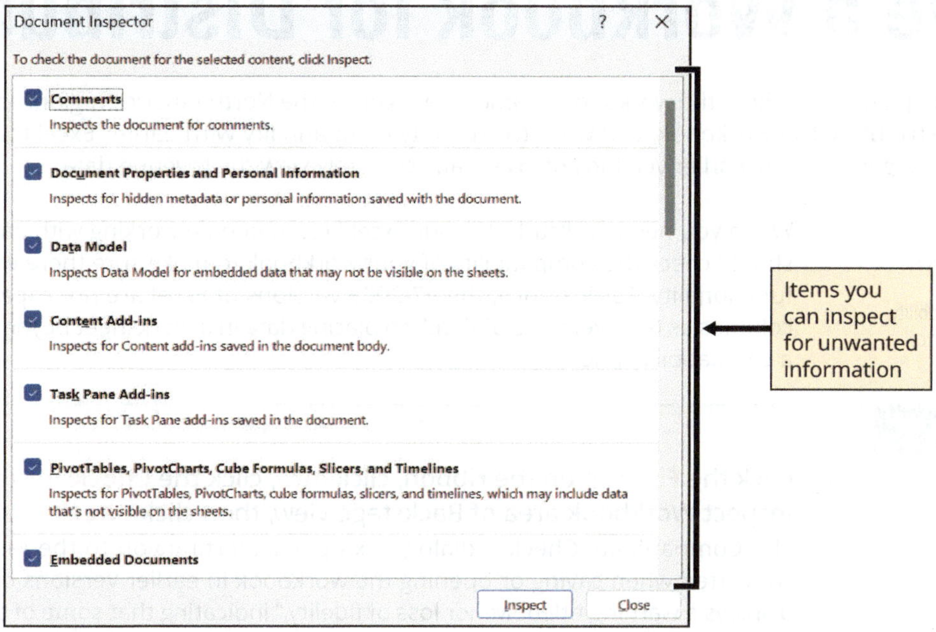


**Figure 6-18:** File's Properties dialog box

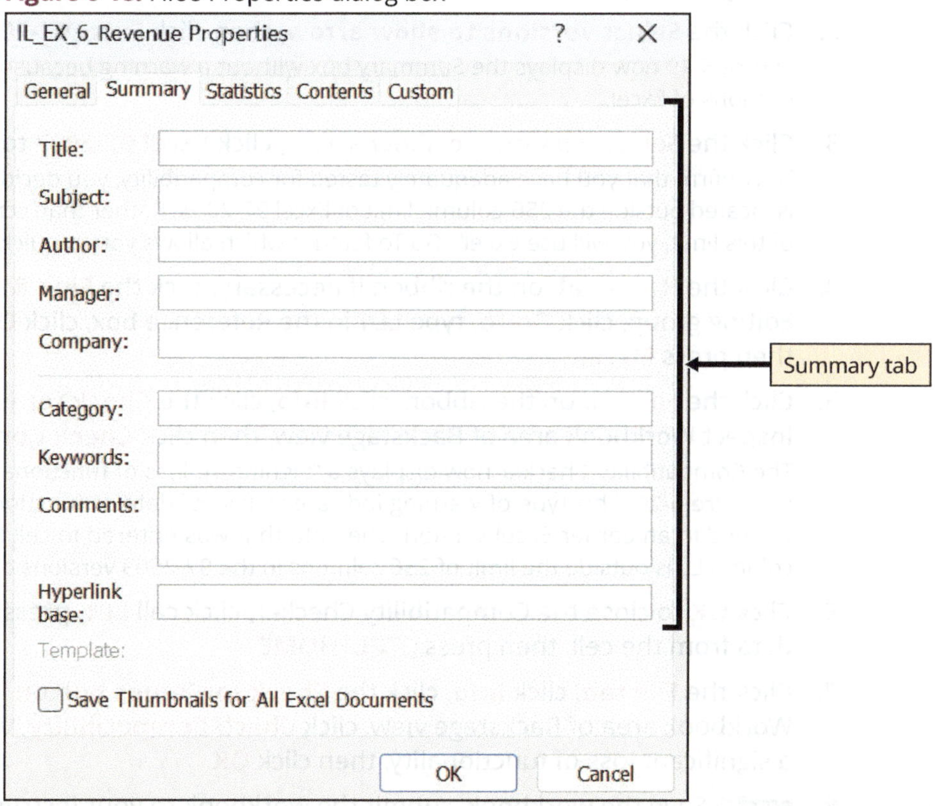


## Adding a worksheet background

You can make your Excel data more attractive on the screen by adding a picture to the worksheet background. To add a worksheet background, click the Page Layout tab on the ribbon, click the Background button in the Page Setup group, choose From a file, Bing Image Search, or a OneDrive account in the Insert Pictures dialog box, click the image file in the next dialog boxes, then click Insert. The image is added, repeating as necessary to fill the background behind the worksheet cells on the screen. A worksheet background will not print with the worksheet.

# Save a Workbook for Distribution

**Case** You plan to distribute the workbook to office managers in the North America region, as Elena requested. Before distributing the workbook, you want to check its compatibility with earlier Excel formats to make sure that managers running earlier versions of Excel can accurately view the revenue data.

**Objectives**
- Check workbook compatibility
- Check compatibility for different Excel versions

When you need to distribute your Excel files to people working with earlier versions of Excel, you should check the compatibility of your workbook to make sure there won't be any loss of data or functionality. For instance, the 97-2003 versions of Excel are not capable of displaying as many columns as later versions of Excel, so placing data in a worksheet beyond those limits would cause a compatibility issue.

## Steps

1. **Click the File tab on the ribbon, click Info, click the Check for Issues button in the Inspect Workbook area of Backstage view, then click Check Compatibility**
   The Compatibility Checker dialog box opens, alerting you to the features that will be lost or converted when saving or opening the workbook in earlier versions of Excel. The Summary box displays a warning titled "Minor loss of fidelity," indicating that some of the worksheet's formatting might either not be available, or it appears differently in earlier versions of Excel. Minor loss of fidelity warnings won't result in lost data or worksheet functionality.
2. **Click the Select versions to show arrow, then click Excel 97-2003 to deselect it**
   Figure 6-19 now displays the Summary box without a warning because it applied only to 97-2003 versions of Excel.
3. **Click the Select versions to show arrow, click Excel 97-2003 to select it, then click OK**
   To confirm that you have adequately tested for compatibility, you decide to add data to a cell that is located outside the 256-column limit of Excel 97-2003. Rather than scrolling to a column outside of this limit, you will use Excel's Go To feature which allows you to quickly move to another cell.
4. **Click the Home tab on the ribbon if necessary, click the Find & Select button in the Editing group, click Go To, type LL1 in the Reference box, click OK, type 1 in cell LL1, then press ENTER**
5. **Click the File tab on the ribbon, click Info, click the Check for Issues button in the Inspect Workbook area of Backstage view, then click Check Compatibility**
   The Compatibility Checker now displays a "Significant loss of functionality" warning, as displayed in Figure 6-20. This type of warning indicates a loss of data or functionality when a workbook is opened in an earlier Excel version. The data that was entered in cell LL1 could be lost because column LL is outside the limit of 256 columns in the 97-2003 versions of Excel.
6. **Click OK to close the Compatibility Checker, click cell LL1, press DEL to remove the data from the cell, then press CTRL+HOME**
7. **Click the File tab, click Info, click the Check for Issues button in the Inspect Workbook area of Backstage view, click Check Compatibility, verify there is no longer a significant loss of functionality, then click OK**
8. **sam Save the workbook, submit the workbook to your instructor as directed, close the workbook, then close Excel**

**Figure 6-19:** Compatibility Checker dialog box

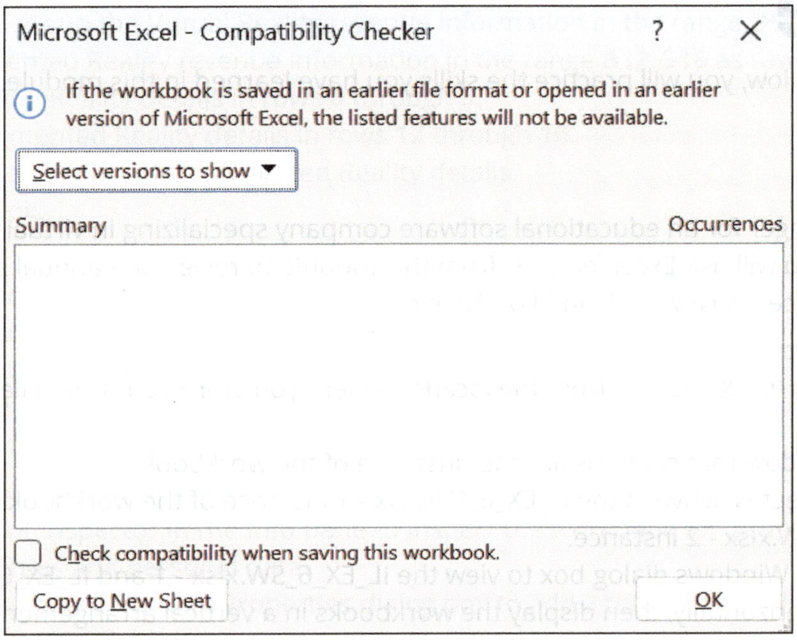


**Figure 6-20:** Significant loss of functionality warning

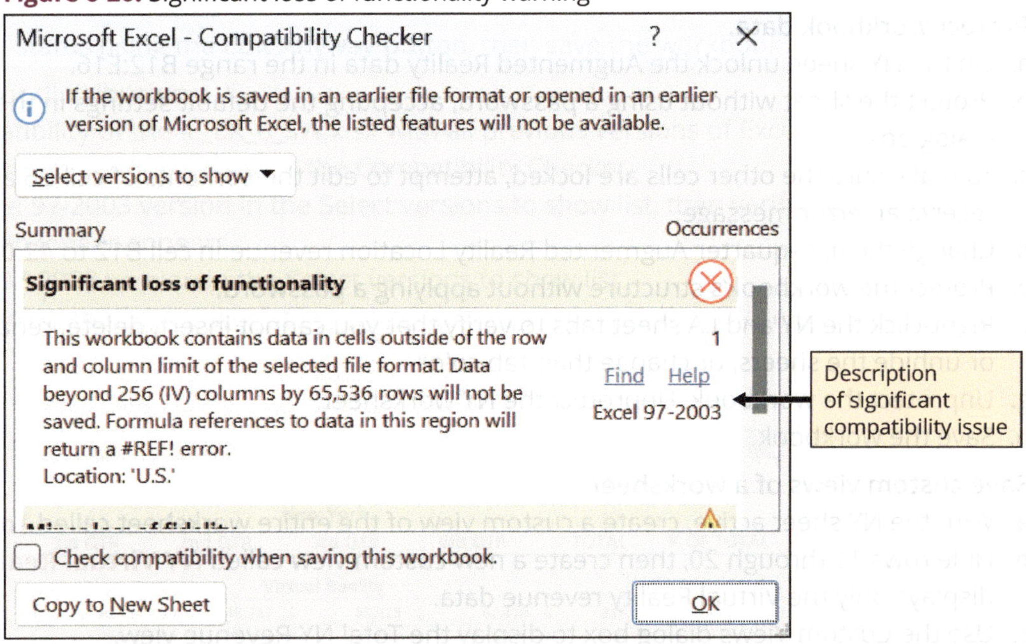


## Exporting a workbook to other file types

You can export Excel workbooks to many other different formats. Clicking File, then clicking Export opens the Export pane, where you can click either Create a PDF/XPS Document or Change File Type. PDFs and XPS files have the advantage of preserving formatting, fonts, and images and making it difficult to change the file. These files can be opened and viewed in free viewers available online. To select this option, click the Create PDF/XPS button in the Create PDF/XPS Document section, click the Save as type box, click the preferred format, then click Publish. If you click Change File Type in the Export pane, you can choose from several file types, including Macro-Enabled Workbook, Excel 97-2003 workbook, Template, OpenDocument Spreadsheet, Text, special types of text files such as CSV and Formatted Text, or a Binary workbook that is optimized for fast loading and saving. Click the format you want, click Save As, then click Save in the Save As dialog box.

## Independent Challenge 1

As the assistant to the VP of International Sales at CL Devices, a medical device company, you analyze the annual sales data for the sales representatives in the North American and European regions. After you complete this year's analysis, you will distribute the workbook to the sales managers for the North American and European regional offices.

a. Start Excel, open IL_EX_6-3.xlsx from the location where you store your Data Files, then save it as **IL_EX_6_CLDevices**.
b. Display the NA and Europe worksheets in their own windows, arrange the two windows vertically, then compare the data in the two windows.
c. Hide the window displaying the Europe sheet. Unhide the Europe sheet window, then close the IL_EX_6_CLDevices - 2 window.
d. Maximize the NA window. Unlock the data in cells B4:D18.
e. Protect the worksheet without using a password. Verify the protection by trying to edit a locked cell, such as F4. Verify that you can edit the data in any unlocked cell, such as B4, but do not change the data.
f. Unprotect the NA worksheet.
g. Protect the workbook without using a password.
h. Verify the protection by trying to change the NA sheet name.
i. Unprotect the workbook.
j. On the NA sheet, create a custom view called **Annual Sales** that displays all the worksheet data. Hide columns F through Q. Create a custom view displaying the data in A1:E18, named **First Quarter Sales**. Display all the sales data using a custom view. Display only the first-quarter sales data using a custom view. Use a custom view to view all the sales data for the year.
k. Insert a hyperlink in cell A1 on the NA worksheet to cell A1 on the Company Information worksheet. Add a ScreenTip that reads **Company Information**, then test the hyperlink.
l. On the NA worksheet change the font size of the text in cell A1 to 15.
m. Use the Document Inspector to inspect the workbook for issues, then remove all document properties and personal data. Add a title property of **CL Devices Sales** and the words **medical devices** as keywords. Mark the workbook as final, then remove the final status.
n. Check the compatibility of the workbook with all previous Excel versions.
o. On the Europe worksheet, group the sales data by quarters. (**Hint**: Group the monthly data by columns; do not include the employee ID or the quarter totals. Create a total of four groups.) Use the outline buttons to collapse the monthly details and display only the quarter totals. Compare your screen to **Figure 6-22**.
p. Group the three worksheets, add your name to the center footer section of the worksheets, then add 1.25" custom margins to the top of the worksheets.
q. Preview the worksheets, ungroup the worksheets, then save the workbook.
r. Submit the IL_EX_6_CLDevices file to your instructor, close the workbook, then close Excel.

**Figure 6-22**

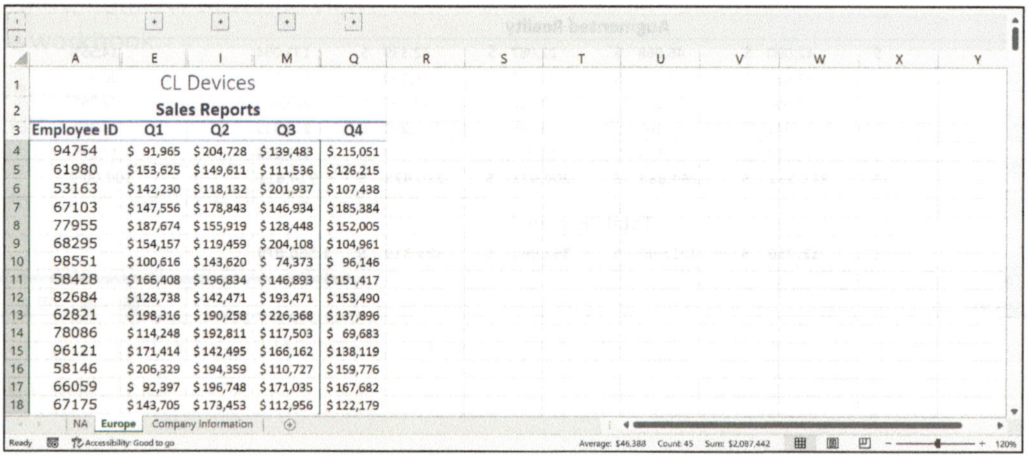

| | A | E | I | M | Q |
|---|---|---|---|---|---|
| 1 | CL Devices | | | | |
| 2 | Sales Reports | | | | |
| 3 | Employee ID | Q1 | Q2 | Q3 | Q4 |
| 4 | 94754 | $ 91,965 | $ 204,728 | $ 139,483 | $ 215,051 |
| 5 | 61980 | $ 153,625 | $ 149,611 | $ 111,536 | $ 126,215 |
| 6 | 53163 | $ 142,230 | $ 118,132 | $ 201,937 | $ 107,438 |
| 7 | 67103 | $ 147,556 | $ 178,843 | $ 146,934 | $ 185,384 |
| 8 | 77955 | $ 187,674 | $ 155,919 | $ 128,448 | $ 152,005 |
| 9 | 68295 | $ 154,157 | $ 119,459 | $ 204,108 | $ 104,961 |
| 10 | 98551 | $ 100,616 | $ 143,620 | $ 74,373 | $ 96,146 |
| 11 | 58428 | $ 166,408 | $ 196,834 | $ 146,893 | $ 151,417 |
| 12 | 82684 | $ 128,738 | $ 142,471 | $ 193,471 | $ 153,490 |
| 13 | 62821 | $ 198,316 | $ 190,258 | $ 226,368 | $ 137,896 |
| 14 | 78086 | $ 114,248 | $ 192,811 | $ 117,503 | $ 69,683 |
| 15 | 96121 | $ 171,414 | $ 142,495 | $ 166,162 | $ 138,119 |
| 16 | 58146 | $ 206,329 | $ 194,359 | $ 110,727 | $ 159,776 |
| 17 | 66059 | $ 92,397 | $ 196,748 | $ 171,035 | $ 167,682 |
| 18 | 67175 | $ 143,705 | $ 173,453 | $ 112,956 | $ 122,179 |

# Independent Challenge 2

As the executive assistant to the CEO of a large U.S. retailer, you need to review sales data for the different geographical classifications of the stores. With two years of sales data in a workbook, you will create summary information, including subtotals for each classification. The final report will be distributed to the executive leadership.

a. Start Excel, open IL_EX_6-4.xlsx from the location where you store your Data Files, then save it as **IL_EX_6_Stores**.
b. Group the Current and Previous worksheets.
c. With the worksheets grouped, add a row at the top of the worksheet with the title **Annual Sales** merged and centered across columns A through E.
d. Format the title in row 1 using the Title cell style. Format the column headings in row 2 using the Heading 3 cell style.
e. Ungroup the worksheets. Arrange the worksheets as necessary to verify that both have the same title row and worksheet formatting. When you are finished, close the second window instance.
f. On the Current worksheet, sort the data in A to Z order on the Classification field.
g. On this sheet, use a command in the Outline group to create subtotals for the net sales and net sales per square foot for each region. (**Hint**: In the Subtotal dialog box, choose Classification in the At each change in list and add subtotals to both the Net Sales and Net Sales/Sq Ft fields.) Widen column D to fully display the net sales totals.
h. Inspect the workbook and remove all document properties and personal information. Add the keywords, or tags, **classifications** and **sales** to the workbook's summary properties.
i. Freeze the first two rows of the Current worksheet. Scroll down to row 37 to verify the first two rows appear at the top of the screen. Unfreeze the rows.
j. Check the compatibility of the workbook with earlier versions of Excel.
k. Group the two worksheets. With the worksheets grouped, change the custom top margin to .5".
l. With the worksheets grouped, add a header that includes your name in the left section and a code for the sheet name in the center section.
m. Ungroup the worksheets, then prepare the workbook for distribution by marking it as final. Save the workbook, close the workbook, reopen the workbook, and enable editing.
n. Use the outline symbols on the Current worksheet to display only the classification totals and the grand total. Compare your Current worksheet to **Figure 6-23**.
o. Preview the worksheets, save the workbook, submit the workbook to your instructor, then close Excel.

**Figure 6-23**

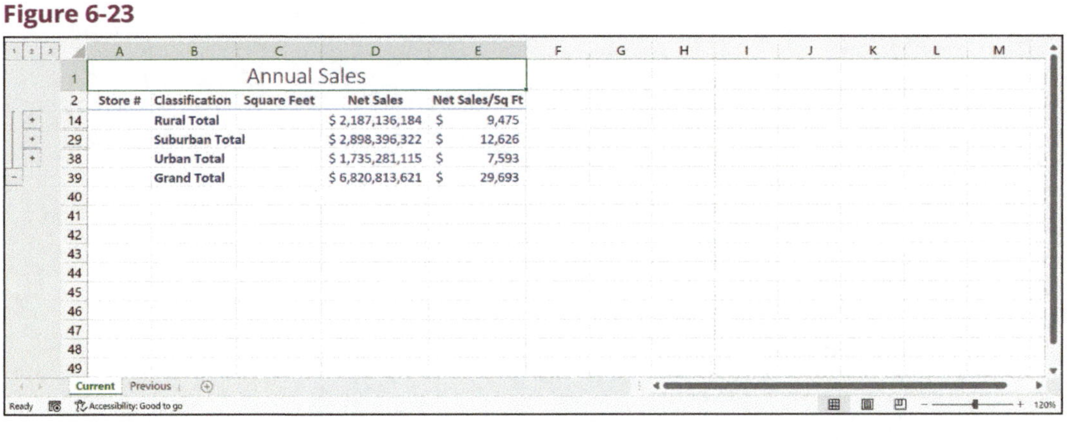

# Visual Workshop

Open IL_EX_6-5.xlsx from the location where you store your Data Files, then save it as **IL_EX_6_Commercial**. Use the skills you learned in this module to modify the Vacancies worksheet so the content and formatting match **Figure 6-24**. The text in cell A1 is a hyperlink to cell A1 in the Company Info worksheet. (**Hint**: The data in the range A3:J15 has subtotals added to Q1 and Q2, using the average function for each change in city.) Enter your name in the center footer section, save the workbook, submit your work to your instructor as directed, close the workbook, then close Excel.

**Figure 6-24**

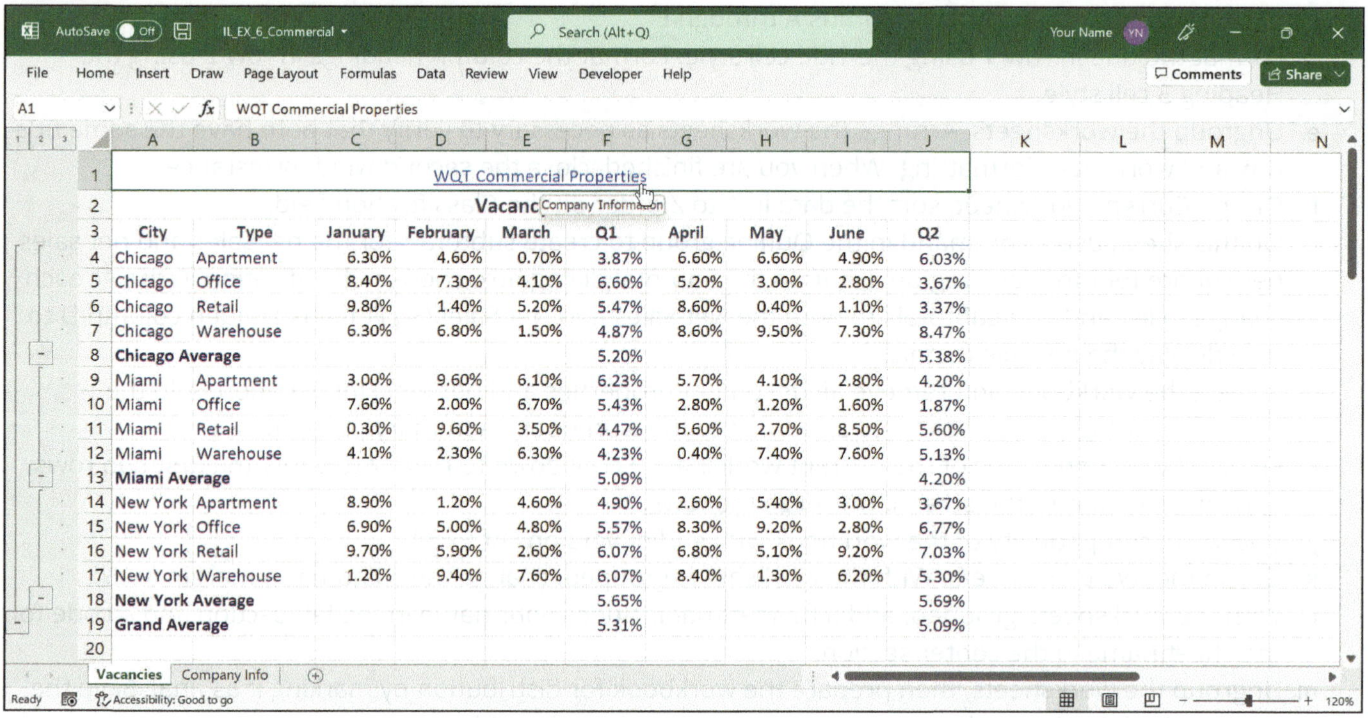


| | A | B | C | D | E | F | G | H | I | J |
|---|---|---|---|---|---|---|---|---|---|---|
| 1 | WQT Commercial Properties | | | | | | | | | |
| 2 | Vacanc | | | | | | | | | |
| 3 | City | Type | January | February | March | Q1 | April | May | June | Q2 |
| 4 | Chicago | Apartment | 6.30% | 4.60% | 0.70% | 3.87% | 6.60% | 6.60% | 4.90% | 6.03% |
| 5 | Chicago | Office | 8.40% | 7.30% | 4.10% | 6.60% | 5.20% | 3.00% | 2.80% | 3.67% |
| 6 | Chicago | Retail | 9.80% | 1.40% | 5.20% | 5.47% | 8.60% | 0.40% | 1.10% | 3.37% |
| 7 | Chicago | Warehouse | 6.30% | 6.80% | 1.50% | 4.87% | 8.60% | 9.50% | 7.30% | 8.47% |
| 8 | **Chicago Average** | | | | | 5.20% | | | | 5.38% |
| 9 | Miami | Apartment | 3.00% | 9.60% | 6.10% | 6.23% | 5.70% | 4.10% | 2.80% | 4.20% |
| 10 | Miami | Office | 7.60% | 2.00% | 6.70% | 5.43% | 2.80% | 1.20% | 1.60% | 1.87% |
| 11 | Miami | Retail | 0.30% | 9.60% | 3.50% | 4.47% | 5.60% | 2.70% | 8.50% | 5.60% |
| 12 | Miami | Warehouse | 4.10% | 2.30% | 6.30% | 4.23% | 0.40% | 7.40% | 7.60% | 5.13% |
| 13 | **Miami Average** | | | | | 5.09% | | | | 4.20% |
| 14 | New York | Apartment | 8.90% | 1.20% | 4.60% | 4.90% | 2.60% | 5.40% | 3.00% | 3.67% |
| 15 | New York | Office | 6.90% | 5.00% | 4.80% | 5.57% | 8.30% | 9.20% | 2.80% | 6.77% |
| 16 | New York | Retail | 9.70% | 5.90% | 2.60% | 6.07% | 6.80% | 5.10% | 9.20% | 7.03% |
| 17 | New York | Warehouse | 1.20% | 9.40% | 7.60% | 6.07% | 8.40% | 1.30% | 6.20% | 5.30% |
| 18 | **New York Average** | | | | | 5.65% | | | | 5.69% |
| 19 | **Grand Average** | | | | | 5.31% | | | | 5.09% |
| 20 | | | | | | | | | | |

# Working with Images and Integrating with Other Programs

## Case

Jamia Arias, the CEO of Bayside, would like to create a networking consulting division in the company. To add this expertise quickly, Jamia is considering acquiring a company specializing in networking. Jamia has four companies under consideration in different geographical regions of the United States. Jamia needs to analyze the revenue data for the four firms to evaluate their potential value to Bayside. To help with her assessment, she asks you to create data exchanges between Excel and other data sources.

## Module Objectives

After completing this module, you will be able to:

- Describe a data exchange
- Import data using Get & Transform tools
- Transform data with the Power Query editor
- Import Access data
- Import HTML data
- Link worksheet data to a Word document
- Link an Excel chart to a PowerPoint slide
- Insert a graphic file in a worksheet

## Files You Will Need

Support_EX_7-1.txt
Support_EX_7-2.xlsx
Support_EX_7-3.accdb
Support_EX_7-4.htm
IL_EX_7-5.docx
IL_EX_7-6.pptx
Support_EX_7-7.jpg
Support_EX_7-8.txt
Support_EX_7-9.xlsx
Support_EX_7-10.accdb
Support_EX_7-11.htm
IL_EX_7-12.docx
IL_EX_7-13.pptx
Support_EX_7-14.jpg
Support_EX_7-15.xlsx
Support_EX_7-16.txt
Support_EX_7-17.accdb
Support_EX_7-18.jpg
Support_EX_7-19.htm
IL_EX_7-20.docx
Support_EX_7-21.txt
IL_EX_7-22.pptx

# Describe a Data Exchange

**Case** To support her business analysis of the four networking companies under consideration for acquisition, Jamia asks you to use the following guidelines to plan data exchanges between Excel and external data sources.

**Objectives**
- Explain the steps for data exchange
- Explain how the Get & Transform tools are used to import and transform data

When importing external data into Excel, the Get & Transform tool is the default method. You can also exchange data between Microsoft 365 apps by linking and embedding objects. The first step in a data exchange involves planning what you want to accomplish.

## Details

**To exchange data:**

- **Identify the data you want to exchange, its file type, and, if possible, the app used to create it**
  Whether the data you want to exchange is a database file, a worksheet, an HTML file, a text file, or another source, it is important to identify its **source program**, the program used to create the data you are linking or embedding, and its file type. Once you identify the source program, you can determine options for exchanging the data with Excel.

- **Determine the app with which you want to exchange data**
  Besides knowing which program created the data you want to exchange, you must also identify the program that will receive the data, called the **destination program**. This determines the procedure you use to perform the exchange.

- **Determine the method of your data exchange**
  The **Get & Transform** tools, previously called **Power Query**, are a set of Business Intelligence tools used to connect and import external data into Excel. Workbooks, database files, text files, and HTML files are among the many data sources that can be imported using a tool in the Get & Transform group on the Data tab. Imported data is often in an unstructured format, and the Get & Transform tools allow you to transform it into a more desirable format for use in Excel. For example, you can remove columns, remove rows, split a column, perform arithmetic calculations, or change data types in Get & Transform's Power Query Editor before you load the data into an Excel worksheet. The Power Query Editor records and saves these editing steps as part of the data so they can be applied when the workbook data is refreshed with new data. **Figure 7-1** displays data to be imported into the Power Query Editor. Each request for data is called a **query**, and you may have multiple queries in a workbook.

  Another method of data exchange is a technology called **object linking and embedding (OLE)**, which lets you share information among the Microsoft 365 apps, copying from a source file and pasting, embedding, or linking into a destination file. The data to be exchanged, called an **object**, may consist of text, a worksheet, or any other type of data. This method, used when Excel data needs to be imported into another Microsoft 365 app, involves copying Excel data and pasting it in other applications. The copied data can be linked or embedded in the destination file. When you **embed**, you simply insert a copy of the original object into the destination document; you can later, if necessary, edit this embedded data separately from the source document. You **link** data when you want the information you insert to be updated automatically if the data in the source document changes. **Figure 7-2** displays an Excel chart that is linked to a PowerPoint slide. You will use object linking when pasting Excel data in other applications so any changes in the Excel data will be updated in the destination files.

**Figure 7-1:** Data to be imported in the Power Query Editor

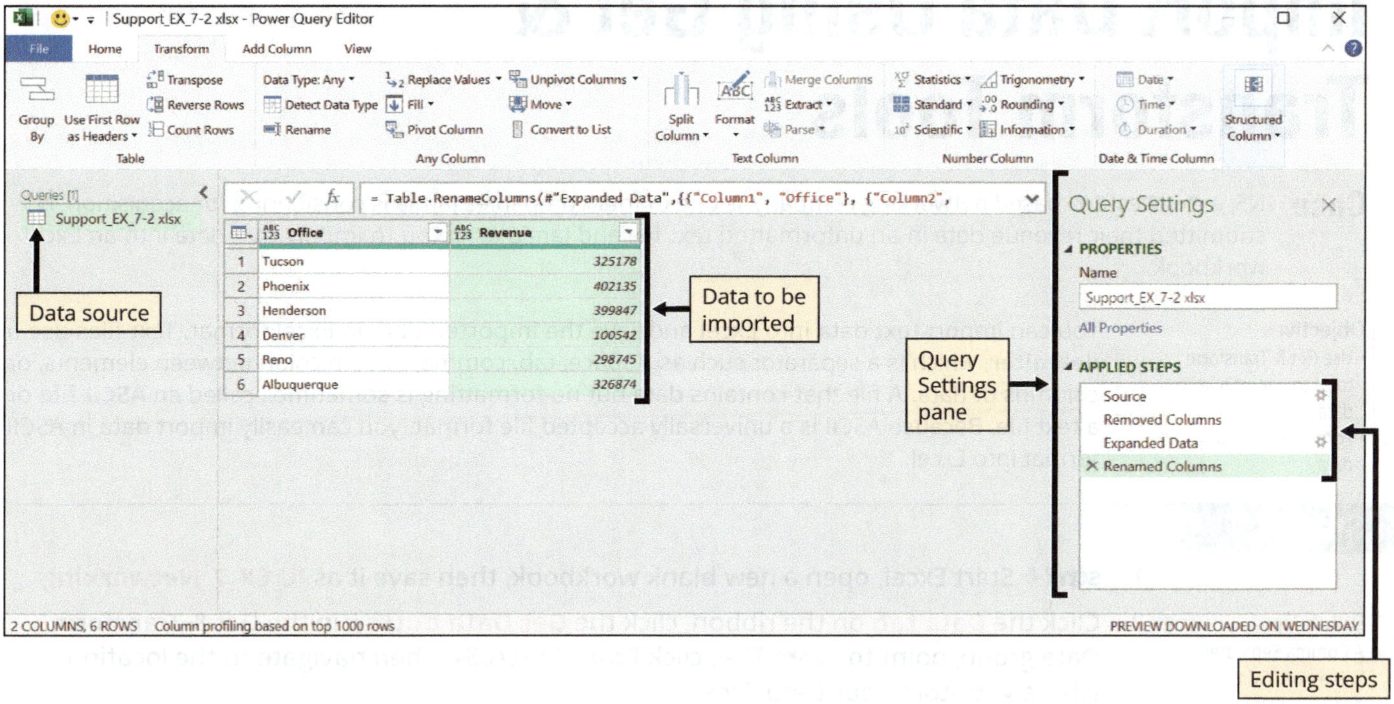


**Figure 7-2:** Excel chart linked to a PowerPoint slide

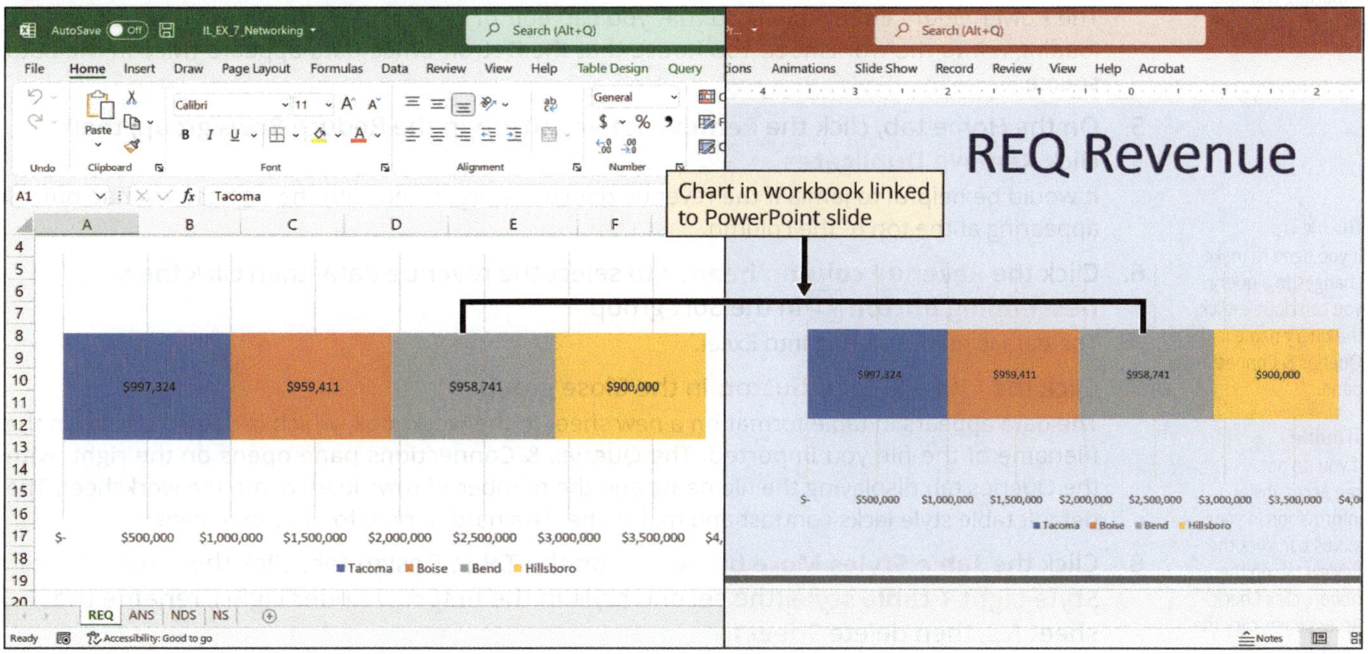

# Import Data Using Get & Transform Tools

**Case** NS, a midwestern-based networking company, is one of four companies Jamia is considering for acquisition. NS submitted their revenue data in an unformatted text file and Jamia asks you to import that data into an Excel workbook.

**Objectives**
- Use Get & Transform tools to import text data
- Format imported data

You can import text data into Excel and save the imported data in Excel format. Text files use a **delimiter**, which is a separator such as a space, tab, comma, or semicolon between elements, or columns of data. A file that contains data but no formatting is sometimes called an **ASCII file** or a text file. Because ASCII is a universally accepted file format, you can easily import data in ASCII format into Excel.

## Steps

**Quick Tip**
A Comma Separated Values, or CSV, file is a text file that uses commas to separate data. CSV files have the extension .csv and are imported using the same steps as importing text files with .txt extensions.

**Quick Tip**
If you need to make changes to a query you can double-click the query name in the Queries & Connections pane.

**Trouble**
If you do not see Accessibility information in your status bar, click the Review tab on the ribbon, click Check Accessibility, click the Keep accessibility checker running while I work check box to add a checkmark, then close the Accessibility pane.

1. **sam Start Excel, open a new blank workbook, then save it as IL_EX_7_Networking**
2. **Click the Data tab on the ribbon, click the Get Data button in the Get & Transform Data group, point to From File, click From Text/CSV, then navigate to the location where you store your Data Files**
   The Import Data dialog box displays only text files.
3. **Click Support_EX_7-1 if necessary, then click Import**
   A preview of the data is displayed in the Support_EX_7-1.txt dialog box, as displayed in **Figure 7-3**.
4. **Click the Transform Data button at the bottom of the dialog box**
   The Power Query Editor opens so that you can edit or reorganize the data if necessary before loading it into the worksheet. You notice that the Detroit office data appears twice in the data source.
5. **On the Home tab, click the Remove Rows button in the Reduce Rows group, then click Remove Duplicates**
   It would be helpful to Jamia if the revenue data were organized with the highest revenue offices appearing at the top of the column.
6. **Click the Revenue column header to select the revenue data, then click the Sort Descending button in the Sort group**
   The data is ready to bring into Excel.
7. **Click the Close & Load button in the Close group**
   The data appears in table format on a new sheet in the workbook, which is named based on the filename of the file you imported. The Queries & Connections pane opens on the right, with the Queries tab displaying the file name and the number of rows loaded into the worksheet. The default table style lacks contrast and makes the data hard to read for a screen reader.
8. **Click the Table Styles More button on the Table Design tab, click the White, Table Style Light 1 table style (the second style in the first row under Light), rename the sheet NS, then delete Sheet1**
9. **Format the data in column B in the Accounting style with the $ symbol and no decimal places, confirm the Accessibility message in the status bar is Good to go, click cell A1, then save your work**
   **Figure 7-4** displays the worksheet with the data you imported into Excel.

**Figure 7-3:** Preview of data from text file

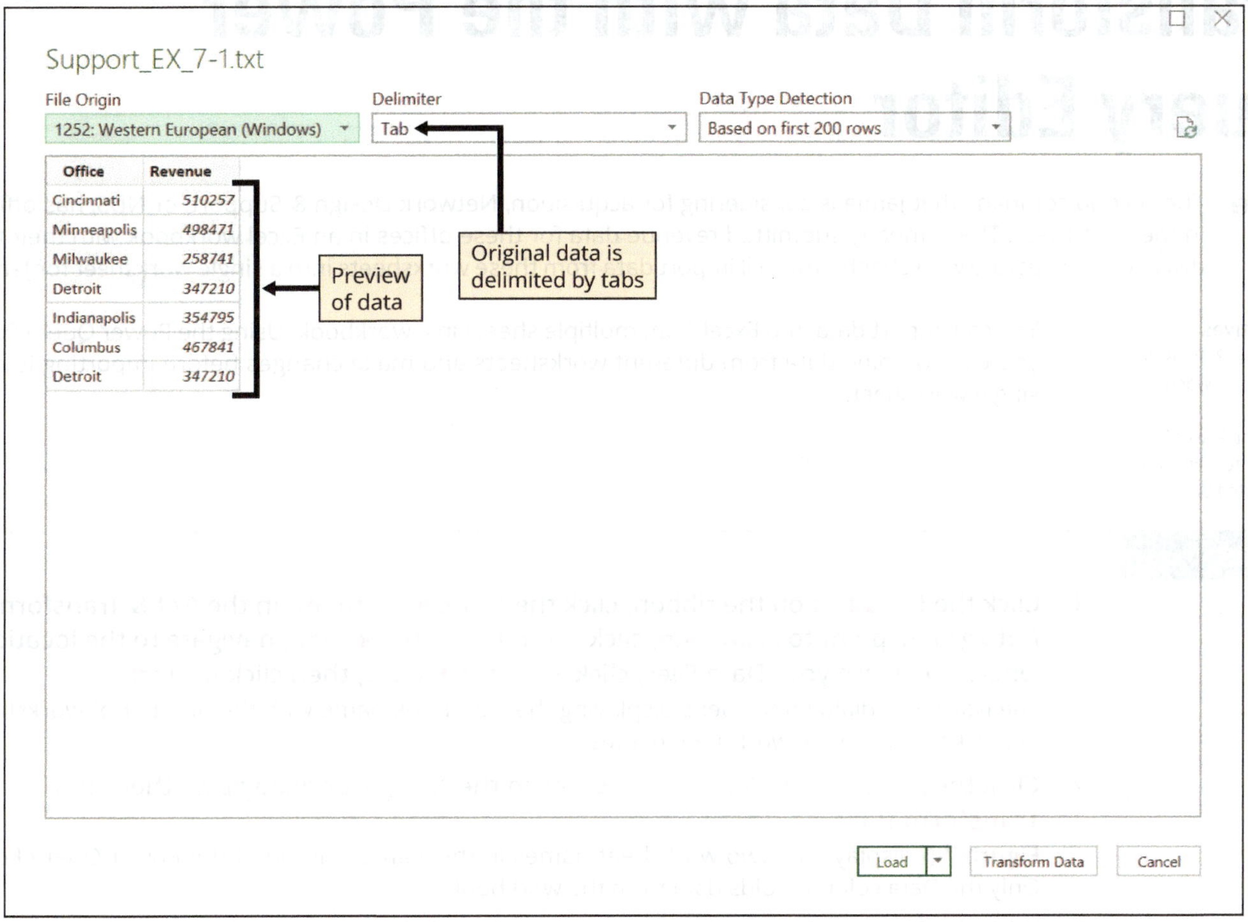


**Figure 7-4:** Worksheet with imported and formatted text file data

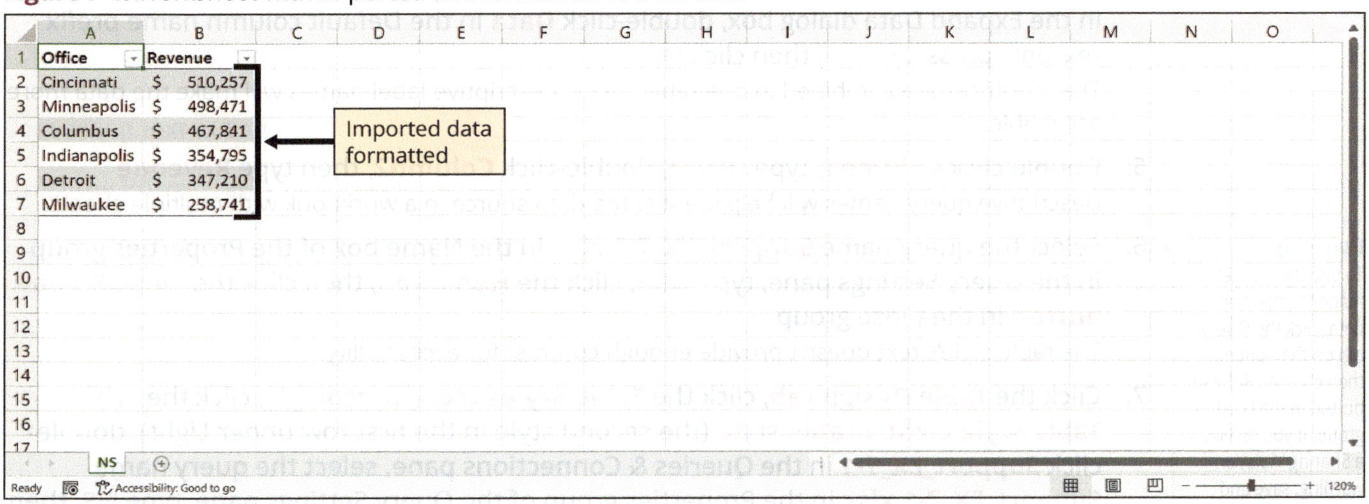

# Import Access Data

**Case** Jamia received revenue data in an Access file from a southeastern-based networking company, ANS. Jamia asks you to import this table into the Excel workbook containing the revenue for the other companies.

**Objectives**
- Use Get & Transform to import a database table
- Use the Power Query Editor to transform imported data

You can import data from a database table created in a database program into Excel. A **database table** is a set of data organized using columns and rows. A **database program** is an application, such as Microsoft Access, designed specifically for managing large amounts of data organized in tables. To import data from an Access table into Excel you will use the Get & Transform tool.

## Steps

1. Click the **Data tab** on the ribbon, click the **Get Data button** in the Get & Transform Data group, point to **From Database**, click **From Microsoft Access Database**, then navigate to the location where you store your Data Files
2. Click **Support_EX_7-3**, then click **Import**
3. Click **Revenue** below the Support_EX_7-3.accdb folder in the Navigator dialog box, click **Transform Data**, then in the Power Query Editor with the ID column selected click the **Remove Columns button** in the Manage Columns group on the Home tab of the ribbon
   You can add columns to analyze the data before bringing it into Excel.
4. Click the **Add Column tab**, click the **Conditional Column button** in the General group, in the Add Additional Column dialog box, double-click **Custom** in the New column name box, type **Relative Revenue**, click the **Column Name arrow**, click **Revenue**, click the **Operator arrow**, click **is greater than**, type **700000** in the Value box, type **Above Average** in the Output box, then type **Below Average** in the Else box
   Compare your Add Conditional Column dialog box to **Figure 7-7**.
5. Click **OK**
   The revenue for each office is evaluated as above or below average in the new column. The data is ready to bring into Excel.
6. Select the query name **Revenue** in the Properties group of the Query Settings pane, type **ANS**, click the **Home tab**, then click the **Close & Load button** in the Close group
   The Access data is imported into the worksheet as a table, and the Queries & Connections pane confirms that six rows were loaded using the Projected Revenue query.
7. Click the **Table Styles More button** on the Table Design tab, click the **White, Table Style Light 1 table style** (the second style in the first row under Light), format the data in column **B** in the Accounting style with the $ symbol and no decimal places, then click cell **A1**
   Your formatted worksheet should match **Figure 7-8**.
8. Save your work

**Trouble**
If a yellow information bar displays the preview age, you can click Refresh to display the most current view of the data.

**Quick Tip**
You can delete rows in the data by clicking the Remove Rows button in the Reduce Rows group of the Home tab.

**Figure 7-7:** Add Conditional Column dialog box

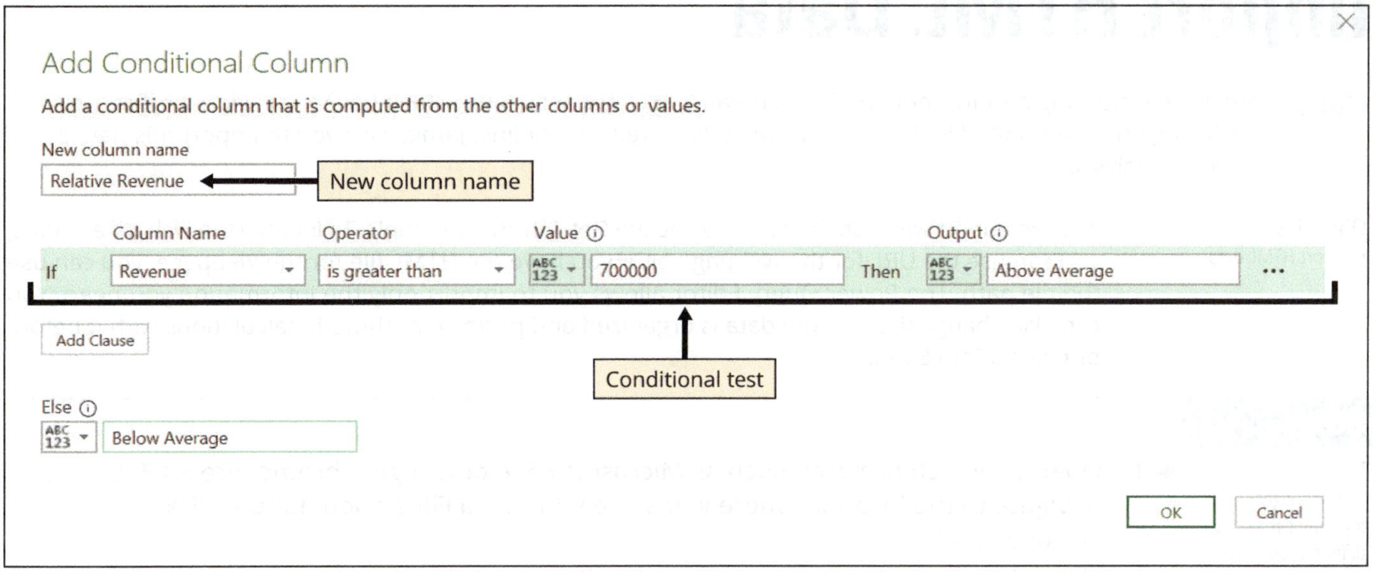


**Figure 7-8:** Formatted worksheet with imported data

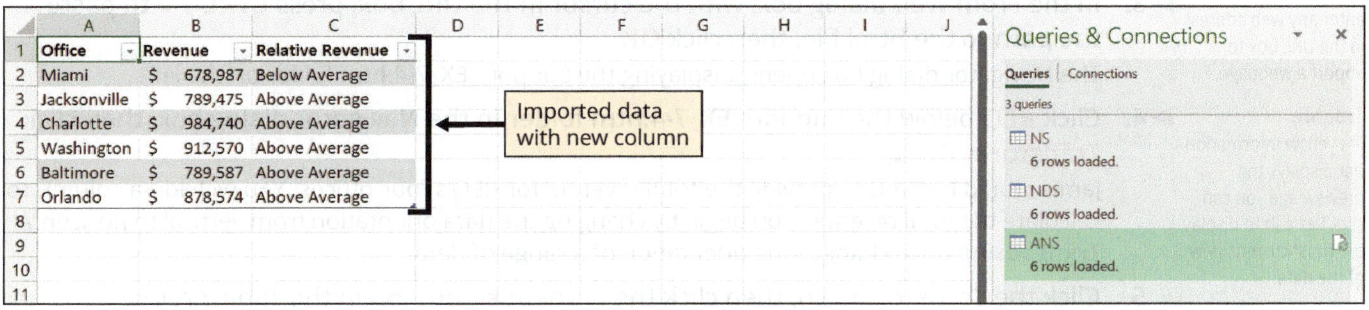

# Import HTML Data

**Case** Jamia is considering a fourth networking company, REQ, for acquisition. REQ has four regional offices in the Pacific region of the United States. After viewing REQ's revenue online, Jamia asks you to import this data into Excel for analysis.

**Objective**
• Import HTML data

You can import web data into Excel using the Get & Transform tools. To identify the web data source, you can use the URL for the webpage or, if you have the HTML file for the webpage, you can use the file path. The Power Query Editor allows you to import only the information you need. You can also change the way the data is organized and perform arithmetic calculations with it before bringing it into Excel.

## Steps

**Trouble**
The webpage formatting may differ on your screen depending on your default web browser.

**Quick Tip**
If you have an internet connection, you can enter any web address in the URL box to import a webpage.

**Trouble**
If a yellow information bar displays the preview age you can click Refresh to display the most current view of the data.

1. **Open your web browser, such as Microsoft Edge or Google Chrome, press CTRL + O, navigate to the location where you store your Data Files, then double-click Support_EX_7-4**
   The webpage opens in your web browser. It displays the REQ revenue data, as displayed in **Figure 7-9**.
2. **Select the file path in the address bar, press CTRL + C to copy the file path, activate the IL_EX_7_Networking workbook, click the Data tab on the ribbon, click the Get Data button in the Get & Transform Data group, point to From Other Sources, then click From Web**
3. **In the From Web dialog box, with the cursor in the URL box, press CTRL + V to paste the path to the html file, then click OK**
   The Navigator dialog box opens, displaying the Support_EX_7-4.htm folder on the left.
4. **Click REQ below the Support_EX_7-4.htm folder in the Navigator dialog box, then click Transform Data**
   Jamia would like you to provide the total revenue for REQ's four offices. You will add a column to calculate the total revenue. You begin by changing the data orientation from vertical to horizontal. **Transposing data** changes the orientation of a range of data.
5. **Click the Transform tab, then click the Transpose button in the Table group**
   The revenue for the offices is arranged horizontally. Before adding a column to total the revenue for the four offices, you need to remove the column headers assigned by the Power Query Editor.
6. **Click the Home tab, click the Use First Row as Headers button in the Transform group, click the Hillsboro column header, click the Add Column tab, then click the Custom Column button in the General group**
7. **In the Custom Column dialog box, select Custom in the New column name box, type Total Revenue, click after = in the Custom column formula box, double-click Tacoma in the Available Columns box, type +, double-click Boise in the Available Columns box, type +, double-click Bend in the Available Columns box, type +, double-click Hillsboro in the Available Columns box, then click OK**
   3813475 is displayed in the new Total Revenue column.
8. **Click the Home tab, click the Close & Load button in the Close group, click the Table Design tab, click the Table Styles More button on the Table Design tab, click the White, Table Style Light 1 table style (the second style in the first row under Light), then format the data in row 2 in the Accounting style with the $ symbol and no decimal places**
   Compare your worksheet to **Figure 7-10**.
9. **Close the Queries & Connections pane, close your web browser, then save the workbook**

**Figure 7-9:** Webpage with REQ revenue data

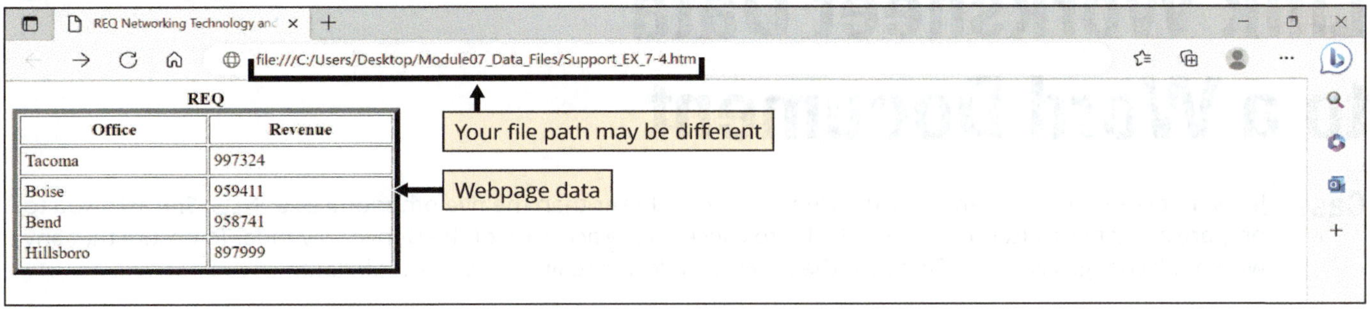


**Figure 7-10:** Imported and formatted HTML data

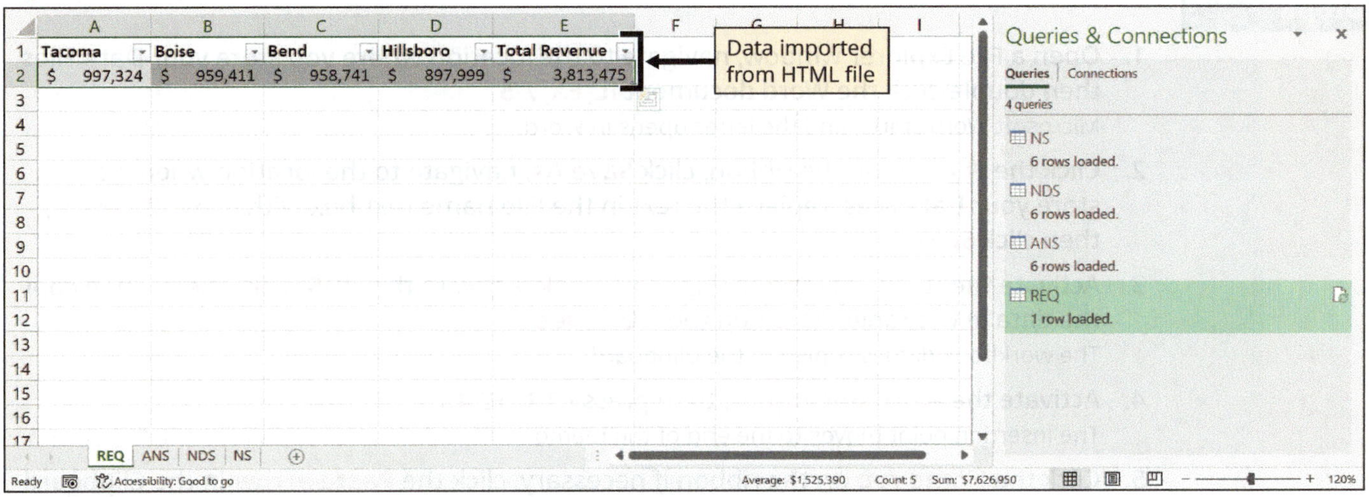


## Importing Web data

You can import a locally stored HTML file directly into an Excel workbook by clicking the File tab in Excel, clicking Open, clicking Browse, selecting All Files in the Open dialog box, browsing to the HTML file, then clicking Open. You can also import web data by selecting the data on the webpage, right-clicking any cell in the selected range, clicking Copy on the shortcut menu, then pasting the copied data in a worksheet.

# Link Worksheet Data to a Word Document

**Case** Jamia notices that the revenue for the Denver office is lower than the five other offices at NDS. She asks you to prepare a business letter to the CFO at NDS to check on the accuracy of the Denver revenue. To ensure that any workbook changes will be reflected in the letter, you decide to link the workbook data.

**Objectives**
- Link data to a Word document
- Update linked data

There are times when you want to import Excel data into a Word file. You can choose to embed the data, which places a copy of the worksheet data in the Word document. If you instead choose to link the worksheet data, the link contains a connection to the workbook so that any changes you make to the workbook are reflected in the linked object.

## Steps

1. **Open a File Explorer window, navigate to the location where you store your Data Files, then double-click the Word document IL_EX_7-5**
   Microsoft Word starts, and the letter opens in Word.
2. **Click the File tab on the ribbon, click Save As, navigate to the location where you store your Data Files, replace the text in the File name text box with IL_EX_7_Letter, then click Save**
3. **Activate the IL_EX_7_Networking workbook, activate the NDS worksheet, then copy the data in the range A1:B7 on the NDS sheet**
   The workbook data is copied to the Clipboard.
4. **Activate the Word document, then press CTRL+END**
   The insertion point moves to the end of the memo.
5. **Click the Home tab on the ribbon if necessary, click the Paste arrow in the Clipboard group, then click the Link & Use Destination Styles button under Paste Options**
6. **Select the table data, click the Layout tab on the ribbon, in the Table Column Width box in the Cell Size group type 1.2, then press ENTER**
   Compare your screen to **Figure 7-11**
7. **Activate the IL_EX_7_Networking workbook, press ESC if necessary to deselect the data, on the NDS worksheet click cell B5, type 400542, then click the Enter button ✓ on the formula bar**
8. **Activate the IL_EX_7_Letter document, select the table if necessary, right-click the table, then click Update Link**
   The table data is updated to reflect the change in the linked Excel workbook, as displayed in **Figure 7-12**.
9. **Click the Insert tab on the ribbon, click the Header button in the Header & Footer group, click Edit Header, type your name in the Header area, click the Close Header and Footer button in the Close group, save the Word document, close the document, submit the Word file to your instructor, then close Word**

**Figure 7-11:** Word document with linked worksheet data

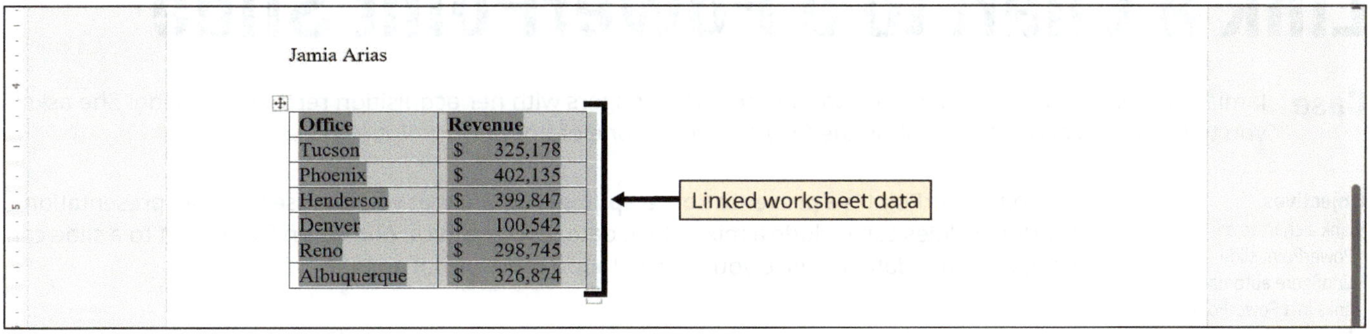

Jamia Arias

| Office | Revenue |
|---|---|
| Tucson | $ 325,178 |
| Phoenix | $ 402,135 |
| Henderson | $ 399,847 |
| Denver | $ 100,542 |
| Reno | $ 298,745 |
| Albuquerque | $ 326,874 |



**Figure 7-12:** Word document with updated table data

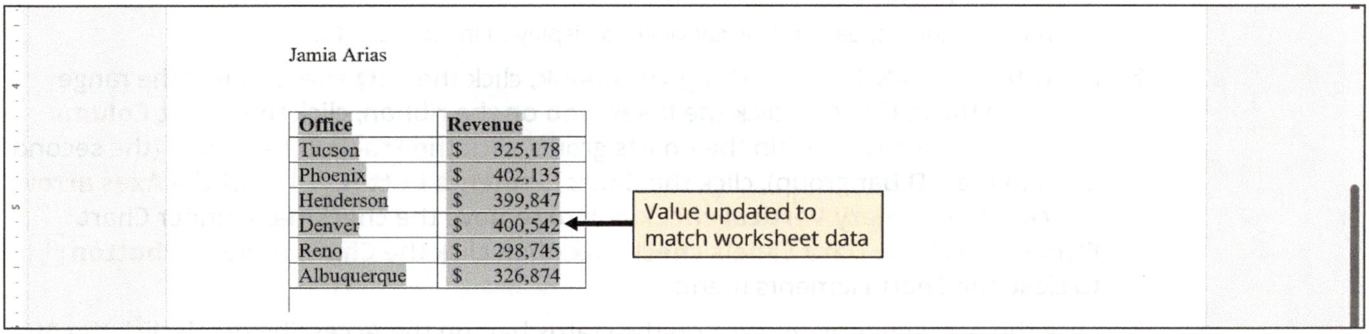

Jamia Arias

| Office | Revenue |
|---|---|
| Tucson | $ 325,178 |
| Phoenix | $ 402,135 |
| Henderson | $ 399,847 |
| Denver | $ 400,542 |
| Reno | $ 298,745 |
| Albuquerque | $ 326,874 |



## Managing and breaking links

When you open a Word document containing linked data, a message box opens asking if you want to update the linked data. You can manage this default behavior by clicking the File tab on the ribbon, clicking Info, then clicking Edit Links to Files in the right pane. The Links dialog box opens, allowing you to change a link's update method from the default setting of automatic to manual. The Links dialog box also allows you to change the link source, permanently break a link, open the source file, or manually update a link. If you send your linked files to another user, the links will be broken because the linked file path references the local computer where you inserted the links. Because the file path will not be valid on the recipient user's device, the links will no longer be updated when the user opens the destination document. To correct this, recipients who have both the destination and source documents can use the Links dialog box to change the link's source in the destination document to their own device. Then the links will be automatically updated when they open the destination document in the future. If you are managing links in an Excel workbook you can click the Data tab, then click the Edit Links button in the Queries & Connections group to open the Edit Links dialog box.

# Link a Chart to a PowerPoint Slide

**Case** Jamia is preparing a presentation for Bayside senior managers with her acquisition recommendation. She asks you to link an Excel chart illustrating the REQ revenue to one of her PowerPoint slides.

**Objectives**
- Link a chart to a PowerPoint slide
- Configure automatic links in a PowerPoint file

Microsoft PowerPoint is a **presentation graphics** program that you can use to create presentations. PowerPoint slides can include a mix of text, data, and graphics. Adding an Excel chart to a slide can help to illustrate data and give your presentation more visual appeal.

## Steps

1. Open a File Explorer window, navigate to the location where you store your Data Files, double-click the PowerPoint file **IL_EX_7-6**, then save the file as **IL_EX_7_ManagementPresentation**
   The presentation appears in Normal view, as displayed in **Figure 7-13**.
2. Activate the **IL_EX_7_Networking workbook**, click the **REQ sheet**, select the range **A1:D2** on the REQ sheet, click the **Insert tab** on the ribbon, click the **Insert Column or Bar Chart button** in the Charts group, click the **Stacked Bar chart** (the second chart in the 2-D Bar group), click the **Chart Elements button**, click the **Axes arrow**, click the **Primary Vertical check box** to remove the checkmark, under Chart Elements click the **Data Labels check box**, then click the **Chart Elements button** to close the Chart Elements menu
3. Click the **Accessibility checker** on the status bar, on the Accessibility tab click the **Alt Text button** in the Names group, type **REQ Annual Revenue by Office** in the text box, click the **Close button**, then click again to close the Accessibility pane
   You will make a few more changes to the chart before bringing it into the presentation.
4. Delete the **chart title**, move the **chart** until its upper-left corner is at the upper-left corner of cell **A4**, resize the chart until its lower-right corner is at the lower-right corner of cell **I19**, then change the worksheet orientation to landscape if necessary
5. Right-click the **Chart Area** outside of the plot area, click **Copy** on the shortcut menu, then click the **PowerPoint program button** on the taskbar to display the presentation
6. Click **Slide 2** in the Thumbnails pane, right-click **Slide 2** in the Slide pane, click the **Home tab** on the ribbon if necessary, click the **Paste Options arrow** in the Clipboard group, then click the **Use Destination Theme & Link Data button** in the Paste Options group
   The bar chart from Excel illustrating the projected revenue is added to the slide and linked to the workbook.
7. Click the **File tab** on the ribbon, click **Info**, click **Edit Links to Files** at the bottom of the right pane, in the Links dialog box click the **Automatic Update check box** to add a checkmark, close the dialog box, click the **Back button** at the top of the pane, then in the presentation click the **Save button** on the title bar
   Any links in this presentation will now be automatically updated if the source file changes.
8. Switch to **Excel**, on the **REQ sheet** type **900,000** in cell **D2**, then click the **Enter button** on the Formula bar, click the **PowerPoint program button** on the taskbar to display the presentation, then compare your slide to **Figure 7-14**
9. With slide 2 activated, click the **Insert tab** on the ribbon, click the **Header & Footer button** in the Text group, add a checkmark in the **Footer check box**, type your name in the **Footer text box**, click **Apply**, save and close the presentation, submit the PowerPoint file to your instructor, then close PowerPoint

**Trouble**
If Copy is not displayed on the shortcut menu, you may have clicked the Plot area rather than the Chart area. Right-clicking the white area surrounding the bar displays the Copy command on the menu.

**Quick Tip**
You can click the Use Destination Theme & Embed workbook button to place a copy of, or embed, the chart object; you can edit an embedded object by double-clicking it.

**Figure 7-13:** Presentation in Normal view

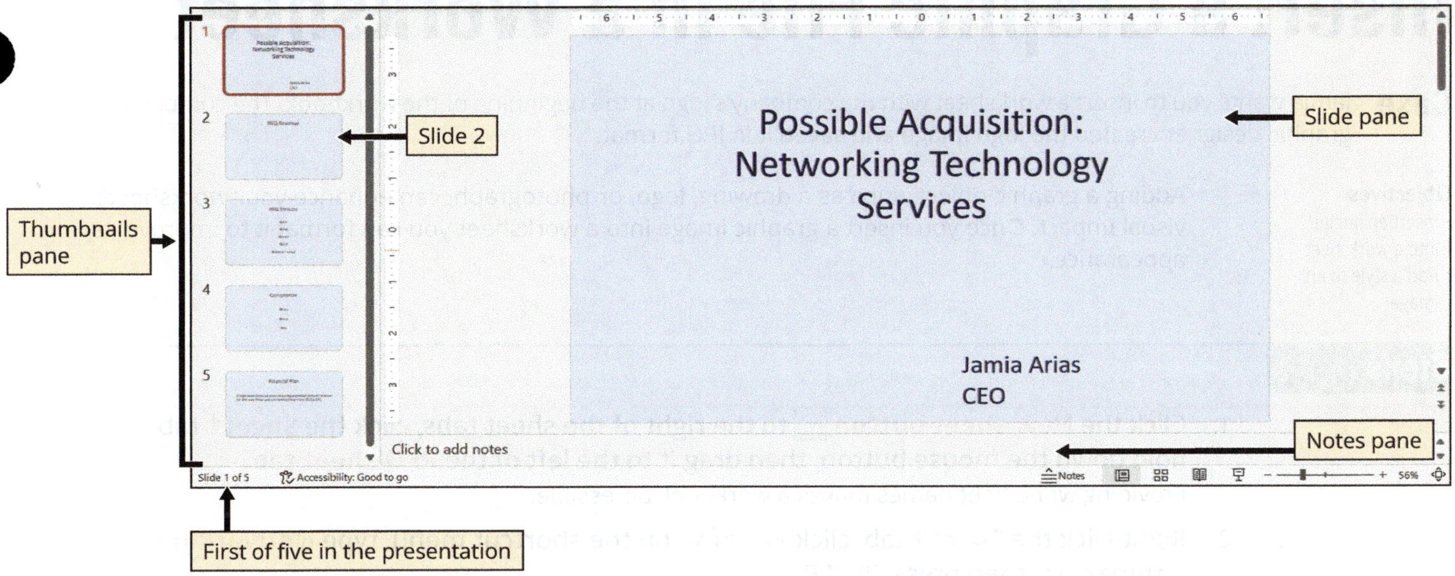


**Figure 7-14:** Completed slide

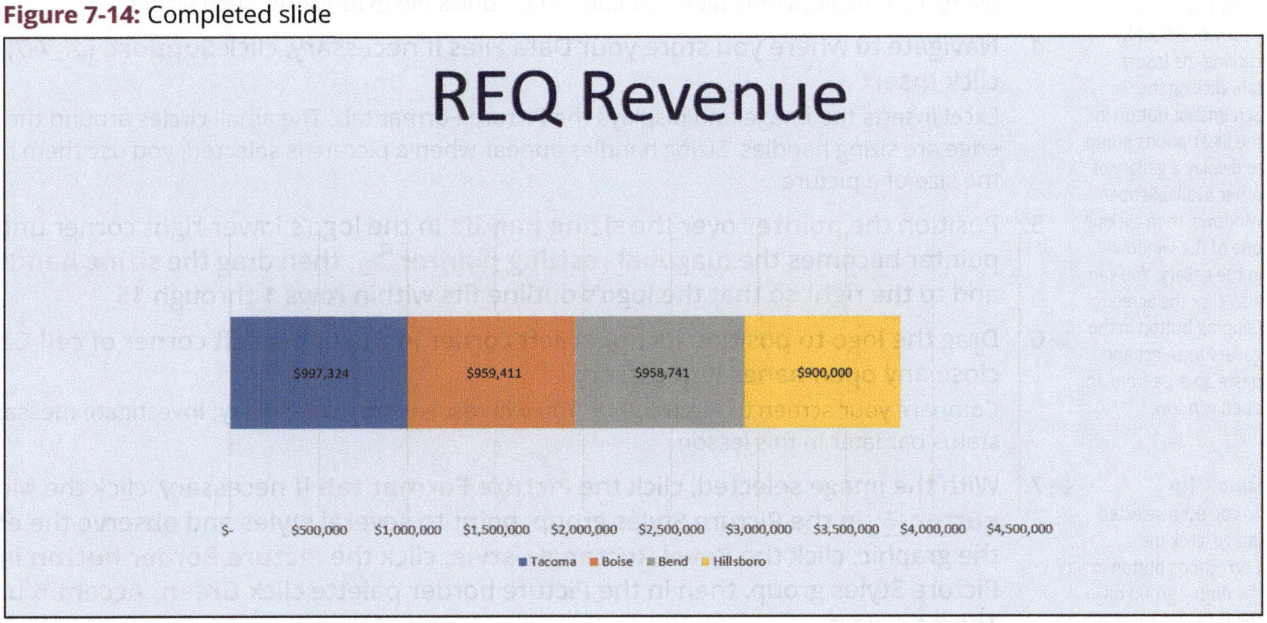

# Insert a Graphic File in a Worksheet

**Case** Jamia wants you to insert a worksheet with the company's logo at the beginning of the workbook. The company's graphic designer created the logo image and saved it in JPG format.

**Objectives**
- Insert an image into a worksheet
- Add a style to an image

Adding a graphic object, such as a drawing, logo, or photograph, can enhance your worksheet's visual impact. Once you insert a graphic image into a worksheet you can format it to improve its appearance.

## Steps

1. **Click the New sheet button ⊕ to the right of the sheet tabs, click the Sheet1 tab, hold down the mouse button, then drag it to the left of the REQ sheet tab**
   Providing worksheet names makes a workbook accessible.
2. **Right-click the Sheet1 tab, click Rename on the shortcut menu, type Networking Companies, then press ENTER**
3. **Click the Insert tab on the ribbon, click the Illustrations button, click the Pictures button in the Illustrations group, then click This Device**
   The Insert Picture dialog box opens. Because you specified that you want to insert a picture, the dialog box displays only files that contain graphics file extensions, such as .jpg.
4. **Navigate to where you store your Data Files if necessary, click Support_EX_7-7, then click Insert**
   Excel inserts the image and displays the Picture Format tab. The small circles around the picture's edge are sizing handles. Sizing handles appear when a picture is selected; you use them to change the size of a picture.
5. **Position the pointer over the sizing handle in the logo's lower-right corner until the pointer becomes the diagonal resizing pointer ⤡, then drag the sizing handle down and to the right so that the logo's outline fits within rows 1 through 15**
6. **Drag the logo to position its upper-left corner in the upper-left corner of cell C2, then close any open panes if necessary**
   Compare your screen to Figure 7-15. You will resolve the Accessibility: Investigate message in the status bar later in this lesson.
7. **With the image selected, click the Picture Format tab if necessary, click the More button in the Picture Styles group, point to several styles and observe the effect on the graphic, click the Bevel Rectangle style, click the Picture Border button in the Picture Styles group, then in the Picture border palette click Green, Accent 6 under Theme Colors**
8. **Click the Alt Text button in the Accessibility group, type Bayside Logo in the Alt Text box, click the Close button ☒ to close the Alt Text pane Compare your worksheet to Figure 7-16.**
9. **sam ↑ Select the five worksheets to group them, click the Insert tab, click the Header & Footer button in the Text group, on the Header & Footer tab, with the insertion point in the center section of the Header click the Sheet Name button in the Header & Footer Elements group, click the Go to Footer button in the Navigation group, enter your name in the center footer section, click the Normal button on the Status Bar, ungroup the worksheets, save the workbook, close the workbook, close Excel, then submit the workbook to your instructor**

**Quick Tip**
You can insert a screenshot of an open window, on your worksheet by clicking the Insert tab, clicking the Screenshot button in the Illustrations group to display a gallery of other available open windows, then clicking one of the windows in the gallery. You can also click the Screen Clipping button in the gallery to select and paste an area from an open window.

**Quick Tip**
To correct a selected image, click the Corrections button in the Adjust group on the Picture Format tab, then click an option in the Sharpen/Soften or Brightness/Contrast section.

**Quick Tip**
You can copy the formatting of an image by selecting the image, clicking the Format Painter button in the Clipboard group of the Home tab, then clicking the image to apply the formatting.

**Figure 7-15:** Resized and repositioned logo

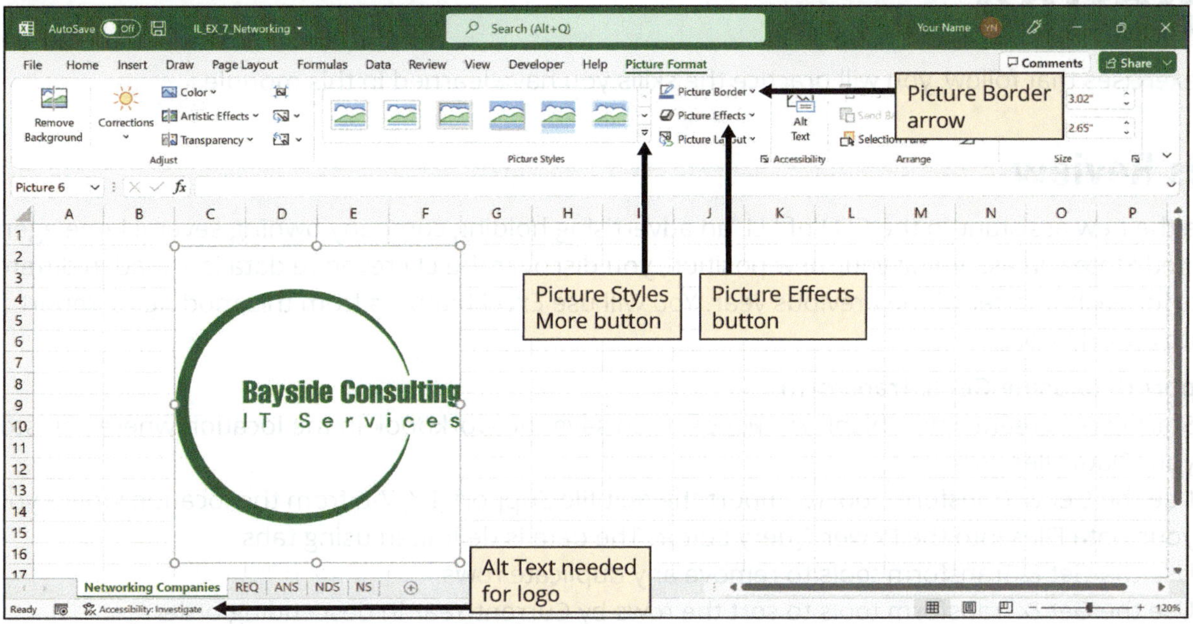


**Figure 7-16:** Worksheet with formatted picture

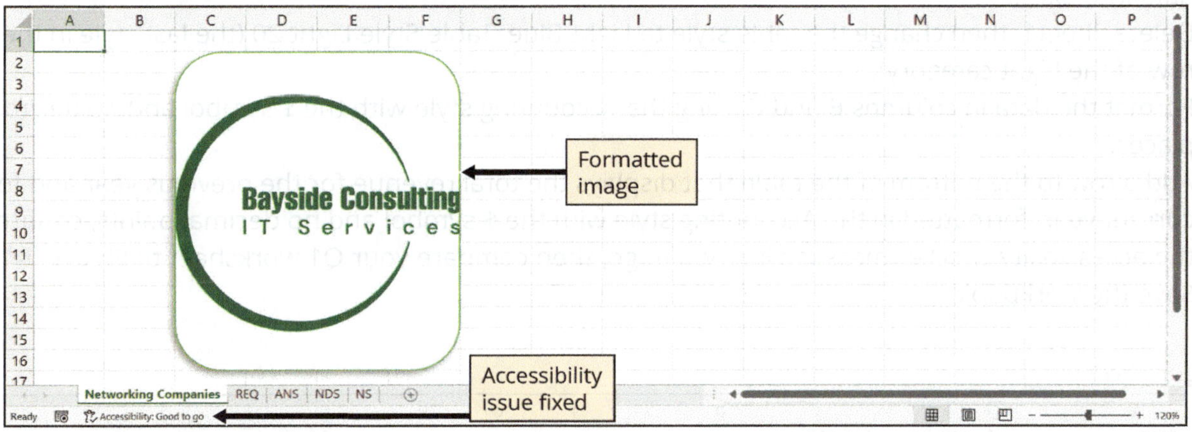


## Working with SmartArt graphics

SmartArt graphics provide another way to visually communicate information. Each SmartArt type communicates a kind of information or relationship, such as a list, process, or hierarchy, and includes appropriate layouts. To insert a SmartArt graphic into a worksheet, click the Insert tab, then click the SmartArt button in the Illustrations group. In the Choose a SmartArt Graphic dialog box, choose from eight SmartArt types: List, Process, Cycle, Hierarchy, Relationship, Matrix, Pyramid, and Picture. There is also a link for SmartArt available on Office.com. The dialog box describes the type of information that is appropriate for each selected layout. After you choose a layout and click OK, a SmartArt object appears on your worksheet. You can enter text directly in the placeholders or use the SmartArt text pane. You can change the layout by selecting the SmartArt, then clicking a different layout in the Layouts group on the SmartArt Design tab.

You can add shapes to a SmartArt graphic by first clicking the shape where you want the added shape to appear, clicking the Add Shape arrow in the Create Graphic group of the SmartArt Design tab, then selecting the desired position. Also in the Create Graphic group are the Promote and Demote buttons, which you can use to increase or decrease the level of a selected shape. The SmartArt Design tab lets you choose color schemes and styles for your SmartArt. You can add shape styles, fills, outlines, and other shape effects to SmartArt graphics using choices on the Format tab. You can change the size of a SmartArt shape by selecting the shape, then clicking the Larger button or the Smaller button in the Shapes group on the Format tab. You can align multiple SmartArt graphics at once by selecting them, clicking Align in the Arrange group on the Format tab, then selecting the alignment option.

# Practice

In the exercises that follow, you will practice the skills you have learned in this module.

## Skills Review

You are the new assistant to the CFO of LLI, an advertising holding company owning several large agencies in the United States. In assuming your new position, you discover the LLI revenue data is stored in different file formats for each quarter of the previous year. You will use Excel features from this module to import all the data into a workbook.

1. **Import data using Get & Transform.**
   a. Start Excel, create a new blank workbook, then save the workbook in the location where you store your Data Files as **IL_EX_7_LLI**.
   b. Use the Get & Transform tool to import the text file Support_EX_7-8 from the location where you store your Data Files into the Power Query Editor. The data is delimited using tabs.
   c. Use the Get & Transform tools to remove any duplicate rows.
   d. Use the Get & Transform tools to sort the rows by Current Year in descending order.
   e. Use the Properties box in the Power Query Editor to rename the query Q1, then load the revenue data into Excel.
   f. Delete Sheet1, then change the table style to Light Blue, Table Style Light 20 (the last style in the third row of the Light category).
   g. Format the data in columns B and C using the Accounting style with the $ symbol and no decimal places.
   h. Add a row to the bottom of the table that displays the total revenue for the previous year and for the current year, formatted in the Accounting style with the $ symbol and no decimal points, confirm that the accessibility checker message is Good to go, then compare your Q1 worksheet to **Figure 7-17**.
   i. Save the workbook.

**Figure 7-17**

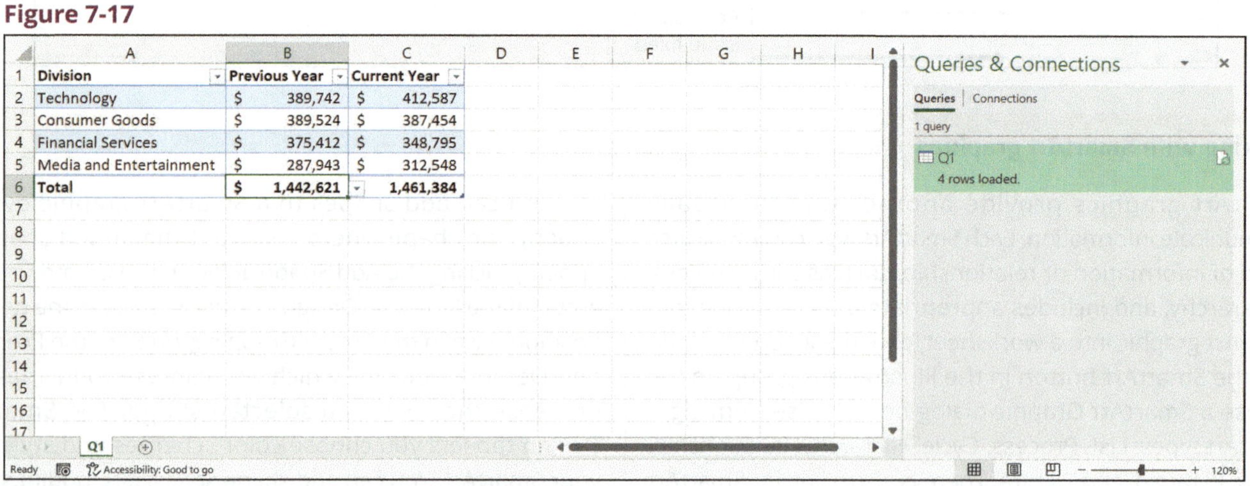


2. **Transform data with the Power Query Editor.**
   a. Use the Get & Transform tool to import the data from both worksheets of the Support_EX_7-9 workbook from the location where you store your Data Files into the Power Query Editor. (**Hint**: You need to click the Support_EX_7-9.xlsx folder in the Navigator dialog box.)
   b. In the Power Query Editor, delete all the unnecessary columns. (**Hint**: You need to delete all columns other than the Data column.)

c. Use the Expand button in the Structured Column group on the Transform tab to combine the data on both sheets into one table. Delete the Column name prefix in the Expand Data dialog box.
d. Change the Column1 label to **Division**, the Column2 label to **Previous Year**, and the Column3 label to **Current Year**.
e. Use the Properties box to change the query name to **Q2**, then load the data into the Excel workbook.
f. Change the table style to Light Blue, Table Style Light 20 (the last style in the third row of the Light category).
g. Format the data in columns B and C using the Accounting style with the $ symbol and no decimal places.
h. Add a table total row that displays the revenue for both the previous year and the current year, confirm that the accessibility checker message is Good to go, compare your screen to **Figure 7-18**, then save the workbook.

**Figure 7-18**

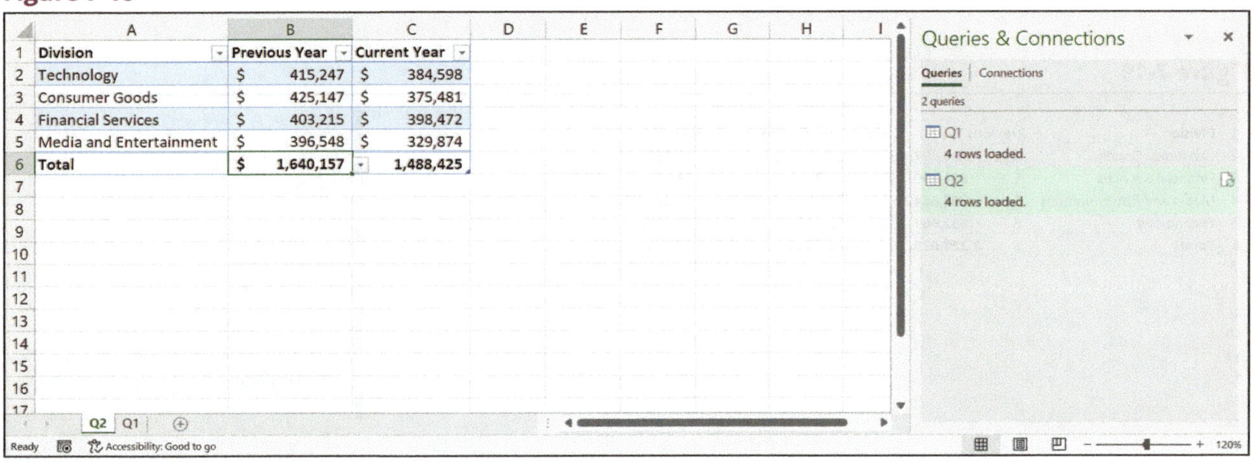


**3. Import Access data.**

a. Use the Get & Transform tool to import the data on the Q3 table in the Access Data File Support_EX_7-10 from the location where you store your Data Files into the Power Query Editor. Close the message about the age of the preview, if necessary.
b. Delete the **ID** column.
c. Use the Add Conditional Column dialog box to add a conditional column named **Performance Evaluation** that evaluates whether the Current Year column is greater than 500,000. Display High-Performing if this evaluation is true, otherwise leave the new column cell blank.
d. Load the data into the Excel workbook.
e. Change the table style to Light Blue, Table Style Light 20 (the last style in the third row of the Light category).
f. Format the data in columns B and C using the Accounting style with the $ symbol and no decimal places.
g. Add a table total row that displays the revenue for both the previous year and the current year, format the totals using the Accounting style with the $ symbol and no decimal places, delete any other total row calculations, confirm that the accessibility checker message is Good to go, then save the workbook.

**4. Import HTML data**

a. Open the file Support_EX_7-11 in your browser, copy the file path in the address bar, then use the Get & Transform tool to import the Q4 table data from the Web file into the Power Query Editor using the copied file path. (**Hint**: You need to paste the path to the html file in the URL box in the From Web dialog box.)

## Skills Review (Continued)

b. In the Power Query Editor, add a custom column named **Growth in Dollars** that calculates the difference in revenue from the previous year to the current year. (**Hint**: The formula in the dialog box should be = [Current Year] – [Previous Year].) Close the message about the age of the preview, if necessary.

c. Load the data into the Excel workbook, then change the table style to Light Blue, Table Style Light 20 (the last style in the third row of the Light category).

d. Format the data in columns B, C, and D using the Accounting style with the $ symbol and no decimal places.

e. Add a table total row that displays the revenue for the Previous Year, Current Year, and Growth in Dollars columns, using the Accounting style with the $ symbol and no decimal places, then confirm that the accessibility checker message is Good to go.

f. Compare your screen to **Figure 7-19**, then save the workbook.

**Figure 7-19**

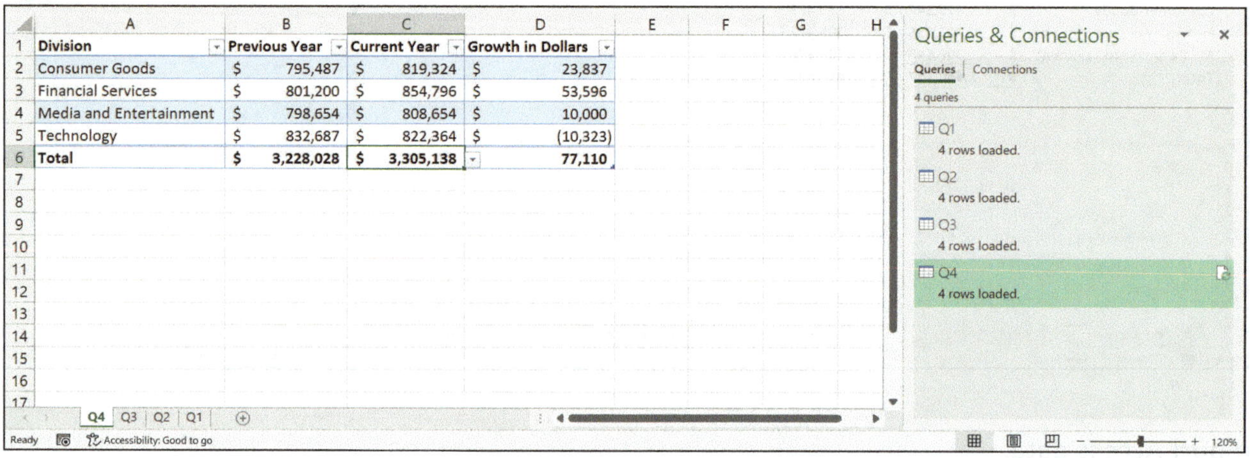


5. **Link worksheet data to a Word document.**

a. Activate the Q3 sheet, copy the range A1:C6.

b. Open the Word file IL_EX_7-12 from the location where you store your Data Files, then save it as **IL_EX_7_LLIMemo**.

c. At the end of the memo body, use the Paste menu to paste the copied worksheet data by linking and using destination styles. Widen the Previous Year and Current Year columns if necessary to display the values on one line.

d. Note that the consumer goods' current year value is currently $489,254. Switch to Excel, on the Q3 worksheet of the IL_EX_7_LLI workbook, then change the value in cell C5 to **$495,000**.

e. Activate the IL_EX_7_LLIMemo document in Word, update the linked data, then verify that the current year's consumer goods value has changed to $495,000, as displayed in **Figure 7-20**. (**Hint**: To update the link, right-click the table in the memo, then click Update Link.)

f. Use a tool on the Insert tab of the ribbon to edit the header, enter your name in the header, save your changes to the IL_EX_7_LLIMemo document, preview the memo, close the document, then close Word.

**Figure 7-20**

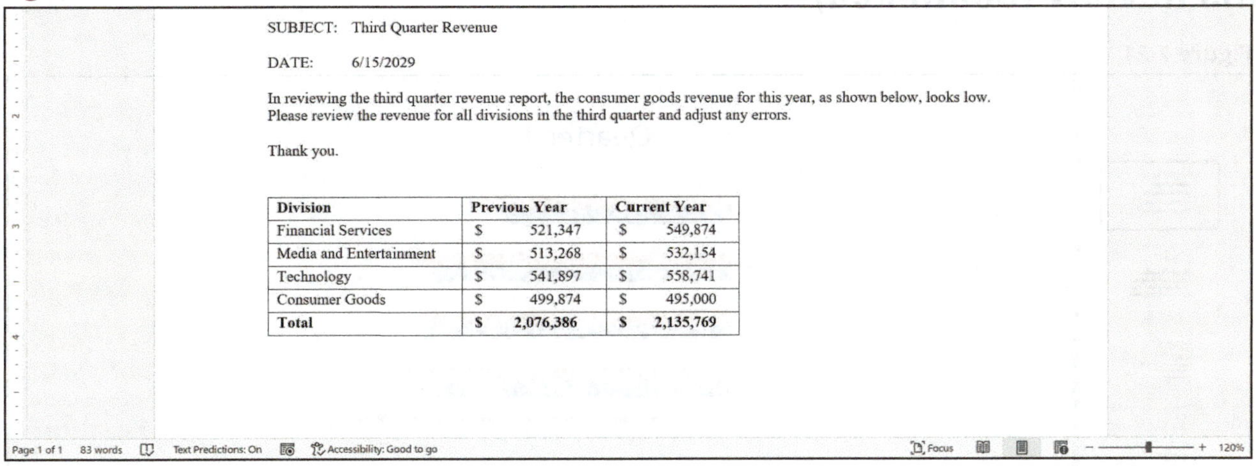

SUBJECT: Third Quarter Revenue

DATE: 6/15/2029

In reviewing the third quarter revenue report, the consumer goods revenue for this year, as shown below, looks low. Please review the revenue for all divisions in the third quarter and adjust any errors.

Thank you.

| Division | Previous Year | Current Year |
|---|---|---|
| Financial Services | $ 521,347 | $ 549,874 |
| Media and Entertainment | $ 513,268 | $ 532,154 |
| Technology | $ 541,897 | $ 558,741 |
| Consumer Goods | $ 499,874 | $ 495,000 |
| **Total** | **$ 2,076,386** | **$ 2,135,769** |



6. **Link an Excel chart to a PowerPoint slide.**
   a. Open the PowerPoint presentation IL_EX_7-13 from the location where you store your Data Files, then save it as **IL_EX_7_LLIPresentation**.
   b. Switch to Excel, activate the Q1 worksheet in the IL_EX_7_LLI workbook, then using the data in the range A1:C5, create a clustered bar chart (**Hint**: The first chart in the Recommended Charts list). Delete the chart title, then move and resize the chart so its upper-left corner is at the upper-left corner of cell A8 and its lower-right corner is at the lower-right corner of cell E22.
   c. Add the Alt Text **Quarter 1 Revenue**.
   d. Copy the chart, activate the PowerPoint file, then display Slide 2, Quarter 1. (**Hint**: Click slide 2 in the Thumbnails pane.)
   e. Link the copied chart to Slide 2, using the theme of the destination file. Move the mouse pointer over the Financial Services Current Year bar to see that the Financial Services current year revenue is $348,795.
   f. Open the Info pane on the File tab, then edit the file's links to automatically update. Return to the presentation.
   g. Switch to Excel, then on the Q1 worksheet change the Financial Services Current Year amount in cell C4 to **$400,000**. Notice in the bar chart that revenue for the current year's financial services is now $400,000.
   h. Activate the IL_EX_7_LLIPresentation file, then verify the current year's financial services in the chart on Slide 2 change to $400,000. If the Accessibility message in the status bar is Investigate, add the Alt Text **Quarter 1 Revenue**.
   i. Enlarge the chart and re-center it, if necessary, under the title.
   j. Use a tool on the Insert tab to add a footer containing your name to all of the slides. (**Hint**: Use the Apply to all check box.) Compare your slide to **Figure 7-21**.
   k. Save the presentation, close the presentation, then close PowerPoint.

# Skills Review (Continued)

**Figure 7-21**

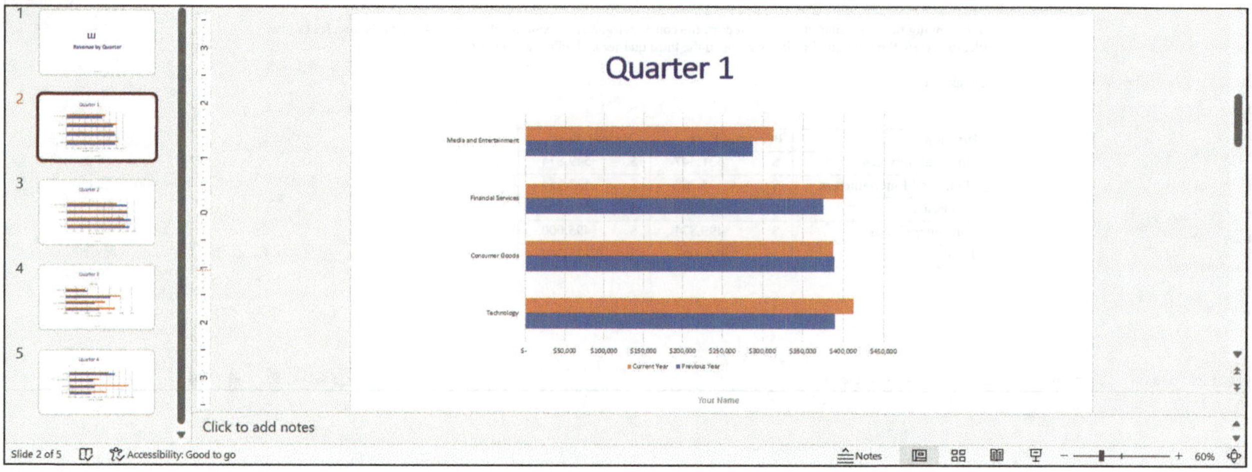


7. **Insert a graphic file in a worksheet.**
   a. Activate the Q2 worksheet in the IL_EX_7_LLI file. Select rows 1 through 4, then insert four blank rows above row 1 to create space for an image.
   b. In rows 1 through 4, insert the picture file Support_EX_7-14.jpg from the location where you store your Data Files.
   c. Resize and reposition the logo as necessary to make it fit in rows 1 through 4, centered across Columns A through C.
   d. Add the Alt Text **LLI Logo** to the picture.
   e. Apply the Center Shadow Rectangle Picture Style (the first style on the left in the third row), then change the picture border color to Red in the Standard colors.
   f. Further resize and reposition the picture so that both the image and the border fit in the first four rows. **Figure 7-22** displays the completed worksheet.
   g. Group the worksheets, change the orientation of the worksheets to landscape, add the sheet name to the center section of the header, add your name to the center section of the footer, preview the workbook, ungroup the worksheets, save and close the workbook, then submit the workbook to your instructor.

**Figure 7-22**

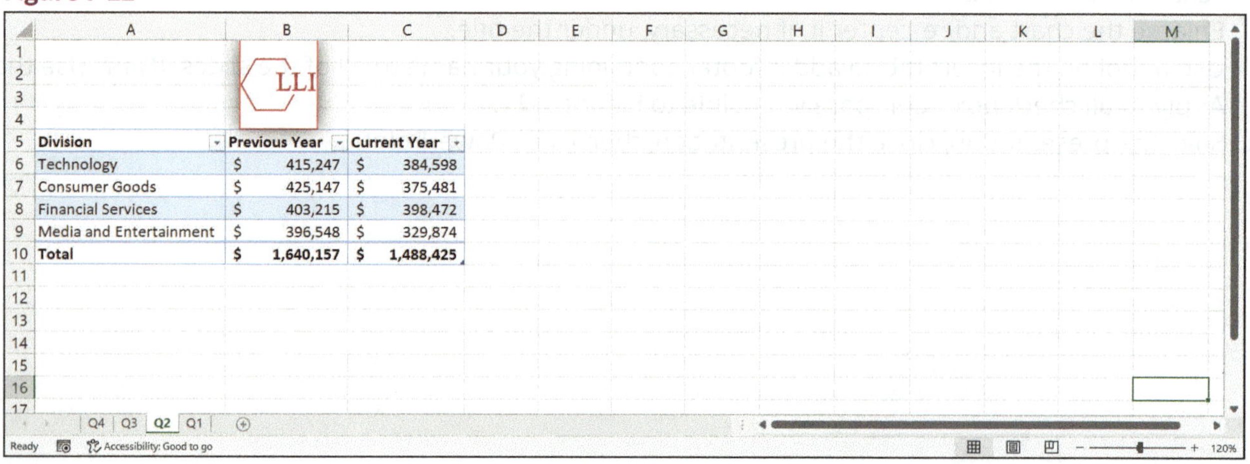

| Division | Previous Year | Current Year |
|---|---|---|
| Technology | $ 415,247 | $ 384,598 |
| Consumer Goods | $ 425,147 | $ 375,481 |
| Financial Services | $ 403,215 | $ 398,472 |
| Media and Entertainment | $ 396,548 | $ 329,874 |
| **Total** | **$ 1,640,157** | **$ 1,488,425** |

## Independent Challenge 1

As a junior analyst in the telecom infrastructure investments group of a private equity firm, you manage the broadband, data center, and telecom-tower sectors. You have received annual revenue reports from these sectors and need to bring them all together in an Excel workbook for analysis.

a. Start Excel, create a new workbook, then save it as **IL_EX_7_TRQ** in the location where you store your Data Files.
b. Use the Get & Transform tool to import the data from both worksheets of the Excel workbook file Support_EX_7-15 into the Power Query Editor.
c. Delete all columns except for the Data column, then expand the Data column to display all columns of data without using a default column name prefix. (**Hint**: In the Expand Data dialog box, remove Data in the column name prefix textbox.)
d. Rename the column headers as follows: Column1: **Office**, Column2: **Quarter 1**, Column3: **Quarter 2**, Column4: **Quarter 3**, Column5: **Quarter 4**.
e. Rename the query **Broadband**, load the data into Excel, then delete Sheet1.
f. Format the table with the table style Light Blue, Table Style Light 16 (the third style from the left in the third row under Light), then format the data in cells B2:E5 using the Accounting style with the $ symbol and no decimal places.
g. Use the Get & Transform tool to import the data from the tab-delimited text file Support_EX_7-16 into the Power Query Editor. Delete any duplicate rows then rename the query **Data Center**. Load the data into the Excel workbook.
h. Format the table with the table style Light Blue, Table Style Light 16, then format the data in cells B2:E5 using the Accounting style with the $ symbol and no decimal places.
i. Use the Get & Transform tool to import the data from the Tower table in the Access file Support_EX_7-17 into the Power Query Editor.
j. Delete the first column, then load the data into Excel.
k. Format the table with the table style Light Blue, Table Style Light 16, then format the Tower data in cells B2:E5 with the Accounting style with the $ symbol and no decimal places.
l. On the Tower worksheet, insert four blank rows at the top of the worksheet.
m. Insert the image file Support_EX_7-18 and resize it to fit in rows 1 through 4.
n. Apply the Center Shadow Rectangle Picture Style (first style on the left in the third row), then change the picture border color to White, Background 1 under Theme colors. Resize the picture to fit the image and the border in the first four rows. Move the picture so it appears centered above the worksheet data.
o. Add Alt Text of **Annual revenue report for tower sector** to the picture.
p. Compare your Tower worksheet to **Figure 7-23**.

**Figure 7-23**

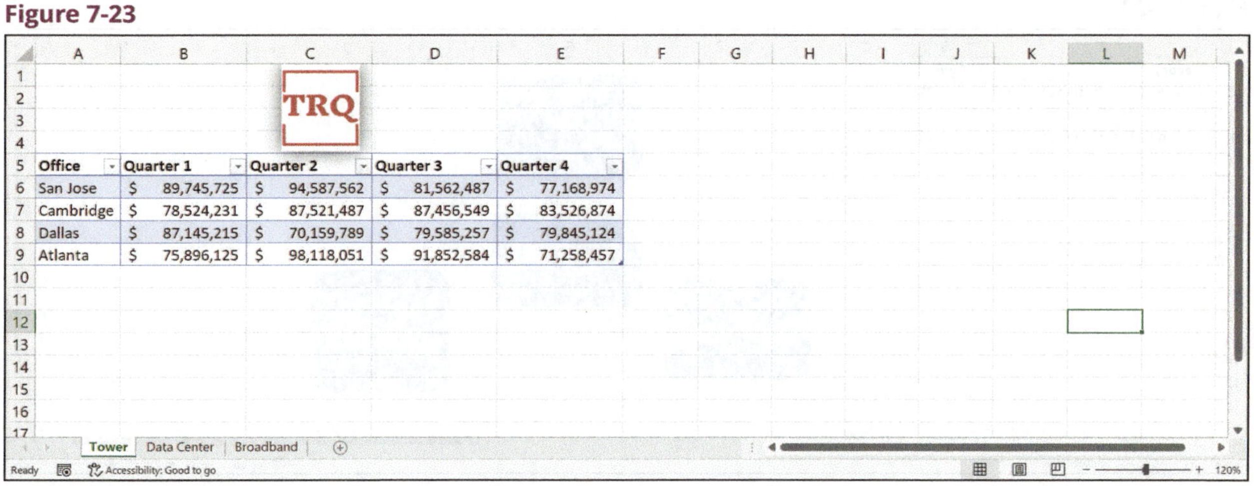

## Independent Challenge 1 (Continued)

q. Group the worksheets, add the sheet name to the center section of the header, add your name to the center section of the footer, preview the workbook, ungroup the worksheets, save and close the workbook, then submit the workbook to your instructor.

## Independent Challenge 2

You are the assistant director of HR at an EV startup. The HR Department uses short, frequent employee satisfaction surveys to assess the organizational health of the company. The results of a recent three-question survey focused on management are stored in an html file and you will import this data into Excel for analysis.

a. Start Excel, create a new workbook, then save it as **IL_EX_7_Survey** in the location where you store your Data Files.
b. Use the Get & Transform tool to import the Survey table from the web file Support_EX_7-19 into the Power Query Editor using the file's URL.
c. Delete any duplicate rows, then load the data into Excel.
d. Delete Sheet1, format the table with the table style Light Blue, Table Style Light 16 (the third style from left in the third row under Light), then format the data in cells B2:B4 using the Percent Style format.
e. Copy the range A1:B4, open the Word file IL_EX_7-20 from the location where you store your Data Files, then save it as **IL_EX_7_SurveyMemo**.
f. At the end of the memo body, paste the copied worksheet data by linking it and using destination styles.
g. Switch to Excel, then change the value in cell B2 to **72%**.
h. Activate the IL_EX_7_SurveyMemo document in Word, then update the linked data.
i. Enter your name in the header of the memo, save your changes, then close Word.
j. Activate the Excel workbook, on the Survey sheet click any cell outside the data, then insert a SmartArt graphic, choosing the Radial Cluster graphic in the Relationship category. (**Hints**: Click the Insert tab on the ribbon, then click the SmartArt button in the Illustrations group. The Radial Cluster graphic is in the seventh row of the Relationship category, second from the left.)
k. Close the Queries & Connections pane, then move the SmartArt graphic to line up the upper-left corner with the upper-left corner of cell D1.
l. Add the Alt Text, **Results of management culture survey** to the SmartArt graphic.
m. Add the imported survey data into the SmartArt graphic using Management Culture as the center of the graphic and the three categories as outside shapes. Resize the text in the SmartArt to 12, then resize the shapes to fit the larger text. (**Hint**: Press ENTER to move to the next line in a shape.)
n. Compare your chart to **Figure 7-24**.

**Figure 7-24**

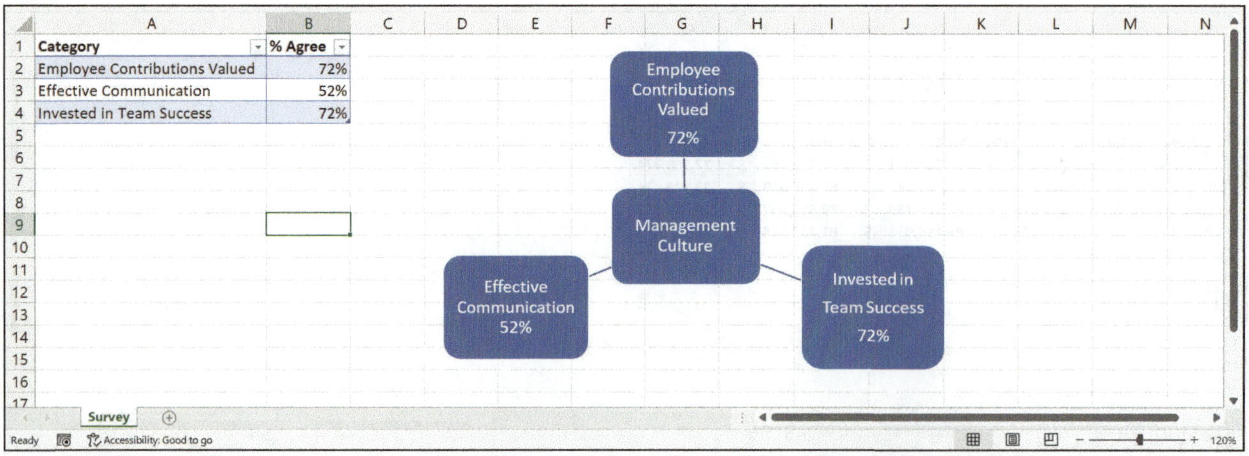

o. Change the SmartArt style to Polished (The first style in the 3-D section).

p. Change the SmartArt colors to Colorful – Accent Colors (The first color option in the Colorful Category. (**Hint**: Use the Change Colors tool on the SmartArt Design tab.)

q. Resize the SmartArt graphic proportionally to line up the lower-right corner with the lower-right corner of cell J15, then compare your worksheet to **Figure 7-25**.

r. Enter your name in the worksheet footer, change the orientation to landscape, preview the workbook, save and close the workbook, then submit the workbook to your instructor.

**Figure 7-25**

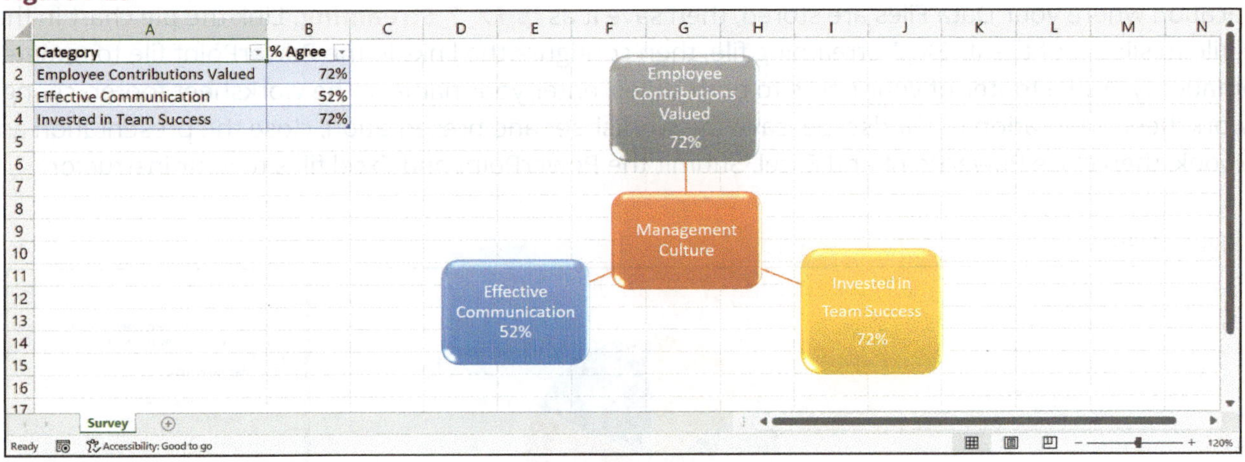

# Visual Workshop

Create a new blank workbook in Excel, then save the workbook in the location where you store your Data Files as **IL_EX_7_Media**. Using the text file Support_EX_7-21, create the 2-D pie chart displayed in **Figure 7-26**. (**Hints**: Use the Power Query Editor to remove duplicate data; after loading the data into Excel, format it using the Percent Style; remove Sheet1 from the workbook; remove the table style using the None style in the Table Styles gallery; the column headers are not part of the chart data; the data labels display the category names and percentages on the outside end of the data series; the legend and the chart title are removed; and the Alt Text is **User age demographics**.) Open the PowerPoint file IL_EX_7-22.pptx from the location where your Data Files are stored, then save it as **IL_EX_7_Streaming**. Link the pie chart in the Excel file to slide 2 of the IL_EX_7_Streaming file, then configure the links in the PowerPoint file to update automatically. Add a footer of your name to both slides, enter your name in the worksheet footer, change the worksheet orientation to Landscape, save the worksheet and presentation, close the presentation and workbook, then close PowerPoint and Excel. Submit the PowerPoint and Excel files to your instructor.

**Figure 7-26**

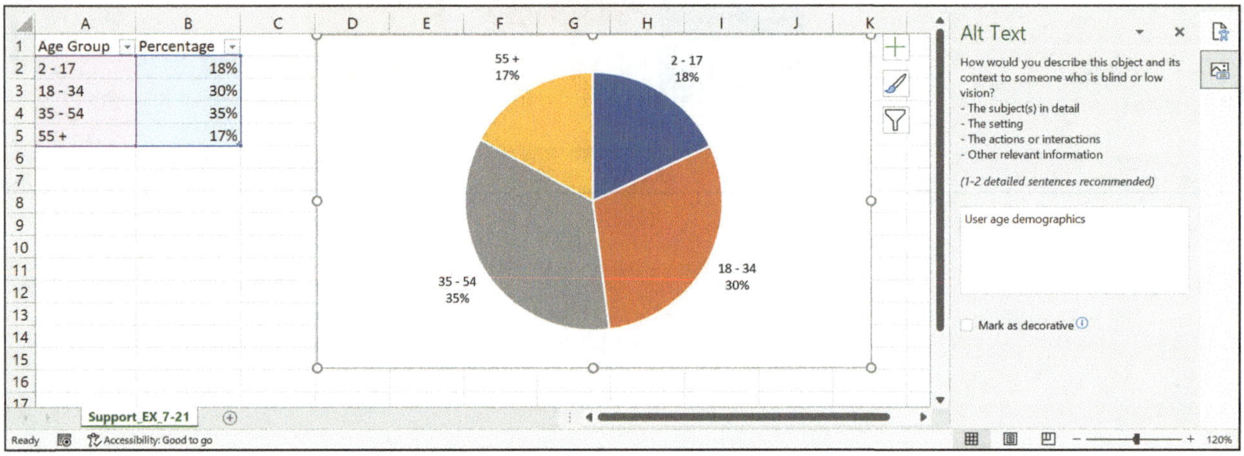

# Analyzing Data with PivotTables

## Case

Bayside uses PivotTables to analyze company data. Zahra Khan, the manager of the Southern U.S. offices, is preparing for a meeting with the company's VP of Finance. Zahra asks for your help in summarizing last quarter's employee business expenses by type, office, and division. You will create a PivotTable to summarize this data and illustrate the information graphically using a PivotChart.

## Module Objectives

After completing this module, you will be able to:

- Plan and design a PivotTable report
- Create a PivotTable report
- Change a PivotTable's summary function and design
- Filter PivotTable data
- Change the organization of PivotTable data
- Create a PivotChart report
- Update a PivotTable report
- Extract information from a PivotTable

### Files You Will Need

IL_EX_8-1.xlsx
IL_EX_8-2.xlsx
IL_EX_8-3.xlsx
IL_EX_8-4.xlsx
IL_EX_8-5.xlsx

# Plan and Design a PivotTable Report

**Case** Zahra asks you to design a PivotTable to display last quarter's business expense information for its offices in the South. You begin by reviewing guidelines for creating PivotTables.

**Objectives**
- Explain the function of PivotTable components
- Explain the six steps in designing a PivotTable

The PivotTable Report feature lets you summarize large amounts of worksheet data in a compact table format. Then you can freely rearrange, or "pivot," PivotTable rows and columns to explore the relationships within your data. Before you begin creating a PivotTable report (often simply called a PivotTable), you need to review the data and consider how a PivotTable can best summarize it.

## Details

**Before you create a PivotTable, think about the following guidelines:**

- **Review the source data**
  Before you can effectively summarize data in a PivotTable, you need to understand the source data's scope and structure. The source data does not have to be defined as a table, but it should be in a table-like format; that is, it should have column headings and the same type of data in each column, and it should not have any blank rows or columns. To create a meaningful PivotTable, ensure that at least one of the fields has repeated information so that the PivotTable can effectively group it. Also, be sure to include numeric data that the PivotTable can total for each group. The data columns represent categories of data, which are called fields, just as in a table. You are working with expense information that Zahra received from Bayside's Southern office managers, displayed in **Figure 8-1**. Information is repeated in the Employee ID, Division, Office, and Type columns, and numeric information is displayed in the Amount column, so you can summarize this data effectively in a PivotTable.
- **Determine the purpose of the PivotTable**
  The purpose of your PivotTable is to summarize expense information by type and office across various divisions.
- **Identify the fields you want to include**
  You want your PivotTable to summarize the data in the Division, Office, Type, and Amount columns, so you need to include those fields in your PivotTable.
- **Determine which field contains the data you want to summarize and which summary function you want to use**
  The Bayside offices are organized into four divisions, Cloud Services, IT Consulting, Security Consulting, and Support. You want to summarize expense information by summing the amount field for each type by office and division. You'll do this by using the Sum function.
- **Decide how you want to arrange the data**
  The PivotTable layout you choose determines the information you want to communicate. Division values will appear in the PivotTable columns, type and office values will appear in rows, and the PivotTable will summarize amount figures, as displayed in **Figure 8-2**.
- **Determine the location of the PivotTable**
  You can place a PivotTable in any worksheet of any workbook. Placing a PivotTable on a separate worksheet makes it easier to locate and prevents you from accidentally overwriting parts of an existing sheet. You decide to create the PivotTable as a new worksheet in the current workbook.

**Figure 8-1:** Expense data

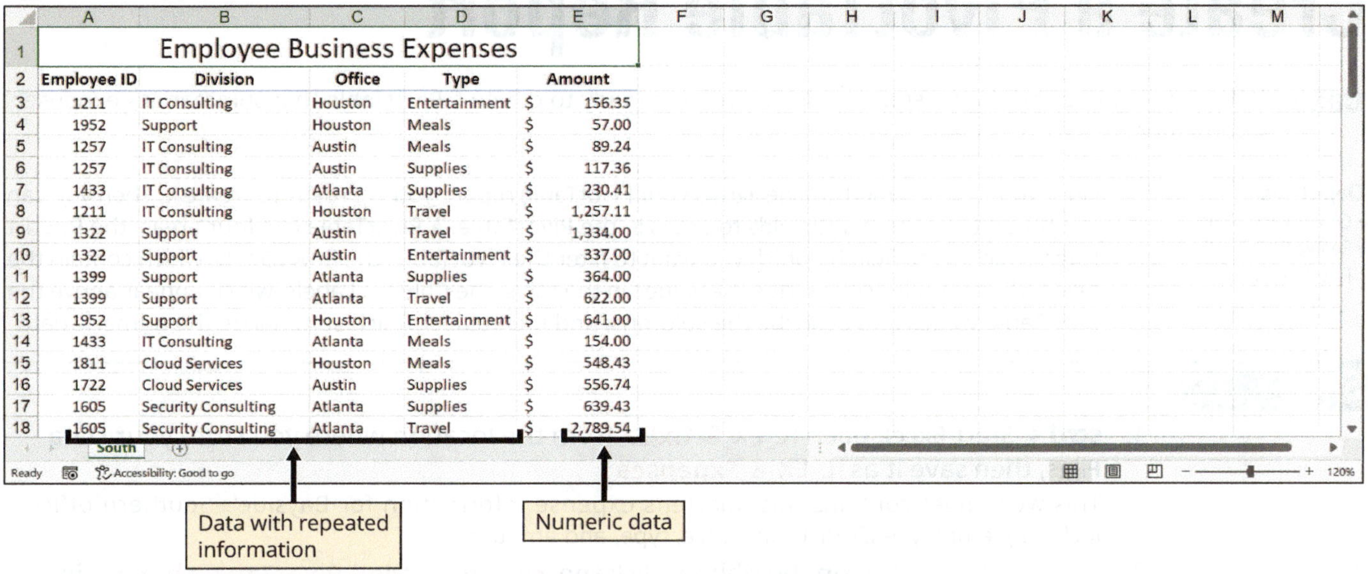

| | A | B | C | D | E |
|---|---|---|---|---|---|
| 1 | Employee Business Expenses | | | | |
| 2 | Employee ID | Division | Office | Type | Amount |
| 3 | 1211 | IT Consulting | Houston | Entertainment | $ 156.35 |
| 4 | 1952 | Support | Houston | Meals | $ 57.00 |
| 5 | 1257 | IT Consulting | Austin | Meals | $ 89.24 |
| 6 | 1257 | IT Consulting | Austin | Supplies | $ 117.36 |
| 7 | 1433 | IT Consulting | Atlanta | Supplies | $ 230.41 |
| 8 | 1211 | IT Consulting | Houston | Travel | $ 1,257.11 |
| 9 | 1322 | Support | Austin | Travel | $ 1,334.00 |
| 10 | 1322 | Support | Austin | Entertainment | $ 337.00 |
| 11 | 1399 | Support | Atlanta | Supplies | $ 364.00 |
| 12 | 1399 | Support | Atlanta | Travel | $ 622.00 |
| 13 | 1952 | Support | Houston | Entertainment | $ 641.00 |
| 14 | 1433 | IT Consulting | Atlanta | Meals | $ 154.00 |
| 15 | 1811 | Cloud Services | Houston | Meals | $ 548.43 |
| 16 | 1722 | Cloud Services | Austin | Supplies | $ 556.74 |
| 17 | 1605 | Security Consulting | Atlanta | Supplies | $ 639.43 |
| 18 | 1605 | Security Consulting | Atlanta | Travel | $ 2,789.54 |



**Figure 8-2:** PivotTable report based on expense data

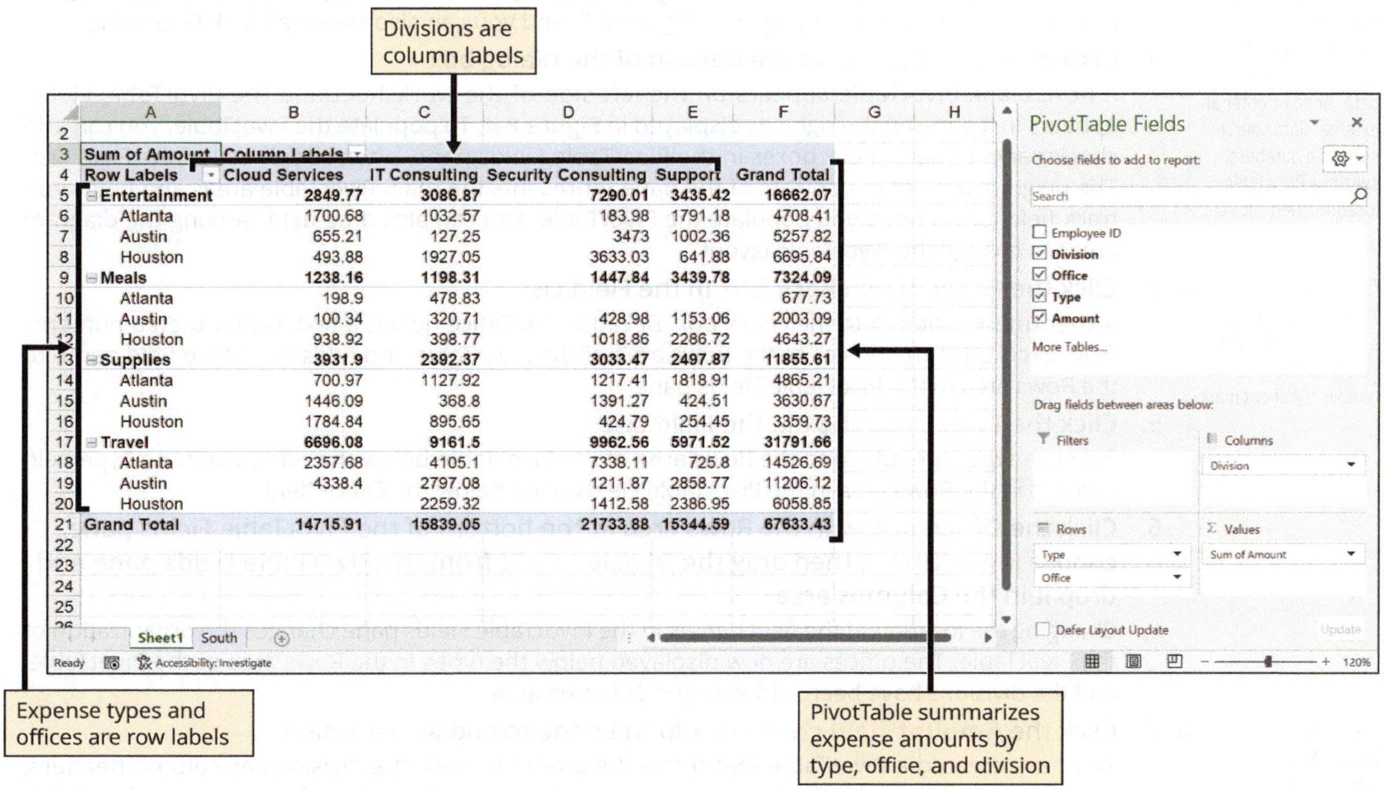

| | A | B | C | D | E | F |
|---|---|---|---|---|---|---|
| 3 | Sum of Amount | Column Labels | | | | |
| 4 | Row Labels | Cloud Services | IT Consulting | Security Consulting | Support | Grand Total |
| 5 | **Entertainment** | **2849.77** | **3086.87** | **7290.01** | **3435.42** | **16662.07** |
| 6 | Atlanta | 1700.68 | 1032.57 | 183.98 | 1791.18 | 4708.41 |
| 7 | Austin | 655.21 | 127.25 | 3473 | 1002.36 | 5257.82 |
| 8 | Houston | 493.88 | 1927.05 | 3633.03 | 641.88 | 6695.84 |
| 9 | **Meals** | **1238.16** | **1198.31** | **1447.84** | **3439.78** | **7324.09** |
| 10 | Atlanta | 198.9 | 478.83 | | | 677.73 |
| 11 | Austin | 100.34 | 320.71 | 428.98 | 1153.06 | 2003.09 |
| 12 | Houston | 938.92 | 398.77 | 1018.86 | 2286.72 | 4643.27 |
| 13 | **Supplies** | **3931.9** | **2392.37** | **3033.47** | **2497.87** | **11855.61** |
| 14 | Atlanta | 700.97 | 1127.92 | 1217.41 | 1818.91 | 4865.21 |
| 15 | Austin | 1446.09 | 368.8 | 1391.27 | 424.51 | 3630.67 |
| 16 | Houston | 1784.84 | 895.65 | 424.79 | 254.45 | 3359.73 |
| 17 | **Travel** | **6696.08** | **9161.5** | **9962.56** | **5971.52** | **31791.66** |
| 18 | Atlanta | 2357.68 | 4105.1 | 7338.11 | 725.8 | 14526.69 |
| 19 | Austin | 4338.4 | 2797.08 | 1211.87 | 2858.77 | 11206.12 |
| 20 | Houston | | 2259.32 | 1412.58 | 2386.95 | 6058.85 |
| 21 | **Grand Total** | **14715.91** | **15839.05** | **21733.88** | **15344.59** | **67633.43** |

# Create a PivotTable Report

**Case** With the planning and design stage complete, you are ready to create a PivotTable that summarizes expense information.

**Objectives**
- Create a PivotTable
- Reorganize PivotTable data

Once you have planned and designed your PivotTable report, you are ready to create it. Then you can **populate** it, meaning add fields to areas in the PivotTable. A PivotTable has four areas: the Report Filter, which is the field by which you want to filter the PivotTable; the Row Labels, which contain the fields whose labels will describe the values in the rows; the Column Labels, which appear above the PivotTable values and describe the columns; and the Values, which summarize the numeric data.

## Steps

1. **sam Start Excel, open IL_EX_8-1.xlsx from the location where you store your Data Files, then save it as IL_EX_8_Expenses**
   This worksheet contains this quarter's expense information for Bayside's Southern offices, including employee ID, division, office, type, and amount.

2. **Click the Insert tab on the ribbon, click the Recommended PivotTables button in the Tables group, then click each of the recommended layouts on the left side of the Recommended PivotTables dialog box, scrolling as necessary**
   The Recommended PivotTables dialog box displays recommended PivotTable layouts that summarize your data, as displayed in **Figure 8-3**, and you can also create a blank PivotTable.

   **Quick Tip**
   To create a blank PivotTable without reviewing recommended ones, click the PivotTable button in the Tables group, verify your data range or enter an external data source such as a database, specify a PivotTable location, then click OK.

3. **Click Blank PivotTable at the bottom of the dialog box**
   A new, blank PivotTable appears on the left side of the worksheet and the PivotTable Fields appears in a pane on the right, as displayed in **Figure 8-4**. To populate the PivotTable, you can add checkmarks to field check boxes in the PivotTable Fields pane, often simply called the Field List. The diagram area at the bottom of the pane represents the main PivotTable areas and helps you track field locations as you populate the PivotTable. You can also drag fields among the diagram areas to change the PivotTable layout.

4. **Click the Office field check box in the Field List**
   A checkmark is added to the check box. Because the Office field is a text, rather than a numeric, field, Excel adds the offices to the Rows area of the PivotTable and adds the Office field name to the Rows area in the PivotTable Fields pane.

   **Quick Tip**
   To remove a field from a PivotTable, click the field's check box to remove the check mark.

5. **Click the Type check box in the Field List**
   Expense types are added to the Rows area of the PivotTable below the offices and the Type field name is in the Rows area in the PivotTable Fields pane below the Office field.

6. **Click the Office arrow in the Rows area at the bottom of the PivotTable Fields pane, choose Move Down, then drag the Division field from the PivotTable Fields pane and drop it in the Columns area**
   Changing the location of the field names in the PivotTable Fields pane changes the organization of the PivotTable. The offices are now displayed below the types in the Rows area of the PivotTable, and the divisions have been added to the Columns area.

7. **Click the Amount field check box in the pane to add a checkmark**
   You have created a PivotTable that totals the amounts, with the divisions as column headers, and types of expenses and offices as row labels. Sum is the Excel default function for data fields containing numbers, so Excel automatically calculates the sum of the amounts. The PivotTable indicates that travel expenses were almost twice the entertainment expenses and more than four times the meals expenses, as displayed in **Figure 8-5**.

   **Trouble**
   In your PivotTable, if the order of Type fields doesn't match the order shown in Figure 8-5, click the Row Labels arrow in cell A4, then click Sort A to Z.

8. **Click the Collapse button [−] to the left of the Entertainment label**
   The office details for the entertainment type are no longer visible. When you have two levels of data in the rows or columns area, you can drill down and drill up in the data to expand or collapse the second-level field details below the top field.

9. **Click the Expand button [+] to the left of the Entertainment label, change the name of Sheet1 to PivotTable, then save the workbook**
   Renaming an unnamed worksheet to a relevant sheet name improves the accessibility for all users and changes the accessibility investigate message to Good to go.

**Figure 8-3:** Recommended PivotTables dialog box

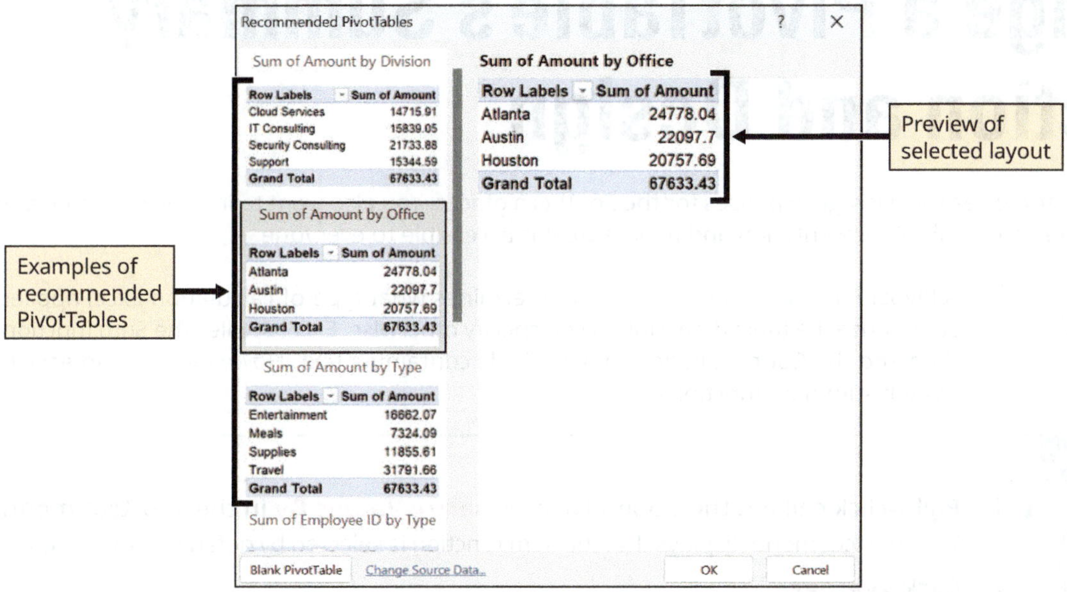


**Figure 8-4:** Empty PivotTable ready to receive field data

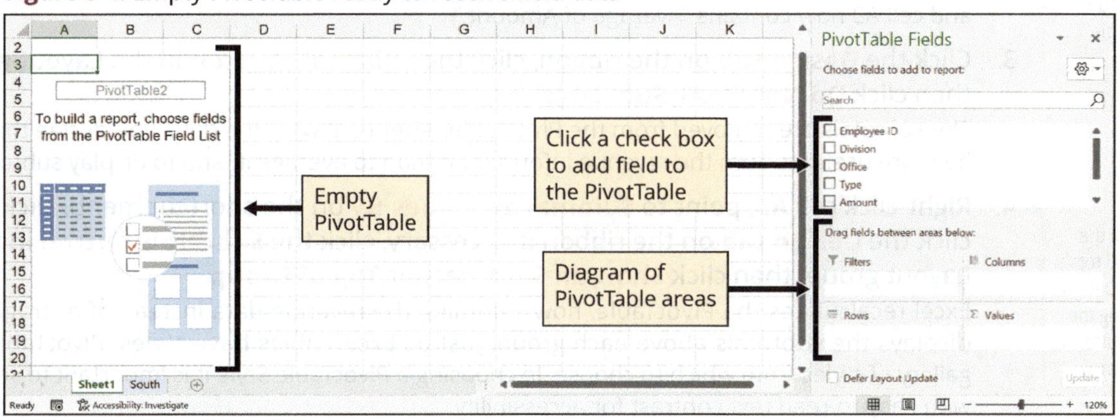


**Figure 8-5:** New PivotTable with fields in place

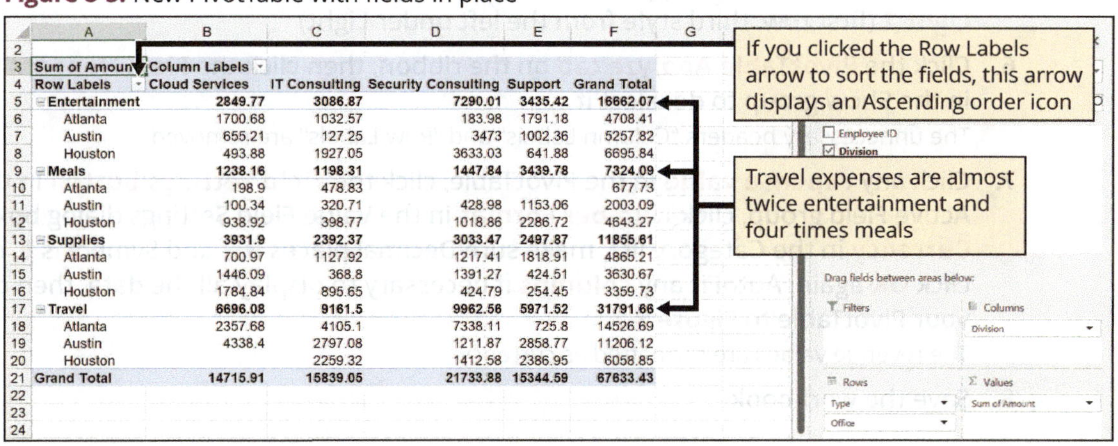


## Changing a PivotTable layout

The default layout for PivotTables is Show in Compact Form; the row labels are displayed in a single column, and the second-level field items (such as the offices in the Bayside example) are indented for readability. You can change the layout of your PivotTable by clicking the Design tab, clicking the Report Layout button in the Layout group, then clicking either Show in Outline Form or Show in Tabular Form. The tabular form and the outline form display each row label in its own column. The tabular and outline layouts take up more space on a worksheet than the compact layout.

# Change a PivotTable's Summary Function and Design

**Case** You want to see the average expenses for the Southern offices. You also want to improve the appearance of the PivotTable for Zahra's presentation and make sure it is accessible to everyone.

**Objectives**
- Change a PivotTable's summary function
- Format a PivotTable

A PivotTable's **summary function** determines what type of calculation Excel applies or uses to summarize the table data. Unless you specify otherwise, Excel applies the Sum function to numeric data and the Count function to data fields containing text. However, you can easily change the default summary functions.

## Steps

**Quick Tip**
You can also change the summary function by clicking the Field Settings button in the Active Field group on the PivotTable Analyze tab.

**Quick Tip**
You can control the display of grand totals by clicking the Design tab, then clicking the Grand Totals button in the Layout group.

1. **Right-click cell A3, then point to Summarize Values By in the shortcut menu**
   The shortcut menu displays that the Sum function is selected by default, as displayed in **Figure 8-6**.
2. **Click Average**
   The data area of the PivotTable displays the average expenses for each division by type and office, and cell A3 now contains "Average of Amount."
3. **Click the Design tab on the ribbon, click the Subtotals button in the Layout group, then click Do Not Show Subtotals**
   The subtotals are removed from the PivotTable. After reviewing the data, you decide that it would be more useful to sum the revenue information than to average it, and to display subtotals.
4. **Right-click cell A3, point to Summarize Values By on the shortcut menu, click Sum, click the Design tab on the ribbon if necessary, click the Subtotals button in the Layout group, then click Show all Subtotals at Top of Group**
   Excel recalculates the PivotTable, now summing the revenue data instead of averaging it, and displays the subtotals above each group. Just as Excel tables have styles, PivotTables have a gallery of styles from which to choose. In choosing a PivotTable Style it is important to select styles with easy-to-read text contrast for accessibility.
5. **Click the More button in the PivotTable Styles gallery, then click White, Pivot Style Light 2 (first row, third style from the left under Light)**
6. **Click the PivotTable Analyze tab on the ribbon, then click the Field Headers button in the Show group to deselect it**
   The unnecessary headers "Column Labels" and "Row Labels" are removed.
7. **Click any expense value in the PivotTable, click the Field Settings button in the Active Field group, click Number Format in the Value Field Settings dialog box, click Currency in the Category list, make sure Decimal places is 2 and Symbol is $, click OK, click OK again, AutoFit any columns if necessary to display all the data, then compare your PivotTable to Figure 8-7**
   The revenue values are formatted as currency.
8. **Save the workbook**

**Figure 8-6:** Shortcut menu displaying Sum function selected

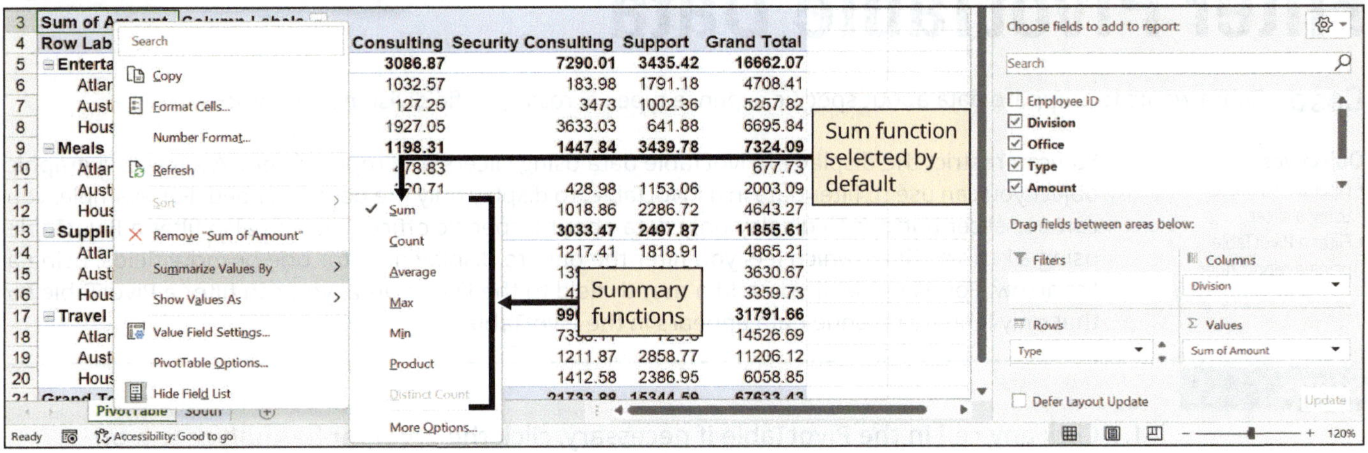


**Figure 8-7:** Formatted PivotTable

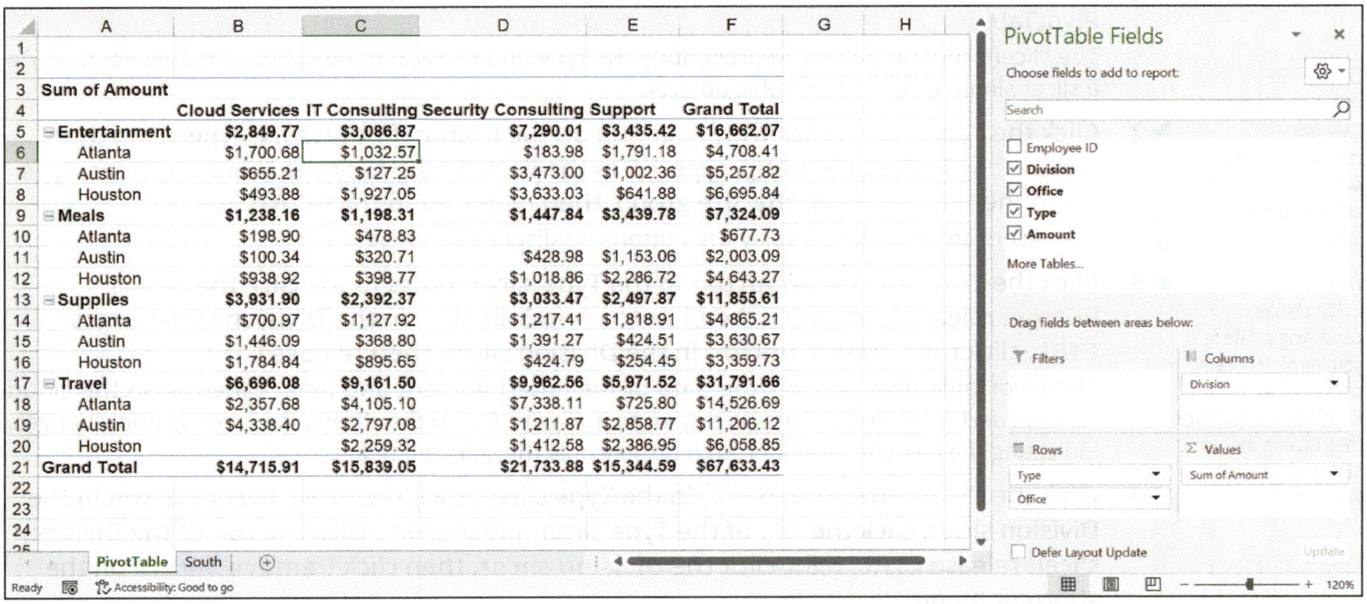

| Sum of Amount | Cloud Services | IT Consulting | Security Consulting | Support | Grand Total |
|---|---|---|---|---|---|
| Entertainment | $2,849.77 | $3,086.87 | $7,290.01 | $3,435.42 | $16,662.07 |
| Atlanta | $1,700.68 | $1,032.57 | $183.98 | $1,791.18 | $4,708.41 |
| Austin | $655.21 | $127.25 | $3,473.00 | $1,002.36 | $5,257.82 |
| Houston | $493.88 | $1,927.05 | $3,633.03 | $641.88 | $6,695.84 |
| Meals | $1,238.16 | $1,198.31 | $1,447.84 | $3,439.78 | $7,324.09 |
| Atlanta | $198.90 | $478.83 | | | $677.73 |
| Austin | $100.34 | $320.71 | $428.98 | $1,153.06 | $2,003.09 |
| Houston | $938.92 | $398.77 | $1,018.86 | $2,286.72 | $4,643.27 |
| Supplies | $3,931.90 | $2,392.37 | $3,033.47 | $2,497.87 | $11,855.61 |
| Atlanta | $700.97 | $1,127.92 | $1,217.41 | $1,818.91 | $4,865.21 |
| Austin | $1,446.09 | $368.80 | $1,391.27 | $424.51 | $3,630.67 |
| Houston | $1,784.84 | $895.65 | $424.79 | $254.45 | $3,359.73 |
| Travel | $6,696.08 | $9,161.50 | $9,962.56 | $5,971.52 | $31,791.66 |
| Atlanta | $2,357.68 | $4,105.10 | $7,338.11 | $725.80 | $14,526.69 |
| Austin | $4,338.40 | $2,797.08 | $1,211.87 | $2,858.77 | $11,206.12 |
| Houston | | $2,259.32 | $1,412.58 | $2,386.95 | $6,058.85 |
| Grand Total | $14,715.91 | $15,839.05 | $21,733.88 | $15,344.59 | $67,633.43 |

### Using the Show buttons

To display and hide PivotTable elements, you can use the toggle buttons in the Show group on the PivotTable Analyze tab. For example, clicking the Field List button hides or displays the PivotTable Fields pane. Clicking the +/– button hides or displays the Expand and Collapse Outline buttons, and clicking the Field Headers button hides or displays the Row and Column Label headers on the PivotTable.

# Filter PivotTable Data

**Case** Zahra wants to compare data about specific expense types across specific divisions and offices.

**Objectives**
- Filter a PivotTable using a slicer
- Filter a PivotTable using a report filter

You can restrict the display of PivotTable data using slicers and report filters. A **slicer** is a graphic object you can use to filter data in a PivotTable, to display only the data you need. For example, you can use slicer buttons to display only data about a specific office. You can also filter a PivotTable using a **report filter**, which lets you filter the data to display data for one or more fields, using a list arrow. For example, if you add a month field to the Filters area, you can filter a PivotTable so that only January revenue data appears in the PivotTable.

## Steps

1. **Click any cell in the PivotTable if necessary, click the PivotTable Analyze tab on the ribbon if necessary, click the Insert Slicer button in the Filter group, in the Insert Slicers dialog box click the Type check box and the Division check box to add checkmarks to both fields, click OK, then drag both slicers to the right of the PivotTable**

   The slicers contain buttons representing the type and division names. You can move and resize a slicer similarly to other graphic objects.

2. **Click the Type slicer, click the Slicer tab on the ribbon if necessary, type 1.5 in the Height box in the Size group, type 1.5 in the Width box, click the Division slicer, type 1.5 in the Height box in the Size group, then type 1.75 in the Width box**

   The slicers are resized to display the buttons, as displayed in **Figure 8-8**.

3. **Click the Entertainment button in the Type slicer, press CTRL, click the Meals button, release CTRL, click the Cloud Services button in the Division slicer, press CTRL, click the Support button in the Division slicer, then release CTRL**

   The PivotTable displays only the data of the entertainment and meal expenses in the cloud services and support divisions, as displayed in **Figure 8-9**. In the slicers, the Filter symbol changes, indicating the PivotTable is filtered to display only the selected fields.

4. **Click the Clear Filter button in the Type slicer, click the Clear Filter button in the Division slicer, click the top of the Type slicer, press CTRL, click the top of the Division slicer, release CTRL, right-click the Division slicer, then click Remove Slicers on the shortcut menu**

   The filters are cleared and the slicers are removed.

5. **In the PivotTable Fields pane, click the Office field arrow in the Rows area, then click Move to Report Filter in the list that opens**

   The Office field moves to cell A1, and a list arrow and the word "(All)" appears in cell B1. The list arrow lets you filter the data in the PivotTable by Office. "(All)" indicates that the PivotTable currently displays data for all offices.

6. **Click the cell B1 list arrow, click Atlanta, click OK, then save your work**

   The PivotTable filters the expense data to display the Atlanta office data only, as displayed in **Figure 8-10**. The Office field list arrow changes to a filter symbol. A filter symbol also appears to the right of the Office field in the PivotTable Fields pane, indicating that the PivotTable is filtered and summarizes only a portion of the PivotTable data.

**Quick Tip**
You can add a slicer style, edit a slicer caption, and change the button order using the buttons and options on the Slicer tab.

**Quick Tip**
In PivotTables containing a date field, you can filter data by date by clicking the PivotTable Analyze tab, then clicking the Insert Timeline button in the Filter group.

**Trouble**
If the PivotTable Fields pane is not visible, click the PivotTable Analyze tab, then click the Field List button in the Show group.

**Figure 8-8:** Slicers for Type and Division fields

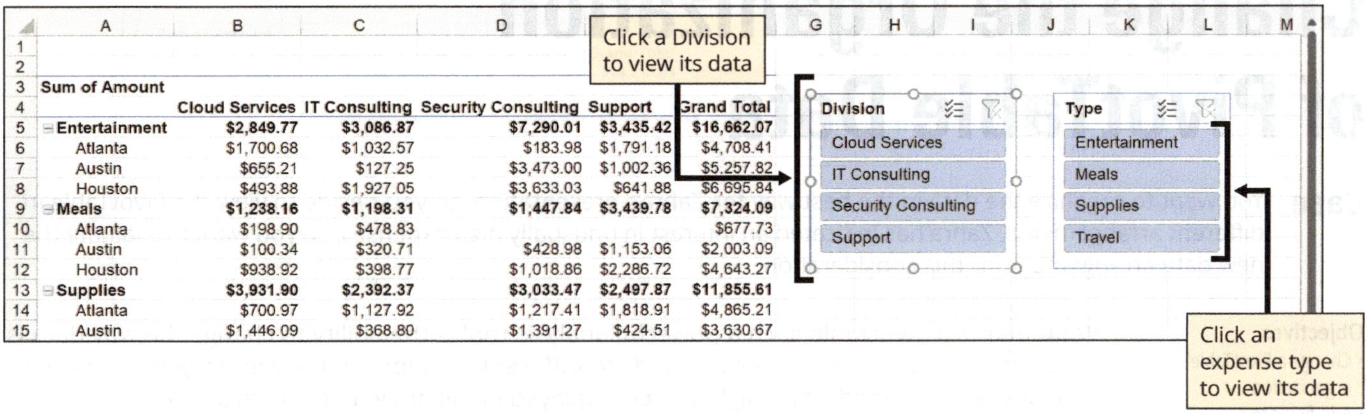


**Figure 8-9:** PivotTable filtered by Type and Division

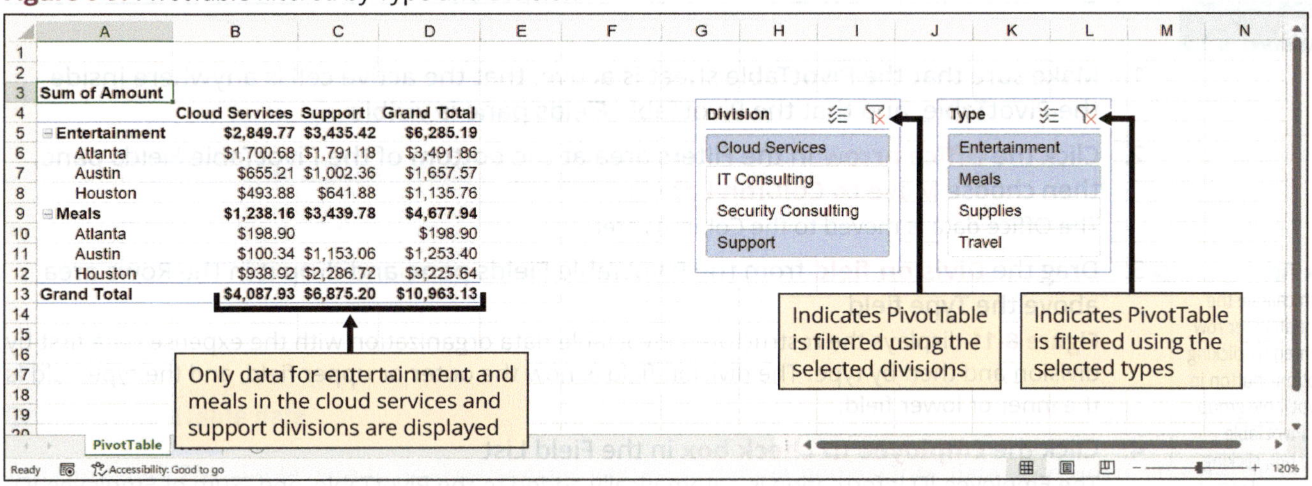


**Figure 8-10:** PivotTable filtered by Atlanta office

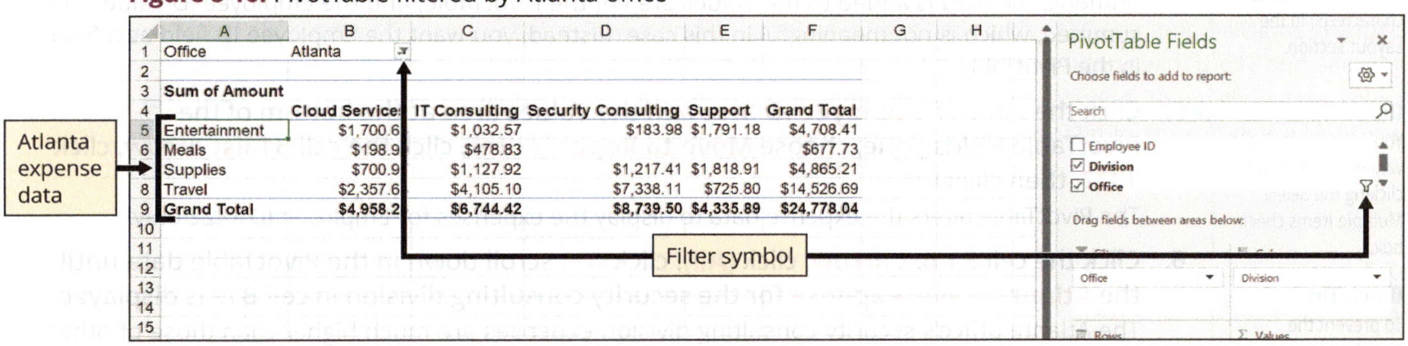


## Filtering PivotTables using multiple values

Instead of using slicers to display multiple values when filtering a PivotTable report, you can use a report filter. Slicers are generally easier to work with because they offer visual methods of filtering and can be moved around a worksheet, but there may be times you want to use a report filter, which is displayed in a fixed cell. After clicking a field's report filter list arrow in the top section of the PivotTable Fields pane or in cell B1 on the PivotTable itself, click the Select Multiple Items check box at the bottom of the filter selections. You can then select multiple values for the filter. For example, selecting quarters 1 and 2 as the report filter in a PivotTable with quarters displays all the data for those quarters. You can also select multiple values for the row and column labels by clicking the PivotTable Analyze tab, clicking the Field Headers button in the Show group, clicking the Row Labels list arrow or the Column Labels list arrow in cells A4 and B3 on the PivotTable, then selecting the data items that you want to display.

# Create a PivotChart Report

**Case** For her presentation, Zahra asks you to chart the expenses for all divisions in the Atlanta office.

**Objectives**
- Create a PivotChart
- Format a PivotChart

A **PivotChart report** is a chart that you create from data or from a PivotTable that lets you summarize and rearrange data to explore new relationships. **Table 8-1** describes how the elements in a PivotTable report correspond to the elements in a PivotChart report. When you create a PivotChart directly from data, Excel automatically creates a corresponding PivotTable report. If you change a PivotChart report by filtering the charted elements, Excel updates the corresponding PivotTable report to display the new data values. You can move the fields of a PivotChart using the PivotChart Fields List window; the new layout will be reflected in the PivotTable.

## Steps

1. **Click the Division arrow in the Rows area at the bottom of the PivotTable Fields pane, choose Move to Report Filter in the menu that opens, click the cell B2 list arrow, click Support, then click OK**
   All expense types for the support division in all offices are displayed in the PivotTable. You want to create the PivotChart from this PivotTable information.
2. **Click any cell in the PivotTable if necessary, click the PivotTable Analyze tab on the ribbon, then click the PivotChart button in the Tools group**
   The Insert Chart dialog box opens and displays a gallery of chart types.
3. **Click the Clustered Column chart if necessary, then click OK**
   The PivotChart appears on the worksheet, as displayed in **Figure 8-14**. The chart has field buttons that let you filter a PivotChart in the same way you do a PivotTable.
4. **Click the Office arrow on the chart, click Select All to deselect the selections, click the Atlanta checkbox, then click OK**
   Only the Atlanta support expense data is displayed in the chart.
5. **Click the PivotChart to select it if necessary, click the Design tab on the ribbon, click the Move Chart button in the Location group, click the New sheet option button, type PivotChart in the text box, then click OK**
6. **Click the Division field button at the top of the PivotChart, click All, click OK, right-click the PivotChart area, click Edit Alt Text, enter Atlanta expenses for all divisions, then click the Close button ☒ in the Alt Text pane**
   The chart is accessible and represents the Atlanta office's expenses for all divisions as displayed in **Figure 8-15**.
7. **Click the Design tab, click the Quick Layout button in the Chart Layouts group, click Layout 3, click the Chart Title element to select it, change the title to Atlanta Expenses, then click the Enter button ✓ in the formula bar**
   You can format a PivotChart by adding a chart style.
8. **Click Style 5 in the Chart Styles group, then save the workbook**
   **Figure 8-16** displays the formatted PivotChart report with the Atlanta office's expenses.

**Quick Tip**
You can change a PivotChart's type by clicking the Change Chart Type button in the Type group on the Design tab.

**Quick Tip**
You can drill up or down fields in a PivotChart using buttons to expand or collapse the second-level field details.

**Trouble**
Your screen may display View Alt Text rather than Edit Alt Text.

**Trouble**
If the chart title isn't selected, pressing ENTER will place a blank line in the title box.

**Figure 8-14:** PivotChart with support expenses

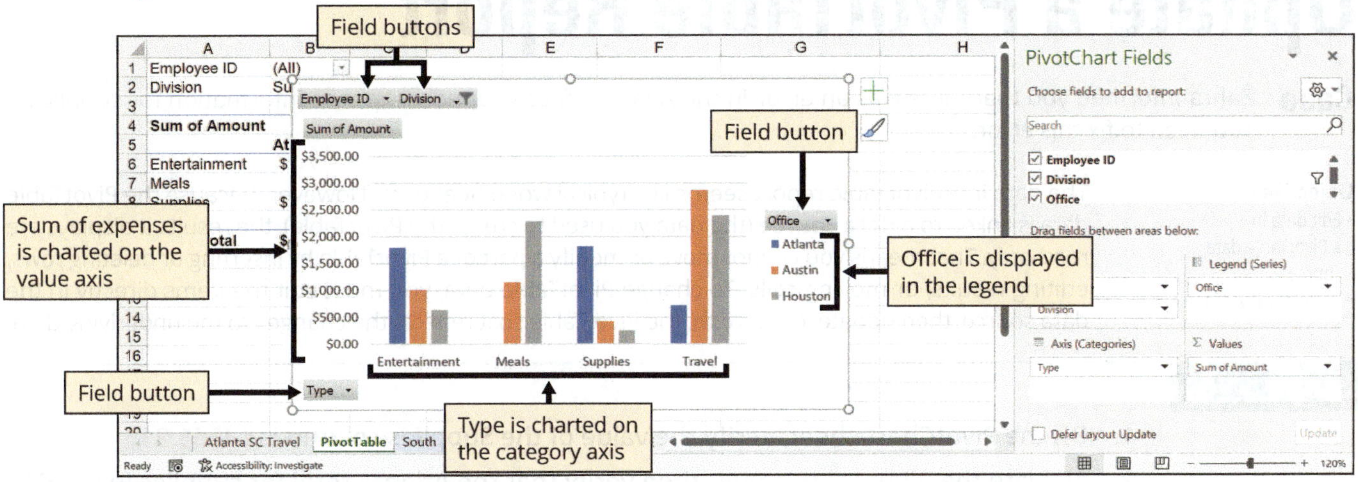


**Figure 8-15:** PivotChart displaying the Atlanta office's expenses

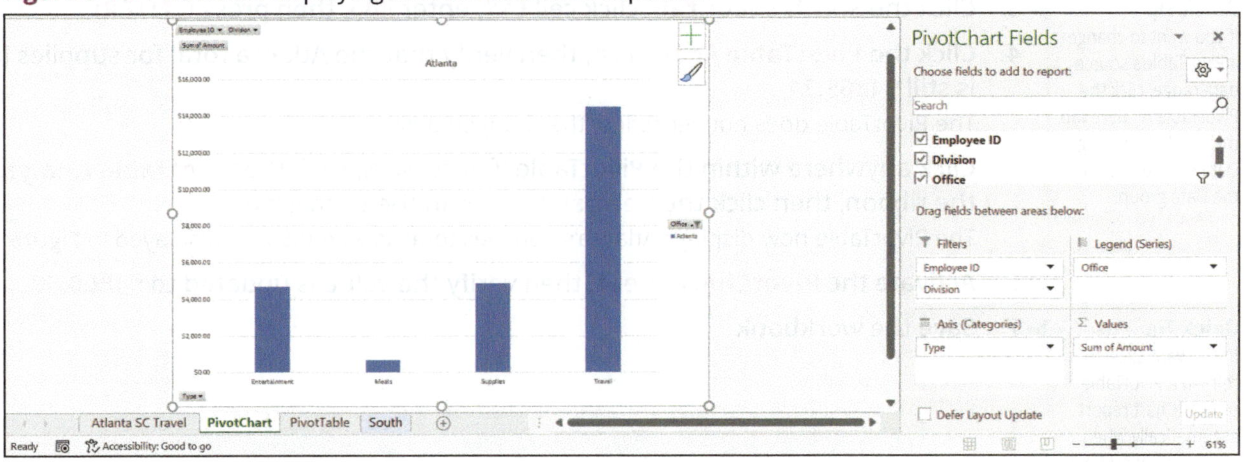


**Figure 8-16:** Formatted PivotChart report

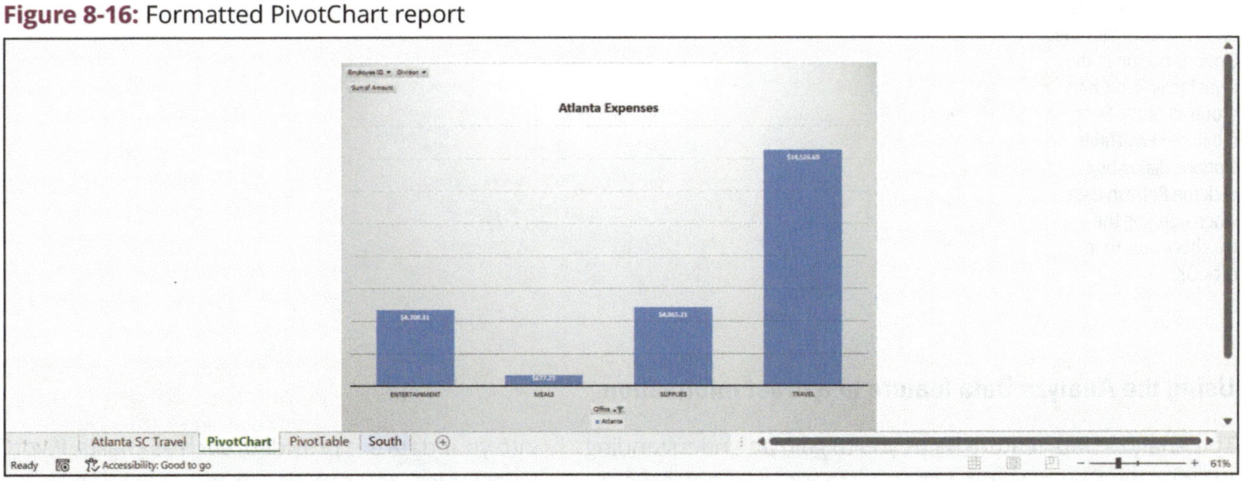


**Table 8-1:** PivotTable and PivotChart elements

| PivotTable items | PivotChart items | fields from lesson |
| --- | --- | --- |
| Row labels | Axis fields | Entertainment, Meals, Supplies, Travel |
| Column labels | Legend fields | Atlanta, Austin, Houston |
| Report Filters | Report Filters | Employee ID, Division |

# Update a PivotTable Report

**Case** Zahra informed you that there was an error in the Atlanta office's support expense information for supplies. You need to fix this error.

**Objectives**
- Edit data in a PivotTable data source
- Refresh a PivotTable

The data in a PivotTable report seems like typical worksheet data. However, because the PivotTable data is linked to a **data source** (the data you used to create the PivotTable), the results it displays are read-only. That means you cannot move or modify a part of a PivotTable by inserting or deleting rows, editing results, or moving cells. To change PivotTable data, you must edit the items directly in the data source, then update, or **refresh**, the PivotTable so it reflects the changes to the underlying data.

## Steps

1. **On the PivotChart sheet, verify the value of the Supplies column is $4865.21**
2. **Activate the PivotTable sheet, then verify that the Atlanta total for supplies in cell C8 is $4865.21**
3. **Click the South sheet tab, click cell E11, enter 300, then press [ENTER]**
4. **Click the PivotTable sheet tab, then verify that the Atlanta total for supplies in cell C8 is still $4865.21**
   The PivotTable does not yet reflect the changed data.
5. **Click anywhere within the PivotTable if necessary, click the PivotTable Analyze tab on the ribbon, then click the Refresh button in the Data group**
   The PivotTable now displays Atlanta's Supplies total as $4800.59, as displayed in **Figure 8-17**.
6. **Activate the PivotChart sheet, then verify the value is updated to $4800.59**
7. **Save the workbook**

**Quick Tip**
If you want to change a PivotTable's source data range, click the PivotTable Analyze tab, then click the Change Data Source button in the Data group.

**Quick Tip**
If you want Excel to refresh a PivotTable or PivotChart report automatically when you open a workbook, click the PivotTable/PivotChart Analyze tab on the ribbon, click the Options button in the PivotTable/PivotChart group, click the Data tab in the PivotTable Options dialog box, click the Refresh data when opening the file check box, then click OK.

### Using the Analyze Data feature to extract information

The Analyze Data feature helps you to gain an understanding of your data by providing charts, trends, and patterns. To access this information, select a cell in the table or data range, click the Analyze Data button in the Analysis group on the Home tab, then review the options provided in the Analyze Data pane. Many options for acquiring new insights into your data are provided, such as charts, PivotCharts, and PivotTables. You can also enter a question about your data or use suggested questions in the Analyze Data pane. The Analyze Data feature will answer your question and create a PivotTable and/or PivotChart on a new worksheet displaying the data organized to answer the question.

**Figure 8-17:** Updated PivotTable report

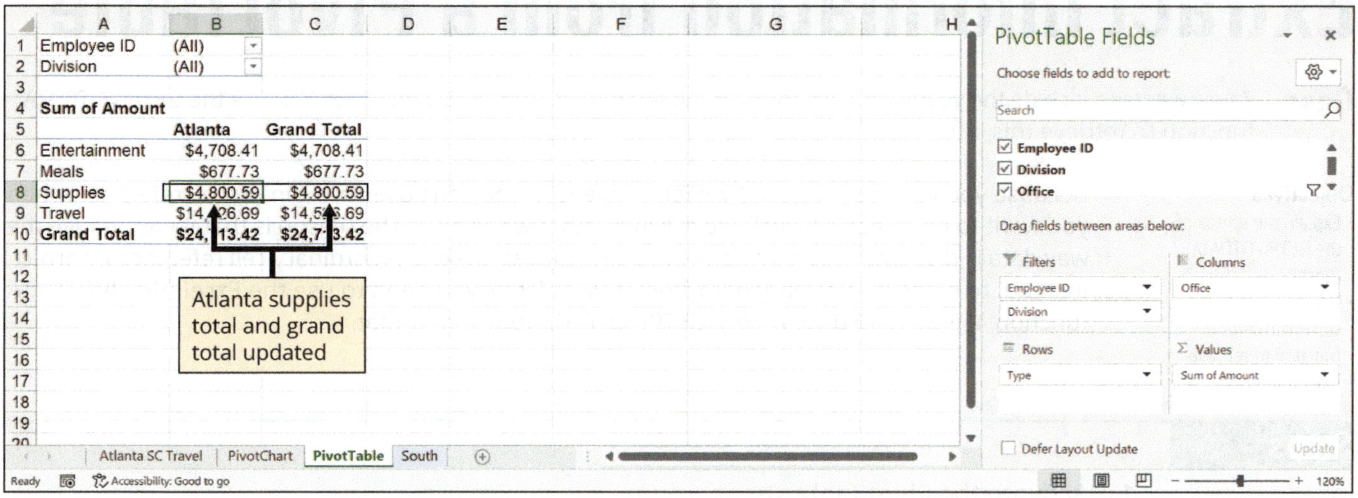


## Adding a calculated field to a PivotTable and a PivotChart

You can use formulas to analyze PivotTable and PivotChart data in a field by adding a calculated field. A calculated field appears in the PivotTable's or PivotChart's Field List and can be manipulated like other PivotTable fields. To add a calculated field, click any cell in the PivotTable, click the PivotTable Analyze tab, click the Fields, Items, & Sets button in the Calculations group, then click Calculated Field. The Insert Calculated Field dialog box opens. Enter the field name in the Name text box, click in the Formula text box, click a field name in the Field list that you want to use in the formula, then click Insert Field. After entering the formula in the Insert Calculated Field dialog box, click Add, then click OK. The new field with the formula results appears in the PivotTable and the PivotChart, and the field is added to the PivotTable and PivotChart Fields List pane. **Figure 8-18** displays a calculated field named Increase added to a PivotTable that calculates a 5% increase (using the formula = Amount*1.05).

**Figure 8-18:** PivotTable with calculated field

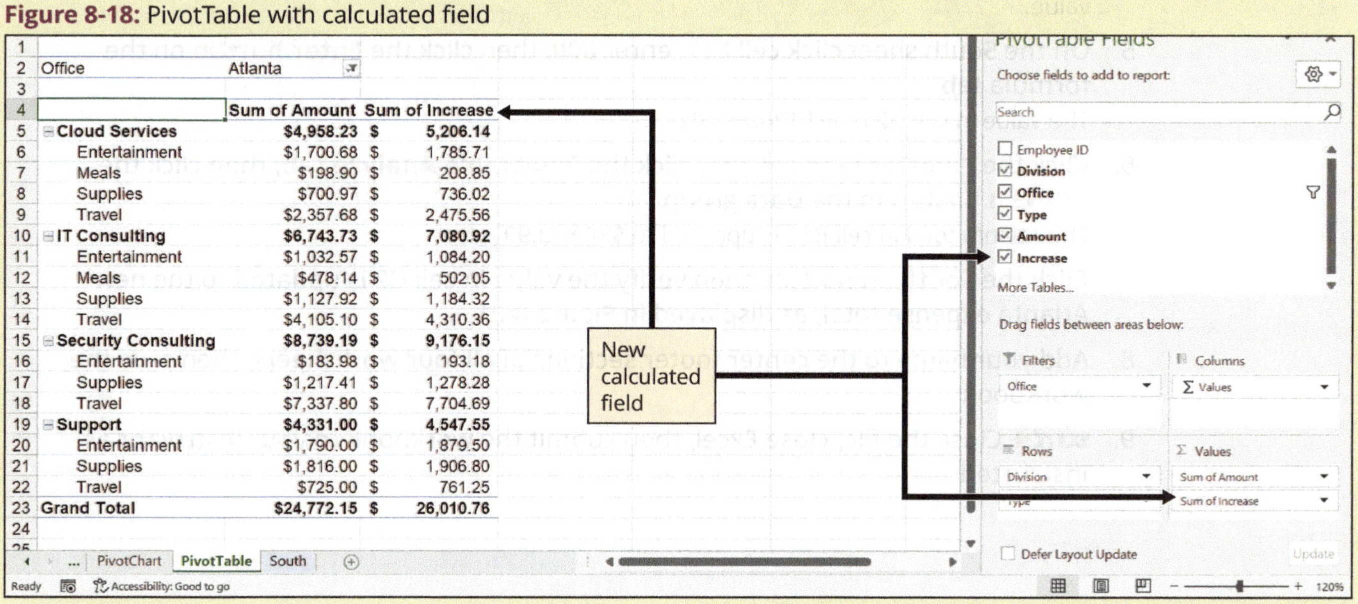

# Extract Information from a PivotTable

**Case** Zahra wants to include the yearly expense total for the Atlanta office in the South sheet. You use the GETPIVOTDATA function to retrieve this information.

**Objectives**
- Explain the syntax of the GETPIVOTDATA function
- Use the GETPIVOTDATA function to retrieve information

Because you can rearrange a PivotTable so easily, you can't use an ordinary cell reference when you want to reference a PivotTable cell in another worksheet. The reason is that if you change the way data is displayed in a PivotTable, the data moves, making an ordinary cell reference incorrect. Instead, to retrieve summary data from a PivotTable, you need to use the Excel GETPIVOTDATA function. **Figure 8-19** displays the GETPIVOTDATA function format.

## Steps

1. **Activate the PivotTable sheet**
   The revenue figures in the PivotTable are filtered to display only the Atlanta expenses.
2. **Activate the South sheet, click cell G1, type Total Atlanta Expenses, click the Enter button ✓ on the formula bar, click the Home tab on the ribbon if necessary, click the Align Right button ≡ in the Alignment group, click the Bold button B in the Font group, then adjust the width of column G to display the new label**
3. **Click cell G2, type =, click the PivotTable sheet tab, click cell B10 on the PivotTable, then click the Enter button on the formula bar**
   Cell B10 on the PivotTable contains the data you want to display on the South sheet. The GETPIVOTDATA function, along with its arguments, is inserted in cell G2 of the South sheet as displayed in **Figure 8-20**. You want to format this total.
4. **Click the Accounting Number Format button $ in the Number group**
   The current expense total for the Atlanta office is $24,713.42. This is the same value displayed in cell B10 of the PivotTable. The Atlanta office notifies you of a correction to the Atlanta supplies value.
5. **On the South sheet click cell E17, enter 800, then click the Enter button on the formula tab**
   The value in cell G2 is still $24,713.42.
6. **Click the PivotTable sheet tab, click the PivotTable Analyze tab, then click the Refresh button in the Data group**
   The Atlanta total in cell B10 is updated to $24,873.99
7. **Click the South sheet tab, then verify the value in cell G2 is updated to the new Atlanta expense total, as displayed in Figure 8-21**
8. **Add your name to the center footer sections of all four worksheets, then save the workbook**
9. **sam Close the file, close Excel, then submit the workbook to your instructor as instructed**

**Figure 8-19:** Format of GETPIVOTDATA function

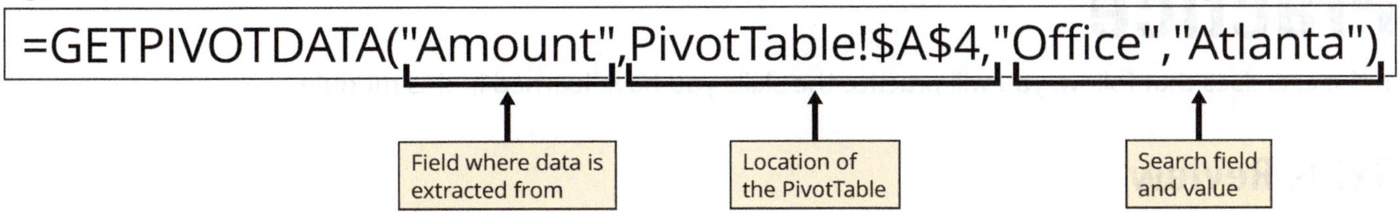


**Figure 8-20:** GETPIVOTDATA function in the South sheet

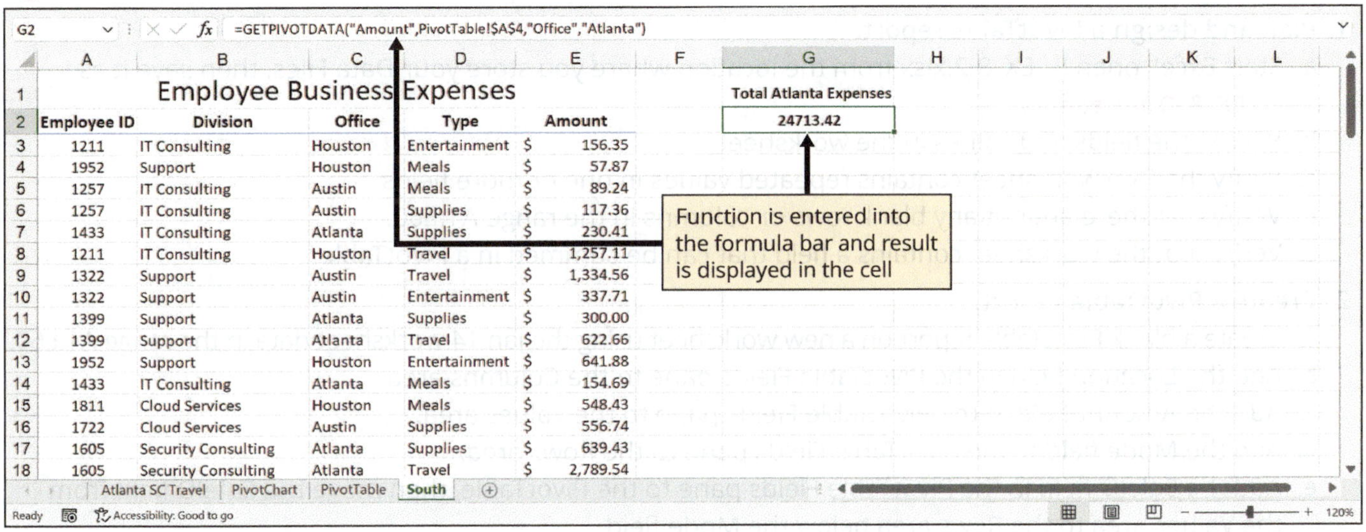


Employee Business Expenses

| Employee ID | Division | Office | Type | Amount |
|---|---|---|---|---|
| 1211 | IT Consulting | Houston | Entertainment | $ 156.35 |
| 1952 | Support | Houston | Meals | $ 57.87 |
| 1257 | IT Consulting | Austin | Meals | $ 89.24 |
| 1257 | IT Consulting | Austin | Supplies | $ 117.36 |
| 1433 | IT Consulting | Atlanta | Supplies | $ 230.41 |
| 1211 | IT Consulting | Houston | Travel | $ 1,257.11 |
| 1322 | Support | Austin | Travel | $ 1,334.56 |
| 1322 | Support | Austin | Entertainment | $ 337.71 |
| 1399 | Support | Atlanta | Supplies | $ 300.00 |
| 1399 | Support | Atlanta | Travel | $ 622.66 |
| 1952 | Support | Houston | Entertainment | $ 641.88 |
| 1433 | IT Consulting | Atlanta | Meals | $ 154.69 |
| 1811 | Cloud Services | Houston | Meals | $ 548.43 |
| 1722 | Cloud Services | Austin | Supplies | $ 556.74 |
| 1605 | Security Consulting | Atlanta | Supplies | $ 639.43 |
| 1605 | Security Consulting | Atlanta | Travel | $ 2,789.54 |

**Figure 8-21:** South worksheet displaying updated Atlanta expenses total

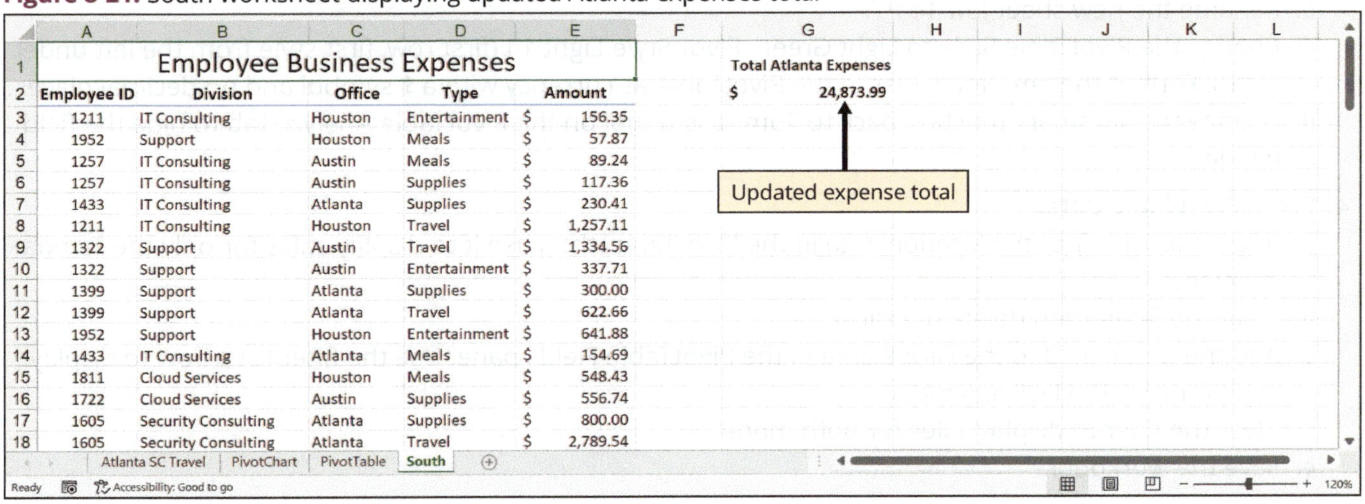


Employee Business Expenses

| Employee ID | Division | Office | Type | Amount |
|---|---|---|---|---|
| 1211 | IT Consulting | Houston | Entertainment | $ 156.35 |
| 1952 | Support | Houston | Meals | $ 57.87 |
| 1257 | IT Consulting | Austin | Meals | $ 89.24 |
| 1257 | IT Consulting | Austin | Supplies | $ 117.36 |
| 1433 | IT Consulting | Atlanta | Supplies | $ 230.41 |
| 1211 | IT Consulting | Houston | Travel | $ 1,257.11 |
| 1322 | Support | Austin | Travel | $ 1,334.56 |
| 1322 | Support | Austin | Entertainment | $ 337.71 |
| 1399 | Support | Atlanta | Supplies | $ 300.00 |
| 1399 | Support | Atlanta | Travel | $ 622.66 |
| 1952 | Support | Houston | Entertainment | $ 641.88 |
| 1433 | IT Consulting | Atlanta | Meals | $ 154.69 |
| 1811 | Cloud Services | Houston | Meals | $ 548.43 |
| 1722 | Cloud Services | Austin | Supplies | $ 556.74 |
| 1605 | Security Consulting | Atlanta | Supplies | $ 800.00 |
| 1605 | Security Consulting | Atlanta | Travel | $ 2,789.54 |

# Practice

In the exercises that follow, you will practice the skills you have learned in this module.

## Skills Review

You are the assistant director of sales at QWE, a restaurant ownership group with three casual dining restaurants in Florida. To help understand the effectiveness of a one-day online sales promotion, you will summarize the day's sales data using a PivotTable and PivotChart.

1. **Plan and design a PivotTable report.**
   a. Start Excel, open IL_EX_8-2.xlsx from the location where you store your Data Files, then save it as **IL_EX_8_OnlineSales**.
   b. Review the fields and values in the worksheet.
   c. Verify that the worksheet contains repeated values in one or more fields.
   d. Verify that there are not any blank rows or columns in the range A1:E60.
   e. Verify that the worksheet contains a field that can be summed in a PivotTable.
2. **Create a PivotTable report.**
   a. Create a blank PivotTable report on a new worksheet using the Jan 14 worksheet data in the range A1:E60.
   b. Add the Location field in the PivotTable Fields pane to the Columns area.
   c. Add the Amount field in the PivotTable Fields pane to the Values area.
   d. Add the Mode field in the PivotTable Fields pane to the Rows area.
   e. Add the SaleID field in the PivotTable Fields pane to the PivotTable, then move the SaleID field from the Values area to the Rows area below the Mode field.
3. **Change a PivotTable's summary function and design.**
   a. Change the PivotTable summary function to Average.
   b. Rename the new sheet **Jan 14 PT**.
   c. Change the PivotTable Style to Light Green, Pivot Style Light 14 (first row, first style from the left under Light). Format the amount values in the PivotTable as currency with a $ symbol and no decimal places.
   d. Change the summary function back to Sum. Use a tool on the PivotTable Analyze tab to hide the field headers.
4. **Filter PivotTable data.**
   a. Add a slicer to filter the location data in the PivotTable, then use it to display sales for only the Tampa location.
   b. Clear the filter, then delete the slicer.
   c. Add the Mode field to the Filters area in the PivotTable Fields pane. Use the filter list arrow to display sales for only the Delivery mode.
   d. Clear the filter to display sales for both modes.
   e. Save the workbook.
5. **Change the organization of PivotTable data.**
   a. In the PivotTable Fields pane, drag the Location field from the Columns area to the Rows area above the SaleID field.
   b. Drag the SaleID field from the Rows area to the Filters area below the Mode field.
   c. Drag the Mode field to the Columns area.
   d. Add the Gratuity field to the Values area below the Amount field. (**Hint**: The Amount field label is "Sum of Amount.")
   e. Format the gratuity values in the PivotTable as currency with a $ symbol and no decimal places. (**Hint**: The Gratuity field label is "Sum of Gratuity.")
   f. Compare your completed PivotTable to **Figure 8-22**, then save the workbook.

**Figure 8-22**

| | A | B | C | D | E | F | G |
|---|---|---|---|---|---|---|---|
| 1 | | | | | | | |
| 2 | SaleID | (All) | | | | | |
| 3 | | | | | | | |
| 4 | | **Delivery** | | **Pick-up** | | **Total Sum of Amount** | **Total Sum of Gratuity** |
| 5 | | **Sum of Amount** | **Sum of Gratuity** | **Sum of Amount** | **Sum of Gratuity** | | |
| 6 | Miami | $556 | $86 | $1,428 | $188 | $1,984 | $274 |
| 7 | Orlando | $949 | $199 | $541 | $114 | $1,489 | $313 |
| 8 | Tampa | $2,714 | $589 | $660 | $188 | $3,373 | $778 |
| 9 | **Grand Total** | **$4,218** | **$875** | **$2,629** | **$490** | **$6,847** | **$1,365** |
| 10 | | | | | | | |

6. **Create a PivotChart report.**
   a. Use the existing PivotTable data to create a Clustered Column PivotChart.
   b. Move the PivotChart to a new worksheet, named **PivotChart**.
   c. Apply the Quick Layout, Layout 1, to the PivotChart. Add the title **Online Promotion** to the chart.
   d. Use a command on the PivotChart Analyze tab to hide the field buttons in the chart, then add the Alt Text **Online Promotion Sales for Three Locations** to the chart.
   e. Compare your PivotChart with **Figure 8-23**, then save the workbook.

7. **Update a PivotTable report.**
   a. Activate the Jan 14 PT sheet, then note the Miami total for delivery in cell B6.
   b. Activate the Jan 14 sheet, then change the Amount value in cell B3 to **$110**.
   c. Refresh the PivotTable, then verify that the Miami total for delivery increased to $576 on both the PivotTable and the PivotChart.
   d. Save the workbook.

**Figure 8-23**

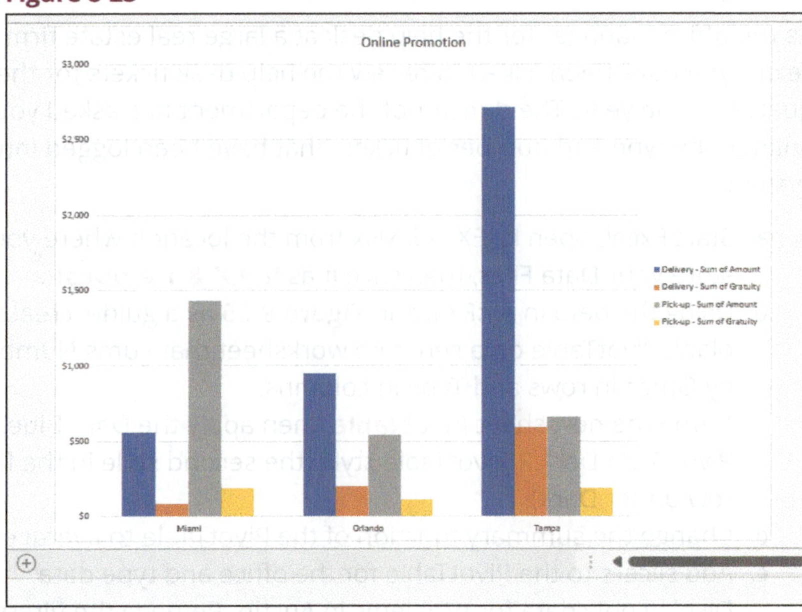


8. **Extract information from a PivotTable.**
   a. In cell G1 of the Jan 14 sheet, enter the text **Total Promotion Sales**, then format the label in cell G1 in bold and left-aligned.
   b. In cell G2 of the January Expenses sheet, type **=**, switch to the Jan 14 PT sheet, click the cell that contains the grand total for the sales amount in cell F9, then press ENTER.
   c. Review the GETPIVOTDATA function that was entered in cell G2, then format the value in cell G2 in Accounting Number format and no decimal places.
   d. Compare your Jan 14 sheet to **Figure 8-24**.
   e. Add your name to the center footer sections of the three worksheets, save the workbook, close the workbook, then close Excel.
   f. Submit the workbook to your instructor.

## Skills Review (Continued)

Figure 8-24

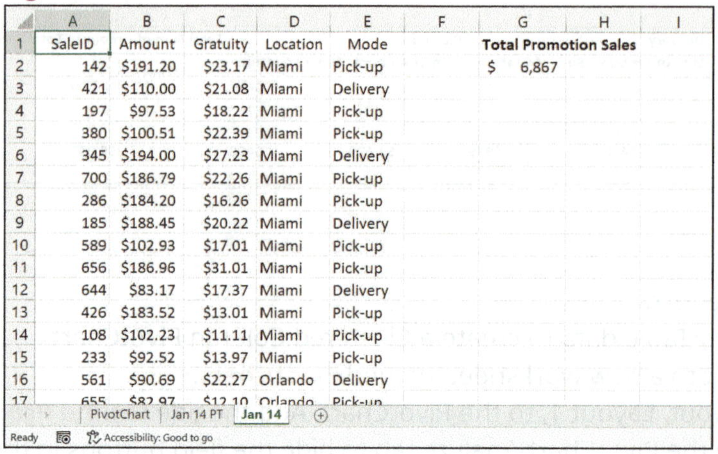

| | A | B | C | D | E | F | G | H | I |
|---|---|---|---|---|---|---|---|---|---|
| 1 | SaleID | Amount | Gratuity | Location | Mode | | Total Promotion Sales | | |
| 2 | 142 | $191.20 | $23.17 | Miami | Pick-up | | $ 6,867 | | |
| 3 | 421 | $110.00 | $21.08 | Miami | Delivery | | | | |
| 4 | 197 | $97.53 | $18.22 | Miami | Pick-up | | | | |
| 5 | 380 | $100.51 | $22.39 | Miami | Pick-up | | | | |
| 6 | 345 | $194.00 | $27.23 | Miami | Delivery | | | | |
| 7 | 700 | $186.79 | $22.26 | Miami | Pick-up | | | | |
| 8 | 286 | $184.20 | $16.26 | Miami | Pick-up | | | | |
| 9 | 185 | $188.45 | $20.22 | Miami | Delivery | | | | |
| 10 | 589 | $102.93 | $17.01 | Miami | Pick-up | | | | |
| 11 | 656 | $186.96 | $31.01 | Miami | Pick-up | | | | |
| 12 | 644 | $83.17 | $17.37 | Miami | Delivery | | | | |
| 13 | 426 | $183.52 | $13.01 | Miami | Pick-up | | | | |
| 14 | 108 | $102.23 | $11.11 | Miami | Pick-up | | | | |
| 15 | 233 | $92.52 | $13.97 | Miami | Pick-up | | | | |
| 16 | 561 | $90.69 | $22.27 | Orlando | Delivery | | | | |
| 17 | 655 | $82.97 | $12.10 | Orlando | Pick-up | | | | |

PivotChart | Jan 14 PT | Jan 14

Ready Accessibility: Good to go

## Independent Challenge 1

As the office manager for the help desk at a large real estate firm in Texas, you have been asked to review the help desk tickets for the first quarter of the year. The director of the department has asked you to analyze the type and number of tickets that have been logged into the system.

a. Start Excel, open IL_EX_8-3.xlsx from the location where you store your Data Files, then save it as **IL_EX_8_HelpDesk**.
b. Using the data in A1:F73, and **Figure 8-25** as a guide, create a blank PivotTable on a separate worksheet that sums Number by Office in rows and Type in columns.
c. Name the new sheet **PivotTable**, then apply the Dark Blue, Pivot Style Dark 2 PivotTable style (the second style in the first row under Dark).
d. Change the summary function of the PivotTable to average.
e. Add slicers to the PivotTable for the office and type data. Display only data for problems in Austin. Remove the filters and remove the slicers.
f. Add the Area field to the Rows area under the Office field.
g. Add the Tier field to the PivotTable, then move the Tier field from the Values area to the Filters area of the PivotTable.
h. Add the Month field to the Columns area under the Type field.
i. Move the Month field from the Columns area to the Rows area under the Office and Area fields.
j. Display only the PivotTable data for Tier 2 tickets.
k. Change the summary function of the PivotTable back to sum, then display the PivotTable data for all tiers.
l. Add a slicer for the Office field to display the data for only the Houston office. Delete the slicer but do not remove the filter.
m. Hide the field headers in the PivotTable, then compare your PivotTable to **Figure 8-26**.

Figure 8-25

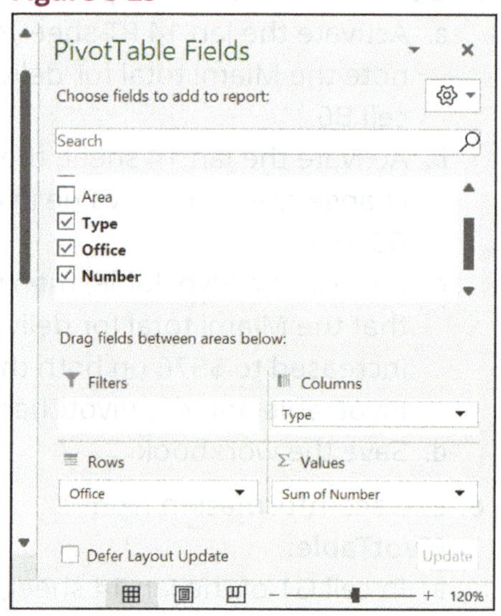


Figure 8-26

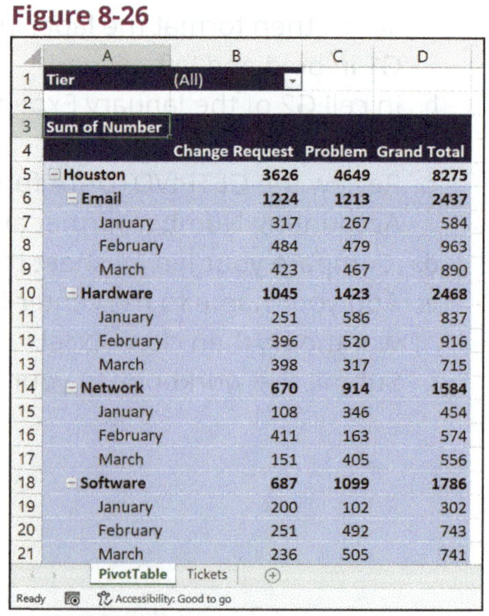

| | A | B | C | D |
|---|---|---|---|---|
| 1 | Tier | (All) | | |
| 2 | | | | |
| 3 | Sum of Number | | | |
| 4 | | Change Request | Problem | Grand Total |
| 5 | Houston | 3626 | 4649 | 8275 |
| 6 | Email | 1224 | 1213 | 2437 |
| 7 | January | 317 | 267 | 584 |
| 8 | February | 484 | 479 | 963 |
| 9 | March | 423 | 467 | 890 |
| 10 | Hardware | 1045 | 1423 | 2468 |
| 11 | January | 251 | 586 | 837 |
| 12 | February | 396 | 520 | 916 |
| 13 | March | 398 | 317 | 715 |
| 14 | Network | 670 | 914 | 1584 |
| 15 | January | 108 | 346 | 454 |
| 16 | February | 411 | 163 | 574 |
| 17 | March | 151 | 405 | 556 |
| 18 | Software | 687 | 1099 | 1786 |
| 19 | January | 200 | 102 | 302 |
| 20 | February | 251 | 492 | 743 |
| 21 | March | 236 | 505 | 741 |

PivotTable | Tickets

Ready Accessibility: Good to go

n. Create a clustered column PivotChart that displays the ticket numbers. Move the PivotChart to a new sheet named **PivotChart**.

o. Apply Quick Layout 3 to the PivotChart. Edit the chart title to **Houston First Quarter Help Desk Tickets**.

p. Add the Alt Text **Houston First Quarter Help Desk Tickets** to the chart, then compare your chart to **Figure 8-27**.

**Figure 8-27**

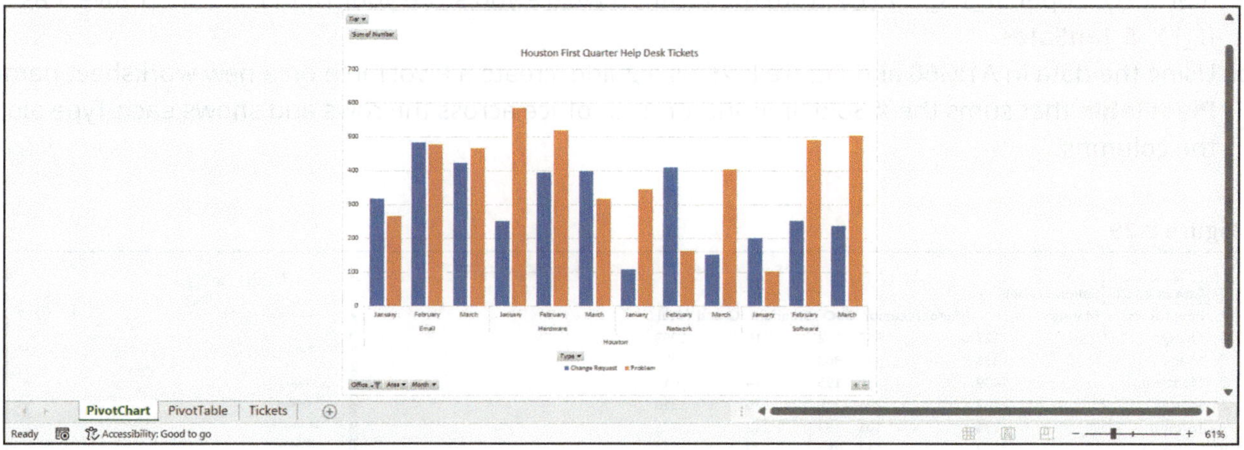


q. Activate the Tickets sheet and change the number in cell F3 to **500**. Update the PivotTable to reflect this change.

r. Activate the Tickets sheet, enter **Total Houston Tickets in First Quarter** in cell H1, then format the label in cell H1 in bold and left-aligned.

s. Use the GETPIVOTDATA function to display the grand total number of Houston tickets in cell H2, then compare your Tickets sheet to **Figure 8-28**.

t. Add your name to the center section of the three worksheet footers, then save the workbook.

u. Close the workbook, then close Excel. Submit the workbook to your instructor.

**Figure 8-28**

| | A | B | C | D | E | F | G | H | I | J | K |
|---|---|---|---|---|---|---|---|---|---|---|---|
| 1 | Tier | Month | Area | Type | Office | Number | | **Total Houston Tickets in First Quarter** | | | |
| 2 | 1 | February | Email | Change Request | Austin | 335 | | 8291 | | | |
| 3 | 1 | February | Email | Change Request | Houston | 500 | | | | | |
| 4 | 2 | February | Email | Change Request | Dallas | 486 | | | | | |
| 5 | 2 | February | Software | Change Request | Austin | 245 | | | | | |
| 6 | 2 | February | Software | Change Request | Houston | 251 | | | | | |
| 7 | 2 | February | Software | Change Request | Dallas | 456 | | | | | |
| 8 | 2 | February | Hardware | Change Request | Austin | 511 | | | | | |
| 9 | 1 | February | Hardware | Change Request | Houston | 396 | | | | | |
| 10 | 1 | February | Hardware | Change Request | Dallas | 597 | | | | | |
| 11 | 2 | February | Network | Change Request | Austin | 276 | | | | | |
| 12 | 2 | February | Network | Change Request | Houston | 411 | | | | | |
| 13 | 1 | February | Network | Change Request | Dallas | 558 | | | | | |
| 14 | 1 | February | Email | Problem | Austin | 593 | | | | | |
| 15 | 1 | February | Email | Problem | Houston | 479 | | | | | |
| 16 | 1 | February | Email | Problem | Dallas | 141 | | | | | |
| 17 | 2 | February | Software | Problem | Austin | 131 | | | | | |
| 18 | 1 | February | Software | Problem | Houston | 492 | | | | | |
| 19 | 1 | February | Software | Problem | Dallas | 283 | | | | | |
| 20 | 1 | February | Hardware | Problem | Austin | 564 | | | | | |
| 21 | 1 | February | Hardware | Problem | Houston | 520 | | | | | |

PivotChart | PivotTable | **Tickets**

Ready | Accessibility: Good to go

## Independent Challenge 2

You are the assistant to the sales manager of an international semiconductor company with sales offices in the United States and Canada. The company sells four types of semiconductors to businesses: memory chips, microprocessors, standard chips, and complex systems-on-a-chip (SoCs). The January sales data has been provided to you in a worksheet and you want to use this data to create a PivotTable that analyzes and charts the sales for each type of semiconductor.

a. Start Excel, open IL_EX_8-4.xlsx from the location where you store your Data Files, then save it as **IL_EX_8_JanSales**.
b. Using the data in A1:G60 and **Figure 8-29** as a guide, create a PivotTable on a new worksheet named **PivotTable** that sums the # Sold amount for each office across the rows and shows each Type along the columns.

**Figure 8-29**

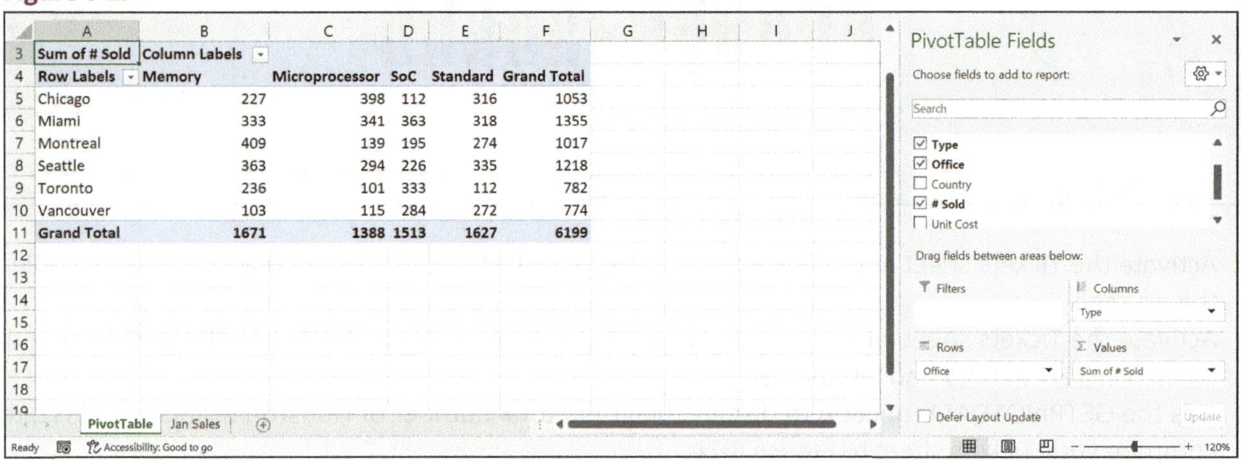


c. Group the Canadian offices (**Hint**: Select the Montreal, Toronto, and Vancouver headings in Column A, then click the Group Selection button in the Group group on the PivotTable Analyze tab.)
d. Rename the Group1 label **Canada**. (**Hint**: Enter the new name in the cell with the Group1 label.)
e. Group the three offices in the United States (Chicago, Miami, and Seattle), then name this new group **U.S.**.
f. Collapse both the Canada and U.S. groups.
g. Turn off the grand totals for the Rows. (**Hint**: Click the Grand Totals button in the Layout group on the Design tab, then click On for Columns Only.)
h. Add the Unit Cost field to the PivotTable below the # Sold field.
i. Use **Figure 8-30** as a guide to add a calculated field named **Sale Amount** to the PivotTable that multiplies the # Sold field by the Unit Cost field. (**Hint**: Click the Fields, Items, & Sets button in the Calculations group on the PivotTable Analyze tab.)
j. Remove the Unit Cost and # Sold fields from the PivotTable, then format the sale amount values using the Currency format with the $ symbol and no decimal places.
k. On the JanSales worksheet, change the value for the # Sold for the Memory type in Chicago, in cell F6, to **50**. Update the PivotTable to reflect this increase in sales.
l. Expand the grouped U.S. and Canada data, then add a Type slicer to the PivotTable. Use the slicer to display the sales for the Memory type only.

**Figure 8-30**

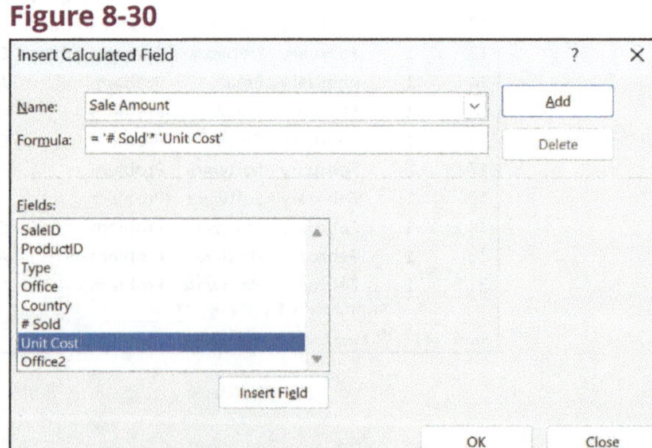

m. Resize the slicer to display the buttons in two columns that are each .2" height and 1.29" width. (**Hint**: Use the Buttons group on the Slicer tab.)
n. Change the slicer caption to **Semiconductor Type**. (**Hint**: Use the Slicer group on the Slicer tab.)
o. Change the slicer object size to 1" height and 2.8" width. (**Hint**: Use the Size group on the Slicer tab.)
p. Add a slicer style of Light Blue, Slicer Style Dark 1 (first style from the left under Dark), then move the slicer below the PivotTable.
q. Clear the filter but do not remove the slicer, remove the field headers, then compare your PivotTable to **Figure 8-31**.

**Figure 8-31**

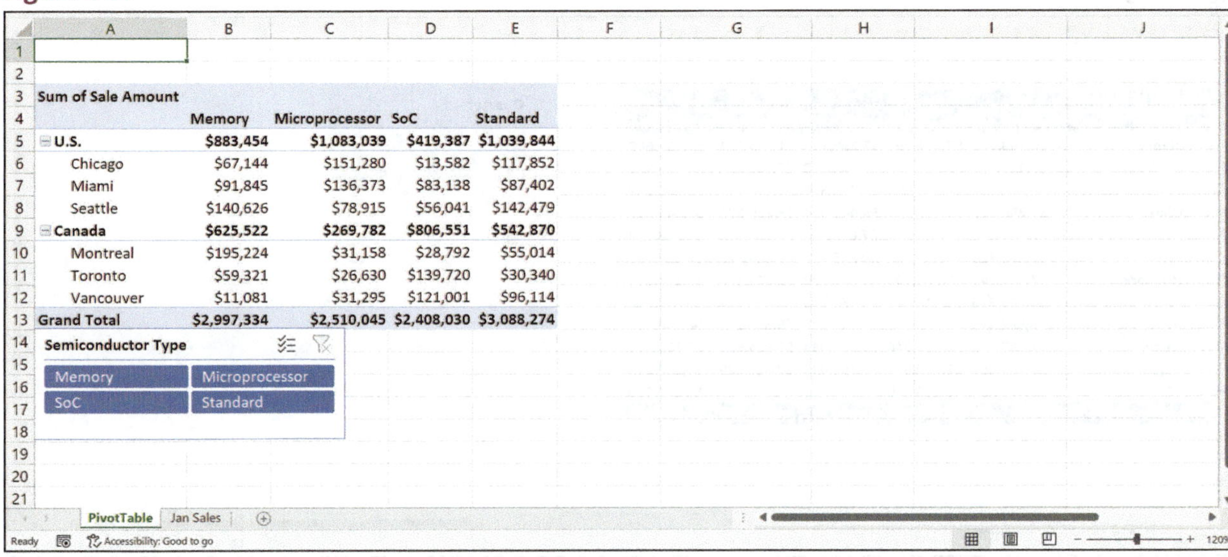

| | A | B | C | D | E |
|---|---|---|---|---|---|
| 1 | | | | | |
| 2 | | | | | |
| 3 | Sum of Sale Amount | | | | |
| 4 | | Memory | Microprocessor | SoC | Standard |
| 5 | U.S. | $883,454 | $1,083,039 | $419,387 | $1,039,844 |
| 6 | Chicago | $67,144 | $151,280 | $13,582 | $117,852 |
| 7 | Miami | $91,845 | $136,373 | $83,138 | $87,402 |
| 8 | Seattle | $140,626 | $78,915 | $56,041 | $142,479 |
| 9 | Canada | $625,522 | $269,782 | $806,551 | $542,870 |
| 10 | Montreal | $195,224 | $31,158 | $28,792 | $55,014 |
| 11 | Toronto | $59,321 | $26,630 | $139,720 | $30,340 |
| 12 | Vancouver | $11,081 | $31,295 | $121,001 | $96,114 |
| 13 | Grand Total | $2,997,334 | $2,510,045 | $2,408,030 | $3,088,274 |



r. Collapse the grouped U.S. and Canada data, then create a stacked column PivotChart for the sales data for the four types. (**Hint**: Choose the first Stacked Column Chart type in the dialog box.)
s. Move the PivotChart to a new sheet, then name the chart sheet **PivotChart**.
t. Apply a quick layout of Layout 3 to the PivotChart, then add a title of **U.S. and Canada Sales** to the chart.
u. Add the Alt Text **U.S. and Canada Sales for 4 Types of Semiconductors**, then compare your PivotChart to **Figure 8-32**.
v. Add your name to the center section of the three worksheet footers, save the workbook, close the workbook, then close Excel. Submit the workbook to your instructor.

**Figure 8-32**

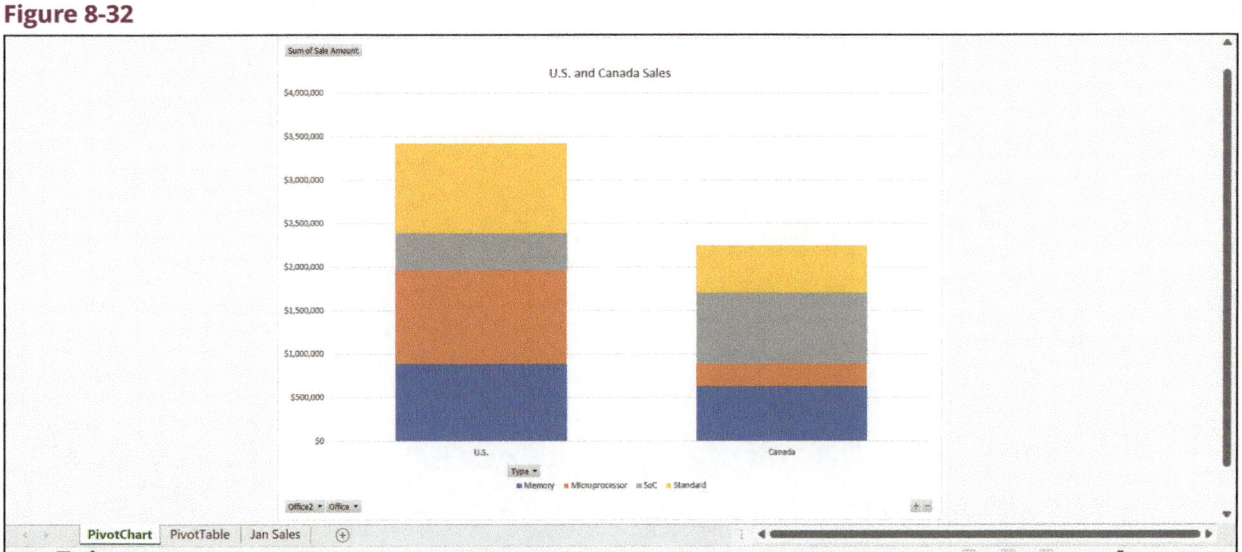

# Visual Workshop

Open IL_EX_8-5.xlsx from the location where you store your Data Files, then save it as **IL_EX_8_YearSales**. Using the data on the Sales worksheet, create the PivotTable and slicer displayed in **Figure 8-33** on a new worksheet named **PivotTable**. Format the table, slicer, and data as necessary to match the figure. (**Hint**: The PivotTable has been formatted using the Dark Blue, Pivot Style Dark 2 Pivot Style.) Add your name to the PivotTable footer, then save the workbook. Close the workbook, close Excel, then submit the workbook to your instructor.

**Figure 8-33**

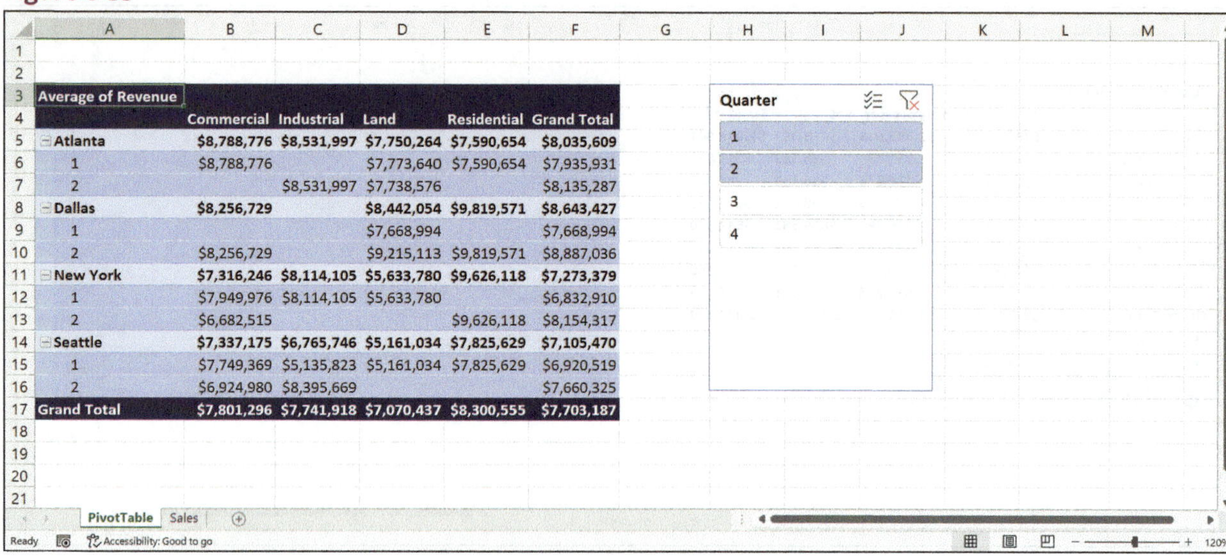

| Average of Revenue | Commercial | Industrial | Land | Residential | Grand Total |
|---|---|---|---|---|---|
| Atlanta | $8,788,776 | $8,531,997 | $7,750,264 | $7,590,654 | $8,035,609 |
| 1 | $8,788,776 | | $7,773,640 | $7,590,654 | $7,935,931 |
| 2 | | $8,531,997 | $7,738,576 | | $8,135,287 |
| Dallas | $8,256,729 | | $8,442,054 | $9,819,571 | $8,643,427 |
| 1 | | | $7,668,994 | | $7,668,994 |
| 2 | $8,256,729 | | $9,215,113 | $9,819,571 | $8,887,036 |
| New York | $7,316,246 | $8,114,105 | $5,633,780 | $9,626,118 | $7,273,379 |
| 1 | $7,949,976 | $8,114,105 | $5,633,780 | | $6,832,910 |
| 2 | $6,682,515 | | | $9,626,118 | $8,154,317 |
| Seattle | $7,337,175 | $6,765,746 | $5,161,034 | $7,825,629 | $7,105,470 |
| 1 | $7,749,369 | $5,135,823 | $5,161,034 | $7,825,629 | $6,920,519 |
| 2 | $6,924,980 | $8,395,669 | | | $7,660,325 |
| Grand Total | $7,801,296 | $7,741,918 | $7,070,437 | $8,300,555 | $7,703,187 |

# Automating Worksheet Tasks

## Case

Carlos Alvaro, the HR Director at Bayside, is in the process of evaluating the job performance of the company's technicians. As part of this assessment, Carlos will consider the annual billing revenue and the evaluation review for each technician. Carlos asks you to create macros to format the data in the technicians' billing reports, calculate the annual billing total, and evaluate whether a job promotion needs to be awarded.

## Module Objectives

After completing this module, you will be able to:

- Plan a macro
- Enable a macro
- Create a macro
- Run a macro
- Edit a macro
- Create a button for a macro
- Create a command button
- Create a form control

## Files You Will Need

IL_EX_9-1.xlsx
IL_EX_9-2.xlsx
IL_EX_9-3.xlsx
IL_EX_9-4.xlsx
IL_EX_9-5.xlsx

# Plan a Macro

**Case** You need to create a macro to format the technicians' billing worksheets and calculate their total billings for the year. You work with Carlos to plan the macro.

**Objectives**
- List the steps to create a macro
- Determine the storage location for a macro

A **macro** is a named set of instructions, written in the Visual Basic programming language, that performs tasks automatically in a specified order. You can create macros to automate Excel tasks that you perform frequently. You don't need to know the Visual Basic language to create a macro, because instead of writing code you can simply record a series of actions using the macro recorder built into Excel. When recording a macro, the sequence of actions in a macro is important, so you need to plan the macro carefully before you begin recording.

## Details

**To plan a macro, use the following guidelines:**

- **Assign the macro a descriptive name**
  The first character of a macro name must be a letter; the remaining characters can be letters, numbers, or underscores. Letters can be uppercase or lowercase. Spaces are not allowed in macro names; use underscores instead. You can press SHIFT+HYPHEN ( - ) to enter an underscore character. You decide to name the macro FormatTotal. **Table 9-1** displays a list of macros that could be created to automate other common tasks in Bayside spreadsheets.
- **Write out the steps the macro will perform**
  This planning helps eliminate careless errors. After a discussion with Carlos, you write down a description of the new FormatTotal macro, as displayed in **Figure 9-1**.
- **Decide how you will perform the actions you want to record**
  You can use the mouse, the keyboard, or a combination of the two. For the new FormatTotal macro, you want to use both the mouse and the keyboard.
- **Practice the steps you want Excel to record, and write them down**
  During your meeting with Carlos, you write down the sequence of actions to include in the macro.
- **Decide where to store the macro**
  Macros can be stored in an active workbook, in a new workbook, or in the **Personal Macro Workbook**, a special workbook that can contain macros that are available to any open workbook; it opens whenever you start Excel to make macros available at any time but is hidden by default. You decide to store the macro in the active workbook.

**Figure 9-1:** Handwritten description of planned macro

**Macro to format worksheet and calculate the annual billing total**

| | |
|---|---|
| Name: | FormatTotal |
| Description: | Formats worksheet and calculates the annual billing |
| Steps: | 1. AutoFit column A<br>2. Select row 2 and insert blank row<br>3. Select row 1 and insert blank row<br>4. Enter Bayside Promotion Report in cell A1<br>5. Enter Billing Status: in cell C2<br>6. Enter Post-Review Job Position: in cell C3<br>7. Autofit column C<br>8. Enter Total in cell A17<br>9. Use the AutoSum button in cell B17 to calculate total<br>10. Format B5:B17 in Currency, zero decimals |

**Table 9-1:** Possible macros and their descriptive names

| description of macro | descriptive name |
|---|---|
| Enter a frequently used division, such as Technology | TechDiv |
| Enter a frequently used company name, such as Bayside | Company_Name |
| Print the active worksheet on a single page, in landscape orientation | FitToLandscape |
| Add a footer to a worksheet | FooterStamp |
| Add a total to a worksheet | AddTotal |

# Create a Macro

**Case** You are ready to create a macro that totals the revenue values in column B and formats the active worksheet. You create this macro by recording your actions.

**Objectives**
- Change a macro storage location
- Create a macro by recording steps

The easiest way to create a macro is to record it using the Excel Macro Recorder. You turn the Macro Recorder on, name the macro, enter the keystrokes, and select the commands you want the macro to perform, then stop the recorder. As you record the macro, Excel automatically translates each action into program code that you can later view and modify.

## Steps

**Quick Tip**
You can also click the Record Macro button in the Code group on the Developer tab or the Record Macro button on the left side of the status bar to record a macro.

**Trouble**
If you make a mistake when recording a macro, click the Stop Recording button in the Macros group, click the Macro button, click the macro name in the Macro dialog box, click Delete, click OK to confirm the deletion, then begin the macro steps again.

**Quick Tip**
You can also click the Stop Recording button in the Code group on the Developer tab or the Stop Recording Macro button on the left side of the status bar to stop recording a macro.

1. **Click the Create Macro sheet tab, click the View tab on the ribbon, then click the Record Macro button in the Macros group**
   The Record Macro dialog box opens, as displayed in **Figure 9-4**. The default name Macro1 is selected. You can either assign this name or enter a new name. This dialog box also lets you assign a shortcut key for running the macro and assign a storage location for the macro.
2. **Type FormatTotal in the Macro name text box, if the Store macro in box does not display "This Workbook," click the Store macro in list arrow, click This Workbook, type your name in the Description text box, then click OK**
   The dialog box closes, and the Record Macro button is replaced with a Stop Recording button. Take your time performing the following steps. Excel records every keystroke, menu selection, and mouse action that you make, not the amount of time you take to record them.
3. **Click the Home tab, with A1 as the active cell, click the Format button in the Cells group, click AutoFit Column Width, click the row 2 heading button, click the Insert button in the Cells group, click the row 1 heading button, then click the Insert button in the Cells group**
4. **Click cell A1, type Bayside Promotion Report, click the Enter button on the formula bar, click cell C2, type Billing Status:, click the Enter button on the formula bar, click cell C3, type Post-Review Job Position:, then click the Enter button on the formula bar**
5. **With cell C3 as the active cell, click the Format button in the Cells group, then click AutoFit Column Width**
6. **Click cell A17, type Total, click the Enter button on the formula bar, click cell B17, click the AutoSum button in the Editing group, then click the Enter button on the formula bar**
7. **Select the range B5:B17, right-click the range, click Format Cells on the shortcut menu, in the Category list of the Number tab in the Format Cells dialog box click Currency, in the Decimal places box select the existing text, type 0, then click OK**
8. **Click the View tab, click the Stop Recording button in the Macros group, then save the workbook**
   **Figure 9-5** displays the result of the actions you took while recording the macro.

**Figure 9-4:** Record Macro dialog box

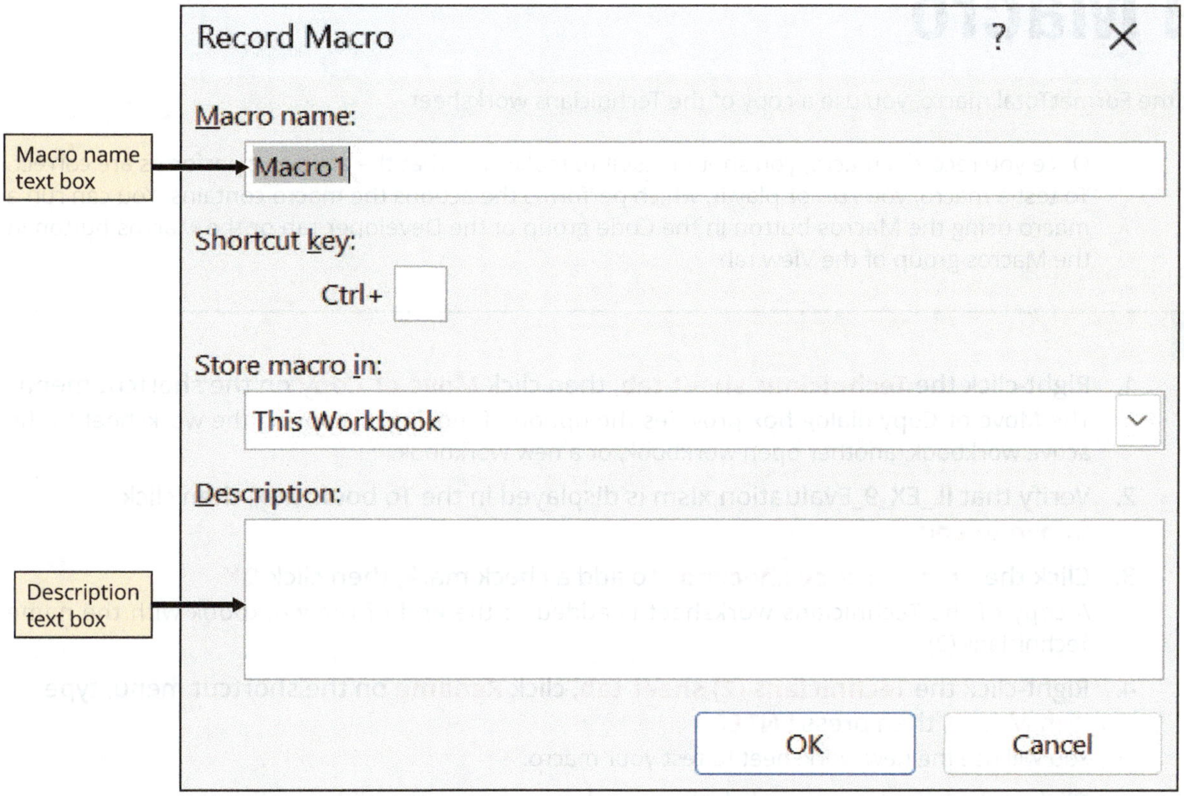


**Figure 9-5:** Worksheet with new data and formatting

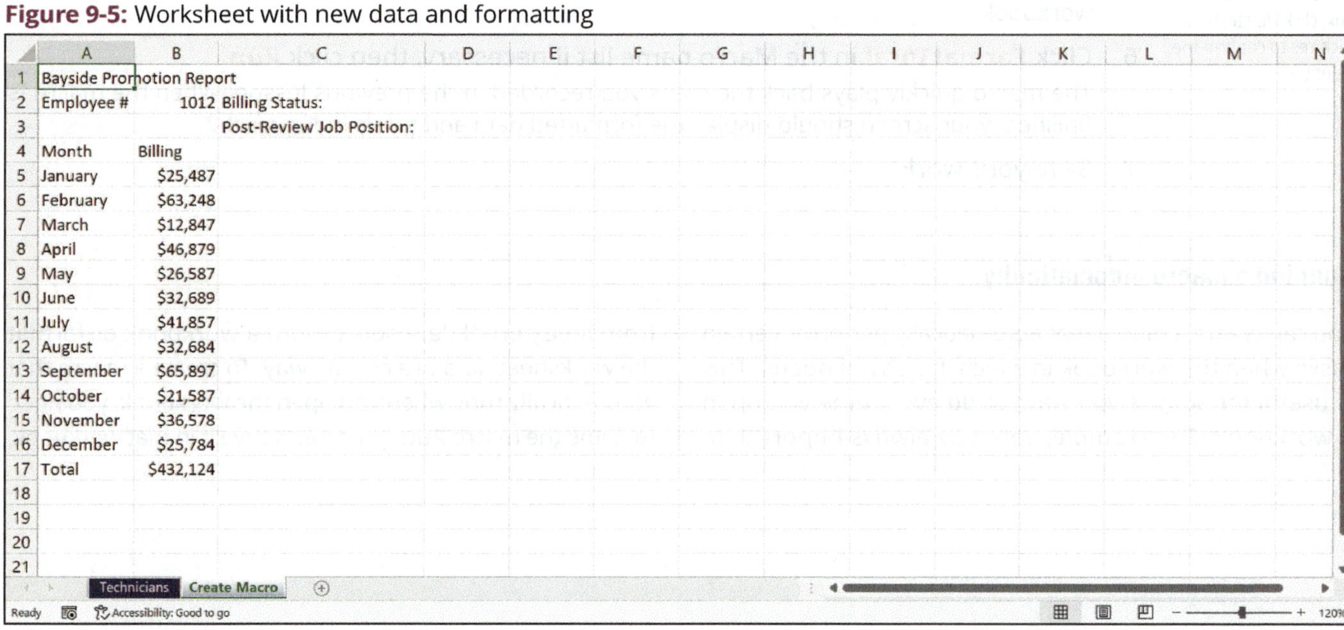

| | A | B | C |
|---|---|---|---|
| 1 | Bayside Promotion Report | | |
| 2 | Employee # | 1012 | Billing Status: |
| 3 | | | Post-Review Job Position: |
| 4 | Month | Billing | |
| 5 | January | $25,487 | |
| 6 | February | $63,248 | |
| 7 | March | $12,847 | |
| 8 | April | $46,879 | |
| 9 | May | $26,587 | |
| 10 | June | $32,689 | |
| 11 | July | $41,857 | |
| 12 | August | $32,684 | |
| 13 | September | $65,897 | |
| 14 | October | $21,587 | |
| 15 | November | $36,578 | |
| 16 | December | $25,784 | |
| 17 | Total | $432,124 | |

# Run a Macro

**Case** To test the FormatTotal macro, you use a copy of the Technicians worksheet.

**Objectives**
- Display macros in a workbook
- Run a macro using the Macro dialog box

Once you record a macro, you should test it to make sure that the actions it performs are correct. To test a macro, you **run** or play it, which performs the actions the macro contains. You can run a macro using the Macros button in the Code group of the Developer tab or the Macros button in the Macros group of the View tab.

## Steps

1. **Right-click the Technicians sheet tab, then click Move or Copy on the shortcut menu**
   The Move or Copy dialog box provides the option of moving or copying the worksheet to the active workbook, another open workbook, or a new workbook.
2. **Verify that IL_EX_9_Evaluation.xlsm is displayed in the To book: box, then click (move to end)**
3. **Click the Create a copy checkbox to add a check mark, then click OK**
   A copy of the Technicians worksheet is added to the end of the workbook with the name Technicians (2).
4. **Right-click the Technicians (2) sheet tab, click Rename on the shortcut menu, type Run Macro, then press ENTER**
   You will use the new worksheet to test your macro.
5. **Click cell A1 if necessary, click the Developer tab on the ribbon, click the Macros button in the Code group, click the Macros in list arrow, then click This Workbook**
   The Macro dialog box, displayed in **Figure 9-6**, displays all the macros contained in the current workbook.
6. **Click FormatTotal in the Macro name list if necessary, then click Run**
   The macro quickly plays back the steps you recorded in the previous lesson. When the macro is finished, your screen should display the formatted data and totals in **Figure 9-7**.
7. **Save your work**

**Quick Tip**
To delete a macro, click the macro name in the Macro dialog box, click Delete, then click Yes to confirm the deletion.

### Running a macro automatically

You can create a macro that automatically performs certain tasks when the workbook in which it is saved opens. This is useful for actions you want to do every time you open a workbook. For example, you may always import data from an external data source into a workbook or format the worksheet data in a certain way. To create a macro that automatically runs when you open the workbook, you need to name the macro Auto_Open and save it in that workbook.

**Figure 9-6:** Macro dialog box

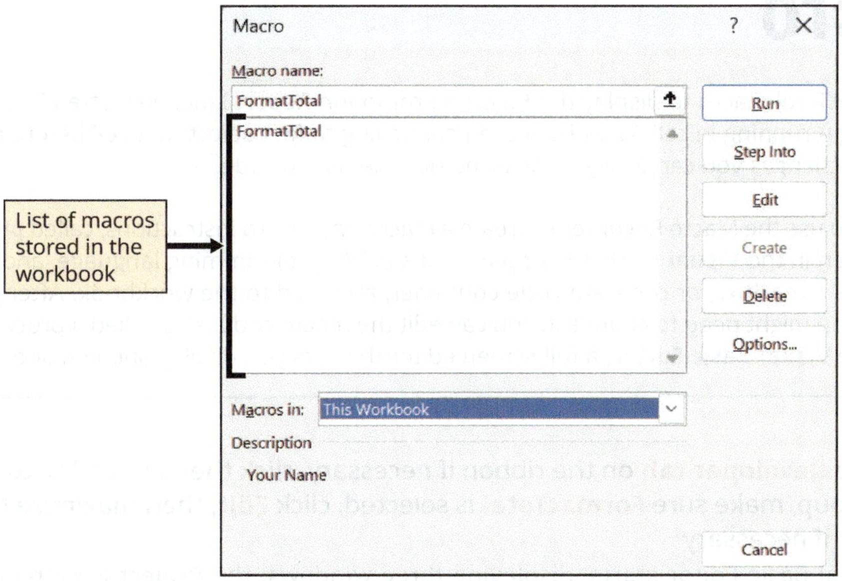


**Figure 9-7:** Result of running FormatTotal macro

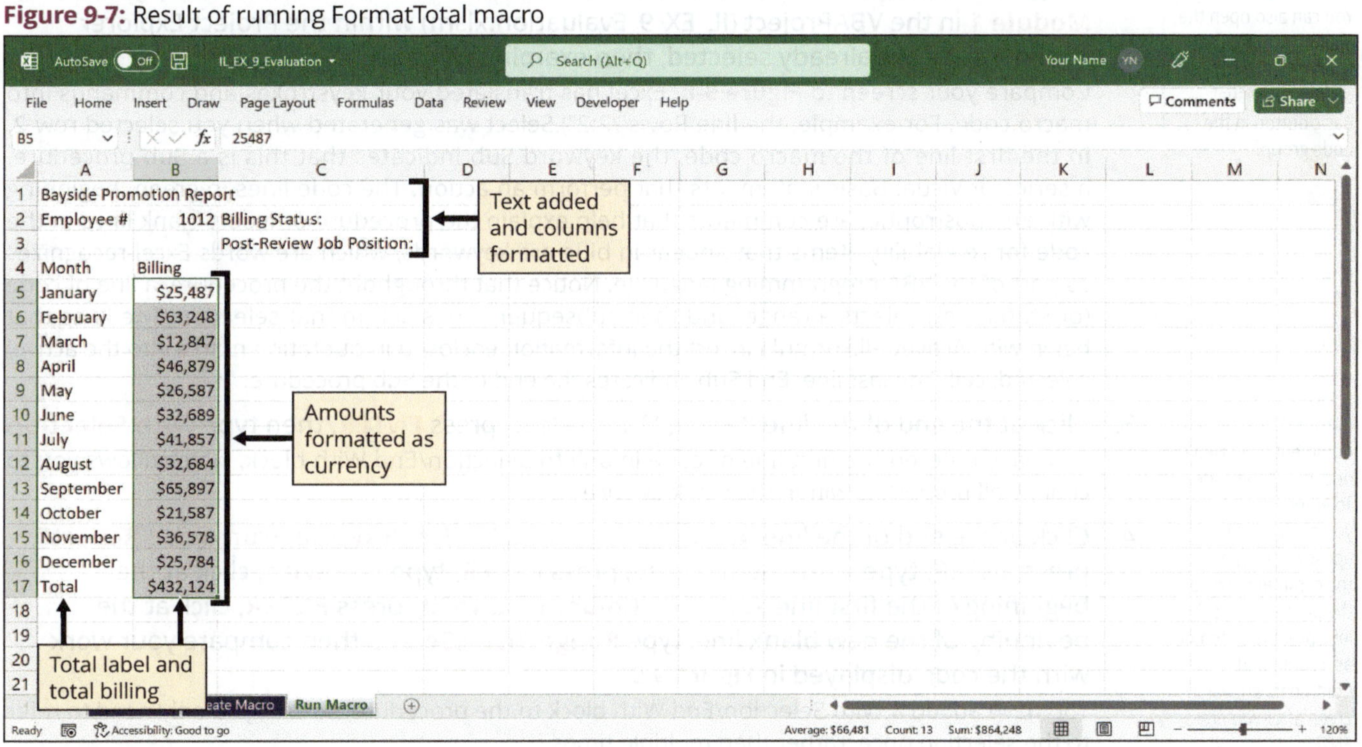


## Creating a main procedure

A sequence of VBA statements is called a procedure. For this reason, macros are often referred to as procedures. When you routinely need to run several macros one after another, you can save time by executing them in one procedure. This type of procedure, which contains multiple procedures that run sequentially, is referred to as a **main procedure**. To create a main procedure, you type a **Call statement**, a Visual Basic statement that retrieves the procedure, using the format Call *procedurename*, where *procedurename* is the name of the procedure or macro you want to run. For example, Call FormatTotal in a main procedure would run the FormatTotal macro.

# Edit a Macro

**Case** Carlos wants the FormatTotal macro to display the Bayside Promotion Report label formatted in bold. He also wants the macro to begin running in cell A1 without the user having to first select that cell before running the macro. These are small changes you can easily make by editing the macro code.

**Objectives**
- Describe the Visual Basic Editor window
- Edit a macro using VBA

When you use the Macro Recorder to create a macro, the macro instructions, called **program code**, are written in the **Visual Basic for Applications (VBA)** programming language, and the macro is stored as a **module**, or program code container, attached to the workbook. After you record a macro, you might need to change it. You can edit the macro code, also called a procedure, directly using the **Visual Basic Editor**, a full-screen editor that lets you display and edit lines of code.

## Steps

**Trouble**
If the Properties window does not appear, click the Properties Window button.

**Quick Tip**
You can also open the Editor by clicking the Developer tab, then clicking the Visual Basic button in the Code group.

**Quick Tip**
Comments are used to document VBA code. To enter a comment, you must type an apostrophe (') before the comment text so the program doesn't interpret the statement as a command. Comments appear in green after you press ENTER.

**Quick Tip**
You can return to Excel without closing the module by clicking the View Microsoft Excel button on the Visual Basic Editor toolbar.

1. **Click the Developer tab on the ribbon if necessary, click the Macros button in the Code group, make sure FormatTotal is selected, click Edit, then maximize the Code window, if necessary**
   The Visual Basic Editor starts, displaying three windows: the Project Explorer window, the Properties window, and the Code window.
2. **Drag the left edge of the Project Explorer window to expand it if necessary, click Module 1 in the VBAProject (IL_EX_9_Evaluation.xlsm) within the Project Explorer window if it's not already selected, then examine the steps in the macro**
   Compare your screen to **Figure 9-8**. Excel has translated your keystrokes and commands into macro code. For example, the line Rows("2:2").Select was generated when you selected row 2. In the first line of the macro code, the keyword Sub indicates that this is a Sub procedure, a series of Visual Basic statements that perform an action. The code lines in green, beginning with an apostrophe, are comments that help explain the procedure or insert blank lines in the code for readability. Items that appear in blue are keywords, which are words Excel recognizes as part of the VBA programming language. Notice that throughout the procedure, a line of code (or statement) selects a range, and then subsequent lines act on that selection. The lines that begin with ActiveCell.Formula insert the information enclosed in quotation marks into the active, selected, cell. The last line, End Sub, indicates the end of the Sub procedure.
3. **Click at the end of the line Range("A1").Select, press ENTER, then type With Selection**
   You have entered the first line of code in a With Selection/End With block, which allows you to change all properties within the block at once.
4. **Click at the end of the line ActiveCell.FormulaR1C1 = "Bayside Promotion Report", press ENTER, type .Font.Bold = True, press ENTER, type End With, click at the beginning of the first line Selection.Columns.AutoFit, press ENTER, click at the beginning of the new blank line, type Range("A1").Select, then compare your work with the code displayed in Figure 9-9**
   You have added a With Selection/End With block to the procedure, so that you only need to refer to the selection once, rather than multiple times.
5. **Click File on the menu bar, then click Close and Return to Microsoft Excel**
   You want to test the FormatTotal macro to make sure the macro reflects the change you made using the Visual Basic Editor.
6. **Right-click the Technicians sheet tab, click Move or Copy on the shortcut menu, click (move to end), click the Create a copy checkbox, click OK, then rename the Technicians (2) sheet tab to Edit Macro**
7. **Click the Macros button in the Code group on the Developer tab, make sure FormatTotal is selected, then click Run**
   The Bayside Promotion Report label is formatted in bold in cell A1, as displayed in **Figure 9-10**.
8. **Save the workbook**

**Figure 9-8:** Visual Basic Editor

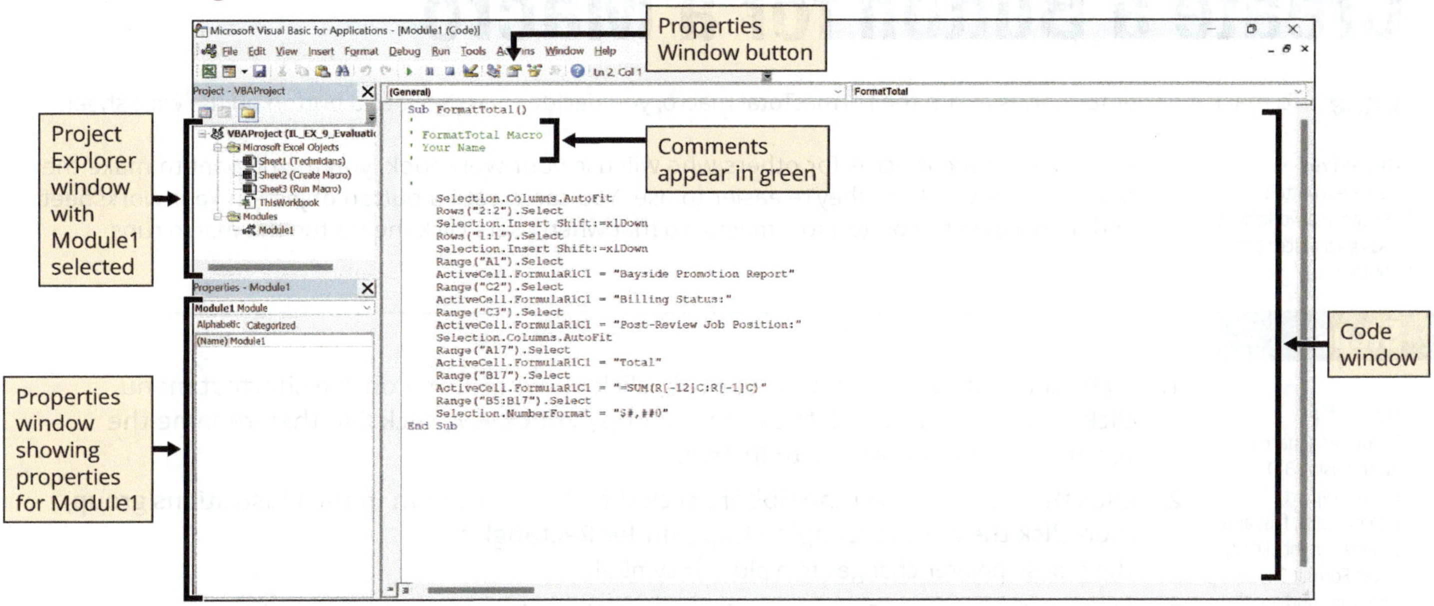


**Figure 9-9:** Edited Visual Basic code

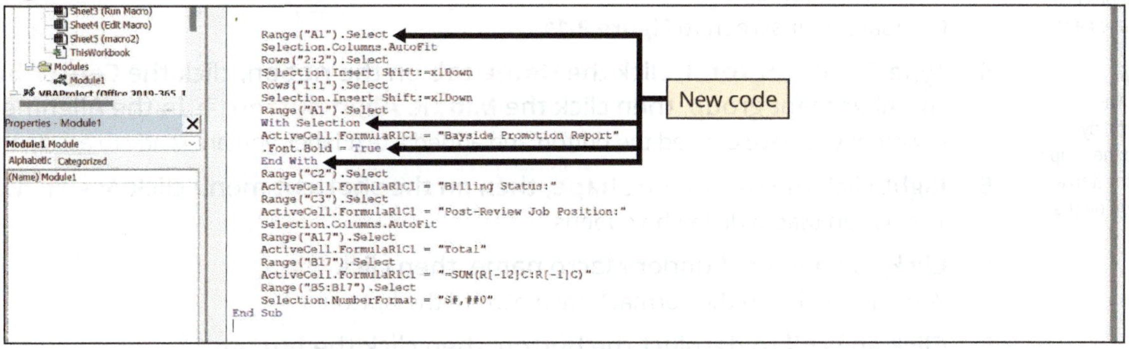


**Figure 9-10:** Result of running the edited FormatTotal macro

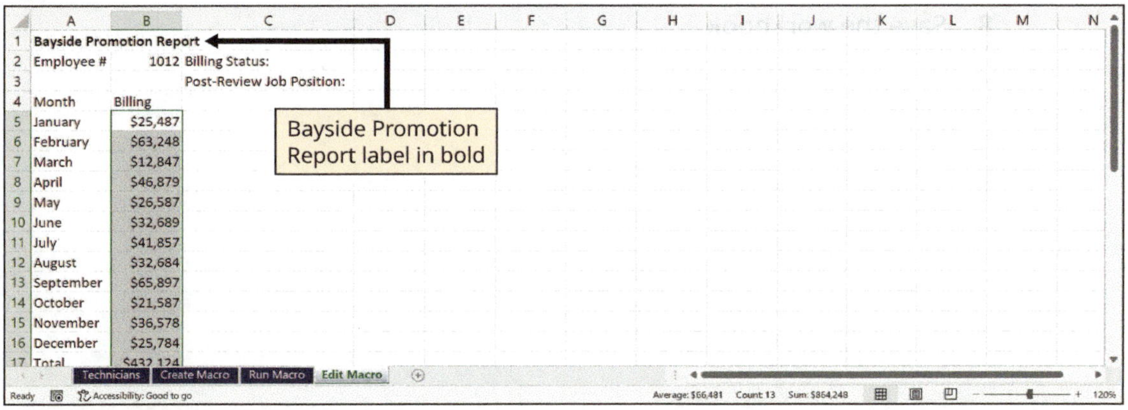


## Using relative referencing when creating a macro

By default, Excel records absolute cell references in macros, but you can record a macro's actions based on the relative position of the active cell by clicking the Use Relative References button in the Code group before recording the action. For example, when you create a macro using the default setting of absolute referencing, bolding the range A1:A3 will always bold that range when the macro is run. However, if you click the Use Relative References button when recording the macro before bolding the range, then running the macro will not necessarily result in bolding the range A1:A3. The range that is bolded will depend on the location of the active cell when the macro is run. If the active cell is F1, then the range F1:F3 will be bolded. Selecting the Use Relative References button highlights the button name, indicating it is active, and it remains active until you click it again to deselect it.

# Create a Button for a Macro

**Case** To make it easier for Carlos to run the FormatTotal macro, you decide to assign it to a button on the worksheet.

**Objectives**
- Create a button shape in a worksheet
- Assign a macro to a button

When you create macros for others who will use your workbook, you might want to make the macros more visible so they're easier to use. You can create a button object on your worksheet and then assign the button to a macro, so that when users click the button the macro runs.

## Steps

**Quick Tip**
To format a macro button using 3-D effects, clip art, photographs, fills, and shadows, right-click it, select Format Shape from the shortcut menu, then select the desired options in the Format Shape pane.

**Quick Tip**
You can move a shape button by pointing to the shape and dragging it to a new location on the worksheet.

1. **Right-click the Technicians sheet tab, click Move or Copy on the shortcut menu, click (move to end), click the Create a copy checkbox, click OK, then rename the Technicians (2) sheet tab to Button**
2. **Click the Insert tab on the ribbon, click the Shapes button in the Illustrations group, then click the first rectangle shape under Rectangles**
   The mouse pointer changes to a plus + symbol.
3. **Click at the upper-left corner of cell A16, then drag the pointer to the lower-right corner of cell B17**
   Compare your screen to **Figure 9-11**.
4. **Type Format & Total, click the Home tab on the ribbon, click the Center button in the Alignment group, then click the Middle Align button in the Alignment group**
   Now that you have created the button and added a text label, you are ready to assign the macro to it.
5. **Right-click the rectangle shape, then on the shortcut menu click Assign Macro**
   The Assign Macro dialog box opens.
6. **Click FormatTotal under Macro name, then click OK**
   You have assigned the FormatTotal macro to the button.
7. **Click any cell to deselect the button, then click the button**
   The FormatTotal macro runs. Compare your worksheet **Figure 9-12**.
8. **Save the workbook**

**Figure 9-11:** Button shape

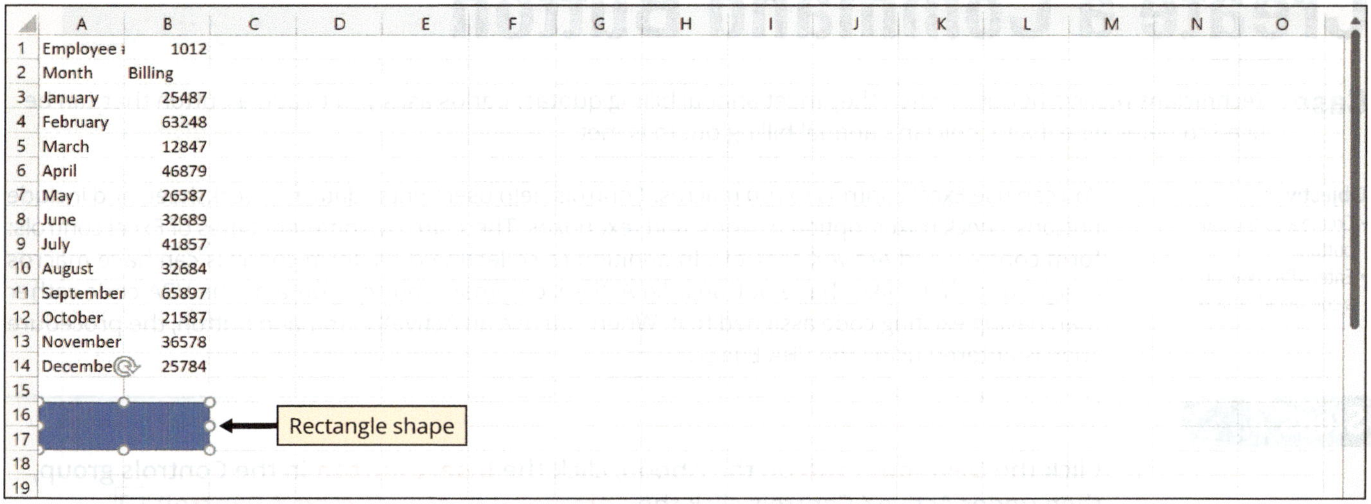


**Figure 9-12:** Result of clicking the macro button

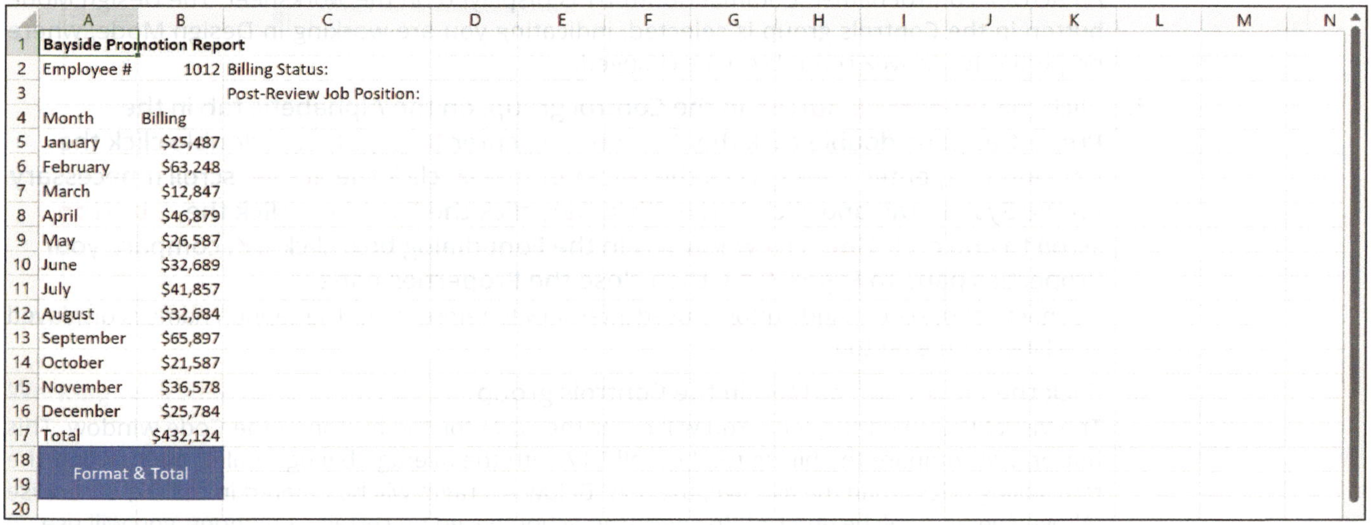


## Copying a macro to another workbook

If you would like to use a macro in another macro-enabled workbook, you can copy the module to that workbook using the Visual Basic Editor. To do so, open both the source workbook (the one containing the macro) and the destination workbook (the one where you want to use the macro). Open the Visual Basic Editor by clicking the Visual Basic button in the Code group on the Developer tab, then verify that macros are enabled in each workbook. In Project Explorer, drag the module that will be copied from the source workbook to the destination workbook.

# Practice

In the exercises that follow, you will practice the skills you have learned in this module.

## Skills Review

You are the assistant to the CFO at a computer chip company that sells chips for engineering, scientific, graphics, AI, and gaming applications. Your customers include both enterprises (large companies) and individual consumers. You regularly review the quarterly sales reports for the divisions in the four offices and evaluate their performance relative to the previous year's average quarterly sales.

1. **Enable a macro.**
   a. You need to plan a macro that enters an Average label in cell B22, a formula in cell C22 that averages the first quarter sales in the range C2:C21, center aligns the labels in the first row, formats the sales in currency format with zero decimal places, and autofits the widths of columns A and B.
   b. Write out the steps the macro will perform, and plan to store the macro in the workbook where you will use it.
   c. Start Excel, open IL_EX_9-2.xlsx from the location where you store your Data Files, then save it as a macro-enabled workbook named **IL_EX_ 9_FirstQuarter**. (**Hint**: The file will have the file extension .xlsm.)
   d. Use the Excel Options feature to display the Developer tab if it does not appear on the Ribbon.
   e. Using the Trust Center dialog box, enable all macros.
2. **Create a macro.**
   a. Activate the Create Macro sheet.
   b. Open the Record Macro dialog box, name the new macro **Average**, store it in the current workbook, and enter your name in the Description text box.
   c. Begin recording the macro.
   d. Enter the label **Average** in cell B22.
   e. Use AutoSum to enter a function in cell C22 that averages the range C2:C21.
   f. Center the labels in A1:C1.
   g. Format the range C2:C22 in currency with zero decimal places.
   h. Autofit the widths of columns A and B.
   i. Stop the recorder, select cell A1, then save the workbook.
3. **Run a macro.**
   a. Copy the FirstQuarter sheet, move it to the end of the workbook sheets, then rename the new sheet **Run Macro**.
   b. With the Run Macro sheet active, use the Macro dialog box to display macros in "This Workbook."
   c. Run the Average macro.
   d. Select cell A1, then confirm that the macro steps were completed correctly.
   e. Save the workbook.
4. **Edit a macro.**
   a. Copy the FirstQuarter sheet, move it to the end of the workbook sheets, then rename the new sheet **Edit Macro**.
   b. With the Edit Macro sheet active, open the Macros dialog box, then open the Average macro for editing.
   c. In the Visual Basic window, add the following two lines to the top of the macro code below the comments:

```
Range("A1:C1").Select
Selection.Font.Bold = True
```

d. Use the Close and Return to Microsoft Excel command on the File menu to return to Excel.
e. Test the Average macro, verifying that the labels in the first row are in bold font.
f. Select cell A1, then save the workbook.

5. **Create a button for a macro.**
   a. Copy the FirstQuarter sheet, move it to the end of the workbook sheets, then rename the new sheet **Button**.
   b. Using the first rectangle shape under Rectangles on the Shapes palette, draw a rectangle in the range A24:B24.
   c. Label the button with the text **Average Sales**, then center and middle align the text on the button.
   d. Assign the Average macro to the button, then test the button.
   e. Confirm that the macro steps were completed correctly, select cell A1, then save the workbook.

6. **Create a command button.**
   a. Enter the label **First Quarter Sales** in cell D2 and autofit the width of column D.
   b. Add an ActiveX command button control in cell D3.
   c. Add a caption to the button with the text **Sales Performance**, add a name with the text **SalesPerformance**, and change the BackColor property to Active Title Bar.
   d. Add the Alt Text **If average sales < 6000 then below average, otherwise above average** to the button. (**Hint**: Click the Accessibility checker in the status bar to display the accessibility pane.)
   e. Resize the button and the width of column D to display the button in the range D3:D4.
   f. Select the button if necessary, then enter the macro code displayed in **Figure 9-20** in the Visual Basic code window. (**Hint**: Remember to use the list arrow at the upper left of the VBA Editor to select the SalesPerformance command object.)

**Figure 9-20**

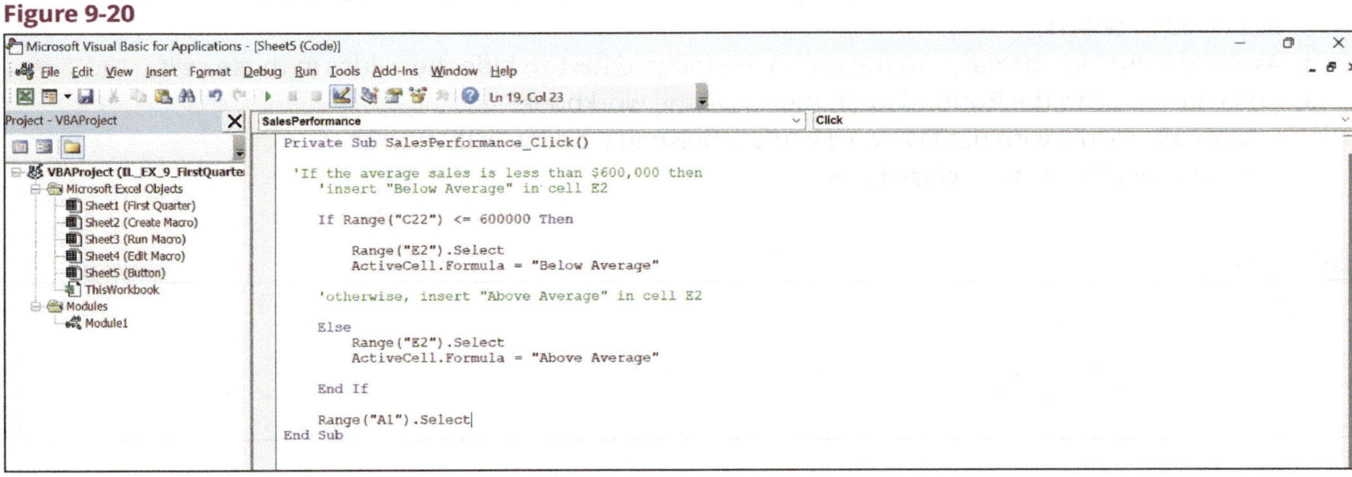


   g. Return to the worksheet, then test the Sales Performance button. (**Hint**: Remember to deselect the Design Mode button before testing the button.)
   h. Verify that "Above Average" is displayed in cell E2, autofit the width of column E, then save the workbook.

7. **Create a form control.**
   a. Add a form control check box in cell D6.
   b. Change the label of the check box to **Consumer**.
   c. Format the check box to enter the cell link of G1.
   d. Assign a new macro named **Consumer** to the check box and enter the Visual Basic code displayed in **Figure 9-21**.

## Skills Review (Continued)

**Figure 9-21**

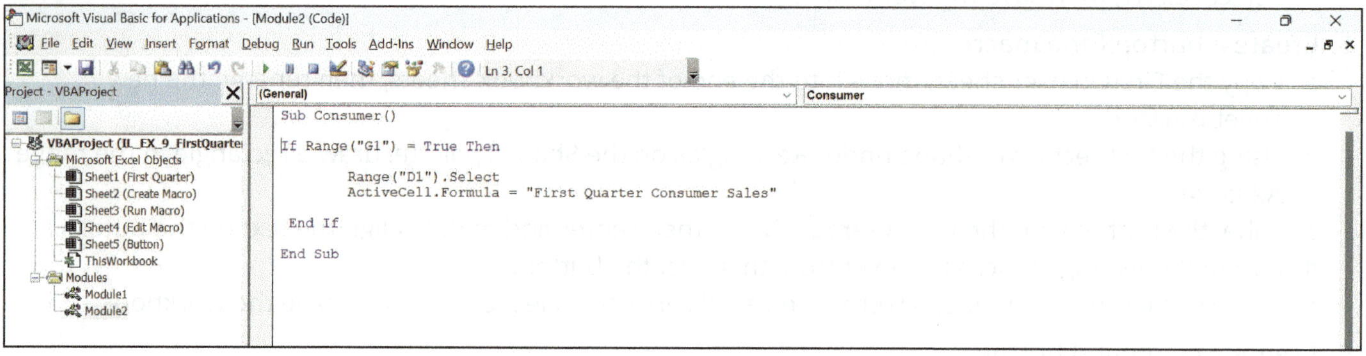


e. Return to the worksheet, deselect the check box, then select it.
f. Verify that the text "First Quarter Consumer Sales" is displayed in cell D1. Verify that "True" is displayed in cell G1.
g. Delete the contents in cells G1 and D1.
h. Add a form control check box in cell D8.
i. Change the label of the check box control to **Enterprise**.
j. Format the check box to enter the cell link of H1.
k. Assign a new macro named **Enterprise** to the check box control and enter the Visual Basic code displayed in **Figure 9-22**.
l. Return to the worksheet, deselect the check box, then select it.
m. Verify that the text "First Quarter Enterprise Sales" is displayed in cell D1. Verify that "True" is displayed in cell H1.
n. Assign the custom format **;;;** to the text in the range G1:H1 to hide the values in those cells.
o. Add your name to the Button footer, then save the workbook.
p. Disable all macros with notification if you are finished working with macros.
q. Close the workbook, then close Excel.

**Figure 9-22**

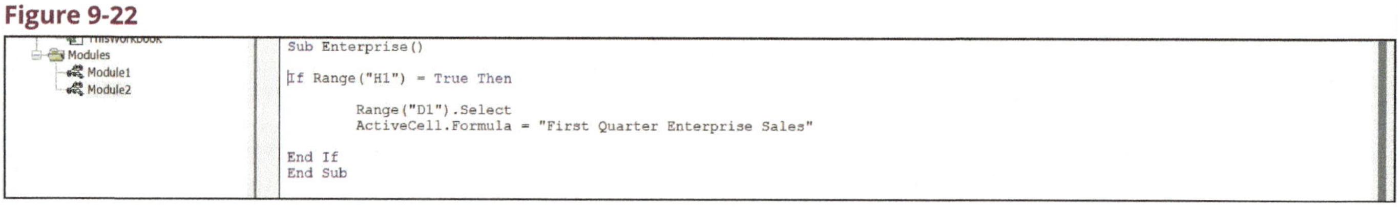


## Independent Challenge 1

As an IT team leader at Perez and Hassan Consulting Group, you develop methods to help your team associates work more efficiently. Your team requested an Excel macro that performs the following:

- Calculates the annual revenue from quarterly reporting worksheets
- Adjusts the column widths to display all worksheet data
- Determines whether the team is eligible for a performance bonus
- Enters the office location in the worksheet header

Plan the steps for this macro, which you will save with the current workbook.

a. Start Excel, open IL_EX_9-3.xlsx from where you store your Data Files, then save it as a macro-enabled workbook called **IL_EX_ 9_PandH**.
b. Check your macro security setting on the Developer tab to be sure that all macros are enabled.
c. On the Create Macro sheet of the workbook, create a new macro named **AnnualSales**, enter your name in the macro description, then save it in the current workbook. Record a macro that accomplishes the following:
   - Enters a label of **Annual Total** in cell F2
   - Enters a formula in cell F3 to calculate the pharmaceuticals total for the four quarters
   - Copies the formula in cell F3 to the range F4:F6
   - Enters a formula in cell F7 to calculate the total for the range F3:F6
   - Formats the values in the range F3:F7 in currency format without decimals
   - Enters a label of **Total of All Divisions** in cell E7 and right aligns the label in the cell
   - Bolds the labels in the range A3:A6 and cell A1
   - AutoFits column F to display all the column data
   - Merges and centers the company name in cell A1 over columns A through F
   - Remember to stop recording when you are finished
d. Copy the Quarterly Sales worksheet and place the copied worksheet at the end of the workbook's sheets. Name the new worksheet **Edit Macro**, then edit the AnnualSales macro to also bold the range B2:F2. Place the new code at the bottom, just above the End Sub line.
e. With the Edit Macro sheet active, run the AnnualSales macro and verify that the labels in cells B2:F2 are formatted in bold.
f. Copy the Quarterly Sales worksheet and place the copied worksheet at the end of the workbook's sheets. Name the new worksheet **Button**, then create a button on the new worksheet in the range A8:B9, using the first Rectangle shape tool. Label the button **Annual Totals**. Center and middle align the button label.
g. Assign the AnnualSales macro to the new button, then test the button.
h. Insert an ActiveX command button in the range A11:B12. Using the Properties panel, change the name of the button to **Bonus** and the caption of the button to **Check for Bonus**.
i. Add the Alt Text **Check for bonus if annual sales > = $10,000,000** to the button named Bonus. (**Hint**: Click the Accessibility checker in the status bar to display the accessibility pane.)
j. Enter the ActiveX command button code displayed in **Figure 9-23**. (**Hint**: Don't forget to select the Bonus button in the VBA window by clicking the list arrow at the top of the code window.)

**Figure 9-23**

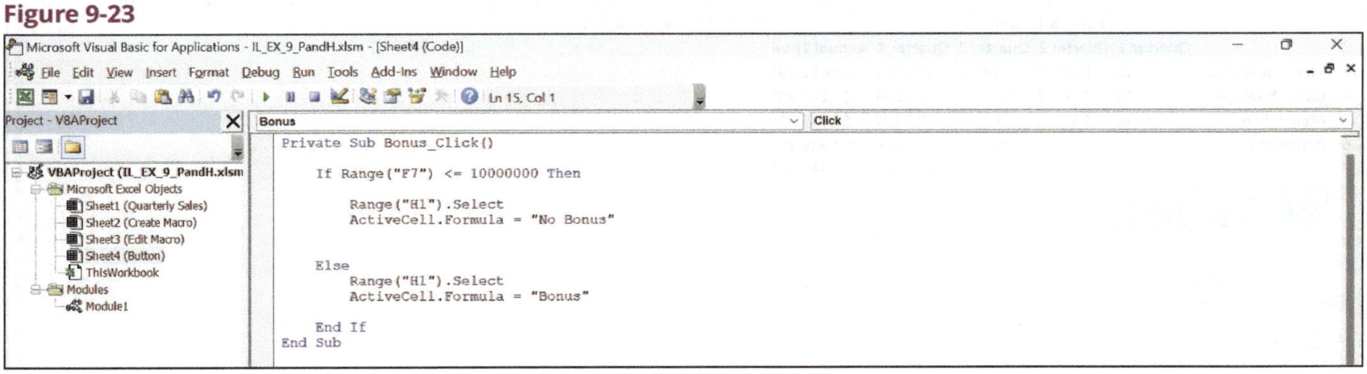

# Independent Challenge 1 (Continued)

k. Return to the Button worksheet and click the Check for Bonus button to display the bonus status for the current year. (**Hint**: Don't forget to deselect Design Mode before using the button.)

l. In cells A14 and A16, create two form control check boxes, the first named **New York** and the second named **Los Angeles**. Assign cell K1 as the cell link for the first check box and cell K2 as the cell link for the second check box. (**Hint**: If clicking the Properties button doesn't open the Format Control dialog box, right-click the check box, then click Format Control in the shortcut menu.)

m. Name the macro assigned to the first check box **NY**, then enter the check box code displayed in **Figure 9-24** for the first check box.

**Figure 9-24**

```
Sub NY()
If Range("K1") = "True" Then

  ActiveWindow.View = xlPageLayoutView
    With ActiveSheet.PageSetup
      .CenterHeader = "New York Office"
    End With
    Range("A1").Select
    Application.Wait (Now + TimeValue("0:00:02"))
    ActiveWindow.View = xlNormalView

Else

If Range("K2") = "True" Then
ActiveWindow.View = xlPageLayoutView
    With ActiveSheet.PageSetup
      .CenterHeader = "Los Angeles Office"
    End With
    Range("A1").Select
    Application.Wait (Now + TimeValue("0:00:02"))
    ActiveWindow.View = xlNormalView
End If
End If
End Sub
```

n. Name the macro assigned to the second check box **LA**, then enter the check box code for the second check box by copying the code between the lines Sub NY () and End Sub for the first check box and pasting it in the code window for the second check box between the Sub LA () and End Sub lines.

o. Make sure both check boxes aren't checked, exit Design Mode, if necessary, then check the New York check box. Verify that "New York Office" is displayed in the worksheet header. Delete True from cell K1, then click the Los Angeles check box. Verify that "Los Angeles Office" is displayed in the worksheet header. Format the range K1:K2 to hide the values then compare your worksheet to **Figure 9-25**.

p. Enter your name in the worksheet footer. Save the file, disable all macros with notification if you are finished working with macros, close the workbook, then close Excel.

**Figure 9-25**

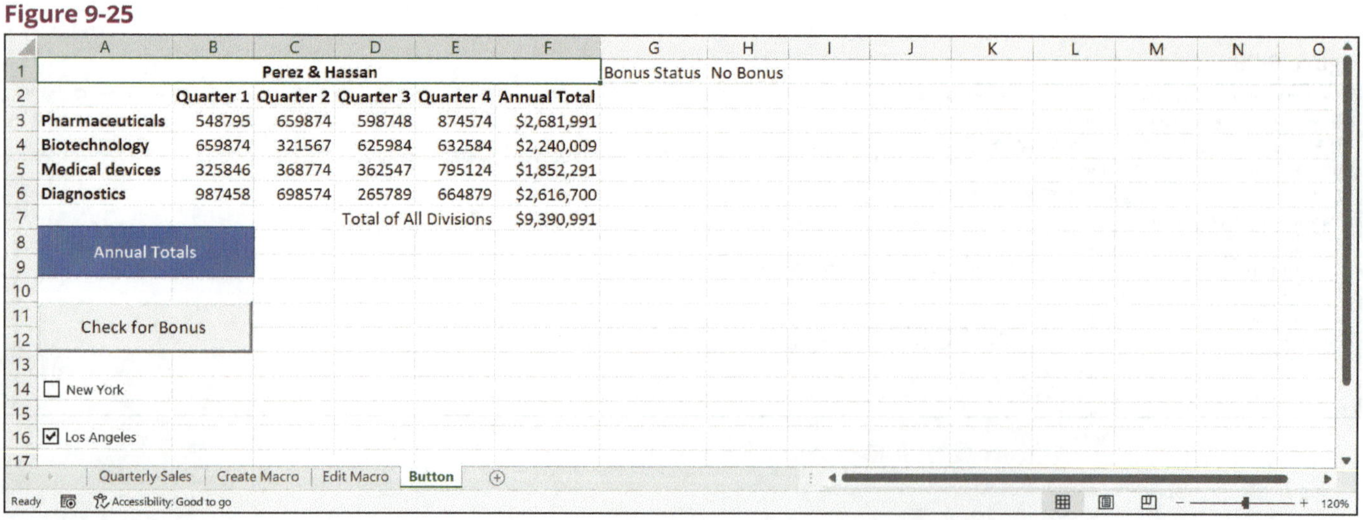

| | A | B | C | D | E | F | G | H |
|---|---|---|---|---|---|---|---|---|
| 1 | Perez & Hassan | | | | | | Bonus Status | No Bonus |
| 2 | | Quarter 1 | Quarter 2 | Quarter 3 | Quarter 4 | Annual Total | | |
| 3 | Pharmaceuticals | 548795 | 659874 | 598748 | 874574 | $2,681,991 | | |
| 4 | Biotechnology | 659874 | 321567 | 625984 | 632584 | $2,240,009 | | |
| 5 | Medical devices | 325846 | 368774 | 362547 | 795124 | $1,852,291 | | |
| 6 | Diagnostics | 987458 | 698574 | 265789 | 664879 | $2,616,700 | | |
| 7 | | | | Total of All Divisions | | $9,390,991 | | |

## Independent Challenge 2

You are an assistant to the dean at a state university. As part of your work, you analyze enrollment data for the school's divisions. The CFO is developing next year's budget and needs the enrollment data for the past two years. You will create macros to analyze the enrollment change in each division and calculate the average change for all enrollment at the University. (Note: Remember to disable all macros when you are finished working with them.)

a. Start Excel, open IL_EX_9-4.xlsx from where you store your Data Files, then save it as a macro-enabled workbook called **IL_EX_ 9_Enrollment**.

b. Check your macro security setting on the Developer tab to be sure that all macros are enabled.

c. Activate the Create Macro sheet, record a macro with the name **Change**, store the macro in this workbook, and then add your name to the description
The macro should do the following:
   - Calculate the change in enrollment in column D. (**Hint**: To calculate the change, subtract the year 1 amount from the year 2 amount, and then divide that result by the year 1 amount; =(C5-B5)/B5 is the formula that you need to enter.)
   - Format the values in column D as percentages with two decimals.
   - Format the label in cell A1 in Title style.
   - Center align the headings in the range A4:D4.
   - Add an Average label in cell C10 formatted as right aligned.
   - Enter a formula in cell D10 to calculate the average of enrollment changes in column D.

d. Copy the Enrollment worksheet and place the copied worksheet at the end of the workbook's sheets. Name the new worksheet **Run Macro**.

e. With the Run Macro sheet active, run the Change macro using the Macro dialog box and verify the macro results are correct.

f. Copy the Enrollment worksheet and place the copied worksheet at the end of the workbook's sheets. Name the new worksheet **Edit Macro**.

g. With the Edit macro sheet active, edit the Change macro to insert code that formats the ranges A4:D4 and C10:D10 as bold. To do this, add the following lines before the End Sub line:

```
Range("A4:D4").Select
Selection.Font.Bold = True
Range("C10:D10").Select
Selection.Font.Bold = True
```

h. Test the change macro on the Edit Macro sheet to verify that it runs correctly and that the ranges appear in bold format.

i. With the Edit Macro sheet active, create a command button (ActiveX Control) in the range B11:B12.

j. Using the Properties panel, change the name of the button to **Hide** and the caption of the button to **Hide Division Details**, then resize the button to fully display its name.

k. Add the Alt Text **Hide the Divisions worksheet** to the button. (**Hint**: Click the Accessibility checker in the status bar to display the Accessibility pane.)

l. Enter the code for the new button as displayed below. (**Hint**: Don't forget to select the Hide button in the VBA window by clicking the list arrow at the top of the code window.)

```
Sheets("Divisions").Select
ActiveWindow.SelectedSheets.Visible = False
```

m. Create a second command button (ActiveX Control) in the range D11:D12.

n. Using the Properties panel, change the name of the button to **Show** and the caption of the button to **Show Division Details**.

o. Add the Alt Text **Show the Divisions worksheet** to the button.

## Independent Challenge 2 (Continued)

p. Enter the code for the button as displayed below. (**Hint**: Don't forget to select the Show button in the VBA window by clicking the list arrow at the top of the code window.)

```
Sheets("Enrollment").Select
Sheets("Divisions").Visible = True
```

q. Align the tops of the buttons. (**Hints**: Because these are ActiveX controls, you must be in Design Mode to select multiple buttons. With the buttons selected, click the Align button in the Arrange group on the Shape Format tab, then click Align Top.)

r. With the buttons selected in Design Mode, change their sizes to **.5"** for the shape height and **1.5"** for the shape width. (**Hint**: Use the Size group on the Shape Format tab.)

s. Exit Design Mode, then test the Hide Division Details button and verify that the Divisions sheet is hidden. Activate the Edit Macro sheet, then test the Show Division Details button and verify the Divisions sheet is now displayed.

t. Compare your Edit Macro worksheet to **Figure 9-26**.

u. Change the name of the Edit Macro sheet to **Final**, enter your name in the Final worksheet footer, save the workbook, close the workbook, close Excel, then submit the workbook to your instructor.

**Figure 9-26**

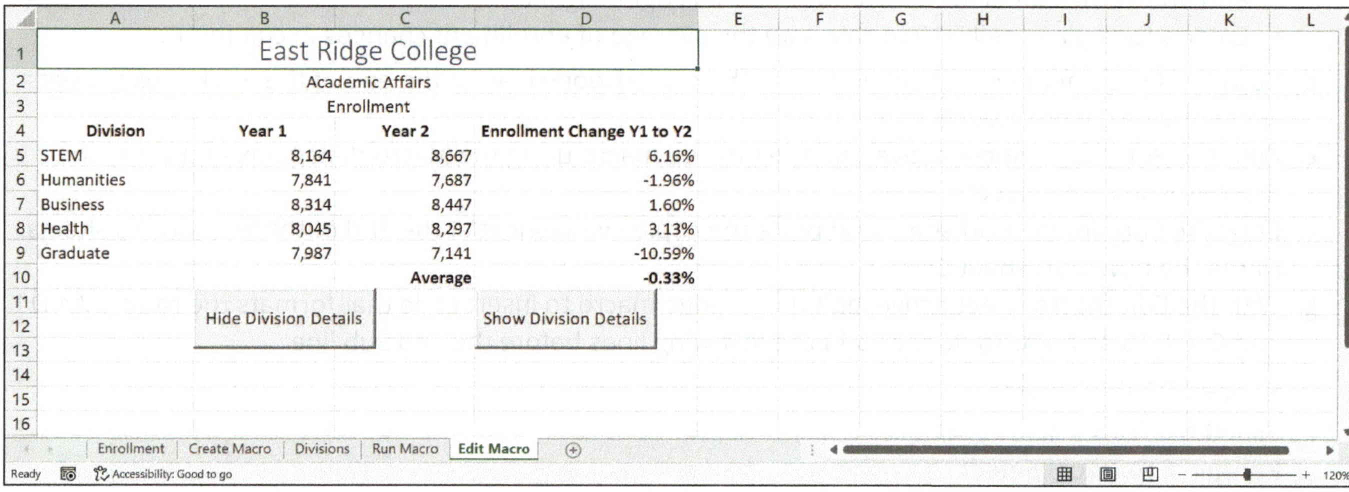

# Visual Workshop

Start Excel, open IL_EX_9-5.xlsx from the location where you store your Data Files, then save it as a macro-enabled workbook called **IL_EX_9_Inventory**. Using **Figure 9-27** as a guide, on the Quarterly Inventory sheet record a macro named **Format**, stored in the workbook, that performs the following actions:

- Adds a row at the top of the worksheet
- Inserts a label of **ACE Automotive Supplies** in cell A1, formatted with the Heading 1 cell style and merged and centered across columns A through E
- Calculates values in column E by multiplying cost by quantity
- Applies the Currency format with two decimal places to the values in columns C and E
- Center aligns the headings in row 2
- Uses conditional formatting to add the 3 Symbols (Uncircled) icon set to the values in the Quantity column
- Ends with cell A1 as the active cell

Add a button labeled **Format** to the Test Macro sheet, assign the Format macro to the button, and test the button. Add your name to the footers of both worksheets, save the workbook, close the workbook, submit the workbook to your instructor, then close Excel. (Note: Remember to enable all macros before beginning this Visual Workshop, and to disable them when you are finished.)

**Figure 9-27**

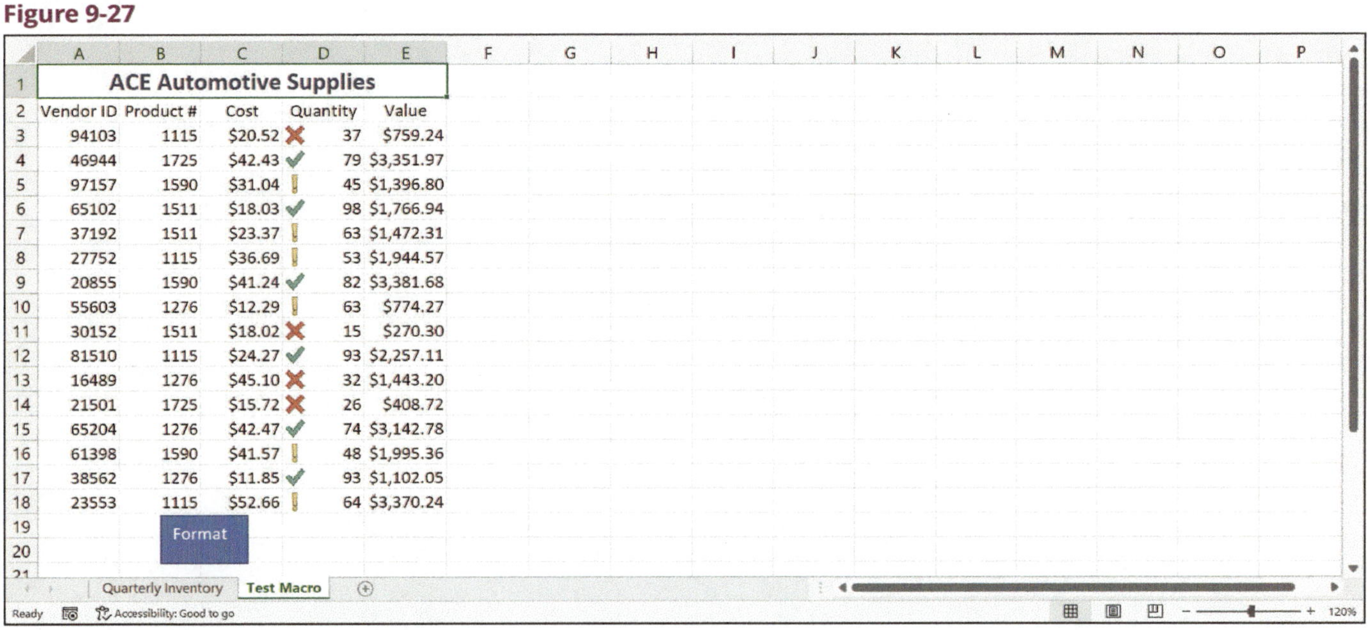

ACE Automotive Supplies

| Vendor ID | Product # | Cost | Quantity | Value |
|---|---|---|---|---|
| 94103 | 1115 | $20.52 | 37 | $759.24 |
| 46944 | 1725 | $42.43 | 79 | $3,351.97 |
| 97157 | 1590 | $31.04 | 45 | $1,396.80 |
| 65102 | 1511 | $18.03 | 98 | $1,766.94 |
| 37192 | 1511 | $23.37 | 63 | $1,472.31 |
| 27752 | 1115 | $36.69 | 53 | $1,944.57 |
| 20855 | 1590 | $41.24 | 82 | $3,381.68 |
| 55603 | 1276 | $12.29 | 63 | $774.27 |
| 30152 | 1511 | $18.02 | 15 | $270.30 |
| 81510 | 1115 | $24.27 | 93 | $2,257.11 |
| 16489 | 1276 | $45.10 | 32 | $1,443.20 |
| 21501 | 1725 | $15.72 | 26 | $408.72 |
| 65204 | 1276 | $42.47 | 74 | $3,142.78 |
| 61398 | 1590 | $41.57 | 48 | $1,995.36 |
| 38562 | 1276 | $11.85 | 93 | $1,102.05 |
| 23553 | 1115 | $52.66 | 64 | $3,370.24 |

# Worksheet Management

## Case

Elena Fuentes, Bayside's Vice President of Finance, wants to ensure consistency and accessibility in revenue workbooks at Bayside. She asks you to use Excel's tools and options to help Bayside employees work efficiently in a customized environment and ensure all employees can access revenue data.

## Module Objectives

After completing this module, you will be able to:

- Create and apply a template
- Create a custom AutoFill list
- Customize a theme
- Use comments
- Use notes
- Change Excel default settings
- Use a password to protect a workbook
- Create accessible workbooks

## Files You Will Need

IL_EX_10-1.xlsx
IL_EX_10-2.xlsx
IL_EX_10-3.xlsx
IL_EX_10-4.xlsx
IL_EX_10-5.xlsx

# Use Comments

**Case** You think one of the quarterly revenue values in the worksheet may be incorrect, so you decide to add a comment about it. You also want to add a question for Elena about a quarterly revenue value that is significantly higher than the revenue for the other quarters. The replies to the comments in the worksheet will be displayed when the workbook is sent back to you.

**Objectives**
- Insert a new comment
- Display worksheet comments
- Respond to a comment

**Threaded comments** are worksheet comments that contain a Reply box directly below the original comment, allowing you to discuss workbook data with others. When you sort or copy and paste cells, any comments attached to them move to the new location. In PivotTable reports, however, the comments do not move with the worksheet data.

## Steps

1. Click the **File tab** on the ribbon, click **Options**, click **Advanced** in the Excel Options list, scroll to the **Display** section, in the **For cells with comments, show:** section click the **Indicators only, and comments and notes on hover option button** to select it if necessary, then click **OK**
   The other options in the "For cells with comments, show:" area allow you to display comments and notes with their indicators or no comments, notes, or indicators.
2. On the U.S. sheet click cell **B10**, click the **Review tab** on the ribbon, then click the **New Comment button** in the Comments group
   The Comment box opens, as displayed in **Figure 10-10**. Excel automatically includes the current user name at the beginning of the comment; this is the name of the user currently logged in to Windows. The **user name** is the name that appears in the User name text box of the Excel Options dialog box.
3. Type **Is this figure correct? It seems low.**, click the **Post button** [▶], then click outside the Comment box
   A dark pink triangle appears in the upper-right corner of cell B10, indicating that a comment is attached to the cell.
4. Place the pointer over cell **B10**
   The comment appears next to the cell with the Reply box. When you move the pointer or click outside of cell B10, the comment disappears.
5. Right-click cell **E7**, click **New Comment** on the shortcut menu, type **Is this increase due to the new online marketing campaign?**, click the **Post button** [▶], then click outside the Comment box
6. Click cell **A1**, then click the **Show Comments button** in the Comments group
   **Figure 10-11** displays the two comments in the Comments pane.

**Quick Tip**
To delete a comment in a selected cell, click the Delete button in the Comments group.

7. In the Comments pane, select the **comment in cell B10**, click the **Next Comment button** in the Comments group, with the comment in cell E7 selected, type **Not sure - we are still waiting for 4th quarter sales analytics.** in the Reply box, click the **Post button**, then close the Comments pane
   You can move to a previous comment by clicking the Previous Comment button in the Comments group.

**Trouble**
Your screen may show Post rather than Save to save the change; this is not a problem.

8. Move the pointer over cell **B10**, click **Edit** in the Comment box, type **Elena -** at the beginning of the comment in the Comment box, then click **Save**
   After saving your file the user name for comments may change to Author.
9. Save the workbook

**Figure 10-10:** Comment box

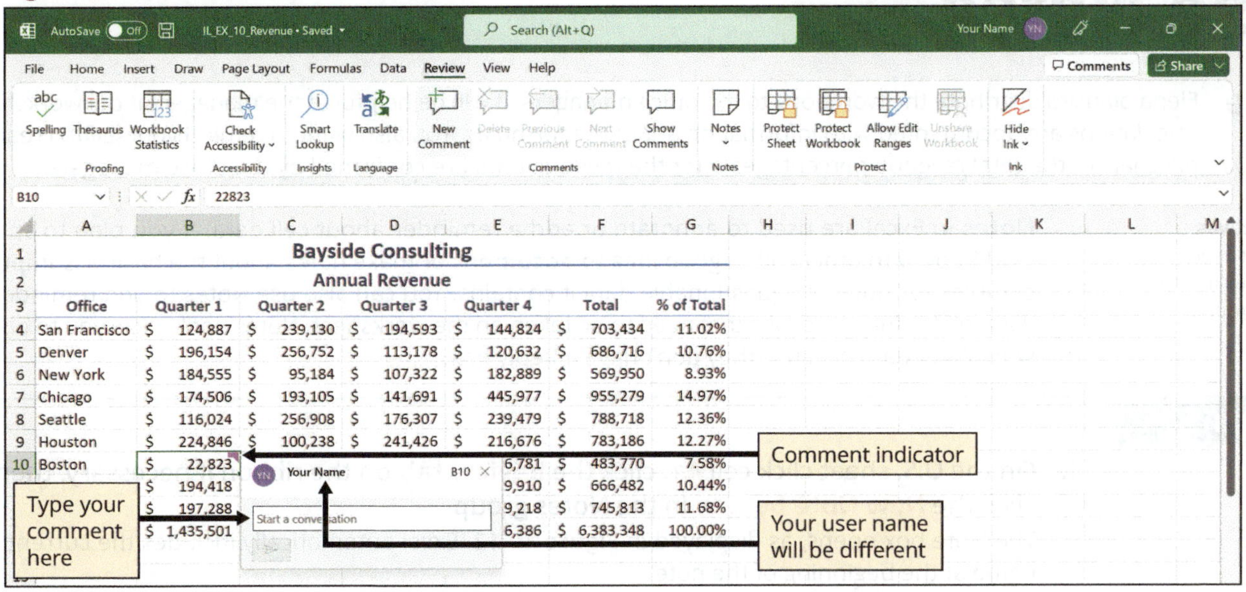


**Figure 10-11:** Comments pane

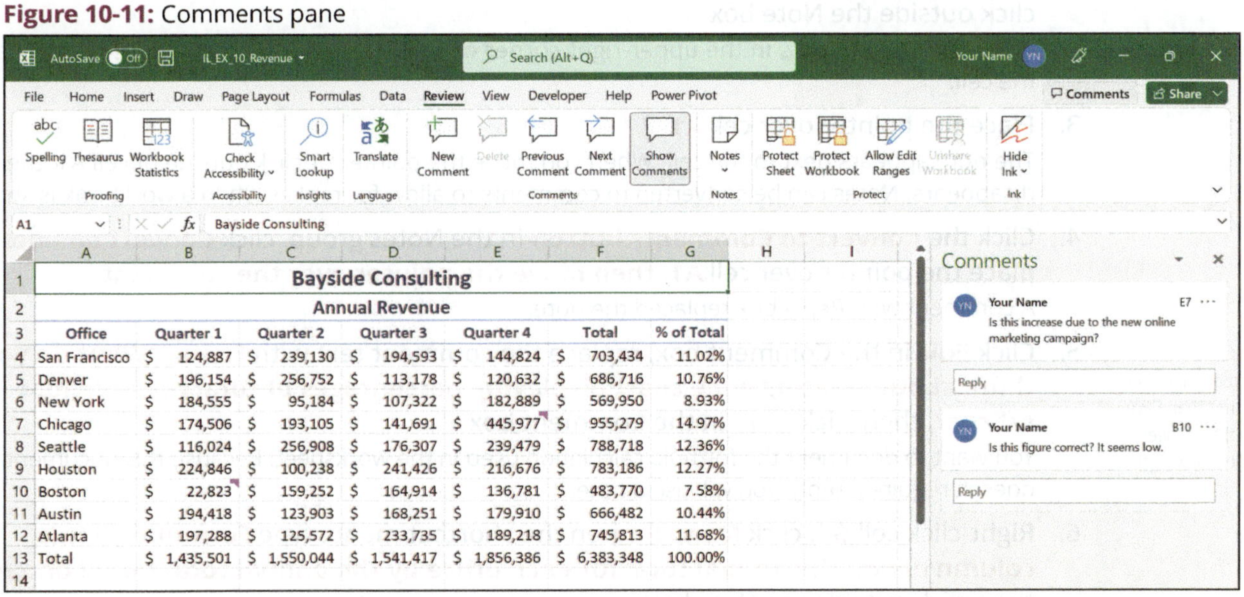


### Co-authoring by sharing an Excel workbook

If you have a subscription to Office 365, you can co-author a workbook with others to collaboratively add and edit data. When you co-author, the names of the people you are working with and the changes they made are displayed on the worksheet. When a file is saved to OneDrive, AutoSave is enabled so the workbook is automatically saved as you and other people make changes.

To share your workbook, click the Share button in the upper-right corner of the screen, then click Share in the menu. In the Share dialog box, you can upload your workbook to a OneDrive account and provide a name for the workbook. The Share dialog box allows you to enter the email addresses, names, or the group of your co-authors. Clicking the Can edit arrow allows you to choose whether the recipients will be able to view or edit the workbook. After entering an optional message, click Send to email a link to the workbook on OneDrive. You can also copy a link to the workbook by clicking the Copy link button. When a recipient clicks the link, the workbook opens in Excel for the web. A copy of the workbook can be downloaded to use in the Excel desktop app by clicking File, clicking Save As, then clicking Download a Copy. You can also use the Share dialog box to email a copy of the file as a workbook or PDF file using the options in the Attach a copy instead area.

# Use Notes

**Case** Elena plans to distribute the workbook to the office managers. It will be helpful to the managers if the worksheet calculations are documented with information about the formulas. You also want to remind yourself to create a pie chart of the total revenue percentages after the revenue data are confirmed by the office managers.

**Objectives**
- Insert a note
- Convert notes to comments

**Notes** in Excel are used to annotate or add a reminder about cell data. If you plan to share a workbook with others, it's a good idea to **document** or make notes about the basic assumptions, complex formulas, or questionable data it contains. You can also use Notes to add reminders to yourself for future actions that need to be taken on the worksheet. Notes don't allow you to discuss worksheet data because they don't have a Reply box.

## Steps

1. **On the U.S. sheet click cell A1, click the Review tab on the ribbon if necessary, then click the New Note button in the Notes group**
   The Note box opens, as displayed in **Figure 10-12**. Excel automatically includes the current user name at the beginning of the note.
2. **Type Create a pie chart displaying percentages of total revenue for offices., then click outside the Note box**
   A red triangle appears in the upper-right corner of cell A1, indicating that a note is attached to the cell.
3. **Place the pointer over cell A1**
   The note appears next to the cell. When you move the pointer or click outside of cell A1, the note disappears. Notes can be converted to comments to allow for replies when a workbook is shared.
4. **Click the Convert to Comments button in the Notes group, click Convert all notes, place the pointer over cell A1, then move the pointer over the comment**
   A comment with Reply box replaced the note.
5. **Click Edit in the Comment box, replace the comment text with Elena – What do you think about creating a pie chart displaying percentages of total revenue for offices?, then click Save in the Comment box**
   You want to document the formula calculation used in the worksheet. Because this documentation doesn't require a reply, you will use a note.

   **Trouble**
   Your screen may show Post rather than Save to save the change; this is not a problem.
6. **Right-click cell G3, click New Note on the shortcut menu, type Formulas in this column divide the annual total for each office by the annual total for all offices., then click outside the Note box**
7. **Click the Show All Notes button in the Notes group, then drag the lower-right corner of the Note box to the right to fully display the note if necessary**
   **Figure 10-13** displays the note on the screen.
8. **Click the Show All Notes button in the Notes group, then save the workbook**
   The note is no longer displayed on the screen.

**Figure 10-12:** Note box

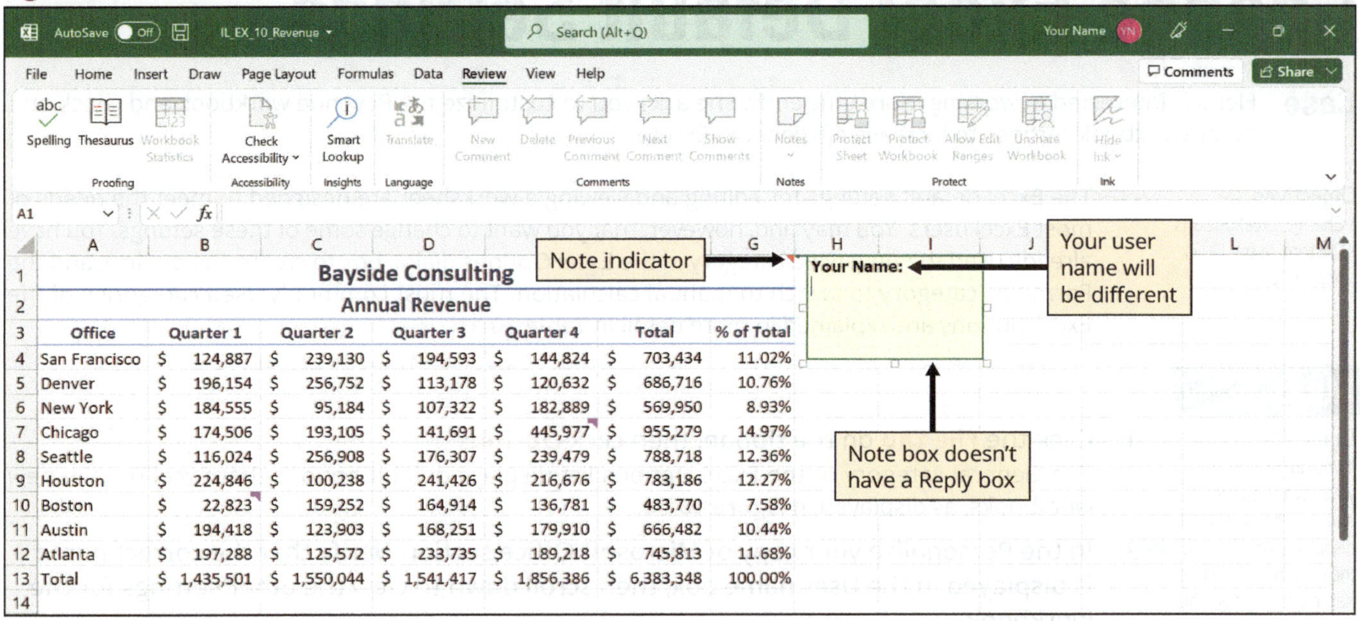


**Figure 10-13:** Note displayed on screen

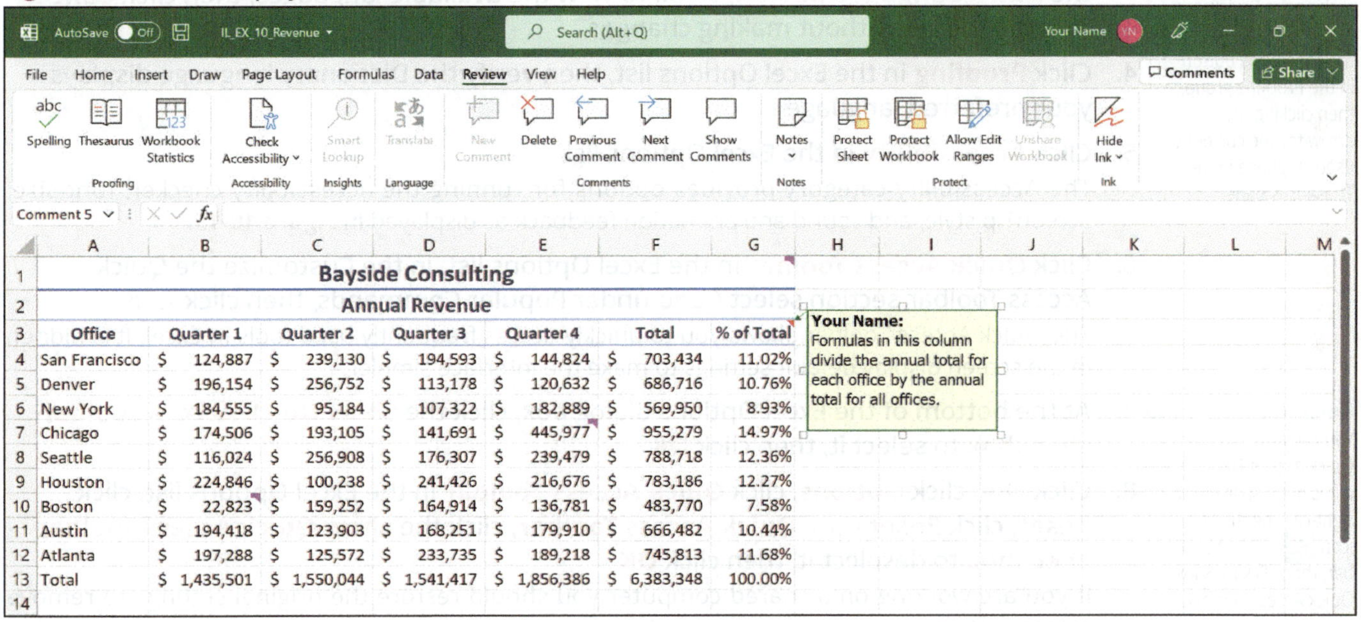

# Change Excel Default Settings

**Case** Elena is interested in working more efficiently. She asks you to customize the Revenue workbook and check on other workbook settings to increase efficiency in Excel.

**Objectives**
- Change Excel options
- Customize the Quick Access Toolbar

The Excel default settings for editing and viewing a worksheet are designed to meet the needs of most Excel users. You may find, however, that you want to change some of these settings. You have already used the Advanced category in the Excel Options dialog box to create custom lists and the Formulas category to switch to manual calculation. The most commonly used categories of the Excel Options are explained in more detail in **Table 10-1**.

## Steps

**Quick Tip** If you are working on your own computer and your name is not displayed, you can edit the contents of the User name box to reflect the correct information.

**Quick Tip** You can change the thesaurus language by clicking the Review tab on the ribbon, clicking the Thesaurus button in the Proofing group, then clicking the arrow for the currently used language in the Thesaurus pane.

**Quick Tip** You can also add the Quick Access Toolbar if it is not displayed by right-clicking the Save icon on the title bar, then clicking Show Quick Access Toolbar.

1. **Click the File tab on the ribbon, then click Options**
   The General category of the Excel Options list displays default options that Excel uses in new workbooks, as displayed in **Figure 10-14**.
2. **In the Personalize your copy of Microsoft Office section, verify that the correct name is displayed in the User name box, then scroll down to view the other settings for the workbook**
3. **Click Language in the Excel Options list, verify your preferred language is listed in the Office authoring languages and proofing section of the Excel Options dialog box, click the Add a Language button, scroll to view the available languages, then click Cancel to close the list without making changes**
4. **Click Proofing in the Excel Options list, then verify the Dictionary language displays your preferred language**
5. **Click Accessibility in the Excel Options list**
   The Accessibility category provides options for running the accessibility checker, font size, ScreenTip style, and sound and animation feedback as displayed in **Figure 10-15**.
6. **Click Quick Access Toolbar in the Excel Options list, in the Customize the Quick Access Toolbar section select Redo under Popular Commands, then click Add**
   The Quick Access Toolbar allows you to quickly access frequently used tools in Excel. It is hidden in the screen display default settings to make the interface simpler.
7. **At the bottom of the Excel Options dialog box, click the Show Quick Access Toolbar checkbox to select it, then click OK**
8. **Click File, click Options, click Quick Access Toolbar in the Excel Options list, click Reset, click Reset only Quick Access Toolbar, click the Show Quick Access Toolbar checkbox to deselect it, then click OK**
   If you are working on a shared computer you should restore the original settings to remove customizations.

### Tracking changes in a workbook

You can track changes to a workbook when you want to display what changes are being made to it from the present point onward. To use this feature, you can add the Track Changes button to the ribbon. To do so, right-click the ribbon, click Customize the Ribbon, right-click Review, click Add New Group, click New Group (Custom), click the Choose Commands from the arrow, click Commands Not in the Ribbon, click Track changes (Legacy) in the list of commands, click Add, then click OK. You can use the Highlight Changes command to specify what types of changes to track. Note that this legacy feature is not compatible with certain newer features in Excel, such as uploading to OneDrive, as this method of working collaboratively on workbooks has been replaced by co-authoring.

**Figure 10-14:** General category of Excel options

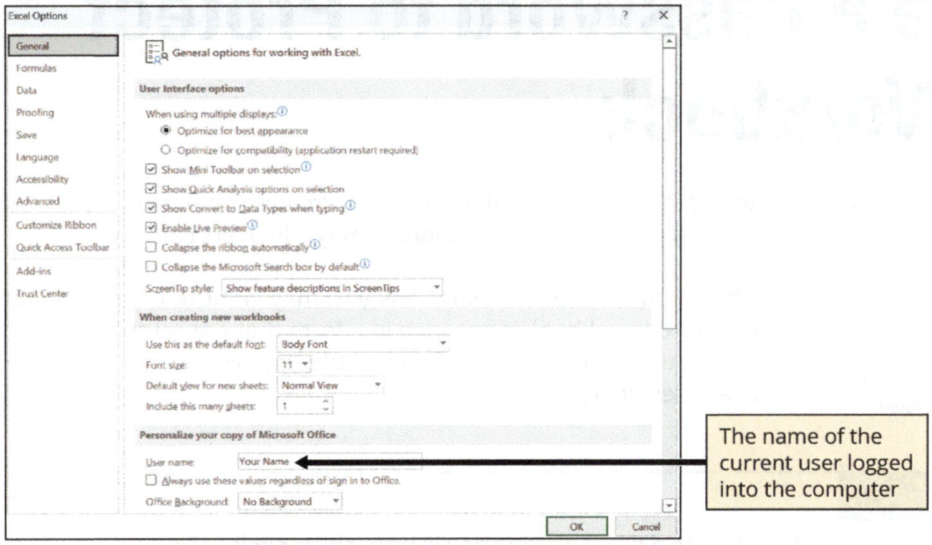


**Figure 10-15:** Accessibility category of Excel options

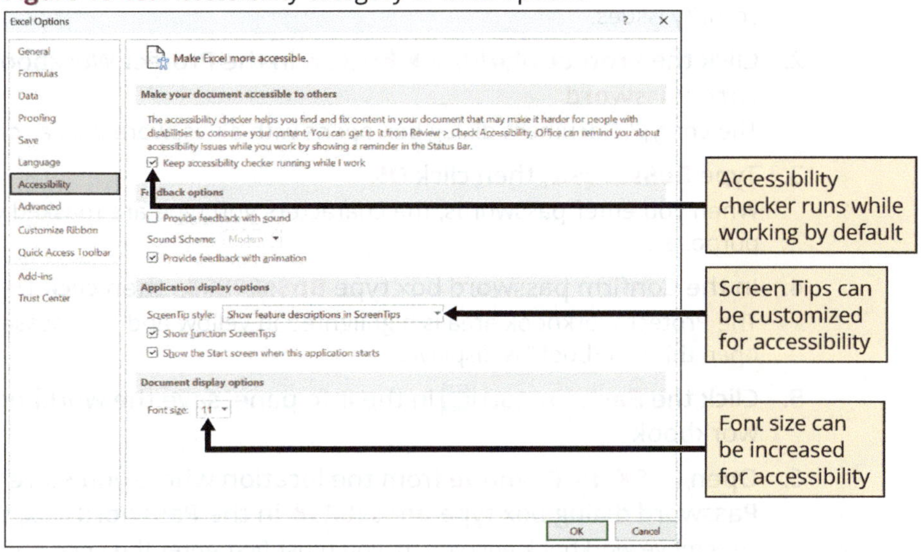


**Table 10-1:** Categories of Excel options you can change

| category | allows you to |
|---|---|
| General | Change the user name, customize default settings of new workbooks, enable LinkedIn features, and customize the user interface |
| Formulas | Control how the worksheet is calculated, how formulas appear, and error-checking settings and rules |
| Data | Control how data is analyzed and imported |
| Proofing | Control AutoCorrect and spell-checking options |
| Save | Select a default format and location for saving files, and customize AutoRecover settings |
| Language | Control the languages displayed and add additional languages and proofing tools |
| Accessibility | Specify options for workbook accessibility features and checking |
| Advanced | Set options for pen settings, create custom lists, and customize editing and display options |
| Customize Ribbon | Add commands, tabs, and groups to the Ribbon |
| Quick Access Toolbar | Add commands to the Quick Access Toolbar |
| Add-Ins | Install Excel Add-in programs such as Solver and Analysis ToolPak |
| Trust Center | Change Trust Center settings to protect your Excel files and your computer |

# Use a Password to Protect a Workbook

**Case** Elena asks you to put the workbook with revenue information on one of Bayside's servers. You decide to encrypt the workbook with a password so only authorized Bayside users can open it.

**Objectives**
- Use a password to encrypt a workbook
- Delete a password on an encrypted workbook

When you distribute a workbook you may want to encrypt it with a password to protect it. An encrypted workbook is encoded in a form that only authorized people with a password can read. For security, it is a good idea to include uppercase and lowercase letters, numbers, and special characters in a password.

## Steps

1. **Click the File tab on the ribbon, then click Info**
   The Info pane displays information about your file. It also includes tools you can use to check for security issues.
2. **Click the Protect Workbook button in the Protect Workbook area, then click Encrypt with Password**
   The Encrypt Document dialog box opens with a Password box, as displayed in **Figure 10-16**.
3. **Type BbSs2029&, then click OK**
   When you enter passwords, the characters you type are masked with bullets (• • •) for security purposes.
4. **In the Confirm password box type BbSs2029&, then click OK**
   The Protect Workbook area is highlighted in yellow and the message "A password is required to open this workbook" is displayed.
5. **Click the Back button in the Info pane, save the workbook, then close the workbook**
6. **Open IL_EX_10_Revenue from the location where you store your Data Files, in the Password dialog box type BbSs2029& in the Password box, then click OK**
   To remove workbook encryption, you must first enter the encryption password, to verify that you are qualified to make changes.
7. **Click the File tab on the ribbon, click Info, click the Protect Workbook button in the Protect Workbook area, then click Encrypt with Password**
   **Figure 10-17** displays the Encrypt Document dialog with the masked password.
8. **In the Password box select the masked password, press DEL, then click OK**
   The password is removed from the Workbook, and encryption is turned off.
9. **Click the Back button in the Info pane, then save the workbook**

**Figure 10-16:** Encrypt Document dialog box

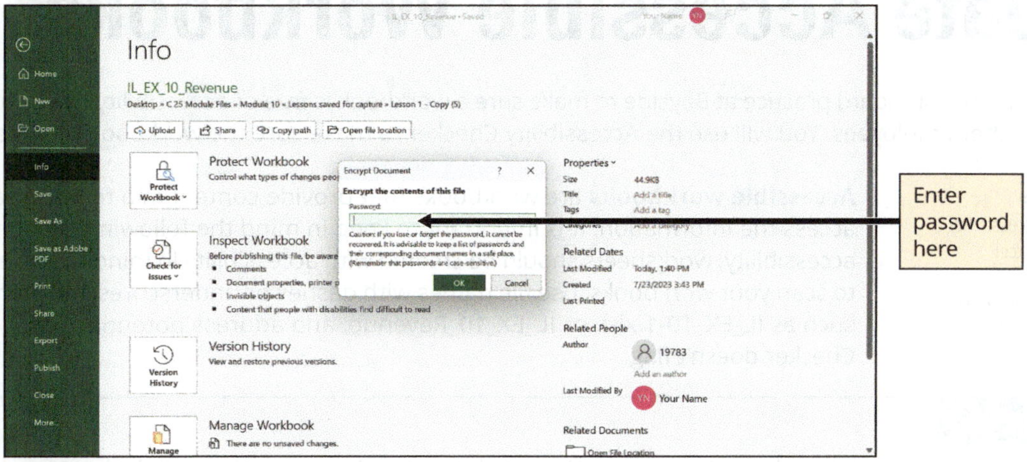


**Figure 10-17:** Masked password

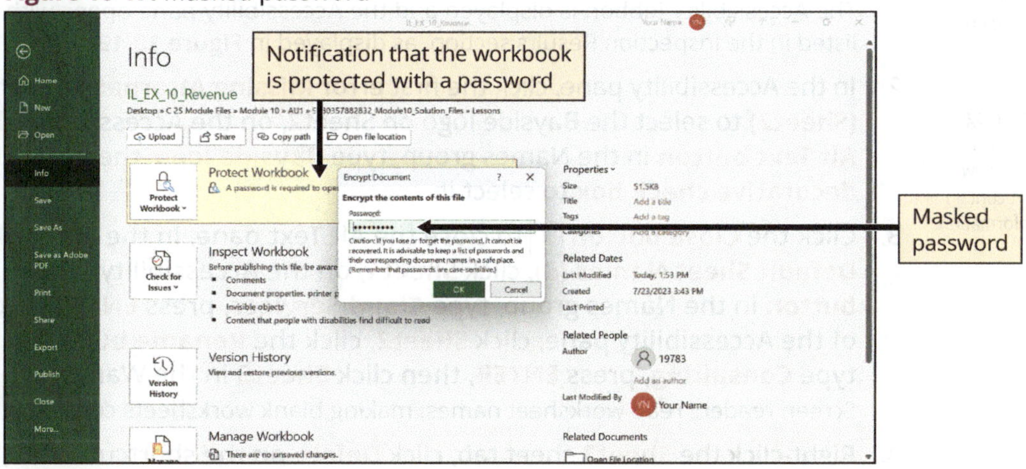


## Working with a previous version of an Excel workbook

When you save your Excel files on OneDrive, AutoSave is automatically turned on, meaning that it will save versions of your workbook while you make changes without needing to use the Save command. The older saved versions can be restored if you make errors in newer versions using Version history by clicking the File name on the title bar, clicking Version History, then clicking the desired version in the Version History pane. **Figure 10-18** displays two versions of a workbook. After your desired version opens, you can click the Restore button above the formula bar to save the file.

**Figure 10-18:** Version History pane

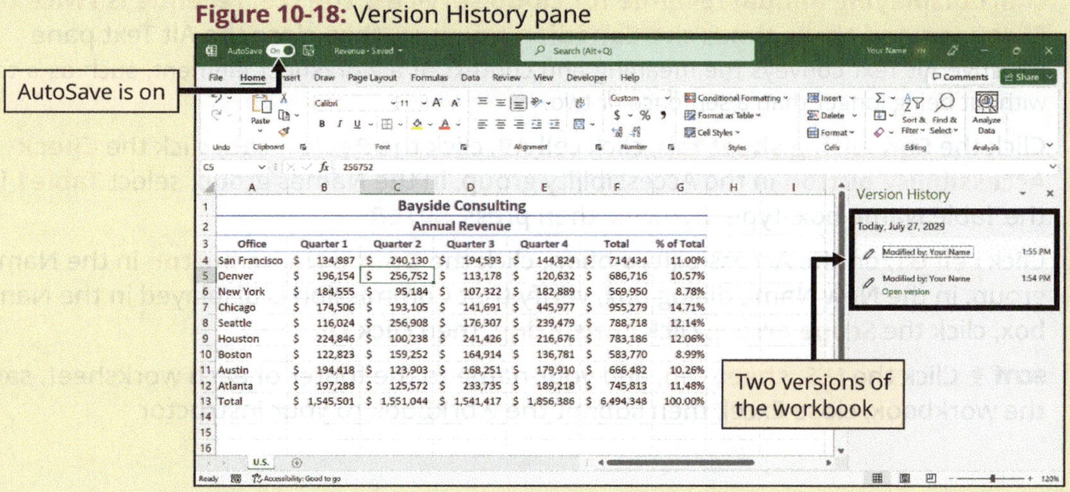

# Create Accessible Workbooks

**Case** It is the standard practice at Bayside to make sure a workbook is free of accessibility issues before sharing it with other employees. You will use the Accessibility Checker to make sure the workbook is accessible to everyone.

**Objectives**
- Identify accessibility issues in Excel workbooks
- Fix accessibility issues in a workbook

**Accessible workbooks** are workbooks that provide content in a format that allows everyone to access the information. It is important to keep in mind the following best practices for workbook accessibility: worksheets should be created with accessibility in mind; use the Accessibility Checker to scan your workbooks; use file names with dashes or underscores between words and numbers such as IL_EX_10-1.xlsx or IL_EX_10_Revenue; and address potential issues that the Accessibility Checker doesn't flag.

## Steps

**Quick Tip**
High contrast between the content and the background is more accessible.

1. **With the U.S. sheet active, click the Review tab, then click the Check Accessibility button in the Accessibility group**
   The Accessibility Ribbon is displayed and the Accessibility pane opens with the workbook issues listed in the Inspection Results section, as displayed in **Figure 10-19**

**Quick Tip**
Identifying an image as decorative lets a screen reader know that it doesn't contain important information.

2. **In the Accessibility pane, click the first error Missing Alternative text (1), click Picture 2 (Sheet2) to select the Bayside logo on Sheet2, on the Accessibility ribbon, click the Alt Text button in the Names group, type Bayside logo, then click the Mark as decorative check box to select it**
3. **Click the Close button ☒ to close the Alt Text pane, in the Accessibility pane, click Default Sheet Names (3), click Sheet1, on the Accessibility Ribbon, click the Rename button in the Names group, type Cloud Services, press ENTER, in the Warnings box of the Accessibility pane, click Sheet2, click the Rename button in the Names group, type Consulting, press ENTER, then click Sheet3 in the Warnings box**
   Screen readers read worksheet names, making blank worksheets confusing
4. **Right-click the Sheet3 sheet tab, click Delete on the shortcut menu, then click the U.S. sheet tab**
   The message in the status bar is now "Good to go" as displayed in **Figure 10-20**. Screen readers begin reading worksheets at cell A1 and can encounter a problem if the cell is blank.
5. **Click the Close button to close the Accessibility pane, click the Cloud Services sheet tab, click the row 1 heading, then on the Home tab, click the Delete button in the Cells group**

**Trouble**
Your screen may display View Alt Text rather than Edit Alt Text; this is not a problem.

6. **With the Cloud Services sheet active, right-click the Cloud Services Revenue pie chart, click Edit Alt Text on the shortcut menu, replace the existing text with Pie chart displaying annual revenue for cloud services. The U.S. revenue is twice the European and three times the Canadian revenue, then close the Alt Text pane**
   Effective Alt Text conveys the meaning and context of a worksheet element, such as a table, without being longer than a sentence or two.

**Quick Tip**
It is also a good practice to name cells used in formula calculations.

7. **Click the Consulting sheet tab, click cell A9, click the Review tab, click the Check Accessibility button in the Accessibility group, in the Names group, select Table1 in the Table Name box, type Invoices, then press ENTER**
8. **Click cell G1, on the Accessibility ribbon, click the Define Name button in the Names group, in the New Name dialog box, verify that Commission is displayed in the Name box, click the Scope arrow, click Consulting, then click OK**
9. **sam Click the U.S. sheet tab, add your name to the footer of each worksheet, save the workbook, close Excel, then submit the workbook to your instructor**

**Figure 10-19:** Accessibility ribbon and pane

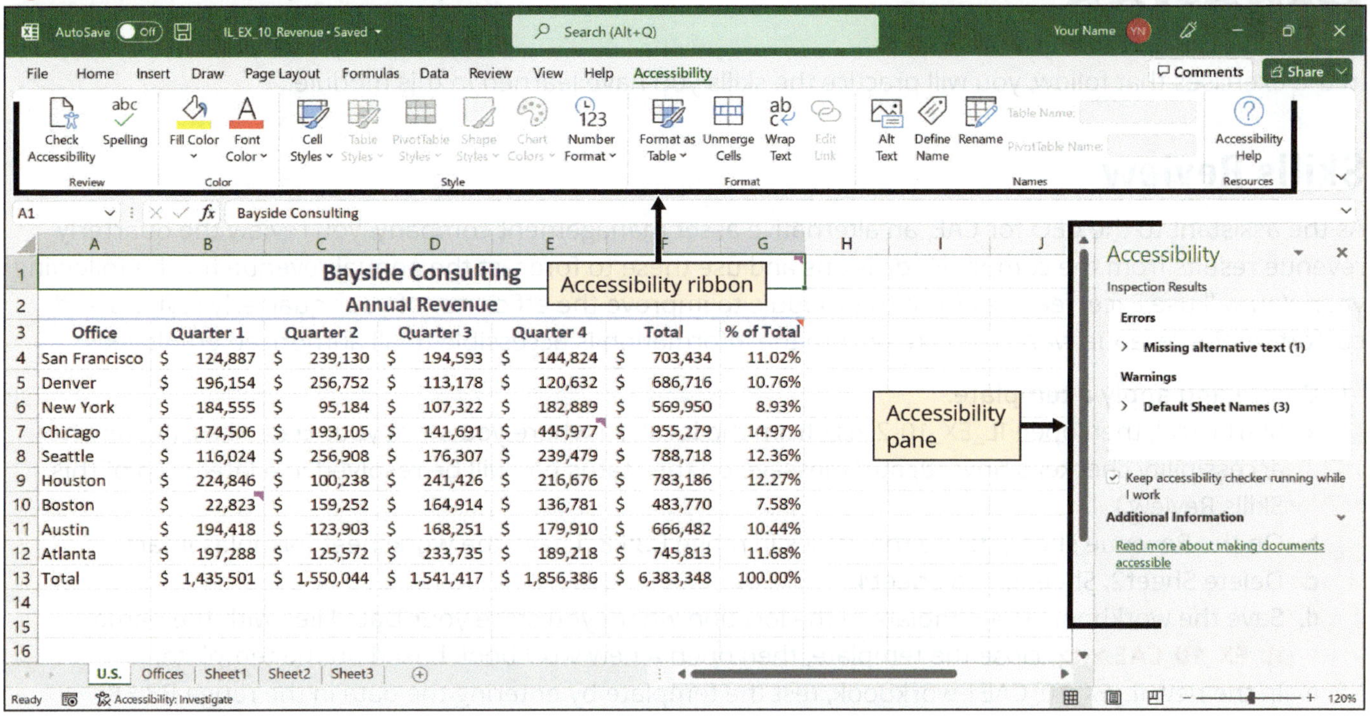


**Figure 10-20:** Workbook free of accessibility issues

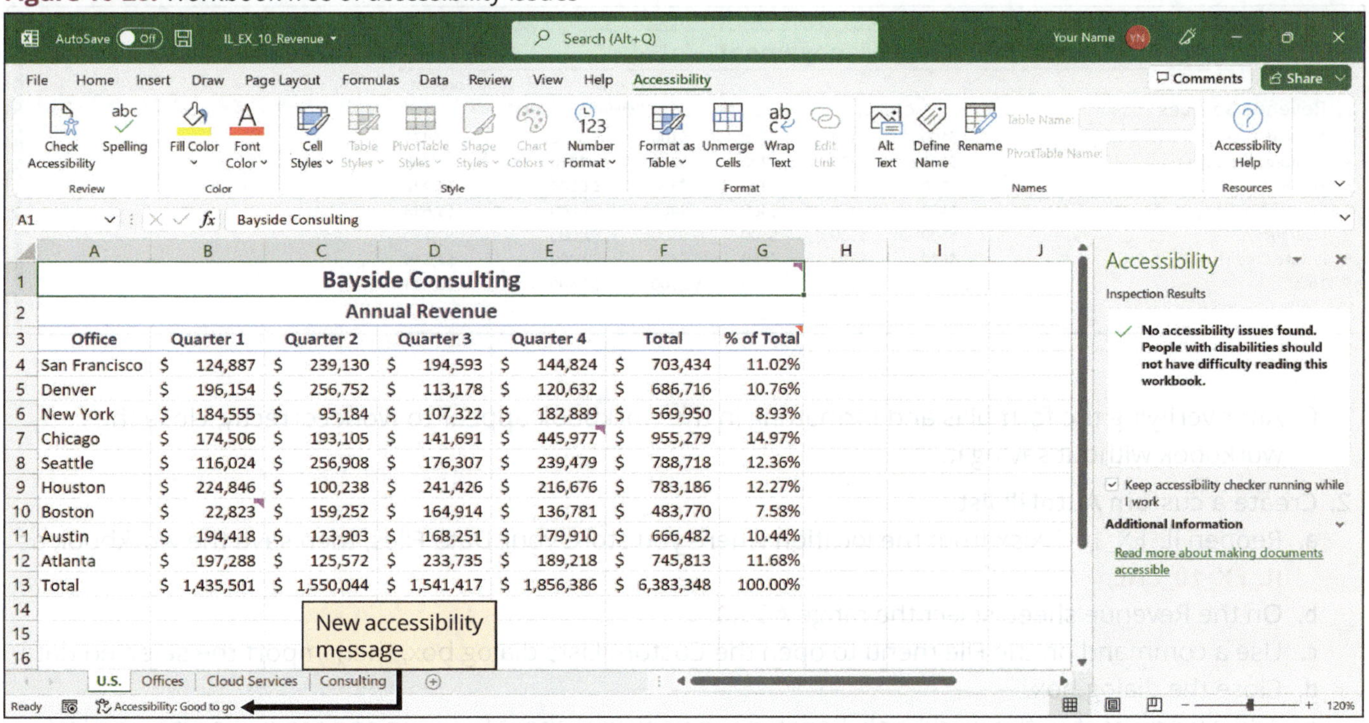

# Practice

In the exercises that follow, you will practice the skills you have learned in this module.

## Skills Review

As the assistant to the CEO for CAE, an alternative asset management company, you review the quarterly revenue results from the company's divisions and use these to forecast the annual revenue for the following year. You will use Excel features from this module to improve the efficiency of your quarterly reviews and customize the revenue worksheets to ensure the information is accessible to all authorized employees.

1. **Create and apply a template.**
   a. Start Excel, then open IL_EX_10-2.xlsx from the location where you store your Data Files. (Note: The accessibility checker's "investigate" message on the status bar will be resolved in a later step of this Skills Review.)
   b. On the Revenue sheet, delete the values in range B3:E8. Leave the worksheet formulas intact.
   c. Delete Sheet2, Sheet3, and Sheet4.
   d. Save the workbook as a template in the location where you store your Data Files with the name **IL_EX_10_CAE.xltx**, close the template, then open a new workbook based on the template.
   e. In the new IL_EX_10_CAE1 workbook, test the template by entering the data in the range B3:E8, displayed in **Figure 10-21**.

**Figure 10-21**

| | A | B | C | D | E | F | G | H | I | J | K |
|---|---|---|---|---|---|---|---|---|---|---|---|
| 1 | CAE Asset Management | | | | | | | | Growth | 6% | |
| 2 | Revenue Sources | Quarter 1 | Quarter 2 | Quarter 3 | Quarter 4 | Annual Revenue | Revenue Forecast Next Year | | | | |
| 3 | Advisory Fees | $100 | $100 | $100 | $100 | $400 | $424 | | | | |
| 4 | Realized Investments | $200 | $200 | $200 | $200 | $800 | $848 | | | | |
| 5 | REIT Funds | $300 | $300 | $300 | $300 | $1,200 | $1,272 | | | | |
| 6 | Renewable Energy Funds | $400 | $400 | $400 | $400 | $1,600 | $1,696 | | | | |
| 7 | Insurance | $500 | $500 | $500 | $500 | $2,000 | $2,120 | | | | |
| 8 | Private Credit | $600 | $600 | $600 | $600 | $2,400 | $2,544 | | | | |
| 9 | Total | $2,100 | $2,100 | $2,100 | $2,100 | $8,400 | $8,904 | | | | |
| 10 | | | | | | | | | | | |

   f. After verifying the formulas and formatting in the workbook appear to work correctly, close the workbook without saving it.

2. **Create a custom AutoFill list.**
   a. Reopen IL_EX_10-2.xlsx from the location where you store your Data Files, then save the workbook as **IL_EX_10_CAE**.
   b. On the Revenue sheet, select the range **A3:A8**.
   c. Use a command on the File menu to open the Custom Lists dialog box, then import the selected data.
   d. Close the dialog box.
   e. Add a worksheet to the workbook. Rename the new worksheet **Sources** and move it so it is the last worksheet in the workbook, located after Sheet4. On the Sources worksheet, enter **Advisory Fees** in cell A1.
   f. Use the fill handle to enter the custom list through cell A6, then widen column A to fully display the sources.
   g. Open the Custom Lists dialog box again, delete the custom list you just created, then save the workbook.

3. **Customize a theme.**
   a. Activate the Revenue sheet, display the Page Layout tab on the ribbon, then use the Create New Theme Colors dialog box to change the Accent 6 color to Orange, Accent 2, Darker 50% (sixth color from left in the last row of Theme Colors).
   b. Name the new theme color palette **CAE**, then save it.
   c. Use the Create New Theme Fonts dialog box to change the Body font to **Calibri Light**. Save the new theme font set as **CAE**.
   d. Save the current theme as **CAE**, then compare your worksheet to **Figure 10-22**.

**Figure 10-22**

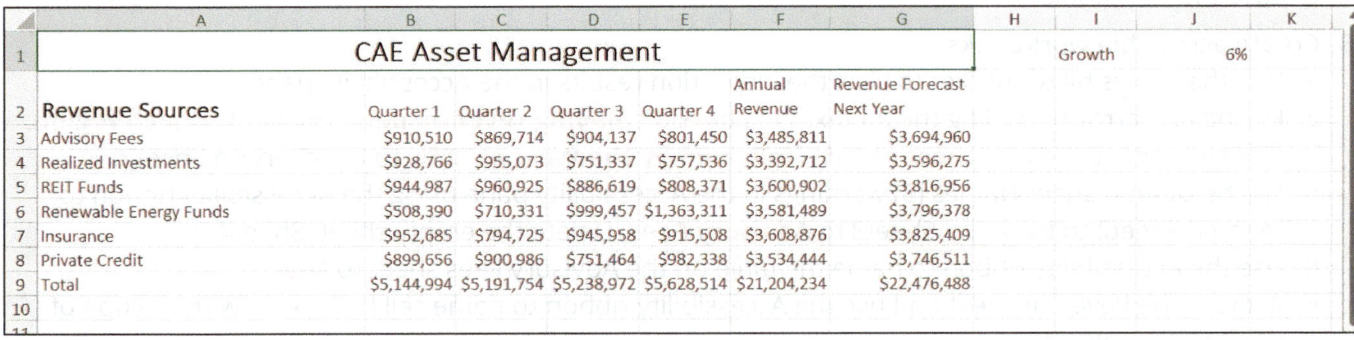

| | A | B | C | D | E | F | G | H | I | J | K |
|---|---|---|---|---|---|---|---|---|---|---|---|
| 1 | CAE Asset Management | | | | | | | | Growth | 6% | |
| 2 | Revenue Sources | Quarter 1 | Quarter 2 | Quarter 3 | Quarter 4 | Annual Revenue | Revenue Forecast Next Year | | | | |
| 3 | Advisory Fees | $910,510 | $869,714 | $904,137 | $801,450 | $3,485,811 | $3,694,960 | | | | |
| 4 | Realized Investments | $928,766 | $955,073 | $751,337 | $757,536 | $3,392,712 | $3,596,275 | | | | |
| 5 | REIT Funds | $944,987 | $960,925 | $886,619 | $808,371 | $3,600,902 | $3,816,956 | | | | |
| 6 | Renewable Energy Funds | $508,390 | $710,331 | $999,457 | $1,363,311 | $3,581,489 | $3,796,378 | | | | |
| 7 | Insurance | $952,685 | $794,725 | $945,958 | $915,508 | $3,608,876 | $3,825,409 | | | | |
| 8 | Private Credit | $899,656 | $900,986 | $751,464 | $982,338 | $3,534,444 | $3,746,511 | | | | |
| 9 | Total | $5,144,994 | $5,191,754 | $5,238,972 | $5,628,514 | $21,204,234 | $22,476,488 | | | | |
| 10 | | | | | | | | | | | |

   e. Verify that the custom CAE color palette is listed in the Theme Colors list, the CAE font set is listed in the Theme Fonts list, and the theme is listed in the Themes list, then delete each custom setting.
   f. Return to the Office theme, then save the workbook.

4. **Use comments.**
   a. On the Revenue sheet, insert a comment in cell A6 that reads **Renewable energy had the largest growth this year. We may need to invest more in that sector.**.
   b. Click anywhere outside the Comment box to close it.
   c. Edit the comment in cell A6 to add the sentence **Are we projecting more than 6% growth for next year?** to the end of the existing comment.
   d. Add a reply to the comment in cell A6 that reads **We should project 8% growth for next year.**.
   e. Display all worksheet comments in the Comments pane then close the Comments pane.
   f. Save the workbook.

5. **Use notes.**
   a. Insert a note in cell E5 that reads **REIT funds dropped off in the 4th quarter.**.
   b. Convert the note in cell E5 to a comment, then edit the comment to add **What should we forecast for next year?** to the end of the comment.
   c. Insert a note in cell G2 that reads **Formulas in this column are calculated by multiplying the growth of 6% in cell J1 by the annual revenue in column F and adding that amount to the annual revenue.**. Resize the Note box to display the note text.
   d. Display the note on the screen then turn off the display of notes.
   e. Save the workbook.

6. **Change Excel default settings.**
   a. Use the General category of the Excel Options dialog box to verify the correct user name is displayed.
   b. Use the Language category of the Excel Options dialog box to verify the Office authoring languages and proofing languages are set correctly for your Excel workbook.
   c. Use the Accessibility category of the Excel Options dialog box to verify the accessibility checker is running while you work.

## Skills Review (Continued)

d. Use the Quick Access Toolbar category of the Excel Options dialog box to add the Open button to the Quick Access Toolbar.

e. Reset all customizations of the workbook to the defaults.

**7. Use a password to protect a workbook.**

a. Encrypt the workbook with the password **CcAaEe2029$**.

b. Save and close the workbook.

c. Open the workbook using the password.

d. Delete the password.

e. Save the workbook.

**8. Create accessible workbooks.**

a. Run the accessibility checker to view the inspection results in the Accessibility pane.

b. Fix the first error by adding the Alt text **Pie chart displaying revenue percentages for each region. The Northeast is the highest at 35%, followed by the West at 28%.** to the chart on Sheet2.

c. Fix the Default Sheet Names (3) warnings in the Accessibility pane using the Accessibility ribbon to rename Sheet2 to **REIT** and Sheet3 to **Advisory Fees**. Delete the empty sheet, Sheet4.

d. Use the Accessibility ribbon to name the table on the Advisory Fees sheet to **Fees**.

e. Activate the Revenue sheet and use the Accessibility ribbon to name cell J1 **Growth** with a scope of the **Revenue sheet**.

f. Verify the accessibility message in the status bar is "Good to go" as displayed in **Figure 10-23**.

**Figure 10-23**

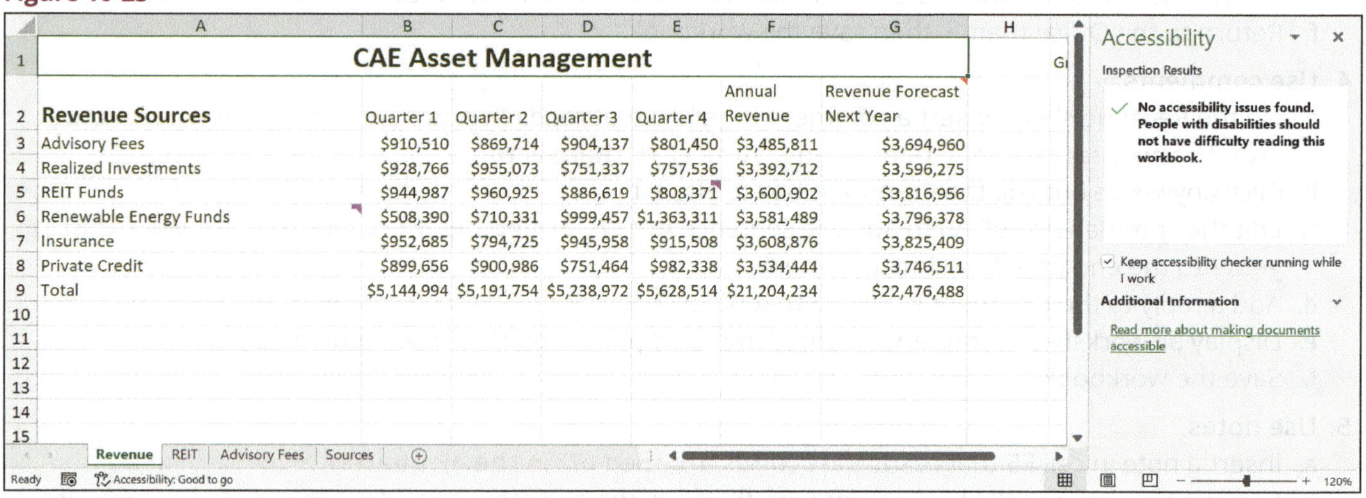

| | A | B | C | D | E | F | G |
|---|---|---|---|---|---|---|---|
| 1 | CAE Asset Management | | | | | | |
| 2 | Revenue Sources | Quarter 1 | Quarter 2 | Quarter 3 | Quarter 4 | Annual Revenue | Revenue Forecast Next Year |
| 3 | Advisory Fees | $910,510 | $869,714 | $904,137 | $801,450 | $3,485,811 | $3,694,960 |
| 4 | Realized Investments | $928,766 | $955,073 | $751,337 | $757,536 | $3,392,712 | $3,596,275 |
| 5 | REIT Funds | $944,987 | $960,925 | $886,619 | $808,371 | $3,600,902 | $3,816,956 |
| 6 | Renewable Energy Funds | $508,390 | $710,331 | $999,457 | $1,363,311 | $3,581,489 | $3,796,378 |
| 7 | Insurance | $952,685 | $794,725 | $945,958 | $915,508 | $3,608,876 | $3,825,409 |
| 8 | Private Credit | $899,656 | $900,986 | $751,464 | $982,338 | $3,534,444 | $3,746,511 |
| 9 | Total | $5,144,994 | $5,191,754 | $5,238,972 | $5,628,514 | $21,204,234 | $22,476,488 |



g. AutoFit the width of Column A, add your name to the center footer sections of the four sheets, save the workbook, close the workbook, then submit the workbook to your instructor.

h. Close Excel.

## Independent Challenge 1

As assistant to the CFO at URR, a data storage company, you prepare the profit worksheets using the revenue and expense quarterly data. You will use Excel features to make the analysis easier to manage each quarter and ensure the profit information is accessible to all who need to access it.

a. Open IL_EX_10-3.xlsx from the location where you store your Data Files.

b. Delete the revenue and expense data in columns B and C, leaving the labels and the total and profit formulas. Delete Sheet2 and Sheet3. Save the workbook as a template with the name **IL_EX_10_URR** in the location where you store your Data Files, then close the template.

c. Open a new workbook based on the IL_EX_10_URR. Enter test data of your choosing for revenue and expenses, then check the results to verify the template is calculating the profits and totals correctly. Close the IL_EX_10_URR1 workbook without saving it.
d. Re-open IL_EX_10-3.xlsx from the location where you store your Data Files, then save it as **IL_EX_10_URR**. (Note: The accessibility checker's "investigate" message on the status bar will be resolved in a later step of this exercise.)
e. On the Profit sheet create a custom list based on the offices in the range A4:A7. Test the custom AutoFill list beginning at cell A1 on a new worksheet named **Offices**. Position the Offices sheet at the end of the workbook after Sheet3. Use the Custom Lists dialog box to delete the custom list from your computer. Do not delete the list of offices on the Offices sheet.
f. On the Profit sheet, add a comment to cell C6 that reads: **Does this include the investment in new equipment?**.
g. Edit the comment in cell C6 to read: **Does this include the investment in new servers?**.
h. Add a note to cell D8 that reads: **Find out how this compares to last year's third quarter profits.**.
i. Convert the note in cell D8 to a comment, then edit the comment to read: **How does this compare to last year's third quarter profits?**.
j. Reply to the comment in cell C6 with **Yes, that expense is included.**.
k. Display the comments in the Comments pane and compare your Profit worksheet to **Figure 10-24**.

**Figure 10-24**

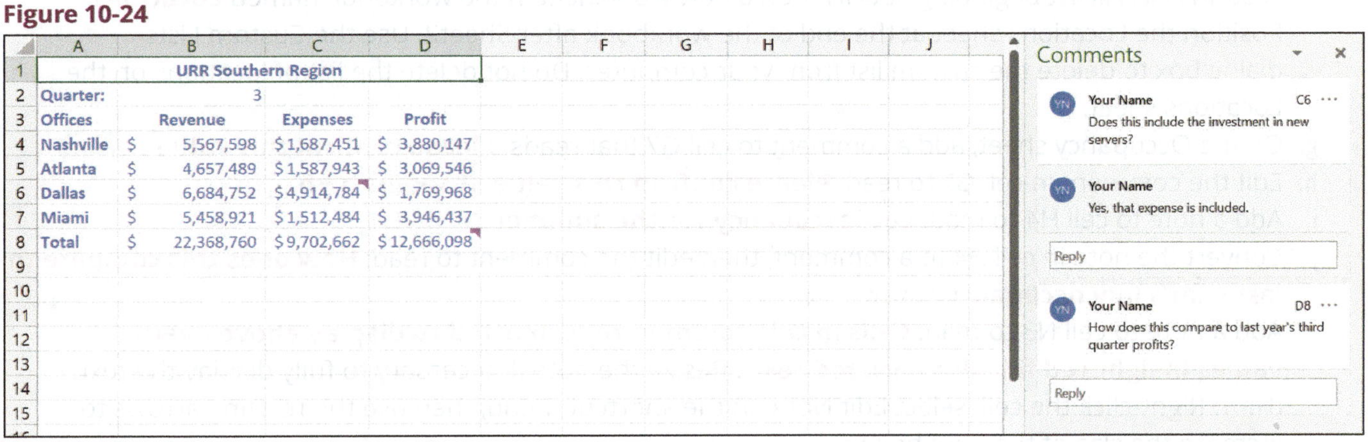


l. Close the Comments pane, then use the Excel Options dialog box to review the user name and the dictionary language.
m. Add the Spelling command to the Quick Access Toolbar. Test the new button, then reset all customizations of the workbook to the defaults.
n. Encrypt the workbook with the password **UuRr2029$**. Test the password by saving the workbook, closing the workbook, and then opening the workbook. Remove encryption from the workbook.
o. Use the Accessibility checker and Accessibility Ribbon to fix the accessibility errors and warnings using these guidelines:
   - The Alt text for the chart on Sheet2 is: **Nashville's 3rd quarter profits. August is the highest followed by July and September with the lowest.**
   - The name for Sheet2 is: **Nashville**
   - Delete the empty sheet, Sheet3
p. Add your name to the center section of all three worksheet footers, then save the workbook.
q. Close the workbook, exit Excel, then submit the workbook to your instructor.

# Independent Challenge 2

As the assistant to the CEO of an international hotel collection, you prepare annual occupancy reports for the company's regional properties. These reports are created annually so creating a template will simplify this process. You will also use Excel features to make your future analysis more efficient and make sure the workbooks are accessible to all employees.

a. Start Excel, then open IL_EX_10-4.xlsx from the location where you store your Data Files.
b. Delete the values in the ranges B4:M7. Delete Sheet2. Save the workbook as a template with the name **IL_EX_10_Occupancy** in the location where you store your Data Files, then close the template.
c. Open a new workbook based on the template, verify the template is calculating the formulas correctly by entering test data, then close the IL_EX_10_Occupancy1 workbook without saving it.
d. Re-open IL_EX_10-4.xlsx from the location where you store your Data Files, then save it as **IL_EX_10_Occupancy**. (Note: The accessibility checker's "investigate" message on the status bar will be resolved in a later step of this exercise.)
e. Review the spelling correction settings in the Proofing category of the Excel Options dialog box. Click the AutoCorrect Options button, then review the entries in the Replace and With columns in the AutoCorrect dialog box. Close the AutoCorrect dialog box without making any changes. Review the AutoRecover save time setting in the Save category of the Excel Options.
f. On the Occupancy sheet create a custom list based on the locations in the range A4:A7. Test the custom AutoFill list beginning at cell A1 on a new worksheet in the workbook named **Locations**. Position the Locations sheet at the end of the workbook after Sheet2. Use the Custom Lists dialog box to delete the custom list from your computer. Do not delete the list of locations on the Locations sheet.
g. On the Occupancy sheet, add a comment to cell G7 that reads: **Please confirm this value.**.
h. Edit the comment in cell G7 to read: **Please confirm this value. It seems high.**.
i. Add a note to cell H4 to read: **Low occupancy for the summer.**.
j. Convert the note in cell H4 to a comment, then edit the comment to read: **How does this compare to last year's July occupancy rate?**.
k. Add a note to cell N3 to read: **Cells in this column are formatted to display above average values in light red fill with dark red text.**. Resize the note if necessary to fully display the text. (**Hint**: Right-click the cell, select Edit Note on the shortcut menu, then use the resizing arrows to increase the size of the note box.)
l. Reply to the comment in cell H4 with **Last year's July occupancy was 60%.**.
m. Display the comments in the Comments pane, then close the Comments pane.
n. Create a new theme color named Occupancy by changing the Accent 1 color to Blue, Accent 5 (the first row of the Theme colors).
o. Create a new theme font named Occupancy by changing the Heading font to Calibri.
p. Save the current theme as Occupancy, verify the custom Occupancy color palette is listed in the Theme Colors list, the Occupancy font set is listed in the Theme Fonts list, and the theme is listed in the Themes list. Delete each custom setting, then return to the Office theme.
q. Add the Quick Print command to the Quick Access Toolbar. Use the Customize the Quick Access Toolbar dialog box to change the toolbar position to below the ribbon. Change the position back to above the ribbon and hide the Quick Access Toolbar. Reset the customizations of the Quick Access Toolbar to the default.
r. Encrypt the workbook with the password **OCCocc497!**. Test the password by saving the workbook, closing the workbook, and then opening the workbook. Remove encryption from the workbook.

s. Use the accessibility checker and Accessibility ribbon to fix the accessibility errors and warnings using these guidelines:
   - Sheet2 name: **Reservations**
   - Change the table style on the Reservations sheet to Light Blue, Table Style Light 2. (**Hint**: Use the Format as Table button in the Format group of the Accessibility ribbon.)
   - Name the table on the Reservations sheet **Reservation_Details**.
   - Name cell H1 on the Reservations sheet Loyalty_Discount with a scope of the Reservations sheet.

t. Activate the Occupancy worksheet and compare it to **Figure 10-25**.

**Figure 10-25**

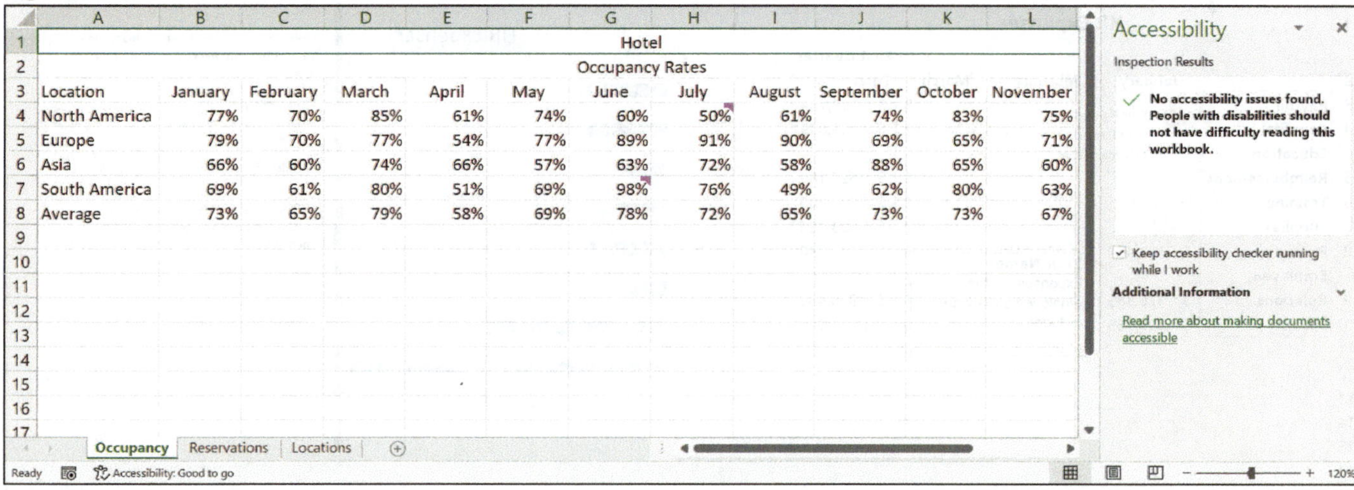

Hotel
Occupancy Rates

| Location | January | February | March | April | May | June | July | August | September | October | November |
|---|---|---|---|---|---|---|---|---|---|---|---|
| North America | 77% | 70% | 85% | 61% | 74% | 60% | 50% | 61% | 74% | 83% | 75% |
| Europe | 79% | 70% | 77% | 54% | 77% | 89% | 91% | 90% | 69% | 65% | 71% |
| Asia | 66% | 60% | 74% | 66% | 57% | 63% | 72% | 58% | 88% | 65% | 60% |
| South America | 69% | 61% | 80% | 51% | 69% | 98% | 76% | 49% | 62% | 80% | 63% |
| Average | 73% | 65% | 79% | 58% | 69% | 78% | 72% | 65% | 73% | 73% | 67% |



u. Add your name to the center section of the three worksheet footers, then save the workbook.

v. Close the workbook, close Excel, then submit your workbook to your instructor.

# Visual Workshop

Open IL_EX_10-5.xlsx from the location where you store your Data Files, then save it as **IL_EX_10_HR**. Add a note and comment and address accessibility issues so your screen matches **Figure 10-26**. Add your name to the center section of the worksheet footer, then save the workbook. Close the workbook, close Excel, then submit the workbook to your instructor.

**Figure 10-26**

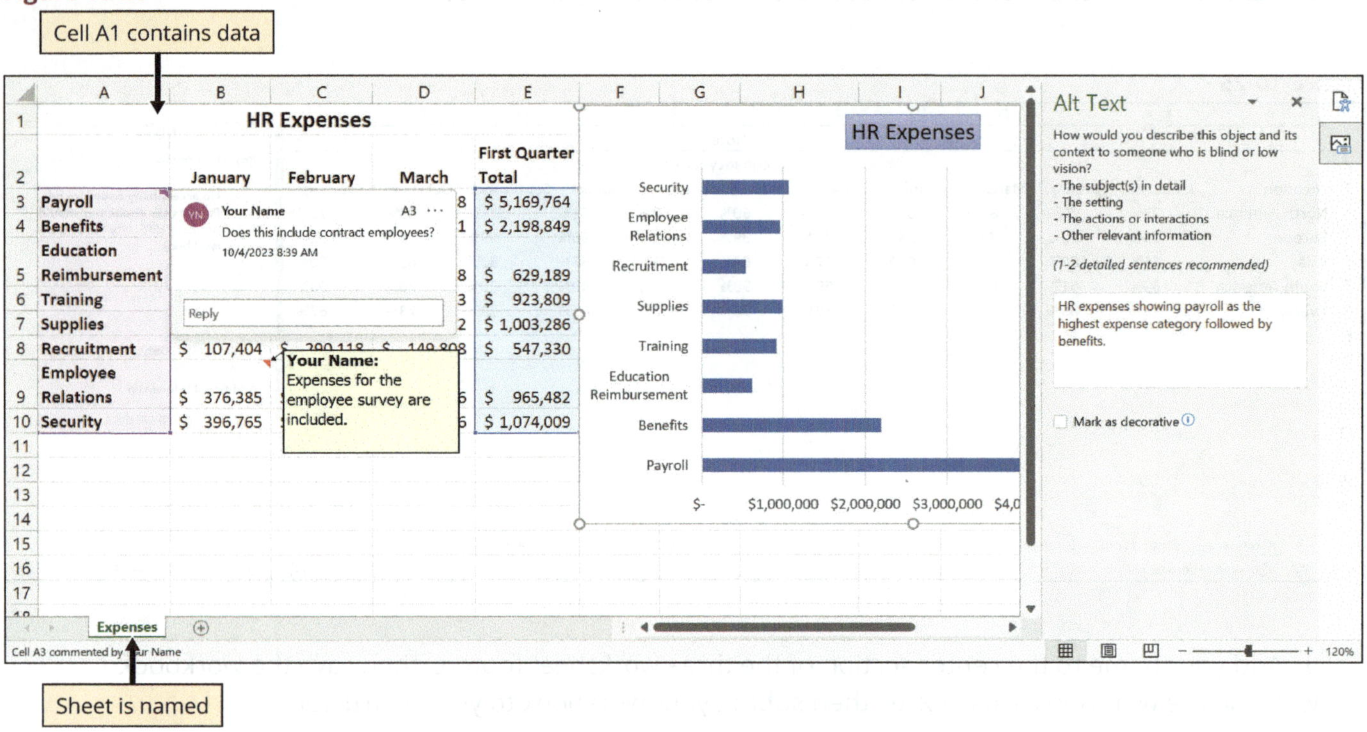

# Using Formulas and Functions

## Case

Elena Fuentes, Bayside's Vice President of Finance, uses Excel formulas and functions to analyze and consolidate employee compensation and bonus data across the company's regions and divisions. Because management is considering adding a new networking division in the South, Elena asks you to format and summarize additional employee data from the current Southern offices. To help plan for this expansion, she also asks you to estimate the financing options for acquiring a networking division.

## Module Objectives

After completing this module, you will be able to:

- Distribute data over multiple columns
- Format data using text functions
- Use dynamic array functions
- Calculate values based on conditions
- Find values based on conditions
- Create formulas using named ranges
- Consolidate worksheet data
- Audit a worksheet
- Use the PMT function

### Files You Will Need

IL_EX_11-1.xlsx
IL_EX_11-2.xlsx
IL_EX_11-3.xlsx
IL_EX_11-4.xlsx
IL_EX_11-5.xlsx

# Distribute Data Over Multiple Columns

**Case** As part of an effort to retain employees, Elena is reviewing the non-salary compensation for Bayside employees. She asks you to use employee data from the Human Resources Department to summarize the bonus payouts and the cost of implementing a bonus for employee longevity. The imported employee data appears in a single column.

**Objective**
- Separate data into columns

You often need to distribute data in a column over multiple columns. For instance, when you import data from an outside source, such as another program or the Internet, multiple data fields may be imported in a single column, and therefore difficult to work with. You can distribute the data into separate columns using the Flash Fill feature. **Flash Fill** observes patterns in data you enter and automatically fills or formats it in adjacent cells based on those patterns. Flash Fill sometimes detects the pattern as you enter data but more often it needs to be manually applied.

## Steps

1. **sam** Start Excel, open **IL_EX_11-1.xlsx** from the location where you store your Data Files, then save it as **IL_EX_11_South**
2. On the Employees sheet click cell **B3**, type **21547**, press **TAB**, in cell C3 type **IT Consulting**, press **TAB**, in cell D3 type **atlanta**, press **TAB**, in cell E3 type **ga**, press **TAB**, in cell F3 type **7157**, press **TAB**, in cell G3 type **8**, then click the **Enter button** in the formula bar
   You manually separated the data in cell A3 into the adjacent cells, as displayed in **Figure 11-1**, by entering the correct data in each cell. You can now use Flash Fill to complete the rows below based on this example.
3. Click cell **B3**, click the **Fill button** in the Editing group on the ribbon, then click **Flash Fill**
   The employee numbers from column A are copied into the range B4:B13.
4. Click cell **C3**, click the **Fill button** in the Editing group, then click **Flash Fill**
   The divisions from Column A are copied into the range C4:C13.
5. Click cell **D3**, click the **Fill button** in the Editing group, then click **Flash Fill**
   Four of the cities in column D are missing. Flash Fill sometimes interprets the data pattern differently than you might expect. In this case, the division names in column C that include both one and two-word labels may be the cause of the issue in later columns. Corrections can be manually applied to the data when these problems occur.
6. Click cell **D4**, type **houston**, then click the **Enter button**
   The corrections are automatically made for the support division's city entries in cells D7, D8, and D9.
7. Click cell **E3**, click the **Fill button** in the Editing group, click **Flash Fill**, click cell **E4**, type **tx**, click the **Enter button**, click cell **F3**, click the **Fill button** in the Editing group, click **Flash Fill**, click cell **F4**, type **6784**, click the **Enter button**, click cell **G3**, click the **Fill button** in the Editing group, click **Flash Fill**, click cell **G4**, type **5**, then click the **Enter button**
8. Widen column **C** to fully display the data, compare your work to **Figure 11-2**, then save your work

**Figure 11-1:** Worksheet with first row of data separated into columns

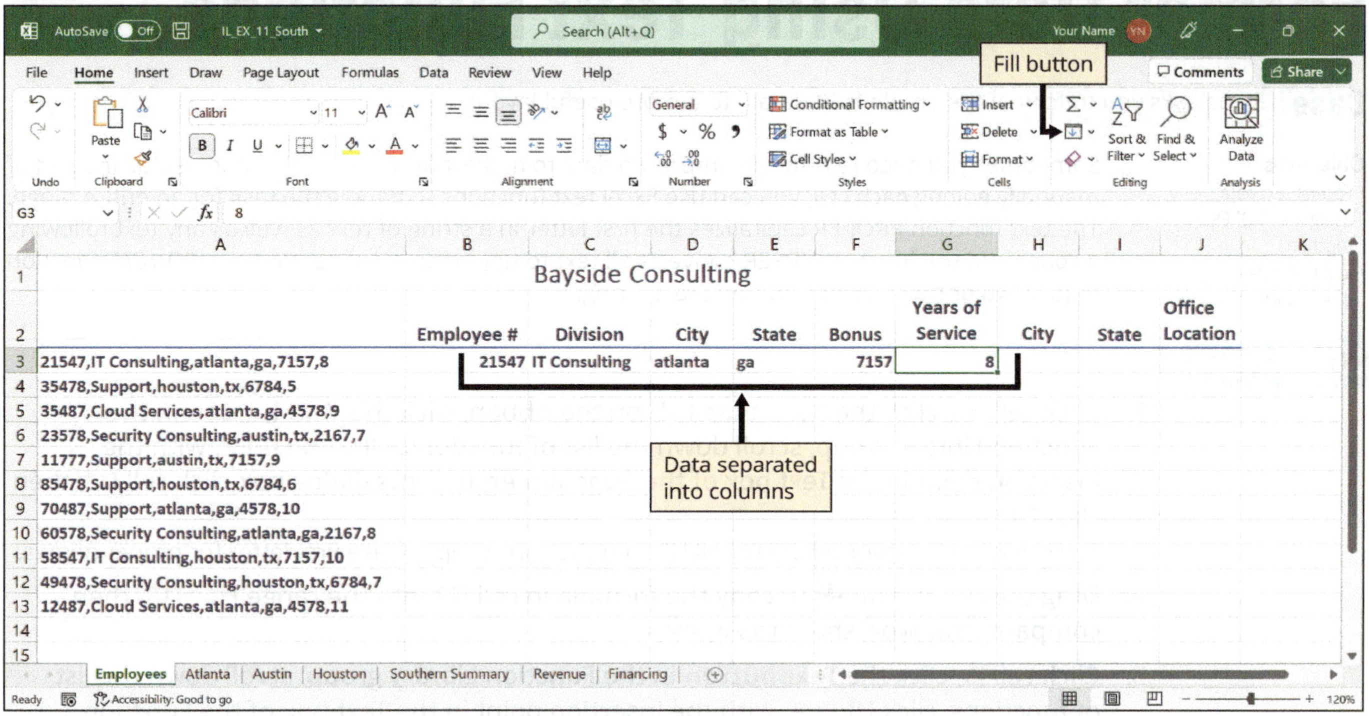


**Figure 11-2:** Worksheet with data in columns

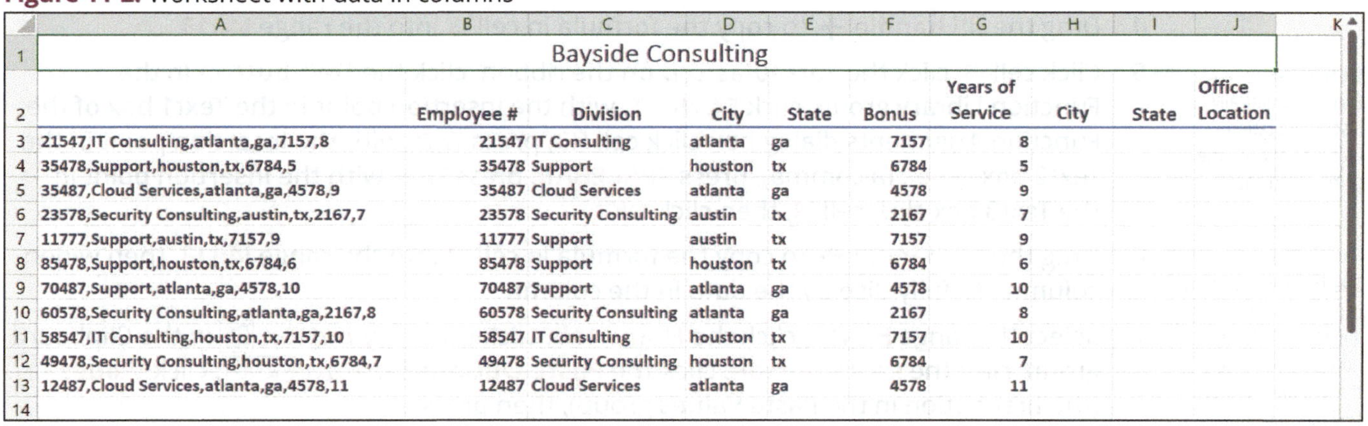


## Working with Excel series

You can use Excel fill series to generate worksheet data based on linear or growth trends. For example, if you want to review payments for a range of interest rates between 4% and 5%, you can fill a worksheet series with interest rates increasing by a desired amount. To fill the series, enter the starting percentage in a cell, click the Home tab on the ribbon, click the Fill button in the Editing group, click Series, in the Series dialog box select the Rows or Columns option button indicating where the results will be placed, verify the Linear option button is selected in the Type category, in the Step value box enter the increase amount for each subsequent value, in the Stop value box enter the final amount, then click OK. In a linear series, the step value is added to the starting value and then added to each successive value until the stop value is reached. If you want to increase values by a constant percentage, you need to use a **growth trend**. In a growth trend, the starting value is multiplied by the step value and then each successive value is multiplied by the step value. To create a growth trend, select the Growth option button in the Type category of the Series dialog box, enter the growth amount in the Step value box, then click OK. For example, if you wanted a sales target to increase by 20 percent each year, you would enter 1.2 in the Step value box.

# Format Data Using Text Functions

**Case** Elena asks you to format the employees' data into a more useful layout.

**Objectives**
- Format text data using the PROPER function
- Join text data using a text function

Sometimes you need to reformat imported data to make it understandable and useful. Instead of manually editing each cell, you can use Excel text functions to handle the task for an entire range. The text function PROPER capitalizes the first letter in a string of text as well as any text following a space and the function UPPER converts all text to uppercase. You can use the CONCAT function to join two or more strings into one text string.

## Steps

1. **Click cell H3, click the Formulas tab on the ribbon, click the Text button in the Function Library group, scroll down the list of functions, click PROPER, with the insertion point in the Text box of the Function Arguments dialog box click cell D3, then click OK**

   The city is copied from cell D3 to cell H3 with the correct uppercase first letter for proper names.

2. **Drag the fill handle + to copy the formula in cell H3 into the range H4:H13, then compare your worksheet to Figure 11-3**

3. **Click cell I3, click the Text button in the Function Library group, scroll down the list of functions, click UPPER, with the insertion point in the Text box of the Function Arguments dialog box click cell E3, then click OK**

   The state abbreviation is displayed in cell I3 with the correct uppercase letters.

4. **Drag the fill handle + to copy the formula in cell I3 into the range I4:I13**

5. **Click cell J3, click the Formulas tab on the ribbon, click the Text button in the Function Library group, click CONCAT, with the insertion point in the Text1 box of the Function Arguments dialog box click cell H3, press TAB, with the insertion point in the Text2 box type , (a comma), press SPACEBAR, press TAB, with the insertion point in the Text3 box click cell I3, then click OK**

**Quick Tip**
Excel automatically inserts quotation marks to enclose the comma and space.

6. **Drag the fill handle + to copy the formula in cell J3 into the range J4:J13, then widen column J to fully display the data in the column**

**Quick Tip**
The TEXTJOIN function can also be used to join strings of text; however, you enter the delimiter in the Delimiter box of the Function Arguments dialog box rather than in the Text box.

7. **Select the range H3:J13, click the Home tab, click the Copy button in the Clipboard group, click the Paste button, click the Paste Options button (Ctrl), click Values (the first option in the Paste Values group), then press ESC**

   The formulas have been replaced with their values, allowing you to delete the cells used in the formulas.

8. **Select columns D and E, hold CTRL, select columns H and I, click Delete in the Cells group, select cell A1, compare your worksheet to Figure 11-4, then save your work**

**Figure 11-3:** Cities with Proper formatting

| | | | | | | | | | | | |
|---|---|---|---|---|---|---|---|---|---|---|---|
| 1 | Bayside Consulting | | | | | | | | | | |
| 2 | | Employee # | Division | City | State | Bonus | Years of Service | City | State | Office Location |
| 3 | 21547,IT Consulting,atlanta,ga,7157,8 | 21547 | IT Consulting | atlanta | ga | 7157 | 8 | Atlanta | | |
| 4 | 35478,Support,houston,tx,6784,5 | 35478 | Support | houston | tx | 6784 | 5 | Houston | | |
| 5 | 35487,Cloud Services,atlanta,ga,4578,9 | 35487 | Cloud Services | atlanta | ga | 4578 | 9 | Atlanta | | |
| 6 | 23578,Security Consulting,austin,tx,2167,7 | 23578 | Security Consulting | austin | tx | 2167 | 7 | Austin | | |
| 7 | 11777,Support,austin,tx,7157,9 | 11777 | Support | austin | tx | 7157 | 9 | Austin | | |
| 8 | 85478,Support,houston,tx,6784,6 | 85478 | Support | houston | tx | 6784 | 6 | Houston | | |
| 9 | 70487,Support,atlanta,ga,4578,10 | 70487 | Support | atlanta | ga | 4578 | 10 | Atlanta | | |
| 10 | 60578,Security Consulting,atlanta,ga,2167,8 | 60578 | Security Consulting | atlanta | ga | 2167 | 8 | Atlanta | | |
| 11 | 58547,IT Consulting,houston,tx,7157,10 | 58547 | IT Consulting | houston | tx | 7157 | 10 | Houston | | |
| 12 | 49478,Security Consulting,houston,tx,6784,7 | 49478 | Security Consulting | houston | tx | 6784 | 7 | Houston | | |
| 13 | 12487,Cloud Services,atlanta,ga,4578,11 | 12487 | Cloud Services | atlanta | ga | 4578 | 11 | Atlanta | | |
| 14 | | | | | | | | | | |
| 15 | | | | | | | | | | |

Cities in Proper format

Employees | Atlanta | Austin | Houston | Southern Summary | Revenue | Financing

Ready · Accessibility: Good to go · Count: 11 · 120%

**Figure 11-4:** Worksheet with data formatted using Text functions

| | A | B | C | D | E | F |
|---|---|---|---|---|---|---|
| 1 | Bayside Consulting | | | | | |
| 2 | | Employee # | Division | Bonus | Years of Service | Office Location |
| 3 | 21547,IT Consulting,atlanta,ga,7157,8 | 21547 | IT Consulting | 7157 | 8 | Atlanta, GA |
| 4 | 35478,Support,houston,tx,6784,5 | 35478 | Support | 6784 | 5 | Houston, TX |
| 5 | 35487,Cloud Services,atlanta,ga,4578,9 | 35487 | Cloud Services | 4578 | 9 | Atlanta, GA |
| 6 | 23578,Security Consulting,austin,tx,2167,7 | 23578 | Security Consulting | 2167 | 7 | Austin, TX |
| 7 | 11777,Support,austin,tx,7157,9 | 11777 | Support | 7157 | 9 | Austin, TX |
| 8 | 85478,Support,houston,tx,6784,6 | 85478 | Support | 6784 | 6 | Houston, TX |
| 9 | 70487,Support,atlanta,ga,4578,10 | 70487 | Support | 4578 | 10 | Atlanta, GA |
| 10 | 60578,Security Consulting,atlanta,ga,2167,8 | 60578 | Security Consulting | 2167 | 8 | Atlanta, GA |
| 11 | 58547,IT Consulting,houston,tx,7157,10 | 58547 | IT Consulting | 7157 | 10 | Houston, TX |
| 12 | 49478,Security Consulting,houston,tx,6784,7 | 49478 | Security Consulting | 6784 | 7 | Houston, TX |
| 13 | 12487,Cloud Services,atlanta,ga,4578,11 | 12487 | Cloud Services | 4578 | 11 | Atlanta, GA |
| 14 | | | | | | |
| 15 | | | | | | |

Employees | Atlanta | Austin | Houston | Southern Summary | Revenue | Financing

Ready · Accessibility: Good to go · 120%

## Working with other text functions

Other useful text functions include LOWER, SUBSTITUTE, LEN, RIGHT, LEFT, and MID. LOWER converts text to all lowercase letters, SUBSTITUTE replaces text in a text string, and LEN displays the number of characters in a string of text. For example, if cell A1 contains the text string "Tomorrow is Friday", then =LOWER(A1) would produce "tomorrow is friday"; =LEN(A1) would result in 18; and =SUBSTITUTE(A1, "Friday", "Saturday") would result in "Tomorrow is Saturday."

You can also use functions to display one or more characters at certain locations within a string. Use RIGHT to find the last characters with the syntax =RIGHT(string, # characters), where # is the number of characters you want to display, such as the last 3. Similarly, use LEFT to find the first characters with the syntax =LEFT(string, # characters), or MID to display the middle characters with the syntax =MID(string, starting character, # characters).

# Use Dynamic Array Functions

**Case** Elena asks you to add a list of divisions to the Atlanta worksheet and shorten the name of the Security Consulting division to Security.

**Objectives**
- Use the UNIQUE array function to extract unique values
- Describe spill ranges
- Change array range values

Dynamic array formulas can be inserted using dynamic array functions. An **array** is a row, column, or a combination of rows and columns of values. Dynamic array formulas can return arrays of changing size so when you add more data, the array expands. These adjacent cells with results outside the cell where the formula is entered are referred to as a **spill range**. Selecting a cell in the spill range displays the formula in the formula bar and a border around the range. The formula can only be changed in the cell where it was entered; after making a change, the spill range updates. Dynamic array formulas will also update array results if the underlying data changes. If an output range is blocked by non-empty cells, a #SPILL! error displays. A spilled range can be referenced in functions using the spilled range operator (**#)** after the range. For example, you can reference the spilled range in cells A1:A9 using A1#. **Table 11-1** lists a sample of dynamic array functions that can be used in worksheets.

## Steps

1. **Click the Atlanta sheet tab, then click cell A33**
2. **Click the Formulas tab on the ribbon, click the Lookup & Reference button in the Function Library group, scroll down the list of functions, then click UNIQUE**
3. **In the Function Arguments dialog box, with the cursor in the Array box, select the range B3:B31, then click OK**

   The unique divisions are extracted from column B using the dynamic array function UNIQUE. The spill range begins in cell A33. When changes are made to the data referenced in an array formula, the spill range will update.
4. **Select the range B3:B31, click the Home tab on the ribbon, click the Find & Select button in the Editing group, then click Replace**
5. **In the Find what box, type Security Consulting, press TAB, in the Replace with box type Security, click Replace All, click OK, then click Close**

   In addition to the division name changes in column B, Security Consulting is changed to Security in cell A36. **Figure 11-5** displays the updated spill range.
6. **Click cell B33, click the Formulas tab on the ribbon, click the Lookup & Reference button in the Function Library group, scroll down the list of functions, then click SORT**
7. **In the Sort Function Arguments dialog box, type A33# in the array box, then click OK**

   A33# uses the spill range operator # to refer to the spilled range beginning in cell A33. The division list is sorted using the data in the range A33:A36.
8. **Select the sorted list of divisions in the range B33:B36, right-click the selected range, click Copy, right-click cell G3, click Values (V) in the Paste Options section (the second option from the left), then press ESC**
9. **Save your work**

**Table 11-1:** Array functions

| function | description |
|---|---|
| FILTER | Extracts data based on defined criteria |
| RANDARRAY | Generates an array of random numbers |
| SEQUENCE | Generate an array of sequential numbers |
| SORTBY | Sorts a range of cells by a different range or array |
| TRANSPOSE | Arranges vertical data horizontally and horizontal data vertically Switch or rotate cells |

**Figure 11-5:** Worksheet with an updated list of divisions

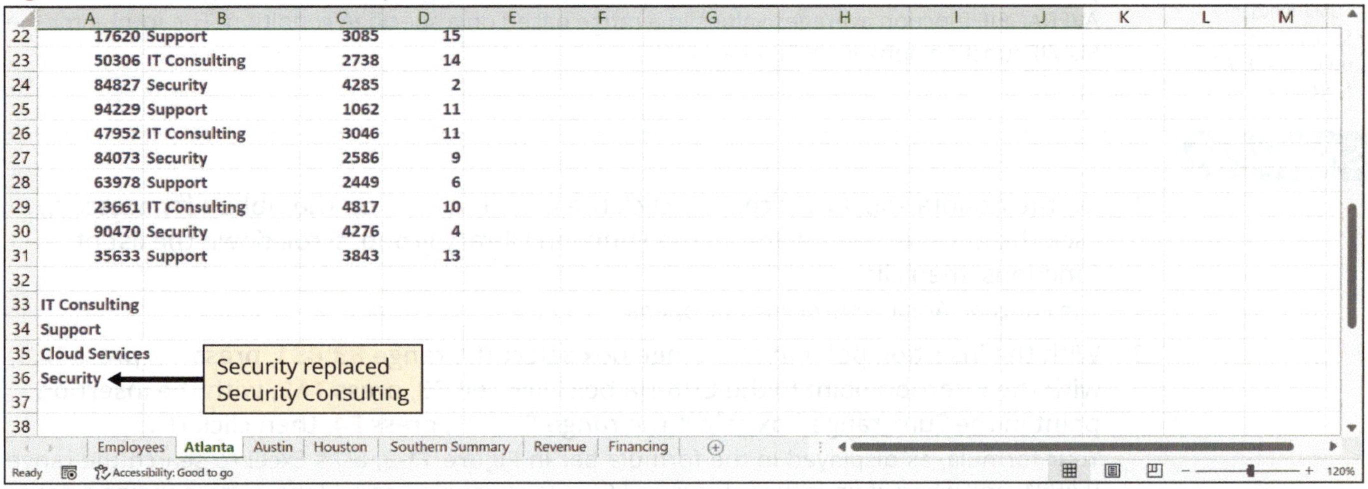


## Using array formulas

In addition to using dynamic array functions to insert formulas in a worksheet, you can enter dynamic formulas with your own operators and range of cells. For example, **Figure 11-6** displays the revenue results in column D for the formula =B2:B9*C2:C9 entered in cell D2. The formula is only entered in cell D2 and the results automatically spill down to cell D9.

**Figure 11-6:** Worksheet with spilled results of dynamic array formula

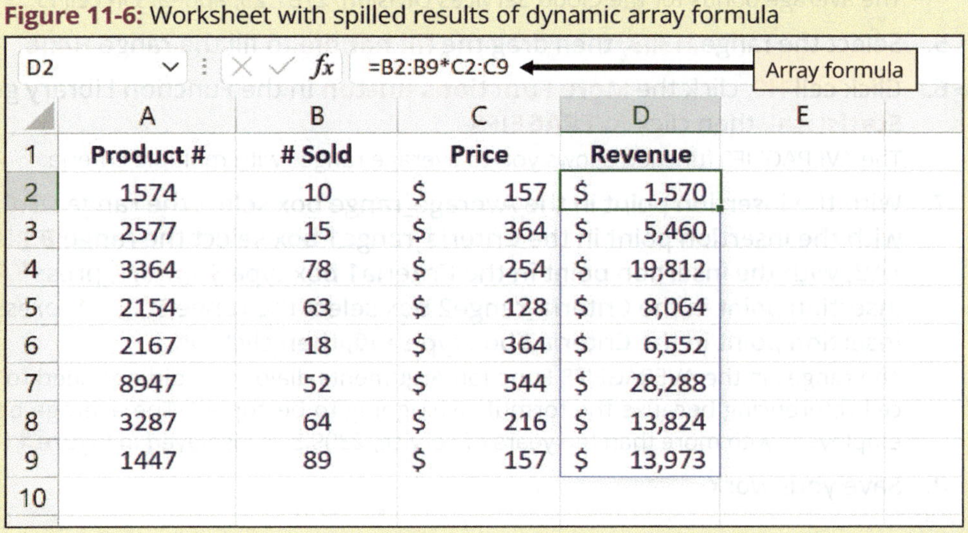

# Calculate Values Based on Conditions

**Case** Elena asks you to analyze the Atlanta office's bonus data to provide her with information about each division, including bonus information for senior support employees.

**Objectives**
- Total data using the SUMIF function
- Summarize data using the AVERAGEIF function

You can use Excel functions to sum and average data in a range based on criteria, or conditions, you set. The SUMIF function totals only the cells in a range that meets the given criteria. The AVERAGEIF function averages values in a range based on a specified condition. The format for the SUMIF function appears in **Figure 11-7**.

## Steps

1. **On the Atlanta sheet click cell H3, click the Formulas tab on the ribbon if necessary, click the Math & Trig button in the Function Library group, scroll down the list of functions, then click SUMIF**
   The Function Arguments dialog box opens.
2. **With the insertion point in the Range box select the range B3:B31, press F4, press TAB, with the insertion point in the Criteria box click cell G3, press TAB, with the insertion point in the Sum_range box select the range C3:C31, press F4, then click OK**
   Your formula, as displayed in the formula bar in **Figure 11-8**, asks Excel to search the range B3:B31, and where it finds the value in cell G3, Cloud Services, to add the corresponding amount from column C. The result, the total bonus for the Cloud Services Division, is displayed in cell H3.
3. **Click cell I3, click the More Functions button in the Function Library group, point to Statistical, then click AVERAGEIF**
4. **With the insertion point in the Range box select the range B3:B31, press F4, press TAB, with the insertion point in the Criteria box click cell G3, press TAB, with the insertion point in the Average_range box select the range C3:C31, press F4, then click OK**
   The average bonus for the Cloud Services Division, 2781.25, appears in cell I3.
5. **Select the range H3:I3, then drag the fill handle to fill the range H4:I6**
6. **Click cell H9, click the More Functions button in the Function Library group, point to Statistical, then click AVERAGEIFS**
   The AVERAGEIFS function allows you to average ranges with multiple criteria.
7. **With the insertion point in the Average_range box select the range C3:C31, press TAB, with the insertion point in the Criteria_range1 box select the range B3:B31, press TAB, with the insertion point in the Criteria1 box type Support, press TAB, with the insertion point in the Criteria_range2 box select the range D3:D31, press TAB, with the insertion point in the Criteria2 box type >10, then click OK**
   The ranges in the AVERAGEIFS Function Arguments dialog box did not need to include absolute cell referencing because the formula isn't going to be copied. The average bonus for support employees with more than ten years of service, 2309.5, is displayed in **Figure 11-9**.
8. **Save your work**

**Quick Tip**
To sum ranges with multiple criteria, you can use the SUMIFS function.

**Figure 11-7:** Format of SUMIF function

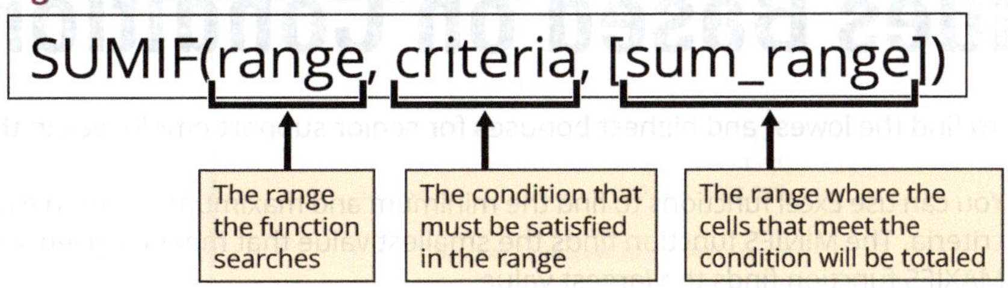


**Figure 11-8:** SUMIF function in the formula bar

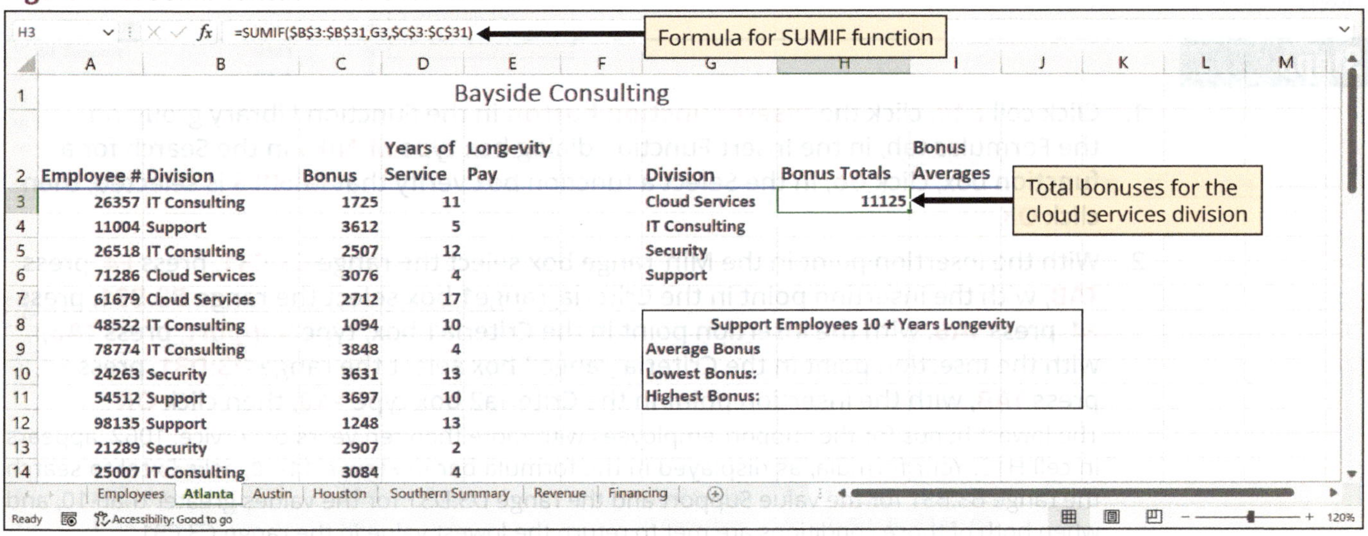


**Figure 11-9:** Worksheet with AVERAGEIFS function result

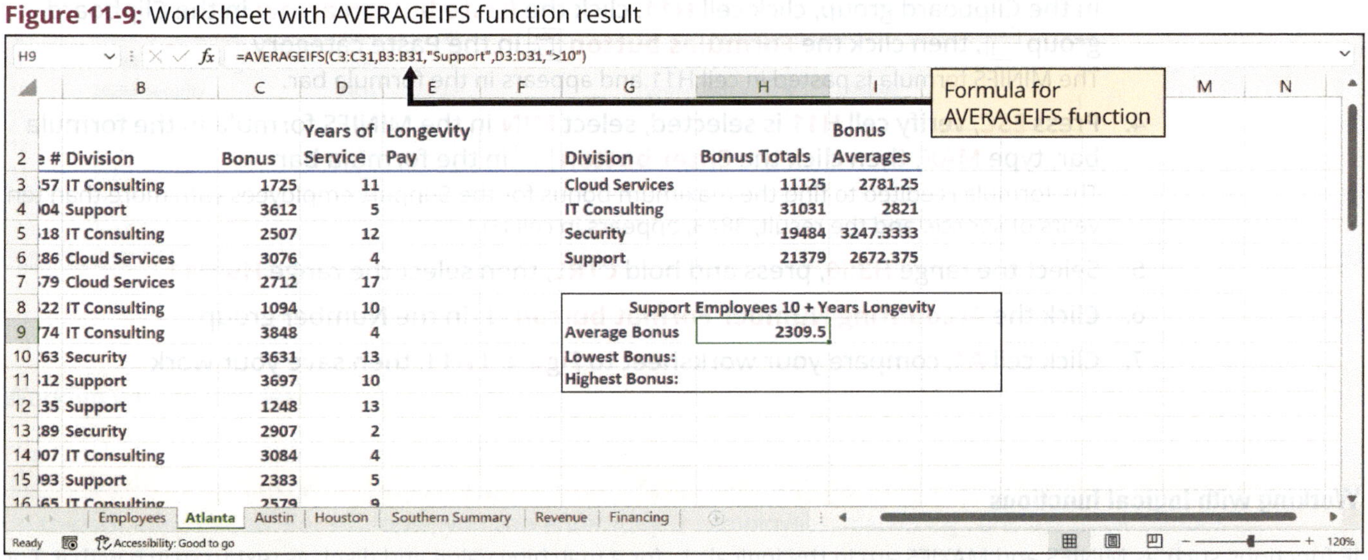

# Create Formulas Using Named Ranges

**Case** Elena asks you to calculate the longevity pay for each employee. Employees with 15 or more years of longevity receive $3000, those with between 10 and 15 years receive $2000, and employees with five or more years receive $1000. You will use a range name and formula to construct a formula to calculate the longevity pay.

**Objectives**
- Assign names to cell ranges
- Build formulas using named ranges

To make your worksheet easier to follow, you can assign names to cells and ranges. Then you can use the names in formulas to make them easier to build and to reduce formula errors. Cell and range names can use uppercase or lowercase letters as well as digits but cannot have spaces. After you name a cell or range, you can define its **scope** or the location in a worksheet where you want the range to be recognized. When defining a name's scope, you can limit its use to a worksheet or make it available to the entire workbook. When used in formulas, names become absolute cell references by default.

## Steps

**Quick Tip**
You can also create range names by selecting a cell or range, typing a name in the Name Box, then pressing ENTER; you can then select a name in the Name box to move to that range in the worksheet.

**Quick Tip**
You can use the New Name dialog box to define a custom function using the LAMBDA function. For example, entering Profit_3_Percent in the Name box and =LAMBDA(rev, rev*1.03) in the Refers to box allows you to use the function Profit_3_Percent in your worksheet to calculate three percent profit amounts for revenue values.

1. **On the Atlanta sheet select the range D3:D31, click the Formulas tab on the ribbon, then click the Define Name button in the Defined Names group**
   The New Name dialog box opens with Years_of_Service in the Name box, as displayed in **Figure 11-12**. The name was taken from the column heading above the selected range and Excel added underscores (_) in place of the spaces between the words because range names cannot contain spaces.
2. **Click the Scope list arrow, click Atlanta, then click OK**
   You accepted the name assigned to the selected range and limited the scope of the name to the Atlanta sheet.
3. **Click the Name Manager button in the Defined Names group**
   The name that has been assigned is listed in the Name Manager dialog box, as displayed in **Figure 11-13**. The Name Manager can be used to create, delete, and edit names in a workbook.
4. **Click Close to close the Name Manager dialog box, click cell E3, click the Logical button in the Function Library group, then click IFS**
   The IFS function tests one or more conditions and returns a value that corresponds to the first TRUE condition. If the first condition is false, the function evaluates the second condition and continues in this manner. Because the IFS function returns a value that corresponds to the first condition, you will begin the logical tests for the formula with the largest value in the Years_of_Service range.
5. **With the insertion point in the Logical_test1 box click the Use in Formula button in the Defined Names group, click Years_of_Service, type >=15, press TAB, with the insertion point in the Value-if-true1 box type 3000, press TAB, with the insertion point in the Logical_test2 box click the Use in Formula button, click Years_of_Service type >=10, press TAB, with the insertion point in the Value-if-true2 box type 2000, press TAB, with the insertion point in the Logical_test3 box click the Use in Formula button, click Years_of_Service, type >=5, press TAB, with the insertion point in the Value-if-true3 box type 1000, press TAB, with the insertion point in the Logical_test4 box click the Use in Formula button, click Years_of_Service, type >0, press TAB, with the insertion point in the Value-if-true4 box type 0, then click OK**
   The IFS function returns the value that meets the *first* condition, so the function checks the range first for values greater than or equal to 15, and where it finds those values it enters 3000 for the longevity pay, then the function checks the range for values greater than or equal to 10, then for values greater than or equal to 5, and finally for values greater than 0, entering the appropriate value in each result cell.
6. **Click cell E32, click the Home tab, click the AutoSum button [Σ] in the Editing group, then press ENTER**
7. **Select the range E3:E32, click the Accounting Number Format button [$] in the Number group, then click the Decrease Decimal button [.00→.0] twice**
   Compare your work with **Figure 11-14**.
8. **Save the workbook**

**Figure 11-12:** New Name dialog box

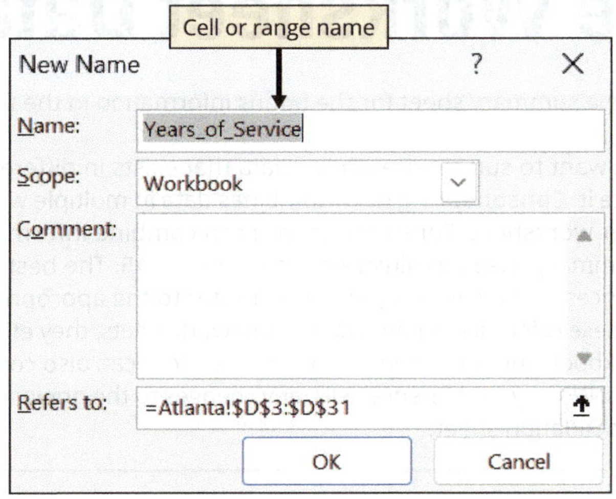


**Figure 11-13:** Name Manager dialog box

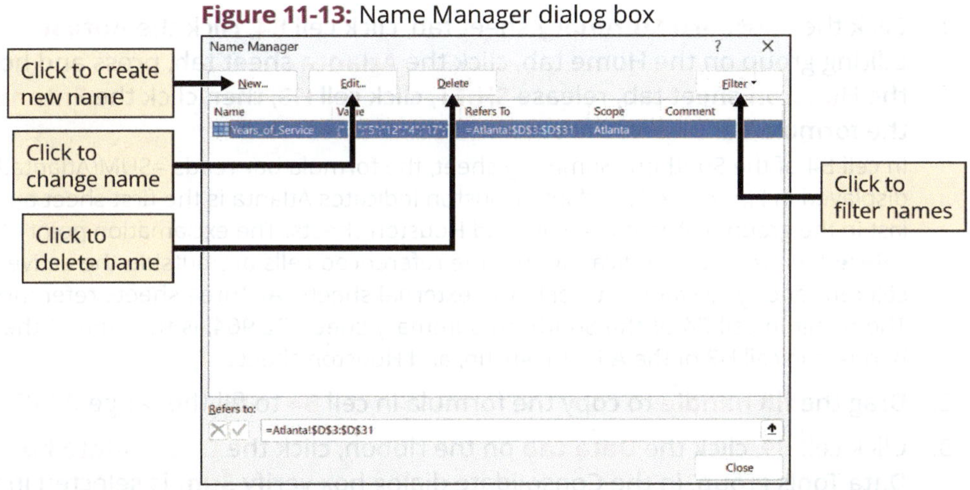


**Figure 11-14:** Worksheet with longevity pay information

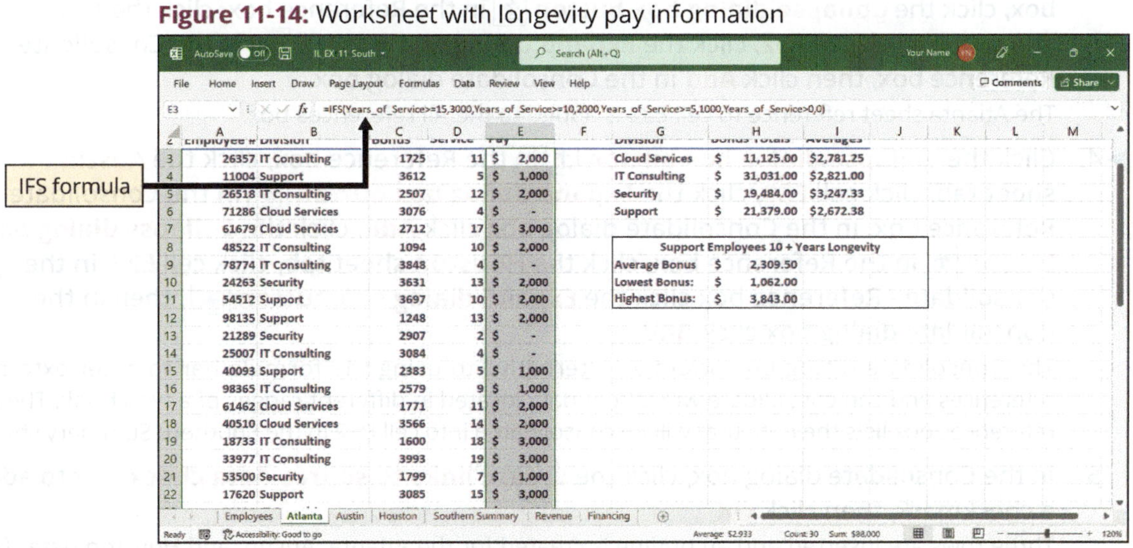


## Using formulas to conditionally format data

You can use a formula to format worksheet data by entering it in a conditional formatting rule. To create a conditional formatting rule with a formula, select the cells you want to format, click the Home tab on the ribbon, click the Conditional Formatting button in the Styles group, then click New Rule. In the New Formatting Rule dialog box, click Use a formula to determine which cells to format, enter the formula in the Format values where this formula is true box, click the Format button, choose a format, then click OK.

# Consolidate Worksheet Data

**Case** Elena asks you to prepare a summary sheet for the bonus information in the three Southern offices.

**Objectives**
- Consolidate data on multiple sheets in the same location
- Consolidate data on multiple sheets in different locations

When you want to summarize similar data that exists in different sheets or workbooks, you can consolidate it. **Consolidating data** combines data in multiple worksheets and displays the results on another worksheet. For example, you can combine information from three different sheets on one summary sheet, as illustrated in **Figure 11-15**. The best way to consolidate data is to add cell references in the summary sheet that refer to the appropriate ranges on the various sheets. Because these references span two or more worksheets, they effectively create another dimension in the workbook and are called **3-D references**. You can also consolidate, or **link** data, from other workbooks. When you reference cells, any changes to the original values are automatically reflected in the consolidation sheet.

## Steps

1. **Click the Southern Summary sheet tab, click cell B4, click the AutoSum button in the Editing group on the Home tab, click the Atlanta sheet tab, press and hold SHIFT, click the Houston sheet tab, release SHIFT, click cell H3, then click the Enter button ✓ in the formula bar**

   In cell B4 of the Southern Summary sheet, the formula bar reads =SUM(Atlanta:Houston!H3), as displayed in **Figure 11-16**. Atlanta:Houston indicates Atlanta is the first sheet and Houston is the last in the group of Atlanta, Austin, and Houston sheets. The exclamation point ( ! ) is an **external reference indicator**, indicating that the referenced cells are outside the active sheet; H3 is the cell reference you want to total in the external sheets. All three sheets reference the same cell. The result in cell B4 of the Southern Summary sheet, 32,964, is the sum of the Cloud Services' bonuses in cell H3 of the Atlanta, Austin, and Houston sheets.

2. **Drag the fill handle to copy the formula in cell B4 to fill the range B5:B7**

3. **Click cell B9, click the Data tab on the ribbon, click the Consolidate button in the Data Tools group, in the Consolidate dialog box verify Sum is selected in the Function box, click the Collapse dialog box button in the Reference box, click the Atlanta Sheet tab, click cell E32, click the Expand dialog box button in the Consolidate - Reference box, then click Add in the Consolidate dialog box**

   The Atlanta sheet reference to cell E32 is added to the All references box.

**Quick Tip**
You can also directly enter a formula to consolidate data, such as entering =SUM(Atlanta!E32+Austin!E30+Houston!E27) in cell B12 of the Southern Summary worksheet.

4. **Click the Collapse dialog box button in the Reference box, click the Austin sheet tab, click cell E30, click the Expand dialog box button in the Consolidate - Reference box, in the Consolidate dialog box click Add, click the Collapse dialog box button in the Reference box, click the Houston sheet tab, click cell E27, in the Consolidate - Reference box click the Expand dialog box button, then in the Consolidate dialog box click Add**

   The Consolidate dialog box offers an alternative to using the formula bar to enter external references and can consolidate worksheet data located in different ranges of a workbook. The All references box lists the data that will be consolidated into cell B12 in the Southern Summary sheet.

5. **In the Consolidate dialog box, click the Create links to source data check box to add a checkmark, then click OK**

   Three rows are inserted and an outline is created for the Atlanta, Austin, and Houston data. The longevity pay total for all three offices, $94,000, is displayed in cell B12.

**Quick Tip**
You can click the level 2 Outline Symbol button 2 to display the total details and the level 1 Outline Symbol button 1 to hide the details.

6. **Click the expand outline button +**

   The total is expanded, displaying the totals from the individual offices in the range B9:B11.

7. **Click cell A9, type Atlanta, press ENTER, type Austin in cell A10, press ENTER, type Houston in cell A11, press ENTER, compare your worksheet to Figure 11-17, then save the workbook**

**Figure 11-15:** Consolidating data from three worksheets

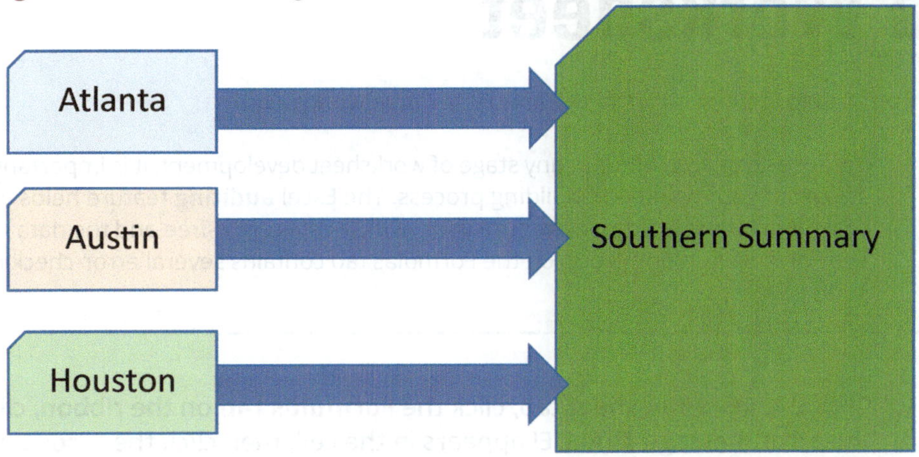


**Figure 11-16:** 3-D reference in formula

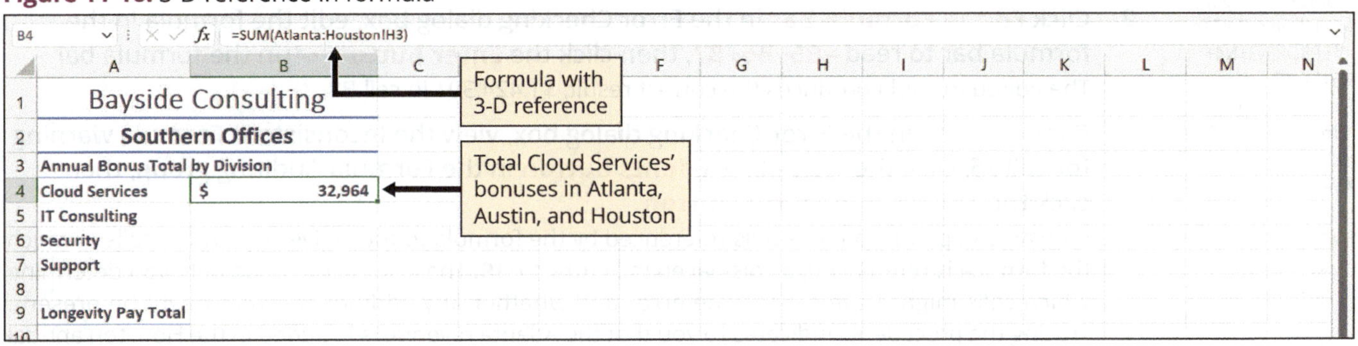


**Figure 11-17:** Southern Summary worksheet with totals

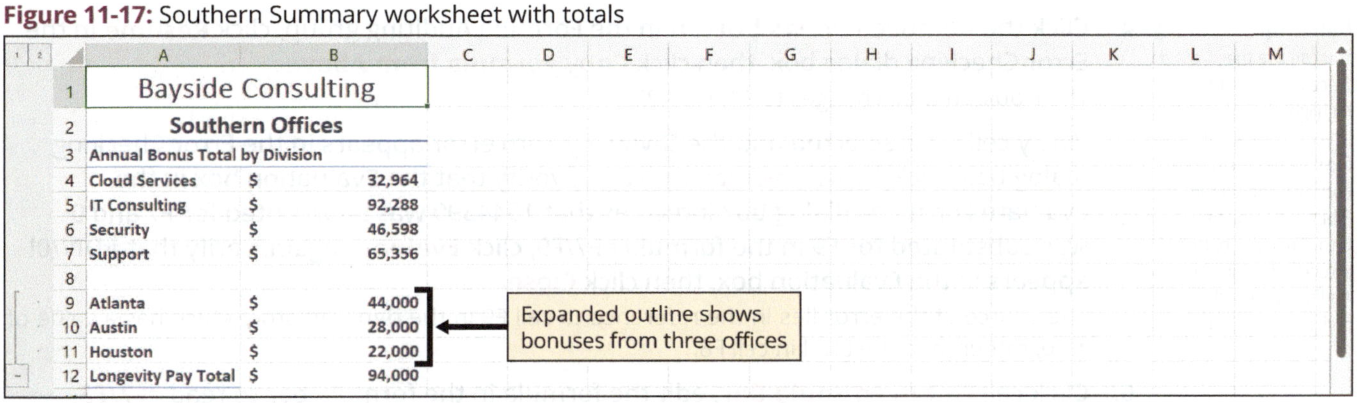

# Audit a Worksheet

**Case** Elena asks you to help identify errors in the annual revenue worksheet.

**Objectives**
- Locate formula errors
- Correct formula errors

Because errors can occur at any stage of worksheet development, it is important to include auditing as part of your workbook-building process. The Excel **auditing** feature helps you track errors and check worksheet logic to make sure your worksheet is error-free and the data is arranged sensibly. The Formula Auditing group on the Formulas tab contains several error-checking tools to help you audit a worksheet.

## Steps

**Quick Tip**
You can use the IFERROR function to display a custom message if there is an error in a formula; for example, editing the formula in cell N7 to =IFERROR(N3+N4+N5+N6, "Error in Formula") displays "Error in Formula" in cell N7 rather than #VALUE!.

1. **Click the Revenue sheet tab, click the Formulas tab on the ribbon, click cell B8, verify the error message #VALUE! appears in the cell, then click the Error Checking button in the Formula Auditing group**
   The Error Checking dialog box opens and alerts you to a data type error. This error is a result of cell B4, which contains text, having been included in the formula, as displayed in **Figure 11-18**.
2. **Click Edit in Formula Bar in the Error Checking dialog box, edit the formula in the formula bar to read =B5+B6+B7, then click the Enter button ✓ in the formula bar**
   The edited formula produces the correct result, $1,424,301 in cell B8.
3. **Click Resume in the Error Checking dialog box, view the Inconsistent Formula warning for cell F6, click the Trace Precedents button in the Formula Auditing group, then click the Trace Dependents button**
   Blue arrows point from the cells referenced by the formula to the active cell, and to cells in which the formula is referenced, as displayed in **Figure 11-19**. These **tracer arrows** help you determine which cells might have caused the error and whether any additional errors might be present. Tracing the precedents indicates to you that the Atlanta revenue is included in the Houston annual total formula. Tracing the dependents indicates that this formula error affects the formulas in cells F8 and G6.

**Quick Tip**
You can use the Trace Error tool to highlight the cells used to calculate a formula by clicking the Formulas tab on the Ribbon, clicking the Error Checking button arrow in the Formula Auditing group, then clicking Trace Error.

4. **Click the Remove Arrows button in the Formula Auditing group, click Resume in the Error Checking dialog box, then click Copy Formula from Above**
   The Houston total changes to $1,449,423.
5. **Verify cell G7 is selected and the Divide by Zero error appears in the Error Checking dialog box, click Show Calculation Steps, verify that the Evaluation box in the Evaluate Formulas dialog box indicates that 1544399 was substituted for F7 and 0 was substituted for F9 in the formula =F7/F9, click Evaluate again, verify that #DIV/0! appears in the Evaluation box, then click Close**
   The source of the error lies in the reference to cell F9 in the denominator, which has a value of zero, rather than the total in cell F8.
6. **Click cell Edit in Formula Bar, edit the formula in the formula bar to read =F7/F8, press F4, then click the Enter button ✓**
   The value in cell F8 changes to 33.97%.
7. **Click Resume in the Error Checking dialog box, verify the error checking is complete as indicated in the message in Figure 11-20, click OK, then save the workbook**

### Circling invalid data

If you enter data validation criteria into your worksheet data, you can locate data that doesn't satisfy that criteria by clicking the Data tab on the ribbon, clicking the Data Validation arrow, then clicking Circle Invalid Data. Red circles appear around cells that are not consistent with data validation criteria. To clear the circles on the worksheet, click the Data Validation arrow, then click Clear Validation Circles.

**Figure 11-18:** Error Checking dialog box

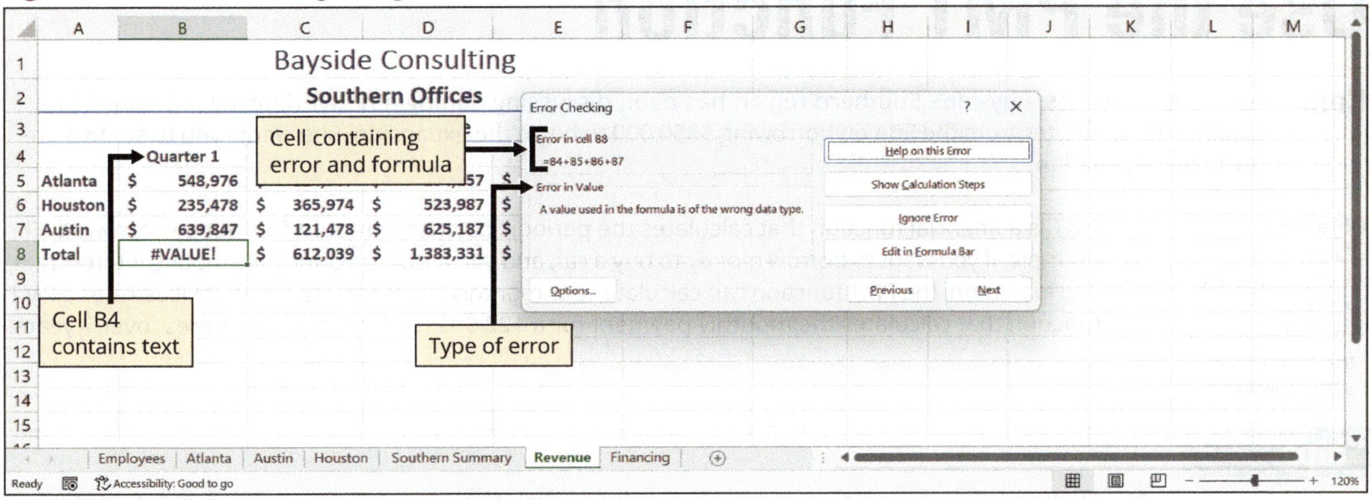


**Figure 11-19:** Worksheet with tracer arrows

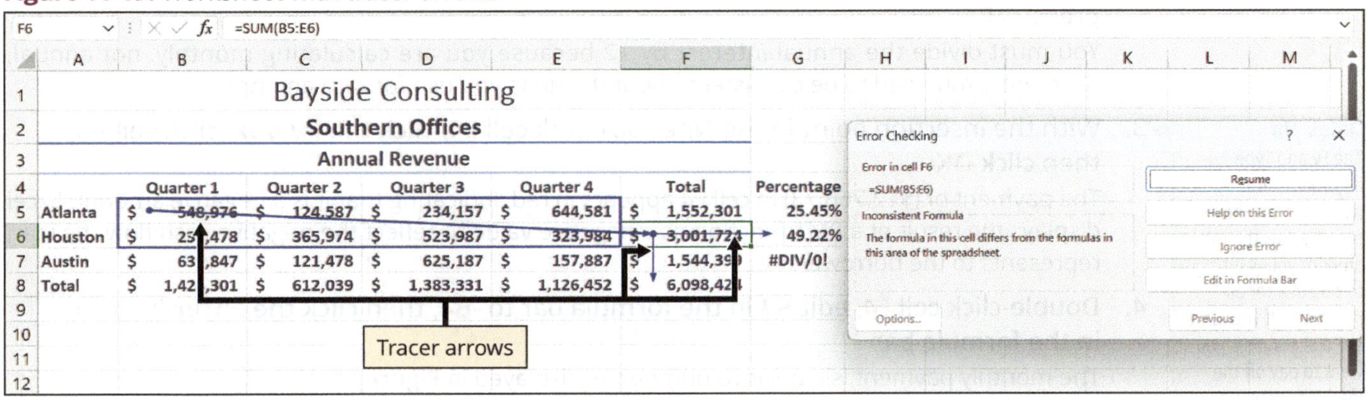


**Figure 11-20:** Final error check results

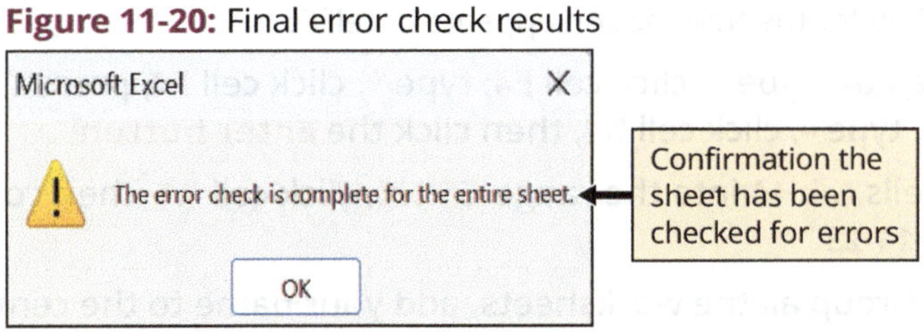


## Watching formulas

As you edit your worksheet, you can watch the effect that cell changes have on selected worksheet formulas. Select the cell or cells that you want to watch, click the Formulas tab on the ribbon, click the Watch Window button in the Formula Auditing group, click Add Watch in the Watch Window, then click Add. The Watch Window lists the workbook name, the worksheet name, the cell address you want to watch, the current cell value, and its formula. As cell values that "feed into" the formula change, the resulting formula value in the Watch Window changes. To delete a watch, select the cell information in the Watch Window, click Delete Watch, then close the Watch Window.

# Use the PMT Function

**Case** For several months, Bayside's Southern region has been discussing adding a networking division. Elena has obtained three quotes from the SBA on borrowing $850,000 to begin the expansion. She wants you to summarize the loan information.

**Objectives**
- Calculate monthly payments using the PMT function
- Edit the PMT function to display payments as a positive value

PMT is a financial function that calculates the periodic payment amount for money borrowed. For example, if you want to borrow money to buy a car, and you know the principal amount, interest rate, and loan term, the PMT function can calculate your monthly payment. **Figure 11-21** illustrates a PMT function that calculates the monthly payment for a $22,000 car loan at 6.7% interest over 7 years.

## Steps

1. **Click the Financing sheet tab, click cell F4, click the Financial button in the Function Library group on the Formulas tab, scroll down the list of functions, then click PMT**
2. **With the insertion point in the Rate box click cell D4 on the worksheet, type /12, then press TAB**

   You must divide the annual interest by 12 because you are calculating monthly, not annual, payments. You need to be consistent about the units you use for rate and nper.
3. **With the insertion point in the Nper box click cell E4, click the Pv box, click cell B4, then click OK**

   The payment of ($12,766.73) in cell F4 appears in red, indicating that it is a negative amount. Excel displays the result of a PMT function as a negative value to reflect the negative cash flow the loan represents to the borrower.
4. **Double-click cell F4, edit B4 in the formula bar to -B4, then click the Enter button ✓ in the formula bar**

   The monthly payment is a positive number as displayed in **Figure 11-22**.
5. **With cell F4 selected, drag the fill handle + to fill the range F5:F6**

   A monthly payment of $12,485.22 for the second option appears in cell F5. A monthly payment of $11,177.39 for the third option appears in cell F6.
6. **Click cell G4, type =, click cell E4, type *, click cell F4, press TAB, in cell H4 type =, click cell G4, type –, click cell B4, then click the Enter button**
7. **Copy cells G4:H4 into the range G5:H6, click cell A1, then compare your worksheet to Figure 11-23**
8. **sam Group all the worksheets, add your name to the center section of the grouped footer, ungroup the worksheets, save the workbook, submit the workbook to your instructor, close the workbook, then close Excel**

**Quick Tip**
The Fv and Type arguments are optional: Fv is the future value, the total amount you want to obtain after all payments. If you omit it, Excel assumes you want to pay off the loan completely, so the default Fv is 0. Type indicates when the payments are made; 0 is the end of the period, and 1 is the beginning of the period. The default is the end of the period.

### Working with other financial functions

You can use the FV (Future Value) function to determine the amount of money a given monthly investment will amount to, at a given interest rate, after a given number of payment periods. The syntax is FV(rate,nper,pmt,pv,type), where *rate* is the interest paid by the financial institution, *nper* is the number of periods, and *pmt* is the amount you deposit. For example, suppose you want to invest $2,000 every month for the next 12 months into an account that pays 4% a year. You can enter the function =FV(.04/12,12, −2000), and Excel returns the value $24,444.93 as the future value of your investment. You can use the NPER function to determine the number of payment periods required for a loan or investment. For example, if you want to take out a loan for $25,000 at an interest rate of 7% with payments of $500 monthly, you can enter =NPER(7%/12,500, −25000) and Excel returns the value 59.29. You can use the PV function to find the present value of a loan or an investment. For example, if you have an investment that will pay you an amount of $100 for 8% per month over 20 years, you can enter =PV(8%/12,12*20,100) and Excel returns a value of $11,955.43, the present value of that investment.

**Figure 11-21:** Example of PMT function for a car loan

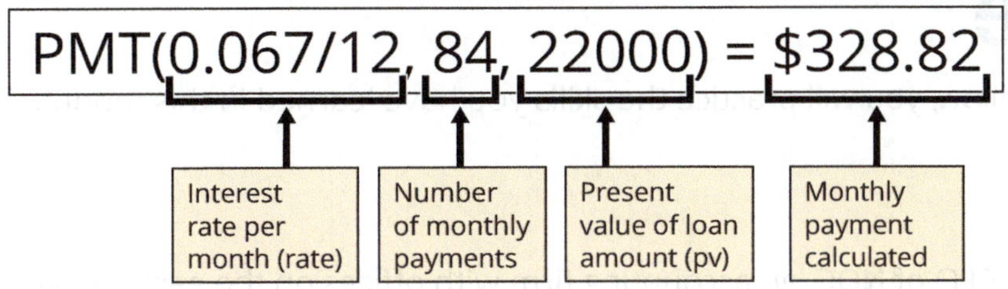


**Figure 11-22:** PMT function calculating a monthly loan payment

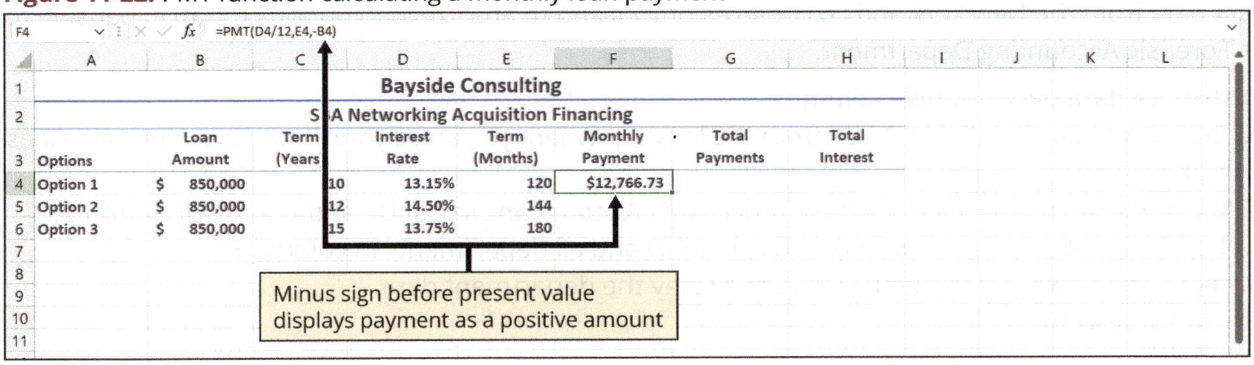


**Figure 11-23:** Completed worksheet

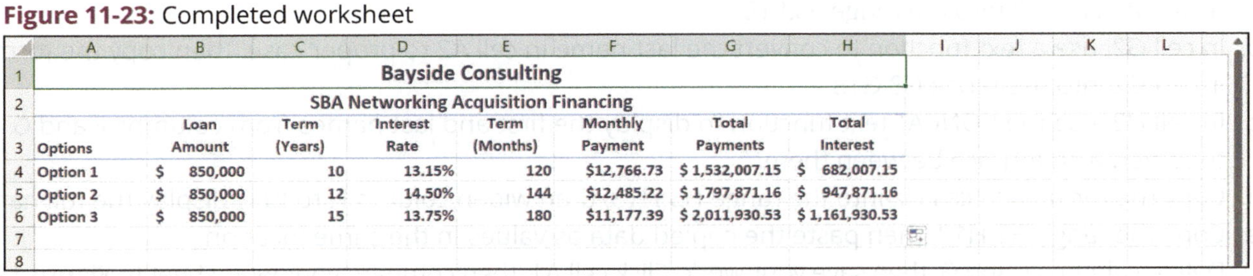


## Using the LET function to name calculation results

When working with formulas, it is sometimes helpful to store intermediate calculations, values, or name definitions. The LET function assigns names to these calculations. These names reside only inside the function and are not permanently stored. They can improve the readability of a function. For example, in **Figure 11-24**, the LET function stores the sum of the four quarters using the variable annual and then uses this variable in the IF formula to check if it is greater than 20000, making the employee eligible for a bonus.

**Figure 11-24:** LET function

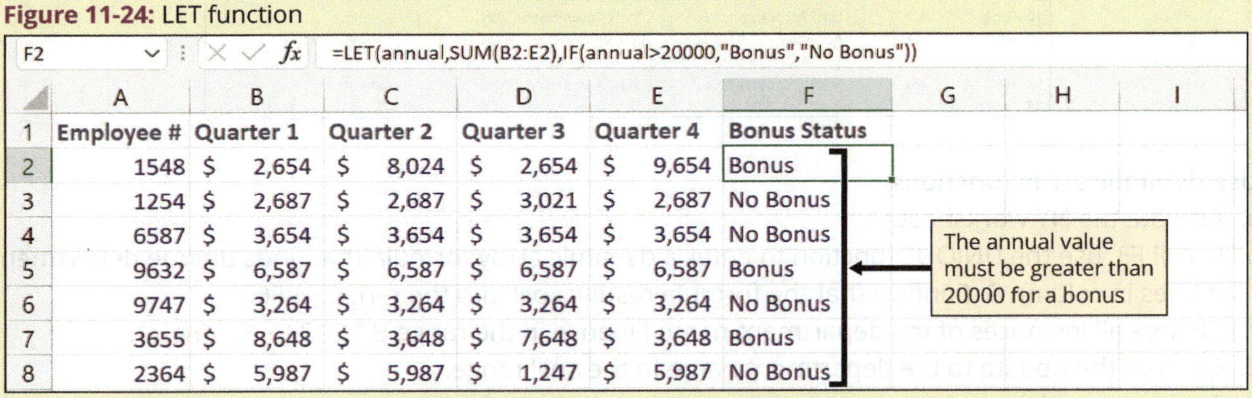

# Practice

In the exercises that follow, you will practice the skills you have learned in this module.

## Skills Review

As the assistant to the CFO of NQC, an accounting firm with offices on the east and west coasts of the United States, you review employee and department data monthly. You also review proposals for new debt the company is considering for major expenses. You will use Excel formulas and functions to review the January data from the New York and Los Angeles offices and to analyze loan options for an expansion to add a Forensic Accounting Department.

1. **Distribute data over multiple columns.**
   a. Start Excel, open IL_EX_11-2.xlsx from the location where you store your Data Files, then save it as **IL_EX_11_NQC**.
   b. On the New Employees worksheet, enter **Staff Accountant** in cell D2 and **Financial** in cell E2.
   c. Use Flash Fill to enter all positions in column D and all departments in column E.
   d. Increase the width of column D to fully display the department data.
   e. Save your work.
2. **Format data using text functions.**
   a. In cell F2, use a text function to convert the name in cell B2 to proper name format, then copy the formula in cell F2 into the range F3:F13.
   b. In cell G2, use a text function to convert the last name in cell A2 to proper case, then copy the formula in cell G2 into the range G3:G13.
   c. In cell H2, use the CONCAT text function to display the first and last names from columns F and G together, with a space between them.
   d. Copy the formula in cell H2 into the range H3:H13, then widen column H to fully display the full names.
   e. Copy the range H2:H13, then paste the copied data as values in the same location.
   f. Delete columns F and G, then save your work. Click cell A1, then compare your worksheet to **Figure 11-25**.

**Figure 11-25**

A1 fx Last Name

| | A | B | C | D | E | F | G |
|---|---|---|---|---|---|---|---|
| 1 | Last Name | First Name | Placement | Position | Department | Name | |
| 2 | ascollilo | amina | Staff Accountant, Financial | Staff Accountant | Financial | Amina Ascollilo | |
| 3 | chau | brunilda | Accounting Clerk, Cost | Accounting Clerk | Cost | Brunilda Chau | |
| 4 | cruz | mai | Junior Accountant, Auditing | Junior Accountant | Auditing | Mai Cruz | |
| 5 | desir | keri | Senior Accountant, Tax | Senior Accountant | Tax | Keri Desir | |
| 6 | kullolli | liness | Staff Accountant, Financial | Staff Accountant | Financial | Liness Kullolli | |
| 7 | mezias | corina | Accounting Clerk, Auditing | Accounting Clerk | Auditing | Corina Mezias | |
| 8 | moun | candida | Accounting Clerk, Cost | Accounting Clerk | Cost | Candida Moun | |
| 9 | shu | daria | Junior Accountant, Financial | Junior Accountant | Financial | Daria Shu | |
| 10 | vong | ari | Staff Accountant, Tax | Staff Accountant | Tax | Ari Vong | |
| 11 | wilson | troy | Accounting Clerk, Tax | Accounting Clerk | Tax | Troy Wilson | |
| 12 | nunez | isandra | Senior Accountant, Auditing | Senior Accountant | Auditing | Isandra Nunez | |
| 13 | stelk | jade | Staff Accountant, Cost | Staff Accountant | Cost | Jade Stelk | |
| 14 | | | | | | | |

3. **Use dynamic array functions**
   a. Activate the NY worksheet.
   b. In cell F3, use the UNIQUE function to enter a dynamic array formula that finds unique department names in column B. Confirm that the formula results spill into the range F4:F6.
   c. Change all instances of the department name Finance in the range B3:B13 to **Financial**.
   d. Confirm the update to the department name in the spill range.
   e. Save your work.

4. **Calculate values based on conditions.**
   a. In cell G3, use the SUMIF function to total the expenses of employees in the Auditing Department. (**Hint**: Use absolute cell references for the ranges.)
   b. Copy the formula results in cell G3 into the range G4:G6.
   c. In cell H3, use the AVERAGEIF function to average the expenses of employees in the Auditing Department. (**Hint**: Use absolute cell references for the ranges.)
   d. Copy the formula results in cell H3 into the range H4:H6.
   e. Format the range G3:H6 with the Accounting Number format using two decimal places.
   f. Widen columns G and H as necessary to fully display the values in the columns.
   g. Save your work.
5. **Find values based on conditions.**
   a. In cell K4, use the MINIFS function to find the lowest expenses of employees in the Cost Department with more than 200 billable hours. Use absolute cell references for the ranges in the formula.
   b. In cell K5, use the MAXIFS function to find the highest expenses of employees in the Cost Department with more than 200 billable hours. (**Hint**: You can copy the formula in cell K4 and edit it for MAXIFS.)
   c. Format cells K4 and K5 with the Accounting Number format using two decimal places.
   d. Save your work.
6. **Create formulas using named ranges.**
   a. On the NY sheet, name the range C3:C13 **Billable_Hours**, and limit the scope of the name to the NY worksheet.
   b. In cell E3, use the IFS function and the named range Billable_Hours to enter the text:
      - **Exceeds Expectations** for billable hours greater than or equal to 200.
      - **Meets Expectations** for billable hours greater than or equal to 160.
      - **Below Expectations** for billable hours greater than or equal to zero.
   c. Confirm the formula results spill into the range E4:E13.
   d. Widen column E to fully display the formula results.
   e. Save your work.
   f. Compare your worksheet to **Figure 11-26**.

**Figure 11-26**

| | A | B | C | D | E | F | G | H | I | J | K | L | M |
|---|---|---|---|---|---|---|---|---|---|---|---|---|---|
| 1 | January | | | | | | | | | | | | |
| 2 | Employee # | Department | Billable Hours | Expenses | Review | Department | Total Expenses | Average Expenses | | Cost Department | | | |
| 3 | 9922 | Auditing | 168 | $ 2,355 | Meets Expectations | Auditing | $ 3,678.00 | $ 1,839.00 | | More Than 200 Billable Hours | | | |
| 4 | 8733 | Cost | 210 | $ 1,991 | Exceeds Expectations | Cost | $ 6,077.00 | $ 1,519.25 | | Lowest Expenses | $ 1,441.00 | | |
| 5 | 4036 | Financial | 150 | $ 1,078 | Below Expectations | Financial | $ 4,156.00 | $ 1,385.33 | | Highest Expenses | $ 1,991.00 | | |
| 6 | 8033 | Tax | 176 | $ 1,985 | Meets Expectations | Tax | $ 3,666.00 | $ 1,833.00 | | | | | |
| 7 | 3716 | Tax | 140 | $ 1,681 | Below Expectations | | | | | | | | |
| 8 | 2525 | Auditing | 199 | $ 1,323 | Meets Expectations | | | | | | | | |
| 9 | 5142 | Financial | 204 | $ 1,531 | Exceeds Expectations | | | | | | | | |
| 10 | 1458 | Financial | 155 | $ 1,547 | Below Expectations | | | | | | | | |
| 11 | 1632 | Cost | 185 | $ 1,025 | Meets Expectations | | | | | | | | |
| 12 | 7090 | Cost | 201 | $ 1,441 | Exceeds Expectations | | | | | | | | |
| 13 | 6275 | Cost | 210 | $ 1,620 | Exceeds Expectations | | | | | | | | |
| 14 | Totals | | 1998 | $ 17,577 | | | | | | | | | |
| 15 | | | | | | | | | | | | | |

7. **Consolidate worksheet data.**
   a. Activate the Summary sheet.
   b. In cell B3, use the AutoSum function to total cell G3 on the NY and LA sheets.
   c. Copy the formula in cell B3 into the range B4:B6.

## Independent Challenge 1 (Continued)

**Figure 11-30**

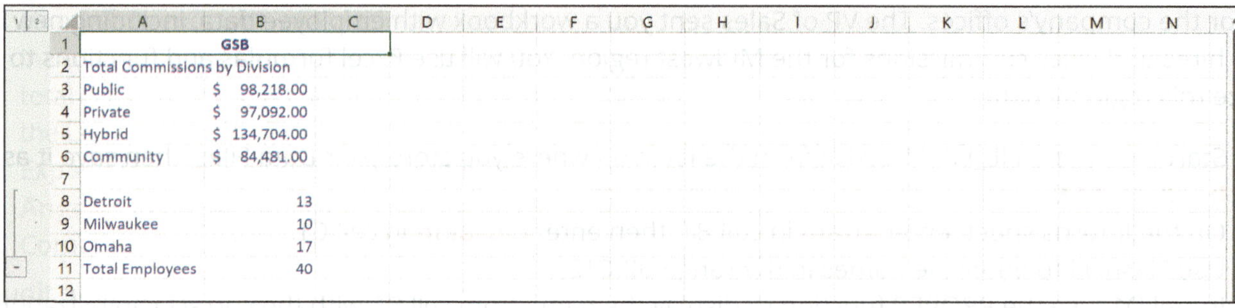

| | A | B |
|---|---|---|
| 1 | GSB | |
| 2 | Total Commissions by Division | |
| 3 | Public | $ 98,218.00 |
| 4 | Private | $ 97,092.00 |
| 5 | Hybrid | $ 134,704.00 |
| 6 | Community | $ 84,481.00 |
| 7 | | |
| 8 | Detroit | 13 |
| 9 | Milwaukee | 10 |
| 10 | Omaha | 17 |
| 11 | Total Employees | 40 |
| 12 | | |

## Independent Challenge 2

As an assistant to the CFO of MBX Streaming Services, you use Excel formulas and functions to analyze sales data. You will review the first quarter sales and profit calculations and provide options for financing new equipment.

a. Start Excel, open IL_EX_11-4.xlsx from the location where you store your Data Files, then save it as **IL_EX_11_MBX**.

b. On the Reps sheet, enter **badawi** in cell B2, enter **faith** in cell C2, then enter **subscriptions** in cell D2.

c. Use FlashFill to enter the names and departments in the range B3:D20.

d. In cell E2, use a text function to display the last name from cell B2 with the correct capitalization for proper names.

e. In cell F2, use a text function to display the first name from cell C2 with the correct capitalization for proper names.

f. In cell H2, use a text function to display the department from cell D2 with the correct capitalization for proper names.

g. Copy the formulas in the range E2:F2 into the range E3:F20, then copy the formula in cell H2 into the range H3:H20.

h. In cell G2, use a text function to join the text in cell F2 with the text in cell E2, including a space between the names, then copy the formula in cell G2 into the range G3:G20.

i. Use **Figure 11-31** as a guide to enter a text formula in cell I2 that displays the first character of the text in cell C2, then copy then copy the formula in cell I2 into the range I3:I20.

j. In cell J2, use a text function to join the following text:

   Text1: **I2**
   Text2: **"."**
   Text3: **B2**
   Text4: **"@company.com"**

k. Copy the formula in cell J2 into the range J3:J20.

l. Copy the data in the range E2:J20, then paste the selection as values in the same range. Delete columns A through F and column I. Widen columns A, B, and C as necessary to fully display the data in those columns.

m. Use the UNIQUE function in cell E2 to enter a dynamic array formula that finds unique department names in column B. Confirm that the formula results spill into the range E3:E4.

**Figure 11-31**

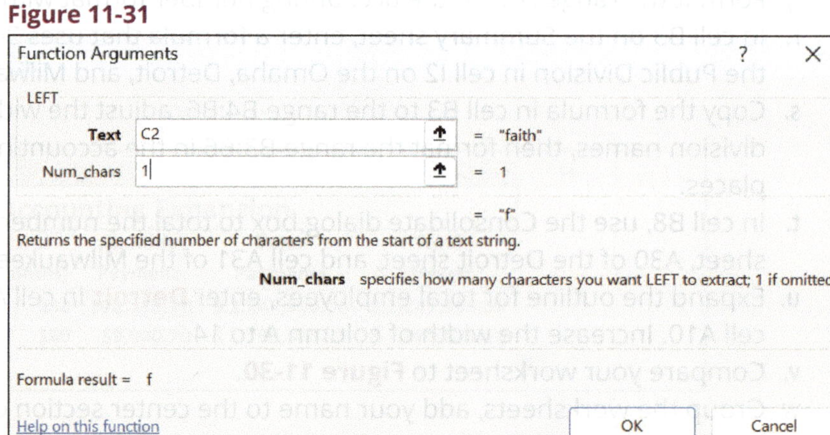

n. Change the department name Content to Content Licensing in the range B2:B20, then confirm the update to the department name in the spill range. Widen columns B and E to fully display the department names.

o. On the Sales sheet, name the range containing the sales in column D **Sales** with a scope of the workbook. Use the named range and an IFS function in cell E2 to calculate a bonus based on the sales in cell D2 following the criteria:

  Equal to or greater than 65000, 10000
  Equal to or greater than 50000, 7000
  Equal to or greater than 40000, 4000
  Equal to or greater than 30000, 1000
  Equal to or greater than 0, 0

p. Format the bonus values with the Accounting Number format using zero decimal places.

q. On the Profit sheet, use the Error Checking dialog box to locate formula errors. If you wish, use the Trace Precedents feature to help locate the source of the errors. Remove all tracer arrows if necessary, then correct all formula errors.

r. On the Loan sheet, use an array formula in cell B5 to calculate the down payments in the range B5:F8. (**Hint**: The array formula is A5:A8*B4:F4.)

s. Format the range B5:F8 with the Accounting Number format using zero decimal places.

t. Enter **600000** in cell B11, enter **120000** in cell B12, then calculate the amount financed in cell B13 by subtracting the down payment from the equipment cost.

u. Enter a formula in cell B16 that calculates the monthly payment for the amount financed in cell B13 and the interest rate and term in cells B14:B15, then display the payment as a positive value.

v. Format the range B11:B13 with the Accounting Number format using zero decimal places. Compare your worksheet to **Figure 11-32**.

**Figure 11-32**

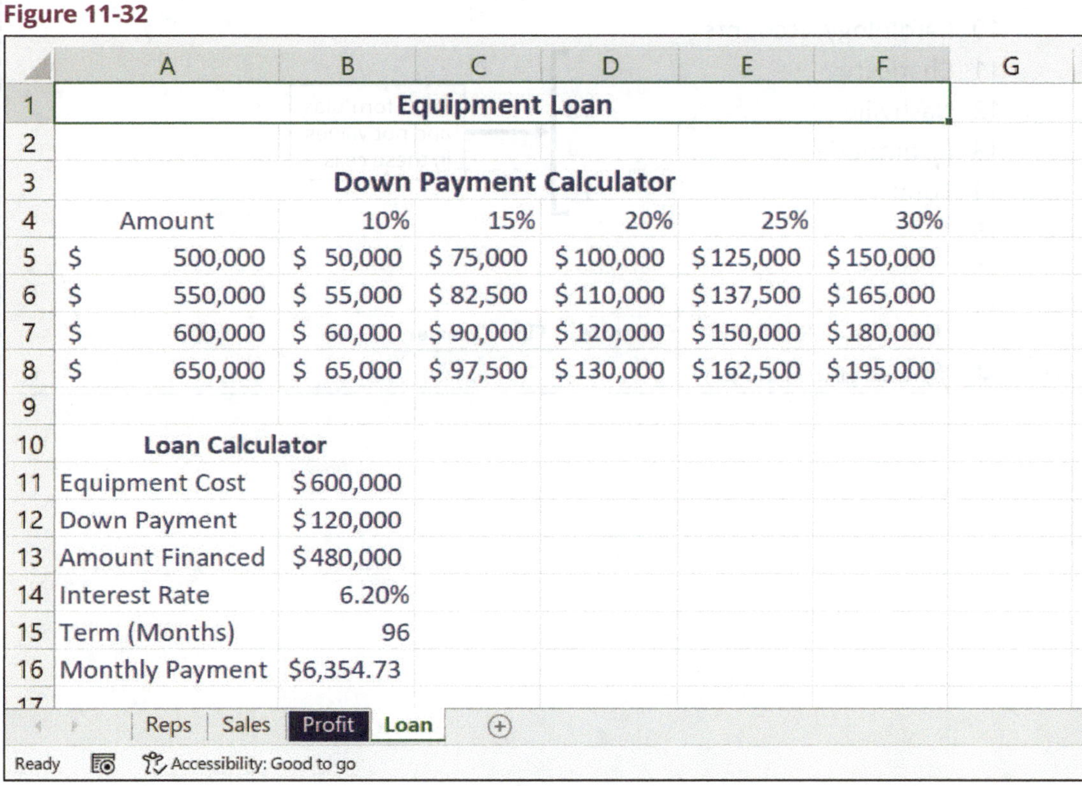


w. Group the four worksheets, enter your name in the worksheet footer, ungroup the worksheets, save the workbook, then submit it to your instructor.

x. Close the workbook, then close Excel.

## Visual Workshop

Open IL_EX_11-5.xlsx from the location where you store your Data Files, then save it as **IL_EX_11_Southern**. Use the data in the Nashville, Richmond, and Charlotte worksheets to create summary information on the First Quarter worksheet displayed in **Figure 11-33**. The outstanding balance data are in the same location on all three worksheets. The number of cardiology accounts for each location appears in different locations on the three worksheets. (**Hint**: You need to calculate the total outstanding balance for each department in the range G2:G7 on the Nashville sheet before totaling the outstanding balance totals on the First Quarter sheet.) If your formulas result in errors, use the auditing features to find and correct errors in the worksheet. Enter your name in the Nashville and First Quarter worksheet footers, save the workbook, submit it to your instructor, then close Excel.

**Figure 11-33**

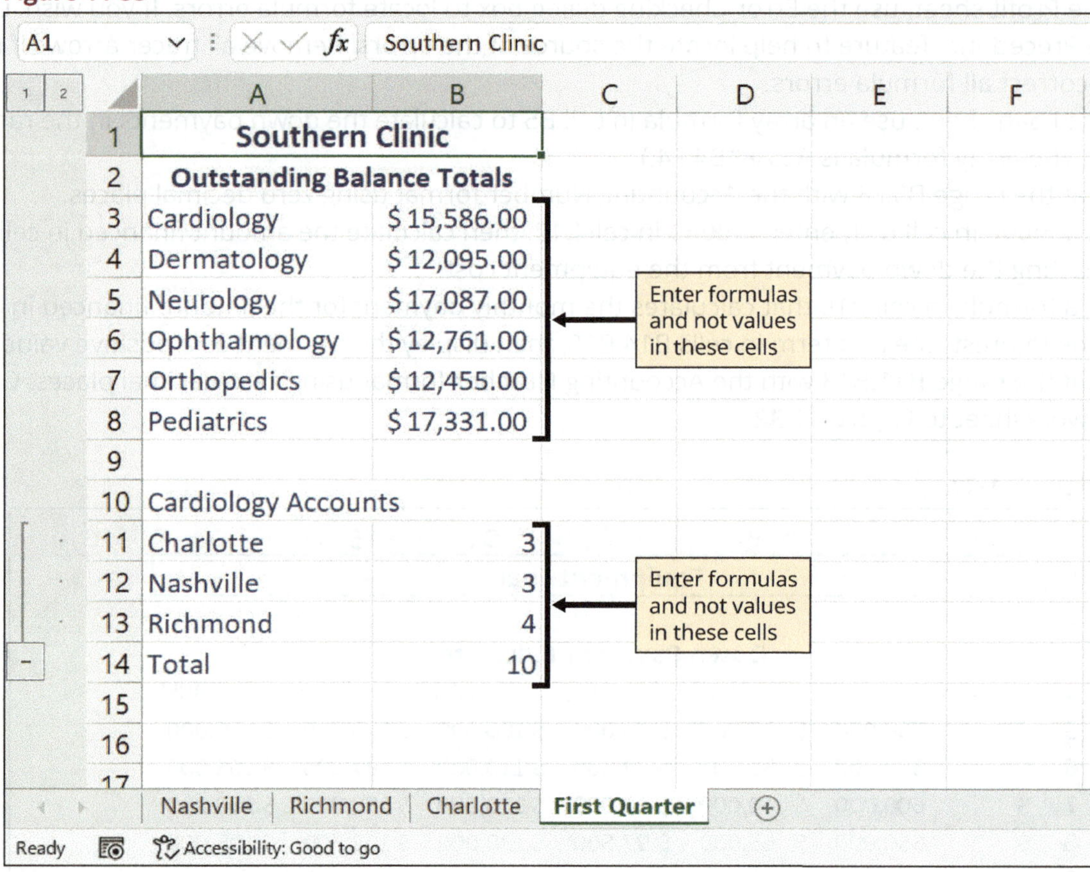

# Performing What-if Analysis

## Case

Elena Fuentes, Bayside's Vice President of Finance, uses what-if analysis to analyze regional data and forecast revenue. You will help Elena complete this analysis using the data analysis tools and add-ins in Excel.

## Module Objectives

After completing this module, you will be able to:

- Describe what-if analysis
- Use Scenario Manager to manage scenarios
- Create a scenario summary
- Create a data table
- Use Goal Seek to find input values
- Use Solver to define and solve a problem
- Manage data using a data model
- Analyze data using Power Pivot

## Files You Will Need

IL_EX_12-1.xlsx
IL_EX_12-2.xlsx
IL_EX_12-3.xlsx
IL_EX_12-4.xlsx
IL_EX_12-5.xlsx

# Describe What-if Analysis

**Case** Elena has received projected revenue and project data from Bayside's division directors. She has also received management data from the Human Resources Department. Elena created a worksheet model to perform an initial what-if analysis with this data, as displayed in **Figure 12-1**. Elena thinks the support revenue projections for the first quarter months should be higher. You first review the guidelines for performing what-if analysis.

**Objectives**
- Summarize guidelines for performing what-if analysis
- Define what-if analysis terminology

By performing what-if analysis in a worksheet, you can get immediate answers to questions such as "What happens to profits if we sell 25 percent more of a certain product?" or "What happens to monthly payments if interest rates rise or fall?" A worksheet you use to perform what-if analysis is often called a **model** because it acts as the basis for multiple outcomes or sets of results. To perform what-if analysis in a worksheet, you change the value in one or more **input cells** (cells that contain data instead of formulas), then observe the effects on dependent cells. A **dependent cell** usually contains a formula whose resulting value changes depending on the values in the input cells. For more robust data analysis, you can use Power Pivot, an Excel add-in, to create a Pivot Table from multiple tables to obtain answers to what-if questions.

## Details

**When performing what-if analysis, use the following guidelines:**

- **Understand and state the purpose of the worksheet model**
  Identify what you want to accomplish with the model. What problem are you trying to solve? What questions do you want the model to answer for you? Elena's worksheet model is designed to total Bayside revenue projections for the four divisions during the first quarter and to calculate each division's percentage of the total quarterly revenue. It also calculates total revenues and percentages for each month within the first quarter.
- **Determine the data input value(s) that, if changed, affect(s) dependent cell results**
  In what-if analysis, changes in the data input cells produce varying results in the output cells. You will use the model to work with the data input values for the Support divisions, in the range B7:D7.
- **Identify the dependent cell(s) that will contain results**
  The dependent cells usually contain formulas, and the formula results adjust as you enter different values in the input cells. The results of the dependent cells formulas appear in the range B8:E8 (the monthly totals and the quarterly total) and E7 (the Support division Quarter 1 total). The cells in the ranges B9:D9 and F4:F7 (the percentages of quarterly revenue) are also dependent cells.
- **Formulate questions you want what-if analysis to answer**
  You must know the questions you want your model to answer before performing a what-if analysis. In the Bayside model, one of the questions you want to answer is: What support revenue target is required to bring the overall support revenue percentage to between 15% and 20%?
- **Determine when to use advanced what-if analysis tools**
  If the answers to your what-if questions require data from multiple tables, you can use Power Pivot. Unlike regular PivotTables that analyze data from a single table, Power Pivot enables you to create PivotTables using fields from multiple tables. You can also perform calculations in Power Pivot. **Figure 12-2** displays a PivotTable created with fields from two tables.

**Figure 12-1:** Worksheet model for a what-if analysis

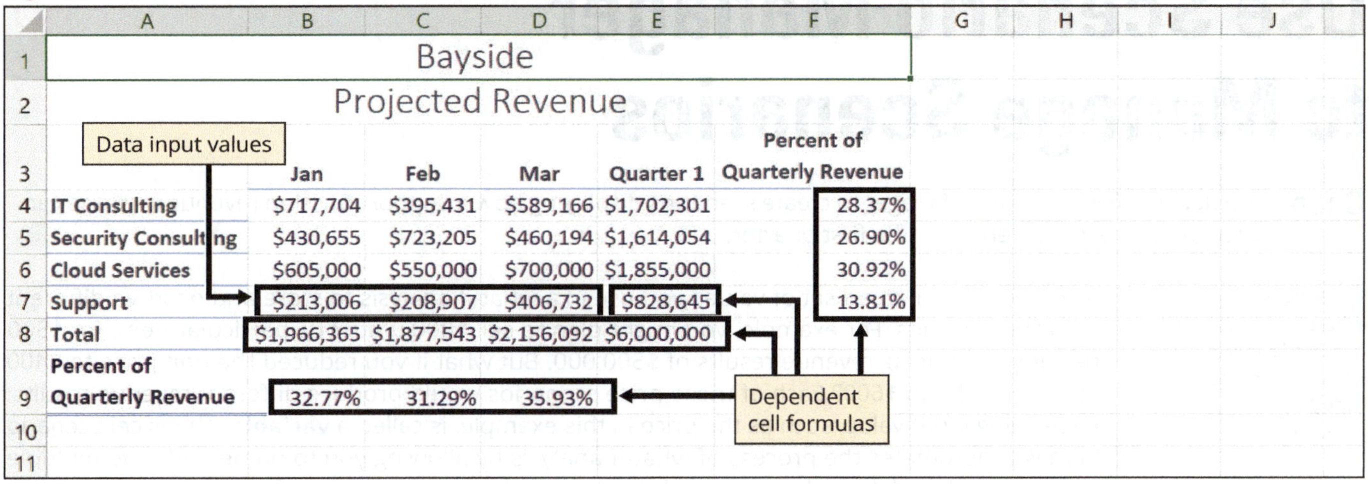

| | A | B | C | D | E | F |
|---|---|---|---|---|---|---|
| 1 | Bayside | | | | | |
| 2 | Projected Revenue | | | | | |
| 3 | | Jan | Feb | Mar | Quarter 1 | Percent of Quarterly Revenue |
| 4 | IT Consulting | $717,704 | $395,431 | $589,166 | $1,702,301 | 28.37% |
| 5 | Security Consulting | $430,655 | $723,205 | $460,194 | $1,614,054 | 26.90% |
| 6 | Cloud Services | $605,000 | $550,000 | $700,000 | $1,855,000 | 30.92% |
| 7 | Support | $213,006 | $208,907 | $406,732 | $828,645 | 13.81% |
| 8 | Total | $1,966,365 | $1,877,543 | $2,156,092 | $6,000,000 | |
| 9 | Percent of Quarterly Revenue | 32.77% | 31.29% | 35.93% | | |



**Figure 12-2:** PivotTable created using fields from two tables

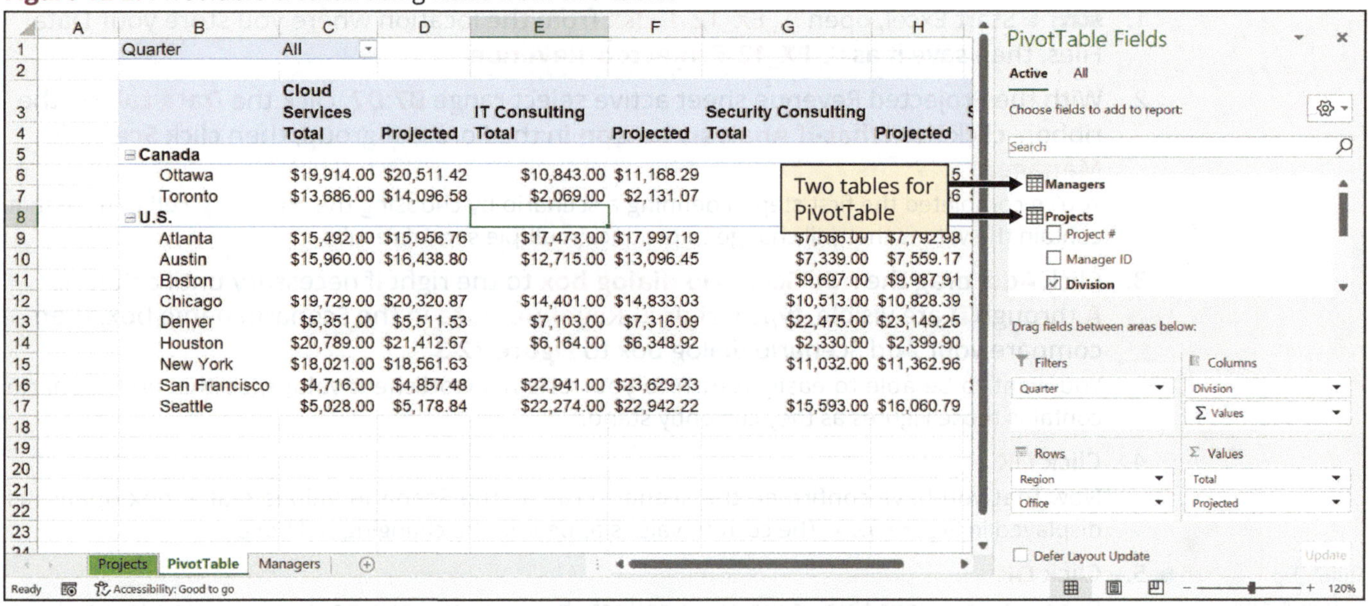

| Quarter | All | | | | | |
|---|---|---|---|---|---|---|
| | Cloud Services Total | Projected | IT Consulting Total | Projected | Security Consulting Total | Projected |
| Canada | | | | | | |
| Ottawa | $19,914.00 | $20,511.42 | $10,843.00 | $11,168.29 | | |
| Toronto | $13,686.00 | $14,096.58 | $2,069.00 | $2,131.07 | | |
| U.S. | | | | | | |
| Atlanta | $15,492.00 | $15,956.76 | $17,473.00 | $17,997.19 | $7,566.00 | $7,792.98 |
| Austin | $15,960.00 | $16,438.80 | $12,715.00 | $13,096.45 | $7,339.00 | $7,559.17 |
| Boston | | | | | $9,697.00 | $9,987.91 |
| Chicago | $19,729.00 | $20,320.87 | $14,401.00 | $14,833.03 | $10,513.00 | $10,828.39 |
| Denver | $5,351.00 | $5,511.53 | $7,103.00 | $7,316.09 | $22,475.00 | $23,149.25 |
| Houston | $20,789.00 | $21,412.67 | $6,164.00 | $6,348.92 | $2,330.00 | $2,399.90 |
| New York | $18,021.00 | $18,561.63 | | | $11,032.00 | $11,362.96 |
| San Francisco | $4,716.00 | $4,857.48 | $22,941.00 | $23,629.23 | | |
| Seattle | $5,028.00 | $5,178.84 | $22,274.00 | $22,942.22 | $15,593.00 | $16,060.79 |

# Use Scenario Manager to Manage Scenarios

**Case** You decide to use Scenario Manager to create scenarios displaying how a Support Division revenue increase can affect total Bayside revenue for the first quarter.

**Objectives**
- Create scenarios to analyze Excel data
- Analyze scenarios using Scenario Manager

A **scenario** is a named set of values you use in a what-if analysis to store and observe different worksheet results. For example, you might plan to sell 1000 units of a particular item, for $500 per unit, producing revenue results of $500,000. But what if you reduced the unit price to $400 or increased it to $600? Each of these price scenarios would produce different revenue results. A changing input value, such as the price in this example, is called a **variable**. The Excel Scenario Manager automates the process of what-if analysis by allowing you to name and save multiple scenarios with variable values in a worksheet.

## Steps

1. **sam Start Excel, open IL_EX_12-1.xlsx from the location where you store your Data Files, then save it as IL_EX_12_Projected_Revenue**
2. **With the Projected Revenue sheet active select range B7:D7, click the Data tab on the ribbon, click the What-If Analysis button in the Forecast group, then click Scenario Manager**
   You've completed the first step in defining a scenario by choosing the **changing cells**, those that contain the values that will change to produce multiple sets of results.
3. **Click Add, drag the Add Scenario dialog box to the right if necessary until columns A through D are visible, type Original Revenue Data in the Scenario name box, then compare your Add Scenario dialog box to Figure 12-3**
   You want to be able to easily return to your original worksheet values, so this first scenario contains those Figures as they currently stand.
4. **Click OK**
   Now that you have confirmed the scenario range, the Scenario Values dialog box opens, as displayed in **Figure 12-4**. The current values appear in the changing cell boxes.

**Quick Tip**
You can delete a scenario by clicking it in the Scenario Manager dialog box, then clicking Delete.

5. **Click OK**
   Because you want this scenario to reflect the current worksheet values, you leave these unchanged.
6. **Click Add, in the Scenario name box type Increase Jan, Feb, Mar by 100000, verify that the Changing cells box reads B7:D7, click OK, in the Scenario Values dialog box, change the value in the $B$7 box to 313006, change the value in the $C$7 box to 308907, change the value in the $D$7 box to 379012, then click Add**
   The second scenario displays the effects of increasing revenue by $100,000 in January, February, and March, and you're ready to add a third scenario.
7. **In the Scenario name box type Increase Jan, Feb, Mar by 200000, click OK, in the Scenario Values dialog box, change the value in the $B$7 box to 413006, change the value in the $C$7 box to 408907, change the value in the $D$7 box to 479012, then click OK**
   The Scenario Manager dialog box lists the three scenarios, as displayed in **Figure 12-5**.

**Quick Tip**
To edit a scenario, select it in the Scenario Manager dialog box, click the Edit button, then edit the Scenario.

8. **Click the Increase Jan, Feb, Mar by 100000 scenario, click Show, notice that the percent of support revenue in cell F7 changes to 17.56%, click the Increase Jan, Feb, Mar by 200000 scenario, click Show, notice that the support revenue percent is now 21.68%, click Original Revenue Data, click Show, then click Close**
9. **Save the workbook**

**Figure 12-3:** Add Scenario dialog box

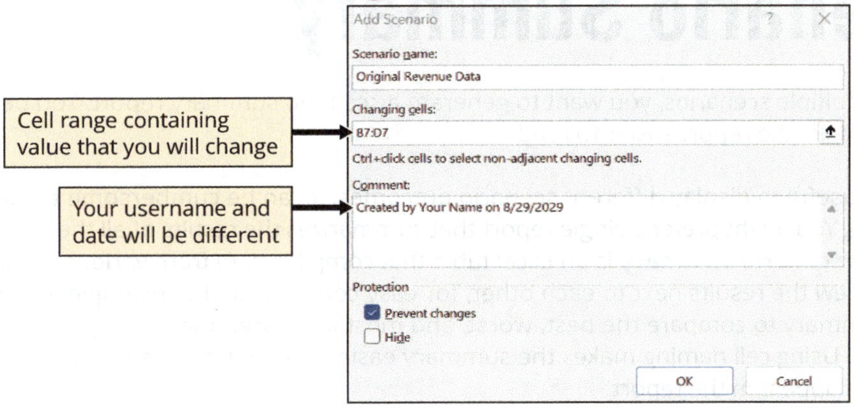


**Figure 12-4:** Scenario Values dialog box

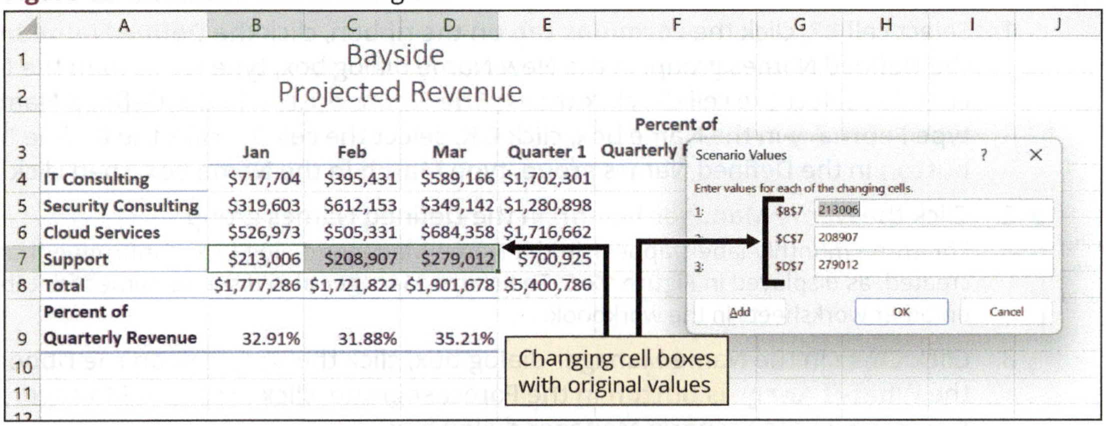


**Figure 12-5:** Scenario Manager dialog box with three scenarios listed

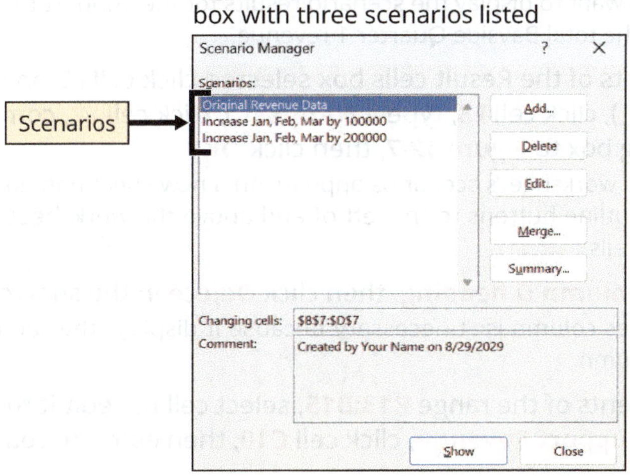


## Merging scenarios

Excel stores scenarios on the worksheet of the workbook in which you created them. To apply scenarios from another worksheet or workbook to the current worksheet, click the Merge button in the Scenario Manager dialog box. The Merge Scenarios dialog box opens, letting you select scenarios from other locations. When you click a sheet name in the sheet list, a message under the sheet list tells you how many scenarios exist on that sheet. To merge scenarios from another workbook, such as those sent to you in a workbook from a coworker, open the other workbook file, click the Book list arrow in the Merge Scenarios dialog box, then click the workbook name and worksheet with the scenarios. When you merge workbook scenarios, it's best if the workbooks have the same structure, so that there is no confusion of cell values.

# Create a Scenario Summary

**Case** Now that you have defined multiple scenarios, you want to generate a scenario summary report. You begin by creating cell names that will make the report easier to read.

**Objectives**
- Display scenarios in a scenario summary report
- Format a scenario summary report

Although it is useful to display different scenario outcomes, it can be cumbersome to view each one separately. You might prefer a single report that summarizes the results of all the scenarios in a worksheet. A **scenario summary** is an Excel table that compiles data from various scenarios so that you can view the results next to each other, for easy comparison. For example, you can use a scenario summary to compare the best, worst, and most likely scenarios for a particular set of circumstances. Using cell naming makes the summary easier to read because the names, not the cell references, appear in the report.

## Steps

1. **Select cell B7, click the Formulas tab on the ribbon, click the Define Name button in the Defined Names group, in the New Name dialog box, type January in the Name box, click OK, select the cell C7, click the Define Name button in the Defined Names group, type February in the Name box, click OK, select the cell D7, click the Define Name button in the Defined Names group, type March in the Name box, then click OK**

2. **Click the Name Manager button in the Defined Names group**
   The three monthly labels appear in the Name Manager dialog box, confirming that they were created, as displayed in **Figure 12-6**. The Name Manager also displays names for tables created on other worksheets in the workbook.

   **Quick Tip** You can also click the Name box list arrow on the formula bar to view cell names.

3. **Click Close in the Name Manager dialog box, click the Data tab on the ribbon, click the What-If Analysis button in the Forecast group, click Scenario Manager, then click Summary in the Scenario Manager dialog box**
   Excel needs to know the location of the cells that contain the formula results you want to display in the report. You want to display the scenario results for the Support total and the percentage of revenue and for the total Bayside Quarter 1 revenue.

4. **With the contents of the Result cells box selected click cell E7 on the worksheet, type a comma (,), click cell E8, type a comma (,), click cell F7, compare your Scenario Summary dialog box to Figure 12-7, then click OK**
   A summary of the worksheet's scenarios appears on a new sheet named Scenario Summary. The report displays outline buttons to the left of and above the worksheet so that you can hide or display report details.

   **Quick Tip** To analyze the results of scenarios, you can create a scenario PivotTable report by selecting the Scenario PivotTable report option in the Report type section of the Scenario Summary dialog box.

5. **Right-click the column D heading, then click Delete in the shortcut menu**
   The Current Values column isn't necessary because it displays the same values as the Original Revenue Data column.

6. **Delete the contents of the range B13:B15, select cell B2, edit it to read Scenario Summary for Support Revenue, click cell C10, then edit it to read Support Total Revenue**

7. **Click cell C11, edit it to read Total Bayside Revenue, click cell C12, then edit it to read Percent Support Revenue**

   **Quick Tip** The scenario summary is not linked to the worksheet. If you change the values in the worksheet, you must generate a new scenario summary.

8. **Widen column C to fully display the names of the Result Cells, right-click the column A heading, click Delete in the shortcut menu, right-click the row 1 heading, click Delete in the shortcut menu, change the page orientation to landscape, then save the workbook**
   The scenario summary is now easier to read and understand, as displayed in **Figure 12-8**.

**Figure 12-6:** Name Manager dialog box displaying names

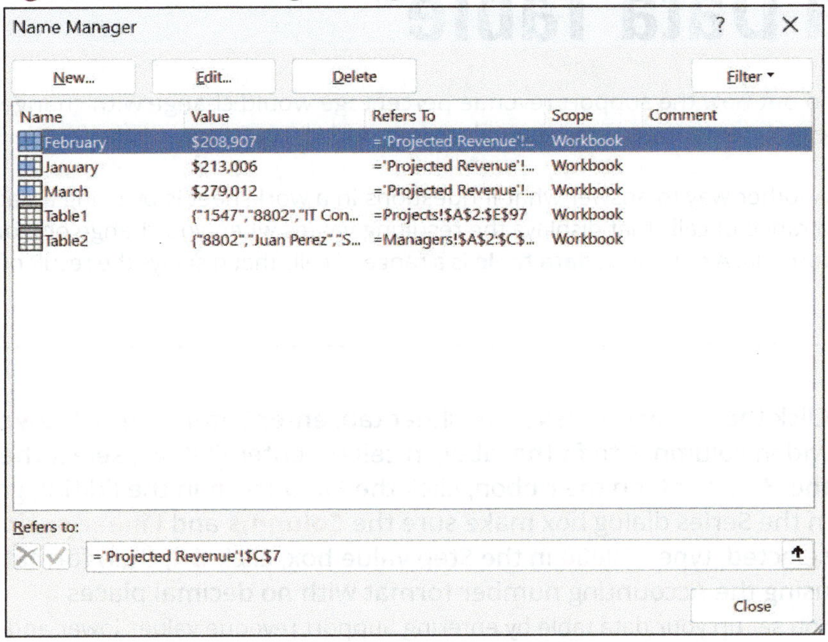


**Figure 12-7:** Scenario Summary dialog box

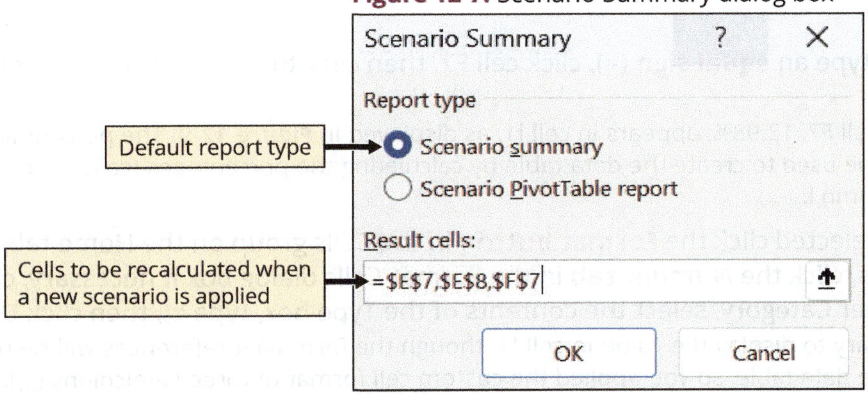


**Figure 12-8:** Completed Scenario Summary report

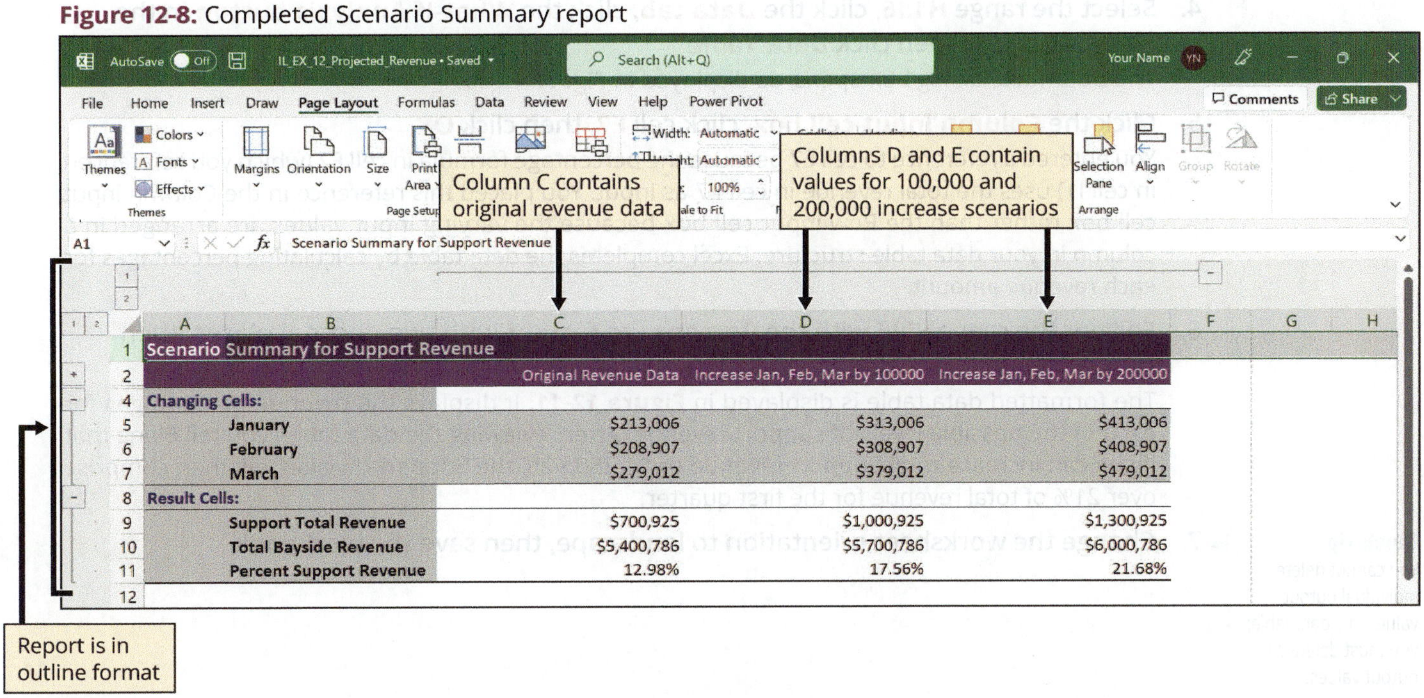

# Create a Data Table

**Case** You want to find out how the support revenue percentage would change with changes to the Support total revenue. You begin by entering a set of possible values, in $150,000 increments, for the Support total.

**Objectives**
- Create a data table structure
- Analyze options using a data table

Another way to answer what-if questions in a worksheet is by using a data table. A **data table** is a range of cells that displays the resulting values when you change one or more input values in a formula. A **one-input data table** is a range of cells that displays the result of varying one input value.

## Steps

1. **Click the Projected Revenue sheet tab, enter Total Support Revenue in cell H1, widen column H to fit the label, in cell H2 enter 650925, select the range H2:H6, click the Home tab on the ribbon, click the Fill button in the Editing group, click Series, in the Series dialog box make sure the Columns and Linear option buttons are selected, type 150000 in the Step value box, click OK, then format the selected range using the Accounting number format with no decimal places**

   You set up your data table by entering Support revenue values lower and higher than the current projection in cell E7. Because the revenue values varied by a constant number, you used a linear series to quickly fill in the amounts. These possible revenue values constitute the **input values** in the data table.

2. **Click cell I1, type an equal sign (=), click cell F7, then click the Enter button ✓ on the formula bar**

   The value in cell F7, 12.98%, appears in cell I1, as displayed in **Figure 12-9**. The percent formula in cell F7 will be used to create the data table by calculating the percentages (called the **output values**) in column I.

**Quick Tip**
You can create your own custom format by clicking a format that resembles the one you want, then customizing it in the Type box.

3. **With cell I1 selected click the Format button in the Cells group on the Home tab, click Format Cells, click the Number tab in the Format Cells dialog box if necessary, click Custom under Category, select the contents of the Type box, type ;;;, then click OK**

   It isn't necessary to display the value in cell I1, though the formula it references will be used in generating the data table, so you applied the custom cell format of three semicolons (;;;), which hides the contents.

4. **Select the range H1:I6, click the Data tab, click the What-If Analysis button in the Forecast group, then click Data Table**

   The Data Table dialog box opens, as displayed in **Figure 12-10**.

5. **Click the Column input cell box, click cell E7, then click OK**

   You entered a reference to cell E7 because the percentage formula in cell F7 (which you referenced in cell I1) uses the total revenue in cell E7 as input. You placed this reference in the Column input cell box rather than the Row input cell box because the varying input values are arranged in a column in your data table structure. Excel completes the data table by calculating percentages for each revenue amount.

6. **Format the range I2:I6 with the Percentage format with two decimal places, then click cell A1**

   The formatted data table is displayed in **Figure 12-11**. It displays the revenue percentages for each of the possible levels of support revenue. After reviewing the data table, you tell Elena that if she can increase total Support revenue to $1,250,925, the Support division will then comprise over 21% of total revenue for the first quarter.

**Quick Tip**
You cannot delete individual output values in a data table; you must delete all output values.

7. **Change the worksheet orientation to landscape, then save the workbook**

Figure 12-9: One-input data table structure

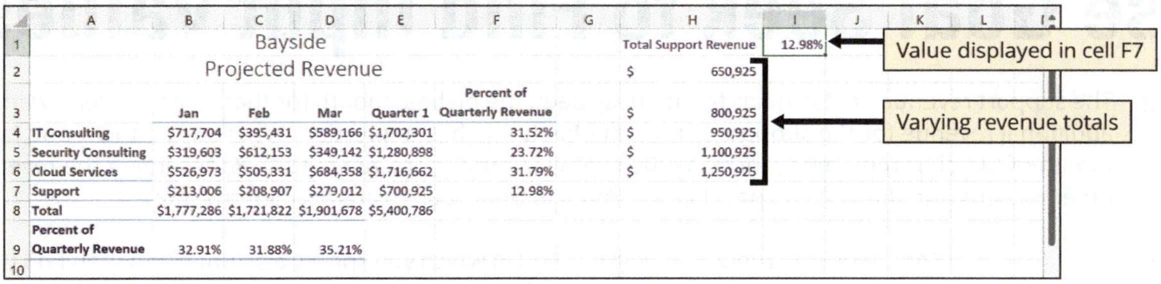


Figure 12-10: Data Table dialog box

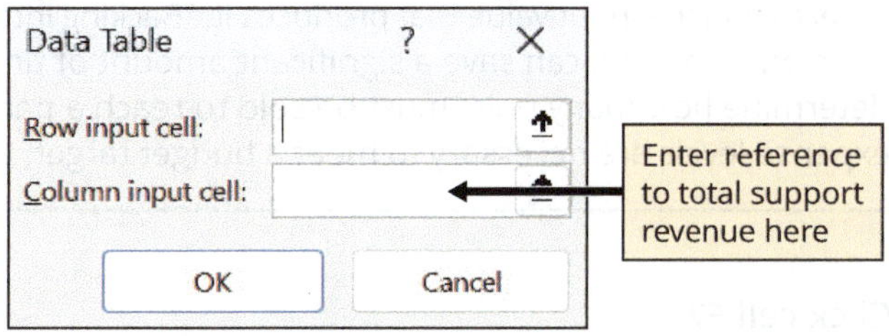


Figure 12-11: Completed data table with resulting values

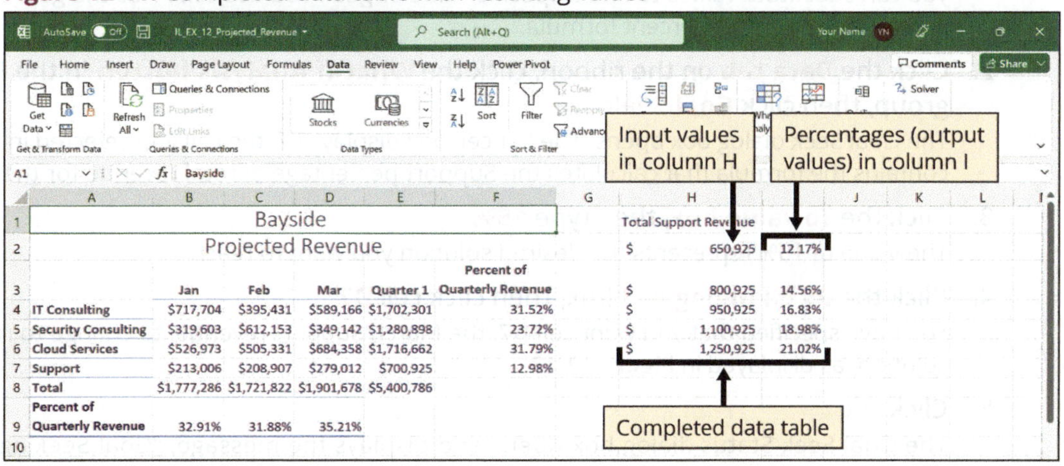


## Creating a two-input data table

A **two-input data table** is a table in which you can vary the results in two cells and display the recalculated results. You could, for example, use a two-input data table to calculate your monthly car payment based on both varying interest rates and varying loan terms, as displayed in **Figure 12-12**. In a two-input data table, different values of one input cell appear across the top row of the table (in this case, different terms), while different values of a second input cell (in this case, different interest rates) are listed down the left column. You create a two-input data table the same way that you create a one-input data table, except you enter both a row and a column input cell. In the example, the two-input data table structure was created by first entering the number of payments in the range B6:D6 and the rates in the range A7:A15. Next, the data table values were created by selecting the range A6:D15, clicking the Data tab, clicking the What-If Analysis button in the Forecast group, then clicking Data Table. In the Data Table dialog box, the row input value is the term in cell B3. The column input value is the interest rate in cell B2. You can check the accuracy of these values by cross-referencing the values in the data table with those in the range B1:B4, where an interest rate of 6.5% for 60 months has a monthly payment of $424.59.

Figure 12-12: Two-input data table

| | A | B | C | D | E |
|---|---|---|---|---|---|
| 1 | Loan Amount | $21,700.00 | | | |
| 2 | Annual Interest Rate | 6.50% | | | |
| 3 | Term in Months | 60 | | | |
| 4 | Monthly Payment: | $424.59 | | | |
| 5 | | | | | |
| 6 | | 36 | 48 | 60 | |
| 7 | 6.00% | $660.16 | $509.63 | $419.52 | |
| 8 | 6.25% | $662.62 | $512.12 | $422.05 | |
| 9 | 6.50% | $665.08 | $514.61 | $424.59 | |
| 10 | 6.75% | $667.56 | $517.12 | $427.13 | |
| 11 | 7.00% | $670.03 | $519.63 | $429.69 | |
| 12 | 7.25% | $672.52 | $522.15 | $432.25 | |
| 13 | 7.50% | $675.00 | $524.68 | $434.82 | |
| 14 | 7.75% | $677.50 | $527.22 | $437.41 | |
| 15 | 8.00% | $680.00 | $529.76 | $440.00 | |
| 16 | | | | | |

# Use Goal Seek to Find Input Values

**Case** The support revenue in March has traditionally been the highest month for that division. Elena wants to project additional revenue for the support division in March and has a question: What support revenue target for the month of March is required to increase the overall support percentage to 15%, assuming the revenues for the other months and divisions do not change? You use Goal Seek to answer her question.

**Objectives**
- Determine input values for a desired result using Goal Seek
- Use Goal Seek to answer questions about data

**Goal seek** is a problem-solving method in which you specify a solution and then find the input value that produces the answer you want. You can think of goal seeking as what-if analysis in reverse. Instead of trying many sets of values to achieve a certain solution, you specify a solution and ask Excel to find the input value that produces it. "Backing into" a solution in this way, sometimes referred to as **backsolving**, can save a significant amount of time. For example, you can use Goal Seek to determine how many units must be sold to reach a particular revenue goal or to determine what expense levels are necessary to meet a budget target.

## Steps

1. **Click cell F7**
   The first step in using Goal Seek is to select a goal cell. A **goal cell** contains a formula in which you can substitute values to find a specific value or goal. You use cell F7 as the goal cell because it contains the Support percent formula.
2. **Click the Data tab on the ribbon, click the What-If Analysis button in the Forecast group, then click Goal Seek**
   The Goal Seek dialog box opens. The Set cell box displays F7, the cell you selected in Step 1, which contains the formula that calculates the Support percentage of total revenue for the quarter.
3. **Click the To value box, then type 15%**
   The value of 15% represents the desired solution you want to reach.
4. **Click the By changing cell box, then click cell D7**
   You have specified that you want cell D7, the March Support revenue, to change to reach the 15% solution, as displayed in **Figure 12-13**.
5. **Click OK**
   The Goal Seek Status dialog box opens and displays the message, "Goal Seeking with Cell F7 found a solution." Cell D7 now displays the amount of $406,732, the revenue necessary to achieve a support percentage of 14.99% (which when rounded up becomes 15%).
6. **Click OK**
   The goal seek solution is displayed in **Figure 12-14**. Changing the revenue amount in cell D7 changes the other dependent values in the worksheet E7, D8, D9, E8, F4:F7.
7. **Click cell A1, then save the workbook**

**Quick Tip**
Before you select another command, you can return the worksheet to its status before the Goal Seek by pressing CTRL+Z.

**Figure 12-13:** Completed Goal Seek dialog box

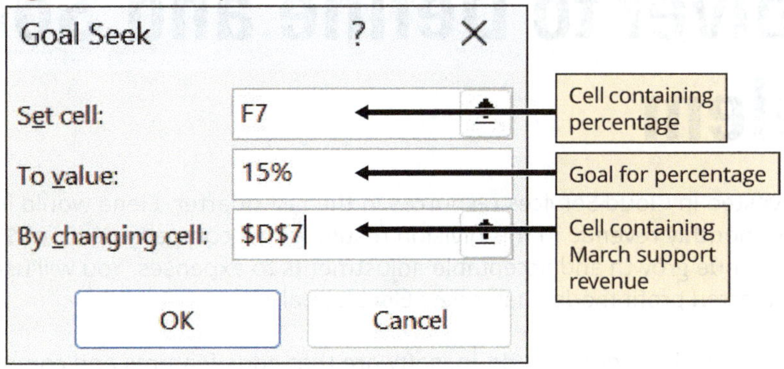


**Figure 12-14:** Worksheet with goal seek solution

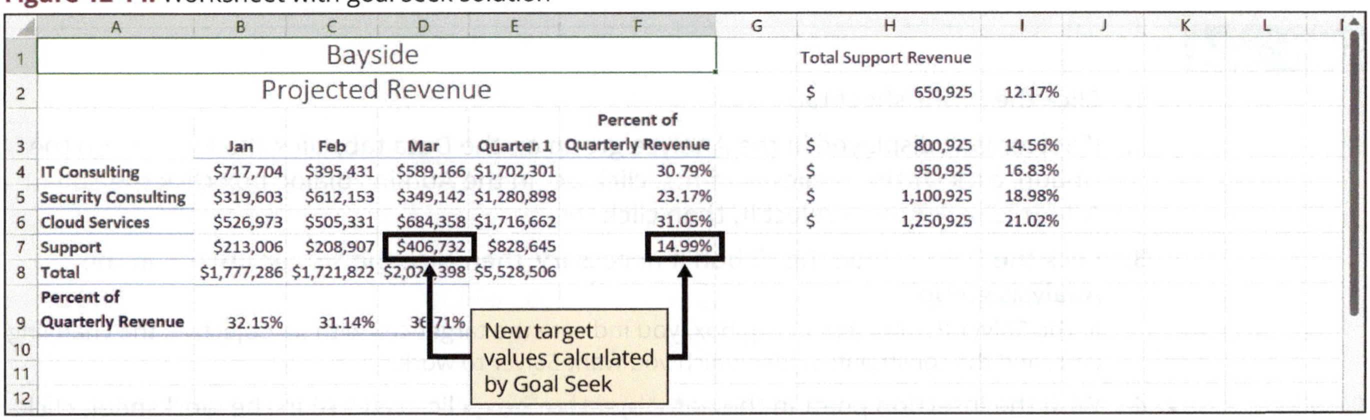


### Predicting data trends with Forecast Sheet

Forecast Sheet is a tool you can use when you have historical time-based data to project future data based on past trends. You can forecast the future of your data related to a timeline by selecting the data, clicking the Data tab, then clicking the Forecast Sheet button in the Forecast group. The Create Forecast Worksheet dialog box opens, where you enter your Forecast End date, then click Create. The new chart displays your values along with the forecasted values and related confidence levels. A data table is also added to the worksheet, displaying the new projected data for the chart.

# Use Solver to Define and Solve a Problem

**Case** Bayside invested in Cloud Services resources in the last quarter. Elena would like a return on this investment with higher monthly revenue in this division resulting in a company profit of $2,500,000. She advised you on expected revenue growth and acceptable adjustments to expenses. You will use these values in Solver to find the best-projected profit model that meets Elena's goal.

**Objectives**
- Add worksheet constraints in Solver
- Use Solver to find the best solution to a problem

Excel Solver is an **add-in**, software that adds features and commands to Excel or another Office app. It must be installed before you can use it. Solver finds the best solution to a problem that has several inputs. The cell containing the formula is called the **target cell**, or **objective**. Solver is helpful when you need to perform a complex what-if analysis involving multiple input values or when the input values must conform to specific limitations, called **constraints**.

## Steps

1. **Click the Profit sheet tab**
2. **If Solver isn't displayed in the Analyze group on the Data tab, click the File tab on the ribbon, click Options, click Add-ins, click Go, in the Add-ins dialog box click the Solver Add-in check box to select it, then click OK**
3. **Click the Data tab on the ribbon if necessary, then click the Solver button in the Analysis group**

   In the Solver Parameters dialog box, you indicate the target cell with its objective, the changing cells, and the constraints under which you want Solver to work.

4. **With the insertion point in the Set Objective box, click cell E16 in the worksheet, click the Value Of option button if necessary, double-click the Value Of box, then type 2,500,000**

   You have specified an objective of $2,500,000 for the total profit.

5. **Click the By Changing Variable Cells box, select the range B7:D7, press and hold CTRL, then select cell B13**

   You have told Excel which cells to vary to reach the goal of a $2,500,000 total profit.

6. **Click Add, with the insertion point in the Cell Reference box in the Add Constraint dialog box, select cell B7 in the worksheet, verify that <= is selected, click in the Constraint box, then type 728000**

   You added the constraint that the January Cloud Services revenue be less than or equal to $728,000. This reflects growth in that revenue value within realistic values.

7. **Click Add, with the insertion point in the Cell Reference box, select cell C7 in the worksheet, verify that <= is selected, click in the Constraint box, type 727000, click Add, with the insertion point in the Cell Reference box, select the cell D7 in the worksheet, verify that <= is selected, click in the Constraint box, type 757000, click Add, with the insertion point in the Cell Reference box, select the cell B13 in the worksheet, click the <= list arrow, click >=, type 4000, click OK, then compare your Solver Parameters dialog box with Figure 12-15**

   These constraints keep the revenue growth and expense reduction within realistic values.

8. **Click Solve**

   Solver found a solution as indicated in the Solver Results dialog box.

9. **With the Keep Solver Solution option selected, click OK, compare your results to Figure 12-16, change the worksheet orientation to landscape, then save your work**

**Quick Tip**
If your Solver Parameters dialog box has entries in the By Changing Variable Cells box or in the Subject to the Constraints box, click Reset All, click OK, then continue with Step 3.

**Quick Tip**
If your solution needs to be an integer, you can select it in the Add Constraint dialog box.

**Figure 12-15:** Solver Parameters dialog box

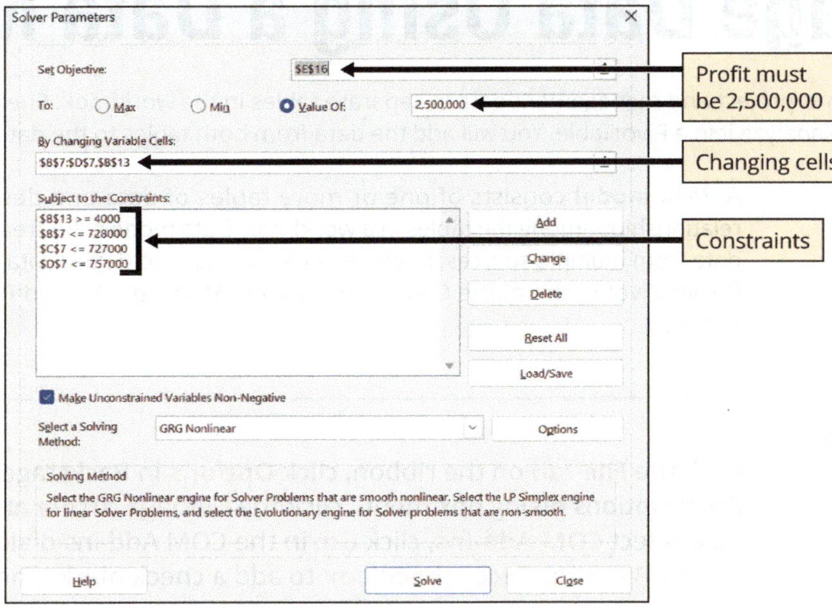


**Figure 12-16:** Solver Solution

| | A | B | C | D | E | F |
|---|---|---|---|---|---|---|
| 1 | Bayside | | | | | |
| 2 | Projected Profit | | | | | |
| 3 | | Jan | Feb | Mar | Quarter 1 | |
| 4 | Revenue | | | | | |
| 5 | IT Consulting | $717,704 | $395,431 | $589,166 | $1,702,301 | |
| 6 | Security Consulting | $319,603 | $612,153 | $349,142 | $1,280,898 | |
| 7 | Cloud Services | $696,773 | $675,131 | $757,000 | $2,128,904 | |
| 8 | Support | $213,006 | $208,907 | $279,012 | $700,925 | |
| 9 | Total Revenue | $1,947,086 | $1,891,622 | $1,974,320 | $5,813,028 | |
| 10 | | | | | | |
| 11 | Expenses | | | | | |
| 12 | Salaries | $1,050,000 | $1,250,000 | $1,000,700 | $3,300,700 | |
| 13 | Office Expenses | $ 4,000 | $ 4,687 | $ 3,641 | $ 12,328 | |
| 14 | Total Expenses | $1,054,000 | $1,254,687 | $1,004,341 | $3,313,028 | |
| 15 | | | | | | |
| 16 | Profit | $893,086 | $636,935 | $969,979 | $2,500,000 | |
| 17 | | | | | | |

## Analyzing data using the Analysis ToolPak

The Analysis ToolPak is an Excel add-in that contains many statistical analysis tools. You can use one of these tools by clicking the Data tab, clicking the Data Analysis button in the Analysis group, selecting the desired analysis tool in the Data Analysis dialog box, clicking OK, entering the input range and other relevant specifications in the data tool's dialog box, then clicking OK. For example, clicking the Descriptive Statistics tool in the Data Analysis dialog box, then selecting Summary statistics generates a statistical report including mean, median, mode, minimum, maximum, and sum for an input range you specify on your worksheet.

## Creating an Answer Report

After Solver finds a solution, you can generate an Answer Report summarizing the target cell information, adjustable cells, and constraints by selecting Answer from three types of reports in the Solver Results window, then clicking OK. The report appears as a separate worksheet named Answer Report 1 with three sections. The top section has the target cell information; it compares the original value of the target cell with the final value. The middle section of the report contains information about the adjustable cells. It lists the original and final values for all cells that were changed to reach the target value. The last report section has information about the constraints. Each constraint you added to Solver is listed in the Formula column, along with the cell address and a description of the cell data. The Cell Value column contains the Solver solution values for the cells. The Status column contains information on whether the constraints were binding or not binding in reaching the solution. Binding constraints indicate all the allocated resource was used or the constraint was pushed to its limit. Non-binding constraints indicate there was an extra resource available after the constraint was met.

# Manage Data Using a Data Model

**Case** Elena has project and management data in separate tables in the workbook. She asks you to bring together the data to analyze it in a PivotTable. You will add the data from both tables to the data model to begin your analysis.

**Objectives**
- Add tables to a data model
- Create relationships between tables
- Update Excel tables in Power Pivot

A **data model** consists of one or more tables of data and describes the data structure and relationships among the tables in a workbook. Data models are created in Power Pivot by combining data from multiple sources. Power Pivot also is used to define data relationships in the data model. Power Pivot is one of the Component Object Model (COM) add-ins that extend the functionality of Excel.

## Steps

**Trouble**
If a Power Pivot tab isn't displayed on your ribbon, right-click a blank area of the ribbon, click Customize the Ribbon on the shortcut menu, click the Power Pivot check box under Main Tabs to select it, then click OK.

1. Click the **File tab** on the ribbon, click **Options** in Backstage view, click **Add-ins** in the Excel Options dialog box menu, click the **Manage arrow** at the bottom of the dialog box, select **COM Add-ins**, click **Go**, in the COM Add-ins dialog box click the **Microsoft Power Pivot for Excel check box** to add a check mark if necessary, then click **OK**

2. Click the **Projects sheet**, click the **Power Pivot tab** on the ribbon, then click the **Add to Data Model button** in the Tables group

   The Power Pivot window opens and the top pane displays data in a table, and the bottom pane displays the calculation area, as displayed in **Figure 12-17**. The Calculation Area button in the View group displays and removes the Calculation area.

3. Click the **Switch to Workbook button** on the Quick Access Toolbar of the Power Pivot window, click the **Managers sheet tab**, on the **Power Pivot tab** click the **Add to Data Model button** in the Tables group, double-click the **Table1 sheet tab** in Power Pivot, type **Projects**, press **ENTER**, double-click the **Table 2 sheet tab**, type **Managers**, then press **ENTER**

   The two tables are now part of the data model.

**Trouble**
You may need to move your mouse over the column header that reads Manager to display the full field name of Manager #.

4. Click the **Design tab** on the ribbon in the Power Pivot window, then click the **Create Relationship button** in the Relationships group, in the Create Relationship dialog box click the **first list arrow** and click **Managers** if necessary, select the **Manager # field** if it is not already highlighted, click the **second list arrow** and click **Projects**, click the **Manager ID field** in the table below Project to highlight it, then click **OK**

   Creating a relationship between tables allows you to access corresponding data from both tables.

5. Click the **Home tab**, then click the **Diagram View button** in the View group

   The two tables and their relationship are displayed, as illustrated in **Figure 12-18**. This is a one-to-many relationship because each Manager # value can be associated with multiple Manager ID rows in the Projects table.

**Quick Tip**
You can open the Power Pivot window from the workbook by clicking the Data tab, then clicking the Go to the Power Pivot Window button in the Data Tools group.

6. Click the **Switch to Workbook button** on the Quick Access Toolbar, click the **Managers sheet tab** if necessary, click cell **B2**, edit the name Juan Perez to **Gabriela Sanchez**, click the **Manage button** in the Data Model group, click the **Data View button** in the View group, then click the **Refresh button**

   The Data Refresh dialog box indicates that the data was successfully updated.

7. Click **Close** in the Data Refresh dialog box, verify that the name Gabriela Sanchez appears instead of Juan Perez in row 2, then save your work

**Figure 12-17:** Power Pivot window

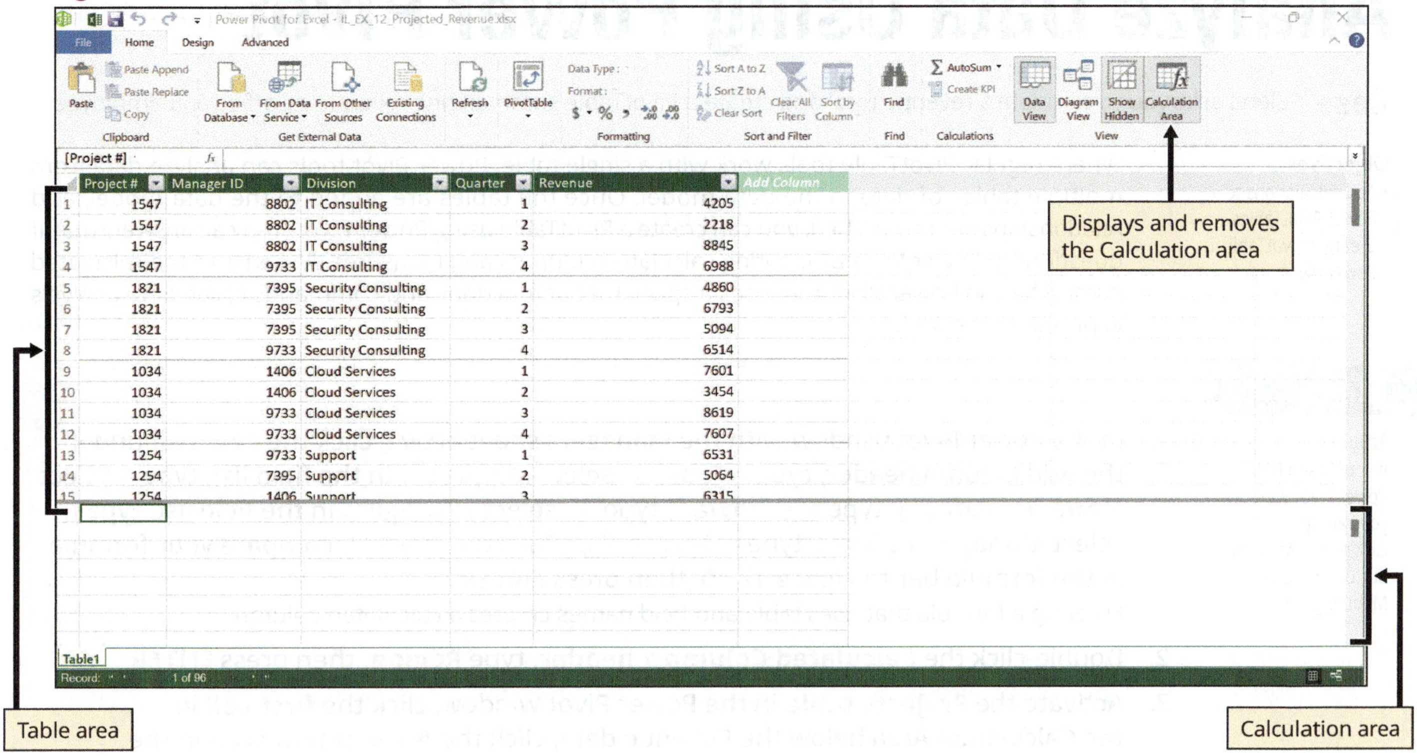


**Figure 12-18:** Diagram of the relationship between tables

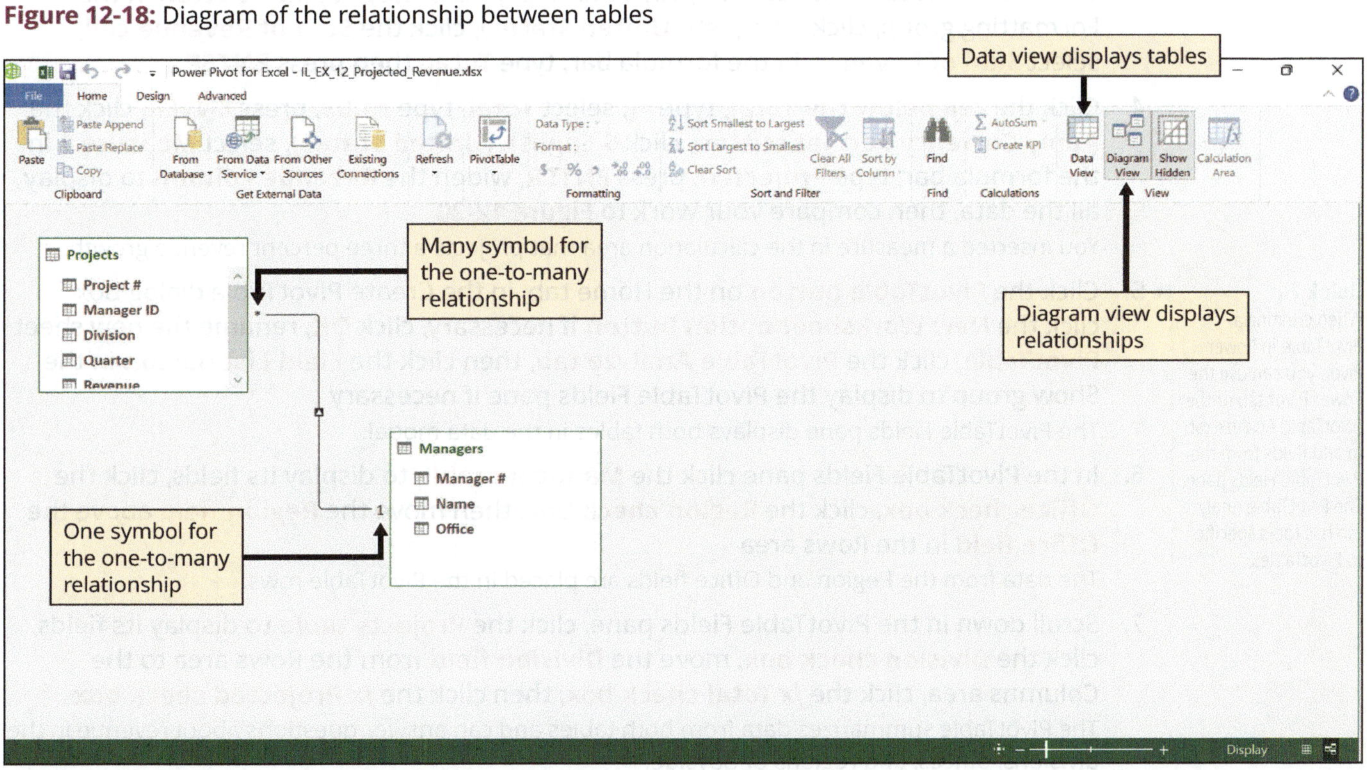

# Analyze Data Using Power Pivot

**Case** Elena asks you to calculate a revenue total and create a PivotTable summarizing revenue by office and employee.

**Objectives**
- Add calculations to Power PivotTables
- Create a PivotTable in Power Pivot

Where regular PivotTable tools work with a single table, Power Pivot tools can analyze data from multiple tables of data in the data model. Once the tables are added to the data model, and relationships are established, you can create a PivotTable using Power Pivot. You can answer what-if questions in Power Pivot by creating calculated columns and measures. A **measure** is a calculated named field in Power Pivot that uses a special set of functions and commands called data analysis expressions, or DAX.

## Steps

**Trouble**
If you closed the Power Pivot window you can open it by clicking the Manage button in the Data Module group.

1. **In the Power Pivot window with the Managers sheet active, click the first cell under the Add Column header, type =IF(OR(M, select Managers in the field list, type [, select Managers[Office], type ="Ottawa",, type M, select Managers in the field list, type [, select Managers[Office], type ="Toronto"), "Canada" ,"U.S."), compare your formula in the formula bar to Figure 12-19, then press ENTER**
   Entering a formula that uses table and field names creates a calculated column.
2. **Double-click the Calculated Column 1 header, type Region, then press ENTER**
3. **Activate the Projects table in the Power Pivot window, click the first cell in the Calculation Area below the Revenue data, click the AutoSum button in the Calculations group, click the Apply Currency Format button $ in the Formatting group, click $ English (United States), click the Revenue column header to select the revenue data in that column, click the Apply Currency Format button in the Formatting group, click $ English (United States), click the Sum of Revenue cell, select Sum of Revenue in the formula bar, type Total, then press ENTER**
4. **Click the cell below the Total, type =[, select Total, type *1.03, press ENTER, click the Apply Currency Format button, click $ English (United States), select Measure 1 in the formula bar, type Projected, press ENTER, widen the Revenue column to display all the data, then compare your work to Figure 12-20**
   You inserted a measure in the calculation area that projects a three percent revenue growth.

**Quick Tip**
When creating a PivotTable in Power Pivot, you can use the Power Pivot tab or the PivotTable Analyze tab to add fields from the PivotTable Fields pane. The PivotTable Analyze tab has tools specific to PivotTables.

5. **Click the PivotTable button on the Home tab, in the Create PivotTable dialog box click the New Worksheet option button if necessary, click OK, rename the new sheet PivotTable, click the PivotTable Analyze tab, then click the Field List button in the Show group to display the PivotTable Fields pane if necessary**
   The PivotTable Fields pane displays both tables in the data model.
6. **In the PivotTable Fields pane click the Managers table to display its fields, click the Office check box, click the Region check box, then move the Region field above the Office field in the Rows area**
   The data from the Region and Office fields are placed in the PivotTable rows.
7. **Scroll down in the PivotTable Fields pane, click the Projects table to display its fields, click the Division check box, move the Division field from the Rows area to the Columns area, click the *fx* Total check box, then click the *fx* Projected check box**
   The PivotTable summarizes data from both tables and can answer questions about revenue in the divisions, offices, and regions of Bayside.
8. **Click the Field Headers button in the Show group to deselect it, click the Design tab, click the Grand Totals button in the Layout group, then click On for Columns Only, then compare your PivotTable to Figure 12-21**
9. **sam Close the PivotTable Fields pane, group the worksheets, add your name to the center section of the footers, ungroup the sheets, save the workbook, close the workbook, close Excel, then submit the workbook to your instructor as directed**

**Figure 12-19:** Calculated column formula

**Figure 12-20:** Calculation Area with measure

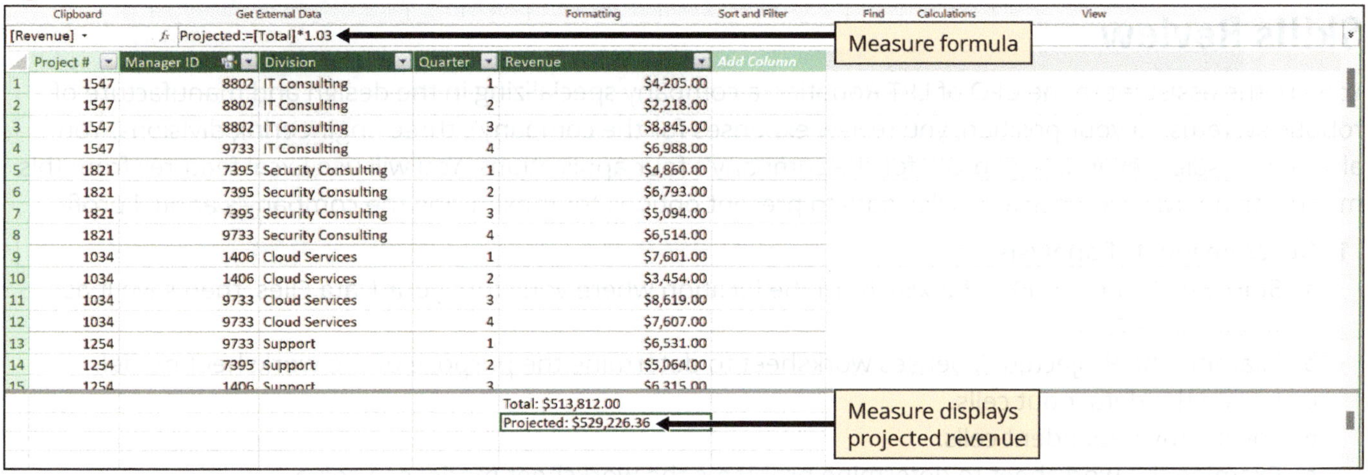


| | Project # | Manager ID | Division | Quarter | Revenue |
|---|---|---|---|---|---|
| 1 | 1547 | 8802 | IT Consulting | 1 | $4,205.00 |
| 2 | 1547 | 8802 | IT Consulting | 2 | $2,218.00 |
| 3 | 1547 | 8802 | IT Consulting | 3 | $8,845.00 |
| 4 | 1547 | 9733 | IT Consulting | 4 | $6,988.00 |
| 5 | 1821 | 7395 | Security Consulting | 1 | $4,860.00 |
| 6 | 1821 | 7395 | Security Consulting | 2 | $6,793.00 |
| 7 | 1821 | 7395 | Security Consulting | 3 | $5,094.00 |
| 8 | 1821 | 9733 | Security Consulting | 4 | $6,514.00 |
| 9 | 1034 | 1406 | Cloud Services | 1 | $7,601.00 |
| 10 | 1034 | 1406 | Cloud Services | 2 | $3,454.00 |
| 11 | 1034 | 9733 | Cloud Services | 3 | $8,619.00 |
| 12 | 1034 | 9733 | Cloud Services | 4 | $7,607.00 |
| 13 | 1254 | 9733 | Support | 1 | $6,531.00 |
| 14 | 1254 | 7395 | Support | 2 | $5,064.00 |
| 15 | 1254 | 1406 | Support | 3 | $6,315.00 |
| | | | | Total: $513,812.00 | |
| | | | | Projected: $529,226.36 | |

**Figure 12-21:** PivotTable created using Power Pivot

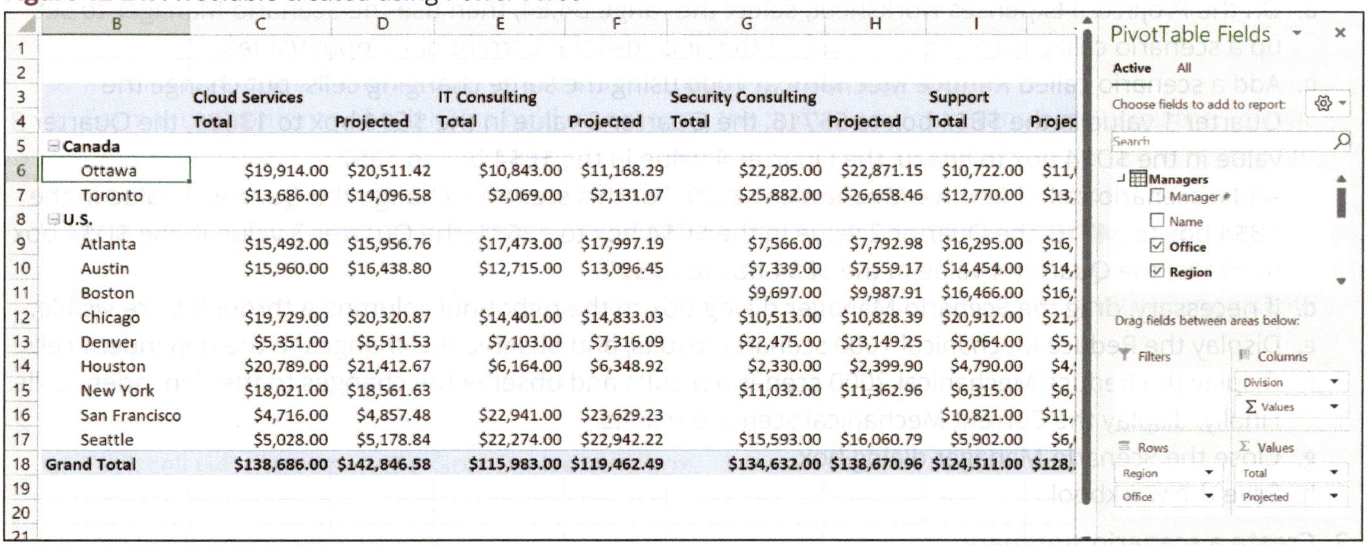


| | B | C | D | E | F | G | H | I | |
|---|---|---|---|---|---|---|---|---|---|
| 3 | | Cloud Services | | IT Consulting | | Security Consulting | | Support | |
| 4 | | Total | Projected | Total | Projected | Total | Projected | Total | Projec |
| 5 | Canada | | | | | | | | |
| 6 | Ottawa | $19,914.00 | $20,511.42 | $10,843.00 | $11,168.29 | $22,205.00 | $22,871.15 | $10,722.00 | $11, |
| 7 | Toronto | $13,686.00 | $14,096.58 | $2,069.00 | $2,131.07 | $25,882.00 | $26,658.46 | $12,770.00 | $13, |
| 8 | U.S. | | | | | | | | |
| 9 | Atlanta | $15,492.00 | $15,956.76 | $17,473.00 | $17,997.19 | $7,566.00 | $7,792.98 | $16,295.00 | $16, |
| 10 | Austin | $15,960.00 | $16,438.80 | $12,715.00 | $13,096.45 | $7,339.00 | $7,559.17 | $14,454.00 | $14, |
| 11 | Boston | | | | | $9,697.00 | $9,987.91 | $16,466.00 | $16, |
| 12 | Chicago | $19,729.00 | $20,320.87 | $14,401.00 | $14,833.03 | $10,513.00 | $10,828.39 | $20,912.00 | $21, |
| 13 | Denver | $5,351.00 | $5,511.53 | $7,103.00 | $7,316.09 | $22,475.00 | $23,149.25 | $5,064.00 | $5, |
| 14 | Houston | $20,789.00 | $21,412.67 | $6,164.00 | $6,348.92 | $2,330.00 | $2,399.90 | $4,790.00 | $4, |
| 15 | New York | $18,021.00 | $18,561.63 | | | $11,032.00 | $11,362.96 | $6,315.00 | $6, |
| 16 | San Francisco | $4,716.00 | $4,857.48 | $22,941.00 | $23,629.23 | | | $10,821.00 | $11, |
| 17 | Seattle | $5,028.00 | $5,178.84 | $22,274.00 | $22,942.22 | $15,593.00 | $16,060.79 | $5,902.00 | $6, |
| 18 | Grand Total | $138,686.00 | $142,846.58 | $115,983.00 | $119,462.49 | $134,632.00 | $138,670.96 | $124,511.00 | $128, |

## Using Excel 3-D Maps

Excel 3D Maps, is a COM add-in that helps to visualize worksheet data in 3-D formats. Data should be organized in a table for mapping and include at least one geographic value. If you want to view data over time you need to include at least one date or time field. To insert a Power Map into a worksheet, click the Insert tab, then click 3D Map in the Tours group. The 3D Maps window opens with its own ribbon containing a Home tab, a Tour pane on the left displaying Tour 1, an automatically created Tour with a single scene, a Field List displaying the fields available to map, and a Layer pane on the right with areas for map locations, height, category, and time. A tour is a list of maps in the 3D Map and each map is a scene. Most often 3D Maps contain several scenes that make up an animation offering different points of focus of the data. You can create a new scene by clicking the New Scene button in the Scene group and you can use the Layer Pane to change the way the data displays on the map. The data is displayed in a column chart by default, but you can select stacked column, clustered column, bubble, heat map, or region. When you save your workbook, 3D Map tours and scenes are saved.

# Skills Review (Continued)

6. **Use Solver to define and solve a problem.**
   a. Activate the Profit sheet, then open the Solver Parameters dialog box.
   b. Select cell F21 (the total profit) as the objective cell, with a target value of **4,500,000**.
   c. Select cells B5:E5 and B15 as the changing cells.
   d. Specify that cell B5 <= **1300000**, cell C5 <= **1320000**, cell D5 <= **1250000**, cell E5 <= **1250000**, and cell B15 >= **600000**.
   e. Use Solver to find a solution. Keep the solver solution, then compare your worksheet to **Figure 12-24**.

**Figure 12-24**

| | A | B | C | D | E | F | G | H |
|---|---|---|---|---|---|---|---|---|
| 1 | | [illegible] Robotics | | | | | | |
| 2 | | Projected Profit by Application | | | | | | |
| 3 | | **Quarter 1** | **Quarter 2** | **Quarter 3** | **Quarter 4** | **Total** | | |
| 4 | **Revenue** | | | | | | | |
| 5 | Medical | $1,224,146 | $1,207,053 | $1,103,325 | $1,204,621 | $4,739,147 | | |
| 6 | Assembly | $1,402,831 | $955,790 | $913,091 | $1,300,394 | $4,572,106 | | |
| 7 | Packing | $1,020,221 | $1,069,730 | $906,181 | $1,022,470 | $4,018,602 | | |
| 8 | Dispensing | $1,135,348 | $1,061,795 | $1,193,994 | $1,125,142 | $4,516,279 | | |
| 9 | **Total Revenue** | $4,782,546 | $4,294,368 | $4,116,591 | $4,652,627 | $17,846,134 | | |
| 10 | | | | | | | | |
| 11 | **Expenses** | $ 314,723 | $ 255,043 | $ 406,855 | $ 209,282 | $ 1,185,903 | | |
| 12 | Payroll | $ 540,640 | $ 452,513 | $ 124,042 | $ 158,023 | $ 1,275,218 | | |
| 13 | Benefits | $ 453,970 | $ 576,025 | $ 102,055 | $ 305,273 | $ 1,437,323 | | |
| 14 | Training | $ 531,183 | $ 228,332 | $ 194,283 | $ 699,493 | $ 1,653,291 | | |
| 15 | Supplies | $ 647,070 | $ 347,186 | $ 722,976 | $ 322,482 | $ 2,039,714 | | |
| 16 | Recruitment | $ 563,369 | $ 366,157 | $ 639,139 | $ 271,623 | $ 1,840,288 | | |
| 17 | Employee Relations | $ 712,086 | $ 173,716 | $ 123,913 | $ 695,235 | $ 1,704,950 | | |
| 18 | Security | $ 393,529 | $ 759,370 | $ 669,677 | $ 386,871 | $ 2,209,447 | | |
| 19 | **Total Expenses** | $ 4,156,570 | $ 3,158,342 | $ 2,982,940 | $ 3,048,282 | $ 13,346,134 | | |
| 20 | | | | | | | | |
| 21 | **Profit** | $625,977 | $1,136,026 | $1,133,651 | $1,604,345 | $4,500,000 | | |

Scenario Summary | Projected Expenses | **Profit** | Sales | Employees

Ready | Accessibility: Good to go

7. **Manage data using a data model.**
   a. Activate the Sales sheet, then use Power Pivot to add the worksheet data to the data model.
   b. Switch to Worksheet view, activate the Employees sheet, then use Power Pivot to add the worksheet data to the data model.
   c. In Power Pivot, rename the Table1 sheet **Sales**, then name the Table2 sheet **Employees**.
   d. Use a command on the Design tab in the Power Pivot window to create a relationship between the Emp# field in the Employees table and the Employee ID field in the Sales table.
   e. View the relationship between the tables in Diagram View and verify it is one to many, illustrating that one employee in the Employees table can have many sales in the Sales table.
   f. Return to the workbook in Worksheet view, then on the Employees sheet, change the contents of cell B2 to **Amina Levy**.
   g. Return to the data model in Power Pivot, use the Home tab to return to the Data View, activate the Employees sheet if necessary, then refresh the worksheet data. (**Hint**: To return to the data model in Power Pivot, click the Manage button in the Data Model group.)
   h. Widen the Name and Title columns to fully display the data in those columns.

8. **Analyze data using Power Pivot.**
   a. On the Employees sheet in the Power Pivot window, in the first cell under the Add Column header, enter a calculated column formula that uses table and field names to enter "Management" for the entries of Sales Manager or Account Manager in the Title column and "Representative" for all other titles. (**Hint**: The function is: =IF(OR(Employees[Title]="Sales Manager",Employees[Title]="Account Manager"),"Management","Representative".)
   b. Rename the Calculated Column 1 header, **Position**.
   c. Activate the Sales sheet in the Power Pivot window, then in the first cell in the calculation area below the Revenue data use the AutoSum button on the Home tab of the Power Pivot window to total the revenue.
   d. Widen the Revenue column to fully display the Sum of Revenue, change the label from Sum of Revenue to **Total**, then format the Total value using the $ English (United States) Currency format and two decimal places.
   e. In the cell below Total in the calculation area, insert a measure that projects a four percent revenue growth, change the Measure 1 label name to **Projected**, then format the Projected value using the $ English (United States) Currency format and two decimal places.
   f. Create a PivotTable on a new worksheet, name the sheet **PivotTable**, then create a PivotTable that adds the Application field from the Sales table to the Columns area, the Total and Projected fields from the Sales table to the Values area with the Total field on top, the Department field from the Employees table to the Rows area, and the Position field from the Employees table to the Rows area above the Department field.
   g. Use a tool on the Power Pivot Analyze tab to hide the Field Headers, display grand totals only for the columns, then compare your PivotTable to **Figure 12-25**.
   h. Group the worksheets, add your name to the footer of the worksheets, ungroup the worksheets, save and close the workbook, submit the workbook to your instructor, then close Excel.

**Figure 12-25**

| | Assembly | | Dispensing | | Medical | | Packing | |
|---|---|---|---|---|---|---|---|---|
| | Total | Projected | Total | Projected | Total | Projected | Total | Projected |
| **Management** | | | | | | | | |
| Inside Sales | $318,675.00 | $331,422.00 | $182,207.00 | $189,495.28 | $190,901.00 | $198,537.04 | $182,204.00 | $189,492.16 |
| Outside Sales | $173,801.00 | $180,753.04 | $266,052.00 | $276,694.08 | $138,552.00 | $144,094.08 | $235,185.00 | $244,592.40 |
| **Representative** | | | | | | | | |
| Inside Sales | $67,232.00 | $69,921.28 | $302,461.00 | $314,559.44 | $279,520.00 | $290,700.80 | $284,407.00 | $295,783.28 |
| Outside Sales | $463,544.00 | $482,085.76 | $444,405.00 | $462,181.20 | $494,887.00 | $514,682.48 | $386,406.00 | $401,862.24 |
| **Grand Total** | **$1,023,252.00** | **$1,064,182.08** | **$1,195,125.00** | **$1,242,930.00** | **$1,103,860.00** | **$1,148,014.40** | **$1,088,202.00** | **$1,131,730.08** |

# Independent Challenge 1

You are the assistant to the CFO at DYN Data Centers located in the Southeast United States. You are reviewing the first quarter revenue projections for the data center locations. As part of your assessment, you will forecast the effect on the company's first-quarter revenue if the Charlotte location's revenue estimates increase.

a. Start Excel, open IL_EX_12-3.xlsx from the location where you store your Data Files, then save it as **IL_EX_12_DYN**.
b. Create cell names for cells B4:D4 based on the labels in cells B3:D3 (do not create a cell name for cell E4), using the Create Names from Selection dialog box.
c. Use Scenario Manager to set up a scenario called **Current Revenue** that includes the current January, February, and March revenue values for Charlotte.

## Independent Challenge 1 (Continued)

d. Use Scenario Manager to add a scenario called **Increase Revenue 100000** by changing the January value for Charlotte to **528984**, the February value for Charlotte to **390747**, and the March value for Charlotte to **515874**.
e. Use Scenario Manager to add a scenario called **Increase Revenue 200000** by changing the January value for Charlotte to **628984**, the February value for Charlotte to **490747**, and the March value for Charlotte to **615874**.
f. View each scenario and confirm that it performs as intended, then display the Current Revenue scenario.
g. Generate a scenario summary titled **Charlotte Options**. Use cells E4, F4, and E8 as the Result cells.
h. Delete the Current Values column in the report, the notes at the bottom of the report, row 1, and column A.
i. Change the label in cell A1 to **Scenario Summary for Charlotte Revenue Increases**.
j. Edit cell B9 to read **Total Charlotte Revenue**, edit cell B10 to read **Charlotte Percentage of Total Revenue**, edit cell B11 to read **Total Revenue**, increase the width of column B to fully display the labels, then rename the worksheet **Charlotte Revenue Increases**.
k. Compare your worksheet to **Figure 12-26**.

**Figure 12-26**

| | A | B | C | D | E |
|---|---|---|---|---|---|
| 1 | Scenario Summary for Charlotte Revenue Increases | | | | |
| 2 | | | Current Revenue | Increase Revenue 100000 | Increase Revenue 200000 |
| 4 | Changing Cells: | | | | |
| 5 | | January | $428,984 | $528,984 | $628,984 |
| 6 | | February | $290,747 | $390,747 | $490,747 |
| 7 | | March | $415,874 | $515,874 | $615,874 |
| 8 | Result Cells: | | | | |
| 9 | | Total Charlotte Revenue | $1,135,605 | $1,435,605 | $1,735,605 |
| 10 | | Charlotte Percent of Total Revenue | 16.50% | 19.99% | 23.19% |
| 11 | | Total Revenue | $6,883,258 | $7,183,258 | $7,483,258 |
| 12 | | | | | |

l. Activate the Revenue sheet, use Goal Seek to find the February revenue for Charlotte that produces an interest rate of 18% for that location, then accept the Goal Seek solution.
m. Compare your worksheet to **Figure 12-27**.

**Figure 12-27**

| | A | B | C | D | E | F |
|---|---|---|---|---|---|---|
| 1 | DYN Data Centers | | | | | |
| 2 | Projected Operating Revenue | | | | | |
| 3 | | January | February | March | Total Revenue | Percent of Revenue |
| 4 | Charlotte | $428,984 | $416,339 | $415,874 | $1,261,197 | 17.99% |
| 5 | Nashville | $571,525 | $586,355 | $695,208 | $1,853,088 | 26.44% |
| 6 | Tampa | $737,315 | $777,123 | $762,809 | $2,277,247 | 32.49% |
| 7 | Atlanta | $549,283 | $563,489 | $504,546 | $1,617,318 | 23.08% |
| 8 | Total | $2,287,107 | $2,343,306 | $2,378,437 | $7,008,850 | |
| 9 | Percent of Revenue | 32.63% | 33.43% | 33.93% | | |
| 10 | | | | | | |

n. Group the worksheets, enter your name in the center footer section of the grouped worksheet, then save the workbook.
o. Close the workbook, then submit the workbook to your instructor.

## Independent Challenge 2

As the assistant to the director of a lab at a research hospital, you have been asked to evaluate the options for purchasing a new imaging machine for the lab. You will use Excel's What-If Analysis tools to explore the best financing options for this equipment purchase.

a. Start Excel, open IL_EX_12-4.xlsx from the location where you store your Data Files, then save it as **IL_EX_12_Lab**.
b. With the MRI sheet active, open Solver, then use the Set Objective options to set the Break-Even in Years in cell B6 to a value of **6**.
c. In Solver, use the Estimated Patients Annually and Bill per Session, in cells B3:B4, as the changing cells.
d. Add a constraint to Solver specifying the Estimated Patients Annually in cell B3 must be an integer. (**Hint**: Choose int as the operator in the Add Constraint dialog box.)
e. Add a second constraint specifying that the Estimated Patients Annually in cell B3 must be less than or equal to **1200**.
f. Add a third constraint specifying that the Bill per Session in cell B4 must be less than or equal to **1250**.
g. Generate a solution using Solver and accept Solver's solution. Compare your worksheet to **Figure 12-28**.

**Figure 12-28**

| | A | B | C | D |
|---|---|---|---|---|
| 1 | MRI Purchase | | | |
| 2 | Purchase Price | $ 8,000,000 | | |
| 3 | Estimated Patients Annually | 1067 | | |
| 4 | Bill per Session | $ 1,250 | | |
| 5 | Annual Billing | $ 1,333,333 | | |
| 6 | Break-Even in Years | 6.000000053 | | |
| 7 | | | | |

h. Activate the Loan sheet. Enter **6%** in cell D2, use the value in cell D2 to fill the range D3:D9 with a linear series using **.25%** as the step value, then format the range D2:D9 as Percentage with two decimal places.
i. Enter **72** in cell E1, then use the value in cell E1 to fill the range F1:I1 with a linear series using **12** as the step value.
j. Reference the monthly payment amount from cell B4 in cell D1, and format the contents of cell D1 so they are hidden.
k. Generate a two-input data table, using cells D1:I9, that displays the effect of varying interest rates and loan terms on the monthly payments. (**Hint**: Use cell B3, Term in Months, as the Row input cell, and cell B2, the Annual Interest Rate, as the Column input cell.)
l. Format the range E2:I9 as currency with two decimal places and a $ sign, then compare your worksheet to **Figure 12-29**.
m. Group the two worksheets, then enter your name in the center section of the grouped footer.
n. Save the workbook, close the workbook, submit the workbook to your instructor as directed, then close Excel.

**Figure 12-29**

| | A | B | C | D | E | F | G | H | I | J | K | L | M |
|---|---|---|---|---|---|---|---|---|---|---|---|---|---|
| 1 | Loan Amount | $8,000,000.00 | | | 72 | 84 | 96 | 108 | 120 | | | | |
| 2 | Annual Interest Rate | 7.70% | | 6.00% | $132,583.10 | $116,868.44 | $105,131.44 | $96,046.00 | $88,816.40 | | | | |
| 3 | Term in Months | 72 | | 6.25% | $133,529.23 | $117,829.60 | $106,107.96 | $97,038.05 | $89,824.08 | | | | |
| 4 | Monthly Payment | $139,096.97 | | 6.50% | $134,479.44 | $118,795.49 | $107,089.86 | $98,036.12 | $90,838.38 | | | | |
| 5 | | | | 6.75% | $135,433.71 | $119,766.11 | $108,077.12 | $99,040.18 | $91,859.29 | | | | |
| 6 | | | | 7.00% | $136,392.05 | $120,741.44 | $109,069.74 | $100,050.21 | $92,886.78 | | | | |
| 7 | | | | 7.25% | $137,354.45 | $121,721.48 | $110,067.69 | $101,066.20 | $93,920.83 | | | | |
| 8 | | | | 7.50% | $138,320.90 | $122,706.21 | $111,070.96 | $102,088.13 | $94,961.42 | | | | |
| 9 | | | | 7.75% | $139,291.39 | $123,695.62 | $112,079.55 | $103,115.97 | $96,008.50 | | | | |
| 10 | | | | | | | | | | | | | |

# Visual Workshop

Open the file IL_EX_12-5.xlsx from the location where you store your Data Files, then save it as **IL_EX_12_OfficeExpenses**. View the one-to-many relationship in the file's data model. Use **Figure 12-30** as a guide to calculate total expenses and a projected expense increase of 5% in the Expenses table in the Power Pivot window. Update the office for Employee ID # 5468 in the Employee table to **Columbus** and refresh the Employee table in the Power Pivot window. Then, using the data model, create the PivotTable displayed in **Figure 12-31**. When you are finished, add your name to the center footer section of the PivotTable sheet, save the workbook, submit the workbook to your instructor as directed, then close Excel.

**Figure 12-30**

| | Expense ID | Category | Amount | Client Category | Employee ID | Manager ID | Add Column |
|---|---|---|---|---|---|---|---|
| 1 | 8841 | Entertainment | $2,311.00 | Government | 1254 | 8185 | |
| 2 | 1113 | Meals | $153.00 | Corporate | 3257 | 6700 | |
| 3 | 4652 | Supplies | $1,008.00 | Insurance | 5468 | 4858 | |
| 4 | 3428 | Travel | $2,528.00 | Foundations | 5487 | 6951 | |
| 5 | 7609 | Entertainment | $1,946.00 | Government | 9654 | 2978 | |
| 6 | 7008 | Meals | $185.00 | Foundations | 3254 | 6270 | |
| 7 | 2847 | Supplies | $356.00 | Government | 1254 | 8185 | |
| 8 | 3511 | Travel | $1,531.00 | Corporate | 3257 | 6700 | |
| 9 | 4352 | Entertainment | $2,335.00 | Insurance | 5468 | 4858 | |
| 10 | 3551 | Meals | $428.00 | Foundations | 5487 | 6951 | |
| 11 | 4376 | Supplies | $507.00 | Government | 9654 | 2978 | |
| 12 | 9337 | Travel | $1,451.00 | Foundations | 3254 | 6270 | |
| 13 | 8051 | Entertainment | $1,980.00 | Government | 1254 | 8185 | |
| 14 | 9524 | Meals | $2,611.00 | Corporate | 3257 | 6700 | |
| 15 | 8628 | Supplies | $2,012.00 | Insurance | 5468 | 4858 | |
| | | | Total: $31,222.00<br>Projected: $32,783.10 | | | | |

Expenses | Employee

Record: 1 of 24

**Figure 12-31**

| | A | B | C | D | E | F | G | H |
|---|---|---|---|---|---|---|---|---|
| 1 | | | | | | | | |
| 2 | | | | | | | | |
| 3 | | | Total | | | Projected | | |
| 4 | | | Cincinnati | Cleveland | Columbus | Cincinnati | Cleveland | Columbus |
| 5 | | **Corporate** | | | | | | |
| 6 | | Meals | | $2,764.00 | | | $2,902.20 | |
| 7 | | Travel | | $2,043.00 | | | $2,145.15 | |
| 8 | | **Foundations** | | | | | | |
| 9 | | Meals | $328.00 | | $1,034.00 | $344.40 | | $1,085.70 |
| 10 | | Travel | $3,795.00 | | $3,674.00 | $3,984.75 | | $3,857.70 |
| 11 | | **Government** | | | | | | |
| 12 | | Entertainment | | $4,353.00 | $4,291.00 | | $4,570.65 | $4,505.55 |
| 13 | | Supplies | | $1,558.00 | $996.00 | | $1,635.90 | $1,045.80 |
| 14 | | **Insurance** | | | | | | |
| 15 | | Entertainment | | | $3,366.00 | | | $3,534.30 |
| 16 | | Supplies | | | $3,020.00 | | | $3,171.00 |
| 17 | | **Grand Total** | $4,123.00 | $10,718.00 | $16,381.00 | $4,329.15 | $11,253.90 | $17,200.05 |
| 18 | | | | | | | | |

# Index

## Special Characters

# D



# E



# F